The Nuclear Deception

Also by Servando González

BOOKS

Arte: realismo o realidad
Historia de las artes visuales
(with Armando Ledón)
Historia herética de la revolución fidelista
(published in Mexico as Fidel Castro para
herejes y otros invertebrados)
Observando
The Secret Fidel Castro

MULTIMEDIA

Real History of "The Horse": A HyperComic
How to Create Your Own Personal Intelligence Agency
The Riddle of the Swastika: A Study in Symbolism
Popol Vuh: An Interactive Educational Game
Hypertext for Beginners

INTERNET SITES

Castromania: The Fidel Watch
Tyrant Aficionado
The Swastika and the Nazis
Memoirs of a Computer Heretic

The Nuclear Deception
Nikita Khrushchev and the Cuban Missile Crisis

Servando González

Spooks Books
An Imprint of InteliBooks *Publishers*
Oakland, California

All rights reserved. Copyright © 2002 by Servando González

No part of this book may be reproduced or transmitted in any form or by any means, graphic, electronic or mechanical, including photocopying, recording, taping or by any information storage or retrieval system, without permission in writing from the publisher, except by a reviewer, who may quote short passages in a review.

Cataloging-in-Publication Data

González, Servando, 1935-

The nuclear deception : Nikita Khrushchev and the
Cuban missile crisis / Servando González.
p. cm.

Includes bibliographical references and index.

ISBN 0-9711391-5-6 (soft cover)

1. Cuban missile crisis. 2. United States—Foreign relations—Cuba. 3. Soviet Union—Foreign relations—United States. 4. Soviet Union—Foreign relations—Cuba. 5. United States—Foreign relations—1959-1962. I. Title. II. González, Servando, 1935-

Cover design: Damion Gordon/BTP GRAPHX
Cover illustration: Servando González

Second Printing, May 2003.
This book was printed in the United States of America
To order additional copies of this book, contact:

InteliBooks
www.InteliBooks.com
orders@intelibooks.com

In memoriam
Sherman Kent (1903-1986)

Contents

Acknowledgements *xi*
Preface *xiii*
Questions and More Questions xiii
This Elusive Thing We Call "History" xiv
Objectivity and the Historian xvi
A Non-Conventional Approach to History xviii
Note on Style and Sources xx

Introduction 22
The Official Story 22

PART ONE: Living With a Goat

One: Khrushchev's Lies 29
Khrushchev Speaks 29
Fidel Tells his Version of the Story 33
Khrushchev's Schemes 36

Two: Castro's Unexplainable Rush to Communism 40
Latin America and the Soviets 41
The Cuban Communists and Fidel 43
The Russians are Not Coming 49
Fidel Pulls a Fast One 50
Communist "Infiltration" Continues 51
Finally, the Russians are Coming 53
Suddenly, Fidel Becomes a "Marxist" 55

Three: Khrushchev's Problems 58
The U.S.S.R. and Latin America 58
Figuratively Speaking... 63
Khrushchev Backs Fidel 66
Khrushchev Enters Muddy Waters 71
Underdevelopment... But Just a Little 77
Che Guevara's Economic Idealism 80
The Ruble Stops Here 82

Four: Coup d'État Khrushchev-Style 88
The "Escalante Affair" 88
The DGI and the Russians 93
The Enigmatic Kudryavtsev 94
The Revolutionary Instructors and the Rebel Army 97
Castro's Victory 102

Five: Khrushchev's Plan 106
Nikita Gets an Idea 106
Khrushchev's Plan in Action 109
"Deception" and "Stealth" 113
Khrushchev Sends Clear Signals 116
Khrushchev's "Errors" 119

Six: Khrushchev's Spy 124
Penkovsky: the CIA's Greatest Success 124
Was Penkovsky a Soviet Plant? 126
The KGB and Disinformation 129
Penkovsky: a Soviet Deception Exercise? 132

Seven: Khrushchev's Failure 136
None So Blind... 137
McCone's "Hunch" and the "Photographic Gap" 139
Confusion in Moscow 141
Khrushchev's "Miscalculations" 143

Eight: The Trigger-Happy Tyrant 149
Fidel's Extraordinary Love for Nuclear Missiles 150
Castro's Attempt to Destroy New York 154
The Russians See Nothing, Do Nothing 154
Who Pushed the Button? 156
Franqui's Bizarre Story 158
Khrushchev and Castro's Even More Bizarre Stories 160

Nine: Khrushchev's Goat 162
A Letter Written in Terror 162
Khrushchev Got Cold Feet 165
Khrushchev's Appeasement Rituals 168

PART TWO: This is *Not* a Missile

Ten: **A Missile is a Missile is a Missile** *177*
Is "Photographic Evidence" Evidence at All? *177*
Missiles and Signs of Missiles *180*
Strategic Missiles as Symbols *186*
The Treachery of Intelligence Images *188*
A Logical Conclusion *191*

Eleven: **Starry-eyed Historians VS. Hard-nosed Spies** *193*
Are Historians too Gullible to Write Spy Stories? *194*
Historians and Intelligence Analysts *196*
The Spy With a Multiple Personality Disorder *198*

Twelve: **The Blight, Allyn, Welch, *et al.*, Paper Mill** *203*
Scholars and Intelligence Services *204*
The National Security "Archive" *210*
The Value of Documents *212*
Documents, or Images of Documents? *213*
The Outoboros of American Politics *215*
Scholars, or Spies? *217*
Oral History; But Whose? *219*
Dezinformatsia, Inc. *220*

PART THREE: Was There Ever a Cuban Missile Crisis?

Thirteen: **Decision-Making in the Kremlin and in the White House** *227*
Decision-Making and Decision-Makers *228*
Rational and Irrational Decision-Making *229*
Khrushchev's Pet Plan *232*
Unsound Theories *235*
Kennedy's "Irrational" Behavior *237*
Little Brother Was Watching Them *243*
Eyeball to Eyeball Machismo *244*

Fourteen: **The Missile Crisis that Never Was** *247*
What is a "Crisis"? 248
The Notorious September Estimate   251
Was the Cuban Crisis a Real Crisis?   256
Awareness   257
Decision-Making Time   259
Threat   260
The Incredibly Shrinking Nuclear Warheads   263
The Metamorphosis of the Soviet Missiles   267
Kennedy's Politics   271
How Close to the Brink?   273
Was the Crisis a Pseudo-event?   275

Epilogue: **More Questions Than Answers** *278*
The "Lessons" of the Cuban Missile Crisis   279
The Aftermath of the Crisis   282
Two, Three... Many Vietnams   286
A Few Conclusions   291
A Personal Note   293

Appendixes
Appendix 1: The Evaluation of Information   295

Notes *297*
Select Bibliography *395*
Index *421*

In Place of a Colophon *431*

Acknowledgements

This book owes a great deal to a great many. I have been assisted in this study by a host of great men and women who have stood beside me and gone before me in this endeavor. These I do now gratefully acknowledge.

To the librarians of The Latin American Library at Tulane University, The Hoover Institution Library and Archives, The John F. Kennedy Library, The San Francisco State University Library, The University of San Francisco Library, and The University of Southern Alabama Library in Mobile.

To Carlota Caulfield, for her critical readings and suggestions. To Franco Gonzalez and Stacy McKenna for their help in polishing my English, proofreading the manuscript and invaluable suggestions and criticism.

To Marcelo Fernández-Zayas, a true expert in the field of intelligence and espionage, for long, clarifying conversations over the phone on some of the subjects I deal with in this book.

To Jorge Luis Machado, of the Hoover Institution Library and Archives, for his invaluable help in finding some hard-to-find graphic materials.

To Lorenzo Cañizares, for calling my attention about some important subjects. To Ismael Lorenzo, for helping me find a book almost impossible to find. To Jesús Barquet, for sending me important printed materials.

To Neil Jensen, editor of *Sumeria*, for publishing an article of mine, several years ago, parts of which now appear in this book.

To Assistant Director for National Estimates and Chairman of the Board of National Estimates Sherman Kent, deputy chairman Abbot Smith, and board member John Huizenga, former chief of the Soviet Affairs section of the Office of National Estimates, for having had the honesty, courage and integrity to put their jobs on the line by standing for what they believed was right. They were the true heroes of the Cuban missile crisis.

To those whose names I cannot provide, because of their work in the shadow world of intelligence and espionage. All those who spoke with me have been promised anonymity in return for their secret thoughts, but I recognize my debt to them.

To the United States of America and the American people, for accepting me as a citizen of this great nation and allowing me to express my controversial ideas without fear of reprisals or censorship. I hope that, faced with the choice, the American people never make the mistake of renouncing freedom in exchange for promised security.

To all of these I wish to say thank you. But the responsibility for ideas expressed in this book is strictly my own. Thus, the views presented here do not necessarily represent the views of any of the persons or institutions I have mentioned above.

PREFACE

There is an important element missing when there is unanimity of viewpoint.

—Robert F. Kennedy. *Thirteen Days.*

You can either start with fiction or with documentary. But whichever one you start with, you will inevitably find the other.

—Jean-Luc Goddard.

The event known as the Cuban missile crisis, to many people the greatest of all Cold War crises, is a milestone in the history of the Cold War. Some analysts have even concluded that what was called the Cold War ended in 1962 with the Cuban missile crisis.[1] "Generations to come," praised *Time* magazine, "may well count John Kennedy's resolve as one of the decisive moments of the 20th Century."[2] Yet, there is perhaps no single event in recent history as puzzling as this one.

There are many questions that still remain unanswered.[3] Why did Khrushchev risk so much? What was his ultimate purpose? Why did he withdraw so fast? Why did he not retaliate at other sensitive points, like Berlin? Why did President Kennedy not seize the heaven-sent opportunity to get rid of Castro? Why did the Americans permit the shootdown of a U-2 plane over Cuba without taking retaliatory actions? Who shot down the U-2, and under what conditions did it happen? Why did Kennedy allow the Soviet ships to leave Cuba without boarding them, to physically verify that the canvas-covered objects on deck were actually missiles and their nuclear warheads on their way back to the U.S.S.R.?

Questions and More Questions

The main questions of the crisis have eluded satisfactory answers, first, because most of the analysts who have studied it have neglected the true Cuban role in the event, particularly the Russo-Cuban relations prior to the crisis; secondly, because a set of preconceived notions —like the one that assumes that Khrushchev was full of love for Fidel— have acted as a smoke screen, blurring the whole picture; and, finally, because the fundamental question about the crisis, namely, why Khrushchev installed strategic nuclear missiles in Cuba, has been erroneously formulated. Consequently, it has been impossible to find the right answer to a question when the question itself is wrong. As a matter of fact, it seems as if those who have studied the Cuban missile crisis have carefully avoided simple answers and searched for complex ones, probably overlooking that the principle *explicanda non sunt multiplicanda praeter necessitatem*, better known as Occam's razor, is still a practical way to find answers to complex problems.

Almost all the information I have used in my analysis of the Cuban missile crisis is in the public record. The amount of information available in primary sources and the scholarly studies it has generated is overwhelming. Half of the book is plain history, but half of it is a no-man's land between politics, intelligence and espionage, and sheer speculation. There are extensive notes throughout the book, and they are as important as the main text itself.

Also, an important basis of the study has been the insight obtained when I was an officer in the Cuban armed forces. As an officer of the Cuban army, I had the privilege to participate in the crisis from the less known angle: the Cuban point of view (or, better, in order to avoid confusion by those who equal Cuba to Castro, I would say from the point of view of a Cuban). I have had discussions and conversations with many of my ex-colleagues in the army, sharing our memoirs, though for obvious reasons I cannot mention names because many of them are still in Cuba and some are still in the Cuban army.

I do not pretend to have certain knowledge of matters of which there is no available documentation. Most of the evidence, however, seems to point in the direction I have tried to indicate and away from the more familiar picture on the subject: on good Khrushchev trying to help his poor friend Fidel from the piratical actions of American imperialism (Soviet view), or on courageous Kennedy, angered by Russian perfidy, trying to get rid of Communist Castro (American view).

I assert my belief that there are no certain facts in history. The only fact, if any, that we are certain of is that for no historical event do we possess *all* the documentation; nor are we assured that the documentation that has been released into the public domain can be accepted blindly as entirely trustworthy. This may be due to bureaucratic "erosion," or a matter of deliberate disinformation.[4] "All sources are suspect," wrote A.J.P. Taylor, adding that "little of the raw materials of history was devised for the use of historians; and that little is often the least reliable."[5]

This Elusive Thing We Call "History"

As Edward H. Carr has shown in his excellent *What is History?*,[6] the art of the historian does not merely consist of finding the facts, since everything that happens may be considered a fact, but in *selecting* the facts which, consciously or unconsciously, he believes are significant for his study.

In other words, historians emphasize the facts they believe are important, while neglecting the ones they feel are not. This emphasis can be made consciously, as in the case of Marxist historians, who fit history into the preconceived pattern of economic relations, or unconsciously, as in the case of historians who are determined by the conviction that history is a rational process. Irrationalities and oddities, then, will be played down or forgotten. Therefore, everything depends on the facts which a historian selects from the infinite number that are available, and on the emphasis he gives to those facts, and the result is the pattern "seen" by the historian, which may be explicit or implicit in his narrative. Thus, there is no *objective* history, any more than there is no *objective* journalism.

Proof of the above is that most books and papers about the Cuban missile crisis give no importance, or totally ignore, a key event in the series of events that lead to the crisis: the expulsion, following Castro's orders, of Soviet ambassador Sergei Kudryavtsev from Cuba in May, 1962. I contend that the Cuban missile crisis cannot be fully understood without a serious analysis of Kudryavtsev's activities in Cuba prior to the crisis.

I have a skeptic's attitude towards historical conclusions based on "facts." I firmly believe that there are no objective conclusions in history. All historical conclusions based on "facts" are impregnated with theories, which are contaminated with beliefs and political ideologies.

In the first place, historians usually differ about what they consider a fact. Secondly, conclusions based on facts can differ not only because of the selection of the facts but also because of the way they are analyzed. Third, many historians seem to ignore that, particularly in recent history, some of the "facts" have been left in for the sole purpose of disinformation.[7] Finally, even though this book is full of new or lesser known facts about the crisis, my major emphasis has been on the interpretation of the facts, including those that are known and at first sight seem irrelevant. There are times when retrospective analysis from back files or from sources that had long been available but never fully exploited, can turn up more information than expected. The facts may not change, but the analyst will see them in a new light. The real problem lies in the fact that if an analyst is not looking for a particular clue amid thousands of bits of information he will not find it. Thus, information judged insignificant or misinterpreted at the time it was found, but now still available, is there, before all those who have eyes to see it.

Intelligence services agree that the most difficult aspect of the intelligence business is not the collection of raw data, but its interpretation and transformation into usable intelligence. Many outsiders believe that intelligence consists mainly in stealing the bad guys' secrets. Most of the job of intelligence, however, consists in using your experience to evaluate information you already know. Not all intelligence involves cloak and dagger spooks or high tech espionage. A vast amount of the information that later becomes intelligence proper comes from open sources —monitoring of foreign broadcasts, close reading of the press, attendance at commercial and scientific conferences, study of officially released statistics and, above all, books— all of which, added to the information from secret sources, becomes raw material for the production of intelligence.

Not having been trained in intelligence and espionage, most scholars who have studied the missile crisis have made the common mistake of accepting raw data —i.e., documents, oral interviews, etc.— as intelligence. They apparently ignore that finding documents or interviewing participants in an event is data collection, and data is not true intelligence. Some people mistakenly call the product of these activities "raw intelligence," but this is a contradiction in terms. Intelligence is the sum of the conclusions based on raw data after it has been processed, analyzed and evaluated by qualified intelligence analysts.

Conscious of the pitfalls described above, in writing this book I have tried to use to some extent a new research and analysis methodology I have developed over the years for the study of contemporary or recent history. This methodology, which I call "historical tradecraft,"[8] is a combination of the research methodology of the historian with that of the intelligence analyst. The main guiding principle of the historical tradecraft approach is that in the field of intelligence and espionage things are seldom what they seem.[9] This is a new research and analysis tool, and I am still in the process of learning how to use it, therefore, some inconsistencies in its use may appear in this work. Also, though I see it as a promising tool, its effectiveness still needs to be evaluated.[10]

Objectivity and the Historian

When a historian works with documents he is constantly concerned with whether important" or "key" documents have been lost, suppressed or falsified. In fact, the addition or subtraction of a particular single document could easily cast an entirely different light on the problem under study. One may wonder how much of the most vital information is still classified? How much of it is not even classified because it was never written out, but transmitted verbally so as to leave no traceable sources? Even worse, how many of the "declassified" documents are actually forgeries?

It transpires in the works of most of the American scholars who have studied the Cuban missile crisis that they assume that the participants really meant what they said and said what they felt. They seem to forget that deception is a way of life among political leaders. As the Italian semiologist Umberto Eco observed, man is the only animal who tells lies.[11]

While studying recent American history, I found out that it seems as if there are two main currents of historical knowledge in the United States: a visible one, expressed openly in scholarly works and divulged by the press, and another one, a subterranean or underground history, rarely expressed openly except by the most revisionist historians, but that in fact molds the opinions and influences the decisions of America's leading politicians. When the chips are down, everybody in the high echelons of power and government in the United States is apparently convinced, as Robert Kennedy seemingly was,[12] that the USS *Maine* battleship was not sunk by a Spanish mine, that the Lusitania was allowed to be sunk by a German submarine, that Roosevelt knew in advance of the Japanese attack on Pearl Harbor, that the Tonkin Gulf incident was a fabrication concocted by Johnson to escalate the Vietnam war, that the Korean Airlines flight 007 was on a spy mission... etc. And this hidden knowledge is always present at decisionmaking time and directly influences the decisions made by our leaders.[13]

Historians, like everybody else, tend to see what they expect to see —dishonest historians see what it is convenient to see.[14] Historic objectivity is inevitably blurred by the innate biases built into human perception, and maybe this fact constitutes the historian's best asset. As Albert Szent-Georgi has remarked, "discovery consists of seeing what everybody has seen, but nobody has thought."

Philosopher Joseph Jastrow pointed out that the mind is a belief-seeking rather than a fact-seeking apparatus. Most experts, says Nobel Prize winner Richard Feynman, don't know more than the average person. They may act as though they are engaged in real science, they may do studies, follow some methodologies and sometimes have results, but they are actually practicing what he calls "cargo-cult science."[15] Reading some historian's account, one gets the impression that, whichever decision Kennedy had taken during the Cuban missile crisis, they would eventually have found a "scientific" explanation to prove that it was the best decision ever taken by the brightest man we ever had.

Political science scholars have been trying for years to add technical sophistication to the arsenal of political science. Once this is achieved, and only then, they argue, "can it discriminatingly validate its plethora of great ideas and separate the attractive hypothetical speculation from the confirmed, evidence supported proposition."[16] In other words, political science must aim for objectivity. But, then, what is objectivity?

Objectivity has been described as the attempt to collect, collate, evaluate, and interpret all data relevant to a specific topic in an attempt to be as unbiased and unprejudiced as possible in approximating truth or reality.[17] The definition itself, however, proves to be elusive. First of all, it states that one must collect *all* relevant data, but, which data is relevant?; and according to what criteria? Besides, most of the time it is impossible to collect all the data one considers relevant. Secondly, the data must be interpreted, that is, filtered through the analyst's own biases and prejudices. Therefore, there will never be true objectivity. In fact, no one can claim objectivity when observing social phenomena or when analyzing historical events. Everything observed is distorted by the observer's mind. The human mind directs the observer's attention to see what he wants to see. Everything we observe approximates reality according to our own preconceived notions, and it is not reality itself. The social sciences deal with human phenomena and not with physical phenomena *per se*.

Some attempts have also been made to reduce the amount of subjectivity in historical and political analysis, and increase their objective aspects through the use of mass data, game simulations, and statistics. Those efforts have come mainly from the behaviorist scientists. They argue that with proper analysis, large samples, and proper tabulation, the behavior of the actors of historical events can be not only analyzed, but also predicted. The problem with the quasi-scientific laws of behaviorism is that they neglect the human factor, with all its subjective elements, including rationality and, particularly, irrationality. In order to avoid this pitfall I have followed in my research the principle of studying the political leaders or decision groups, the men who make the decisions, instead of focusing on the nation as the unit of analysis. This explains why I prefer to talk about Khrushchev, Kennedy, or Castro rather than about the Soviet Union, the United States, or Cuba. Ultimately, it is individuals who make foreign policy decisions, and knowing something about such individuals singly and in groups may give us a better understanding of the foreign policy behavior of their nations.[18]

As Professor Adam B. Ulam rightly observed a long time ago, no alternative theory had been presented explaining Soviet motives for the Cuban move, nor the bizarre character of the Soviet actions on Cuba.[19] In the purest Sherlock Holmes style, I have seized several apparently unexplainable characteristics of the event and I have used these features as criteria against which to test my hypothesis about Khrushchev's hidden motives and goals. My explanation of the events presents a clear advantage: it provides a coherent picture of this jigsaw puzzle of history called the Cuban missile crisis without having to resort to assumptions or to the totally baseless theory that Khrushchev was an incompetent fool.

A Non-Conventional Approach to History

I think that an event as bizarre as the Cuban missile crisis could only have happened in the Caribbean, a region on Earth where the surreal is a common occurrence in everyday life. The Cuban missile crisis is just another episode of what Cuban writer Alejo Carpentier calls *"lo real maravilloso"* (the marvelous-real). But let me warn you: though I affirm that this is a fantastic story, I am not equating the fantastic with the imaginary. In fact the whole Cuban missile crisis affair proves once more that reality is more fantastic than fiction itself.

Contrary to many versions of historical events, I don't claim that my account is the only and ultimate truth. On the contrary, I advise the reader to rely on the motto: *Omnia dubitatem*. Put in doubt my version of the Cuban missile crisis, but also put in doubt all other versions as well. As writer Anthony Brand pointed out, in doubting everything lies the healthy skepticism that will keep us all, readers and writers alike, relatively honest.[20]

Ideally authors should be objective. That is, they should record what has happened with no hint of bias, no heavy hand of opinion. But such pristine purity is a myth. That is why writer E.B. White said that he who puts pen to paper writes, unavoidably, of himself. Therefore, I am stating very clearly that this is a biased analysis of the Cuban missile crisis. In fact, it is no more biased than all the other books written about the Cuban missile crisis —and probably less biased than some "serious" books written on the subject.

Using the approach described above, I have arrived at some conclusions that widely differ from most of the previous studies on the Cuban missile crisis. In my analysis I have tried to substitute history for myth. If in the process it happens that

I have only substituted myth for myth, nobody —particularly the myth-makers— should point their fingers at me. Let he that is without sin cast the first stone. The big difference between they and I is that I openly proclaim the fact that I am biased. I never try to fool the reader.

All history is unavoidably written from the present. It is almost impossible, therefore, not to project the present to the past, a characteristic which has been called the contamination of the past by the present. It was in that sense that Benedetto Croce said that all history is contemporary.

Due to the immense amount of data generated by even the simplest historical event, historians, in order to decide what to look for, must have a preconceived opinion, a working hypothesis, about the event in question. That, of course, limits their options, but, without that preconceived opinion, how should they be able to select the relevant (for them) data, to permit them to make the internal connections evident among the immense abundance of raw data? Actually, there is no such thing as "bare historical facts." All the facts that enter our knowledge —even "scientific facts"— are filtered by our way of seeing them.[21]

"In no few sense could we say that the nucleus of history is fiction," said Peruvian writer Mario Vargas Llosa. "But there is a fiction that produces monsters, it is the fiction that doesn't see itself as fiction. The greatness of literature is that it expresses things and at the same time doesn't fool us." And then he asks himself: "What is fiction? To what point history is possible? Or, to what point is it simply a branch of fiction?" Because remembrances cast shadows in reality, most historical stories look more as an effort to rectify the past than to preserve it. "Not only fiction is a lie. Not only Literature, but History also is made out of lies that look unavoidable, maybe necessary."[22] Paraphrasing Lord Acton's counsel: "When you perceive a truth, look for the balancing truth," one could say, "when you perceive a lie, look for the balancing lie."

I would also like to warn the reader in advance that, like everybody else, I have a point of view. This is a factual, but opinionated book. But, being myself a searcher for other authors' biases, I don't try to hide my own. In this sense I am sure that this is a book that will make some people uncomfortable.

I am not one of those scholars in the pay-roll of an American think tank because of his ability to tell the establishment what it loves to hear. Neither am I one of those "leftist" intellectuals who criticizes American interventionism but justifies Castro's interventionism and totalitarianism. Nor I am one of those "objective" American scholars who calls Pinochet "dictator" but calls the Cuban tyrant "President." Finally, to make things even more complicated, I am not one of those Cuban-Americans who criticizes human rights violations in Cuba but remains silent before human rights violations in the United States.[23]

Thus, one may wonder, what would be the use of reading a historical account if its author up front claims that it probably is not true, or, at least is not the *whole* truth? I suggest that you can read it for the only reason one should read a book, being of history, fiction or poetry: just for the enjoyment of it. Or, much better, paraphrasing what the Columbia University Press tells in its motto: just for the pleasure of thinking.

In a book that created great controversy among American historians,[24] Peter Novick, a history professor at the University of Chicago, questioned the role and future of historians. Novick affirmed that it is time to stop talking about "historical objectivity." We can't aspire to write definitive history, he said. Therefore, the most we can do is write interesting history.

It is easy to foresee that a book such as this may well spring up more questions than it gives answers. My goal has been to open the greatest possible number of doors to my readers. My main aim is not so much to answer the questions about the Cuban missile crisis but to open a new and fresh debate about the subject.

The reader will notice that I barely mention books written about the crisis in the last fifteen years, particularly the ones based on "declassified" documents, "oral history," or written by scholars who have visited Cuba, and, when I do, it is mostly to criticize them. Nor I included these books in the Select Bibliography at the end of the book. There are important reasons for this.

If one is to believe the scholars who have written these books, in the last fifteen years new evidence has surfaced that challenges previous interpretations of the Cuban missile crisis.[25] The new "evidence," however, consist mainly in "oral history" —which is not history at all but hearsay and opinions told by professional liars and deceivers—[26] and declassified "documents" —which are not documents at all, but photocopies of alleged documents provided by organizations specializing in falsifying documents. Most of these "documents" are kept in an "archive" — which is not an archive at all— researched mostly by "objective scholars" — whose professional integrity probably has been compromised by different intelligence services. I will study this in detail in chapter twelve.

This book has three parts. The first part consists of nine chapters detailing the events which lead to the crisis and its outcome, as well as an analysis of Nikita Khrushchev's motives and intentions for doing what he actually did. A second part, with three chapters, is devoted to the analysis of some theoretical aspects of the crisis from the point of view of semiotics, intelligence, and espionage, and the analysis of the research methodology and the inner motivations of the researchers themselves. The last part, with two chapters and the Epilogue, return to the basic theme of the first chapters, studying the event from some unconventional points of view and attempting to bring some key events of the crisis up to date.

More than another study on the Cuban missile crisis, the book must be seen as a case study depicting the complex Castro-Soviet relations; so complex indeed that professor Maurice Halperin once characterized them as the strange phenomenon of the tail wagging the dog.[27] It is also a critical view of the work of the American intelligence services, the CIA in particular, and the role of some American scholars who, wittingly or unwittingly, are actively collaborating with different intelligence services in the dissemination of disinformation.

Note on Style and Sources

Due to the insufficiency of reliable documentation[28] and because of the impossibility of verification,[29] speculation on American, Soviet and Cuban affairs is unavoidable. As it seems unlikely that neither the United States, Cuba or Russia will truly open their archives to research, the analyst can only make educated guesses based on observable facts. In that sense my book, like all the books that have been written about the Cuban missile crisis, is mainly based on circumstantial evidence. But, as a former CIA analyst once observed, "Intelligence may be defined as the subjective evaluation of ambiguous data."[30]

Primary documentation for the Cuban missile crisis is thus limited to the formal communications between Soviet and American leaders during the weeks following President Kennedy's disclosure of the presence of the missiles in Cuba. Though there have been efforts to analyze Khrushchev's motives and strategies, we are still lacking reliable information on Soviet decision-making during the crisis. In contrast, the decision-making process in Cuba since Castro took power in 1959 is pretty simple: Castro gives orders from his *cojones* and everybody must agree... or else.[31]

INTRODUCTION

> *This is a mystery. Maybe historians will be able to clarify this twenty or thirty years hence. I don't know.*
>
> —Fidel Castro, in an interview with Claude Julien.
> *Le Monde*, March 22, 1963.

If a political-fiction writer would have imagined before October, 1962, a plot for a novel about the deployment of strategic nuclear missiles in Cuba by the Soviet Union, it is almost sure that, sooner or later, he would have discarded the idea because of the low probability for the occurrence of such an event. As it always happens, however, reality outshined literary fiction and Nikita S. Khrushchev, breaking all probability laws, apparently installed the Russian rockets in the Caribbean Island[1] precipitating what history has recorded as the Cuban missile crisis.[2]

The Official Story

Late in the night of October 26, 1962, Nikita S. Khrushchev sent a secret message to President Kennedy in which he agreed to the dismantling —under international control— of the Cuban missile bases, provided that the United States only promise not to invade the Caribbean island. But the cheerful mood at the White House was quickly shattered by a second message, made public in Moscow, in which Khrushchev offered to dismantle the Soviet missiles in Cuba if the U.S. missiles in Turkey, as a sole condition, were to be dismantled.

Following Robert Kennedy's recommendation, the President paid no attention to the second message and responded to the first, and then waited anxiously through the night. Then, shortly after ten o'clock on that Sunday morning, October 28, Moscow released the text of another message from Khrushchev to Kennedy, in which the Soviet leader said he had ordered the work on the Cuban bases to stop and had ordered the missiles to be crated and returned to the Soviet Union under United States verification. The Cuban missile crisis was over. After thirteen days on the brink of holocaust a terrified world sighed relief.

Hundreds of books and papers have been written since that somber day, trying to explain in vain the apparently incomprehensible attitude of the Soviets.[3] Beginning with Robert Kennedy and ending with Nikita Khrushchev, diverse answers have been provided and several explanations have been offered, none of them with too much conviction, to explain the bizarre affair.[4] And today, after all these years, the intriguing questions still remain: Why did Khrushchev risk setting up missile sites in Cuba? What was his purpose? Was this action another instance of Khrushchev's *niekulturnyi*[5] behavior; a kind of international shoe-banging like his 1960 U.N. performance?[6] There is a point, however, in which almost all Western analysts coincide: Nobody has yet understood why Khrushchev acted in such an irrational way.

CIA Director John McCone had hinted in Washington some weeks before, that he suspected the Soviets were deploying nuclear ballistic missiles in Cuba.[7] But it was not until October 15, 1962, that the CIA's top photointerpreter Dino Brugioni analyzed the pictures taken by a U-2 flying over Cuba and discovered that Russian strategic missile sites were being built on the Island.[8] It was not until October 16, however, that President Kennedy was given irrefutable proof that the Soviets were installing ground-to-ground missiles with nuclear capability in the Island. After consulting with his brother Robert, he summoned a group of high staff officials and experts in Cuban and Soviet affairs to the White House. All of them were shocked and confused by the news.[9]

On several occasions, President Kennedy had asked the intelligence community for an evaluation of the Soviet military buildup in Cuba, but apparently no official within the government, probably with the exception of McCone, had anticipated the Russian move. On each of the four times that the U.S. intelligence community emitted its National Estimate,[10] with official reports on Cuba and the Caribbean, they had advised the President that the Russians would not make offensive weapons available to Castro. In the last National Intelligence Estimate, dated the 19th of September, just before the crisis erupted —the now notorious "September estimate"— the United States Intelligence Board (USIB) concluded without reservation that Soviet emplacement of offensive missiles in Cuba was highly unlikely. The estimate pointed out that the Soviet Union had not taken this kind of step with any of its satellites in the past. In fact, the Soviets had never placed strategic nuclear weapons outside its own territorial borders, not in the loyal Communist Eastern Europeans nations, nor in communist China.[11] Both military and civil leaders had believed all along that the Soviet Union would never risk such action, especially after the repeated reassurances, both public and private, the Soviets had given them.[12]

Just a week before, on September 11, the Soviet press agency *TASS* transmitted a long declaration by the Soviet government assuring that the Soviet union had no need for bases abroad, since its Inter-Continental Ballistic Missiles (ICBMs) already enabled it to strike any part of the world. This declaration was meant to be a reply to the announcement by President Kennedy that he would do nothing against Cuba as long as there were no offensive weapons on the island. And now, less than three weeks after, the ugly reality of Russian nuclear weapons a mere ninety miles from American shores was presented as a naked fact to the American leaders.

Kennedy felt that his dignity had been assaulted by a high-class liar. Some American political analysts considered at the time that placing the nuclear missiles in Cuba was "an act of duplicity and of defiance which had no parallel even in the trying years just passed."[13]

Almost immediately, the opinions were polarized. The "hawks" in the group, a great majority at first, considered it was absurd to leave the initiative to the Russians and called for immediate direct military action against Cuba. To the Joint Chiefs of Staff the issue was clear; now was the time to do the job for which they had prepared contingency plans. Cuba I (the Bay of Pigs invasion) had been badly done; Cuba II would not be. The missiles provided the occasion to deal with the issue: clearing the Western hemisphere of Castro's Communism.[14]

All plans were drawn for an invasion of the island which, according to a confidential report submitted by Secretary Robert S. McNamara, would require 250,000 men, 2,000 air sorties against targets in Cuba, and 90,000 Marines and Airborne in the invasion force. One Pentagon estimate of the American casualties put the expected figure over 25,000.[15]

But, finally, President Kennedy's opinion prevailed in convincing the group not to act directly against Cuba, but to fence the island in so as to prevent further deliveries of offensive weapons sent by the Russians. From that moment on, the Russian ships bound for the Island would be intercepted on the high seas and searched by the U.S. Navy and this would continue until the Soviet Union removed her missiles from Cuba.[16] Therefore, instead of taking actions against Cuba, Kennedy took actions against what he considered the cause of evil, the Soviet Union.

The final part of this story is well known. At the last moment, the Soviet ships turned prudently back just before reaching the American limiting perimeter. Khrushchev, who just some hours before had mounted a world-wide campaign against the "American lie" and had sent a letter to President Kennedy refusing to confirm the presence of Soviet nuclear missiles on the island, denouncing at the same time "the folly of degenerate imperialism and American piracy," suddenly got cold feet, did an unexpected about face, and sent the famous message to President Kennedy agreeing to the dismantling of the Cuban missile bases in exchange only for the simple American promise of not invading the island.

Kennedy had pulled off the greatest coup of his career —the first military victory of the nuclear era. It was a victory not only over the Soviet Union, but over many of his own advisers who from the start favored a more militant course of action.[17]

And today, forty years later, it still doesn't make much sense why Nikita Khrushchev gambled into provoking the United States to the point of nuclear war. Did he underestimate Kennedy's personal courage? Did he feel so threatened by American ICBM superiority that he was driven to a desperate act? Did he plan to use Cuba as a cover for ousting the United States from Berlin? Or did he simply believe that only the presence of missiles in Cuba would deter a further American invasion of the Island? Why did Nikita Khrushchev behave in such a weird fashion; first, deploying the missiles in Cuba, and, secondly, taking them out in such a great rush?

Just after the Cuban missile crisis was over, Henry Kissinger wrote that he could not understand why the Soviet Union should have installed strategic nuclear weapons in Cuba. In an article in *The Reporter*, he said it was "difficult to explain Soviet actions except as a colossal blunder. The Russians clearly misjudged the character of the President and the mood of the country ... Given the vulnerability of those bases, it is difficult to understand to what military problem they were addressed."[18]

Until now no one has found a satisfactory answer to the question of why Khrushchev took the unprecedented step of deploying major strategic nuclear weapons —never deployed before on the territory of its East European satellites despite the huge Soviet ground forces there— outside its formal alliance system. So far, the vast literature of the Cuban missile crisis contains no credible diagnosis by President Kennedy or his brother Robert, nor by any of his aides, as to what they thought led the Soviet Premier to try to put nuclear missiles in Cuba in the first place. Sorensen's book on Kennedy lists some possible reasons for Khrushchev's move, but these speculations merely indicate that the Kennedy administration either never resolved the question or didn't want the public to know what they actually knew. In 1982, twenty years after the crisis, a group of former Ex-Comm members made an appraisal of the crisis, and the title of their report, as reported in *The New York Times*, was highly revealing of their state of mind: "Twenty Years After, the Riddles Still Remain."

Today, forty years after the crisis, and after a veritable mountain of books and academic papers have been published, based on "declassified documents," "critical oral history," and shocking revelations by alleged participants in the crisis, the riddles still remain. Khrushchev's real purpose is still as obscure today as it was forty years ago, and no plausible explanation has been offered that can fully explain his hidden motives.[19]

Proof of this is that in early 1987, during the Hawk's Cay conference on the missile crisis, Richard Ned Lebow had to admit, "As I look over the evidence, it becomes less and less clear to me why Khrushchev did this."[20] In the same volume Robert S. McNamara stated, "I think the main puzzle we face in the Cuban episode is this: What in God's name did Khrushchev think he was doing? I'm not sure I have any idea, and I'm not sure we will ever find out."[21] Theodore Sorensen, another participant in the crisis, still cannot understand Khrushchev's motives: "The only honest answer I have is: 'I don't know now, and I didn't know then.' None of us knew. We could only speculate about what Khrushchev was up to."[22] Arnold Horelick, the author of an important book on the crisis,[23] confessed "I just don't know." ... "I've thought about this question since 1962, and I have concluded that there is no entirely plausible explanation of why the Soviets did what they did."[24]

The only thing that seems certain, however, is that there is a consensus that Khrushchev had gambled and lost. Whatever his plan had been, it had failed, and failed rather grandly.[25]

PART ONE

Living With a Goat

Chapter 1

Khrushchev's Lies

The first person from the Soviet side to provide an explanation for the strange event we know as the Cuban missile crisis was Alexei Kosygin, the Vice-Premier of the Soviet Union, when he spoke to a small inner circle of the Soviet Communist Party and government. In his speech, Kosygin said that the Cubans had asked the U.S.S.R. for missiles because they feared for the safety of their country. Though, after his fall, Khrushchev was accused of lying and concocting "hairbrained schemes," the official Soviet version of the event still was that, in view of the constant threat of American intervention, the U.S.S.R. and Cuba reached an agreement in the second half of 1962, by which the Soviet Union would place powerful means of defense in Cuba, including missiles and medium-range bombers.[1]

Khrushchev Speaks

When Nikita Khrushchev spoke some days later to the Supreme Soviet, on December 12, he added nothing to what Kosygin already said, but he stressed the fact that the Soviet Union had saved Cuba from American aggression.[2] In his lengthy report, Khruschev stated that the missiles were sent to Cuba solely at the request of the Cubans, exclusively for their protection. Apparently Khrushchev was so interested in spreading his own version of the event that he even went as far as spending thousands of dollars of their always badly needed hard currency to have his speech printed in more than ten prominent foreign newspapers.

But not everybody agrees with Khrushchev's version of the story. Harvard's Soviet specialist Adam Ulam goes as far as to call Khrushchev's assertion that the Cubans requested the missiles "a clumsy lie."[3] Ulam considers the claim that the missiles were meant to defend Cuba to be "laughable."[4] The explanation advanced by Khruschev that the missiles were intended solely or primarily to deter a U.S. attack on Cuba has also been examined in detail and rebutted by crisis scholars Arnold Horelick, Myron Rush,[5] Roger Hilsman,[6] and Adam B. Ulam.[7]

Notwithstanding all evidence on the contrary, however, a barrage of disinformation spread by "oral history" and new declassified "documents," mostly surfaced on several conferences about the crisis, has reinforced the notion that Khrushchev's main goal was to protect Castro and his revolution. According to authors Lebow and Stein, "Almost every Soviet official who claims any knowledge of the missile deployment insists that one of its important objectives was to protect Fidel Castro and his revolution,"[8] adding that "Khrushchev derived enormous personal satisfaction from his assistance to Cuba."[9] But, as I will show below in detail, in order to believe Khrushchev's story one also has to believe that the Soviet Premier was either a fool, a kook, or a masochist, and there is no evidence that he was any of these.

It was not too long after Khrushchev's speech to the Supreme Soviet, however, that the contradictions of his argument became clear for all to see. From the very beginning, Khrushchev's version of the facts seemed foolish. Furthermore, it did not explain the bizarre methods he used to get the missiles into Cuba, or his paralyzing terror when he was caught in the act, or the sudden rush to bring them out, or his secret negotiations with Kennedy behind Castro's back.

It is evident that to achieve the limited political objectives he claimed, Khrushchev need not have invested so heavily nor risked so much. If his sole aim was to defend Cuba from the American "imperialists," as he declared in his report, he could have achieved that with much more effectiveness by other simpler means, so it is obvious that his real purpose had little or nothing to do with his claimed aim.

During the course of the Ex Comm meetings, several hypotheses, some of them overlapping and some inconsistent, were offered trying to answer why Khrushchev had made such a drastic and dangerous departure from the usual Soviet practice. One of the hypotheses was that Khrushchev conceived the move to use the island as a barter. According to this hypothesis, the Soviet chairman placed the strategic missiles in Cuba as a bargaining chip to obtain leverage on the U.S. to be used later in a summit meeting or in a U.N. confrontation with President Kennedy. During the crisis there was also wide-spread speculation that Khrushchev attempted to set up a "horse trade" with the U.S. through his Cuban venture —missiles in Cuba for missiles in Turkey.

A careful evaluation of the details of the Russian operation, however, casts heavy doubts upon this hypothesis. First, it is questionable that the Soviet Union would have accepted the cost and risk of such a delicate and complex operation just to force an exchange of the U.S. missiles in Turkey. It is almost sure that Khrushchev already knew a year before that the phasing out of the American missiles in Turkey had been under consideration long before the crisis.[10] The Soviet intelligence must have been aware that the Kennedy administration had decided the previous year to remove the American missiles from Turkey. Anyway, they were obsolete, clumsy liquid-fuel rockets. The American plan was to replace them with missile-bearing Polaris submarines stationed in the Mediterranean.[11]

The second of Khrushchev's messages, in which he offered to swap the Soviet missiles in Cuba for the U.S. missiles in Turkey presented President Kennedy with a strange and ironic situation: he had already decided the previous year to remove them. The wisdom of risking a nuclear war over the removal of missiles that were soon to be removed is questionable; unless we assume that the proposition was no more than a smoke-screen laid by Khrushchev to divert attention from his real objective, now in jeopardy.

It is more likely that the exchange proposal was an improvised position to cover unexpected unfavorable contingencies, but it was not what he had expected after the culmination of the Cuban venture. A fact supporting this possibility is that Khrushchev even failed to prepare the Soviet media for it. On the same day that his exchange proposal to Kennedy appeared in the first page of *Izvestia*, a commentary on an inside page stated: "There are those in the U.S.A. who speculate that in exchange for denying Cuba the ability to repel American aggression, one might 'give up' some American base close to Soviet territory... Such 'proposals,' if you can call them that, merely serve to betray the unclean conscience of the authors."[12] It is useful to keep in mind that *Izvestia's* editor was Khrushchev's son-in-law Alexei Adzhubei, one of his closest collaborators, obviously involved to some extent in the Cuban venture. Therefore, barter was not Khrushchev's initial aim.

According to another hypothesis, the Soviet Union had discovered its strategic inferiority and wanted to close the missile gap. Placing missiles so near American shores would give the Russian rockets a real advantage over the American ones.

The Russians, however, could not effectively use their missiles in Cuba until after they had already fired their intercontinental ballistic missiles from the Soviet Union. The time advantage the U.S.S.R. supposedly had achieved by deploying strategic missiles just off the American coast was meaningless, because an initial rocket salvo fired from the Soviet Union would undoubtedly trigger a devastating American retaliation both on Cuba and the Soviet Union even before the ICBMs from Russia could hit the American soil. On the other hand, even a rocket salvo fired from Cuba alone, which lacked the capacity for totally destroying the U.S. retaliatory capabilities, would bring a devastating counterblow to the Soviet Union. Therefore, in order to hit their targets simultaneously, the Soviet artillerymen would have to calculate the firing time of their missiles very carefully: first, firing the long-range missiles in the Soviet Union, then, the intermediate-range missiles also in the Soviet Union, and, only later, the medium-range missiles in Cuba —a feat almost impossible for the Russians to reach given the state of their technological development at that time.[13] Only in that way could the Russians stand any chance of crippling America's second-strike capability, but this obviously would wipe out any time advantage in having Russian missile bases ninety miles from the U.S. mainland.[14] Therefore, missile power could not have been Khrushchev's goal.

Another theory explains that the action was part of Cold War politics. The Soviet Premier believed that Americans lacked the will to risk nuclear war and, confronted with the *fait accompli* of Soviet missiles in Cuba they could do nothing except complain to the U.N. If such a thing were to happen, the U.S. would appear weak and irresolute to the world and that would cause, in the long run, the American allies to doubt the value of the Americans' word and to seek accommodation with the Soviets. If this test of American will succeed, Khrushchev could move the Soviet forces into West Berlin and ultimately increase Soviet penetration in Latin America.

One must wonder, however —as Robert McNamara, former Secretary of Defense and advocate of this hypothesis has wondered— why did Khrushchev need to further poke the firmness of American intentions after the stormy American stand in Berlin in 1961? Furthermore, the size of the alleged Soviet missile deployment was disproportionate with a mere political probe. The choice of Cuba as the location for a probe was so militarily disadvantaged for the Russians that this sole consideration suffices to discard this hypothesis.

According to another hypothesis that wholly agrees with Khrushchev's own explanation, the Soviet Union had ample reasons for wanting to protect Cuba from an American attempt to invade the island. "We had no other way of helping them meet the American threat except to install our missiles on the island...," explained Khrushchev.[15] Yet, the facts seem to indicate that the deploying of strategic nuclear weapons in Cuba was the less suited method if deterrence from a major U.S. attack was the Soviet goal. First, because tactical weapons could have made the job much better and with less cost. And, second, because a better solution would have been the presence of a sizeable contingent of Soviet troops in Cuba so that the U.S. would think twice about attacking the Island to avoid a large number of casualties. These Soviet forces would have been close to the military strength of the allied forces in West Berlin.[16]

Moreover, if Khrushchev's aim was to protect the Island, he could have achieved that with much greater effectiveness by associating Cuba with the Warsaw Pact or by signing a defense treaty, like the one signed in 1964 with East Germany which specified that any armed attack against one of the contracting parties would oblige the other to give immediate military assistance. Khrushchev was fully aware that the missiles could not be used against a U.S. invasion because a Soviet transgression of the nuclear threshold in response to an American use of conventional lower levels of violence would be wildly irrational since it would mean virtually the destruction of the Soviet Union and probably of the whole Soviet block. Moreover, Soviet Medium-Range Ballistic Missiles (MRBMs), even with their alleged range, could not reach either New York or Chicago.[17]

Therefore, it was obvious that the Soviet leader intended for the missiles to accomplish more complex tasks than the defense of the Castro regime as he claimed, and his real motives had little or nothing to do with this aim. On the other hand, in the Spring of 1962 the tensions in CubanSoviet relations were harsh, characterized by the removal of Aníbal Escalante and other old Communists, the expulsion of the Soviet ambassador from Cuba and the recall of the Cuban ambassador to the Soviet Union, which brought the two countries close to a break in diplomatic relations. Furthermore, far from being an asset for the Soviets, the Island, thanks mainly to Castro's crazy policies, had become a liability. Cuba's growing social and economic problems and Castro's adventuristic international policy were highly embarrassing for the Russians. All of the above, added to Khrushchev's growing suspicions about Castro's true allegiances and motives, made it highly improbable that the Soviet Premier had selected precisely that moment to send the missiles to Cuba to protect Fidel from an American invasion.

Fidel Tells His Version of the Story

After the crisis was over, Castro unexpectedly dropped by the University of Havana on several occassions and engaged in informal conversations with the students. In some of those exchanges he affirmed that, if he could, he would have beaten up Khrushchev. When some students asked him why the Russians took the missiles back to Russia, he answered with evident irony: "Those *señores* (gentlemen, as opposed to the friendly "comrades") asked us permission to install them here, and we agreed. We don't know why they brought them in, and we don't now either why they took them out."[18]

Moreover, Castro himself made sure that all Cubans got the point. On October 29th, Cubans finally learned of the agreement between Kennedy and Khrushchev —at least officially, because most of them already knew about it via the *Voice of America*. Castro's official newspaper, *Revolución,* read, printed with big letters on page one: "Khrushchev orders missiles withdrawn from Cuba." The newspaper also published the text of the exchange of letters between Khrushchev and Kennedy, unknown until then in Cuba, and the dispatches of the news agencies from the start of the crisis to its end, never published by the Cuban press before. Obviously, the publication of that information was not a personal initiative of Carlos Franqui, editor of *Revolución*, but of an angry Fidel who in that way defined for the people the degree of his responsibility for the negotiations in which he had not participated.[19] In Havana, pro-Soviet posters were torn off in rage from walls. Both militiamen and "spontaneous" conga[20] dancers marched through Havana's streets intoning: *"Nikita mariquita; lo que se da no se quita"* ("Nikita, you little sissy; what one gives, doesn't take back"), berating Khruschev and the Soviets for leaving them in the lurch.

Castro, though deeply angered, refrained for some time from distressing his Soviet "allies" even more by not disagreeing openly with their version of how the missile affair had started. However in January, 1963, adding to Khrushchev's further embarrassment, he gave his first version of the episode, categorically denying that Cuba had ever asked for "strategic arms" to be installed on the Island and advancing his own account of the episode. According to Castro, far from having asked for missiles, the Soviets told him to ask for them.[21]

Later, in February, during a dinner given for Claude Julien of the French newspaper *Le Monde*, he asserted that, far from asking Moscow for missiles, the Soviet Union had foisted them on Cuba for the alleged purpose of "strengthening international socialism." In March, *Le Monde* published Julien's interview with Castro and almost immediately the Cuban authorities issued a document denying that

Castro had given the interview to Julien, but not denying Castro's key phrases quoted by the French journalist. According to Julien, Castro's words were: "Moscow offered them to us... Such is the truth even if other explanations are provided elsewhere...," adding that for him Khrushchev's intentions were "a mystery."[22] In *Le Monde's* March 22 installment of his interview, Castro was quoted as saying: "What support did we get during the [U.S.] blockade last October when we were on the edge of a major conflict? Where were big mass demonstrations in our favor noticed? What did the revolutionaries of Europe and Latin America do? Only the Venezuelans reacted then. But the big parties that call themselves revolutionaries did not budge. They are not revolutionaries, but bureaucrats. They are satellites." Castro's harsh criticism now extended to the pro-Soviet communist parties all around the world.

Later that same year, Fidel gave more details to French journalist Jean Daniel about how the Russians had warned him that the Americans were about to invade the Island and told him that the only way to freeze them up was to build missile sites. Daniel's interview with Fidel appeared in *L'Express* and in *The Washington Post,* and shows very well how the Russians managed to persuade the Cuban leader into thinking that the U.S. was about to launch an attack on Cuba. Castro's words to Daniel are so important that they deserve to be quoted in detail:

> Six months before the installation of these missiles in Cuba, we had an accumulation of information telling us of new preparations for an invasion of the island, preparations undertaken by the CIA, whose directors were mortified by the failure of the Bay of Pigs and by the fact that they saw themselves as ridiculous in the eyes of the world and ill treated by the American Government.
>
> We knew also that the Pentagon would lend its authority to the CIA preparations, but we had our doubts as to the state of mind of the President. Some even believed that it was only necessary to alert him, to alarm him, to cause the project to fail.
>
> Then, one day, the son-in-law of Khrushchev, Alexei Adzhubei, came to visit us before going to Washington.[23] Upon his arrival in the U.S., Adzhubei was received by the chief of the American Government and they spoke, above all, about Cuba. One week after this interview, we received in Havana a copy of Adzhubei's report to Khruschev.
>
> It was the copy of this report that started everything. What had Kennedy said to Adzhubei? Listen well to this. It is very important. He had said that the new situation in Cuba was intolerable for the United States and that the American Government had decided to tolerate it no longer.
>
> He had said that pacific coexistence had been deeply compromised by the fact that Soviet influence in Cuba altered the balance of power, destroyed the accepted equilibrium and (now Castro spoke detaching each syllable),

KENNEDY HAD REMINDED THE RUSSIAN THAT THE UNITED STATES HAD NOT INTERVENED IN HUNGARY, which evidently was a way of exacting Russian nonintervention in the event of an invasion.

Obviously the term "invasion" was not pronounced, and Adzhubei, uninformed at that time, could not draw the same conclusions as we did. But when we had communicated to Khrushchev all our previous information, they began to interpret the Kennedy-Adzhubei conversation in our sense and they set about gathering information. At the end of the month, the Russian and Cuban governments became certain that a landing in Cuba might happen at any moment. This is the truth.

What should we do? How could we be warned of the invasion? In Khrushchev we found the same preoccupations as we had. He asked us what we wanted. We answered him: arrange that the United States understands that to attack Cuba is to attack the Soviet Union. How to accomplish this aim? After these questions the discussions and planning began.

We thought of a proclamation, of an alliance, of classic military assistance. The Russians explained to us that they had a double preoccupation: save the Cuban revolution (meaning, their Socialist honor in the world) and at the same time avoid a world conflict. In their opinion, if we settled for conventional armaments, the United States might not hesitate before invading. In that case, Russia would retaliate and it would mean an inevitable world war.

. . .

Under these conditions, how could the Cubans refuse to share the risks taken to save us? It is, on the whole, a question of honor! No? You believe that honor does not count in politics? That we are romantics? Perhaps. Why not? In any case, we are militants.

Briefly, we agreed on the installation of missiles. Moreover, it must be said that for us Cubans, it did not make much difference whether we died by a conventional bomb or by a hydrogen one. But all the same, we did not play with world peace. It is the United States who played with peace using war as a blackmail to stifle revolutions.

Then, in the month of June, 1962, my brother Raúl and Che Guevara went to Moscow to discuss the arrangements for installing the missiles. The convoy arrived by sea three weeks later. The United States managed to learn that it contained armaments, of course, but it took them two months to discover that the armaments were missiles. Two months —that is more than we had calculated. For it is evident that it was a question of intimidation and not of committing an aggression.[24]

When Lee Lockwood asked Fidel in 1965 about the time the decision was taken, and upon whose initiative it was, to install Soviet nuclear missiles in Cuba,

Castro answered: "Naturally the missiles would not have been sent in the first place if the Soviet Union had not been prepared to send them. But they wouldn't have sent [them] either if we had not felt the need for some measures that would unquestionably protect the country."[25] But Castro didn't mention to Lockwood that what really made him think about the necessity to take measures against a U.S. aggression was the copy of Adzhubei's report on his talk with Kennedy.

In 1984, Castro brought up the subject again. This time he said to Tad Szulc that the crisis of 1962 was born from a conviction by both the Cuban and the Soviet governments that the U.S. was preparing to invade Cuba with its own forces. "We took it up with the Soviets," Castro said. "They had already made great commitments to us, and they asked our opinion. We told them —though we didn't speak of missiles— that it was necessary to make it clear that an invasion of Cuba would mean war with the Soviet Union... it could be a military pact." ... "Then they proposed the missiles," he added. "The installation of medium-range missiles was analyzed among other measures."[26]

I seems, however, that Castro is not yet convinced that Cuba's protection was Khrushchev's main motive. In a book published in 2001, but initially published in a slightly different version in 1995, Carlos Lechuga, Cuba's ambassador to the United Nations at the time of the crisis, expresses his belief that "So, there are three different stories concerning the birth of an idea which was *officially declared* to have been devised to help Cuba defend itself against attack by the United States.[27] Given the facts that Lechuga lives in Cuba, that he is in good standing with Castro, and that Ocean Press, the book's publisher, is a front for the Cuban intelligence services, one can safely surmise that Lechuga is only expressing Castro's suspicions that Khrushchev's true motives were other than Cuba's defense.

But we know beyond a reasonable doubt that the Americans were not going to invade the island —at least at that time— and that the Soviets were fully aware of it. Therefore, Adzhubei's report on Kennedy's remarks about Hungary was nothing but a fabrication. The false report was Khrushchev's pretext to dangle in front of Fidel the mouth-watering bait of powerful weapons within his easy reach, and the power-hungry *Comandante* swallowed the bait, hook, line, and sinker.

Khrushchev's Schemes

Most analysts agree that the Soviet Premier's decision to install strategic missiles capable of carrying nuclear warheads in Cuba must have been taken some time around May 1962, during a visit he made to Bulgaria on May 14-20, 1962. If one is to believe Khrushchev, during the visit,

> One thought kept hammering away at my brain: what will happen if we lose Cuba? I knew it would have been a terrible blow to Marxism-Leninism. It would gravely diminish our stature throughout the world, but especially

in Latin America. If Cuba fell, other Latin American countries would reject us, claiming that for all our might the Soviet Union hadn't been able to do anything for Cuba except to make empty protests to the Unites States.[28]

By that time, Raúl Castro, Cuban Minister of Defense and Fidel's brother, was in Moscow, and was informed of the decision to send missiles to Cuba. Most likely he was not told precisely what type of missiles the Russians would install, and surely he wasn't told what their real purpose was. At that moment the Cubans lacked the technological knowledge and sophistication to ask questions about the characteristics of the missiles. They were probably told that the Russians would simply supply some defensive missiles, the details of which they did not need to be worried about because they were to be under Russian control first before the Cubans got the necessary training to operate them.

At the end of August, 1962, Che Guevara was hurriedly dispatched to Moscow. Undoubtedly the Cubans were puzzled and concerned about what was taking place in their own land. On that occasion a Soviet communiqué acknowledged that in order to protect Cuba from "aggressive imperialist threats," the Soviet government would send armament to the Island and military technical specialists to train Cuban servicemen.

In view of the increasing concern in the United States over the volume of Russian military shipments to Cuba, President Kennedy issued a statement in September saying that American intelligence sources had learned that the Russians were setting up in Cuba "anti-aircraft defense missiles with a slant range of twenty-five miles," radar installations, etc., and that they were also sending military technicians to the Island. But the President stressed that, as far as he knew, no Soviet bases or "offensive ground-to-ground missiles" had been or were being installed. "Were it be otherwise," he said, "the gravest issue will arise."[29]

That same day, the Soviet ambassador Anatoly Dobrynin conveyed through Attorney General Robert Kennedy a most unusual message from Premier Khrushchev to President Kennedy. In it the Soviet leader promised that he would not stir up any international crisis before the American congressional elections in early November. One week later the Soviet press agency *TASS* published an official release corroborating the Soviet policy of not transferring nuclear weapons to other nations. According to *TASS*, the Soviet weapons were so powerful and its rockets so accurate that the Soviet Union did not need to search for sites for them beyond its borders.[30]

The more one examines the evidence about the missile crisis of 1962, the more obvious it becomes that Khrushchev lied to everyone involved. First of all he lied to Fidel Castro, when he told him about the necessity to defend Cuba against an imminent invasion, when he knew very well that no U.S. invasion was about to happen at that moment. Neither did he have the least intention of backing Castro's military adventures in third world countries. Khrushchev also failed to explain that the United States had been prepared to attack Cuba not despite the presence of

Soviet missiles, but precisely because the missiles were there.[31] In fact, the Soviet weapons provoked rather than deterred an American aggression.

Not even the Chinese failed to notice the inconsistencies in Khrushchev's arguments. A September 1963 statement by a spokesman of the Chinese government asserted that,

> Although the tension in the Caribbean sea stemmed from the U.S. imperialist policy of aggression against Cuba and although there has been a continuing danger of an invasion of Cuba by the U.S. imperialists, nevertheless, before the Soviet Union sent rockets into Cuba, there did not exist a crisis of the United States using nuclear weapons in the Caribbean sea and of a nuclear war breaking out. If it should be said that such a crisis did arise, it was a result of the rash action of the Soviet leaders.[32]

Later that year, in a particularly bitter attack in *Ren-Min-Rih-Bao* on November 19, 1963, the Chinese communists accused Khrushchev of "nuclear fetishism," and of "recklessly playing with nuclear weapons." They also said that the Soviet Premier was guilty of "fawning before imperialist nuclear blackmail."

Khrushchev also lied to Kennedy, whom he had promised not to annoy during the 1962 election campaign, and to whom he had given his word never to send offensive weapons to Cuba. And, finally, he lied to his own people, by telling them the false information about an imminent U.S. attack on Cuba.

To top it off, most military experts agreed at the time that, from a purely strategic point of view, a missile base in Cuba would have had almost no effect in the Russo-American balance of power and would not have given the Russians even a short-term advantage. And, last but not least, placing those dangerous weapons so near the trigger-happy Fidel was very risky indeed, even if from Havana the missiles could not reach Moscow.

It is not necessary to be a military expert to recognize that Polaris-type missiles carried by submarines —like the ones the Russians were beginning to deploy in their subs— were much more difficult to detect and destroy than the missiles allegedly deployed in Cuba. The Americans themselves had come to acknowledge that non-hardened fixed launching pads, like the ones the Russians were building in Cuba, were greatly exposed to enemy attack, and, as I mentioned above, it was well known a year before the missile crisis that the U.S. had decided to eliminate the outdated, clumsy liquid-fuel missiles from Turkey and replace them with missile-bearing Polaris submarines. Had Soviet missiles fired from Cuba struck the United States there would have been retaliation not only against the firing base but against the Soviet Union itself. It was therefore absurd, and Khrushchev must have known it, to believe that those weapons could have been used in a local Cuban-American conflict without affecting the U.S.S.R.

Moreover, Soviet behavior during the crisis evidences that Khrushchev did not even expect the kind of American response his action elicited —a menacing posture directed not against Cuba, but against the Soviet Union. Yet, it is impossible to think that Khrushchev believed that President Kennedy was going to accept his bold move with crossed hands. Therefore, if he was not expecting a U.S. action against the Soviet Union, nor a do-nothing policy, what were his expectations about the possible actions Americans would take vis-à-vis his provocative move?

Almost all the scholars who have studied the Cuban Missile Crisis coincide in asserting that, with his foolish behavior, Khrushchev placed in American hands the long sought pretext for an invasion of Cuba. But, taking into account that Nikita Sergeevich Khrushchev was anything but a fool, the only explanation left that makes all the pieces in this puzzle fit to conform a sensible pattern, is that he placed the missiles in Cuba because he wanted the Americans to invade Cuba and become his unwitting accomplices in overthrowing Fidel Castro.

The idea that Khrushchev's move was a trap set to catch the American President is not new. In fact it was just one more among the several hypotheses advanced by some Ex Comm members at the very beginning of the crisis. Apparently, however, the idea seemed too far-fetched to be credible and it was soon discarded.[33] Moreover, dubious information surfaced in recent years as a result of meetings where alleged participants in the crisis revealed new, incredible "facts," as well as information from alleged declassified documents, seem to deny this explanation of Khrushchev's actions. Anyway, I will use it as a working hypothesis and in the course of this book I will develop my arguments following these lines.

According to my hypothesis, Khrushchev's purpose was two-fold: first, to get rid of the troublesome Fidel without being blamed himself for it. Secondly, to place the Americans in a very difficult position before the world and their own consciences, after an attack by the U.S., a big and powerful nation, against such a small country as Cuba. Even more important, the eventual discovery after an American invasion that there were no nuclear warheads in Cuba, and that the missiles were actually dummies, would have left the Americans with egg smeared all over their faces, instantly making them the laughing stock of the whole world.

An American invasion of Cuba could have solved Khrushchev's *Fidelista* problem and, making good use of the American discredit on his behalf, would have inherited *Fidelismo,* but without the troublesome Fidel —exactly the same way that, some years later, Fidel himself got rid of Che and inherited *Guevarismo* without the troublesome Guevara.

Chapter 2

Castro's Unexplainable Rush to Communism

> *"All right," said the cat; and this time it vanished quite slowly, beginning with the end of the tail, and ending with the grin, which remained some time after the rest of it had gone.*
>
> —Lewis Carroll. *Alice's Adventures in Wonderland.*

The Cuban revolution is a very strange political phenomenom. Hugh Thomas mentioned the intriguing characteristics of the revolution that took place in Cuba, one of the richest countries in Latin America, where a Marxist regime was established seemingly because of the will of a single man, who is a very untypical Marxist.[1]

One of the American writers who initially studied the Castro phenomenon with the most insight is Theodore Draper. He began one of his studies on the Castroist revolution with the significant phrase: "Who is Fidel Castro? What is he?"[2] Even Herbert Mathews, the *New York Times* journalist that helped Fidel to became known worldwide, affirmed in a letter to Draper: "Castro is an enigma."[3] Carlos Franqui, a former close associate of Castro and the editor of *Revolución* — for some years the official *Fidelista* newspaper—, wrote that after the rebel army took Havana in 1959, "... as far as ideology was concerned, nothing was clear, and Fidel was the greatest enigma of all."[4]

The enigma subsisted. Twenty-five years after Castro took power in Cuba, Professor Michael Erisman, in an insightful analysis of Castro's foreign policy, claimed that Castro "is undoubtedly one of the most intriguing figures of the twentieth century."[5] Professor Herbert S. Dinerstein, in a book about the Cuban missile crisis, rightly asserted that "In presenting so many different facets to the public view, Castro creates the puzzle of who the real Castro is."[6] Like Alice's Cheshire cat, Fidel Castro has disappeared behind his grin, and the grin has almost completely blurred the cat behind it.

Latin America and the Soviets

Before Castro's take-over of Cuba in 1959 and his stormy love affair and later shotgun wedding to the Soviet Union, the Kremlin's strategies in Latin America were characterized by caution. A reason for this was the relative weakness of their puppet communist parties in Latin America and the lack of an industrial proletariat, a necessary condition —according to Marxist dogma— to the development of revolutionary movements. Anyway, there is no doubt that Stalin would not have enjoyed any communist experiment in Latin American, particularly one out of his total control. During the war years, the Russians considered that good relations with the United States was much more important than communist advances in Mexico, Venezuela, Chile or Cuba.

Another reason was that the Soviet Union was relatively weak in those days. To the Soviets, recognition by the United States, access to American technology and industrial equipment, and American help in World War II, were much more important to Moscow than relatively minor communist successes in an area mostly under the control of the U.S., where Washington had long ago claimed a predominant interest and influence.[7]

Even when a revolutionary climate developed in Mexico in the 1930's, and the local Communists thought about making a grab for power, the Russians then gave no support to strike for political control on their own. During these low-profile years, the Soviet Press reported the activities of Latin American communist parties without too much fanfare. The tiny American Communist Party was suffered by the Americans as a bothersome fact of life —like pollution and taxes— but a communist state in the Americas, the Russian leaders apparently believed, would surely have created an undesirable disturbance in the American political body.

The Soviets knew of the growing current of anti-Americanism among Latin American members of the intelligentsia, as well as the chronic social and economic problems of the continent and the growing importance of Wall Street investments in the region. But, notwithstanding the potential for creating trouble for the Americans in their own back yard, they continued to follow their cautious policy even after World War II, despite the Cold War and the changing power configuration in Latin America.

On November 7, 1933, the Cuban communists attempted a small revolution of their own and established a full-fledged "Soviet" of farmers and workers in the Oriente province, in the eastern part of Cuba. Peasants seized the land they had been working on, and a mini-communist regime backed by a militia of "red guards" took control. This communist experiment lasted for several months, but ended in failure. The Kremlin leaders were not pleased with the attempt.

Paradoxically, it was Fulgencio Batista —the same dictator Castro overthrew in January 1, 1959, and that way opened the road for Castro to grab power— who in his first term in the presidency legalized the Communist party in Cuba. Batista even allowed the Cuban Communists to found a newspaper called *Noticias de Hoy*, (known to most people simply as *Hoy*) which began publication on May, 1938. Some months later, in September, Batista legalized the Communist party for the first time in the history of the country.

In the coming years, the communists advanced a lot in Cuba. In the elections of 1940 ten communists were elected to the Chamber of Deputies, and a communist was elected mayor of Santiago de Cuba, the Island's second largest city. During WWII, the collaboration between Batista and the communists became even closer, and the dictator, as a way of recognition for their support, appointed in 1943 some communists to his Cabinet. Moreover, Batista allowed the communists to infiltrate and eventually control a large segment of the labor movement and to exert some power in the Ministry of Labor.[8] Thus, one fnds that before Castro took power in 1959 a cohesive and skilled communist party already existed in Cuba. But, though they were highly skilled in labor and political activities, and worked under a strict party discipline and ideological unity, they were apparently happy with their meager gains and never evidenced any enthusiasm to the idea of taking the political power in Cuba by means of democratic elections and much less by armed violence.

As late as 1954, the overthrow of Arbenz's communist-oriented government in Guatemala, largely the result of the CIA's dirty work acting as a hidden hand to protect the business interests of the unscrupulous Dulles brothers and their powerful friends, brought only a feeble reaction from Moscow. This prudence and restrain, however, began to disappear after Soviet space successes surprised and shocked the world in 1957 and Nikita S. Khrushchev launched his campaign of "Sputnik diplomacy" on a global basis. But even then the Kremlin did not consider Latin America as a prime political target, or "ripe for revolution." The Kremlin politicians instead set out to expand Soviet presence in the area by attempting to project an image of international respectability; an image of the Soviet Union as a great economic power possessing a well-developed industrial machine with advanced technology capable of accomplishing great feats in space and willing — through the development of normal trade and cultural relations— to share peacefully these accomplishments with other nations. Apparently, Khrushchev's goal was to prove the effectiveness` of Communism as a political and economic formula in the eyes of the developing nations, or, as he liked to say, "To demonstrate before the world the superiority of Communism over Capitalism."[9]

If one follows closely the Soviet policy toward Latin America, certain conclusions can be drawn. First of all, the area did not have top priority for the Soviets during most of this period, though they had stood ready to take advantage of any favorable development. Second, until 1960 they had had only modest success in their attempts. The turn of events in Cuba gave them an unexpected opportunity to extend Soviet influence, but it was not clear that they wanted to assume the responsibilities —either economic or political— foisted upon them by the unexpected events.[10]

Before 1959, Soviet objectives in Latin America seem to have been twofold. On one side, the Kremlin's short-term political objectives had been focused at increasing the number of countries extending diplomatic recognition to the U.S.S.R. and to increase its trade with the countries of the area. On the other side, and sometimes in direct conflict with the former, a close look at the party literature at the time shows that the Soviet's longer-run objectives had remained what they always had been: to gain, under the name of the Marxist ideology, influence and control on the Latin American republics of the hemisphere.

The Cuban Communist Party, though politically strong, ideologically had languished for a long time in the usual Latin American Communist style. In mid 1958, with Fidel Castro still in the Sierra Maestra mountains fighting his guerrilla war against Batista's troops, the Cuban Communists, after totally ignoring Castro for many long months, made secret contact with him. At that moment Castro's forces consisted of no more than a few hundred men and he was far from reaching the victory, but Batista's days seemed numbered and Castro was becoming —with the help of the American government and mainstream media— the symbol of the resistance against Batista's dictatorship.[11]

Under such circumstances the Cuban communists, who had shown their opportunistic inclinations before, realized that a closer alliance with the man who was rapidly becoming a major player in the fight against Batista was the intelligent thing to do. Bearing in mind the strict discipline of the pro-Soviet Cuban Communist party, one may assume that this alliance was authorized and perhaps even suggested by Moscow, particularly at a time of Soviet alliances with nationalistic movements and leaders such as Nasser in Egypt, Sukarno in Indonesia, Nkrumah in Ghana, Sekou Toure in Guinea and the FNL in Algeria. The sure thing is that Moscow gave the green light to the PSP, and from mid-1958 on the communists began supporting Castro.

The Cuban Communists and Fidel

It was widely known in Cuba that the *ñángaras* (Cuban nickname for the local Communists) had never been among Castro's friends. More than a problem of personal affinities, this attitude was the direct result of their blind adherence to Moscow's brand of Communism. So, one may assume that they were the first to be surprised at the triumph of a revolution without the guide of the sacrosanct Communist party.

Moreover, the previous relations between Castro and the communists had never been friendly, to say the least. Coinciding with Castro's attack on the Moncada garrisons in Santiago de Cuba on July 26, 1953, some members of the PSP hierarchy were also in Santiago attending a semiclandestine meeting. As soon as Batista was informed of the attack he accused the usual suspects: the communists.

When they knew of Batista's accusation, the communists rushed to explain that they had been in Santiago just by chance, for the sole purpose of celebrating the birthday party of Blas Roca, one of the members of the PSP's political bureau. One of them, Joaquín Ordoqui, distinguished himself above the rest by his vituperous abuse on Fidel. A few days later the PSP issued a public statement criticizing Castro's actions and repudiating his "putschist attempt" —putschist is communist parlance for fascist— as a desperate form of adventurism, typical of bourgeois circles lacking in principles and implicated in gangsterism.

The communists had strong reasons to be very angry with Castro. The attack on the Moncada barracks in 1953 brought difficult days for the Cuban communists. Batista suppressed their publications immediately after the attack, and the party itself was subsequently outlawed. As a result, the Cuban communists became even more resentful of Castro, and the PSP issued a statement —published in the *Daily Worker,* and circulated it clandestinely in Cuba because *Hoy*, the party's newspaper, had been banished— stating,

> We oppose the actions of Santiago de Cuba and Bayamo.[12] The putchist methods which were used are characteristic of bourgeois groups. This is an adventurous attempt to conquer military bases. The heroism manifested by the participants is wrong and unproductive; at its roots are mistaken bourgeois conceptions...
>
> The whole country knows who had organized, directed, and led the actions against the barracks. The line of the PSP and the mass movement has been and is: Fight against the Batista tyranny and then unmask the putchists and adventurers of the bourgeois opposition which act against the interest of the people! The PSP considers it necessary to bring the masses together in a united front against the government so as to find a democratic way out of the Cuban situation, to resurrect the constitution of 1940, to secure civil liberties, hold general elections and form a government of the national democratic front.
>
> In its fight, the PSP bases its support on the masses and condemns the putchist adventurism which is directed against the fight of the masses and against the democratic solution which the people desire.[13]

The communists had enough reasons for not trusting Castro. Though Fidel had some acquaintances among the Communists at the University of Havana, he was never known to be a communist himself. Moreover, many people, including the Cuban Communists, saw him as a fascist sympathizer or, at least an anticommunist, and their feelings were not based on hearsay but on facts.

In 1956, as a result of an article which appeared in *Bohemia,* a leading Cuban magazine, written by Luis Dam, a Spanish Republican in exile, Castro became involved in a controversy over the accusation that he was a Communist. According to Dam, the Mexican police had evidence that Castro was a member of the Communist Party.[14]

In his typical fashion, Castro quickly answered back in the next issue of *Bohemia* with an impassioned article he titled *"¡Basta ya de mentiras!"* (No more lies!). According to Castro, "Naturally the accusation of my being a Communist was absurd in the eyes of all who knew my public path in Cuba, without any kind of ties with the Communist Party." And added,

> I totally denounce Mr. Luis Dam's report where he says, 'Incidentally, the Federal Security Police affirms that Fidel is a member of the Communist Party.' Captain Gutiérrez Barros himself read me the report forwarded to the President of Mexico after a week of minute investigation; among its observations it was categorically affirmed that we had no ties whatsoever with Communist organizations. An extract of the report was published in all newspapers. I have before me *Excelsior* of June 26, page 8, column 6, paragraph 5, where it reads as follows: 'The Federal Bureau of Security emphasized that the 26th of July group has no Communist ties nor receives help from the Communists.'

Castro continued his diatribe accusing the Batista government of plotting against him and also reminding the Cuban Communists of their past collaboration with the Cuban dictator,

> The intrigue is ridiculous besides and without the least foundation because I have been a militant in only one political party, and that is the one founded by Eduardo Chibás.[15] What moral authority, on the other hand, does Mr. Batista have to speak of Communism, when he was the Communist Party's presidential candidate in the elections of 1940; if his electoral posters took shelter under the hammer and the sickle; if his pictures beside Blas Roca and Lázaro Peña[16] are still around; if half a dozen of his present ministers and trusted collaborators were well-known members of the Communist Party?[17]

Reminding the Cuban Communists of their past collaboration with the Cuban dictator was the worse attack they could receive. And even worse was Castro's innuendo, insinuating that they were still collaborating with Batista. As Theodore Draper rightly pointed out, it is really very hard to think of a Communist justifying himself in such bizarre way.[18]

Yet one can't blame the Communists for being so critical of Castro. Notwithstanding theories on the contrary, there is a great deal of evidence pointing to the fact that Castro was never a Marxist or a Communist. Javier Felipe Pazos, who met Fidel at the Sierra Maestra mountains, expressed his total disbelief in the theory that Castro was a Communist and that the revolution was a Communist conspiracy from the beginning.[19]

According to Carlos Franqui, not even Che Guevara considered Fidel to be a Communist at the times of the Sierra Maestra struggle. In a letter Che wrote in 1957, he asserted that he considered Fidel's movement motivated by the eagerness of the bourgeoisie to free itself from the economic chains of imperialism. And Che added that he always considered Fidel to be "an authentic left-wing bourgeois leader, although his figure is glorified by personal qualities of extraordinary brilliance that set him far above his class."[20] Franqui also rightly points out that neither the ideas nor the language of *History Will Absolve Me* —Castro's political statement at the Moncada trial— reveals a clandestine communism.[21]

Apparently some American officers agreed with Franqui. Soon after Fidel Castro's rise to power in 1959, Allen W. Dulles, the crafty Director of Central Intelligence, told a Senate committee at a secret briefing that the Cuban leader did not have any Communist affiliations. According to a 900 page declassified report released on March 27, 1982, Mr. Dulles said after Fidel Castro took power in Cuba: "We do not think that Castro himself has any Communist leanings,"... "We do not believe Castro is in the pay of or working for the Communists."[22]

The fact is that there is no evidence that any of Castro's followers was a Communist. They would follow Castro alone, and they would continue to follow him in blind faith up to the point of utter defeat, convinced of what they regarded as his almost supernatural powers.[23] While still in the Sierra Maestra, Castro repeatedly expressed democratic and anti-Communist opinions.[24] Of course, dealing with Fidel Castro one must always keep in mind that he is an accomplished liar.[25]

Faced with the 1961 announcement by Castro that he always had been a Marxist at heart, some authors have tried to prove the point *a posteriori,* though apparently with different intentions. Author Lionel Martin affirms that the Moncada's leadership nucleus studied Marxism together, and draws a chain of Marxist ideology around various leaders of the 26th of July Movement who themselves had some Marxist education and were involved with the Communists. As part of his argument that Castro was a Marxist since his university days, Martin claims that he was quite friendly with fellow students Leonel Soto, Alfredo Guevara, Flavio Bravo and Luis Más Martín, all members of the Communist youth organization.[26] But the argument is fallacious, because it is also known that Fidel was quite friendly with some homosexuals at the university, and there is no evidence that he was a homosexual himself.

Nathaniel Weyl claims that young Castro was recruited by an international Communist cell, and stresses Castro's student involvement with radical politics.[27]

The Russians Are Not Coming

On January 10, 1959, K. E. Voroshilov, in the name of the Soviet Union, officially recognized the new government of Cuba.[37] But the Castro government did not reciprocate. Still Cuba established no official relations with the Soviet Union.

When Castro took over the office of prime minister on February 16, 1959, the PSP was disappointed again. They were neither included in the new government nor were they permitted to expand their control in the labor unions. In fact, during the first six months of the new regime, little trace of the Communists was detectable in the revolutionary coalition, and known Communists had no official posts in either the primary or secondary echelons of government.[38]

Granted, after the triumph of the revolution on January 2, 1959, only one of the old political parties, the PSP, had been allowed to operate legally and officially. But the Communists were not in a pleasant position. They had no official representation in the new formed government; and it was evident that Fidel Castro and most of his people didn't trust them and felt some bitterness toward them. Some Communists even feared that a public rupture between Fidel and the Communists was a strong possibility.[39]

To make things worse, on May 21 Castro made a speech in which still held an openly anti-Communist position:

> Our revolution is neither capitalist nor Communist. What matters to us, who are attached to a humanist doctrine, are the people, and we mobilize all our energies for the good of the majority. We want to free mankind of every dogma; we want to make the economy and society free without terrorizing or forcing anyone. Today's world situation confronts us with the choice between capitalism which starves people and communism which solves their economic problems but suppresses their freedoms which are dear to them. ... Capitalism sacrifices the human being, communism with its totalitarian conceptions sacrifices human rights. We agree neither with the one nor the other. ... Our revolution is not red but olive green. It bears the color of the rebel army from the Sierra Maestra.[40]

The Communists were justifiably upset, and did not let Castro's attacks go unanswered. Aníbal Escalante, a senior PSP leader, accused Fidel of "ideological confusion." Subsequent polemics between the Communist and anti-Communist members of the M-26-7 were openly conducted in the pages of *Hoy,* the PSP newspaper, and *Revolución*, the official M-26-7 organ during all the spring and summer months of 1959.

On May 25-28, 1959, the PSP had a plenary session of its central committee, and its conclusions were openly critical of the policies Castro was following:

We are a small country that lies in the immediate vicinity of the U.S. The imperialist influence has deformed our economy; we are therefore dependent on imports when it comes to feeding our people. In view of these circumstances, all leftist-extremist tendencies and all excessive measures on the part of the Revolution, all attempts to ignore the realities and the concrete difficulties facing Cuba have to be sharply opposed.[41]

Seemingly concerned about Fidel's intentions,[42] the PSP also asked from the revolutionary leaders a profound revolutionary consciousness, a great firmness of conviction, and an invincible determination (that apparently they had strong doubts Fidel had), as well as a great flexibility and skill in tactics.[43]

Not only the relations between Fidel and the Cuban Communists was strained. In foreign policy too, Castro continued to hold the Soviet Union at arms length. At the end of January, Roberto Agramonte, foreign minister of the Cuban revolutionary government, declared that relations with Russia remained unchanged, that is, nonexistent. Writing in *Hoy*, Carlos Rafael Rodríguez, the main PSP ideologue, strongly criticized the Castro government for not having diplomatic relations with the Soviet Union.[44]

Fidel Pulls a Fast One

The available record proves that the Cuban Communists never trusted Fidel.[45] They were so cautious that in January 1959, after Castro's triumph, they sent a letter to President Urrutia in which they simply called for the restoration of the democratic-bourgeois Constitution of 1940 and for minor agrarian reforms. But at no time did they ever attempt, either before or after Fidel's victory, to force him into a more radical posture, and, paradoxically, in almost all PSP publications they made an effort —obviously following Moscow's suggestions— to moderate the revolutionary ardor of Fidel and his men to avoid a confrontation with the United States. This moderate behavior was in line with the prevailing strategy of the Soviet Union at the time.

In the first months of 1959, after Fidel's victory over Batista, Nikita Khrushchev was already working in the preparatory phase of his carefully planned visit to the United States. His greatest desire was to see all Communist parties throughout the world promoting his newly created concept of pacific coexistence. Of course, there was nothing intrinsically wrong in the PSP's participation in a patriotic struggle to rid Cuba of a corrupt dictator. But the last thing Khrushchev needed was for the Cuban Communists to undertake a revolutionary course that might give the Americans a motive to doubt his good intentions. For Khrushchev, Castro was just another case of a bourgeois nationalistic leader with a radical posture and confused ideas who would eventually accommodate himself to the United States. Both the Soviet and the PSP leaders feared that if Castro followed Arbenz's example, he would share his fate. Therefore, the Cuban Communists' caution was more than justified.

Continuing this cautious policy, in February 27, 1959, the Communists adopted a mild program proposing an agrarian reform in which cooperatives were relegated to the last place. But then, on May 17, less than three months later, Fidel made cooperatives the most important point of his proposal for an agrarian reform—which was immediately approved and implemented. This action left the Communists totally confused. Fidel's revolutionary program in the Sierra Maestra never went beyond the overthrow of Batista's dictatorship and the formation of a corruption-free democratic government. Consequently, the Communists were very surprised by what they considered to be Fidel's reckless behavior.

In fact the Agrarian Reform Law dictated by Fidel was much farther reaching than anybody previously expected. The Communists were against such radical change because they did not feel Cuba was ready. Blas Roca, the PSP's Secretary General, felt himself compelled to declare, "... the measures adopted by the revolutionary government and its laws are not of a Communist character. There is not a single Communist in the government, although the Communists render it wholehearted support and uphold it against counter-revolutionary attacks."[46]

In the Spring of 1959 the internal political situation in Cuba was still unclear, but it was evident that the old PSP Communists were gaining new positions at the expense of Castro's 26th of July Movement. But , though at that time they had already made great advances, the Communists had run into strong resistance in Fidel's Rebel Army ranks and especially within his cabinet, whose anti-Communist members were so upset that they were expressing their views in the open. By that time the 26th of July Movement had split into two well-defined pro- and anti-Communist factions.

Communist "Infiltration" Continues

When Fidel returned to Cuba in May of 1959 from a trip to South America he found widespread discontent and dissention among his own people against Communist "infiltration." The problem had reached such proportions that it had been exposed to the public by *Revolución,* the 26th of July Movement's official newspaper, and an ongoing dispute between the Communists and their critics was being printed in the newspaper's pages. Finally, Fidel moved to rebuff the Communists and bluntly and angrily dissociated himself again from the Communist party and its ideas and programmes.

In an effort to settle things, Fidel made a major speech on May 8 in which he tried to convince the Cubans that he was not a Communist. On May 21 he said publicly:

> The tremendous problem faced by the world is that it has been placed in a position where it must choose between capitalism, which starves people, and communism, which resolves economic problems, but suppresses the liberties so cherished by man. Both Cubans and Latin Americans cherish and foster a revolution that may meet their material needs without sacrificing those liberties.[47]

Following the same lines, Che Guevara addressed a letter in June to the influential magazine *Bohemia* in which he declared that although he hated anti-communism, he had never been a Communist. "If I were a Communist," he claimed, "I would not hesitate to shout it from the rooftops."[48]

When some of his people from the M-26-7 approached him to protest against the schemes and advances of the PSP, Fidel feigned surprise, blamed Raúl or Che Guevara or broke out into a tirade against the PSP Communists. But in practice he did nothing to intervene against the PSP, and those who protested soon found themselves out of favor with Castro himself.[49]

After his unexpected victory over Batista in January, 1959, Castro was given even more coverage in the American press and was hailed in the United States as the hero who brought an end to a corrupt and backward Latin American dictatorship. But Castro got nothing beyond the expressions of sympathy of the American public and a statement of approval from the U.S. government. Apparently there was the unstated assumption that Castro would become a democratic Latin American leader, in the style of Costa Rica's José Figueres, and little thought seems to have been given either to the social and political character of his government, or to the long-range implications of such a dramatic change. Apparently the Americans were unaware of the increasing anti-American feelings developing in Castro's Cuba. The logical reaction when they finally discovered it, was that a strong anti-Castro sentiment began growing in the United States. Similarly, in Cuba anti-Americanism soon became the *leit-motiv* of Castro's propaganda, while at the same time the non-Communist leaders in the new government were being politically and physically eliminated.

Things continued deteriorating to the point that, on October 20, 1959, Fidel had to send Major Camilo Cienfuegos, one of the Rebel Army's most popular leaders after Fidel himself, to detain Huber Matos, a highly respected Rebel Army major and 26th of July Movement member in charge of Camagüey province, accusing him of plotting against the government. Matos' only guilt actually was that he had tendered his resignation as a result of his concern about Communists having taken command of key positions in the government and in the Rebel Army ranks.

The detention of Huber Matos brought on a major governmental crisis. As a result of Fidel's order to detain Matos, Manuel Ray and Faustino Pérez, both Cabinet members, also tendered their resignations in protest. On November 26, a wide-ranging ministerial reshuffle was carried out. That same month Fidel placed Che Guevara in charge of the National Bank, replacing Felipe Pazos.

On December 14, after a Stalinist-type show-trial in which Fidel himself provided "evidence" for the prosecution, Huber Matos was sentenced to twenty years hard labor. From then on anticommunism became a serious political crime in Fidel's Caribbean paradise. With the imprisonment of Huber Matos, Fidel made it clear that his previous guaranties of political freedom would not be honored. Contrary to his claims during his short-lived "humanist" phase, living in Castro's Cuba would soon mean neither bread nor freedom.

Finally, the Russians are Coming

After a visit to Mexico as the head of a Soviet industrial exhibition, Anastas Mikoyan, the Soviet vice-premier came to Havana on February 4, 1959, and thus became the first Soviet leader to visit Cuba to see for himself the curious revolutionary phenomenon taking place in the sunny Caribbean Island. Favorably impressed by the newborn revolution, he signed the first Soviet-Cuban trade agreement on February 13 of that year.

Notwithstanding the Cubans' impatience to fall in love with Moscow at first sight, during his visit to Cuba, Mikoyan was very careful not to say anything about resuming diplomatic ties with Havana. In fact the joint Cuban-Soviet statement was unusually restrained inasmuch as it omitted the usual condemnations of imperialism or any criticism against the United States. Instead there was some soothing language about the United Nations and the ritual phrases of coexistence, cooperation, and friendship of all peoples of the world. In the document the two countries agreed "to consider at an opportune moment the question of resuming diplomatic relations on terms of complete equality and independence."[50] And even after Mikoyan's return to Moscow, the Soviet leaders cautiously applied no pressure to re-establish diplomatic relations with Cuba. This Soviet behavior was strange, because since the beginning of 1959 they were apparently pressing the Cubans for resuming relations between the two countries. It seems that Khruschev already had become suspicious of Castro's true intentions.

Soon after Mikoyan's departure, Che Guevara took his second pilgrimage throughout the Eastern European Communist countries in search for Soviet-Bloc commitments to give Cuba large scale credits to build basic industries. The Soviets and their cherished friends offered the Cubans millions of dollars of "generous socialist help." In the meantime Che and a group of revolutionary leaders, undoubtedly following Castro's orders, began to prepare the Cuban public opinion for the rupture of the traditional economic and political links with the United States.

On May of that same year, Blas Roca, one of the PSP leaders, went to Moscow and had a special meeting with Nikita Khrushchev. Apparently Roca's briefing about the bizarre events in Cuba dissipated some of the Russian leader's doubts and suspicions about Fidel, and the Cuban Communists were given a green light to proceed with their rapprochement with Castro. *Hoy,* the PSP's official organ, published a letter sent by Blas Roca from Moscow in which he stated: "Cuba cannot be economically blockaded by the U.S. imperialists."[51]

Finally, on May 8, 1960, Cuba reestablished diplomatic relations with the U.S.S.R., and on July 9, Khrushchev surprised the world by stating in a speech: "I should like to draw attention to the fact that the United States is obviously planning perfidious and criminal steps against the Cuban people."[52] And Khrushchev continued his speech by offering to buy from Cuba all the sugar the U.S. was about to stop purchasing. In his usual way Khrushchev boasted:

> It should be borne in mind that the United States is now not at such inaccessible distance from the Soviet Union... Figuratively speaking, if need be the Soviet artillerymen can support the Cuban people with their rocket fire, should the aggressive forces in the Pentagon dare to start intervention against Cuba.[53]

On July 6, 1960, President Eisenhower cut the balance of the Cuban sugar quota for 1960. But just three days later, on July 9, the Russians agreed to buy all the Cuban sugar the United States refused to take and might refuse to buy in the future. The following day Che Guevara declared in a mass meeting: "Cuba is a glorious island in the middle of the Caribbean protected by the rockets of the mightiest power in History."[54] Apparently the Cubans had taken Khrushchev's boast at face value, not taking into account that big nations usually show friendliness for small ones, especially when the small ones are fighting their adversaries.

The long-term perspectives of Castro's rapprochement with the Russians were not very promising. Khrushchev was convinced that the U.S., which had never tolerated hostile neighbors, would not permit the creation of a Communist outpost ninety miles from her frontiers. What might be a clear advantage for the Kremlin could only be a handicap for a young socialist revolution trying to rebuild the economy of its country on a diversified basis. But there had always been a streak of the megalomaniac in Castro's makeup, and he may have believed the flattering words addressed to him in Moscow.[55]

Of course Fidel was dead wrong: Nikita Khrushchev never believed even for an instant that the Soviet Union could commit nuclear suicide in defense of a small island lost in the Caribbean. In any event, the way that his speech about the Soviet nuclear umbrella was interpreted in Havana, where it generated great excitement and joy, may have caused him to begin fearing that his Cuban love-affair might pull the Soviet Union in undesired directions.

In the meantime, the Americans were greatly alarmed and some important voices had already began calling Castro a "Soviet agent" and a "prisoner of Khrushchev." But at that moment no one better than Khrushchev himself had realized that if Fidel was in some sense his prisoner, he was no less a prisoner in Castro's friendly net. And, on top of it, the Cubans, with their political naivete, continued waving under the American's noses the imaginary rockets Khrushchev gave them on July. From that time on, Khrushchev began to learn the hard way that the newcomers were to be no easy associates to the motherland of communism.

In the Autumn of 1960, Che Guevara made a three-month trip to the Communist countries. After the usual stop in Moscow, where he declared the solidarity of the Cuban revolution with the Declaration of the 81st Communist parties, he surprised his hosts by going to Peking, China, where he spent two weeks. After such tactless behavior Che was never to be a Russian favorite any more.

By the end of 1960, the socialization of all major branches of the Cuban economy was practically an accomplished fact, but the word "Socialism" was still very rare in official government declarations. In November, Carlos Rafael Rodríguez, the PSP leading ideologue, stated that he feared that a premature bid of the Communists for greater power would alienate the Cuban people, possibly arouse the wrath of the Fidelistas and almost certainly cause military intervention by the U.S.[56]

Suddenly, Fidel Becomes a "Marxist"

During 1960, Castro continued raising the PSP Communists to more powerful positions and began protecting them on the grounds that loyalty to the revolution and unity were the two chief needs of the country. By late 1959, the Cuban delegation to the United Nations had begun to separate itself from the rest of the Latin American countries in order to pursue a "neutral" line that corresponded more often than not with that of the Communist bloc. By December, Secretary of State Christian Herter complained about the difficulty of even communicating with the Cuban government, let alone doing anything to alleviate the existing "unhappy" relations.[57] From that time on the events in Cuba's convoluted political life began developing at a vertiginous speed.

In a speech after the air attack that initiated the Bay of Pigs invasion, Fidel proclaimed for the first time that the Cuban revolution was a democratic and socialist one. Even with the qualifier word democratic attached to the word socialist, the term created shock and confusion in Moscow. Khrushchev, who initially felt some sympathy for the Cuba leader, was now angered by Fidel's arrogance, lack of discipline, and his use of pressure tactics to force his unilateral decisions upon the Soviet leaders.

Finally, on December 2, 1961, Fidel again surprised Khrushchev by delivering the famous speech in which, after admitting his bourgeois prejudices, he declared that he had always been a Marxist-Leninist at heart.[58] Fidel began his speech at about midnight on December 1 and finished it at 5:00 a.m. on December 2. Author Loree Wilkerson, who wrote a good analysis of Castro's speech, observed that Fidel's self-analysis in this speech presents the picture of a man desperately trying to modify his past so that it would conform to the present.[59]

Castro's confession of Marxist faith was an unpleasant surprise to the Soviet leadership. It was also viewed with extreme suspicion by the Soviet intelligence analysts in charge of Cuba. Their suspicion was understandable, because an evaluation of Castro's claims may have produced something close to an E-5 —that is, source unreliable, accuracy of information improbable. (See Appendix 1) Evidently, Fidel Castro was trying to create for himself, *a posteriori,* what in intelligence parlance is known as a "legend," a false biography or cover story, supplied mostly to illegals and sleepers,⁶⁰ enabling them to live undetected within a foreign country under a false identity. The Soviets were not alone in their misgivings about Castro's claims. Fidel's non-Communist affiliation had been so widely accepted in international circles that his speech caused a sensation abroad.⁶¹

In January, 1962, Fidel confessed to a French journalist that, even though he had never read beyond page 370 of the first volume of Marx's *Capital,* he had always been a Marxist. Hugh Thomas said that Castro must be therefore the first Marxist-Leninist leader who had scarcely read any of the works of the Master and who scarcely allowed more than a few words and few expressions taken from Marxism to enter his vocabulary.⁶² Thomas' remark is highly accurate. An analysis of Castro's speeches shows that, while giving lip service to Marxism, true Marxist terminology and concepts are totally alien to him.

By the end of 1960, Fidel had apparently taken the unilateral decision of making a fusion with the Communists —perhaps instead of a fusion we may call it more properly an absorption. But though his decision was not officially exposed until the Summer of 1961, it seems reasonable to think that he began his drift toward the capture of the Communists in the very beginning of 1959, because all the internal crisis in his regime that year were related with his rapprochement with the Communists.

Finally, after his insincerely humble admission of ideological underdevelopment and his tribute to the old PSP leaders, Fidel pledged allegiance to the "collective leadership" of the new party he had in mind, product of the fusion of the PSP and the 26th of July Movement but almost completely in the hands of the old PSP party —or so the Communists believed. After this sudden change of their leader's ideology, the members of the 26th of July Movement divided themselves into two well defined groups: those who expressed their discontent in various ways, and those who, in typical Cuban turncoat fashion, claimed to have been Marxists all the time without knowing it, and paid allegiance to the old PSP Communists — whom they knew were actually in Castro's hands.

By late 1961, the campaign on behalf of communism was led by Fidel himself and in Cuba it became a political crime to express any critical opinion against the PSP. Faster than a speeding bullet, Fidel had metamorphosed himself from an anti-Communist into a non-Communist; from a non-Communist into an anti- anti-Communist; and from an anti- anti-Communist into a Communist, all before the astonished eyes not only of the Cuban and American anti-Communists, but of the Cuban and Soviet Communists as well.

The rest of the story of Castro's "communism" is well known, and I am not going to repeat it here. With the benefit of hindsight, however, it seems that the main reason for Castro's confession of Marxist faith was to sugarcoat the pill he wanted the Soviets to swallow. Proof of it is that after the collapse of the Soviet Union, references to Marxism in his speeches are more and more close to zero, and Marxism as official ideology of his revolution has seen a dramatic decline. Marxism is no longer a subject of study at Cuban universities, and the few professors of Marxist studies who complained about it have been quietly separated from their teaching duties, expelled from Castro's "Communist" party, and ostracized.

Chapter 3

Khrushchev's Problems

Don't look a gift Horse[1] in the mouth.
—Popular saying.

During his visit to the United States to attend the 14th General Assembly of the United Nations, Nikita S. Khrushchev said nothing at all in defense of the Cuban revolution. He remained imperturbable when the Americans attacked Fidel Castro calling the Cuban leader "Communist." At that moment Khrushchev's only commitment was limited to pounding his shoe on his desk to awaken the delegates who had fallen asleep after two hours of speech by the young Cuban revolutionary.

As Khrushchev later admitted in his memoirs, the Soviet Union had little contact with Cuba and therefore very limited knowledge of what was happening on the Island. By the end of 1958, Khrushchev was hardly optimistic about a successful anti-Batista revolution in Cuba. In an interview he gave to a Brazilian journalist in November, 1958, he remarked that everybody remembered the tragic fate of Guatemala.[2] It was not until after Castro's surprising victory that the Soviet readers began to hear about the dramatic events developing in the distant Caribbean Island.[3]

The U.S.S.R. and Latin America

It was not until November, 1959, that Moscow considered the necessity to place a *TASS* correspondent working full time in getting news from Cuba. One of the first tenuous signs of Soviet interest in Cuba came in the shape of a Moscow Radio broadcast of late October, 1959, attacking the United States and repeating Castro's version of the leaflet "bombing" of Havana.[4]

But the scanty coverage of Cuban events in the Soviet press continued reiterating the lessons of Guatemala and the possibility that the United States could attempt to unseat Castro either by a coup d'état or by overt intervention.[5] Soviet behavior at the time evidences that, until the advent of the Cuban revolution, Latin America in general and the Caribbean in particular, as an area fully under the control of American power, was not a major field of attention for the Soviet Union.[6]

The Soviet policy towards Latin America since WWII shows that the area was not by any means top priority for the Soviet Union, though they had stood ready to take advantage of any favorable development. Until 1960 they had had only very modest success in their attempts for political control. Prior to 1959 the U.S.S.R. had diplomatic relations with only three Latin American countries: Argentina, Mexico and Uruguay.

Given the preponderant American military and political power in Latin America and the Caribbean, the area had remained low as a potential zone for Soviet influence even during the optimistic Khrushchev years after 1954.[7] The overthrow of the Arbenz government in Guatemala led the Soviet Union, the United States, and the Latin American Communists to the same conclusion: The United States was the dominant force of political developments in Latin America as a whole and particularly in the Caribbean. Hence, the Soviet Union lost interest in the area, and the Communists of that continent were confirmed in their belief that a passive strategy of waiting was the best.[8]

Granted, most Sovietologists agree that after Stalin's death Moscow moved from its position of indifference in supporting new nationalist movements to one of relatively great interest. But this change in strategy towards third world change also implied a shift in geographical priorities. It was only thanks to Khrushchev's personality and energy that this new vision won over Stalin's xenophobic posture toward the third world. Asia, Africa, Latin America and the Middle East suddenly took on greater importance to the Soviets.

This Soviet change in attitude toward developing countries became apparent at the 20th Party Congress. In his speech to the Congress, Khrushchev not only established conditions for a dynamic and more flexible Soviet foreign policy toward third world countries but also outlined what he considered were basic changes in the international system. These key international changes, according to comrade Khrushchev, were bringing the third world into a pivotal strategic role, and its main characteristics were: (a) the rise of the mighty world camp of Socialism, (b) the existence of a large number of non-Communist developing countries opposed to war, with population totalling hundreds of millions of people, (c) the development of a powerful labor movement in capitalist countries, and (d) an international peace movement devoted to the goal of peaceful coexistence. These conditions — affirmed Khrushchev— allowed the Marxists to adopt new tactics without risking nuclear war and also permitted the Soviets to expand their power and influence throughout the third world not by way of violent revolution but by pacific ways of trade, foreign aid, and diplomacy.

Early in July, 1955, at a closed plenum of the Central Committee of the Communist Party, Khrushchev laid out the new goals of Soviet policy. He stated that the temporary stabilization of capitalist forces in Europe meant that all efforts to push westward were futile and should be halted. Khrushchev concluded that, in the future, the Soviet Union should avoid conflict and reduce tensions with the West, make some compromises to settle outstanding problems in marginal areas, and initiate an ideological offensive to penetrate the third world.[9]

By the mid fifties, however, the Soviets had begun to develop some interest in the area. First Deputy Premier Anastas Mikoyan's visit to Mexico appeared to reinforce the interest in Soviet developments that had become increasingly evident in many parts of Latin America. Chile, too, announced that it was sending a commercial delegation to the U.S.S.R. and hoped to restore trade relations with the Soviet Union. In Latin America, as elsewhere in the western world, the "relaxation of tensions" that had begun with Khrushchev's visit to the United States already seemed to be encouraging the emergence of new attitudes toward the Communist powers.[10]

As Soviet spokesmen never tired of pointing out, the expansion of Soviet communist power in the years after WWII was among the outstanding developments of all modern history. Even the most determined anti-communist could not disagree when Premier Khrushchev recalled that Socialism —as he preferred to call the Soviet system in its current state of development— was no longer a precarious experiment confined to the territory of the Soviet Union but a "mighty world force" that had profoundly modified the global balance of power and brought about a wholly new "correlation of forces" between the Soviet camp and those who opposed its expansion.[11] The Soviet ideologues expected to make great advances in the underdeveloped world as it decolonized. They hoped that the communists —particularly the pro-Soviet communists— would lead the nationalist rebellions and convert their countries into Communist states.

Proof that the U.S.S.R.'s repeated offers of expanded trade with Latin American countries were not falling on deaf ears were clearly showing. On October 19, 1959, Brazil informed the decision of sending a trade mission to the Soviet Union in the hope of finding an alternative source to the United States for importing petroleum and equipment as well as an outlet for some of its surplus coffee production. Although the Brazilian-Soviet diplomatic relations were not formally restored, the three year agreement was regarded as the most significant Soviet penetration of the Latin American market so far.[12]

A Still more notable mark of Soviet interest in Latin America was the ten-day visit of Mikoyan to Mexico on November 18-28, 1959. Though the nominal objective of Mikoyan's visit was to open a Soviet exhibition in Mexico City, Moscow's most successful salesman also took time to tour the country extensively and he offered credits to the Mexican petroleum monopoly for the purchase of supplies and equipment in the Soviet Union.[13]

The keynote of the Twenty-First Congress of the Communist Party of the Soviet Union, held in Moscow from January 25 to February 5, 1959, was struck by the successful launching on January 2 of the "cosmic rocket" known as "Lunik." In his seven-hour report on January 27, Khrushchev declared:

> There are no forces in the world that now could re-establish Capitalism in our country or crush the socialist camp. ... The capitalist encirclement

no longer exists for our country. There are two world social systems: capitalism, living out his day, and socialism, filled with growing, vital forces and enjoying the support of the working people of all lands. ... The forces of socialism are mighty and they grow every day. The future belongs to them.[14]

Khrushchev continued predicting that by 1965 the U.S.S.R. and the other members of the "World Socialist System" would actually be producing half of the world's industrial output. By 1970 or earlier, Khrushchev asserted, the U.S.S.R. would have surpassed the United States in both total and per capita production.[15] Even under the most favorable circumstances, however, the realization of such a program would be possible only if peace was maintained; and Khrushchev promised that every effort would be made to preserve and strengthen international peace and security in line with the established Soviet policy of promoting "peaceful coexistence," an end to the "cold war," and a general relaxation of international tensions.

Evidently, Khrushchev's version of Marxism ruled out the necessity of violent struggle or war as the motor for revolutionary change. In his view, the Socialist system would in the long run overtake and outproduce the West, and in this way it would demonstrate its superiority above Capitalism, and this would occur not by violent confrontation but via a pacific emulation, during an extended period of pacific coexistence. In fact, Khrushchev's idea was not totally new. In 1954, when Georgi M. Malenkov took the first steps in the rebuttal of Stalin's policies, he acknowledged that nuclear war would have catastrophic consequences not only for the West, but also for the Soviet Union. This change in attitude was reflected later by Khrushchev at the 20th Party Congress.

Khrushchev's famous "secret speech" of 1956 denouncing Stalin had the unexpected outcome of provoking a severe ideological crisis which shook international Communism. To counteract its effects the Soviet leaders began a drive for stabilization within the Communist movement. Since 1956, Khrushchev and other authorized Soviet spokesmen increasingly insisted that because of the growing advantages of the inherent superiority of their system, "socialism" would not only win out in the world-wide competition with capitalism but might even be able to do so without going through the "final" military struggle with the opposing forces that Lenin and other Soviet theorists had earlier pictured as an inevitable prelude to its triumph.[16] Yet, it is useful to keep in mind that it was only the man and the methods that had changed since Stalin's death, not the ultimate objective of total world control.

There is ample evidence to support the point of view that it was quite unlikely that the Soviets had any master blueprint for world conquest. Nothing evidences that such a master plan existed or that they had any rigid timetables. Nevertheless, the Soviet leaders tended to be patient opportunists and were always ready to grab anything that dropped in their laps, and Khrushchev was no exception to the rule.[17]

The successful seizure of power by Castro in Cuba took place in an unanticipated manner. The unexpected Cuban events took even the Kremlin's most visionary ideologues by surprise and put them in an uncomfortable ideological conundrum.

Faced with the pressing need of having to explain the unexplainable, they quickly elaborated out of Marxist nothingness the new concept of "national democracy" in order to carve a niche to put Castro's unexplainable and unclassifiable revolution in. The Kremlin ideologues defined "national democracy" as an intermediate stage in the development of a revolutionary movement, in which an oppressed people had broken loose the chains from "imperialist oppression" and had taken cover under Moscow's tutelage.

Even if a national democracy was a state with a status of a junior associate of Moscow, it was not only after a prolonged stage of "socialist construction" that it could reach full membership status of the Soviet bloc. But the "national democracy" concept, though encouraged by the Soviet ideologues, proved to be short-lived. To Moscow's embarrassment, Castro unexpectedly rejected the pre-socialist stage of "national democracy" status and, claiming that he had been a Marxist from the cradle, demanded Cuba's full membership in the Soviet bloc as a grown up Communist state.

One may guess that Castro's unsolicited advances were not welcomed in the Kremlin. But Khrushchev found himself with his hands tied in relation to Castro. Contrary to Soviet bloc european countries, linked to the Soviet Union in a geographically tight territory, Cuba was so distant that it was almost impossible for the Soviets to impose their will by force on Castro in the event of a political dissidence or disagreement. This was probably the first time Nikita Khrushchev questioned himself about the wisdom of his hasty decision to back Fidel Castro.

For the petrified Soviet gerontocratic leadership, the Cuban revolution represented at first the opportunity of a great emotional and ideological revitalization. Out of nowhere a backward Latin American country had broken the American sphere of political and economic influence and was willing to follow the Soviet leadership. This was such an unexpected turn of events that they were not going to lose even if they had doubts about Castro and his followers. Finally, after overcoming some initial reluctance, the Russians accepted the newcomers. Some of them said that the Cuban revolution, made them feel young again.[18] A few days after the missile crisis Mikoyan told Dean Rusk:

> You Americans must understand what Cuba means to us old Bolsheviks. We have been waiting all our lives for a country to go Communist without the Red Army, and it happened in Cuba. It makes us feel like boys again![19]

Yet, when Fidel Castro dangled his succulent bait in front of Khrushchev's mouth, the Soviet Premier apparently had second thoughts about swallowing it hook, line and sinker. Khrushchev feared that the U.S.S.R. would become overextended and its power would spread too thin —in fact, if Castro were an agent provocateur and not what he purported to be, that would be a good plan to debilitate the Soviet Union from within.

There are reasons to believe that the problem of whether and how to embrace Castro's revolution caused considerable debate and concern in Moscow. Even in Khrushchev's "liberal" era of multiple innovations, the idea of extending support to a regime headed by a mad political adventurer who was neither likely to be reliable nor subject to Soviet control was undoubtedly debatable.

In February, 1960, Soviet First Deputy Minister Anastas Mikoyan paid a ten day visit to Cuba, ostensibly to open a Soviet exhibition. Once in Cuba, he had long talks with Castro and with other high ranking Fidelistas, and on February 13 the first Cuban-Soviet Trade and Economic Aid Agreement was signed. Under this agreement, publicized as a great economic achievement in the state-controlled Soviet press, the U.S.S.R. promised to buy one million tons of Cuban sugar in each of the next five years and extended an initial credit of one hundred million dollars to Cuba.[20]

Figuratively Speaking...

It was only after Mikoyan's visit to Cuba and his favorable impression of what he saw and what the old pro-Soviet Communists of the Partido Socialista Popular (PSP) may have told him, that the Soviets considered a careful rapprochement with Castro. Three months later, on May 8, 1960, full diplomatic relations were established and, from then on, Moscow's newspapers began printing almost every day enchanted articles about the sunny Caribbean Island rediscovered by the Armenian Columbus Anastas Mikoyan. Every official speech included flattering remarks about the Cuban revolution. In the meantime, Soviet ideologues and Marxist scholars were at pains trying to classify Castro's strange revolution from the point of view of Marxism-Leninism.[21]

When Castro seized the American-owned oil refineries in Cuba on July 7, 1960, after their refusal to refine Russian crude oil, President Eisenhower cut U.S. imports of Cuban sugar by 700,000 tons. Two days later Khrushchev delivered a speech in which he announced that the Soviet Union would buy more Cuban sugar, at a price above the prevailing rate on the world market.

Soviet oil began to enter Cuba in April, 1960, and in May, with the reestablishment of diplomatic relations with the Soviet Union, the policy of non-recognition established by Batista in 1952 was reversed. Events now began to move precipitously; but their nature and speed were attributed to American initiatives and Cuban reactions to them.

And suddenly, on July 9, 1960, Khrushchev, perhaps under the influence of good Soviet vodka,[22] went a step further and firmly requested the United States to keep her hands off Cuba and, exploding in anger, backed his statement with the now famous threat of the "figurative" Soviet nuclear missiles:

It should not be forgotten that the United States is not now at such inaccessible distance from the Soviet Union as it used to be. Figuratively speaking, in case of need, Soviet artillerymen can support the Cuban people with their rocket fire if the aggressive forces in the Pentagon dare to launch an intervention against Cuba. (Stormy applause). And let them not forget in the Pentagon that, as the tests have shown, we have rockets capable of landing directly on a precalculated square at a distance of 13,000 kilometers [around 8,000 miles].(Applause).[23] This, if you wish, is a warning for those who would like to settle international issues by force and not by reason. (Applause).[24]

The precise nature of the Soviet military commitment to Cuba in Khrushchev's speech of July 9, was later to be questioned, and the Soviets themselves immediately moved to de-emphasize the Soviet Premier's promise of "figurative" rocket support of Cuba. Moreover, it is important to remember that Khrushchev's statement about missile support for Cuba was made in the tense period following the U-2 incident and the fiasco of the Paris Summit Conference. But, soon after, Khrushchev apparently made up his mind and back-pedalled.

When Cubans began to rattle the Soviet "figurative" missiles, Khrushchev moved to rest importance to his promise of "figurative" rocket support of Cuba.[25] Just three days after the "figurative" offer, Khrushchev said at a press conference that, "We don't need bases in Cuba. We have bases in the Soviet Union, and we can hit anything from here."[26] A week later, on July 16, *TASS* published an authoritative statement entitled "The Monroe Doctrine Ended Long Ago and Can No Longer Help the Imperialist Colonizer." But, despite the eloquent title, the Soviet commitment in the event of an armed intervention against Cuba was limited to the promise that, "Relying on its power, the Soviet Union will give Cuba the necessary assistance." The "figurative" rockets had suddenly disappeared from the picture.

When in September, 1960, a journalist in New York asked Khrushchev point-blank: "Is it true that you stated that in case of a United States intervention against Cuba, the U.S.S.R. would strike the United States?," he evasively replied: "More or less true..." but immediately added, "You need not worry... Since America is not going to attack Cuba, there can be no danger."[27]

After Khrushchev's figurative *boutade* about the missiles, Castro tried to compromise him further into a more formal commitment, but the clever Nikita Sergeevich went no further with it. Then, in September, 1960, in a five-hour tirade before the U.N. General Assembly, Castro voiced almost every charge against the United States which had ever been voiced by the Soviets and added quite a few of his own crop. He alluded in his speech to the threatening statement directed at Cuba by Admiral Arleigh Burke, Commander of the U.S. naval base at Guantánamo, and, in a direct allusion to the Soviet missiles, pointed out the danger of nuclear war if such a threat were to turn into direct action.[28] It is believed, however, that during a private meeting the two leaders had in New York, Khrushchev refused Castro's request for further references to missile support.[29]

Khrushchev's "missile rattling" about Cuba was not the first case of such bluffings. He had threatened the West before with rockets over Suez, over the landings in Lebanon and Jordan, and over Berlin. But his threats had a very distinctive characteristic. In 1956 the Soviet Premier threatened Britain and France with long-range missiles at the time of the Suez crisis, but not before he was certain that the crisis was effectively over. When the Matsu-Quemoy crisis of the fall of 1958 erupted, Soviet support came in the form of two threatening letters from Khrushchev to Eisenhower. But Khrushchev's guarantees and promises of help to Communist China were extended only after it had become clear that the United States was not going to intervene in the affair and the threat of war was gone.[30]

On August 23, 1958, the Chinese began a bombardment of Quemoy, one of the smaller islands close to China, held by the Nationalists. The attack stopped after a month and a half. Though during the crisis the chinese propaganda spoke of an assault and landings on the island, the Soviet press pointedly ignored such statements and de-emphasized the possibility of war. It was only after the shelling had stopped and the crisis had ended that serious Russian warnings were issued to the United States, and even then the warnings were soon modified to make them less threatening.

On September 7, Khrushchev declared in a letter to President Eisenhower that an attack on the People's Republic of China was an attack on the Soviet Union, apparently suggesting an automatic Soviet response to any attack on China. But, soon after, comments appeared in the Soviet press suggesting that aid would only be "considered" and "offered as necessary," stating also that the Chinese had everything necessary to repel the aggression by themselves. It was only on September 19, when the danger of a serious confrontation had clearly passed, that a nuclear threat was invoked.[31] In his life as a Russian leader, Khrushchev gave abundant proof that he was deeply addicted to the calculated risk —particularly if it implied no risk at all.

The day after the Bay of Pigs invasion began, Khrushchev sent President Kennedy a message appealing to him to call a halt to the aggression. The tone of the message, however, was not in accordance to the man who some months earlier had boasted with apocalyptic visions. This one was a lot more conciliatory,

> As for the U.S.S.R., there must be no mistake about our position. We will extend to the Cuban people and its government all the necessary aid for the repulse of the armed attack on Cuba. ... We are sincerely interested in the relaxation of international tensions, but if others go in for its aggravation, then we will answer them in full measure. In general it is impossible to carry on affairs in such a way that in one area the situation is settled and the fire is put out, and in another area a new fire is lit.[32]

The fact is that when the invasion began, Castro wired Russia for help or at least for open solidarity. But Khrushchev ignored him until the Cuban militia, to his utter surprise, had definitely beaten the invaders.[33]

Khrushchev's shoe-pounding on his desk at the General Assembly was nothing more than an ambiguous statement of support for Fidel. But the Cuban leader wanted more. That same month Fidel sent Carlos Franqui, the editor of *Revolución*, the official Castroist newspaper, to Moscow with the pretext of interviewing Khrushchev. But the true objective of the trip was to find out how the Soviet leader could pass from figurative language to direct statements. Franqui spent several hours in the Kremlin going over the subject with Khrushchev, but the most he obtained from the shrewd peasant was a solomonic statement, which was interpreted in contradictory fashion by the press services of the United States and the rest of the world.[34]

The New York Times informed on November 19, 1960, that the Soviet leaders were reported as trying to convince Premier Fidel Castro to moderate his violent attacks upon the United States, and in particular to stop rattling the Soviet nuclear missiles. Apparently Khrushchev had second thoughts about the responsibilities he had assumed with regard to Cuba. Obviously, Moscow's relations with Washington, especially with the new administration of President-elect John F. Kennedy, counted more for Khrushchev than the Cuban problem as such.

Castro finally got it. On November 8 he told the Cuban people that they must defend themselves and not go to sleep with the knowledge of Soviet protection.[35] Almost immediately *Hoy*, the Cuban Communists' organ, denied that Khrushchev had told Cuba to quit rattling rockets; *TASS* had merely repeated what the Soviet official position was: if Cuba was attacked by the United States, it might face Soviet rockets.[36]

Khrushchev Backs Fidel

Even if the rocket threat was a bit exaggerated to be credible, Khrushchev now seemed to be sincerely backing the Cuban revolutionaries. Why such a sudden change in his attitude towards Cuba? Why this sudden interest in the remote Caribbean Island under the direction of a mad adventurer? The answers lie in the new posture of Khrushchev. Fought to a stalemate in Europe, embarrassed in Asia by the obviously aggressive instincts of Red China, and kept busy in the Middle East, the Premier apparently felt that the Soviet Union had grown enough in resources to try an adventure somewhere else. No longer fearful of their encirclement by the democracies, the Russians were genuinely confident at that moment in history that they were the encircling ones. Hence the new interest in areas which once seemed to Moscow remote and unpromising.[37]

The possibility of taking control over the Cuban revolution, outscoring the United States in its own backyard at relatively little expense and with little risk tempted Khrushchev to intervene in an area where the U.S.S.R. had no direct interest nor the possibility of military influence. Cuba, which unexpectedly had dropped on his lap, seemed to Khrushchev a place where he may score easy and spectacular successes, but, at the same time, a place where in the long run may become costly and dangerously involved. A Soviet leader more cautious than Khrushchev might well had found the excessive American incapacity to deal with Castro extremely suspicious. But Khrushchev's gambling instincts and the prospect of scoring a point, both before the American and the Chinese, irresistibly pulled him to accept the gambit, forgetting in the process than in politics, particularly in international politics, nothing comes for free and every gain has a price, and that eventually the Soviet Union would be inextricably involved into dangerous problems at a heavy expense.[38]

The new phenomenon that Soviet official terminology called "wars of national liberation" offered the Soviet Union an opportunity to expand its influence without the risks involved in direct Soviet military expansion. Furthermore, in the unlikely eventuality of a war of national liberation which eventually failed, the U.S.S.R. could not lose nor it could be considered a blow to Soviet prestige. The Soviets had realized that it was better to have some control over non-Communist countries, ruled by nationalist revolutionaries friendly to the Soviet Union, than full control over Communist ones.[39] Actually, an American intervention of Cuba now, when the loss of a Sovietcontrolled Communist state was not an issue, would be less costly to the Soviet Union than after the Soviets had made larger commitments, or after a pro-Soviet Communist regime had been established.[40]

Another reason for the sudden change in attitude was that the Soviets had not foreseen the victory of traditional Communist parties in Latin America and had all sorts of reservations about parties herded by Johnny-Come-Lately "communists" like Castro. Rather than a violent, revolutionary change, they preferred a long transition from coalition governments to Communism, and indeed favored an extended period of national democracy in which many social elements participated.[41] As long as the situation was one which might be called "creeping revolution," the Soviet commitment, economic and military, could be kept within the bounds of what they were willing to invest. But once a country labeled itself Communist, the Soviets options would become very limited. Hence the Soviet Union's preference for a gradual transition in Latin American countries, as opposed to such rapid communization as in the case of Cuba.[42] But the Soviets were not free to follow their preferences, especially if they wanted to maintain their influence over revolutionary movements in the third world, particularly having the Chinese as partial sponsors threatening the Soviet influence.

Another possible answer for the Soviet change of attitude could have been that, notwithstanding all the negative information about Fidel's tumultuous and foggy past provided by the old PSP leaders and by the Soviet intelligence services, the Fidelistas apparently had genuine progressive aspirations and Fidel himself seemed to be turning pinkish every day. Yet, at the same time, Fidel's attitude seemed highly suspicious to the Russians. Was he undergoing a real conversion to Communism or was he only a clever simulator?

Though the essential feature of Castro's revolution was its anti-Americanism and he was repeating almost every day the familiar slogan of "Yankee Imperialism," frequently heard in Latin America for over half of a century, nothing indicated that he had leftist ideas, nor that he professed Marxist ones. Was Castro trying to join the Communist community to pursue his own particular ambitions?

There were other considerations which inclined Khrushchev to maintain a cautious attitude. The Kremlin's experience with self-made revolutions that had been made without Soviet guidance or support had shown them that these regimes insisted in pursuing policies independent from those of the Soviet Union and were difficult to control. In addition, Castro, though initially having endorsed the Soviet "peaceful coexistence" policy line, also made clear that he believed in the Cuban model of violent revolution as the only suitable one for Latin America and the third world, as clearly expressed in the Second Declaration of Havana.[43]

But the above mentioned considerations were not the only ones that allowed for Khruschev's mental reservations about Fidel and his "socialist" revolution. Despite Castro's claims that most participants in the revolution "...were young men with a modest, working class background; workers and peasants, the sons of working people, employees...,"[44] the facts pointed in another direction. Though Castro's guerrilla forces consisted mainly of peasant soldiers who had joined Castro in the mountains, most of the officers were middle class professionals and former students of the University of Havana. Also, in the cities and in the countryside revolutionary-minded intellectuals, not workers or peasants, had been the ones who took the lead, followed by ample sections of the middle and professional classes. The revolutionary nucleus led by Fidel himself was mostly composed of *declassé* middle-class revolutionaries, that is, members of the bourgeoisie who were totally alienated from their own class —or so they believed.[45]

Furthermore, Fidel not only believed Fidelismo to represent the only correct revolutionary strategy for Latin America, but he also aspired to the leadership of the revolutionary movements in the region. This attitude not only brought the Cuban leader into a collision course with the Kremlin, but also with the pro-Soviet Communist parties in Latin America which supported Khrushchev's line. The Soviet Premier was far from enthusiastic about the prospect of a Fidel Castro whose ambitions had gone even further than Cuba and envisioned himself as a new Bolívar. Remembering what had happened with Tito and Mao, Khrushchev did not want to create another major Communist rebel leader.

Moreover, though giving lip service to his allegiance to the Soviet Union, Castro was carefully maintaining a neutralist position in the Sino-Soviet dispute. Cuba signed a trade and credit agreement with the Chinese in December, 1960, and Castro was receiving a warm endorsement from Peking for his radical position on revolution.[46]

Professor Maurice Halperin observed that, apart from Fidel's complex personality, three circumstances, absent in Soviet relations with other Communist countries gave a distinctive character to Cuban-Soviet relations: First, geography, second, politico-ideological considerations, and, third, world image. By a rare historic coincidence, the year that Fidel came to power in Cuba marked the beginning of the Sino-Soviet dispute.[47] From 1960 until his demotion in 1964, the course of Khrushchev's career was dominated by the Chinese quarrel, made public to the Communist Parties of the world at the secret Moscow Conference of November, 1960.[48] From 1960 onwards it is quite impossible to understand Khrushchev's foreign policy except in the light of his life-and death struggle with China.[49] In all of Khrushchev's moves, whether in domestic policies or in foreign affairs, it is easy to detect his anxiety at what the Chinese reaction might be.[50]

The growing rift between Moscow and Peking stimulated competition for control of the international movement. The rivalry required both major contenders to try to win supporters in every third world country and within every Communist party all around the world, encouraging the formation of rival factions and even splits into separate party organizations. The Chinese were questioning nothing less than Moscow's role as a leader in the Communist movement and the revolutionary peoples of the world.[51]

Despite the fact that Khrushchev's old peasant instinct was telling him to distrust Castro's *bona fides,* the Soviet Premier badly needed friends because of the Chinese. Fidel's apparent need for Soviet aid provided Khrushchev with an irresistible opportunity to outwit the Chinese, providing at the same time a heaven-sent opportunity to extend Soviet influence in the Americas.[52]

After Stalin's death, the Eastern European satellites began to be troubled by a good deal of unrest and disorder. Beginning with more and more open expressions of discontent and disillusionment by hitherto loyal communists, the widespread state of turmoil at times erupted into an open uprising —a spontaneous revolt in East Germany in June, 1953, which was sparked by a workers' demonstration and had to be put down by Soviet military forces; a serious strike during the same year in Pilzen, Czechoslovakia; the Poznan riots in the summer of 1956 and the general ferment following these disorders; the subsequent defiance shown by the Polish communists to the Soviet emissaries after the reinstatement of the "revisionist" Gomulka as party chief; and, finally, the Hungarian uprising of October, 1956.[53] Prudence demanded immediate steps to raise the standard of living in the satellite countries as well as in the U.S.S.R. The morale and effectiveness of the Communist parties in the satellites had to be raised by giving greater autonomy and greater opportunity to gain if not popularity at least the acceptance by their own people. The local Stalinists had to be removed or curbed.[54] But now Khrushchev faced a dilemma, because Castro was seemingly becoming himself a Caribbean Stalin.

With all these potential problems hanging around, however, Khrushchev saw the advantages of using Castro's Cuba as a political asset which perhaps might reverse a negative trend. Since the great Communist victory in China and the extension of Communist power into North Vietnam, the international Communist movement had had few gains to boast about. In fact, beginning in the early 1950s the tide of events seemed to turn against the Soviet Union: Tito strengthened Yugoslav independence from Stalin and rebelled against Soviet ideological orthodoxy; the U.S.S.R. and China headed toward a split; Albania joined the Chinese; there was political upheaval and unrest in East Germany, Hungary and Poland; and Communist liberation movements around the world had suffered one defeat after another. If Cuba would go "socialist," however, it would provide fresh evidence to support the Soviet claim that "Socialism" was the true wave of the future.[55]

Contrasting with the moderation of the Soviet line, the Chinese advocated the use of the third world as the place to fight imperialism using all available means — including violent ones. From the early sixties they had begun urging the third world countries to fight "national liberation" wars, taking the revolutionary initiative from Russian hands now tempered by their own internal economic and political problems. It was not lost to the Chinese leaders that Fidel's call for turning the Andes into a Latin American "Sierra Maestra" was closer to Peking's than Moscow's line. Contrary to the Soviet theory which maintained that the main revolutionary struggle was East VS. West, that is, between the Socialist (Communist) camp, headed by Moscow, and the Capitalist camp, headed by the United States, the Chinese claimed that the real conflict was South VS. North; between the oppressed peoples of Asia, Africa, and Latin America and the centers of white man's imperialism, with which they also associated the Russians.[56]

By the Spring of 1960, the PSP leaders had achieved what looked like a close identification with the Cuban leader and continued doing missionary work in Moscow to stress Castro's potential to the world Communist movement. There were indications that, despite his doubts, Khrushchev was attracted not only by Castro's political success at home but also by his anti-Americanism. As time passed, the Cuban communists, as they became aware of the degree to which Castro was in complete control of the Cuban masses, were becoming less fearful of the risks inherent in the headlong pace at which he was driving his revolution. This evolution in their position led Blas Roca, the Secretary General of the PSP, to visit Moscow in the Spring of 1960. There are reasons to believe that his main purpose was to explain to Khrushchev the opportunity available at the doorstep of the United States to further a movement of "national liberation" and to advance the cause of Marxism-Leninism.[57]

The success of Roca's mission to Moscow was assured by the impact on Khrushchev of the U-2 incident which drastically evaporated the "spirit of Camp David" and led to the adoption by the Russians of a bitterly aggressive attitude towards the United States. The restoration of the diplomatic relations between Cuba and the Soviet Union was announced in Moscow on May 7, while Roca was still there.

Soviet public approval of Cuba had begun to be expressed only in the Spring of 1960, following Deputy Premier Mikoyan's visit to Havana in that year and the establishment of diplomatic relations between the two countries. But even then the Soviets invested only modest economic aid to compensate for the cut in U.S. sugar purchases from Cuba.

In July, 1960, President Eisenhower reduced 700,000 tons from the Cuban sugar quota for the remaining of the year. "I believe," asserted the President, "that we could fail in our obligation to our people if we did not take steps to reduce our reliance for a major food product upon a nation which has embarked upon a deliberate policy of hostility toward the United States."[58]

President Eisenhower's total suspension of Cuba's sugar quota caught Khrushchev by surprise. He was unprepared for anything so drastic and was now confronted with far more than he had bargained for when in February he had allowed Mikoyan to use Cuba as a chip to create trouble for the Americans. In order to replace the United States as an importer of Cuban sugar under conditions that would permit the Cubans to survive, the Russian sugar economy would have to be profoundly readjusted. This would require weeks of study, action and negotiations. Before long-term commitments could be made, Khrushchev would need to evaluate future American policy toward Cuba and the risks involved in supporting Castro.[59]

Although Soviet economic aid to Cuba expanded after the termination of the United States sugar purchases and the break in U.S.-Cuban relations on January 3, 1961, Khrushchev still hesitated to fully endorse the Cuban revolution. Neither Castro's proclamation on the eve of the Bay of Pigs invasion that his revolution was "socialist," nor his assertion, in a speech on December 1, 1961, describing himself to be a Marxist-Leninist, evoked any response from Moscow.

Evidently, Castro's strategy was to compromise the Soviet Union by rapidly giving them the impression that he was implementing in Cuba the structures of a Soviet-type state. But even then the ambitious Soviet leaders were not willing to buy. They advised patience and constantly warned Fidel and his people about turning Cuba into a socialist state. All Soviet emissaries, ambassadors, and party officials in Moscow —even Khrushchev himself and Mikoyan— recommended calm and patience. They were all shocked by the accelerated and artificial process of nationalization they saw Fidel engaged in.[60]

The Russians' reluctance to accept Cuba as a full-fledged member of the socialist camp was understandable. Khrushchev was still in doubt about Castro's ability to survive and recognized that Fidel's attempts to identify himself with the socialist bloc were designed to involve the Soviet Union in Cuba's defense against possible U.S. hostile action. But, overcoming his doubts about Fidel, Khrushchev saw a golden opportunity to plant a Soviet satellite at the very doorstep of the United States.

Khrushchev Enters Muddy Waters

After Castro's apparent radicalization by the end of 1959, his alliance with the PSP and his expanding conflict with the United States, Khrushchev's interest in Cuba increased. In Fidel's conflict with the Americans, the Soviet Premier saw a heaven-sent opportunity to recover from his failure to make gains in Berlin and the possibility of using Cuba as a tool for diverting Washington's attention from Europe. The Russians were also still suffering from the embarrassment resulting from the revolt of several Eastern European satellites and Khruschev was now pleased with the possibility of seeing the U.S placed in a similar difficult situation. The intensification of the Sino-Soviet dispute, which increased the pressure in Moscow to support anti-imperialist revolutions, constituted another consideration. The fact that Cuba sought to make initial contacts with Peking raised the possibility of growing Chinese influence in Cuba and, as a result, increased Soviet interest in developments on the Island.

On April 15, after an air raid on Havana prior to the Bay of Pigs invasion, Castro proclaimed the socialist character of the Cuban revolution. But in the flood of Soviet articles and speeches celebrating the victory of *Playa Girón* (Cuban name for the Bay of Pigs invasion) not a single word, not one allusion, was given to Fidel's new self-appointed political path. Fidel's decision, as always, had been quite unilateral; he had not asked his ideological fathers in Moscow for approval. Of course, Khrushchev was very irritated with this *fait accompli* concocted by Fidel alone.

But, far from waiting for signs of acceptance from the Kremlin, Fidel pushed the Soviets even further. In a speech delivered as usual without a prepared text, that took him five hours to deliver on the night of December 1-2, 1961, he confessed that he had always been "...a Marxist-Leninist and shall remain one until the last day of my life."[61]

But the Soviet Union and the socialist countries remained silent. A month passed without any reaction from Moscow or other capitals of the socialist camp. When, in the first days of January, 1962, the customary messages commemorating the anniversary of the revolution arrived, not a word appeared about Fidel's instant "socialism" or "Marxism-Leninism."[62]

Despite American accusations, as late as 1962 there was no evidence that Castro's revolution had been seized by external forces, nor that he was a Russian puppet. The facts indicated that the Russians were very carefully keeping their distance from Cuba. When Anastas Mikoyan was in Mexico attending a Soviet trade fair, *Revolución* twice proposed that he extend his journey to Havana.[63] Khrushchev recalled that it was the Cubans who made the offer to Mikoyan in Mexico city, but he was ordered from Moscow to refuse. Though later Khrushchev approved the visit, it is interesting to guess why the initiative appeared in the now openly anti-communist *Revolución* —Castro's newspaper— and not in the PSP's *Hoy*.[64]

Even Arthur Schlesinger, Jr., recognized that Castro was hardly a Soviet puppet and was often nearly as much an embarrassment to Moscow as he was to Washington. Before the forces of the Bay of Pigs invasion had been entirely crushed, Castro came out with a declaration that Cuba would follow a Socialist course. "We had trouble understanding the timing of this statement," affirmed Khrushchev in his memoirs, "Castro's declaration had the immediate effect of widening the gap between himself and the people who were against Socialism, and it narrowed the circle of those he could count on for support against the invasion. As far as Castro's personal courage was concerned, his position was admirable and correct. But from a tactical standpoint, it didn't make much sense."[65]

Notwithstanding Castro's continued and persistent pounding at the Russian gates, the Soviet leader had some serious doubts as to where it might lead in the future. Though his defiance of the United States was according to their interests, the alliance with Castro also presented certain problems. Would they be able to contain Castro's ambitions? How far would he embroil the U.S.S.R. in Latin America and at what cost? Opposition to Castro was already strong among the Latin American Communist parties; they were reluctant to endanger their precarious status by taking up arms and rebelling against their governments. Furthermore, to adopt Castro's tactics would be an abrupt shift to "putschist" and "adventurist" policies, specifically denounced by Lenin and condemned by Khrushchev.[66]

The Soviet response to Fidel's self-invitation to the socialist camp was slow and dubious. In its origins, the Castro regime was non-Communist, and therefore suspect.[67] The Communist party was notable for its absence from the highest circles of the Cuban government; and after all, a warm welcome extended to Cuba would imply some kind of military backing, a step not to be undertaken lightly.

In February, 1960, a new step in Cuban-Soviet relations began with the statements made by Khrushchev sympathizing with Cuban aspirations of political and economic independence. Addressing the Indian parliament, the Soviet Premier expressed the Soviet sympathies "with such nations as Cuba, which is actively fighting to safeguard its national and economic independence."[68] Perhaps Khrushchev did not realize that, by accepting Castro because of his anti-Americanism, he was making the same mistake the U.S. makes most of the time: to embrace allies because of what they oppose, not because of what they propose.

Initially, Castro's first probings in the direction of Moscow were not encouraged in the Kremlin. Beginning in September 1959, the gentle mood of Camp David prevailed for a time while the Soviet Premier explored the possibilities of some kind of limited détente with the United States. Cuba was therefore held at arm's length by Khrushchev.[69]

The next few months after Fidel's "I am a Marxist" speech brought only silence from Russia, and from China as well, on the delicate point of the new-created Marxism-Leninism. The Soviet Union, in its anniversary greetings at the beginning of the year 1962, referred not to a Socialist Cuban society, but only to a "new" one. The trade agreements with both Russia and China for 1962 were still unsigned in March of that year. No accord with Russian general strategy had been reached.[70]

On July 26, 1961, the anniversary of Castro's attack on the Moncada barracks, red flags went up beside the Cuban flag all over the island, supposedly to honor their Russian guest of honor, cosmonaut Yuri Gagarin. The Internationale was replacing the 26th of July March as the new song of the revolution, and the crowd happily chanted: *"¡Fidel!, ¡Jruschov!, ¡Estamos con los dos!"* ("Fidel!, Khrushchev!, We are with you both!"). Advancing a step forward, Che Guevara publicly stated that Cuba was now a part of the socialist world. In September, 1961, however, Cuban President Osvaldo Dorticós pushed harder during a visit to Moscow to obtain official recognition of Cuban Socialist status, but failed.[71]

By the end of 1961 it became evident that things were not going well from Castro's point of view. Cuba's admission to the socialist bloc had not been conceded in Moscow and economic assistance was less than adequate. No signs of revolutionary activity had appeared in Latin America. Almost a year and a half had passed since Fidel had invoked the Andes in his famous prediction, but nothing had happened. The newly created ORI (*Organizaciones Revolucionarias Integradas, Integrated Revolucionary Organizations*) was falling completely under the influence of the stereotyped old-line Cuban Communists. Fidel thought it was time to force Khrushchev into action by playing the highest card of all.

On December 1, 1961, Fidel revealed his old hidden passion for Marxism. His purpose, at least the one that appeared crystal-clear to the Russians,[72] was to push his way into the socialist bloc in order to obtain further economic aid and military backing and to establish, at the Soviets' expense, his primacy as the undisputed revolutionary leader in Latin America. Moreover, as a selfcertified Marxist-Leninist, he could also establish whatever reinterpretation of doctrine he wished against the old pro-Moscow parties, whose subordination to him might have to be reemphasized from time to time.[73]

In retrospect it seems clear that, perhaps drawn by the dynamic of the Soviet-American conflict and the rivalry with China, Khrushchev had engaged in a commitment in Cuba not justified on grounds of ideology or interests, legitimate or illegitimate. The same strange dynamic of the Soviet-American conflict had previously drawn the U.S.S.R. into expansive and dangerous policies, the beneficiaries of which have been such opportunistic leaders as Mao, Tito, and Nasser. Now Castro wanted to add himself to the list.[74]

When in 1961 Castro announced, first, that Cuba was a socialist state, and, later on, that he was a Marxist-Leninist, the Soviet leader was extremely reluctant to acknowledge his claims. There was an important reason for Khrushchev to act that way. From the point of view of ideology, a Soviet concession that Fidel Castro, a non-communist, had created and was ruling over a socialist state without the help of the communist party, would be tantamount to negating a fundamental principle of Marxism-Leninism, namely, that at some point in a revolutionary process the leading role in setting up the new socialist state is inevitably assumed by the "vanguard party of the workers and peasants." This meant a Soviet-controlled Communist party, which in Cuba had been the PSP, the legitimate Marxist-Leninist vanguard for over thirty-five years. Hence, it was not easy for Khrushchev to swallow Fidel's ideologically embarrassing proposition.[75]

It seems that, at least to Khrushchev, after Castro's rush to communism and his pledge of fidelity to Marxism all things seemed ripe for a takeover of the Cuban revolution by old-style Communists. Apparently this is what the PSP leaders believed, so the party's theoreticians began rewriting recent history to show that, from the earliest moments, the anti-Batista struggle had been guided not by Castro's *barbudos* in the mountains, but by the workers in the factories under the leadership of their vanguard, the Communist party.[76] Parallel to this theoretical activity, a practical one to gain power at all levels of the government, and particularly in the intelligence services and the army, was hastily developed.

But Fidel's humility and weakness proved to be deceitful. By the beginning of 1961 mixed signals began to flow from Havana to Cuba's worried benefactors in the Kremlin.

By that time, a great concern about Fidel and the Cubans had developed in the Kremlin. First of all, Cuba was a real economic embarrassment to the Soviets, who made a great mistake in trying to undertake the development of a country whose tastes, needs, aspirations, and economy had been modeled following the American model. Cuba, which Khrushchev initially believed could become a showcase of the Soviet model of development in America, was in fact quickly turning into a showcase of Soviet inefficiency, mainly due to the Cuban leader's inability to make good use of Soviet aid. Furthermore, Cuba was an ideological source of distress due to the propagation of Fidel's "heretical" ideas and his immature propensity to preach to the Soviets about how to conduct things in their own back-yard. Moreover, Fidel's behavior toward the Chinese was creating a new focus of dissent in a field already engaged in internal quarrels. In addition, his front line position in the Latin American anti-imperialist struggle put a question-mark on Khrushchev's thesis of peaceful coexistence, and played right into Mao's hands.

It was hardly a coincidence that on July 26, 1960, only 17 days after Khrushchev's promise of "figurative" rocket support of Cuba, Castro made public a dramatic declaration stating that the Andes mountains would become the Sierra Maestra of all America.[77] Then, on January 31, after Cuba was expelled from the Organization of American States, Castro proclaimed the Second Declaration of Havana, in which the growing differences between the Soviets and the Cuban leader became even more evident.

The violent tone of the Declaration, which evidenced Castro's characteristic writing style, would not correspond to Soviet policy, which at that moment aimed to leave avenues open for an accommodation with the Unites States.[78] The declaration did not mention the usual fashionable Soviet stereotypes of "peaceful coexistence" and "peaceful transition," but instead urged the people of Latin America to follow Cuba's example. The Declaration's main thesis, which proclaimed that the duty of the revolutionary was to make the revolution, was obviously directed against the Latin American Communist parties and their Kremlin masters.

Though the Second Declaration of Havana was aimed at the United States, unlike the first, it was also directed against the Soviet Union.[79] The main thesis of the Declaration was not only a call to arms in all of Latin America against the U.S., but also a direct challenge to the Kremlin's leadership of the revolutionary movements in Latin America.[80] "We know that [eventually] the revolution will triumph in America and the World" —went the Declaration— "but this does not mean that revolutionaries should sit on their doorsteps and wait to see the corpse of imperialism pass by."[81] Obviously Khrushchev was concerned about the possibility of more third world victorious revolutions following Fidel's advice, looking afterwards to the Soviet Union for economic help and military protection.[82]

Castro was an entropic element who had materialized out of the blue to disrupt the delicate homeostasis of the world Communist system. As described by *Time* magazine, Fidel was egotistic, impulsive, immature, disorganized. A spellbinding romantic, he could talk spontaneously for as much as five hours without strain. He hated desks. He used to sleep irregularly or simply forgot to sleep at all, nurturing in revolutionary euphoria.[83] Fidel belonged to a specific mental type of people with strong tendencies for over-simplification. Yet, his rare ability to find simplistic solutions for even the most complex problems, and the radical and solemn tone in which he announced his decisions, even the more absurd and banal ones, constituted a particular attraction for people living in this chaotic world.[84] According to *Time's* confused reporter, Castro had the Cuban moralistic streak in spades, showing no apparent affection for money or soft living. He had to be cajoled into changing his filthy fatigues. His only luxury were 50 cts. Montecristo cigars. Though he had lots of confidence, physical courage, shrewdness and good luck, his vaguely leftist hopes for Cuba's future were not based on a clear political program.[85]

Contrary to Khrushchev, who apparently was sincere in his hate of Capitalism but not of America or the American people, Castro had that specific mental quality called "compulsive determination," which may explain his almost hysterical antipathy for the United States. He hated America and the Americans with a hatred that had more to do with psychiatry than politics.[86]

Fidel has always preferred intuition to reason. When he wants something he has the mental equipment for following a logical argument and answering it. He has above-average reasoning power and a superb eidetic or photographic memory. But this is not his real genius. What impels him mostly is his unlimited faith in his intuition. He seems to have made his greater (and also his worse) decisions of his life in the spur of the moment and on an irrational basis —a characteristic shown also by Adolf Hitler. At most, Castro was seen in the Kremlin as a tropical version of Tito. But Titoism no longer seemed to be a reliable antidote to nationalism, but more as a virus that might induce it.[87]

In a long speech on July 26, 1960, Castro promised "to continue making the nation the example that can convert the Cordillera of the Andes into the Sierra Maestra of the hemisphere."[88] Castro's obsession with military intervention against his Latin American neighbors, though concealed in bombastic rhetoric, was designed to appeal to Latin American aspirations of freedom and justice, and showed his readiness to do anything necessary to extend the power of Castroism. During 1959 he directly intervened or aided in supporting armed invasions of Panama, Nicaragua, Haiti and the Dominican Republic.

Former Minister of Communications Enrique Oltusky recalls that on the very first conversation he had with Che Guevara, they had a strong argument when Oltusky argued that the revolution should go easy and conceal its activities, or the United States would take reprisals. This ignited Che's scorn. Guevara told him that the revolution from "the very outset must develop in a struggle to death with imperialism." "Genuine revolution cannot be concealed," said Guevara.[89]

Khrushchev's insistence in peaceful coexistence and peaceful transition to power was most meaningful in the context of Western Communist parties —precisely those which had the last chance on gaining power.[90] Therefore, if the available evidence is correct, one can safely assume that Khrushchev did not approve of Castro's strategy or his plans regarding the future Latin American revolution. The radicalism of the Second Declaration of Havana was at odds with the Soviet strategy worked out by the 81 communist parties in 1960, and by the 22nd Soviet Party Congress a year later. The Soviet strategy was based on the possibility of realization of socialist revolutions, not via armed struggle but elections, as a first stage towards communism. This strategy was on a collision course with Castro's point of view expressed in the Declaration.

Due to the fact that the allegiance of the national armies of the Soviet bloc countries could not be taken for granted, the most efficient form of security for the Communist regimes was provided by Soviet armed units stationed in the East European "people's democracies" by virtue of the Warsaw Pact alliance. That was not and could not be, however, the case of Cuba, so far apart from the Soviet geopolitical sphere of influence, and with an army controlled by Castro.

Underdevelopment... But Just a Little

When the Soviets began closing ties with Castro they were sure that, because of the paradoxically good economic boom during Batista's final years in power, Cuba was in the best position to emerge as a positive example of the Communist way of development. From that point of view the situation in Cuba differed quite a lot from that of other countries after a revolution. The civil war had done little damage, even in the countryside, and nothing had happened to upset the smooth running of the economy. And they also knew quite well that, although distorted in some way by the American influence, Cuba's economy was very healthy, making the country one of the most developed in all of Latin America.

The nascent Cuban bourgeoisie of the first decades of independence had suffered catastrophically from the economic collapse of the 1920s. In just one year Cuba's national income was cut by 63 percent. Twenty Cuban banks with 334 branches and deposits of 130 million dollars were forced to close and, by 1939, 83 percent of all Cuban deposits was held by foreign banks. It was not until WWII that the Cuban bourgeoisie began to recover. High sugar prices, a direct outcome of the war, refloated the whole economy and huge profits were rapidly accrued to Cuban capitalists in year after year of *vacas gordas* (fat cows). The value of the sugar crop rose from 110 million dollars in 1940 to 256 million in 1942, and to 677 million in 1947. Bank deposits rose from 183.9 million dollars to 727.3 million dollars in 1951, while the proportion of them held by Cuban banks climbed from 16.8 per cent in 1939 to 60.2 percent in 1955.[91]

But the wealth of the Cuban bourgeoisie actually concealed its relative economic weakness. A great percentage of the Cuban economy was controlled by the United States and, even more dangerous to the Island's economic development, Cuban capital was usually interested not in competing but in collaborating with American capital. This resulted in an integration of the Cuban bourgeoisie within the economy of a foreign capitalism.[92]

During the Second World War and the first decade of the Cold War, Cuba prospered with little or no American interference. By the mid-fifties, more than half of the population had become urban, and the per-capita income of Cubans was the fourth highest of all the countries in Latin America. By 1957, less than one third of Cuba's imports came from the United States, and less than one fifth of Cuban exports were destined thereto. On the other hand, it was evident that the half-century of American influence over Cuba had been beneficial rather than disadvantageous —at least from the technocentric point of view so well criticized by Mexican poet Octavio Paz. By 1958, the previous near-monopoly of American control over the sugar industry in Cuba had diminished to the extent that hardly more than one third of the sugar production was in American hands. Cuba ranked among the most advanced countries in Latin America. In 1958 Cubans had one automobile for every thirty-nine inhabitants —more than highly advanced countries such as Sweden or Belgium.

Though the Cubans had been forced to accept a humiliating limited sovereignty after having fought a long, bloody war against Spain and the republic survived through the pillage of corrupt politicians who were protected in the shadows of the United States, the story also has another side. Economically, the Cubans had benefitted from the U.S. By the late fifties Cuba's economy had reached what W.W. Rostow called the "take-off" stage on its road to becoming a fully economically developed nation.[93]

According to statistics published by the National Bank of Cuba for 1956, the income per-capita for Cubans was 336 pesos (1 Cuban peso was equal to 1 U.S. dollar at the time), being the second highest in Latin America. The principal industry was sugar, a highly mechanized industry with efficient sugar mills, a developed railway network and up-to-date ports and highways. In relation to population, the Island was the most heavily capitalized in Latin America.[94]

Pre-Castro Cuba was not underdeveloped or backward like in the so-called Third World countries. It was, on the contrary, among the more highly developed

Latin American countries. Cuba ranked first among Latin American countries in the extent of railway and highway communication. It ranked second in private automobiles in relation to population, and also in energy consumption. It ranked third in life expectancy at birth, radio sets in relation to population and fourth in electricity consumption per-capita. It also ranked fourth in telephones in relation to population, and in the literacy of the population over ten years of age (76 per cent).

Only Mexico, Chile and Brazil outranked Cuba in the value of industrial production. Over two thirds of the population could read and write, a figure only surpassed by the educated nations of the southern tip of South America. One out of every five Cubans was a skilled worker. Cuba ranked third in the number of physicians. The Island had the greatest number of television stations in Latin America. In the whole continent only Americans attended movies more frequently than Cubans.[95] The proud Cubans compared themselves with the United States and not with the rest of Latin America. Like the United States, Cuba was a country of immigrants, who regularly arrived to the Island from the four corners of the world. Save for political reasons, as in the worst times of the Machado and Batista dictatorships, Cubans rarely emigrated.

Before Castro took power in 1959, Cuba was one of the countries of Latin America where the standard of the working masses was particularly high. Hugh Thomas, citing a variety of sources, among them UNESCO's Basic Facts and the UN Statistical Yearbook for 1960-63, observed that Cuba had more tv sets per capita than any other Latin American country —indeed more than Italy— and more automobiles per capita than any other Latin American country except oil-rich Venezuela.

As proof of the hard conditions of the rural population in Cuba, some Castro-friendly authors have cited the fact that only 4 percent of the Cuban peasants ate meat as a regular part of their diet, and that while 11 percent drank milk, less than 2 percent ate eggs, 1 percent fish, 3 percent bread and none ate green vegetables. Though those frequently quoted statistics are true, they don't reflect the real life of Cuban peasantry. In fact, only 4 percent of the Cuban rural population ate *beef* meat, because most Cuban peasants prefer pork and poultry. But there are no statistics about its widespread consumption because it was mainly from pigs and chickens raised for self-consumption of which no statistics were kept by the Department of Commerce because no commercial transactions were involved.[96] Also, the statistics don't reflect the fact that most of the 11 percent of the rural population who drank milk were children. There is a cultural explanation for this. Usually Cuban farmers don't drink milk. For them milk is just for children. In a country where *machismo* was widespread, it was a sign of weakness and effemination to see a grown up man drinking milk.

Granted, it is also true that just a very small percent of the Cuban peasants ate fish, but the picture was not too different in the cities. Some Cuban scholars noticed the fact that Cuba is an island apparently with its back to the sea. Though Cubans love shrimp, lobster, oysters and other types of seafood, they have never been too attracted to fresh fish. This is reflected in the fact that the Cuban kitchen conspicuously lacks good fish recipes. The few Cuban recipes with fish are made paradoxically with dried fish, like *bacalao* (dried cod, traditionally imported from Norway), which Cubans love.

Also, as it is somehow understandable that most Cuban peasants rarely ate bread —bakeries were located in the cities— it is more difficult to explain why they almost ate no vegetables. One explanation may be that, more than dictated by economic conditions, the low vegetable diet of Cuban farmers was poor alimentary habits inherited from the Spanish peasants. Another explanation could be that they ate mostly the vegetables they planted for self-consumption, therefore it was not recorded in official statistics. A most revealing thing, that official statistics seem to ignore, is that in many of the homes of those poor peasants who apparently ate such a limited diet, radios were commonplace. By late 1950s it was not uncommon to see tv antennas on the roofs of many houses, even in neighborhoods considered poor and in the countryside.

In the late fifties the American investments in Cuba had been growing. In 1959, 12% of American investments were concentrated in industry, against 5% in 1929; and 15 % in oil against 1% thirty years before.[97] The Cuban bourgeoisie, however, had displaced with great success the Americans in some sectors of the economy, notably banking and agriculture. In 1929, American investors controlled 69% of Cuban agriculture, against only 36% in 1959. In 1959, Cubans controlled two-thirds of the banks in Cuba.

But, despite its strong economy, which Castro inherited almost intact, no other developing country was creating so many problems for the Russians. It was a strange and comical sight in the history of the Cold War and in the history of Communism, to see the unexpected presence of thousands of stocky Russians and East Europeans sweating profusely under the fierce tropical sun, taken aback by the laziness and the inefficiency of the "revolutionaries" who were supposed to be building socialism with their help.

Che Guevara's Economic Idealism

On August 26, 1961, at a National Convention on Production held in Havana, Che Guevara stated categorically that the revolution faced no crisis in production; far from it, production had never stopped rising from 1959 on. And Che spoke at length about the marvelous future waiting just around the corner for liberated Cuba. By the end of the four-year plan, affirmed Che, Cuba would be the most industrialized country in Latin America, with the highest per capita consumption of steel, cement, electricity, petroleum and tractors. By 1970 Cubans would use as much cloth and as many pairs of shoes as Swedes, and their consumption of food would also be on a level with that of the advanced countries of Western Europe.

But reality paid no attention to the Cuban revolutionary's dreams and problems began to develop in an unexpectedly accelerated way. The plans elaborated by Che Guevara and his friends rapidly proved to be highly unrealistic: Che wanted to change Cuba as swiftly as possible into a heavy industrialized power equipped with the latest technology, such as electronics, steel, plastics, etc., but he failed to take into account such factors as sources of raw materials, economic traditions, markets, manpower, profitability, and the limits to development potential.[98]

The lack of success soon evidenced both in agriculture and industry, and the cause was not the half-heartily enforced American commercial embargo, for it proved to be almost totally ineffective. The real cause of the failures was the mistakes of the Cuban leaders and, particularly, of Castro himself who, with his special kind of madness, refused to heed his Soviet advisors, and engaged the country in the craziest economic projects a human mind could conceive. Cuba's economic difficulties began when Castro unilaterally decided against all advises to make an agrarian revolution in a country that essentially had no agrarian problem and was mainly urban and commercial and tied to the international price system.[99]

It seems that both Castro and Guevara had cherished the idea that the Soviet Union would supply Cuba with complete factories, but forgot to consider the cost of raw materials to be processed in these factories, which sometimes were more costly than the finished products that the factories would have produced.[100] As Theodore Draper has pointed out, the mistakes made by Castro were beyond belief. And his biggest mistake was when he decided to cut back Cuba's sugar production.

In 1952, the year that Fulgencio Batista took power after a coup d'état, Cuba produced 7.2 million tons of sugar. For Cuba, it was better to produce more sugar at a lower price than less sugar at a higher price, because in a competitive market Cuba would keep its lead in the world market, and by keeping prices low, it discouraged the development of competition in the rest of the world. High production meant more sugar to export. Conversely, if the harvest was diminished, the diminished quantity of sugar produced would bring about a price increase and stimulate foreign production —which then would be able to compete with. The country received the same foreign exchange for a high-quantity export at low prices than for a smaller quantity exported at higher prices. The owners of the plantations and mills preferred to control the market and earn more in the long run rather than go for a quick profit and then lose it in a few years.

But, at a Council of Ministers meeting at the end of 1961, Castro surprised everybody when he announced that the next day he was going on television to tell the people to destroy part of their cane fields in order to plant fruits and vegetables. Despite strong criticism from his advisers, Castro proceeded with his plan. The farmers began to plow the cane under and in a few years the harvests were reduced a full 50 percent, from around six million tons to three million. As a direct result of Fidel's instructions, half of the canefields were destroyed, ruining years of work and hundreds of thousands of invested pesos. Castro's mistake increased Cuba's foreign exchange for a brief period of time, but in the long run it proved to be ruinous for the whole Cuban sugar industry and the Island lost its markets to other sugar producers.[101] Not only in the sugar industry, but in the whole Cuban economy, the plans elaborated by Castro worked very badly in practice and, soon after, the Cubans began blaming their Soviet comrades for the disaster.

A few months after the Russians began sending their equipment to Cuba, they discovered that tropical climates require special materials and conditioning that they were not prepared to produce. Normally, Russian equipment was not designed or intended to be used in climates with high heat and humidity. The frustrated Cubans soon began blaming the Russians and their equipment. Given the Cubans' past experience dealing with Western goods and technology, Soviet products seemed rather crude to them.

As early as the beginning of 1962, Soviet intelligence got wind of Che's sharp criticism of the Soviet way of foreign trade and of the merits of their goods.[102] Seemingly, despite the official posture, Soviet aid did not please the Cubans. Criticism became more and more open, not only in Che's Ministry of Industry, but also in the Ministry of Foreign Trade, where the Russians had been nicknamed *"los bolos"* (the coarse ones).[103] Cuba's type of Communism or *socialismo con pachanga*,[104] as Che called it, was certainly disastrous and very expensive for the Russians.

Meanwhile, Castro continued pushing his harebrained plans, and ordered a collectivization of farms and even small commercial and manufacturing enterprises at a pace unequalled even in the Soviet Union, China or Easter Europe. As expected, this quickly affected work productivity and required a large increase in the management which materialized in an increase of government bureaucracy.

A mounting stagnation had settled, first, over agriculture and, soon after, over the entire Cuban economy. In January, 1962, the government announced that some basic foods would be rationed.[105] On March 13, 1962, Fidel was forced to introduce an even more severe rationing on most essential foods.[106] In a tv speech Castro denounced the U.S. economic blockade and blamed it for his decision to ration basic foods. At the same time that he apologized for the lack of promised economic improvements, he blamed both "American imperialism" and the errors of his own regime for the economic problems.[107]

The Ruble Stops Here

By the end of 1961, the worried and annoyed Russians called a halt, and began tightening the screws on Cuba. Soviet advisors appeared at every ministry and immediately began criticizing the Cuban methods. When the Russians made adverse comments about the Cuban efforts on industrialization, the Cubans began muttering that the Soviet Union did not really seek to encourage Cuban industrialization because they wanted the Cubans to depend on the Soviets forever for their purchase of heavy industrial products.

Though the Russians didn't have any concrete proof, some of them suspected that the Chinese were behind the anti-Soviet campaign. Some Soviet officials in Havana told their Cuban friends that Khrushchev was exasperated by the sheer incompetence of the Castro regime. Added to the Soviets' growing bitterness, widespread resentment toward the continuation of large-scale aid to Cuba was also building up among the leaders of the East European Communist satellites.[108]

Reports of Cuban inefficiency and wasteful use of Soviet aid kept reaching Moscow and giving cause for concern. Russian officials at the Soviet embassy in Havana cracked jokes among themselves calling Castro's Cuba *Kubyshka*.[109]

In a rally at the University of Havana in mid-March, 1962, Castro called on the Cuban youth to develop a more intense Communist spirit, and promised a new society in Cuba devoid of individualism —a clear criticism to the Soviet Union.[110] With his usual arrogance and megalomania, Castro had entrusted himself the role of Jiminy Cricket of the Communist world. He was now the most pure Communist in all of the Communist world, and was going to look after the ideological purity of world communism.

In the meantime a galloping inflation had developed in Cuba, contaminating the workers with laziness due to the lack of incentives. Absenteeism among workers reached alarming proportions and declining morale and reduced purchasing power were soon reflected in the poor quality of work. Black market activities flourished through the width and breadth of the Island. Meanwhile, Cuba had been losing professionals through emigration at a high pace —an emigration caused mainly by Castro's own mistakes.[111]

By March, 1962, *Cuba Socialista* published an article by Che Guevara warning the Cubans that in the future they would have to pay for the raw materials for the factories the government had purchased with their own money and not with Soviet credits.[112] On June 4, 1962, while addressing a group of Cuban students who were going back to their country, Nikita Khrushchev advised them to work hard because arms and heroism alone were not enough to solve every difficulty.[113] Apparently the mercurial Khrushchev was running out of patience with Castro, Guevara, and the rest of the lazy, good-for-nothing Cuban "communists."

In the month of April, 1962, the Cuban economy came perilously close to a total breakdown in sugar production. Widespread anti-regime sabotage erupted with the burning of cane and basic industries all along the island.[114] Anti-Castro demonstrations broke out in Havana, Matanzas, Cárdenas and other cities, but were quickly and violently broken up. Several arrests were reported.[115] Rumors began to circulate mentioning Fidel's angry remarks about old PSP Communists and their Soviet masters in connection with the economic problems in Cuba.[116]

Although the U.S.S.R. and even the pro-Soviet Cuban Communist party had almost nothing to do with Castro's rise to power, this initially seemed to have played into Khrushchev' hands. Now, just after a few months had passed, the initial advantage had turned into a very expensive experiment whose final results looked more blurry every day. This in no way was what the Soviet Premier had ever expected. Khrushchev could not afford a dozen Cubas. Just in case, Communist parties in Latin America got orders from Moscow to create trouble, unrest, flareups, and instability, but preventing at the same time the pro-Castro revolutionaries from taking power. If the Soviet Union could not afford more Castro-style revolutions, Khrushchev reasoned, its puppet Communist parties would have to stall Castro-incited revolutionary movements. As a matter of fact this had been the goal of Moscow's Latin American policy for many years: to keep Latin America capitalist —and a headache for Washington. Once we realize this, one can readily understand Latin American Communist tactics. Communists had often supported dictators —like Batista in Cuba— and inevitably had formed alliances with the extreme Right to bring down centrist governments whose programs included even mild reforms. Paradoxically, in the past, the pro-Soviet Communist parties in Latin America had been America's best allies.[117]

As early as mid-1959, the old-guard PSP leaders became rightfully worried about Castro's radical theories and concerned with the secret training of revolutionaries in Cuba for military adventures against Cuba's neighbors.[118] Yet, having mistakenly come to Castro's rescue —if only for the initial bait of exploiting the political propaganda opportunities offered by the U.S.-Cuban dispute— Khrushchev found himself with a non-desired client on his hands which he could not disavow, at least overtly, without incurring in great embarrassment and loss of prestige.[119] Khrushchev simply could not afford to abandon a country like Cuba, unless at the same time the Soviets were prepared to forego its pretensions of leadership of the Communist camp.

Even more, Fidel's popularity in Cuba bordered on madness, and it would be stupid to oppose him politically.[120] Khrushchev found the relationship with Cuba more and more uncomfortable. Irrespective of Castro's self-professed Marxism, Khrushchev would have leaped at the opportunity of establishing a foothold in Cuba, in line with the Soviets' purely national interest in challenging the U.S. influence in Latin America, in undermining the U.S. security, and simply in annoying Americans. But, at the same time, Castro's unpredictable and arrogant behavior and his own goals of hemispheric domination through subversion had the effect of constraining Soviet flexibility in an area where the Russians previously had been trying to compete under the auspices of Khrushchev's theory of pacific coexistence.

Every American attack on Castro provoked a counter attack.[121] The American owned refineries refused to refine Russian crude, so Fidel took over them. Americans suspended the sugar quote, so Fidel nationalized the mills. Americans ordered the economic blockade, so Fidel nationalized U.S. property. Fidel's counter attack was always stronger than the attack that had provoked it.

Yet Fidel's actions worried Khrushchev. In the past, much less provocative actions had brought the U.S. marines into other Latin American nations. Even the PSP and their followers advised Fidel to keep calm, while Khrushchev himself sent several emissaries recommending Fidel to act with moderation. But, instead of paying attention to Khrushchev's advice, Fidel took further radical measures. It became evident that what he wanted was to compromise the Soviets by drawing them into his own personal vendetta with the United States.[122]

Khrushchev had no clear idea why Castro insisted on identifying his revolution as "Marxist-Leninist" and "proletarian." Maybe it was Castro's only way to stay in power forever, otherwise he would have to satisfy his programmatic commitment to general elections and his personal power would be subject to suffrage constraints. But Castro was obviously a man who was ill-disposed to surrender his firm grip on political power in Cuba.

Nikita Khrushchev had a good political instinct and was not going to fool himself. He was fully convinced that Castro would fall sooner or later from some form of U.S. intervention. He was also unwilling to wage a world war just to protect the crazy Fidel,[123] and help him economically until his fall was deemed too expensive and too useless a sacrifice. Thus Khrushchev agreed in principle to a few barter deals but not to massive aid. He had too many closer allies still far from being on their own feet to get involved with that tiny island halfway around the world. But barter deals apparently were not what Fidel was looking-for. Hence, he tried to force Khrushchev to come through with more. The crafty Fidel calculated that if he identified Cuba as a full member of the Socialist camp the Russians would lose immeasurable propaganda points if they let Cuba down. So he declared Cuba a Socialist country and Khrushchev was stuck.[124] But almost from the very moment that Fidel declared that the revolution was Communist everything turned to hell. There was chaos, rationing, imprisonments, persecutions, summary executions, rioting, fear of the military, and the people were beginning to associate all that with the Soviet Union.[125]

In addition, the ideology behind Fidel Castro and his associates seemed to be just a combination of populism, liberating militarism and old-fashioned caudillismo.[126] Fidel was not some cool theoretician, nor a Soviet-style old "survivor" like Molotov or Gromyko. Though he apparently was a sincere visceral hater of the United States and had been involved in violence since his student days at the University of Havana, his emotional profile resembled more that of the Nazi-style street fighter of the 1930s than of a bureaucratic Communist from the Eastern Communist countries. Castro's character was emotionally unstable and unpredictable, and his ideology, which obviously was not Marxism-Leninism, every day seemed more close to fascism.[127] Some people at the Kremlin began expressing doubts about Fidel's mental sanity.

After Kennedy and Khrushchev met in Vienna, U.S. Secretary of State Dean Rusk called a meeting of the Latin American ambassadors to inform them about the meeting. All the Latin American countries were present with the exception of Cuba and the Dominican Republic. According to Rusk, during the Vienna meeting Khrushchev had mentioned to Kennedy that Castro was "unstable." The Mexican ambassador asked Rusk if it was at all possible to interpret the term used by the Russian leader as meaning "politically and mentally unstable." The question gave rise to an uproar of humor among those who were present.[128]

Actually it was now Fidel and his guerrilla activities, more than the U.S., who worried Khrushchev. The Soviet Union could simply not afford a whole bunch of Castros in Latin America. A Fidel-style takeover of Bolivia, Guatemala or the Dominican Republic would drain Russia's funds like quicksand, and the resulting fiasco could only hurt the Soviets and Khrushchev's prestige. The Soviet Premier was not interested at all in Pyrrhic victories.

Henry Kissinger once noted that Castro never asked the U.S. for economic help, as if Cuba's economic progress would offer too limited a scope for his ambitions. In fact, economic progress can be achieved only by slow, painful, and highly technical measures, contrasting with the heroic exertions of the struggle for independence against the colossus from the north. If Castro were to act on the advice of the Russians —and of the Cuban experts on economic development— the best he could have hoped for would be that after some decades he would lead a small progressive country —perhaps a Switzerland of the Caribbean. Compared with the prospect of leading a continental revolution throughout Latin America —and given Castro's paranoid *delusions de grandeur*— this goal would have appeared to him trivial, boring, even unrealistic.[129]

Khrushchev would have wondered how he, who could not control Albania, could control Cuba, even if Cuba would eventually become a fully fledged "people's republic." Geography and logistics made this nearly an impossible task.[130] Khrushchev soon realized that Fidel was never going to be a prisoner of the Cuban Communists nor a puppet of Moscow. Castro was, by character, incapable of accepting orders or even advice. Given his personality and his desire to play a larger role than that of a pawn in bloc policies, he was likely to be an unstable and unpredictable element in Soviet-Cuban relations.

The Soviet Premier also realized that he had completely failed in his efforts to compel Castro to change his policies, thus the Soviet leader must have concluded that the Cuban leader had to be deposed and replaced by an old-line Communist obedient to the Soviet Union. Khrushchev had carefully studied the possibility of getting rid of Castro by force, but, given the Soviet role vis à vis the Third World and the Chinese, he could not resort to direct action or openly threaten him with force. It was less easy, however, to resist the temptation to proceed to his overthrowing by indirect means.

Therefore, Khrushchev instructed Sergei Kudryavtsev, the Soviet Ambassador to Havana, to put in action his secret plan to overthrow Fidel Castro. But unexpectedly, as the Soviets were taking steps to increase their Cuban involvement, and putting pressure on Fidel with the idea of having him gradually replaced by a man more obedient to Moscow's orders, Fidel suddenly fought back and ordered a wholesale purge of the PSP ranks.

Chapter 4

Coup d'État Khrushchev-Style

> ... perhaps we do not know some things about Soviet
> Foreign policy decision-making that we should.
> —Sherman Kent.

The fall of PSP leader Aníbal Escalante and the expulsion of Soviet Ambassador Sergei Kudryavtsev in the Spring of 1962, key events in the Castro-Soviet relations, have not received all the attention they deserve.[1] It is still a mystery why Castro allowed the "old guard" PSP Communists to attain such power and so many important posts in the Cuban government and the Soviet ambassador to control the Cuban intelligence services. Many analysts have speculated that Castro did not know what was happening; that he was powerless to curb the pro-Soviet Communists; that they were helpful to him and he needed their organizational abilities; that it was just Escalante fighting for personal power; that Kudryavtsev was acting on his own; or that it was just a small incident magnified by Castro in one of his frequent bravados directed at gaining leverage over the Russians.[2]

Most of the analysts, however, seem to have misunderstood the real forces behind Escalante and Kudryavtsev, as well as Castro and Khrushchev's hidden motives to behave the way they did during the whole affair. Both the Cuban and Soviet regimes, each for its own reasons, have successfully concealed the essence of this strange story of political intrigue. However, the importance of this story, a key element to understanding what really happened during the Cuban missile crisis, deserves to be recounted in some detail.[3]

The "Escalante Affair"

Soviet leaders historically distrusted and suspected whatever they did not have under absolute control and Nikita S. Khrushchev was no exception to this rule. To the Soviet leaders "spheres of influence" meant something completely different in the framework of their ideology —the ideology of a single-party State— than it means to the West. To them there could be no secure, "friendly" government except a government run by a Communist party under their total control; no sphere of influence, but a sphere of total Soviet rule; no satisfactory percentage of obedience short of 100.⁴

By mid-1961, Khrushchev became extremely angry with Castro's behavior and concerned about his own ability to hold the unpredictable Cuban leader in check. As seen from the Kremlin, Castro was volatile, undisciplined, and most of the time his decisions made no sense at all. His wholesale executions, mass arrests, and terrorist adventures against his Latin American neighbors, together with the spectacle of thousands of Cubans trying to escape the Island, raised the very Stalinist specter Khrushchev was trying to dispel. Moreover, Castro was systematically destroying the Cuban economy⁵ and paid no attention to "suggestions" coming from Moscow. Thus, Khrushchev concluded that he had to be overthrown and replaced with an old-time PSP Communist obedient to Moscow.⁶

After Castro's victory at the Bay of Pigs, some signs became evident to observers of Cuban politics. Though Castro remained in charge of events, many of his followers from the 26th of July Movement and the Rebel Army were quietly disappearing from the limelight. In their places, old Communist members of the PSP appeared everywhere, issuing orders and instructions in their dogmatic way. By mid 1961, Castro's 26th of July Movement, the PSP, the Revolutionary Directorate, and the Rebel Youth casually began to be referred to as the *"Organizaciones Revolucionarias Integradas"* (Integrated Revolutionary Organizations). Soon after, these words appeared in the press as an acronym "ORI." Then it began to be evident, without any official announcement, that the old PSP Communist leaders (and only they) were always referred to as the *dirigentes* (leaders) of the ORI.⁷

Fidel entrusted the main task of setting up the ORI to the PSP and, more specific, to Aníbal Escalante. Escalante was probably the most energetic figure in the old Communist leadership, a man highly regarded in Moscow.⁸ To judge from a speech Escalante made in Peking on October, 1959, one must assume that the PSP leader was of the opinion that, as the Chinese bourgeoisie accepted the revolution and were coopted into it, the same might occur in Cuba, and Castro would later be forced to yield control to the Communists.⁹ Escalante's feelings were apparently shared by other PSP leaders. In an interview with Max Frankel, of *The New York Times*, Carlos Rafael Rodríguez, another senior PSP leader, asserted that the Communists had the power to "shape Premier Castro's thoughts."¹⁰

In a speech given on July 26, 1961, Fidel explained that it was thanks to their unity of purpose that the different groups of revolutionaries had fused together in the Integrated Revolutionary Organizations. Though he gave no details about the composition of this new movement, everybody knew that the old PSP formed the backbone of the ORI, that Aníbal Escalante was in charge of the organization, and that he and all the others were Communist leaders of the old PSP party.¹¹

On September 6, 1961, Revolución printed a brief *TASS* dispatch datelined the same day in Moscow, saying that Nikita Khrushchev, First Secretary of the

Central Committee of the Communist Party of the U.S.S.R., and Presidium members Alexei Kosyguin and Mikhail Suslov had met with Blas Roca, a PSP leader and one of the leaders also of the ORI of Cuba, and that they had held a friendly and cordial conversation. The substance of Roca's conversation with Khrushchev and his colleagues was not revealed in the *TASS* dispatch.

Professor Maurice Halperin, who was living in Havana at the time, affirms that, quite by accident, he was informed by a reliable source that Roca told the Russian leaders that members of the Chinese Embassy in Havana had been attempting to persuade certain elements of the former PSP to overthrow Castro by a military coup.[12] In retrospect, it seems that the Soviets were actually trying to project on to the Chinese the guilty feelings associated with their plans. It is also possible that, by telling some Castroists about the alleged Chinese intentions, the Soviets were just testing the waters to see what their reaction would be to a Soviet coup directed against Castro.

Meanwhile, the strange events continued. During the whole of 1961, Fidel, unnaturally and incredibly, seemed to be humbling himself abjectly before the PSP Communists and praising their virtues.[13] In a television speech on December 2, 1961, Castro explained to his surprised audience that he had always been a Marxist-Leninist by heart and would be so until the last day of his life.[14] "In the future," Fidel added, "Cuba's government will be by 'collective leadership.'" But, as always, Castro's actions did not agree with his words and he continued governing the country as unilaterally as before.

Certainly neither the PSP Communists nor the Russians believed too much of Castro's own confessed Marxism. It was more probable that he was not telling the truth, but apparently he was a little dazzled by power and by his newly-acquired Marxist toy, and he was willing to let the Communists take the initiative. The Communists seized the opportunity, and aimed all their energies at organizing the ORI for their own benefit in order to capture power from within.[15] The Russians were vitally interested in the organization of a pro-Soviet Cuban Communist party and the only trusted and faithful people they had in Cuba were the members of the PSP.

In the meantime, Escalante continued working feverishly to organize the ORI into a carbon copy of their own organization. ORI offices were set up in almost every important town. These offices, in fact, acted merely as fronts for PSP headquarters. Though giving lip-service to Castro, the organization was completely in the hands of Aníbal Escalante and his pro-Soviet PSP comrades —or so the PSP comrades believed.[16]

Escalante felt so confident in his new role, and Castro seemed so mesmerized by Marxism, that soon the PSP key man went a step further and during a speech called the ORI the "backbone of the revolutionary state."[17] Since Castro made no objection about that opportunistic definition, nor did nothing to curtail PSP activities, it seemed as if such behavior had his tacit approval. Faced with that state of affairs, the *Fidelistas* seemed to have fallen into a state of torpor and frustration and had begun to get used to the idea of a revolution stolen by the old PSP Communists.[18]

After Aníbal Escalante became the ORI's Organizational Secretary, he soon established the ORI's First National Directorate, which was a carbon copy, at party level, of the Cuban government. Everywhere that provincial and municipal ORI directories were set up, local secretaries of the PSP were automatically designated as their heads. Within a few months the ORI emerged as Cuba's shadow government, holding all the political power.[19] It seemed as if Escalante had more power than Castro himself. Little by little the *Fidelistas* were quietly removed from positions of influence. People even had the impression that Fidel and his supporters from the Sierra Maestra were willing to assume a subordinate role to the PSP "old guard."

Unknowingly, Cubans were living what later was called "the year of sectarianism."[20] Escalante felt so powerful that when one of his daughters got married he ordered that one of the mansions left by the escaping bourgeoisie that Fidel had set aside for himself, be given to his daughter.[21]

But the PSP Communists did not realize that, instead of having Fidel in their net, they themselves had been caught in Castro's trap. Actually, Castro was playing a risky cat-and-mouse game with the Cuban Communists and their Kremlin masters. He apparently had no scruples about turning over the job of setting up the ORI to Escalante and the PSP because he knew that, despite all appearances, the real power remained in his hands. The enhanced role of the Communists certainly would inspire more confidence in the Kremlin about his own reliability. But it was a long way from this to actually relinquish power to the old Communists. As professor Maurice Halperin has pointed out, power has always been a strictly personal matter for Fidel.[22]

Writing about this period in Castro-Russian relations, Boris Goldenberg expressed the widespread belief that at that time the old PSP Communists controlled "all the positions of power."[23] But Herbert Matthews, who knew Fidel Castro better, pointed out that Goldenberg should have rather said "all but one."[24]

Earlier in the month the public had been informed that the National Directorate, or governing council, of the ORI had been formed. Of its twenty members, half of them were former PSP leaders, and among them was Aníbal Escalante.

In the meantime, Fidel had secretly began contacting several of the purged anti-Communist *Fidelistas* from his 26th of July Movement, and preparing them to confront the pro-Moscow Communists. News circulated that Faure Chomón, a known anti-Communist, had been recalled from his post as Cuban ambassador to the Soviet Union[25] and appointed Minister of Communications. At the same time some key *Fidelista* men, including Faustino Pérez, Marcelo Fernández and Enrique Oltuski, had begun to move out of oblivion and into positions of prominence. All of them were spending a great deal of their time dwelling on the peril of "sectarianism" and grouping the trusted *Fidelistas* again around Fidel.[26]

Shortly after his speech of December 2, 1961, where he announced that he had always been a Marxist-Leninist at heart, Fidel withdrew from public view. The very few times he had been seen, it was in the company of a group of his trusted Sierra Maestra *comandantes,* most of whom had been out of circulation for well over a year, and were now craving for revenge against those whom they considered responsible for their troubles. Rumors circulated about Castro's angry outbursts against the PSP Communists and their Russian masters. *Bolas* (Cuban slang for rumors) raced through Havana that Fidel had been overheard in a restaurant cursing the old-guard Communists; that he had asked a Latin American government (the *bola* had it as Brazil) about the chances of political asylum. At some time, the rumors had been so persistent that the Mexican Ambassador had to deny rumors that Castro had sought asylum in the Mexican Embassy in Havana.[27] A brief appearance of Fidel in Havana's streets brought out more rumors.[28] Finally, Fidel reappeared in public for the first time since the beginning of February.[29]

While the PSP Communists felt confident that Fidel was securely caught in their net, he had in fact decided that the time had arrived to settle matters with the by now universally detested "old Communists" entrenched in the ORI, and to remove whatever illusions remained in the Kremlin that in the foreseeable future they would take over Havana. During a speech that Castro was delivering at the University of Havana on the night of March 13, somebody read a note written by José Antonio Echevarría, one of the martyrs of a group of university students who had attempted to kill Batista, and omitted a reference to God. Fidel seized the opportunity and created an incident.[30] Suddenly, he began mentioning an undetermined "them" as sectarian, myopic and stupid. Though Fidel did not mention who "they" were, it was hardly necessary. Two days later, an editorial in the first page of *Revolución,* most likely written by Castro himself, called for a "War Against Sectarianism." At that moment nobody on the Island knew what "sectarianism" meant, but they were sure it was something bad involving the pro-Soviet Communists of the PSP. On March 16, Fidel charged once more against "them," but now he directly implicated the PSP and the ORI with "sectarianism."[31]

The showdown between Castro and the pro-Soviet Communists came between March 16 and March 22 of 1962. Acting swiftly, Castro moved ruthlessly in to smash the PSP communists at the ORI and their Soviet allies, and covered his rear guard by deploying some of his most trusted followers to key positions. Celia Sánchez, his personal secretary from the Sierra Maestra days, was appointed Minister of the Presidency; Faure Chomón, ex-Cuban ambassador to the U.S.S.R., was nominated Minister of Communications; and Raúl Castro was designated Vice-Premier, a newly created position.

Then, on March 22, all Havana's newspapers published the membership of the ORI Secretariat. Fidel Castro led the list as First Secretary, followed by Raúl, and Che Guevara. The old Sierra *comandantes* were back in charge.[32] On March 24, *Hoy,* edited by PSP leader Blas Roca and until now acting as unofficial organ of the ORI, declared that "Fidel is the soundest Marxist-Leninist in Cuba, the leading representative of the working class and the most dependable of Communists." Apparently, the "old guard" communists got the feeling that Fidel was cooking something big and bad and were back-pedalling fast.

On March 26, Fidel went in for the kill. Addressing the whole nation over radio and tv on the subject of sectarianism, he openly denounced Aníbal Escalante for his actions as the Organizational Secretary of the ORI. In his speech, Fidel made clear that he was associating sectarianism with Soviet-style Communism.[33] Almost immediately, the PSP members began losing their key positions. They were promptly replaced by reliable *Fidelistas.* The monster that Fidel created had served its purpose, eating up other people, observed Carlos Franqui, yet when he saw that the monster might eat him too, he quickly decapitated it.[34]

Some people argued that Castro's public response to Khrushchev's schemes was moderate, yet Fidel knew quite well that the Soviet Premier would not take it lightly. As the man appointed by Khrushchev to take Castro's place after a Soviet-orchestrated coup d'état, Escalante was a key player in the plot, but he did not act alone. The PSP and the Russians had by no means confined themselves to the political sphere of the ORI, as one may wrongly assume after Castro's denunciation of "sectarianism." The Russians knew that Fidel's power resided in the Rebel Army and in the General Directorate of Intelligence (*Dirección General de Inteligencia,* DGI), and it was there where they had focused most of their efforts.

The DGI and the Russians

The DGI (Dirección General de Inteligencia, General Directorate of Intelligence) was originally a branch of the Rebel Army's Counter-Intelligence section, or G2, which later became the Ministry of Interior (Ministerio del Interior, MININT). To head up the G2, Castro appointed a trusted Fidelista, Major Ramiro Valdés, "Ramirito." From the very beginning, the Soviets made every effort to control the DGI and to mold it into their own image.

Under Russian guidance, Ramiro Valdés, better known for his craftiness than for his intelligence, organized an efficient secret police. He also used the assistance of some prominent leaders of the Revolutionary Directorate appointed by Castro himself, such as José Abrahantes, Carlos Figueredo and Julio García Olivera. But the KGB was active and managed to infiltrate into the DGI a large group of PSP members, headed by Osvaldo Sánchez (then working under the cover name of Lieutenant Rafael Suárez), an experienced PSP leader.

Osvaldo Sánchez Cabrera was a senior cadre of the PSP. He had a seat in its national committee, equivalent of the central committee of the Communist Party of the Soviet Union. A seasoned communist militant, Sánchez had traveled several times to the Soviet Union and had lived there for around five years while attending specialized schools in communist ideology, sabotage, political agitation and terrorism. Though some claims that he was a KGB officer have not been proved, it is safe to assume that, at least, he had been recruited as an agent by the Soviet intelligence services.[35]

As early as May, 1959, the CIA reported that Vadim Kotchergin, a Soviet intelligence officer, arrived in Cuba ostensibly on a trade union delegation, but actually to advise the local Communists on methods of penetrating the Castro government.[36] KGB instructors soon began teaching Cubans the craft of intelligence and clandestine operations before they were assigned to overseas posts.[37]

Castro apparently welcomed Soviet expertise and training for the DGI, but he resisted the KGB's schemes to control his intelligence service. He appointed another of his trusted *Fidelistas,* Major Manuel Piñeiro "Barbarroja" (red beard) to head the DGI. Piñeiro had studied at Columbia University in New York and — adding to Russian suspicions— was married to an American dancer. Piñeiro, who had been in Raúl Castro's column and afterwards became chief of the Army in Oriente province, was one of Castro's staunchest supporters.[38]

Alerted by Castro, Piñeiro kept an eye on the KGB colonel working side by side with him at the DGI. PSP members and KGB officers which occupied advisory positions in the DGI were closely watched by Piñeiro and his people, who reported frequently to Castro himself.[39] When Castro decided to put an end to the Soviet political tutelage, the DGI became an important pawn in the game of power between Castro and Khrushchev.

In late 1960, profiting from Valdés' lack of experience, Osvaldo Sánchez, helped by the KGB people, almost managed to displace Valdés and Piñeiro *de facto* from the directorate of the DGI. But the Soviets, like most people and governments, made the mistake of underestimating Fidel's own abilities to hatch a plot. On January 9, 1961, Osvaldo Sánchez' light plane was flying in a clear night along the north coast of the province of Matanzas when an anti-aircraft battery allegedly failed to properly identify his aircraft, and shot it down. Sánchez and his two PSP comrades were fatally injured in the mysterious accident. The Russians, though angry and suspicious, couldn't say or do anything, and were faced with the loss of their key man inside the DGI.[40] When the news arrived in the Kremlin, Khrushchev became justifiably furious with Castro.

The Enigmatic Kudryavtsev

In retrospect, it seems that the final stage of the Soviet-instigated plot to overthrow Castro began in the Fall of 1961, after the return of PSP leader Blas Roca from a meeting with Khrushchev. The pro-Soviet Communists and the KGB, under the efficient direction of Soviet ambassador Sergei Kudryavtsev, moved swiftly.

But, on June 1, 1962, *Prensa Latina,* Castro's official news agency, reported to the world:[41]

> Soviet Ambassador Sergei M. Kudryavtsev visited Premier Maj. Fidel Castro yesterday afternoon for the purpose of saying goodbye, since he

will return to his country soon to take another important post, which he was recently given. Premier Fidel Castro and Ambassador Kudryavtsev held a friendly and cordial conversation touching on several topics, particularly the achievements attained in the development of relations between both countries in political, economic, and cultural fields.

Both the supreme leaders of the revolution and the U.S.S.R. expressed their great satisfaction over the cordial friendship existing between Cuba and the Soviet Union and their absolute certainty that these fraternal relations will develop even more for the good of both countries and world peace.

Ambassador Kudryavtsev gave the Cuban Premier a sincere message for the Cuban people in which he expresses his best wishes for welfare and economic progress in the construction of the socialist state of Cuba.[42]

The reality, however, differed considerably from the "friendly and cordial" description offered by *Prensa Latina*. Unknown to the Cuban public, Kudryavtsev was actually a senior Soviet intelligence officer.[43] The fact that he had been appointed as the first Soviet ambassador to Castro's Cuba is clear evidence of Khrushchev's concerns about the Cuban leader. Kudryavtsev played a key role in the Soviets' first attempt to overthrow Castro by force.[44]

By late 1961, Soviet bids to control the DGI became increasingly bold. Some *Fidelista* agents sent to Moscow for training were recruited by the KGB, but others refused and reported the pitch in detail to Piñeiro.

The Russians, however, were frustrated by their own good work. The KGB had helped to shape an internal security system created by Castro —a network of government informers stretching into every city block, factory, farm, and office to spy on their fellow citizens. Neighborhood committees of watchers (vigilantes) for the Committees for the Defense of the Revolution (*Comités de Defensa de la Revolución,* CDRs), provided watch over each geographical area of the Island.[45] This informant system, a gift of the KGB, became extremely efficient, and accurately informed Castro about the Soviet sponsored machinations against him.[46]

Castro tolerated the intrigue for over a year before he decided to put an end to the Soviet bluff. *The New York Times* reported that rumors ran that, shortly after his "anti-sectarianism" harangue, Castro asked Kudryavtsev to leave. The defeated Russian left Havana hastily, on May 30, 1962. The Western press did not fail to notice that Castro made it a point not to see him off at Havana's airport.[47]

Since his arrival in Havana in 1960, Kudryavtsev had been an influential and conspicuous figure in Cuban politics. Unlike Soviet diplomats in other countries, he never bothered to conceal his power or to limit himself to behind-the-scenes activities. Theodore Draper observed that Kudryavtsev's departure from Cuba was embarrassingly precipitate. Just a few days before, he had made known that he intended to take a vacation in the U.S.S.R. But he left as if he had not been given time to pack his belongings. The Cuban press did not even pay him the customary respects to the past services of a former ambassador.[48]

Some time later Castro confessed that "he had expelled Kudryavtsev"" for having engaged in "open and excessive political activities."[49] But it is an established fact that Soviet ambassadors do not carry out personal policies —particularly when they are also high-ranking intelligence officers. Therefore, we may safely assume that Kudryavtsev had enjoyed the full confidence of Nikita Khrushchev in performing the difficult task of attempting to tame the shrewd Fidel Castro.[50] Proof that Kudryavtsev was following orders is that his career was not affected by his expulsion from Cuba. A few years after Castro expelled him, Kudryavtsev was sent to West Germany (19651967), and later appointed ambassador to Cambodia (1967-1970). In 1971, the indefatigable Kudryavtsev was appointed as the permanent Soviet delegate to UNESCO in Paris —a commonly used cover for Soviet intelligence officers.

Fidel's response to Khrushchev's schemes, at any rate in public, was moderate. He wanted, however, that everybody get the hint. When some days later Castro visited the offices of *Revolución,* he remarked within hearing range of several people, "This Kudryavtsev is bothering me more than Bonsal did."[51]

Years later, in his putative memories, Khrushchev gave a simplistic and naïve account of the reasons why *he* "recalled Kudryavtsev" —who is never mentioned by name. According to Khrushchev, the Soviet Ambassador "turned out to be unsuited for service in a country just emerging from a revolution. One of his problems was that when the situation heated up and the shooting started[52] he demanded that the Cubans give him a special bodyguard."[53] It is very funny just to imagine a tough guy like GRU officer Sergei Kudryavtsev asking the Cubans for a bodyguard —especially a Cuban bodyguard provided by Castro.

Khrushchev ends his version of the Kudryavtsev incident by saying that, "We could see that our ambassador was doing more to harm our relations with Cuba than to help, so we recalled him and made Alekseev ambassador in his place."[54] Of course, Kudryavtsev was not acting on his own as Khrushchev tried to suggest. In fact Khrushchev didn't recall Kudryavtsev; Castro kicked him out the Island together with a group of KGB officers who had been involved in the failed coup d'état.[55]

It seems that Khrushchev's distorted version of Kudryavtsev's behavior in Cuba —which the Soviet Premier most likely never believed— came through the ambassador's competitor, Aleksandr Alexeev, who had fallen in love with Castro and most likely had been recruited by him as a double agent. According to Alexeev, Kudryavtsev was a snob and a physical coward who wore a bulletproof vest. He was also an arrogant man who continuously criticized the Cubans.[56]

But the scanty information available about the secretive Kudryavtsev shows a very different person from the one described by Castro and Alexeev. Sergei Mikhailovich Kudryavtsev (b. 1915) was not a coward or a fool. In his authoritative book *KGB,* John Barron respectfully calls him "the old master of subversion."[57]

The Soviet intelligence officer Castro outfoxed and later expelled from Havana was not a novice in the black arts of intelligence and espionage. The fact that a man of his calibre and experience was deployed in Cuba under a diplomatic cover as the first Soviet ambassador to the Island clearly indicates the importance the Soviets had given to the operation he was running in Cuba: the neutralization and eventual ousting of Fidel Castro.

Kudryavtsev's first mission abroad was to Austria, where he operated from 1937 to 1938. From 1940-41, during the years of the Russo-German pact while Hitler was ruling in Germany, Kudryavtsev continued his career as a young intelligence officer working under a press reporter cover in the Berlin office of the Soviet wire service *TASS*.[58]

A few years later Kudryavtsev surfaced in Turkey (1941-1942). After two years in Turkey he was appointed first secretary of the Soviet Embassy in Ottawa, Canada (1942-1945). While in Canada, he headed the Soviet spy ring exposed by Igor Gouzenko in 1946, which stole Anglo-American nuclear data during WWII.[59] This efficient spy ring is credited for providing the Soviet Union with the know-how to build the atomic bomb.[60] After his expulsion from Canada, Kudryavtsev reappeared in West Germany under the pseudonym Aleksandr Erdberg, where, under a cover job in the Soviet Trade Delegation to Berlin, he was the KGB *rezident* (KGB term for chief of office) from 1945 to 1947.[61] It is believed that he created and directed an efficient Soviet sabotage and espionage network in West Germany.[62] A few years later he was assigned to France (1959-60), and from France he moved to Cuba.

Therefore, despite much badmouthing from both enemies and friends, it seems that, far from being a coward, Kudryavtsev was an efficient and disciplined officer of the Soviet intelligence services who did his best to serve his country and to accomplish the missions assigned to him.[63]

According to author Andrew Tully, "there is some evidence that, while he was operating in Havana, Kudryavtsev created a sabotage and spy school outside Havana,"[64] purportedly to create agents for Castro, though most likely to create and recruit agents to help in overthrowing him. It was not, however, the school Tully mentioned, but the *Escuela Nacional de Instrucción Revolucionaria* (National School of Revolutionary Instruction, ENIR) Osvaldo Sánchez Cabrera, the one that played a cardinal role in Khrushchev's plans. But, rather than a sabotage and espionage center, the Osvaldo Sánchez school was fully devoted to brainwashing and indoctrinating the men the Soviets had planned to use as a 5th column to infiltrate the Rebel Army and eventually use to overthrow Fidel Castro.

The Revolutionary Instructors and the Rebel Army

The creation of the Revolutionary Instructors was another episode in Khrushchev's schemes aimed at his goal of overthrowing Castro and gaining total power in Cuba. When Fidel came down from the Sierra Maestra mountains after Batista escaped on January, 1959, he was one of the most powerful personalities in the new government, but he was by no means the one and only power.

In fact, in the first months after the victory, Castro did not even have control over the moderate wing of the 26th of July Movement, which had a larger following than his own radical faction of the Rebel Army.[65] In the ranks of the 26th of July Movement, the Revolutionary Directorate and even in the Rebel Army, there were men with a strong political appeal who considered themselves equal to Castro.

Ever fearful of potential competitors, Fidel took advantage of the power ambitions of the "old guard" Communists to block his potential rivals from any access to power.[66] The creation of the Popular Militia and the Revolutionary Instructors were steps taken by Castro in a deliberate effort to destroy both the Rebel Army and the 26th of July Movement. To achieve his goal, he used the PSP Communists who, while thinking that they were depriving Fidel of his power, never imagined that they were actually playing into Castro's hands as unwilling instruments in his power game against his rivals in the M-26-7 and the Rebel Army. Both the Russians and the PSP Communists made a big mistake when they thought they had Castro under their thumb.

It was shortly after the victory at the Bay of Pigs that Fidel Castro called for the introduction of "revolutionary instructors" into all units of the Rebel Army.[67] The main function of the newly created political officers was to become the main source of political and ideological indoctrination for the troops. Though at the beginning they were not army officers in the strictest sense, they would act as if they were. Just as it was necessary to have a chief in military matters, reasoned Fidel, it was also necessary to have someone in charge of political matters.[68]

For the implementation of Castro's idea, a big National School of Revolutionary Instructors was hastily established in the former immigration-quarantine camp of Tiscornia, in the picturesque Casablanca hills facing the entrance channel to the Havana bay. It was named "Osvaldo Sánchez" in honor of the PSP leader who had died in an airplane friendly-fire "accident" just a few months before.

The original faculty of the Osvaldo Sánchez school was fully in the hands of the "old guard" communists, members of the PSP. The professors were mostly "old guard" cadres of the PSP and some Republican Spaniards who had fought in the Spanish Civil War against Franco, also Communists or at least long-time sympathizers.[69] The Director of the school was Lt. Carlos Díaz, a former High School teacher and PSP cadre. The Dean of the faculty was Jaime Novomody, a Polish jew, most probably a KGB agent or asset, who came to Cuba during WWII and had attended political indoctrination courses in the U.S.S.R. during the Stalin era. The school was under the control of the newly established Department of Revolutionary Instruction of the Rebel Army, headed by Capt. Sidroc Melquisidec Ramos, a member of the PSP intelligentsia who also wrote poetry.[70]

The courses at the Osvaldo Sánchez school had a duration of six months of full-time, live-in intensive study. The main subjects taught were: Cuban History, Political Economy and Marxist Philosophy. Military training was almost null.[71]

More than a thousand students attended the first course. They came mainly from the Rebel Army and the newly created *Milicias Populares* (Popular Militia), established by Castro in October, 1959, many of them coming right from the battleground after the victory at the Bay of Pigs.

Students at the Osvaldo Sánchez school were officially told that the Revolutionary Instructors in no way constituted a system of dual command and that they were only expected to be second-rank officers in the military units, just below the military commanders. In practice, however, a subtle scheme to brainwash the students was developed. In informal meetings and in lectures they were constantly reminded that, because of the low ideological level of most Rebel Army officers, the Revolutionary Instructors were required to be always alert, looking for signs of ideological deviation among Rebel Army officers. If faced with "traitors," in an emergency situation —they were told— they should not hesitate to detain or even execute the "traitors" and assume command of the units. The lecturers made a point in giving examples of similar actions taken by Soviet Political Commissars in WWII when dealing with old ex-Czarist officers in the Red Army. It seems likely that the Machiavellian Soviet-PSP plan was to use the mostly non-Communist Revolutionary Instructors as unwitting instruments in their coup d'état against Castro.

To the PSP Communists and their Russian friends, the introduction of the Revolutionary Instructors represented a new lever of control over Castro's Rebel Army. Up to that moment the loyalty of the armed forces to the leadership of the revolution had been assured by the personal following of most of the Rebel Army officers to Castro alone. Now the existence of the Popular Militia was a counterbalance to the Rebel Army, and the Revolutionary Instructors were going to be the PSP's fifth column inside the army. The PSP Communists and their Kremlin masters were jubilant while Castro seemed to be foolishly sharpening the butcher's knife for his own neck.

In order to accomplish their goal of taking the levers of power from Castro's hands, the Communists needed hundreds and hundred of middle- and low-level new cadres. But the PSP, particularly in the last years of the Batista government, had shrunk into a relatively small political party. They lacked among their ranks all the reliable men they now badly needed. Therefore, they were forced to quickly find new people who they thought had some sympathy for the PSP or who were, at least, sympathetic to Marxism, and turn them fast into PSP cadres. In order to do that in such a short time they could only trust their political intuition.

The task, however, proved to be more difficult than they previously calculated. The eyes of the PSP Communists turned out to be bigger than their stomachs. As soon at the indoctrination process began, the Revolutionary Instructors began giving trouble to their PSP indoctrinators. Though most of the students at the Osvaldo Sánchez school had a limited educational background, no higher than High School, some of them had university degrees. These were the ones who almost immediately began questioning some of the theoretical basis of Marxism. Moreover, Cubans —a highly individualistic and clever people— in those early days of the revolution had not yet lost their habit of thinking by themselves.

It was not easy for most of the students —especially for those not coming from the PSP ranks— to swallow the cock and bull story that the front line of the anti-Batista struggle had been manned not by Fidel's guerrillas in the mountains but by the workers in the factories under the leadership of the PSP comrades. It was difficult to convince the students that only thanks to the PSP had Fidel's *barbudos* (bearded ones) been able to outflank the enemy.[72]

One conflicting issue in the course, among many others, was the students' acceptance of the validity of Marx's Theory of Value and his concept of surplus value. Most of the students made a sincere effort to understand, but they simply couldn't. There were endless discussions over such theoretical issues as how the *circulation* of goods (as opposed to *production*) added or failed to add extra value to the goods. Some conflicting issues opened Byzantine arguments that lasted for weeks, not only among students, but also among faculty professors. Not even comrade Novomody, with all the power of persuasion backed by his position as Faculty Chairman and his set of doctrinaire "phonograph records" dating from the Stalin era, helped them to reach a plausible consensus.

Finally, comrade Novomody found a Solomonic solution to the problem. Those who understood Marx's Theory of Value were true proletarians at heart. But, those who could not, only were showing their deep-seated bourgeois prejudices. Faced with such explanations of "scientific Marxism" so close to religion, most teachers and students began having a better understanding not only of Marxism, but also about many other things of this new era of Cuban life and politics.

After continuous purges that drastically reduced the number of students, the first promotion of Revolutionary Instructors from the Osvaldo Sánchez school graduated. Soon after, the brand new Revolutionary Instructors —or *Comisarios Políticos* (Political Commissars) the unofficial name by which they were immediately known— arrived in the military units all over the Island.

Almost immediately, conflicts between the Revolutionary Instructors and the military commanders erupted.[73] To be sure, this was in part because of errors made by the instructors themselves —some of them tried to follow too close to the letter the "hints" they had gotten at the school and attempted to exert dual command in the military units— and soon ended in the stockades. But the real problem was the logical resistance made by the military commanders —men hardened in the guerrilla warfare against Batista— to surrender their command to the newcomers, men without strong revolutionary background and with no military training.

By the autumn of 1961, the Osvaldo Sánchez School had graduated about 750 battalion and company revolutionary instructors. They were mainly assigned to the armed forces, though some of them assumed ideological leadership in some other areas in the economy and culture.[74] Khrushchev's trap was almost set to catch Castro. In the meantime, Escalante and a few trusted old PSP cadres continued working feverishly to develop propitiatory conditions for the coup in the armed forces. In a meeting of the provincial assemblies of the ORI, Escalante pointed out the importance of organizing the Party within the ranks of the army.[75]

The most critical problem still faced by the Communists was their growing demand for reliable PSP cadres for all the tasks they needed to accomplish. The faculty of the first course at the Osvaldo Sánchez school was mainly composed of old party cadres who were already holding high level positions in the political apparatus. They commuted daily from their posts to the school in order to teach a few hours, but at the expense of neglecting their main duties. The direction of the school, therefore, was forced to select some of the best students of the first course about to graduate and appoint them as professors for the approaching second course. This selection was based not only on the students' academic achievements, but also on their perceived political views. Some of the new professors were old PSP members of proven Communist militancy, but most of them were not. Soon after, the second course began, with about a thousand students from all over the Island, together with their brand new professors. But this new combination proved in the long run to be highly explosive.

In early 1962, the Rebel Army was far from the standards of what later became Cuba's Revolutionary Armed Forces (*Fuerzas Armadas Revolucionarias*, FAR). Both the Rebel Army and the militia —now with high morale after its baptism of fire at the Bay of Pigs— more resembled a Pancho Villa-style bunch of disorganized armed men than a real army.

Most of the students and the faculty at the Osvaldo Sánchez school carried their side arms —Colt .45 automatics were preferred— everywhere, even to the classrooms when they attended classes. A common view was to see a teacher immersed in explaining a group of students the subtleties of Marxist dialectics while having his Czech 9 mm submachine gun hanging from his shoulder. Some students had powerful Belgian FAL automatic rifles with hundreds of rounds of live ammo in their lockers, as well as American made M-1's, M-2's or M-3's. Some of them even had hand grenades taken from the invaders in the beaches at the Bay of Pigs. And, even more important, what made the combination highly volatile was the fact that the hard-core Communists and PSP members behaved arrogantly and lacked sympathy among the young *Fidelistas*.

On March 31, 1962, Castro gave a speech at the University of Havana during a mass meeting commemorating the fifth anniversary of an attempt to kill Batista. Castro ended his speech with some obscure allusions to the dangers of sectarianism. The meaning of Castro's words may have sounded enigmatic to most of the people who had heard them, but not to the students and professors at the Osvaldo Sánchez school.

Every morning, before attending classes, the faculty held an informal meeting with Chairman Novomody. The main objective was to discuss the most important events of the previous day, particularly Fidel's speeches, which later on would be discussed in class with the students. But the day after Castro's speech with allusions to sectarianism they wouldn't. Novomody stubbornly denied importance to Castro's words and provided other items for discussion. The professors were frustrated and annoyed, but managed to avoid the student's questions in the classrooms. A climate of mounting tension continued growing at the Osvaldo Sánchez school.

Finally, on March 27, during a major television speech, Castro made an open, violent criticism of Aníbal Escalante and of sectarianism. Next day Novomody tried to avoid again the discussion and gave express orders not to make references to Castro's speech. But at that moment the atmosphere was charged. Some students —particularly those coming from the Rebel Army ranks— ostentatiously began carrying their rifles and sub-machine guns all the time. Some professors ignored Novomody's orders and discussed Fidel's words with their students.

The long repressed anti-PSP feelings exploded with force. Students were openly criticizing Escalante and the PSP and condemning sectarianism. The direction of the school feared a direct, and probably violent, confrontation and called for assistance. Captain Sidroc Ramos, of the Army's Department of Instruction promptly arrived and tried to calm down students and professors, but failed. As a last resort, he ordered to disband the second course and to send the hard-core group of dissident students and professors to remote military units in the Sierra Maestra and the Escambray mountains.

Conflict also had reached a peak in the military units who already had Revolutionary Instructors assigned. Rebel Army officers reacted with a show of strength, and the few Revolutionary Instructors who had gained some power lost their command. Many of them ended their short military careers in the stockades.

Castro's Victory

By late March, 1962, Khrushchev may have realized that thus far he had accumulated more liabilities than tangible assets for his somewhat forced Cuban investment. He never anticipated that supplying military aid to Castro and pumping money to keep the Cuban economy afloat —let alone developing it— would turn out to be a very costly business. In addition, the aftermath of the PSP purge coincided with a rise in shortage of consumer goods.

A growing disaffection with the regime and its ally, the Soviet Union, surfaced for the first time. Khrushchev had good reasons to doubt the surviving possibilities of the Castro regime.[76] Moreover, the fall of Escalante and some other "old guard" PSP Communists from the Cuban political scene, added to the expulsion of Kudryatsev, vanished Khrushchev's last hopes of taming the shrewd Fidel.

Things were complicated even further by Fidel's aggressive and unpredictable behavior. It was becoming more and more difficult for the Soviets to deal with him. Faced with American threats, his response was to shake his fists under Kennedy's nose while insisting in an irrevocable guarantee that the Soviet Union come to his rescue if Cuba was attacked.[77]

The Escalante affair was a total victory for Castro. First, he profited from the PSP Communists' lust for power by using them to get rid of his rivals in the Cuban power game. Then, after gaining more power, he used what was left of the revolutionary organizations' key men to get rid of the very Communists who had unknowingly done him such a great service. Later, when the Escalante affair was over, Castro reinstated into key positions the men who remained loyal to him. But for them these were no longer positions won in the struggle against Batista, but rewards bestowed "magnanimously" by Fidel. So indebted, they now owed total obedience to him. In his customary way Fidel had put the factions to fight against each other while remaining on top, watching the bulls from the fence.

In March, 1962, Fidel reasserted his leadership of the revolution. He forced Aníbal Escalante into exile to the Soviet Union, censured and deprived others of their positions and reshuffled his political organization from top to bottom. "Old guard" communists were gradually downgraded and only a few PSP leaders who made a humiliating about face and rushed to pledge total allegiance to Castro were allowed to stay in the government.[78] Only a few of them were included in the 100-member Central Committee of his Communist Party, and only two were admitted to the six-man secretariat. Fidel was now in full political control of Cuba. He never broke up completely with the "old guard'" but now he relied more heavily in persons loyal to himself than on PSP communists.

To Khrushchev, the disastrous Escalante affair was a proof that he was dealing with a furtive, secretive, clever intriguer capable, like himself, of every kind of scheme and lie. Castro, a cynic and cruel man who cared nothing for his friends, had outwitted the Russians and proved to be an even better schemer than Khrushchev. Fidel's Jesuit education was paying off.

The Soviet Premier remembered very vividly how, soon after Castro approached the Soviets for the first time, Khrushchev had the opportunity to experience Castro's arrogance first hand. Khrushchev met Castro for the first time in New York in September, 1960, when both leaders were visiting the United Nations. The Soviet Premier had invited Fidel to a dinner at the Soviet U.N. mission in New York. Castro, as usual, was a half hour late and kept Khrushchev waiting.[79] Witnesses to the incident report that Khrushchev was furious. But, as soon as Castro arrived, Khrushchev's mood changed and was all smiles. Apparently the Soviet leader had fallen victim to Fidel's powers of fascination.[80]

But now the Soviet leader was furious again. Authors Fursenko and Naftali portray a vivid image of Khrushchev's fury and how he breathed fire excoriating Castro after he refused to accept Khrushchev's terms for the solution of the crisis.[81] Khrushchev's furious reaction to Castro's actions during the Escalante-Kudryavtsev affair had been very similar; the only difference was that he had kept his fury to himself because he had a plan to get even with the Cuban leader.[82]

By expelling the Soviet ambassador, Fidel had humiliated Khrushchev[83] and the Soviet Union. Moreover, before kicking Kudryavtsev out of Cuba, he had recalled Ambassador Faure Chomón, who left Moscow on May 5. Though his successor, Carlos Olivares, was appointed twelve days later, he remained in Cuba. So both embassies had no heads of mission for a time.[84]

In the diplomatic field, when two nations recall their respective ambassadors it is an unmistakable sign that the relations between the two countries are at a very low level. Moreover, when, as in the Kudryavtsev case, one of the ambassadors had actually been expelled, not to mention detained, by the host country, a break in diplomatic relations is expected. Therefore, if we discard the idea that Khrushchev was a stupid fool, a kook, or a masochist, it is very difficult to accept his version of the events. Khrushchev's claims that he seized precisely such a moment to offer his "friend" Castro —the same man he had failed to overthrow by force a few days before— nuclear weapons for his defense against the United States was simply a fairy tale for public consumption he decided to use as a cover to hide his true intentions. This was a classic example of Soviet *dezinformatsia*[85] at its best.

The sequel to the Soviet commitment in Cuba had been a calamitous failure. In such circumstances the sensible course for Khrushchev was to cut his losses and get out of the game, particularly considering that the Soviet lines of supply to Cuba were long and extremely vulnerable. But to leave Cuba voluntarily would have been tantamount to an admission of failure and would have involved substantial loss of face.

Yet, there were too many unanswered questions about Fidel Castro that made the Soviet Premier suspicious. Who —may have reasoned Khrushchev— was this son of a wealthy landowner, educated in the best Jesuit schools? Who was this sometime brother-in-law to a wealthy member of Batista's cabinet, heir to a fortune, eligible for the best salons of Havana and Santiago? Who *really* was this privileged darling of the Cuban oligarchs, who had a degree in law —the theology of Capitalism? What were Fidel's true links to William Wieland, a strange U.S. "diplomat," first in Havana, and later in Colombia during the *Bogotazo*? Why had the CIA Station Chief in the U.S. Embassy in Havana been so openly pro-Castro? Why did *The New York Times*, through Herbert Matthews, contribute so much to the spread of the *Fidelista* myth to the world? Was Castro what he purported to be, or was he actually a CIA agent working for the United Sates?[86]

With all these ideas running around in his head, Nikita Khrushchev now tried to find a way to, once and for all, get rid of his Cuban "Communist." But, if Fidel was in his hands, he was no less in the hands of Fidel. After the expelling of Kudryavtsev and the purging of Escalante and several of the "old line" Cuban communists, some members of the PSP, out of fear, began following Fidel's line and had become an instrument of his policies rather than Moscow's. This state of affairs highly irritated Khrushchev. But the Soviet Premier could not afford to openly destabilize the Castro government. The cost in terms of Soviet international prestige vis-à-vis Peking, Washington and the Third World would have been intolerable. Any direct Russian action against Cuba would have led to serious political and ideological consequences for the Soviet Union.

If, however, Castro could be eliminated as a result of American "aggression," then Khrushchev and the U.S.S.R. could retreat from Cuba, their honor relatively untarnished. After an American invasion of the Island, the failure of Communism in Cuba could not be blamed on deficiencies in Soviet-style Communist management of Cuban affairs, but on "Yankee Imperialism."[87]

Therefore, after the failed Kudryavtsev-Escalante coup d'ètat to overthrow the obnoxious Castro, Nikita Sergeevich conceived another plan.

Chapter 5

Khrushchev's Plan

Never attempt to win by force what you might win by fraud.
—Machiavelli's advice to the Prince.

After Fidel beguiled him into a political and ideological quagmire, Nikita Khrushchev conceived a top-secret scheme to, once and for all, get rid of his self-declared Caribbean "communist" without being discredited for doing so. Though he was tempted to get rid of Castro by overt force, the problem was that to do so would have been like shooting himself in the foot. Given Castro's prestige in revolutionary and third world circles, to take unilateral action against him could provoke repercussions that could damage Khrushchev's own policies and perhaps damage the foreign interests of the Soviet Union. Perhaps the Castro problem could have been solved in an easier way, but the Soviet Premier feared the presence of one disturbing factor: Communist China. In the Soviet leader's moves, especially in relation to foreign affairs, some scholars detected his awareness of a disturbing shadow at his elbow; his anxiety at what the Chinese reaction might be.[1] At that particular moment Khrushchev was at the apex of his political career, and had practically unlimited power and the authority to use it as he saw fit, not only at home, but also in foreign affairs. So, he put his plan into action.

Nikita Gets an Idea

Much has been written about who was the originator of the plan of placing what looked like strategic missiles in Cuba. The available evidence seems to indicate that the idea came from Khrushchev himself. French author Michel Tatu believes that Khrushchev was undoubtedly the instigator of the Cuban move.[2] This seems to be supported in the collectively authored Soviet study *International Relations Since the Second World War*. Without directly connecting the remarks to Khrushchev, but with reference to the October 1964 plenary session of the Central Committee which ratified his ouster, the study affirms that the Party with all its strength came out "against hairbrained schemes, premature conclusions and rash, unrealistic decisions and actions, against boasting and idle talk, ..."

The Chinese apparently agreed. According to them, the crisis was the result of the rash action of the Soviet leader who, without consulting anybody, willfully embarked upon a reckless course. The Chinese were not alone, because Fidel Castro shared the same opinion. In 1967, Lee Lockwood asked him: "Do you think that Khrushchev acted in a personal and highhanded manner in the Missile Crisis?" Castro answered: "With regard to us, yes."[3]

For these and other bits of evidence, it is difficult to avoid the conclusion that Khrushchev himself, acting alone with a small group of close collaborators — which may have included Brezhnev and Kosygin— must have formulated the whole plan.[4] He was very careful to keep his scheme to sneak missiles into Cuba a secret from the others in the Politburo. He was especially careful not to reveal what kind of missiles he was sending, nor his real objectives. This was consistent with Khrushchev's past behavior. Whenever problems, domestic or foreign, crowded in upon each other, Khrushchev tried to solve them —or rather to stabilize them— by resorting to dazzling improvisations. More evidence that he acted alone is the fact that during the crisis he did not consult all the Presidium members present in Moscow, nor did he summon to Moscow those who were absent. He apparently consulted mainly with Mikoyan, Brezhnev, Kozlov, Suslov and Kosygin.

When U.S. Ambassador Adlai Stevenson displayed the photographs he claimed were evidence of Soviet missiles in Cuba at the U.N. Security Council meeting on October 25, 1962, Soviet Ambassador Valerian Zorin countered that the photographic evidence was a fake.[5] Apparently at that moment Zorin had not been informed by his government of the facts. Failure to have alerted Zorin by October 25 may have been the result of continued Soviet deception to its own officials, further evidence that the whole scheme was created by Khrushchev alone without consultation with other members of the Party's Central Committee. Khrushchev, apparently against the better judgement of some of his advisers, steamrolled through with his plan to place the missiles in Cuba.

According to Khrushchev's own version, it was during his visit to Bulgaria on May 14-20, 1962, that he conceived the idea of installing strategic missiles in Cuba. Khrushchev was aware that a great part of the American public and a number of political leaders were calling for an invasion of Cuba. The American leaders were hysterical about Castro at the time of the Bay of Pigs and thereafter. The Kennedys seemingly had their Irish up, and were determined to get even with Castro at any cost. Khrushchev had read confidential intelligence reports about Kennedy's resolve to avenge his defeat at the Bay of Pigs and to overthrow the obnoxious Castro. He even knew about a contingency plan for the invasion of Cuba prepared after the Bay of Pigs which had been kept current at the Pentagon since then. Furthermore, Khrushchev knew that, during the days of the Bay of Pigs invasion, 90 percent of the American policy makers and the military favored going to war against Castro. In April, 1961, Kennedy was willing to send American troops to Laos. To Khrushchev it would have been easier for Kennedy to justify to the American people the sending of troops just ninety miles to fight communism in Cuba than sending them halfway around the world.

Contrary to the opinion of most American scholars, the author rejects, by and large, the explanation that Khrushchev underestimated Kennedy's character after the Bay of Pigs episode and their meeting in Vienna. It is evident that Khrushchev planned to set up the missile bases in Cuba with a certain outcome in mind —of course, he never would have dreamed of the actual outcome of the crisis. Even if most Soviet military leaders weren't aware of Khrushchev's real plan, they knew full well that they were in no position to do anything if the United States intervened in Cuba.

Several analysts have concluded that the Soviet Premier's Cuban missile gambit was —at least in part— to trade the missiles in Cuba for a favorable settlement of the Berlin question. They missed the point, however, because they did not see Khrushchev's real objective: to get rid of Castro and discredit the United States. Maybe Berlin would have been a by-product of the effort, but his principal goal was to get rid of Fidel Castro.

According to Samuel L. Sharp, the common mistake that most Western analysts of the Soviet Union made was that they focused their analysis mainly, and sometimes exclusively, on Marxist-Leninist ideology as a key to understanding Kremlin policy. Baffled by the elusive phenomenon of Soviet behavior they found a desperate negative solace in remembering what Winston Churchill said of Soviet policy: "a riddle wrapped in a mystery inside an enigma." Not too many, Sharp points out, seemed to notice that, after disclaiming his ability to predict Soviet behavior, Churchill added: "But perhaps there is a key. That key is Russian national interest."[6] And Russian national interest, as defined by Sharp, was no more than what the Soviet leaders of that time considered to be Russian national interest —which, most likely, was very close to their own interests.

Before the Cuban missile crisis, both American intelligence and Kremlinology experts stressed the fact that no offensive Soviet missiles had ever been stationed outside Soviet territory —not even in Eastern Europe—[7] and that the Soviets evidently recognized that the development of an offensive military base in Cuba might provoke U.S. military intervention. In one of the meetings of the Ex Comm,[8] Sorensen cautioned that there was the possibility that Khrushchev was trying to deliberately incite the Americans into an attack on Cuba to facilitate his moving on Berlin. It seems obvious that, when Khrushchev placed the missiles in Cuba, he gave Kennedy the opportunity for a showdown, not in Berlin, where the Russians had all the strategic advantages, but only ninety miles from the United States, where the Soviets had to operate at the end of a long and vulnerable supply line and the Americans had all the strategic advantages.

Since one cannot know what went into decisions in the Kremlin, it may have been that Khrushchev was actually seeking a confrontation. But if he was, it is scarcely credible that he would have wanted that kind of confrontation in a place so strategically disadvantageous to the Soviet Union. Khrushchev should have recognized, with even the most superficial knowledge of American politics, that no American President —least of all one with Kennedy's character and record—

could tolerate the installation of Russian missiles in Cuba, particularly right before an election.

It should not be forgotten that, whatever way we look at the problem, it was Khrushchev who made the crisis possible by placing what looked like strategic missile bases in Cuba, despite assurances to the contrary and U.S. warnings. Most authors who studied the crisis shortly after the event concluded that Khrushchev's move was counterproductive. As Horelick pointed out, the Soviet weapons provoked, rather than deterred, an American response. Schlesinger noted that, had the Americans been looking for an excuse to smash Castro, they could hardly have found a better one. Sorensen said that the U.S. intelligence experts never doubted that the development of an offensive military base in Cuba might provoke American military intervention. Even Anatoly Gromyko, the Soviet Foreign Minister's son, in an article about the crisis, admitted that the missiles gave the Americans the pretext they had been seeking for so long.

Authors who have studied the crisis more recently have arrived at similar conclusions. "The secret deployment of missiles raised rather than lowered the risks of an American invasion of Cuba," wrote Lebow and Stein.[9] Therefore, if one discards the possibility that Khrushchev was a fool, the unavoidable conclusion is that the only valid reason Khrushchev had to do what could only provoke an American invasion of Cuba, was because he wanted it to happen.

To maximize the effectiveness of the missiles as a provocation, Khrushchev used every possible means to make the Americans believe that, after the installation and further training of Cuban personnel, the missiles would be under Castro's control. This is clearly implied in the Soviets' first statement of the crisis in October 23 in which they affirmed that Cuba alone had the right to decide what kind of weapons were appropriate for its defense. The *Fidelistas* apparently believed it too, because in post-crisis remarks, Che Guevara said that during the crisis the Cubans were prepared, in the event of an American attack, to strike New York, the very heart of the imperium. The author also recalls having heard Castro himself making after the crisis similar statements at the University of Havana.

Khrushchev's Plan in Action

Despite the fact that Khrushchev knew that the U.S. had no intention of invading Cuba, at least at that particular time,[10] he took the necessary steps to ensure that Fidel believed that it was *he* who had asked the Russians for the missiles. Alexei Adzhubei, Khrushchev's son-in-law and the editor of *Izvestia*, was on his way to Washington to interview President Kennedy. But, before traveling to the U.S., Khrushchev ordered him to make a stopover in Havana to tell Fidel some carefully fabricated disinformation concerning the sentiments of the Kennedy Administration towards Cuba and the rumors of an imminent American invasion.[11]

A few days later, after Adzhubei's return to Moscow, an alleged copy of his confidential report to Khrushchev about his meeting with Kennedy was sent to Fidel. In his report, obviously a total fabrication, Adzhubei informed the Soviet

Premier of a remark President Kennedy had made during the interview a few days earlier at Hyannis Port. According to the Soviet version of the interview, Kennedy reminded Adzhubei that the United States had not intervened in Hungary in 1956. This was evidently a subtle means of exacting a pledge of Russian nonintervention should there be an American invasion of Cuba.

In the weeks following Adzhubei's report, the Cubans were spoon-fed a considerable amount of disinformation from alleged Soviet intelligence sources about the imminence of an American invasion of the Island.[12] The news, though false, confirmed a real concern in Castro's mind.[13] At this psychologically critical moment, Khrushchev asked Castro what he needed in order to face the invasion. Castro replied that, as far as he was concerned, anything that could stop the Americans would be good for him.

At that moment, without realizing it, Fidel was caught in Khrushchev's trap —or so Khrushchev believed. Once he solved the problem of getting Castro to ask for the missiles, Khrushchev had to make him believe that the Russians were foolish enough to place them close to his hands. But, to some of the Russians' surprise, after some initial hesitation, Castro gladly accepted the missile offer.

But, if Fidel actually believed Khrushchev's offer, he was dead wrong. The most simple logic dictates that no great power is going to give missiles to any newcomer who just asks for them. The U.S.S.R. installed missiles where it chose, and nowhere else. When Mao asked for missiles, the Soviets turned him down flat. So, who was going to believe that they would give missiles to the unreliable Fidel Castro? But Khrushchev rightly knew he could exploit Fidel's megalomania for his own benefit. He "suggested" to Castro that the Cuban government formally requested the Soviet Union to install a few missiles on the Island to deter an imminent U.S. invasion.

Khrushchev may have guessed that Castro's natural tendency for treachery would make him swallow the tasty nuclear bait. However, just in case Fidel would try to play it rough, the missiles would be accompanied by four battle groups of special ground troops to give the missiles close-in protection —a formidable force of Soviet infantrymen that could have defeated the whole Cuban army in a very short time.[14] Khrushchev was not going to risk Castro overpowering the "nuclear" missile sites and discovering what he was not supposed to discover.

According to Alexeev's account, when Khrushchev called him to the Kremlin to inform him of his new post as Soviet ambassador to Cuba, the Prime Minister asked: "How would Fidel Castro respond if we placed our missiles in Cuba?" According to Alexeev, Khrushchev's question put him in a state of shock, because he could never suppose that Castro would agree to such a thing. Accordingly, Alexeev answered that, in his opinion, Castro "will not accept such a proposal."[15] Alexeev's account proves that Khrushchev, with his peasant instinct, knew Castro much better than his main KGB man in Cuba.

There is circumstantial evidence indicating that Castro's own secret plan contemplated overpowering the missile bases and taking control of them the same way he probably overpowered the SAM battery that shot down Major Anderson's U-2. The fact that this was Castro's plan is evidenced in an interview Che Guevara gave after the crisis to a correspondent of the Communist *Daily Worker* of London. Though the article that was published had been toned down for publication, the *United Press* managed to obtain a copy of the unexpurgated text. In the interview Guevara, as usually acting as Castro's mouthpiece, made an ominous statement: "We would have used them against the very heart of the United States, including New York."[16]

Even at that early time in his political career, a power-seeking paranoid like Fidel Castro may have reached the conclusion that the only true way to be free from political tutelage and in equal terms with the super powers was by having the great equalizer.[17] When Lee Lockwood asked him in 1967 if there were any nuclear missiles hiding in Cuba, his answer was, "*unfortunately,* there are none."[18]

Actually, from the point of view of guaranteeing the defense of Cuba,[19] Khrushchev's proposition may have seemed considerably beyond the Island's needs, but the Soviet Premier was confident that the Cubans lacked the military experience needed to discover the ruse. Yet Fidel was not so easily fooled. From Khrushchev's memoirs one can deduct that Castro initially was reluctant to accept the Soviet Premier's proposal. One is tempted to think that Fidel may have suspected Khrushchev's intentions, since the offer to place nuclear missiles in Cuba had followed so closely on the heels of the embarrassing Escalante-Kudryavtsev affair.

But Castro has always had *delusions de grandeur.* He has always seen himself as the center of the world. Proof of that is his long speech at the U.N. in which, for more than four hours, he explained to the bored delegates his plan to fix not only Cuba, but the whole world.[20]

In order to guarantee that he would "convince" Fidel of the need for nuclear missiles, Khrushchev put some pressure on Castro. In this context, the fact that the Soviet-Cuban commercial agreement for 1962, under discussion since the fall of 1961, was not signed until May 14, may have reflected not only economic bargaining, but politico-military differences as well.[21] Another indication of Soviet pressure is that the Soviet flow of arms to Cuba had been discontinued in early 1962, coinciding with the strain in Cuban-Soviet relations. Arms shipments to Cuba resumed near the end of July and proceeded through the summer at an accelerated pace.[22]

After some initial faked hesitation, Castro agreed to the arrangement though, but not without having set up his own secret plan to outsmart Khrushchev. Knowing Castro's love for the missiles, one may safely assume that his plan contemplated taking over the missiles and materializing his dreams of having nuclear weapons and using them against the United States. Author Andrés Suárez reached the conclusion that "Castro was desperately anxious to get the missiles and that mankind can breathe a little easier because they are no longer within his reach."[23]

Suddenly, as if by magic, the trade agreements that took so long to negotiate were satisfactorily negotiated. Khrushchev chose to momentarily back Castro against his friend Aníbal Escalante, and suddenly began showing signs of having, at least temporarily, accepted Castro's self-proclaimed "socialism." May day slogans at the Red Square acknowledged for the first time that Cuba had "embarked on the path of building socialism."[24]

Carlos Franqui recalled that, after the Soviet promise of nuclear missiles, Fidel seemed to have a blind belief in the Soviet military machine. According to Franqui, "he felt like one of the powerful, as if he was involved in world-changing events. Don't forget," says Franqui, "that Fidel gets his kicks from war and high tension."[25] Franqui also observed that "Fidel behaved as if he was the one in Moscow, showing Khrushchev how things should be done."[26] It seems that Khrushchev's offer of nuclear missiles had fueled Castro's paranoid dreams of destroying the United States.

Evidence shows that the swift easing of tensions in Soviet-Cuban relations that followed the Kudryavtsev-Escalante affair began as a Russian initiative. Keeping in mind, however, that the Soviet Premier was not known to suffer from any masochistic tendencies, nor had he been committed to a mental institution, one must wonder what motivated that sudden and unexpected change. Evidently, Khrushchev's mellowing was part of his plan directed at persuading Fidel into accepting the Trojan horse of the Soviet "missiles."

At the end of August, 1962, Cuban Minister of Finance Ernesto Che Guevara, visited Moscow and concluded a treaty with the U.S.S.R. By it, the Soviet Union forgave all Cuban debts for past arms supplies. According to a *TASS* communiqué of September 2, 1962,

> The Cuban republic addressed the Soviet government with a *request* for help by delivering armaments and sending technical specialists for training Cuban servicemen. ... The Soviet government attentively considered this *request* of the Government of Cuba and an agreement was reached on this question. As long as the above-mentioned quarters continue to threaten Cuba, the Cuban Republic has every justification for taking measures to insure its security and safeguard its sovereignty and independence while Cuba's true friends have every right to respond to this legitimate *request*.[27]

Apparently Raúl Castro had been told in July to "request" some armaments from the Soviets, the nature of which perhaps had not been specified enough. The use of the word "request" three times in the document is proof that the Soviets tried to make clear to everybody that the initiative of asking for the missiles was Cuban.

But then, to his utter surprise, Khrushchev had the opportunity to get a taste of Castro's immense arrogance. The Cuban leader apparently was not happy with the terms of the agreement by which the Soviet Union was going to help Cuba. To

Castro that would be the equivalent of humiliation.[28] For him, nothing less than a mutual Soviet-Cuban defense pact would do. In case of an American attack on the Soviet Union, Castro's forces would defend their Soviet allies, defeat the U.S. and save the U.S.S.R. from the Yankee imperialists.

Castro's reaction may have provoked Khrushchev's anger, but the shrewd Soviet leader perhaps thought that he who laughs last laughs best. He immediately agreed to Castro's foolish request. But Castro was still not happy; he wanted to make the agreement public. He sent Che Guevara and Emilio Aragonés to Moscow to convince Khrushchev that he should disclose the existence of the pact.[29] Khrushchev refused, but told Castro that he would make it public during his visit to the U.N. at the end of the year. Khrushchev was sure that, by that time, Castro would be history, and he would seize the opportunity to denounce the American imperialist for their invasion of Cuba and the overthrowing of the progressive Castro regime.

Now Khrushchev's problem consisted in letting the Americans "discover" the missiles and, at the same time, indirectly let them know that, in the event of an invasion of Cuba, the Soviet response would consist in nothing more than words. Obviously, reasoned Khrushchev, the deployment of what looked like nuclear missiles on Cuban soil would elicit and legitimize a prompt American response — most likely an invasion of the Island.[30]

"Deception" and "Stealth"

According to the official myth, first advanced by the Kennedy administration, immediately accepted by court historians and myth makers, and now repeated over and over by spies and scholars, the main reason for Kennedy's initial violent reaction was the fact that Khrushchev had introduced the missiles in Cuba under a cover of deception and stealth. This accusation runs over most of the documents about the crisis, and was repeated several times during the ExComm meetings. The problem with this argument, however, is that it simply is not true. In reality, not only did the Soviets go to great pains to let the Americans discover the missiles, but the Americans also made a great effort to avoid discovering them.

On July 25, 1962, a heavy Russian freighter docked at Pier 6 in the port of Mariel, a small seafaring town located on the inner side of the Bay of Mariel, on Cuba's north coast, about 30 miles from Havana, in the western part of the island.[31] Four days before, the army had evacuated all of Mariel's residents, even Cuban soldiers and militiamen, within a mile of the waterfront. A heavily armed group of KGB *spetsnatz*[32] soldiers stood on deck. Other Soviet agents kept watch in the harbor.

During the night, under the glare of powerful flood-lights, Soviet troops marched down the gangways and assorted military equipment was hoisted from the ships' decks, placed on heavy trucks covered with tarpaulins, and moved out in night convoys. In the coming weeks other ships followed. Some days later, some foreign correspondents in Havana heard rumors that Soviet soldiers had taken over a former boys' reformatory near the city of Guanajay and were building missile sites not far from the capital.

Soon after, all the townspeople in Mariel and Guanajay and, later, loose-tongued Cubans all over the Island, were whispering about the strange things happening in Pinar del Río. "Judging from the shape, Fidel must be importing palm trees," was the joke running on the streets. Some of the jokes mentioned that Nikita Khrushchev had gone crazy and was actually going to fire the nuclear missiles in Cuba at the American "imperialists."[33]

Khrushchev took for granted that some of the CIA informers and the Cuban exiles, who were leaving the Island by the thousands, would talk in Miami about the strange operation. Obviously the Russians wanted the operation to be an "absolute secret."

A few days before, Soviet Army units had secured a large trapezoidal area in the north central portion of Pinar del Río province, not far from the city of San Cristóbal. According to reports from refugees arriving in Miami, all Cubans had been evacuated from the restricted area.[34] Soon after, Khrushchev's carefully planned "secretiveness" bore its fruit: by mid-September, all Pinar del Río *guajiros* were openly talking about the large missile base the Russians were building not far from the town of San Cristóbal, east of Havana. Khrushchev's "errors" were actually a big finger pointing to the San Cristóbal area.

According to Franqui, the missiles were a sort of public secret:

> ... no one spoke about them openly, but all knew. Fidel later mentioned that only five people were in on the secret: Fidel himself, his brother Raúl, Che Guevara, Ramiro Valdés and President Dorticós. The army, the comandantes, the government, the people, no one knew anything for certain, but they did imagine what was going on. Those living near the bases, of course knew everything.[35]

In the coming weeks other Soviet ships followed. As the summer ended, the roads and highways in Cuba were clogged with military traffic. Troops and heavy equipment were on the move elsewhere. Soviet convoys droned day and night. So heavy was the traffic that the country was suddenly beset with a rash of accidents.[36] Khrushchev took for granted that some of the CIA informers and agents, as well as Cuban exiles who kept fleeing the Island every single day, would tell the Americans in Miami about the ongoing "secret" military operation and mention the big crates so carefully disembarked by the Russians.[37]

From September 1962 on, a string of reports began arriving from U.S. intelligence agents in the field in Cuba and from exiles arriving in Miami indicating the presence of what looked like strategic missiles on the Island. Though most of the reports were not reliable, resulting from the confusion of observers not trained to distinguish between non-strategic anti-aircraft missiles and strategic ones, several reports turned out to be accurate. One came from a former employee at the Hilton hotel in Havana (now renamed Habana Libre), who believed that a strategic missile site was being erected near the town of San Cristóbal in Pinar del Río, and another from someone who had overheard Castro's personal pilot boasting one evening about the nuclear missiles that Cuba was going to get from the Russians.[38] Apparently he was just parroting Fidel's words that very soon the missiles would be in his hands after he had taken them from the Russians.

Though the CIA's sources in Cuba were producing an enormous amount of information —as many as 50 or 100 separate reports a day— no definite or "hard" evidence was provided to support the reports that the Russians were bringing in not only antiaircraft missiles (SAMs, Surface-to-Air Missiles), but also MRBMs (Medium-Range Ballistic Missiles). The most compelling single report, however, came from a former non-commissioned French officer who had served in the American army in Germany. This officer positively *knew* the difference between a SAM and a MRBM. According to his report, he saw on the road huge, multiwheeled tractors transporting Russian missiles under canvas covers. They were, he swore, "bigger, much bigger" than anything the Americans had in Germany.[39]

On August 31, 1962, Senator Kenneth B. Keating of New York charged in the Senate Chamber that he had evidence that there were in Cuba twelve hundred Russian troops as well as "concave metal structures supported by tubing" that appeared destined for a "rocket installation."[40] On September 1, Senator Keating charged again with renewed criticism the Cuban policy of the President. The next day, Keating stepped up his attack on Kennedy's "do nothing" policy and suggested that a mission of the Organization of American States should be sent to Cuba to determine if Soviet missile bases were being erected.[41] On September 6, columnist Walter Trohan mentioned in his well read column at the *Chicago Tribune* Senator Keating's charges about the Kennedy administration's inaction faced with the presence of Soviet missiles in Cuba.[42]

On September 10, 1962, Trohan affirmed that the Russians had already set up 9 out of 12 missile bases they had promised Castro in addition to bombers and fighter planes.[43] Other critical editorials followed in the *Tribune* during September, blaming the President for Khrushchev's actions.[44] Another article questioned the President's logic on the question of what he considered "defensive weapons."[45]

Some senators soon followed Keating's warning about threatening Soviet moves in Cuba. These reports, plus the frustrations which Castro was causing to many Americans, created in the early autumn what one acute observer called "a war party" which demanded immediate military action against Cuba.[46]

Soon after the Russians began shipping their missiles to Cuba, senior officials in the American intelligence became more suspicious. Their intelligence analysts told them that the number of Soviet ships visiting Cuban ports had suddenly and substantially increased and that the Russians didn't allow the Cuban port workers to do any of the unloading, but that they were using their own people to do it once the ships had reached Cuban ports.[47]

One may assume that it took several weeks to plan and coordinate a movement of this magnitude and to re-schedule and assemble the necessary shipping. Since the first of the shipments began to arrive in Cuban ports at the end of July, the latest Khrushchev could have given the green light to his plan was probably June.[48] According to a Defense Intelligence report of 1963, at least 42 IL-28 bombers and an equal number of strategic missiles were brought to Cuba. Nine missile sites were established, six of them with four launchers each for the MRBMs and three of them, fixed sites, for the IRBMs, each designed to include four launching emplacements.[49]

Obviously, a token force of a few conspicuously deployed MRBMs similar to the ones the U.S. had in Italy and Turkey would alone have sufficed to provoke a U.S. demand that the Russians remove them from Cuba. But, by deploying missiles with ranges in excess of several hundred miles, a lot more than needed for local defense, Khrushchev assured himself that the added provocation would stir Americans into action. He wanted badly to stir alarm in the American people and provoke a full retaliatory response against the true source of evil: Castro's Cuba.

Khrushchev Sends Clear Signals

Well aware of the inefficiency displayed by U.S. intelligence during the Bay of Pigs, Khrushchev carefully planned a whole series of "errors," so as to give the Americans unmistakable signals that something important was going on in Cuba.

From September on, almost all Soviet statements stressed that the Soviet Union was in no way going to place strategic missiles in Cuba. In retrospect, it seems clear that Khrushchev was playing a rather complicated game of political semiotics. He was sending open official signals to alarm the American people with the threat of the missiles in Cuba and helping the American decision-makers develop the necessary public support in the event of an invasion of Cuba. At the same time, however, he was sending President Kennedy private signals about the true purpose of the missiles[50] and his lack of appreciation for the bearded Caribbean leader. If, as Khrushchev believed, Kennedy was desperately looking for a good pretext to get rid of Castro, he was giving it to him on a silver platter.

Using the most private channels of communication at the highest levels, Khrushchev sought to assure himself that the Americans were getting the hint. On September 4, Soviet Ambassador Dobrynin gave Attorney General Robert Kennedy a confidential message from the Soviet Chairman. In that message Khrushchev promised that he was not going to create any trouble for the American President during the election campaign, especially since some Congressmen were alarmed with Soviet activity in Cuba.[51]

When Robert Kennedy told Dobrynin of President Kennedy's deep concern about the Soviet buildup in Cuba, the Soviet Ambassador told the Attorney General not to be concerned, for he had been instructed by Soviet Chairman Nikita

Khrushchev to assure the American President that there would be no ground-to-ground offensive weapons placed in Cuba. Furthermore, the Ambassador said, he could assure the President that this military buildup was not of any significance and that Khrushchev would do nothing to disrupt the relationship of the two countries during the period prior to the election. Chairman Khrushchev, he added, liked President Kennedy and did not want to embarrass him.[52] Robert Kennedy told Dobrynin that they were watching the buildup carefully and that he should know it would be of the gravest consequences if the U.S.S.R. placed missiles in Cuba.[53]

We may safely surmise that when Dobrynin informed Khrushchev of his conversation with Robert Kennedy, the Soviet Premier must have felt assured the President got the hint. Knowing the frequency of unmolested U-2 flights over the missile sites, Khrushchev must have believed the Americans had already detected the missile bases in Cuba. The official note sent later by President Kennedy using almost the same words, added to Khrushchev's confidence. After reading the note, the Soviet Premier may have felt assured that President Kennedy would not tolerate the introduction of what Americans believed were strategic nuclear missiles in Cuba. Kennedy's warning expressly mentioned that the introduction of offensive missiles in Cuba would raise the gravest issue. In Khrushchev's mind, the "gravest issue" mentioned by Kennedy could only have meant an invasion of Cuba and the elimination of Fidel Castro.

But, in order to make his signals even more explicit, Khrushchev sent a second personal message to Kennedy on September 6, making it very clear that "Nothing will be undertaken before the American congressional elections that would complicate the internal situation or aggravate the tension in the relations between our two countries..." Later on, a Soviet diplomat engaged in a friendly conversation with some New Frontiersmen[54] dropped "indiscreet" hints about a conversation he had had with Mikoyan and Khrushchev, who told him that the farthest thing he had in mind was to place long-range missiles in Cuba.[55]

"This is a time to lower tensions," Khrushchev had said. "Castro is getting only defensive weapons." Here Mikoyan had interjected: "short-range, surface-to-air missiles for use against planes; in no circumstances would long-range, surface-to-surface missiles go to Cuba."[56] It seems that this was one of those occasions which Khrushchev was known to use so skillfully to amplify his calculated indiscretions.[57] In his book *Leaders,* Nixon noticed that Khrushchev used indiscretions and bombast as tactics.[58]

On September 11, *TASS* released an official Soviet Government statement which contained the following passages:

> The armaments and military equipment sent to Cuba are designed exclusively for defensive purposes and the President of the United States and the American military just as the military of any country knows what means of defense are. How can these means threaten the United States?[59]

TASS also reiterated the Soviet government's well known policy of transfer of nuclear weapons to third nations:

> The government of the Soviet Union authorizes *TASS* to state that there is no need for the Soviet Union to shift its weapons for the repulsion of aggression, for a retaliatory blow, to any other country, *for instance Cuba*. Our nuclear weapons are so powerful in their explosive force and the Soviet Union has such powerful rockets to carry their nuclear warheads, that there is no need to search for sites for them beyond the boundaries of the Soviet Union.[60]

Author Robert Pope made an interesting analysis of the use of the word "designed" in the *TASS* release of September 11.[61] According to his analysis, it is significant that the Soviets had used this word in the translation supplied, implying that the weapons could not be used or were not meant to be used to attack the U.S. Pope points out that the use of the word "designed" suggests that the Russians were taking great pains to try to mislead the American leaders about the real capabilities of the missiles being shipped to Cuba. Pope also explained how careful the Soviets were in rendering official statements into English in their effort to convey the exact meaning intended in the original document. However, if one assumes that the missiles were actually not designed to attack the U.S., but to provoke an American attack on Cuba, this may indicate that, far from trying to mislead the American president, Khrushchev was actually trying to lead him on.

On October 16, Khrushchev had an unexpected meeting with Foy D. Kohler, American Ambassador to Moscow. During the conversation he told the ambassador that he was furious with Fidel Castro for prematurely announcing the agreement with the Soviet Union to build a fishing port in Havana, because it had raised a storm of public suspicion in the United States that what was really going to be built was a submarine base. Khrushchev stated once more that the last thing in the world he wanted to do was to embarrass the President on the eve of elections. By that time Khrushchev must have assumed that Kennedy knew about the missiles in Cuba, or at least had considered that possibility.

The Russian Premier wanted to state as clearly as possible that things in Cuba were not under his control, and, therefore, whatever happened, the Russians were not going to act against the U.S. in the event of an invasion of the Island. Moreover, in order to add credibility to his message, he instructed Penkovsky to report to his controllers that he had inside information that Khrushchev did not plan to apply any pressure on Berlin during the crisis.[62]

On October 24, after President Kennedy denounced the presence of strategic missiles in Cuba, Georgi Bolshakov read the notes of his Moscow talks to Charles Bartlett. The Russian, Bartlett reported later to Robert Kennedy, was clearly puzzled and disturbed, but insisted he could not believe there were long-range missiles on the Island. If that were the case, Bolshakov mentioned, he would be in the position of having being deceived by his own officials.[63]

It seems that Khrushchev wanted to be sure that by now President Kennedy had gotten the hint and that, whatever was going on in Cuba, it was a Cuban problem. Obviously, in the event of an American invasion of the Island the Soviets were not going to interfere. His signals, according to his logic, could not have been more clear.

Thanks to the evidence the Soviets had obtained from Gary Powers' U-2, Khrushchev was fully aware of the high sophistication of the American surveillance techniques. He was absolutely sure that the American intelligence would soon notice the preparations for the construction of the missile sites in Cuba. Why, then, such an apparently stupid lie? Why using "for instance Cuba" as an example?

But, forgetting that for a trained Communist a word is not what you think it says, but what effect it is intended to produce,[64] President Kennedy and his advisers failed —or perhaps avoided— to properly decode Khrushchev's signals and took the Soviet Premier's words at face value. Now, with the benefit of hindsight, it becomes evident that Khrushchev was sending the American President the most clear signals he could have sent without actually tipping his hand.

Khrushchev wanted to be sure that the Americans understood the allusion to Cuba and that, in any event, the Soviets would not intervene to defend missiles that were not "theirs."

Khrushchev's "Errors"

On October 17, the analysts who were studying the U-2 photographs discovered faint scars in the Cuban soil that closely resembled the ones previously seen in the Soviet Union. These scars revealed launch sites under construction for intermediate-range missiles. "These monsters could fly 2,500 miles, placing at their reach almost all big American cities. The intelligence men found three IRBM sites (four missiles each) under construction and another undoubtedly planned." [65]

Many members of the U.S. military were astonished by the openness of Soviet activities in Cuba, particularly knowing that the Russians knew they were under the constant surveillance of American aircraft.[66] What struck every Western intelligence analyst who participated in the Cuban missile crisis was that the missiles had been brought into Cuba and erected without any effort at camouflage or secrecy. Reconnaissance photos of the MRBM sites showed none of the special security measures such as walls or fences typical of these type of installation. Moreover, they were fully exposed to aerial observation.[67]

The aerial photographs released to the public could hardly have been more revealing, to the point that, many years later, some of them were used in the CIA's recruiting brochures to show the Agency's quality work.

The photographs show Soviet military vehicles lined up as if for Saturday inspection, and personnel tents dressed in orderly ranks. Control cables can be seen stretched between the emplacements. The canvass-covered missiles and their prime movers and erectors can be easily identified as the same types that had been photographed in the Moscow military parades in 1959 and 1960. There could hardly have been any mistake about what the Soviets were doing in Cuba.

Both the MRBM's and the IRBM's were above ground and located in soft terrain, very vulnerable to any type of enemy attack.[68] Although a single installation of MRBM could be built in a matter of days, the Russians were progressing very slowly in their installation. They seemed to be in no great hurry, and worked only during daylight hours.[69]

For these and other similar reasons, it is difficult to avoid the conclusion that the plan to deploy what looked like strategic missile sites on Cuban soil was carried out in such a way that they would inevitably be discovered by the Americans. If one assumes that the anti-aircraft SAMs were intended to protect the installations of the strategic missiles, then they should have been installed and ready to shoot at the U.S. planes *before* the strategic missiles arrived.

In fact, as early as the spring of 1962 CIA Director John McCone mentioned his suspicions, allegedly based on a "hunch,"[70] that the Russians eventually might install medium-range missiles in Cuba. The news that the Soviets were installing SAM batteries in Cuba apparently hardened McCone's suspicions and, on August 22, he told President Kennedy and Secretary of Defense McNamara that, in his opinion, the SAMs were being emplaced to protect and hide from air observation the introduction of longer-range strategic missiles.[71] Surprisingly, and apparently contradicting McCone's logical assumptions, the SAM's and other associated anti-aircraft nets only became operational when the construction of the strategic missile sites was well along, and the Soviets employed almost no camouflage at all to hide either set of weapons.

In an effort to justify *a posteriori* one of his more obvious "errors," namely that the anti-aircraft missiles should have been installed before the ballistic missiles so as to close the airspace above them to avoid detection by American spy planes, Khrushchev alleged that this didn't make sense. According to Khrushchev, "there is a limit to the number of missile installations you can put on a tiny sausage-shaped island as small as Cuba."[72] Apparently the Soviet Premier, who never visited the Island, didn't know that Cuba, with around 4,218 square miles, is the largest island not only of the area covered by the Greater Antilles (to which Haiti, Jamaica and Puerto Rico also belong), but of the entire West Indies archipelago — popularly known as "the Caribbean." Contrary to Khrushchev's claims, though long and narrow in some areas,[73] Cuba is not a tiny island. Or perhaps Khrushchev knew that perfectly well, and was just lying.

Furthermore, one of the reasons why the American reconnaissance planes were able to photograph the strategic missile sites was precisely because the SAM batteries didn't shoot at them. According to American intelligence sources at the time, the SAMs weren't operational before October 27, when a Soviet SAM shot down Major Anderson's U-2 while flying over the eastern part of Cuba. There is no solid evidence, however, indicating that the SAMs weren't operational before that date. Actually, all evidence indicates that, though they were operational, they had been ordered not to shoot at the American reconnaissance planes.

Logic indicates that the main —and probably only— purpose of the SAM batteries would have been to protect the strategic missiles sites from early discovery by aerial observation. Since the SAMs could not shoot down planes flying below 10,000 feet, the anti-aircraft missiles could not have been useful against low-flying fighters like the ones the U.S. would have used in the event of an invasion of Cuba.[74] But, defying all logic, SAM crews had been ordered not to shoot at their logical target, the high altitude flying U-2s.[75] Therefore, what was their true purpose? Perhaps their true purpose was to alert clever guys like McCone —or the ones who actually alerted McCone— that something very fishy was going on in Cuba.

Well aware of the apparent inefficiency previously displayed by the U.S. intelligence during the Bay of Pigs invasion, Khrushchev carefully planned a whole series of "mistakes" to send the Americans unmistakable signals that something was going on in Cuba.

One of the most unexplainable[76] Russian "mistakes" was their failure to camouflage the missiles sites previous to their discovery by American spy planes. Allison concluded that this failure may have had a simple answer: stupid bureaucratic procedures in the Soviet Army. Missile sites had never been camouflaged in the Soviet Union, so the construction crews at the sites did what they usually do: emplace missiles according to the installation manuals because somebody forgot to retrain them before they went to work on this mission.[77]

But, knowing the operational procedures of the Soviet Army this explanation seems a bit too simplistic to be credible. First of all, the officers and enlisted men assigned to the job of missile emplacement are normally not common soldiers, but specially trained personnel. Secondly, even with the existence of stupid bureaucratic procedures common to all armies, it is difficult to believe that they had made such a gross mistake, particularly if they were trying to place the missiles in Cuba using deception and stealth as the American official version claimed. Finally, Allison contradicts himself when, just two paragraphs before, he mentions that "The clandestine manner in which the missiles were shipped, unloaded, and transported to construction sites reveals the hand of Soviet intelligence agencies. Secrecy is their standard operating procedure."[78]

According to American intelligence sources, before the crisis, strategic missile sites in the Soviet Union had never been camouflaged. But this argument is fallacious too. After Gary Powers' U-2 was shot down over Russian territory, the flow of photographic information about Soviet missiles stopped. We don't know for sure, but it makes sense that, after discovering the powerful photographic means of the American spy planes, the Soviets may have begun to camouflage the missile sites in the Soviet Union. Also, even if we don't know it with certainty, there are good reasons for believing that, at least in the early sixties, many of the strategic missiles appearing in the photographs of the missile sites in Soviet territory taken by the U-2s were actually dummies —a fact that the U.S. intelligence perhaps suspected, but never mentioned because it was not good for their fear-based business.

The unavoidable conclusion is that, either the crews who emplaced the missiles, their commanders, and the Soviet High Command were total incompetent fools, who knew nothing about secrecy, or the lack of camouflage was as deliberate as the initial emplacement of the missiles.[79] Furthermore, a strong indication that the "bureaucratic procedures" explanation is not true is that the Soviet military literature emphasizing the importance of surprise and deception (*maskirovka*) in warfare is particularly abundant.[80] Consequently, the only logic conclusion one can arrive at is that if the Soviet personnel in charge of installing the missiles did not camouflage them was not because they were incompetent fools, but because they were specifically ordered not to do so. Moreover, the Soviet high command knew that the American U-2s, whose extraordinary capabilities they confirmed when they inspected Gary Powers' plane, were closely watching the Island. For these reasons, it is difficult to avoid the conclusion that the only logical explanation, aside from the Soviets-are-stupid one, is that if they failed to camouflage the missiles it was only because they wanted the Americans to discover them.

In his zeal to make Americans believe his hoax, Khrushchev took care of even the smallest details. For example, the Soviets even sent to Cuba the trucks which would have moved the nuclear warheads to the missile sites.[81] That was a detail the U.S. photo interpreters were not going to miss. Even the concrete arches for the bunkers apparently intended as nuclear storage magazines were prefabricated-cast in the Soviet Union and shipped the whole distance to Cuba.[82] Khrushchev didn't want to run any risks due to Cuban technological failures *in situ*. He wanted the American intelligence to detect and verify that the structures were exactly as the ones the U-2s had photographed in the Soviet Union —most of which were not battle ready because the U.S.S.R., as always, was behind schedule in the production of nuclear warheads.

The lack of adequate camouflage to hide the missile sites from American observation was such a gross mistake that author Anatol Rappoport assumed that the failure of the Russians to hide the missile sites and otherwise to take sufficient measure to prevent premature exposure was due to a plan by which the missile sites were meant to be discovered by American spy planes.[83] Rappoport was not the only one who had reached a similar conclusion. The authoritative *Wall Street Journal* reported during the height of the crisis that "... the authorities here [in the U.S.] almost all accept one key assumption; that Mr. Khrushchev must have assumed that his Cuban missile sites would soon be discovered. The report added that one authority who studied the photographic evidence said that 'The Russians seem almost to have gone out of their way to call attention to them.'"[84]

CIA officer Lyman Kirkpatrick mentioned that "It had been assumed in Washington that the Russians in Cuba were aware of the U-2 flights and that they must have deducted that the Americans were watching the construction." Adding that, "One thing seemed certain. The Russians must understand that the U.S. knew what was going on."[85] Of course, Kirkpatrick added, this assumed; first, that the Russians in Cuba informed Moscow of the U-2 flights; second, that Russian intelligence knew of the quality of U.S. photographic equipment; and, third, that the Americans would be able to determine what was being built.

All the assumptions mentioned by Kirkpatrick proved to be true: first, both the Cubans and the Russians in Cuba informed Moscow of the U-2 flights; second, on May 1, 1960, the Soviets had shot down a U-2 and had studied its cameras in detail; therefore, they knew of the quality of the U.S. photographic equipment; and, third, the Americans had been able to determine what was being built because several month before the crisis Colonel Oleg Penkovsky had given them the operational manual of exactly the same type of missiles the Russians were now deploying in Cuba.

Khrushchev was well aware that the information Penkovsky had provided the Americans about the type of missiles placed in Cuba would allow the CIA to follow the progress of their installation by the hour, which was in the first place the reason why he chose that type of missile (or, to be precise, what *looked like* that type of missile) to be sent to Cuba.

Chapter 6

Khrushchev's Spy

> *And it is by this means that the expendable agent, armed with false information, can be sent to convey it to the enemy.*
> —Sun Tzu.

Many former members of the British intelligence services —and some still in active service— share the opinion that the greatest triumph for British Intelligence since WWII was the recruiting of Colonel Oleg Vladimirovich Penkovsky, an officer of the Soviet Military Intelligence (GRU) who defected in place[1] in 1961.[2] Penkovsky was an opportunistic member of the *nomenklatura* who, through career and marriage, had positioned himself in a place in Soviet society where he had access to secrets that were almost priceless to the West.[3]

CIA Deputy director for intelligence Ray Cline was the man in charge of preparing the intelligence briefings for President Kennedy during the crisis. Cline was convinced that the photointerpreters at the NPIC were able to understand the initial U-2 photographs of strategic missile sites at San Cristóbal only because of previous information supplied by Penkovsky.[4] A detailed memorandum prepared by the CIA on October 19, with detailed information on the MRBM missile sites in Cuba, relied heavily on information provided by Penkovsky. Therefore, "triangulation," positive confirmation by an independent, reliable source of the kind of missiles deployed in Cuba, was possible mainly because of Penkovsky's good work.[5]

Penkovsky: the CIA's Greatest Success

Penkovsky's first successful approach to the British Secret Service was through Greville Wynne, a British businessman who was visiting Moscow. Wynne was also an asset of the British intelligence and had intelligence training. Once the British became convinced of Penkovsky's *bona fides*, as they did perhaps too quickly,[6] the CIA, who previously had refused Penkovsky's advances, took an interest in him. Since then, the Penkovsky case became a joint Anglo-American operation.

In April, 1961, Penkovsky visited London as a member of a Soviet delegation, ostensibly to encourage the expansion of Anglo-Soviet trade in the field of machinery and electronics. While in London, Penkovsky had his first debriefing session on April 20 by two British Secret Service and two CIA officers who questioned him in depth.[7]

Oleg Penkovsky is credited as the single most important spy ever recruited by the American intelligence services in their secret war against the Russians. During the time he collaborated with the Western intelligence services he delivered over 10,000 pages of invaluable Soviet military documents —highly classified training manuals, personal information about Soviet military chiefs, and even detailed specifications of the latest Russian strategic missiles. He also provided reams of documents concerning the Soviet armed forces and their advanced weapons-development programs, in addition to clandestine operational information and doctrine.[8]

After Penkovsky was recruited as a spy for the West, he traveled abroad on three occasions on official duty with high level delegations attending Soviet-sponsored trade exhibitions. Each time, one in Paris and twice in London, he managed to slip away unnoticed from his colleagues and met his American and British controllers for long debriefing and training sessions.[9]

To his first debriefing session Penkovsky brought several highly classified, original Red Army rocket training manuals, which gave detailed information about missiles already in use. He also surprised his case officers when he mentioned that missiles of the same type described in the manuals he had brought would soon after be deployed to Cuba, where they would threaten the United States.[10]

The extraordinary value and high quality of the information Penkovsky provided overcame the initial doubts of the skeptics. Though it is a standard practice in the introduction of a plant to provide him with chicken feed[11] to give the opposition, no intelligence agency in its right mind, reasoned his controllers, would hand over material of such a high quality just to prove the trustworthiness of a penetration.[12] CIA officers who saw the 5,000 negatives —two pages per picture frame— of microfilmed secret documents provided by Penkovsky, were dazzled by the quality and importance of his information.[13]

It was, seemingly, a lucky coincidence that the CIA had an extraordinary large amount of information some months before the crisis about the specific type of missile to be placed in Cuba. The invaluable information Penkovsky provided on the missiles included their range, the steps involved in bringing them to operational readiness and their rate of refire.[14] The take from Penkovsky allowed the CIA to follow the progress of Soviet missile emplacements in Cuba by the hour, and to state with confidence that the missiles threatened almost every major American city. Most scholars who have studied the Cuban missile crisis agree that the information provided by Penkovsky greatly influenced the behavior of President Kennedy during the Cuban missile crisis and was the main reason for his evident confidence in taking a tough stand against Khrushchev by blockading Cuba and insisting that the missiles be withdrawn.

On August 23, 1962, a top secret document entitled "Report on Implications for U.S. Foreign and Defense Policy of Recent Intelligence Estimates," prepared by a special committee of senior intelligence, foreign policy, and defense officials to evaluate the implications of the new intelligence estimates of strategic military capabilities, was sent to President Kennedy. Preparation of the report included the use of closely held materials supplied by Penkovsky, then still and active agent in Moscow.[15] Moreover, the information provided by Penkovsky about the true missile capability of the Soviet Union convinced the U.S. National Security Council that it had been mistaken in believing there was a "missile gap," and that the Soviets were far ahead of the Americans in missile technology development and production.[16]

Colonel Oleg Penkovsky was arrested just before the onset of the Cuban Missile Crisis, and was later tried and executed.[17] The publication of *The Penkovsky Papers,* his alleged memoirs, opened the Soviets to the embarrassment of having the world know that the top levels of their government had been penetrated by a Western spy.[18]

Even more important, Penkovsky's success as a Western agent also helped to patch up and brighten the CIA's image, badly damaged after President Kennedy, in a "leak" to the press, blamed the Agency for the failure of the Bay of Pigs invasion. Robert Kennedy was convinced that the U.S. victory on the Cuban missile crisis, which owed much to Penkovsky's work, was worth all the money spent on the CIA from its creation in 1947 to 1961.[19]

But not everyone in the American and British intelligence services bought Penkovsky's story. James Jesus Angleton, for one, had serious doubts about Penkovsky's *bona fides*.[20] According to Joe Bulik, one of the CIA officers who had an active participation in the Penkovsky case, the last time he saw Angleton, the retired Chief of Counterintelligence told him that every case he had ever worked on inside the Soviet Union over the past seven years had been controlled by the KGB, including the Penkovsky case.[21]

Angleton was apparently not the only one skeptical about Penkovsky. Some members of the British Security Service, MI5, believed that Penkovsky was nothing but a Soviet "plant," the key figure in a Russian disinformation exercise of the highest political consequences.[22] Therefore, let's take a look at the Penkovsky case from the dark side.

Was Penkovsky a Soviet Plant?

In the beginning, Penkovsky was not a CIA spy, but had been recruited by the British intelligence. He had previously tried to approach the CIA in 1955 in Ankara, Turkey, but was turned down flatly because the CIA's Soviet Bloc Division of Clandestine Services was extremely careful not to be taken in by KGB provocateurs and double agents. To the overcautious CIA officers, Penkovsky seemed too good to be true,[23] especially after several recent defeats suffered at the hands of the KGB in Europe at the time. Therefore, the CIA operators were suspicious and understandably reluctant to be duped again.[24]

The facts surrounding Penkovsky's attempts to offer his services to Western intelligence raised grave suspicions.[25] In the late 1960s, he made a visit to the

American Embassy in Moscow, a building that was under constant KGB surveillance, as he must have known given his position in the Soviet intelligence. During the visit he made a cold approach to some American officials, and offered his services. He was interviewed in the embassy's CIA safe room, where he told a CIA officer that he was a senior GRU officer working for the GKNIIR, a joint KGB-GRU organization whose main goal was to steal technical and scientific intelligence from the West.[26] After some discussion and consultation, the CIA officers at the embassy rejected him as an agent provocateur, an obvious Soviet plant.[27]

Some years later, the CIA discovered that the supposedly safe room at the American embassy in Moscow where Penkovsky's interview took place, had been bugged by the KGB. Apparently the equipment had been installed in 1952, when the embassy had been renovated, and the bugs had been operational for almost 12 years. The damage report produced by the CIA's counterespionage and security specialists asserted that during the entire height of the Cold War the Soviet intelligence services had probably intercepted every diplomatic cable between Washington and the embassy, and recorded every single coversation that took place in the building.[28] Therefore, it makes sense to believe that either Penkovsky was a provocation, which explains why he was not detained at the time, or he had been compromised since the very beginning and the KGB began using him as a vehicle to pass disinformation.[29]

A few months after his failed approach at the American Embassy, the Canadian secret services also rejected him. In a Moscow hotel, Penkovsky openly approached a Canadian businessman which happened to have close relations with the Royal Canadian Mounted Police.[30] But, apparently, the Russian colonel had a firm resolve to defect. In another attempt, he approached the British Secret Service through Greville Wynne, who was visiting Moscow on a business trip.[31] The British became all too quickly convinced of Penkovsky's *bona fides* and jubilantly informed the CIA at once about their new recruit.

According to Sir Maurice Oldfield, head of the MI-6, Penkovsky was "The answer to a prayer. What he provided seemed like a miracle, too. That is why for so long he was mistrusted on both sides of the Atlantic." Sir Oldfield seemingly forgot the golden rule of intelligence and espionage work: if it seems too good to be true, it is too good to be true. The Americans, however, apparently forgetting their previous fears, took an interest in the case and the running of Penkovsky became a joint operation for both services from the very beginning.[32]

The first serious doubts about Penkovsky were raised because of his blatant approaches to the Americans and Canadians. These were breaches in tradecraft incredibly clumsy to have been made by a professional intelligence officer with Penkovsky's rank and experience.[33] But there is another piece of evidence that raises serious doubts about his *bona fides*. In order to fulfill his duties as a spy, Penkovsky was provided with a miniature camera to photograph secret documents and slip the films out of the Soviet Union via his contact, Greville Wynne. But, as Wynne's trips to Moscow became less frequent, the wife of Rory Chisholm, Chief of the British Secret Service in Moscow working under a diplomatic cover there, agreed to take on the task. On fourteen occasions Penkovsky met her "accidentally" and handed over films while pretending to talk.[34]

But George Blake, a member of the Secret Service who was caught in the act of betraying his country, some years later declared in an interrogation after his conviction that he had alerted the Soviets about Rory Chisholm before the Secret Service officer had ever left London. It seems most unlikely, therefore, that the KGB, who had the Chisholms under surveillance all the time, had not monitored Penkovsky's suspicious meetings with Mrs. Chisholm from early 1962, and that Penkovsky had not been aware of it.

In fact, there is firm proof that Penkovsky had been under surveillance from an early stage of his dealings with the Western secret services. In November 1962 Greville Wynne was arrested while visiting Budapest, brought to the KGB, and taken to the Lubyanka prison in Moscow. According to his account, the KGB played him a tape recording of one of the earliest conversations he had with Penkovsky in a room of the Ukraine Hotel. If this is true, either Penkovsky's cover had been quickly "blown" after he had been recruited by the British, or he had been a KGB plant from the very beginning.[35]

An argument held at the time by the ones who believed Penkovsky was what he purported to be was that no intelligence agency in its right mind would have sacrificed confidential information of the type and quality provided by Penkovsky just to prove the *bona fides* of a penetration. But a reevaluation made some years later by the MI5 of the information he brought in showed that almost all of it was actually "chicken feed," most likely provided by the Soviet intelligence services to establish confidence in their planted spy so that his major objective could succeed.[36] This, by the way, is standard operating procedure of most intelligence services, including the KGB. British author Chapman Pincher mentions evidence that during WWII the KGB let the Germans sink a heavily laden Soviet troopship to establish the credibility of one valuable agent who had given the Nazis the necessary information to sink the ship.[37]

The technical information Penkovsky provided about the missiles proved later to be several years old. Most of the Soviet Intelligence agents he identified were already known as such in the West. What was most unusual for a defector of his potential was that he did not identify one single Russian spy actually operating in the West. Though he was deputy head of a combined operation of the GRU and the KGB to collect scientific intelligence, he gave no relevant information in that field. Nor did he produce much information about intercontinental missiles or Soviet reconnaissance satellites, which he should have been knowledgeable about, considering his position.[38] Moreover, during the period Penkovsky was active, he failed to give warning to his controllers of the erection of the Berlin Wall in August, 1961.[39]

Some of the information Penkovsky provided turned out to be false. For example, he claimed he had information that Soviet scientists had developed a nerve gas that was twice as effective as anything available to the West. The information sent Americans on a false track, spending huge amounts of money, effort, and time trying to produce something similar. The results ended in total failure.[40]

If one is to believe Penkovsky's CIA controllers, one of the things which helped confirm Penkovsky's *bona fides* was that the missile manuals he gave them were an invaluable tool to identify the type of strategic missiles Khrushchev ordered a few months later to be deployed in Cuba. But this can be decoded with a totally different meaning. According to the CIA's own tradecraft practices, one of the six warning signs which indicate that an enemy deception operation may be under way is "suspicious confirmation." This is the case when a new stream of information from clandestine sources of technical collection seems to reinforce the rationale for or against a U.S. policy initiative.[41] A better description of Penkovsky's activities, which were instrumental in the identification of some objects on Cuban soil which reinforced the American's suspicions that they actually were strategic missiles, can scarcely be made.

It has been repeated over and over that, during the time he collaborated with the Western intelligence services, he delivered over 10,000 pages of invaluable Soviet military documents. That means, at two documents per frame, a total of 5,000 photos[42] taken with a Minox camera. Now, even thinking that he was very fast, and that he had the documents at hand, a very conservative average amount of time for taking each photograph is 3 minutes. That makes a total of 250 hours. But Penkovsky was a full time officer at the GRU, which means that he worked no less than 10 hours a day in his office, plus he had other official duties. How did he manage to have the time to accomplish such a gigantic photographic job? Furthermore, his controllers were surprised by the fact that an incredible 99 percent of the photos were legible,[43] a real feat if one takes into consideration the pressure and fear under which all spy work is done.

It seems that Colonel Penkovsky had a peculiar sense of humor. Shortly after the CIA gave him a Minox camera, he asked for another one, claiming that with the two of them he could double his output. The CIA promptly complied,[44] and the efficient spy kept bringing his oversized catch to his gullible CIA controllers.[45]

The KGB and Disinformation

During a debriefing session, Major Anatoli Golitsyn, a high-ranking KGB officer who defected in 1962, told the CIA of a bizarre plan he heard three years earlier at the KGB. According to Golitsyn, after he had completed an assignment in the KGB, he was looking to move to a more interesting department. In one of his job-seeking activities, he approached a senior officer he knew in the Disinformation Department —a position which would have given him a boost in his career. The officer promised Golitsyn that he would take him on, but explained that he must wait at least a year because a traitor, a certain Colonel Piotr Popov, had been discovered inside the GRU. Until the ramifications of his activities, which affected the KGB, had been thoroughly investigated and rectified, it would not be possible to proceed with a major disinformation exercise against the West, in which there could be a place for Golitsyn.[46]

The Soviet concept of *dezinformatsia* is key in understanding the Penkovsky affair. The KGB defines *dezinformatsia* as the use of misinformation to confuse the enemy and, eventually, to neutralize him.[47] The practical applications of the concept apparently worked so effectively during WWII that its use was expanded afterward, and a whole new Disinformation Department was created inside the KGB.[48] Golitsyn revealed how Aleksandr Shelepin in particular, stressed the use of disinformation while he was the KGB Chairman between 1959 and 1961. Golitsyn firmly believed that the major disinformation operation he heard about was the Penkovsky affair, and that it had succeeded.[49]

Pincher affirmed that some senior officers of the British security and intelligence services believed Golitsyn's conclusions were true. Their view was that Khrushchev's purpose was basically to force President Kennedy into a commitment not to invade Cuba, which was far more important as a center for the spread of communism in Latin America than as a base for missiles.[50] But, as I have shown above, rather than a docile instrument in the hands of Khrushchev, Castro was an unstable power-hungry dictator, intent on spreading in Latin America not Russian Communism, but his own brand of *Fidelismo*. Moreover, Khrushchev could have had little doubt that no American President could really tolerate the presence of Soviet strategic missiles so near American shores. Only a fool would have believed that deploying missiles on Cuban soil would have acted as a deterrent against an American invasion instead of giving the United States an excellent excuse —in the eyes of the world and their own people— to invade Cuba and unseat Castro and his regime.

Oleg Penkovsky and Greville Wynne were tried in Moscow in January, 1963, after the usual propaganda show trial aimed at discrediting the British and the Americans. The Penkovsky trial received worldwide press coverage and the KGB seized the opportunity to expel eight British and five American "diplomats" whom they knew were intelligence officers.

After the trial, it was announced that Penkovsky had been summarily executed by a firing squad. Yet this sounds somewhat strange. The KGB's standard practice is not to execute a traitor immediately after the trial, but to interrogate him over a long period of time before silencing him. Greville Wynne, believed that Penkovsky committed suicide while in prison. There are others, however, who speculate that he may still be alive in the Soviet Union under a different name and enjoying the benefits of an early retirement.[51]

Just the idea that Penkovsky had been a Soviet plant, and that the Russians deliberately surrendered so much valuable information just to allow him to prove his *bona fides*, struck some CIA people as insane. Marchetti vividly remembers "the note of outrage and injury which came into Jack Maury's voice when he described what were to him obtuse, willful, and perverse insinuations that Penkovsky's material was not reliable or important."[52]

There are also many others inside the British and American secret services who cannot bring themselves to the idea that Penkovsky was not what he claimed to be, if only because, having accepted him as the greatest Soviet defector ever, their professional reputations had been linked up to his integrity.[53] But, while some of them still don't believe that Penkovsky was a plant, they believe that Penkovsky had been "blown" soon after he made his first contacts to defect. One significant detail is that after the Penkovsky scandal, nobody criticized Khrushchev —at any rate, in public— for the failure of the Soviet security services to detect that one of their senior officers had been passing top-secret documents to the enemy for more than sixteen months,[54] sometimes in a very clumsy, unprofessional way.[55]

It is known that inside the CIA there were also a few who were skeptical about Penkovsky's true allegiance. His first approach in Ankara was rejected by none other than Richard Bissell, who was at the time the head of the Directorate of Plans (the CIA's clandestine services) and had a low opinion of the value of agents and conventional espionage (HUMINT).[56] Even after the CIA acquired Penkovsky from the British in 1960, Bissell expressed his doubts to Jack Maury, the CIA's Soviet Division chief who personally ran the Penkovsky case from Washington. According to witnesses, Bissell asked Maury, "How do we know this guy is on the level?"[57] Maury found Bissell's skepticism incredible.

Another critic of the Penkovsky operation was James Jesus Angleton, the paranoid head of counterintelligence.[58] Inside the CIA, Angleton was known for the extreme skepticism and boundless suspicion which he brought to his work. Actually, Angleton had been responsible for turning down Penkovsky's overture in 1960, when he initially approached the Americans. Later, after the Russian colonel was recruited by the British services and then offered to the CIA, Angleton continued arguing that Penkovsky was a Soviet plant.[59]

Angleton, whose operating principle departed from the postulate that "there are no friendly services," always suspected that the KGB source of the Penkovsky treachery was British and could well have been a high-level officer of the MI5.[60] The scandal caused some years later by Kim Philby —which ended with his defection to the U.S.S.R. in 1963— and the subsequent investigations of the case which brought hard proof of his life of treachery, confirmed Angleton's suspicions that the British secret services had been penetrated to a great extent by Soviet intelligence.[61] Some years after the Penkovsky affair, Sir Roger Hollis, the former head of the British MI5, was all but convicted posthumously of being a mole[62] himself. Angleton's suspicions about Penkovsky were shared not only by Chapman Pincher, a *Daily Express* journalist who later retired to Australia and wrote several polemic books on the British secret services, but also by Peter Wright, a former Junior Assistant Director of the MI5.

According to Wright, three specific areas of the Penkovsky case made him highly suspicious. The first was the way he was recruited, the second, the particular type of intelligence he provided, and the third, the way he was run by his controllers.[63] I have explained above in some detail the strange way in which Penkovsky was recruited, so let's begin by analyzing the intelligence he provided.

The CIA divided the intelligence provided by Penkovsky into two types: straight intelligence, which they code named ARNIKA, and counterintelligence, which they code named RUPEE. The RUPEE information was mostly about identification of GRU officers, most of which was accurate, but already known to the CIA. What called the attention of Wright is that Penkovsky provided no leads at all to identify Soviet illegals or penetrations of Western intelligence services. According to Wright, it made no sense to him that a man who was doing a job similar to his own and who had spent several years at the top levels of the GRU, and in regular contact with the KGB, had not picked a single trace of information about Soviet secret agents infiltrated in the West.[64]

Regarding ARNIKA, it is now well known that Penkovsky passed over to his controllers thousands of documents dealing with secret Soviet military systems. But Wright noticed two oddities: The first one is that in some instances Penkovsky not merely photographed Top Secret documents, but actually gave his controllers the original documents.[65] This goes against the most elementary rules of tradecraft practiced no only by the Soviet, but by most, if not all, intelligence services around the world. This is even more suspicious coming from a man like Penkovsky, a senior GRU officer who necessarily had been trained in the strict Soviet tradecraft methods and practices.

The second one is that he claimed that some of the most important documents, like the ones which eventually helped the Americans identify the Soviet missiles in Cuba, had been shown to him by his uncle, a senior GRU commander of the Soviet missile forces. Moreover, he said that he had copied the documents during the few moments his uncle had been out of the room.[66] This is totally incredible.

Finally, Wright mentions the sloppy way in which Penkovsky was run by his controllers, both in Moscow and during his frequent visits to the West. Shortly after Penkovsky was allegedly discovered and executed, Wright wrote an internal MI5 report explaining in detail his doubts about the Penkovsky case. As expected, it was received with bouts of outrage.[67]

Penkovsky: a Soviet Deception Exercise?

It is now known that from 1957 to mid-1961 the Soviet government engaged in a deliberate, systematic, and sustained campaign of strategic deception. It produced grossly exaggerated claims regarding the production and deployment of ICBMs and highly inflated statements of the strength and numbers of the Soviet ICBM force vis-a-vis that of the United States. However, if the suspicions about Penkovsky's true role are correct, one wonders why the Soviets used him to dispel the "missile gap" myth. One possible explanation may be that, after the success of their disinformation campaign regarding the "missile gap,"[68] they must have had second thoughts about it, and perhaps realized that an apparent situation of nuclear disequilibrium was potentially dangerous to the U.S.S.R.

Previously, another controversy had erupted among the U.S. intelligence and the military about a so-called "bomber gap" —basically that the Soviets had scores of advanced bombers, much better than the American ones. Actually the American misperception had been motivated by a Soviet deception exercise. During a military parade in Moscow, several squadrons of a new type of bomber flew over the tribune, where military attachés from some western countries were observing them with attention. The ruse had been a new version of an old military trick: marching the same regiment though a clearing over and over. Actually the Soviets had only one squadron of such type of plane.[69]

Khrushchev's bombastic strategic claims and deception, like the ones which gave credit to the "missile gap," created the illusion that the U.S.S.R. was engaged in a serious and successful strategic arms race with the United States. But that false idea proved to be extremely dangerous in the long run, because it had the unwanted effect of stimulating American anxiety and increased the pressure for greater strategic weapons expenditures.

Despite much criticism during his administration, Eisenhower refused to be panicked into a strategic arms race by the threat of a missile gap. Unknown to most critics, the source of Eisenhower's imperturbable attitude was his knowledge of special intelligence estimates of the Soviet missile force and the fact that the U-2s had been conducting secret photographic reconnaissance flights over the U.S.S.R. since 1956. The fact was kept secret until Khrushchev disclosed it in May, 1960, after Gary Powers' plane was shot down deep inside Soviet territory. As a consequence, Eisenhower canceled any further flights over the Soviet Union. So, for a relatively long period of time the U.S. was blind to Soviet missile development until the first spy satellite was successfully launched in late 1962. This situation of information black out meant that the U.S. lacked the technical means for checking Penkovsky's claims that there was no missile gap.

Even more, there are several reasons to believe that the U-2 flights alone could not totally alleviate American concern about the existence of a missile gap or its emergence in the near future. First of all, there is the fact that U-2 photos showing a limited Soviet ICBM deployment did not exclude large-scale production and deployment in the future. Secondly, while acknowledging that U-2 flights had been taking place, the Eisenhower administration never made available to the public specific information regarding the extent to which the U-2 flights had covered Soviet territory and the thoroughness of the information obtained by this method. It is known that the Soviets heavily used decoys to alter their enemy's perception of their true capabilities.

As some leaks indicated, even the experts within the Kennedy administration apparently disagreed in their interpretation of the available data. Some of the experts —most notably the Air Force specialists— had a pessimistic view and brought alarming estimates of Soviet capabilities. Therefore, it is not farfetched to believe that the information Penkovsky gave the Americans which helped dispel the "missile gap" could have actually been disinformation, and that in the early sixties there may have been at least the beginning of a true "missile gap."[70]

Wright speculates that the fact that Soviets were installing in Cuba what, according to Penkovsky, were their most advanced IRBMs helped to confirm to the Americans Penkovsky's claims that the Soviet ICBM capability was very limited.[71] But, as I have mentioned over and over in this book, in the field of intelligence and espionage things are seldom what they seem to be.

Moreover, if one accepts the possibility that the Soviets were worried of an unstable equilibrium due to a missile gap which may appear as a threat to the U.S., it makes no sense to think that they had created a real threat by placing strategic missiles in Cuba. The full impact of the Soviet ruse —if it actually was a ruse— was not felt in the defense policies of the Eisenhower administration. It had a strong effect, though, in the attitudes and defense policies of President Kennedy.

It seems, however, that some administration officials were manipulating the estimates of Soviet capabilities in order to increase public fears of a missile gap. Those fears had been nourished by Khrushchev's dramatic and chilling boasts regarding the growth of the Soviet missile force and his efforts to make political and diplomatic use of these threats. Evidence indicates that, though he profited for some time from his false strategic claims, and he spoke as if the U.S.S.R. was catching up to and even surpassing the U.S. in strategic power, Khrushchev did not in fact engage in a race with the U.S. to deploy ICBMs. Thus, it seems that Khrushchev's plan worked so perfect that in the long run he got caught in his own handiwork and was worried about having overplayed his hand.

In retrospect, it seems clear that Colonel Oleg Penkovsky was but another key element in Khrushchev's dangerous deception game with President Kennedy. The Soviet Premier wanted the Americans to know exactly what type of missiles were supposed to be placed in Cuba, their range, and the danger they posed, and Penkovsky provided them with all the false information they needed.

Now that Khrushchev positively knew that the Americans had discovered the missile sites, he went a step further. The new photographic missions over Cuba brought frightening images. The Russian crews, who previously had been working slowly, only during daylight hours, now were working frantically around the clock, rushing to complete what looked like six sites for MRBMs, four missiles to a site. The photo interpreters at the NPIC allegedly had positively identified the missiles when they spotted what looked like tail fins sticking out under the tarpaulins. They were identical to the fins of the MRBMs they had photographed in Moscow in the May Day parade that very same year.[72]

The pace of construction of the MRBM emplacements was staggering. By the day, by the hour, the emplacements grew under the eye of the U-2's cameras, and it seemed that more canvas-covered objects, which the NPIC photointerpreters kept faithfully identifying as strategic missiles, were becoming ready to fire —or so they claimed.

Chapter 7

Khrushchev's Failure

> *Por eso me pica aquí, y voy a rascarme allá.*
> *(I have an itch here, so I am scratching there.)*
> —Cuban song popular in the 1950s.

Nikita Khrushchev's carefully conceived plans had not counted on the unexpected and incomprehensible behavior of President Kennedy. Seemingly, all reports received in Washington about the strange developments in Cuba aroused less suspicions than Khrushchev thought they should provoke. Even the CIA, which often had been accused of being unnecessarily alarmist, seemed, in this case, rather unimpressed.[1]

Most American analysts seem to agree that the single piece of evidence that initiated the crisis on October 14, 1962, were the photographs taken by an American U-2 reconnaissance plane of a Soviet strategic missile site in Cuba. It has been pointed out, however, that U.S. leaders might have received information three weeks earlier —that is, if a U-2 had flown over the western part of Cuba in the last week of September. But, quite unexplainably, the U-2s were prevented from flying over that part of Cuba, precisely where intelligence reports indicated that the missiles were most likely to be.

Though most alleged sightings coming from Cuban exiles located the missiles in the western part of the Island, the U-2 planes had concentrated their efforts on spying in the *eastern* part of Cuba. It was not until October 9, however, that the interagency Committee on Overhead Reconnaissance (COMOR) gave authorization to fly over the western part of Cuba.

In an effort to explain the unexplainable, a spokesman for the Kennedy administration claimed that a heavy cloud cover prevented getting any photographs of the western part of Cuba until October 14, 1962. According to Official U.S. government statements, photos of that area had not been taken prior to that date because "the weather intervened. Hurricane Ella delayed flights for a week and then a cloud cover blocked high-level surveillance." But this explanation was a total fabrication, because, as meteorological reports clearly pointed out, Ella did not become a hurricane until October 16 —well after the period referred to in the

Kennedy administration's statement.[2] Official Weather Bureau maps show clear weather over Western Cuba most of the time between October 5th and 9th, and good photographic weather in the morning from October 10 to 14. Therefore, the Kennedy administration consciously lied about the issue.

Moreover, the U-2 cameras not only used normal, panchromatic black and white film, but also infrared and other types of specialized film.[3] Photointerpreters can testify that sometimes infrared film is even more useful than panchromatic film, because it penetrates the cloud cover to some extent. In addition, infrared film is also useful in detecting the heat signature of objects on the ground, even the ones covered by camouflage nets. Even more important, the heat signature of an object is one of the best ways to distinguish real objects from dummies. But, surprisingly, in the literature of the crisis no mention is made of the use of infrared film by the U-2s' cameras.

The total Soviet build-up involved several hundred vehicles and a massive sealift to move such a large number of missile trailers, radar vans, fueling trucks, erectors, launchers, personnel carriers, troops and technicians.[4] Roger Hilsman pointed out that, during the month of August alone, nearly 37 Soviet cargo ships arrived in Cuban ports and from July until mid-October, more than 100 shiploads of arms left the U.S.S.R. bound for Cuba.[5] But the Kennedy administration, officially and publicly, took the position that, though it was aware of the military build-up in Cuba, it was strictly defensive.[6]

In shipping the missiles to Cuba, the Kennedy administration accused the U.S.S.R. of stealth and deception. This accusation of deceit runs throughout all official U.S. statements.[7] The evidence indicates, however, that Soviet stealth and deception were faked. Actually, the available record suggests that the Russians went through great pains to let the Americans discover the missiles. The record also indicates that the Soviets sped up their pace of work and camouflaged the missiles only *after* they were pretty sure the Americans had discovered them.

Furthermore, there is no accepted rule of international law that requires nations to publicize their military actions. It is also important to note that neither the U.S.S.R. nor the U.S. were part of a treaty which banned trade in armaments.[8]

None So Blind...

By August, 1962, the word was out in Washington that the Soviets were building missile launchers for weapons already in Cuba. Between August 31 and October 12, 1962, Senator Kenneth Keating, a respected New York Republican, made ten Senate speeches and fourteen public statements about the developments in Cuba. He was merely saying publicly what some rebel members of the American intelligence community, most likely his source of information, were muttering as loudly as they could all around Washington. But, instead of paying attention to the growing concern, White House press secretary Pierre Salinger criticized the television networks for giving Keating and others the air time to express their concerns.

The president's aides systematically ignored the mountains of circumstantial evidence and the declarations of the witnesses. The Kennedy administration, which had placed itself in trouble domestically because of its "do nothing" policy toward Castro's Cuba, tried instead to fence detractors by maintaining that the Soviet weapons build-up in Cuba was defensive in nature and posed no threat to the U.S.[9]

On August, 1962, one of the two U-2s flying regularly over Cuba returned with photographs of Russian SA-2 antiaircraft missiles being unloaded at Cuban docks. In the five weeks between August 24 and October 7, the overflight program was stepped up and seven U-2s were sent to fly over the Island. Each U-2 came back with fresh pictures of more SA-2s. But, to Khrushchev's dismay, who took pains to prolong the unloading operation as much as possible in order to make it easy to detect by the U.S. intelligence, President Kennedy insisted that there was no evidence that the Russians were moving in offensive missiles that could threaten the United States. President Kennedy gave these assurances despite the fact that John McCone had repeatedly mentioned his suspicion that the Soviets were deploying ballistic missiles in Cuba and the SA-2 batteries were just the first step of the operation.[10] In retrospect, it is clear that both the Americans and the Russians had engaged in a subtle cat-and-mouse game; the Russians trying, by every available means, to call the Americans' attention to the missiles, and the Americans doing whatever they could to avoid seeing them.

Despite the fact that all evidence pointed to the province of Pinar del Río in the western part of Cuba as the most likely location for missile sites, a very strange and surreal thing happened: after September 5, no U-2 flights were directed over that part of the Island. It was not until October 14, that a U-2 plane —some claim it was by pure chance[11]— took the now famous photographs of the strategic missile sites under construction.

Though the order to fly the U-2 over Cuba was given on September 4, the flight was delayed until September 14 for unknown reasons.[11] The fact that the Russian missile sites were mainly in the western part of Cuba was so widespread that a *Time* magazine article on September 21, 1962, showed a map of the Island clustered with Soviet ground-to-air missiles, mainly in the western part of Cuba, west and south of Havana. [12]

But, despite all the carefully planned Soviet "indiscretions" —the Mariel evacuations, the fictitious secretiveness, the lack of camouflage, the very long trailers carrying large missiles carelessly covered with tarpaulins, the interminable truck convoys heading west— no U-2 flights were detected by Russian radar over the western part of the Island since the beginning of September. As a matter of fact, the Soviet officers manning the SAM sites had reported a change in the reconnaissance-flight patters, which had unexplainably changed from overflights to peripheral flights.[13] Furthermore, nothing in the normal life of the White House indicated that Kennedy knew about the missiles. At this time Khrushchev must have suspected that something had gone wrong with his plan.

What had really happened was that Khrushchev's plan proved to have big flaws. The Soviet Premier had no real knowledge of the inner workings of American politics. The crisis had caught Kennedy in the midst of a political campaign, and apparently he was more concerned about the Republicans than about the missiles in Cuba. Khrushchev failed to take into account that America was not the Soviet Union and President Kennedy was not necessarily going to act according to his expectations.

McCone's "Hunch" and the "Photographic Gap"

CIA Director John McCone returned from his European honeymoon on September 26 and, on October 4, he attended an urgent meeting of the United States Intelligence Board. During the meeting the members took a careful look at the photographic "mosaic" of the whole Island, but they found no photographic evidence of ICBMs. But then McCone noticed that there were no pictures of the western sector of Cuba taken since September 5. He then ordered that overflights be stepped up and concentrate on that section of Cuba.[14]

The fact that the western part of the Island had not been covered was really strange, because all the information the CIA had received pointed to this area of Cuba as the place where the missiles most likely would be located. One explanation, advanced by the Kennedy administration, was that they feared that the SAM batteries may shoot down a U-2, as it had happened in the Soviet Union and, quite recently, in China. But the western part of Cuba is particularly narrow. Given the wide reach of the U-2 cameras it was not necessary to fly directly over the bases to cover the area. Another explanation, however, may be that President Kennedy was not too interested in discovering the missiles.

A special flight plan was prepared at the meeting to cover the San Cristóbal-Guanajay area, and it was approved by the President on October 10. But the flight was delayed until October 14, allegedly because of poor weather conditions caused by the presence of hurricane Ella.

In his testimony before the Senate Preparedness Subcommittee on March 12, 1963, McCone said he reported his "hunch" about the possibility of strategic missiles in Cuba on August 10. His conclusion was actually based on his suspicion that the SAMs had been deployed to protect the installation of strategic missiles. But his report, he said, remained within the CIA.

"I couldn't understand," he explained to the Senate Subcommittee, "why these surface-to-air missile sites were there, so useless to protect the island against observation from aerial reconnaissance." McCone admitted, however, that his opinion had been based on "intuition" rather than on "hard intelligence." And, though as Director of Central Intelligence he could have ordered that his view be made official and be reported to the President, he never did so.[15]

Talking to journalists at a news conference on February, 1963, McNamara mentioned the socalled "photographic gap" that occurred between September 5 and October 14. According to McNamara, the U-2 missions during that period "didn't relate" to the areas where the Russian missiles were eventually found. That was short of a tacit admission that the CIA had failed to photograph the western half of the Island —the area where all evidence indicated that the missiles were most likely to be— during the six weeks preceding the flight which discovered the long-range missiles.[16]

Those who needed to know had been assured that any missile emplacements would have been discovered by the U-2 reconnaissance flights over Cuba. But they were not told that these flights were bypassing the important areas allegedly to avoid antiaircraft batteries or SAMs already installed by the Soviets. But, early in October, the U-2 flights had been inexplicably canceled after being ordered to fly over the suspect areas in Cuba.

After the crisis, the White House justified this decision by saying that Hurricane Ella had prevented air surveillance, but we know that Ella did not form until October 16. Even before the crisis was over, suspicions arised that the U-2 flights over Cuba had not been scheduled in an optimal manner.[17] Later, in early 1963, the possibility of a "photographic gap" in U-2 coverage of Cuba was examined in detail by the Stennis Committee, but the charges were rejected as "unfounded." However, the Stennis Report curiously ignored the critical questions of the U-2 paths over the Island between September 5 and October 24, merely observing that these flights "completed the coverage of those areas of Cuba which had been spotlighted as required early attention."[18] Yet, during cross examination by Congressmen Minshall and Ford in early February, 1963, Defense Secretary McNamara admitted to the "photographic gap" of some 38 days in U-2 coverage of western Cuba.[19]

Though author Henry Pachter makes no reference to the "photographic gap," he somewhat admits its existence in references to vague hints by administration sources that fearing Soviet SAM emplacements in Cuba, reconnaissance flights during September had been limited to "side ways approaches."[20] Hilsman's 1964 article on the missile crisis gives no further explanation or consequences of the "photographic gap."[21] Even more significantly, in his now classic study of the alleged failures in national intelligence estimates, author Klaus Knorr didn't mention the "photographic gap" nor even the role played by the U-2 in the intelligence gathering during the crisis.[22] Some years later Sorensen remarked that U-2 incidents elsewhere in the world led to a "high-level reexamination of that airplane's use" over Cuba and "some delay in flights," but gave no additional information.[23] Later in 1965, Roberta Wohlstetter suggested that the Kennedy administration knew that the Soviets had operational SAM sites in western Cuba, so they may have been extremely cautious in scheduling U-2 flights over the Island for fear of losing a plane.[24]

Additional disclosures concerning a change in policy governing U-2 flights were made by Elie Abel[25] and Roger Hilsman.[26] Not even Graham T. Allison gave a clear explanation for the failure of U.S. intelligence, due to a "photographic gap," to discover the missiles earlier.

Therefore, the fact remains that on September 10 a high level decision was made and express orders were given, prohibiting direct overflights of western Cuba —the part of the Island where all evidence pointed to the presence of strategic missile sites. This unexplainable decision led to the now famous "photographic gap."

Many years later, NPIC photointerpreter Dino Brugioni offered a much more credible explanation: It was not hurricane Ella that kept the U-2 from flying over the western part of Cuba, "but rather the dereliction, bumbling, and intransigence of [Secretary of State Dean] Rusk and [Assistant to the President for National Security Affairs McGeorge] Bundy."[27] "Because of Bundy and Rusk's stalling actions, there had been no U-2 photos of Cuba for over two weeks.[28]

Confusion in Moscow

Evident signs of confusion in Moscow in the days following the blockade on Cuba further indicate that Khrushchev was not well prepared to cope with this contingency.[29] His behavior after Kennedy's speech evidenced that he was not prepared for, or even expected that kind of American response. Yet, it is naïve to think that the Soviet leader supposed that Kennedy was going to accept his move without reacting vigorously.

Therefore, if he was not expecting a countermove against the Soviet Union, nor a do-nothing response, what could have been his expectations about the probable American answer vis-à-vis the emplacement of Soviet strategic missiles in Cuba? If one discards the Khrushchev-stupid-fool hypothesis,[30] which is nonsense, the only answer is that the Soviet Premier expected a U.S. attack on the missile sites followed by a complete invasion of Cuba —the most logical move the Americans could have made, given the circumstances.

By Thursday evening, October 27, work continued on the sites and the Soviets had not yet admitted the presence of strategic missiles in Cuba at all. However, despite the fact that the Soviet technicians continued working on the sites, the essence of the overall pattern of Soviet behavior indicated that their major goal now was a peaceful settlement of the crisis. Evidence of this pattern of behavior was Khrushchev's letter to Bertrand Russell suggesting a summit meeting; his conciliatory message to U-Thant; and his conversations with the American singer Jerome Hines and with William Knox of Westinghouse.

Other important signs were the indication that the Soviet ships approaching the blockade's limits were slowing down or changing course, and the fact that the Soviet ambassadors in London and Bonn were saying to the British and West German governments that the U.S.S.R. wanted a peaceful resolution to the problem.[31]

Contrary to American suspicions that the Cuban move was related to Berlin, Soviet diplomats, at last beginning to act according to what seemed to be a rational pattern, appeared to be engaged in a studied effort to disassociate Berlin From Cuba.[32] Speaking at Humboldt University in East Berlin, Gromyko did not even mention Cuba. By Friday, Zorin was even assuring other U.N. diplomats that the U.S.S.R. did not take retaliatory action in Berlin to avoid falling into the American "trap."[33]

Arthur Schlesinger mentioned that Averell Harriman had called him and said that the Russian Premier was desperately signaling a desire to cooperate toward a peaceful solution. Khrushchev's behavior, said Harriman, was not the behavior of a man who wanted war, but the actions of a man begging for help to get off the hook.[34]

At 10:00 in the morning of Tuesday the 23rd of October, CIA Director John McCone reported a strange thing to the Ex Comm: no signs of a general alert of the Soviet forces in Cuba or around the globe had been reported.[35] He also said that the Russians were beginning to camouflage the missile sites. Nobody was able to provide an answer explaining why they had waited so long to do so.[36]

As late as Friday, October 26, American intelligence reported from Cuba, from Moscow, and from the United Nations, that the Russians were not ready for war.[37] Surprisingly, even at that late date the Soviets had made no attempt to mobilize their civil defense nor to prepare the population for the eventual use of fallout shelters. This is quite significant, because the Soviets had made a considerable effort to instruct their own civilian population in civil defense and had invested considerably in nuclear shelters.

In an authoritative study of Soviet civil defense, Leon Goure depicts continuous Soviet interest, or at least an absence of neglect, in air defense and atomic defense measures. Goure's analysis is based on a thorough, careful and complete research, based chiefly on Soviet internal publications. The study shows that the Soviets had made a serious effort in the indoctrination of the population in elementary air defense and atomic defense measures, and a shelter program built on the economic margin of house construction and using such resources as subways. In 1962, Goure shows, the Soviets had moved further than the Americans toward providing nuclear shelters for the urban population.[38]

Looking back at the statements made during the crisis, it is apparent that Khrushchev saw events slipping out of his control and acquiring a dynamic of their own, bound on a collision course with the United States. It was almost in desperation that he appealed to President Kennedy to recognize the imminence of a catastrophe and the fact that he, Khrushchev, did not want this disaster, but was unable to prevent it.[39] Moreover, the fact that the Soviets did not consider the use of nuclear shelters during the crisis is a clear indication that Khrushchev never considered a military response to whatever action the U.S. might have taken — which, according to his view, could only have been an invasion of Cuba.

Now, faced with an unexpected dangerous situation, Khrushchev, in a series of actions similar to what Konrad Lorentz calls "appeasement rituals," was showing Kennedy his open hand. But Kennedy either failed to see Khrushchev's signals, or ignored or misread them, and continued to focus his attention on the Soviet Union instead of Cuba where, according to Khrushchev's logic, the real source of the problem resided.

Kennedy's behavior was so surprising that Khrushchev was caught completely off balance and panicked before the possibility of a nuclear confrontation. His sixth sense, which had always told him just how far he could safely go, was now telling him that his Cuban gambit must end.[40] When Khrushchev realized that he had deceived himself about Kennedy's reactions, he retreated and called it a day. Talking to Kennedy, "Chip" Bohlen, about to leave for Paris as U.S. Ambassador, recalled a Lenin adage that Khrushchev was found of quoting: If a man sticks out a bayonet and strikes mush, he keeps pushing. But when he hits cold steel, he pulls back.[41]

Fortunately for the world, Nikita S. Khrushchev was not a madman. Furthermore, he was enough of a political realist to recognize when a gamble had been lost and knew how to employ all of his demagogic arts in patching up the failure.[42] Sorensen recalled how to the American leaders Khrushchev appeared to have been caught off guard, to be maneuvering, to be seeking a consensus among the Kremlin rulers.[43]

Khrushchev's "Miscalculations"

Hardly any of the analysts who have studied the Cuban missile crisis have failed to mention Khrushchev's "miscalculations." According to these authors, the Soviet Premier could hardly have thought of a better way to insure a strong reaction from President Kennedy. By deploying nuclear missiles in Cuba, they reason, Khrushchev placed Kennedy in a position so difficult that, however hard the President might have tried, he could not have found a way to escape irreparable damage either to his personal political interests or to vital American interests. It seems inconceivable that Khrushchev could have ignored that his move would inflict a personal and political humiliation upon Kennedy. If one assumes that these possible consequences escaped Khrushchev's imagination when he planned the operation, it certainly showed poor judgement and his action surely would have been among the most irresponsible.

Let's assume for a moment, however, that the Soviet leader was at least as clever as his American counterpart and that the outcome of his actions did not escape from his attention when he was planning his Cuban move. Once one accepts this assumption, it becomes evident that, from his point of view, the Americans' initial reaction was just what Khrushchev had expected. In fact, Khrushchev's only miscalculation —a logical one given the strong anti-Castro sentiments in both the American people and government— was that he thought Kennedy's response would be directed against the perceived source of danger, Cuba, instead of against the Soviet Union.

As a matter of fact, it was not until his 22nd of October address to the nation that President Kennedy surprisingly informed the American public that his actions would be directed not against Cuba, but against the Soviet Union. The analysis of his previous statements shows that all of them had been ambiguous, and could have been easily interpreted as being directed against Cuba.

Not too long after the crisis ended, President Kennedy observed in a television interview that both the Americans and Khrushchev had made serious miscalculations in the Cuban affair. "I don't think we expected that he would put the missiles in Cuba," the president said, "because it would have seemed such an imprudent action for him to take... he obviously thought he could do it in secret and that the United States would accept it."[44] President Kennedy was right, but for the wrong reasons.

As I mentioned above, the explanation of the events we call the Cuban missile crisis offered in most books, particularly the ones written by American scholars, require a necessary condition to be accepted by the gullible readers: Nikita S. Khruschev was either a kook, or a fool, or both. That condition has materialized in the theory of Khruschev's "miscalculations."

This theory is clearly expressed by Richard Ned Lebow and Janice Gross Stein in their book *We All Lost the Cold War,* so I am quoting them in detail. According to these authors,

> Foreign-policy analysts expect statesmen to have consistent preferences to choose policies most likely to advance their preferences. Khrushchev violated both expectations. He did not choose the appropriate means given his ends, nor did he recognize the contradictions among his objectives. The missile deployment threatened some of his most important foreign-policy goals. It was a singularly inappropriate means of advancing his proclaimed objectives. *The secret deployment of missiles raised rather than lowered the risks of an American invasion of Cuba.* It was illusory for Khrushchev to believe that a missile deployment would compel the United States to move toward détente.[45]

According to the same authors, "Khrushchev's decision reflects this kind of cognitive blindness. Not only was his choice of missile deployment inconsistent with his objectives, but his objectives were contradictory."[46] In their opinion, "He miscalculated badly."[47]

Nobody can blame the politicians who created the miscalculation theory, or the scholars who have nurtured it, for their cognitive blindness, because this theory it is the only one they can use to explain Khrushchev's apparently irrational or foolish behavior —particularly departing from the wrong premise that he sent the missiles to Cuba to protect his friend Fidel Castro and deter an American invasion of the Island. On the other hand, I think that the theory has had so many adherents because it also has served to polish the Americans' egos: the stupid Nikita Khrushchev and the bunch of fools at the Soviet Presidium miscalculated, and were caught in the act by the superior intellects of the Kennedy brothers, McNamara, et al. A Hollywood tale with a happy ending. But let's slightly deflate these people's oversized egos. Amazingly, it was Khrushchev himself who, a priori, refuted in the strongest terms the "miscalculation" theory.

During the stormy meeting the Soviet leader and president Kennedy had in Vienna in June of 1961, Kennedy brought up the issue of the perils of nuclear weapons. He also mentioned the dangers incurred by superpowers involved in pushing social change around the world. Such involvements, Kennedy thought, might lead to miscalculations with catastrophic consequences.[48]

Khrushchev's reaction was immediate: "Miscalculation!," he exploded in anger —or faked anger, in which he was an expert— "All I ever hear from your people and your news correspondents and your friends is that damned word." ... "We don't make mistakes. We will not make war by mistake." ... "You ought to take that word and bury it in cold storage and never use it again."[49]

The problem with the "miscalculation" theory is that its pre-requisite: Khrushchev was either mad, or stupid, or both, is simply not true. His plan was carefully calculated. He would have never been foolish enough to place nuclear weapons so close to Castro's trigger-happy hands. Khrushchev would never have imagined that the Americans were going to ignore for such a long time the presence of his "missiles" in Cuba —particularly after his efforts to make them an easy target for discovery.

He would have never been so stupid as to believe that the Americans would not have reacted violently after the discovery. He knew perfectly well what the Americans' reaction would be after the discovery of the "missiles" in Cuba —or he thought he knew. Khrushchev was convinced that, faced with the discovery of what looked like strategic nuclear missiles on Cuban soil, the American reaction would only have been a quick invasion of the Island and the overthrow of Fidel Castro and his regime. It is in this sense, and only in this sense, that we can properly say that Khrushchev miscalculated badly.

But we cannot blame Khrushchev for his mistake. He was not the only one who miscalculated badly. He was joined in his miscalculation by none others than Dean Acheson, Paul Nitze, John McCone, General Maxwell Taylor, General Curtis Le May,[50] and the rest of the Ex Comm "hawks." He was joined in his miscalculation by the anti-Castro Cubans in the U.S. and by most of the American people. All of them expected that, after the discovery of the missiles, president Kennedy would order an immediate invasion of Cuba. But, for reasons still unknown, all of them miscalculated.

Many people have criticized President Kennedy for his behavior during the crisis: some for overreacting, and others for excessive caution —that is, for not taking advantage of the provocation, invading Cuba and eliminating the missile emplacements and Castro in one single operation.[51] It has been extensively documented that after the Bay of Pigs the Kennedys felt a personal animosity toward

Castro. Therefore, when Khrushchev placed the missiles in Cuba they had the perfect excuse to take revenge, and, in fact, most advisers urged them to seize the opportunity to invade Cuba and smash Castro forever. But, surprisingly, Robert Kennedy himself led the fight against the option to invade, and John Kennedy decided against it.[52]

Even more, from the very beginning President Kennedy seemed to strongly oppose the invasion or even the air strike option. Though he raised the question about the possibility of a surgical air strike, he seems to have accepted now at face value the expert's opinion that the air strike was not feasible —forgetting his own dictum after the Bay of Pigs, "Never rely on experts."[53] Why he didn't question the experts' estimate, which later proved to be wrong, is a question apparently nobody has made. One answer could be that Kennedy, like most leaders, agreed with his experts when their advice supported his own preconceived plans. Though Khrushchev's assumptions were essentially correct and most of the American military favored invading Cuba and overthrowing Castro, Kennedy discarded the invasion option and favored a more flexible response.

During the Berlin crisis, Kennedy shared Dean Acheson's view that it had nothing to do with Berlin; it was a test of American resolve. Now, again with Acheson as a key advisor, Kennedy again took the view that the issue was not primarily Cuba, but another test of American determination. He saw the issue not primarily as one of Cuban-American relations, but as a critical episode in the Cold War.[54] To Khrushchev's dismay, Kennedy always considered the crisis a problem with the Soviets, not with the Cubans.

Among the arguments that allegedly added weight in favor of a blockade rather than an air strike was the risk of hurting the feelings of some members of the Organization of American States (OAS). But, at least from a purely military point of view, a surgical air strike might have been easier and entailed fewer complications than a blockade. Moreover, affirmed its proponents, an air strike would not bring an immediate confrontation with Soviet forces.[55]

Of course, among Kennedy's advisors there were some who had decoded Khrushchev's signals correctly, but the President paid no attention to their opinions. When Kennedy asked General Curtis LeMay how the Russians would react in the event of an attack on Cuba, the general replied, to Kennedy's disappointment, that they would do nothing.[56]

LeMay was not an isolated case. Some of the Ex Comm members at least initially held the view that Khrushchev would pretend that an air strike on Cuba was no affair of the Soviet Union.[57] Moreover, early in the same month that the blockade was declared, Vice-President Lyndon B. Johnson had told at a Democratic dinner meeting that stopping a Soviet ship in the event of a blockade of Cuba would be an "act of war," and added, in reference to the possibility of a blockade, that "some advocates [of a blockade] ... ... have more guts than brain and some don't have either." [58]

Even after McNamara impressively presented the case for a blockade on the afternoon of October 19, the military in the Ex Comm, with some civilian support, continued arguing in favor of a strike.[59] Moreover, the supporters of the air strike argued heavily against the blockade. The blockade, they said, would not neutralize the weapons already within Cuba, nor bring enough pressure on Khrushchev to remove them, permitting work on the sites to continue.[60]

Notwithstanding Sorensen's report to the Ex Comm on Friday morning that the President had reached a decision the night before in favor of a blockade, and should not reopen the discussion, several Ex Comm members began to re-argue the inadequacy of the blockade. The illogical presidential decision had apparently taken some of them by surprise. Someone went further and proposed to take out the bases in a clean and swift operation, confronting the world later with a *fait accompli*. If we committed ourselves to a blockade, someone reasoned, it would be hard, if not impossible, to move thereafter to military action.[61]

Finally, at five o'clock on Monday, October 21, just minutes before his television speech to the nation announcing the discovery of the missiles, President Kennedy had an interview with the congressional leaders and informed them what he had decided to do. Senator Russell of Georgia strongly disagreed, arguing that the blockade would be too slow and risky, and that the only solution was an invasion of Cuba. Senator Fulbright, who just a few months before had opposed an invasion of Cuba, now, to Kennedy's surprise, joined Russell in his criticism.[62]

With the benefit of hindsight, it seems evident that Khrushchev never thought that placing the missiles in Cuba might elicit a strong American response against the U.S.S.R. and much less that it would result in a crisis. Again, it is evident that, in this sense, Khrushchev miscalculated.

But, as most scholars of the crisis apparently believe, his miscalculation was not because he foolishly supposed President Kennedy was not going to react. What really surprised Khrushchev was that Kennedy's response was not directed against Cuba, the focal point of the problem, but against the Soviet Union, so far away and only indirectly responsible. Obviously, the Soviet Premier had not anticipated the blockade, and as a result a great confusion developed within the Kremlin. Soviet diplomats across the world began displaying symptoms of improvisation, as if they had known nothing in advance about the missiles and had no instructions about what to say about them. Even the Soviet Ambassador to the U.S. Anatoly Dobrynin showed all the indications of confusion and ignorance.[63]

When Stevenson clashed with Valerian Zorin at the U.N., the Soviet Ambassador to the U.N. accused the U.S. of using "falsified information" provided by the American intelligence agencies. But when Stevenson proceed to show the delegates the U-2 photos, the Russian's face flushed and he looked startled.[64]

The available record strongly suggests that Khrushchev was caught completely off guard by President Kennedy's address of October 22 announcing his decision not to take action against Cuba, but against the Soviet Union instead:

It shall be the policy of this Nation to regard any nuclear missile launched from Cuba against any nation in the Western Hemisphere as an attack by the Soviet Union on the United States, requiring a full retaliatory response upon the Soviet Union.

Khrushchev's behavior indicates that he was astonished over the belligerent American response against the Soviet Union.[65] It is obvious that he didn't expect that Kennedy was going to misinterpret the clear signals he had been sending in relation with Soviet behavior faced with the American discovery of the missiles. A measure of Khrushchev's surprise was expressed when, in his speech at the 6th Congress of the East German Party in Berlin on January 16, 1963, he said that the act of stationing missiles in Cuba "had the effect of a shock on the imperialists."[66] Actually, the only one shocked was Khrushchev himself.

On the other hand, continuing with the strange behavior he began exhibiting during the Bay of Pigs invasion, John F. Kennedy betrayed for a second time both the Cuban and the American people and allowed Fidel Castro to stay in power. Moreover, after the crisis was over, instead of harassing Castro, a sworn enemy of America, he ordered the FBI, the CIA and other government agencies to harass the anti-Castro Cubans in the U.S. It seems, though, that everyone who expected a honest and patriotic behavior from President John F. Kennedy, and that he was going to stand firm by his principles, miscalculated badly —including Nikita Sergeevich Khrushchev.

Chapter 8

The Trigger-Happy Tyrant

> *I felt "an incredible love" for the nuclear missiles.*
> —Fidel Castro. *Le Monde,* November 24, 1997.

In December 1962, the Hearst-owned *San Francisco Chronicle* and *News Call Bulletin* published a *UPI* cable claiming that Ernesto "Che" Guevara had told a reporter in Havana that "to defend [himself] against aggression" Fidel Castro had planned a nuclear attack on key U.S. cities, including New York. Though the *Chronicle* buried the story on page 16, the *News Call Bulletin* ran a dramatic front-page headline in big, bold letters: "How Castro Plotted Atomic Attack on U.S.!" The *Chronicle* added that "Secretary of State Dean Rusk called Guevara's remark about a nuclear attack 'just talk.'"[1]

But Mr. Rusk was dead wrong. Guevara's remarks should not have been dismissed as "just talk." In an interview Che gave a few weeks after the crisis to Sam Russell, a British correspondent for the *Daily Worker,* Guevara said that "If the missiles had remained, we would have used them all and directed them against the very heart of the United States, including New York."[2] Moreover, in an editorial he wrote during the missile crisis for *Verde Olivo,* the Cuban Armed Forces weekly magazine, Che made his point even more clear, exhorting the Soviets to stand by their commitment to Cuba, no matter what the cost:

> What we contend is that we must walk by the path of liberation even when it may cost millions of atomic victims, because in the struggle to death between two systems the only thing that can be considered is the definitive victory of socialism or its retrogression under the nuclear victory of imperialist aggression.[3]

As in many other occasions, Guevara was acting as a mouthpiece for Castro. It is a matter of public record that Fidel was extremely dissatisfied with the pacific solution of the Cuban missile crisis. The fact that nuclear war had been averted, and the Russians had allegedly received from the American government a pledge for the non-invasion of Cuba, was apparently not very important for Castro. For him the kind of political solutions possible within the parameters of peaceful coexistence were not real solutions. They merely postponed what he believed was an inevitable final confrontation with American imperialism ending with the destruction of the United States and the American people. As always, Castro was itching for a gun fight at the O.K. Corral—in this case the definitive fight, a nuclear one.[4]

Fidel's Extraordinary Love for Nuclear Missiles

Guevara's statement about Castro's plans for a nuclear attack on the United States was written just a few weeks after the end of the Cuban missile crisis of 1962. A careful reading of Khrushchev's memoirs, however, shows that the Soviet Premier was fully aware of Castro's dreams of nuclear power and tried to use them to his advantage.[5] As a matter of fact, there are good reasons for believing that, in order to overcome Castro's initial reluctance to accept the deployment of strategic missiles on Cuban soil, Khrushchev enticed him by dangling a nuclear bait. The Soviet Premier would had suspected that Castro's secret plans would include an attempt to grab the Soviet nuclear missiles and use them against the United States. That is why Khrushchev's plans were carefully laid down to avoid this possibility. Later developments proved Khrushchev right.

Late in the night of October 26, Castro visited the Soviet embassy in Havana and stayed through the early hours of the next day writing a letter to Khrushchev. The most important part of the letter is Castro's efforts to convince Khrushchev that an American invasion of Cuba was imminent, and his request that, in case of such invasion, the Soviet Union should launch a preemptive nuclear attack against the United States. Castro's words were,

> I tell you this because I believe that the imperialists' aggressiveness is extremely dangerous and if they actually carry out the brutal act of invading Cuba in violation of international law and morality, that would be the moment to eliminate such danger through an act of clear legitimate defense, however harsh and terrible the solution would be, for there is no other.[6]

In a letter of October 30, a terrorized Khrushchev refers to Castro's request in very precise terms:

> In your cable of October 27 you proposed that we be the first to launch a nuclear strike against the territory of the enemy. You, of course, realize where that should have led. Rather than a simple strike, it would have been the start of a thermonuclear war.
>
> Dear Comrade Fidel Castro, I consider this proposal of yours incorrect, although I understand your motivation.[7]

A few days later, splitting semantic hairs, Castro emphatically denied that he had ever asked Khrushchev to launch a nuclear attack against the U.S., and explained to the Soviet Premier that what Khrushchev believed he said, even if he said it, was not exactly what he said, even though it was exactly what he meant.[8]

> You base yourself on the alarming news that you say reached you from Cuba and, finally, my cable of October 27. I don't know what news you received, I can only respond for the message that I sent you the evening of October 26, which reached you the 27th. ... And I did not suggest to you, comrade Khrushchev, that the USSR should be the aggressor, because that would be more than incorrect. It would be immoral and contemptible on my part. But from the instant the imperialists attack on Cuba ... the imperialists would be by this act become aggressors against Cuba and against the USSR, and we would respond with a strike that would annihilate them. ... I did not suggest, comrade Khrushchev, that in the midst of this crisis the Soviet Union should attack, which is what your letter seems to say; rather, that following an imperialist attack, the USSR should act without vacillation and should never make the mistake of allowing circumstances to develop in which the enemy makes the first nuclear strike against the USSR. And in this sense, comrade Khrushchev, I maintain my point of view, because I understand it to be a true and just evaluation of a specific situation.[9]

But Khrushchev was adamant. In the Soviet Premier's clear and specific own words, "Castro suggested that in order to prevent our nuclear missiles from being destroyed, we should launch a preemptive strike against the United States."[10] During Castro's visit to the Soviet Union in 1963, Khrushchev brought the subject up again. According to Khrushchev,

> I told Castro "You wanted to start a war with the United States. If the war had begun we would somehow have survived, but Cuba no doubt would have ceased to exist. It would have been crushed into powder. Yet you suggested a nuclear strike!"
> "No. I did not suggest that," replied Castro.
> "How can you say that?" I asked Fidel.
> The interpreter added, "Fidel, Fidel, you yourself told me that,"
> "No!" insisted Castro.
> Then we checked the documents. It was fortunate that Fidel did not tell us this orally, but sent us a message. The interpreter read the document and asked, "How shall I translate this? Here is the word 'war,' here is the word 'blow.'"
> Fidel was embarrassed.[11]

But there is more than meets the eye in the above exchange. As the reader can verify by checking above again, the words "war" and "blow" do not appear in the version of the letter published by *Granma* and reproduced in the National Security Archive Documents Reader. The reason for this is because, in their typical careless fashion, the folks at the National Security Archive had the gall to publish as a true original document an English version —most likely a toned-down forgery— of the original Spanish-written letter Castro sent to Khrushchev.[12]

Despite Castro's denials, his behavior after the crisis seems to confirm Khrushchev's allegation. According to Juan Vivés, a former Cuban intelligence officer who defected to the West, for several years after the missile crisis Castro unsuccessfully tried to build his own Cuban-made missile capable of carrying nuclear weapons. For the ultra secret project he recruited military engineers and professors from Cuban universities. The missile, a sort of primitive V-1 bomb similar to the one developed by the Nazis, would use a MiG-21 jet motor. The testing of the prototypes of the Cuban missile, called *libertadoras* (liberators), was a series of failures, but in 1977 the project was still active. According to Vivés, Castro said that the missiles were not intended as offensive weapons, but that they would be used against the U.S. in case of an American attack against Cuba. Cuban nuclear capability at the time seemed remote, so Castro used to talk about the possibility of using the missiles for bacteriological warfare.[13]

After his missile development projects ended in failure, Castro's nuclear dream was postponed, but not forgotten. In 1989 General Rafael del Pino Díaz, the highest ranking Cuban defector, said that at the time of the Grenada operation in 1983, Castro ordered Cuban MiG 23 pilots to program their computers to attack targets in Florida. Among the selected targets was the Turkey Point nuclear plant, which Castro said had the potential of producing a nuclear disaster larger than Chernobyl.[14] According to Gen. del Pino, Castro's words were: "I don't have nuclear bombs, but I can produce a nuclear explosion."[15]

In another interview, Gen. del Pino claimed that, in 1968, when a group of Cubans were authorized to recover a MiG-17 taken to the U.S. by a defector, Cuban agents secretly made detailed photographs of Homestead Air Force Base in Florida. The base, Gen. del Pino said, had been targeted for an air attack by Cuban planes. The intention of the attack, Castro told the Cuban Air Force officers, was to provoke the United States into an even stronger action "so the Soviet Union would become involved."[16]

Castro's bellicose position during the crisis was revealed later by some of his closest associates. A year after the missile crisis, Che Guevara wrote: "There can be no bargaining, no half measures, no partial guarantees of a country's stability. The victory must be total."[17] A month later, Raúl Castro, head of Cuba's armed forces, reiterated his brother's militant opposition to peaceful coexistence, saying, "We must never establish peaceful coexistence with our enemies."[18]

THE NUCLEAR DECEPTION

According to documents made public in Cuba in August, 1997, in a speech to the Central Committee of Castro's "Communist" Party in 1968, six years after the missile crisis, Castro said he felt "an incredible love" for the nuclear missiles that brought on the crisis, and wanted to keep them even after the Soviets agreed to remove them. Castro admitted to laughing with his advisers even as the possibility of nuclear war loomed, as documents published by the French daily *Le Monde* show.[19]

Le Monde reported that Castro's account of the crisis was provided to the newspaper by Vincent Touze, a French academic and expert on the missile crisis. A few days after the crisis began, at the point when allegedly it had brought the two superpowers closer to a nuclear confrontation than at any other time during the Cold War, Soviet leader Nikita Khrushchev agreed to withdraw the missiles. Castro, who had little control over the situation, said he dearly wanted to keep the missiles, which he saw as a super weapon for any battle against the United States. "We defended these missiles with affection, with an incredible love. We were fighting for the first time almost on equal terms with an enemy that had threatened and provoked us unceasingly," Castro said in his report to the Central Committee of his "Communist" Party.[20]

According to Cuban documents, when Soviet advisers came to Cuba in the summer of 1962 to discuss the installation of the missiles, Castro asked the Kremlin to deploy 1,000 missiles, and became upset when told that only about 40 would be installed. As the tension mounted and it appeared the Soviets would capitulate, Castro argued that a nuclear strike should be launched if the United States were to attack Cuba.

"We didn't envisage lightly the idea we could disappear ... It was a very interesting fact because we were in the antechamber of the holocaust and we were telling jokes," the documents quoted Castro as saying. "Evidently, we knew that we were going to be made to play the role of death, but we were determined to play it," Castro told the Central Committee. Castro said Cuba had placed great faith in the Soviets but soon lost confidence in its ally. He said the Kremlin had botched the situation, which he called a "disaster."

Castro also said he had wanted to inform the United States about the missiles before reconnaissance planes spotted them, but was overruled by Khrushchev. He also professed to be shocked by the fact that they were not camouflaged, and suggested the Soviets had overlooked doing so on purpose. However, Castro admitted his government had been naive, confessing that nobody in the Cuban leadership even knew what nuclear missiles looked like[21] although he accepted the weapons "without hesitation."[22]

In 1975, Castro told Senator George S. McGovern that, during the crisis, he would have taken a harder line than Khrushchev[23] —a fact, carefully kept secret by the Castro-loving American Left, that shows that "nuke 'em" LeMay was not the only kook at large at the time. But, apparently not happy with the Soviet Premier's non-committed answer to his plight, Castro took some specific steps during the crisis to "help" Khrushchev push the button.

Castro's Attempt to Destroy New York

On October 3, 1962, a few days before the onset of the crisis, Castro sent one of his trusted men to New York on a key mission. The man chosen for the job was Roberto Santiesteban Casanova, who had just been appointed to a minor post at the Cuban mission to the United Nations. His diplomatic passport identified him as an "attaché" to the Cuban mission. Santiesteban's professional field, however, was not diplomacy. Quite the contrary, he was an expert in terrorist techniques, having just graduated from a highly secret school of terrorism and subversion, not far from Havana.

As soon as Santiesteban arrived in New York, he contacted the rest of his team, including José Gómez Abad and his wife Elsa, both attachés at the Cuban mission, and José García Orellana, a Cuban immigrant who ran a costume jewelry shop in Manhattan. FBI estimates of how many others were involved in the plot range from twenty-five to fifty people. The secret mission of the terrorist team was to accomplish Castro's orders to blow up a big portion of Manhattan, including the Statue of Liberty, Macy's department store, several subway stations, the 42nd street bus terminal and Grand Central station, as well as several refineries along the New Jersey shore, including the Humble Oil and Refining Company in Linden. To this effect they stored a huge cache of explosives at Garcia's shop.[24]

But the terrorist's plan was too ambitious and included too many people, and soon the FBI got word of it and detained the main conspirators. Had their plan worked out the way it had been conceived, it would undoubtedly have ignited American public opinion and prompted retaliation against Cuba. Had it occurred during the tense days of the crisis, it may have been taken for a Russian preemptive attack on the United States and may have triggered a spasm-like retaliatory strike upon the Soviet Union, with unpredictable consequences. Fortunately, the plan failed. But Fidel Castro is a very resourceful man. After his failed attempt to create a provocation which may have started a nuclear confrontation between the superpowers, Castro pulled another ace from his sleeve.

The Russians See Nothing, Do Nothing

On July 15, 1962, in a high-level meeting at the Sierra del Rosario Mountains in the western province of Pinar del Río, Soviet officers announced to a group of Cuban officers that operation "Corsair" was entering its final phase. The Cubans were concerned about the role of the American intelligence surveillance, but the Russians dismissed their concern and gave the matter no importance.

The Cuban intelligence services were also aware that the CIA was interrogating Cuban refugees at the Opa Locka military base in Florida. The large number of refugees arriving in Miami were providing the CIA with a great deal of information. Castro proposed to stop the emigration flood by eliminating all available means of escape from the island, but the Soviets proposed to leave things unchanged. That way, reasoned the Russians, the CIA would obtain a lot of contradictory information and soon stop relying on the credibility of the refugees. Many of the departing refugees had seen missiles, but, in most cases, these were just antiaircraft SAMs. To the Cubans' dismay, the Soviets even suggested that, instead of trying to hide evidence of the missiles, it was better to let it be obvious. For the first time the Cuban personnel working at the antiaircraft missile sites were granted leaves.

In addition, the Soviets began leaking information about the presence of the missiles in Cuba to anti-Castro organizations and their press in the U.S., particularly in Miami.[25] The person who reported this information concluded that, "ironically, the KGB leaked accurate information about the deployment so as to mask it. By all indications, this strategy was highly effective."[26] Actually, they leaked information not to mask it, but to call even more the Americans' attention about the missiles. To their utmost surprise, however, their strategy was highly ineffective.

The Cubans knew about the high quality of American air surveillance technology. On several occasions, Castro asked the Soviets to give him SAMs, and let his people operate them, but the Russians were reluctant. Although most of the Cubans assigned to the missile bases were engineering students from Havana University, the Soviets only allowed them to operate the radar equipment.

By the beginning of August, the Russians complained to the Cuban government about the lack of discipline and seditious demonstrations of the university students at the missile bases. The Cubans were frustrated and angry by the Russians' inaction in the face of overflying American planes. Fidel himself had to make an inspection visit to the bases in order to calm down the Cubans there. Apparently Fidel convinced everybody, with one important exception: Che Guevara. Major Guevara said that he would only change his opinion if somebody convinced him that the American spy planes flying over Cuba were not jeopardizing the operation. But he finally opted to follow Fidel's orders.[27]

Contrary to the opinion of most American analysts, almost all SAM antiaircraft sites in western Cuba had reached operational status by the beginning of August, 1962. From that early date the Soviets could have fired on the American spy planes if they had wanted to. But it was evident that they did not.

On the morning of October 14, 1962, a U-2 entered Cuban air space and flew over the province of Pinar del Río. The Cubans watched the plane on the radar screens, appalled as the Russians did nothing. Later, Castro complained bitterly about the Russian inaction. Why were the Soviets allowing the American planes to discover the missiles? The Russians had warned him of an imminent U.S. invasion, but now were letting the Americans know about the missiles that were waiting for them. The ever suspicious Fidel smelled a rat.

On October 22, just after President Kennedy's address to the nation, Castro ordered a maximum alert of the Cuban armed forces. While Fidel was mobilizing all military forces, his brother Raúl, chief of the armed forces, warned that an invasion of Cuba would unleash World War III. By October 26, Fidel had lost his patience with the bewildering Russian behavior and unilaterally announced that the Cuban antiaircraft guns would start shooting at American planes, even if the Russian-operated SAMs didn't.

At that crucial hour it was convenient for Khrushchev to have the U.S. believe that the missiles were under Fidel's control. If Americans believed so, they might very well launch a preemptive attack against the sites and follow with an invasion of the Island, confident that there would be no Soviet reprisals.

Following Castro's orders, and disregarding Soviet advice, in the morning of October 27, antiaircraft batteries manned by the Cuban army began firing at American low-flying reconnaissance planes, damaging at least one. As Castro himself told Tad Szulc, "I am absolutely certain that if the low-level flights had been resumed we would have shot down one, two, or three of these planes... With so many batteries firing, we would have shot down some planes. I don't know whether this would have started nuclear war."[28]

But, although Cuban crews were operating anti-aircraft guns, the powerful surface-to-air missiles (SAMs) were under the Soviets' tight control, and the Cubans had no access to the bases and did not know how to operate them. Therefore, though the short-range antiaircraft guns were firing at everything flying over them, the U-2s, flying at an altitude far beyond their fire range, were safe from Castro's antiaircraft batteries.

Then, in the morning of October 27, at the peak of the crisis, a bizarre incident occurred. An American U-2, piloted by Major Rudolph Anderson, Jr., was detected over the eastern part of Cuba and a SAM site at Los Angeles, near Banes, in the Oriente province, fired one or several antiaircraft missiles and shot it down.

Who Pushed the Button?

Several conflicting interpretations have been offered to explain the strange incident of the downing of the U-2. It has been suggested that it may have been an attempt on the part of the Soviet hard-liners to sabotage efforts at a negotiated settlement of the crisis.[29] It has also been suggested that some Russian officer in charge of the antiaircraft battery got nervous and fired the missile without it having been ordered by his superiors. Some American officials have also speculated that the U-2 was shot down by a Soviet SAM fired by an out of control Russian crew.[30] There was even a disinformation attempt, most likely created by the KGB, in which reports from Warsaw mentioned that the battery that shot down the plane had been operated by Chinese technicians.[31]

In any event, the incident took the Russian Premier by surprise, because the officers commanding the SAM batteries had strict orders not to shoot at the U-2s without express authorization from Moscow. Author Ronald Pope noted that in his message of October 28 to President Kennedy, Khrushchev appeared to be making an indirect effort to disclaim responsibility for the shooting down of the U-2: "...through my officers in Cuba I have reports that American planes are conducting

THE NUCLEAR DECEPTION

flights over Cuba."[32] Later, in his spurious memoirs, Khrushchev gave his own version of the event. According to the Soviet Premier, "Castro gave an order to open fire, and the Cubans shot down an American U-2 reconnaissance plane."[33] The evidence indicates, however, that the SAMs were almost certainly under Soviet control. And even if they were not, and the Cubans had managed to momentarily control them, they would not have had time to master the operation of such complex equipment.

Castro, in contrast, has given several different versions of the incident. In 1966 he told Lee Lockwood that the ground-to-air missiles were not in Cuban hands at the time of the missile crisis. In 1975 he repeated the same story to Mankiewicz and Jones, but added some puzzling remarks:

> Q: Who gave the order to fire on that plane? The Soviets or Cuba?
> A [Castro]: The order to shoot at aircraft was given by us. We had control over the antiaircraft guns, and we had one criterion: not to permit aircraft to fly over national territory, because if the planes were allowed to fly it would mean exposing ourselves to surprise attack. On the second day a U-2 flew over, and then was shot down by ground-to-air missiles. Of course, at that time there was no Cuban personnel that could operate these ground-to-air missiles. They were Soviet specialists. But the order to the antiaircraft to open fire was given by the Cuban side.[34]

In his typical cryptic style, Fidel posed a riddle. He gave the order[35] to shoot down the U-2, but the officer manning the SAM battery that shot it down could not have followed his order because he was not under Castro's command. Then, the officer commanding the SAM battery, who was not under Fidel's command, followed Castro's order and fired the missile(s). If the reader has trouble following Castro's logic it is not by chance, but because his explanation has been carefully designed to confuse or, rather, to tell the truth *without specifically telling the truth*.

In a cable Nikita Khrushchev sent to Castro on October 28, in very clear terms he blamed Castro for the incident.[36] In his memoirs, published in 1970, Khrushchev affirms again in very clear terms that it was not the Russians, but the Cubans, who shot down Major Anderson's U-2 plane.[37]

However, a few years later, Khrushchev changed his story and claimed that the plane had been shot down by a Soviet crew —but following Castro's orders: "At one point, Castro ordered our antiaircraft officer to shoot down a U-2 reconnaissance plane." Adding, "We ordered [Gen. Issa A.] Pliyev to obey only orders from Moscow."[38] Apparently Khruschev and Castro joined their efforts to confuse everybody.

Secretary General U-Thant wrote in his memoirs —published in 1978— that, shortly after the event, Fidel told him that the Cubans had shot down Major Anderson.[39] Later, in 1984, Castro revealed to Tad Szulc that the U-2 had been shot down by Soviet surface-to-air missiles, and that the Russians had not coordinated this action with the Cubans. "It is still a mystery how it happened," Castro told Szulc. "We had no jurisdiction and control over Soviet anti-aircraft missile batteries. We couldn't have fired against the U-2. But a Russian there, the battery commander, fired. We didn't want to ask too much about this problem."[40] Some years later, in 1989, Aleksandr Alekseev, former Soviet ambassador to Cuba and a senior KGB officer turned by Castro, said that the U-2 was shot down by a "trigger-happy Soviet air defense commander."[41]

Alekseev's claim, however, is hard to believe. The Soviet military, and especially the Soviet air defense, has rigid standards and operating procedures. Its military doctrine and practice reflects a do-it-by-the-book attitude. No Soviet officer would give such an order unless he was out of his mind or forced to do it. Moreover, in a speech on May 1, 1964, Castro publicly admitted that the Cubans, not the Soviets, had been responsible for shooting down U-2.[42] Therefore, other explanations seem to better fit the picture.

Franqui's Bizarre Story

Carlos Franqui, a Cuban writer who has been in exile for many years, has offered the explanation that it was Fidel himself who, during a visit to a Soviet SAM base, pushed the button that fired the missile. Franqui was the editor of *Revolución*, the 26th of July Movement's official newspaper, and very close to Castro at the time.

Franqui wrote some time ago that Castro himself told him that he had personally pushed the button which launched the missile that shot down the U-2. According to Franqui, Fidel was itching for a nuclear confrontation between the U.S.S.R. and the United States and had been growing restless as the crisis evolved towards a possible agreement between the two superpowers. At some time, wrote Franqui, Fidel "went on to say that if he were in Moscow, he would send the government to the subway, which was supposed to be safe during a nuclear attack."

Then, Franqui told his bizarre version of the shoot down of Major Anderson's U-2. According to Franqui,

> One day, with a look of astuteness on his face I remembered from the guerrilla days, he said, "Now I'm going to find out if they'll invade or not, if this is for real or not." He said nothing more and drove his jeep to Pinar del Río. ... Fidel went to one of the Russian rocket bases, where the Soviet generals took him on a tour of the installation. Just at that moment an American U-2 appeared on the radar screen, flying low over the island. Fidel asked how the Soviets would protect themselves in war if that had been an attack plane instead of a reconnaissance plane. The Russians showed him the ground-to-air missiles and said that all they would have to do would be to push a button and the plane would be blown out of the sky. "Which button?" "This one." Fidel pushed it and the rocket brought

down the U-2. ... The Russians were flabbergasted, but Fidel simply said, "Well, now we'll see if there's a war or not."[43]

Franqui's story, most likely based on hearsay, is hard to believe. First of all, the U-2 was not shot down in Pinar del Río, west of Havana, but in the Oriente province, more than 500 miles east of Havana. Secondly, the type of surface-to-air missile fired by the Russians was an early-type model which requires more than simply pushing a button. Once fired, it is almost impossible for an SA-2 Guideline missile (the type of SAM in Cuba at that time) to hit a target unaided, because it has to be carefully guided by radar until it reaches its target.

Guidance of the earlier models of the SA-2 missile depends on a van-mounted Fan Song radar which acquires the target and feeds target data to a computer. Steering commands generated by the computer are transmitted to the missile over a UHF link vectoring it into the radar beam to intercept the target. The Soviet military technicians manning the missile battery would have to have guided the missile to ensure the hit or they would have easily aborted the shot. Secondly, even if Castro was in Oriente, it is too much of a coincidence that his visit to a missile site occurred during a U-2 overflight. Though U.S. intelligence officials find Franqui's account "intriguing," they point out that, if Castro did push the button, the SA-2 would not have hit the plane unless the Soviets had already been tracking it on radar and taken other steps to ensure the kill. Therefore, the true story has to be, by force, a little more complicated.

Anyway, Franqui's account of the incident may contain at least one grain of truth. According to Seymour Hersh, there is strong evidence that, on October 26, 1962, a Cuban army unit attacked and overran a Soviet-manned SAM base at Los Angeles, near Banes, in the Oriente province, killing many Soviets and seizing control of the site. Hersh based his article on information partly drawn from an interview with former Department of Defense analyst Daniel Ellsberg, who was himself citing classified material from a post-crisis study of the event. The speculation is based on an intercepted transmission from the Soviet base at Los Angeles indicating heavy fighting and casualties. Adrián Montoro, former director of Radio Havana Cuba, and Juan Antonio Rodríguez Menier, a senior Cuban intelligence officer who defected in 1987 and is now living in the U.S., seem to confirm Ellsberg's information.[44]

Though both Castro and the Russians have categorically denied that the attack took place, Raymond L. Garthoff, Special Assistant for Soviet bloc Political/Military Affairs in the State Department during the Kennedy administration, claims that, in fact, beginning on October 28, the Cuban army *did* surround the Soviet missile bases for three days.[45]

The possibility that the SAM bases had been overrun and occupied by Cuban Army units was widely circulated. An article appeared in the *Los Angeles Times* mentioned that, "It now appears from U.S. intelligence decryption that Soviet troops there transmitted a report from Cuba that a 'fire-fight' had occurred in the vicinity of a Soviet SAM site and that some Soviet soldiers had been killed."[46]

Khrushchev and Castro's Even More Bizarre Stories

Messages exchanged between Castro and Khrushchev on October 28, 1962, indicate that something very fishy happened that day. In his message the Soviet premier accused the Cuban leader of shooting down the American plane. Then, Khrushchev warned Castro that such steps "will be used by aggressors to their advantage, to further their aims." In his answer to Khrushchev, Castro explained that he had mobilized his antiaircraft batteries "to support the position of the Soviet forces." Then, Castro added this cryptic remark: "The Soviet Forces Command can give you further detail on what happened with the plane that was shot down."[47]

In 1987 Cuban defector Gen. Rafael del Pino Díaz said that Soviet officers in Cuba were so outraged at Khrushchev's compliance with the American quarantine that they shot down the U-2 without authorization from Moscow. According to del Pino, "the officers wanted to provoke a confrontation."[48] Even the ubiquitous Alexeev also believed for many years that it was the Cubans who had shot down the plane. It was not until fifteen years later that he finally was enlightened by the "truth."[49] Therefore, after so many years of uncertainty and confusion, now the surprising story can be told: Major Anderson's U-2 was shot down by the Russians —not by a Cuban cane cutter from Oriente using a slingshot, as apparently some people had suspected all these years!

Since the only ones who had the know-how to operate the SAM bases were the Russians, and there are no reasons to suspect any Chinese involvement, it is an obvious truism that it was a Russian officer who gave the order to a crew of Soviet Army technicians under his command to fire the anti-aircraft missiles at the U-2. But the problem has never been to discover the obvious, but to find out under what conditions the Soviet officer gave the order. Was he drunk or crazy? Did he give the order under duress, after Castro's army seized control of the site? Or did he give the orders after Castro himself persuaded him to do so?

Rumors I heard from fellow Army officers in Cuba in 1962, just after the Cuban missile crisis, claimed that Castro's mesmerizing powers had been involved in the downing of the U-2. According to the rumors, Castro himself asked the Soviet officer in charge to launch the missile. The officer, notwithstanding his knowledge that his action would be severely penalized, agreed with tears in his eyes by answering "Commander-in-Chief: at your orders!" Adding some credibility to the rumor is the fact that the phrase *"Comandante en Jefe: ¡Ordene!"* became a revolutionary slogan in Cuba just after the missile crisis.

Another key to the possible veracity of the rumor is that, in a letter he wrote to Khrushchev, Castro himself mentioned that the news of the Soviet decision to withdraw the missiles brought tears to the eyes of countless Cuban and Soviet men "who were willing to die with supreme dignity."[50] Giving more substance to this hypothesis is the fact that Castro has hinted it. During a conference on the Cuban missile crisis that took place in Havana, he mentioned that the Soviet generals in Cuba had a strong sense of "solidarity" with the Cubans and regarded the U.S. as their "common enemy."[51] Though the story is perhaps difficult to believe, during his research for his biography of Castro, Tad Szulc discovered that "Cubans and foreigners without number have found it impossible to say no to Fidel."[52]

Anyway, no one can be certain what really happened, and it is not probable that either Fidel or the Russians are going to tell the truth in the foreseeable future. The explanation that an overzealous Soviet officer, acting on his own, gave the order to shoot at the U-2 has become the official line of both Castro and the Russians since the beginning of a series of conferences on the Cuban missile crisis that have been taking place in the U.S., Russia, and Cuba. During one of them, Sergo Mikoyan, whose father Anastas Mikoyan played an important role during the crisis, even named the Soviet officer allegedly responsible for the shooting.[53] But the only thing certain about the U-2 incident in Cuba in 1962 is that most of what has been said about it, particularly during these meetings, is, pure and simply, disinformational hogwash.

In their typical Castro-friendly fashion, Blight, Allyn, and Welch arrive at the conclusion that, "From Khrushchev's perspective, Castro was clearly behaving like a maniac, first by opening fire on American aircraft as the crisis peaked, and then by issuing a call (as Khrushchev understood it) for a preemptive nuclear strike."[54] Well, not only from Khrushchev's —who understood perfectly well what Castro was asking him to do— but from any other imaginable perspective, Castro was behaving like the maniac he is.[55] But, of course, it is not politically correct to accept the unavoidable fact that Fidel Castro, the white, old, rich *macho* man most loved and admired by the American "progressive" left, is a maniac whose ultimate dream was, and still is, the annihilation of the American people.

And here comes another intriguing puzzle of the Cuban missile crisis. When the news that a U-2 had been shot down reached the Ex Comm, most members thought that war was just around the corner. In fact they had decided earlier that if a U-2 were shot down, the SAM battery responsible would be immediately knocked off. "It was the blackest hour of the crisis," Roger Hilsman later recalled.[56]

But, like Khrushchev, most of the Ex Comm members miscalculated: Surprisingly, President Kennedy backpedalled on his promise and decided not to give the order to the U.S. fighters on stand-by to destroy the SAM battery. Adding more to the surrealistic aspects of the story, instead of retaliating in Cuba, as he had agreed, Kennedy ordered in a rush to defuse the missiles in Turkey to be certain that they could not be used without his personal permission —which probably meant never using them.[57] May it have been, one can only guess, that, like the Soviet missiles in Cuba, the American missiles in Turkey had actually been dummies?

Chapter 9

Khrushchev's Goat

> *"Qué hacemos con el loco?"*
> *("What are we going to do wth the madman?")*
> —General Arnaldo Ochoa.

Khrushchev's long letter of Friday, October 26th, had a significant change in tone than those that preceded it in the short span of the crisis. The previous ones had been full of arrogance and threats, but this one was the *cri de coeur* of a humble man bordering desperation.

The tone of the letter, more than the diplomatic proposals it contained, made a deep impression on the ones who read it. Khrushchev obviously intended it to be received like his other personal letters to Kennedy; as an expression of his feelings rather than an official communication. Kenneth O'Donnell, for one, was deeply moved by Khrushchev's anguished fear that he had provoked Kennedy into a fighting mood and a readiness for war against the Soviet Union.

A Letter Written in Terror

Khrushchev's letter of October 26 implicitly agreeing to withdraw the missiles in Cuba, was brought to the American embassy in Moscow by a Soviet official of the American section of the Foreign Ministry —an unprecedented procedure inasmuch as the Americans were usually called to the ministry to receive such type of communications. He arrived somewhat breathless in the embassy's chancery at precisely 5 p.m. As he delivered the letter, he apologized for the absence of the official seal, saying that he had not had time to go by the ministry to have the seal affixed. In contrast with the usual meticulous typing of the Soviet diplomatic notes, this letter contained corrections of typographical errors in the same violet ink and the same handwriting as its signature: N. Khrushchev.[1]

Some people have suggested that when Khrushchev wrote the letter he was so emotionally unstable that the message was almost incoherent.[2] Though the letter was not made public at that time, several rumors circulated as to its tone.[3] According to authors James Daniel and John G. Hubbell, it was "rambling" and "obviously composed under the stress of great emotion."[4] To Elie Abel it was "the nightmare outcry of a frightened man."[5] For Schlesinger, who most likely read it at the time, it was "not ... hysterical," but "gave the impression of having been written in deep emotion."[6] Pachter asserted that the letter was "panicky in tone and confused in content."[7]

After the crisis was over, Rusk showed the letter to the Senate Foreign Relations Committee, and copies were distributed to several allied governments. Despite Washington's denials, some of those who saw it described the letter as "fantastic" —the personal cry of a man anxious above all things to save his country from annihilation.[8]

President Kennedy ordered the letter to be kept secret. The reason given later was that Khrushchev's note betrayed a desperation unworthy of a head of state.[9] Finally, in response to requests from the public, under Executive Order 11652, the Interagency Classification Review Committee took declassifying action on a series of messages exchanged between Kennedy and Khrushchev during the Cuban missile crisis of 1962, including Chairman Khrushchev's letter of October 26, 1962.[10] Included were both the informal translation which was made immediately available to President Kennedy and the official translation, prepared later.

The letter is now part of the public record. Anyone can read it and come to his own conclusions about Khrushchev's state of mind at the moment. After studying it, this author is of the opinion that Khrushchev's almost incoherent and emotional message is a proof that the Soviet Premier was scared to death.

To prove my point, an analysis of Khrushchev's letter is in order. In order to avoid any personal bias, however, I have applied to the analysis of the text the principles of the Theory of Verbal Kinesics as stated by Robert Frank.[11] According to this theory,

> Certain semantic forms, including spatial symbols, universally appear in verbal discourse. These semantic forms represent psycholinguistic tools by which body-environment and body-behavioral responses can be actualized. As such, these forms are symptomatic of underlying psychological states and are isomorphic with parallel behavioral disposition. For example, under periods of stress and fear the frequency of flight or horizontal symbols used by the speaker will increase as the predisposition to actual physical flight increases.[12]

The analysis of the letter[13] shows a preponderance of horizontal metaphors over vertical ones. The beginning of the letter shows only horizontal symbols: "each of us has *set forth* his explanation," (all emphasis added); "I know that war ends only when it *has rolled through* cities and villages, *sowing* death," ... "do you really think that Cuba could *launch* an offensive upon the United States and that even we, together with Cuba, could *advance* against you from Cuban territory?"[14] "You have now declared piratical measures, the kind that were practiced in the Middle Ages when ships *passing through* international waters were attacked," ... "And what *direction* are events taking now?"[15]

In the initial paragraphs of the last page, the document changes its tone and some vertical metaphors appear: "The Soviet Union wants the Cubans *build their life*," "...the constant threat of armed attack and aggression has *hung* and continues to *hang* over Cuba."[16] Then two ambiguous symbols appear: "If people do not *display wisdom*, they will eventually reach the point where they will *clash, like blind moles*," followed by another vertical metaphor, "Mr. President, I appeal to you to *weight* carefully."[17] From that point on up to the end all metaphors are horizontal ones: "If you have done this as the *first step towards* unleashing war." Finally, in what is perhaps the most known part of the letter, a strong horizontal metaphor is repeated: "Mr. President, you and I should not now *pull on the ends of the rope* in which you have tied a knot of war, because the *harder you and I pull*, the tighter this knot will become." "Therefore, if there is no intention of *tightening this knot*, thereby dooming the world to the catastrophe of the thermonuclear war, let us not only relax *the forces straining on the ends of the rope*."[18]

Admittedly, an analysis of this kind is far from perfect, especially when it has not been applied to the original document but to a translation. Still, it is interesting to note that the linguistic analysis agrees with the general opinion of those who saw the letter: it was written in an emotional state, most probably a state of fear, perhaps bordering panic

Western analysts were puzzled by the contradictory character of the two messages received in Washington on Friday evening, October 26, and Saturday morning, October 27. The first of the messages, as we have already seen, seems to have been written in panic and confusion, while the second firmly suggested a swap of missile bases. The most popular explanation for this sudden change of mind in the Kremlin is that Khrushchev broke down on October 26 and, perhaps behind the back of the Politburo, hastily sent his very personal message to Kennedy. Later, forced by the military or whoever wielded more power than him, he was forced to retreat from the surrender letter and return to the original plan, demanding a concession in exchange for the withdrawal of the missiles from Cuba.

Khrushchev's message of October 26 seems to have been hastily written and sent precipitously soon after Friday's American military build-up, the U-2 incidents and Kennedy's "saber-rattling" and hints about the possibility of a military take-over of the White House.

The contradictory content of the two messages sent by Khrushchev to President Kennedy —the secret one received by cable on Friday and the one broadcasted in Moscow on Saturday morning— have been the object of different interpretations and analyses by scholars who have studied it. Pachter's conclusion that the letter received first had been actually written last, makes a lot of sense. It seems that the slow, long-winded letter of the Foreign Ministry carefully prepared and sent through official channels, which arrived in Washington only a few hours after the other letter, most likely had been overtaken by Khrushchev's panicky letter.[19]

While I agree with Pachter's interpretation, I consider the polemic irrelevant.

THE NUCLEAR DECEPTION

The important thing, in which almost all analysts agree, is that the second message was written in the Foreign Office by Kremlin bureaucrats, while the secret one was Khrushchev's hurried and desperate personal plea for peace and sanity. Only Khrushchev himself, probably the only person in the Soviet Union fully aware of all the elements of the situation, could have written such a letter.

In his memoirs, Khrushchev gives his own version of a strange conversation that was reported to him. According to the Soviet chairman, five or six days after the beginning of the crisis —it may have been around the 26th or the 27 of October— Anatoly Dobrynin, the Soviet Ambassador, reported to him that the President's brother, Robert Kennedy, called him to his office and told Dobrynin that he and the President were under severe stress because of the pressure from their own military. The President, Robert Kennedy said, implored Chairman Khrushchev to take into consideration the peculiarities of the American system. Even though the President himself was very much against starting a war over Cuba, an irreversible chain of events could occur against his will. If the situation continues much longer, said Robert Kennedy, the President was not sure if the military would not attempt to overthrow him and seize power. The American army could get out of control. "I don't know how much longer we can hold out against our generals," said Robert Kennedy.[20]

We may never know if Kennedy's fears of being overthrown by the military were true, but one may safely surmise that they were a lie; part of a psychological warfare exercise designed to scare Khrushchev. But, like all disinformational lies, this one had at least a grain of truth. There is a strong evidence supporting the fact that the military observed with worried eyes the actions of the Kennedy administration. As early as january, 1961, Walter Lippmann advised Kennedy to put the military in check. "Once the civilian appointees have the self-confidence to exercise civilian supremacy," wrote Lippmann, "they can and should impose a strict civilian discipline on the statements and speeches issued by the Chiefs of Staff and by local commanders throughout the world."[21]

Though Robert Kennedy himself emphatically denied that the exchange with Dobrynin took place, it is interesting to note that it was precisely on October 27th when an American U-2 plane entered the Soviet airspace and another one was shot down in Cuba.

Khrushchev Got Cold Feet

On October 27, widely considered to be the most critical day of the crisis, notice arrived to the Kremlin that an American U-2 had been shot down over Cuba. But just a few hours later, another incident had occurred. A SAC operated U-2 plane, allegedly on a routine air-sampling nuclear detection mission, apparently made a navigation error, overflew the Chukotski Peninsula in Eastern Siberia, and for a few minutes headed directly toward Moscow. The Soviet radars had picked it up and a few minutes later Soviet fighter planes were in hot pursuit. To complicate things even more, American fighter planes had taken off to help the U-2. Finally, the pilot of the U-2 managed to return to his base without been attacked and the Soviet planes gave up their pursuit.[22]

Some scholars of the missile crisis have seen the incident of the U-2 heading for Moscow rather than Alaska as a clear failure of presidential control.[23] But, with the benefit of hindsight, one can legitimately ask the question, Was the incident really the result of a "navigation error"? Some observers did not fail to notice that throughout the week, beginning with Kennedy's address of October 22, "the U.S. had been trying by direct and indirect means, through overt and not quite covert military alert moves *and intricate psychological warfare hints,* to convince the Soviet Union to remove the missiles from Cuba.[24]

The incident terrified Khrushchev. In a message he sent to President Kennedy he gave his interpretation of the incident:

> An even more dangerous case occurred on October 28,[25] when your reconnaissance aircraft invaded the northern area of the Soviet Union, in the area of the Chukotski Peninsula, and flew over our territory. One asks, Mr. President, how we should regard this. What is this; a provocation? Your aircraft violates our frontier, and this happens at a time as troubled as the one through which we are now passing, when everything has been put in battle readiness. For an intruding U.S. aircraft can easily be taken for a bomber with nuclear weapons, and that can push us toward a fatal step. All the more so because the U.S. government and the Pentagon have long been saying that you continually maintain bombers with atomic bombs in the air. Therefore, you can imagine what kind of responsibility you assume, especially during such anxious time as the present.[26]

By that time, the Soviet intelligence had informed the Kremlin about the evacuation plans for the American President and that a skeleton government had been updated and reviewed. Voice came out that Pierre Salinger had called in a select number of newsmen and told them they had been picked to go to a nuclear shelter with the President in case of a nuclear attack.

Nobody is going to believe that the President cared much for a group of journalists whose newspapers and tv stations would be vaporized in a nuclear attack. Therefore, the only explanation for this apparently foolish behavior is that it was a planted leak, another psychological warfare action directed at scaring the Soviets even more.

Khrushchev must have been terrified by the news. Kennedy had apparently failed to properly decode his signals and, instead of attacking Cuba, was preparing to launch a devastating nuclear attack against the Soviet Union.

The U.S. armed forces went from DEFCON five (peacetime alert) to DEFCON three (war alert), and the strategic Air Command was ordered to DEFCON two (full war footing), only one step away from actual hostilities.[27] Five of the eight divisions of the Army Strategic Reserve were placed on alert. The First Armory Division moved from Texas to Fort Stewart, Georgia. Polaris-armed nuclear submarines left their base in Holy Loch, Scotland, to take up stations at sea within range of the Soviet Union. SAC scattered its B-47 bombers to civilian airfields around the U.S. and kept a major portion of long-range B-52 bombers, loaded with nuclear weapons, in the air. These planes, together with 105 short-range missiles in Europe and 156 intercontinental missiles in the United States, were ready to deliver, at the command of the President, the nuclear equivalent of thirty billion tons of TNT upon the U.S.S.R.[28]

Almost everywhere, emergency military measures were being taken without the slightest attempt at secrecy. The crews of the SAC bombers openly exchanged clear, apocalyptic messages. Following the press services of the White House, American newspapers appeared with headlines announcing an imminent catastrophe. As early as Friday, October 19, General Taylor mobilized the Joint Chiefs of Staff and, the next day, Admiral George Anderson issued special orders alerting the Navy. Warships under the command of Rear Admiral Chester Ward were already tracing a wide ring around Cuba and Marine airplanes were scanning the ocean looking for Soviet surface ships and submarines. McDill Air Force Base, not far from Tampa, began to receive a lot a military aircraft. The USS *Enterprise* hastily steamed out of Norfolk Naval Base with an unknown destination. A great movement of troops and military equipment was reported in all of Florida.

The latest intelligence reports received in the Kremlin indicated that all Polaris nuclear submarines had begun deep runs, apparently to pre-determined launching spots close to the Soviet Union. SAC planes crisscrossed the Atlantic and around the North Pole, with their bomb doors closed as a clear indication that they were carrying nuclear bombs. On the ground other SAC crews waited close to their planes, in the greatest alert in SAC history. All civilian personnel from Guantánamo base was evacuated.

Khrushchev later wrote,

> For some time we felt that there was a danger that the President would lose control of his military, and now he was admitting this to himself. Kennedy's message urgently repeated the Americans' demand that we remove the missiles and the bombers from Cuba. We could sense from the tone of the message that tension in the United States was indeed reaching a critical point.[29]

Now that the crisis was under way, the weakness in Khrushchev's plan became even more evident. He had never imagined the confusion the discovery of the "missiles" would create in Washington, nor the wild assumptions that apparently gripped Kennedy, such as that the missiles were planned to be used for a surprise attack against the U.S. or to tighten the Soviet fist on Berlin. Even more important, he had not foreseen neither the direction nor the strength of Kennedy's response, and he was not ready to face it. Moreover, all signs coming from the White House seemed to indicate that Kennedy was not bluffing[30] and that he meant business —the fact that the U.S. was the only nation who had ever used nuclear weapons in anger always kept creeping into Khrushchev's mind.

The Russian leader was terrorized. "A war psychosis has possessed your minds," he had told William Randolph Hearst, Jr., in 1957. "How many planes in the air? Think of the psychotic state involved. If a signal is given —or if the pilot even thinks a signal has been given— he will fly toward his objective in the Soviet Union."[31]

On August 9, 1961, an Editorial of the *Toronto Globe and Mail* reasoned following the same lines as Khrushchev:

> It is hard to avoid the feeling that there is more danger of the United States applying the fatal spark. Mr. Khrushchev was not exaggerating too much when he spoke of "war psychosis" in the United States. President Kennedy is to a considerable extent a prisoner of this public attitude; his freedom of maneuver is limited. Nor he is entirely the master of his own government. There is always the possibility that in a moment of crisis the wild men in the Pentagon or the Central Intelligence Agency may take matters into their own hands. This is, in fact, the most dangerous of all potentialities in the present situation.[32]

In his memoirs Khrushchev confessed that during the missile crisis the Russians were scared of atomic war.[33] There is no doubt that Khrushchev and other Soviet leaders were badly scared by the sudden prospect of nuclear war.[34] Foreign diplomats in Moscow who saw Khrushchev during the crisis weekend said that he looked extremely tired and worried.

On Sunday morning the word came in that the missiles in Cuba would be withdrawn in return for a simple U.S. pledge not to invade the Island. What had happened? Some American analysts believe that Khrushchev broke down under pressure too quickly. If Khrushchev's goal was to provoke the Americans to invade Cuba, they reasoned, he just had to have waited for two or three more days and Kennedy would have ordered an invasion of the Island. Actually, Khrushchev's quick decision of the withdrawal of the missiles saved Castro from an imminent American invasion.

But the available evidence indicates that this was not the case. Despite the massive build-up of troops and war matériel in Florida, the record points to the contrary. Apparently Kennedy had decided beforehand *not* to invade Cuba and get rid of Castro. Proof of this is that, just a few days before, the Ex Comm had proposed, and Kennedy had approved, a contingency plan to retaliate in kind in the event a U-2 were shot down over Cuba, but when this happened the President backed down and refrained to act.

Khrushchev's Appeasement Rituals

On October 26, Khrushchev sent his first private message to President Kennedy with an implicit solution: he could withdraw the missiles merely in exchange for an American promise not to attack Cuba. At that critical moment, the Russian leader badly needed Kennedy's understanding, because that alone would allow him to argue later that, far from being defeated, he had gotten what he had wanted all along: an American guarantee not to invade Cuba. Fate, a concept alien to Marxists, had placed him almost at the mercy of the American President who, luckily for Khrushchev, was fully aware that the Russian Premier needed to be offered a way out of his problems without losing too much face. For Khrushchev, who obviously never meant to go to war, the main problem, once he realized his defeat, was to prevent any further damage to his own standing. Just three hours after Kennedy received Khrushchev's notification that the missiles would be withdrawn, American low level reconnaissance planes reported that the Soviet crews had stopped the construction of the missile bases and some of them had begun to dismantle the sites.[35]

Khrushchev's seemingly irrational behavior during the crisis only makes sense if one perceives his real purpose in sending the "missiles" to Cuba. Although he was at last forced to put part of the Soviet armed forces in combat readiness by October 23, he was very careful not to generate a crisis atmosphere in Moscow. The pointed public appearances he made throughout the crisis week and his letters to U-Thant and Bertrand Russell were a desperate effort to send Washington the right signals. Averell Harriman certainly grasped the Soviet Premier's mood when he said that Khrushchev was desperately signaling his desire to cooperate in moving toward a peaceful solution.

There is no doubt that Khrushchev wanted to make clear that he had no intention of letting the crisis deteriorate to the point where a nuclear war with the Soviet Union would even become possible just because of the irresponsible behavior of his Caribbean associate. In the type of "appeasement rituals" so aptly described by Austrian ethologist Konrad Lorentz,[36] Khrushchev was now showing Kennedy his bare hands and, at the same time, telling the American president *who* his real enemy was and *where* he should direct his attack.

Most of the analysts who have studied the Cuban missile crisis agree that Khrushchev's prompt withdrawal of the missiles was motivated by the fact that the Soviets knew of American strategic superiority and therefore avoided a fatal nuclear confrontation. In a joint retrospective look at the crisis, however, some American participants expressed their opinion that U.S. strategic superiority, insofar as measurable forces and capabilities were concerned, was of little relevance at the time. This was, at least until 1982, the opinion of Rusk, McNamara, Sorensen, Ball, Bundy and Gilpatrick.[37] According to them, what really affected Khrushchev's decision was American tactical superiority with conventional forces in the Caribbean.

However, even if American forces were superior to those of the U.S.S.R., none of them had the capability to totally destroy their opponent's nuclear arsenal with a first strike and, therefore, both countries had the capability to retaliate, inflicting unacceptable civil damage upon the other. Consequently, the prospect of real victors emerging from a major nuclear confrontation was highly unlikely.[38] Moreover, if Khrushchev knew of American strategic superiority, as he surely did, he knew about it *before* the Cuban missile crisis, not as a result of it. Therefore, this could hardly have been his true motive for the withdrawal of the missiles.

There are good reasons for believing that, contrary to some American analysts' opinion, the main factor which influenced Khrushchev's decision was not U.S. conventional strength in the Caribbean and the possibility of a confrontation in Cuba using conventional forces. In fact, the available record clearly indicates that Khrushchev never considered the possibility of a conventional, localized confrontation with the U.S. What exerted a decisive influence in his hasty decision to order the removal of the missiles in Cuba was the terrifying possibility of a U.S. nuclear attack upon the Soviet Union. The specter of another Hiroshima and Nagasaki made Khrushchev lose his sleep.

It had been discussed in detail at the Ex Comm meeting of Tuesday, October 23, what would be done if a U-2 plane were to be shot down over Cuba. It was agreed that —after obtaining specific permission from the President— bomber and fighter planes, already prepared and ready for the mission, would destroy the offending SAM site. Secretary McNamara said that such an attack could take place within two hours after notification of the firing on one of the American planes.[39]

Then, on October 27, the U-2 was shot down over Cuba. But, though the military and most of he Ex Comm members present in the Saturday afternoon meetings asked for immediate action, President Kennedy, once more, failed to accomplish his promise and refrained from action. Both U-2 incidents were officially ignored and no information was offered to the press.[40]

It seems likely that the main reason why President Kennedy ordered to withhold the information about the shooting down of the U-2 over Cuba may have been because he was under heavy pressure from within his administration to take further action. An announcement like this could have lead to public demands that he fulfill his previous pledge.[41] In fact, when the Ex Comm members got the news that an American U-2 plane had been shot down by a Soviet SAM missile in Cuba, there was almost unanimous agreement that they had to attack early next morning with bombers and fighters to destroy the SAM sites. But, again, like in an Abbot and Costello comedy, Kennedy pulled them back. "We won't attack tomorrow," he said. "We shall try again."[42]

Graham Allison expressed his belief that the Soviets withdrew their missiles just before an American attack. Therefore he draws the conclusion that, had Khrushchev wanted an American strike on the Soviet missiles in Cuba, he could simply have prolonged the crisis a few more days.[43] But Allison fails to notice that Khrushchev's letter promising to withdraw the missiles arrived in Washington just a few hours after the U-2 incident over the Chukotski peninsula. This American "error," added to the ultimatum and the warning of the possibility of a military coup in the U.S. told to the Soviet Ambassador by Robert Kennedy, strained

Khrushchev's already tense nerves.

Also, we should not forget Kennedy's message to Khrushchev at the beginning of the crisis which stated in very clear terms that he did not consider the crisis a Cuban, but a Soviet problem. Consequently, Khrushchev was scared to death. He withdrew the missiles in such a rush because he believed at that moment that the Americans were mad enough to launch an all out preemptive strike directed not against Cuba, but against the Soviet Union.[44] Moreover, despite all claims on the contrary, there is nothing that indicates that, whatever course of action Khrushchev had taken, Kennedy would have ordered a strike on the missile sites in Cuba.

Allison also points out that "the blockade was but the first step in a series of moves that *implicitly* threatened air strike or invasion.[45] But, as he correctly notices, not any of the American official statements during the crisis *explicitly* threatened Castro's Cuba. In fact all of them were direct threats not against Cuba, but against the Soviet Union.

The available record suggests that McNamara's assumptions at the time were correct. Khrushchev's rushed withdrawal of the missiles was not because of the blockade, nor because he feared an air strike or invasion of Cuba in the next hours, but because he was scared to death about the possibility of a devastating American nuclear strike on the Soviet Union. According to McNamara,

> Khrushchev knew without any question whatsoever that he faced the full military power of the United States, including its nuclear weapons. ... We faced that night the possibility of launching nuclear weapons. ... and that is the reason, and the only reason, why he withdrew those weapons.[46]

In a last hour attempt to push Americans into action against Cuba, Khrushchev gave orders to accelerate the process of setting up the missile sites. Construction crews, until now just working by daylight, began working feverishly as if completion of the sites would be needed as fast as possible.[47] This may seem somehow confusing, but, as Edward Jay Epstein pointed out, "even when a deception outlives its usefulness, it can be cloaked in a disguise of ambiguity and confusion."[48] This also explains Khrushchev's later insistence in obtaining from Kennedy a promise not to invade Cuba. Anyway, I have the feeling that Khrushchev never trusted President Kennedy's promises. But successful deception is mostly not a matter of technique, but of the deceiver's intent and the would be deceived's secret wishes. Success comes, therefore, from knowing what the target is likely to do in reaction to certain information and then taking the appropriate steps to indirectly make him react the way we want to.[49]

In order to justify his actions *a posteriori*, Khrushchev argued that, in the morning of October 27, he had received with utmost alarm information from the Cubans and from other sources that a U.S. attack on Cuba would be carried out in the next two or three days. Therefore, he took immediate actions to prevent the attack against Cuba and preserve peace. But it is evident that his alarm was not because of an imminent U.S. invasion of Castro's Cuba, but because he feared that

President Kennedy may order a preemptive nuclear attack against the U.S.S.R. It is not likely that, at that time, Khrushchev still believed Kennedy's threats of invading Cuba and getting rid of Castro.

On October 24, Khrushchev ordered the Soviet ships to stop before reaching the limits of the U.S. blockade and, although he publicly attacked it as a piratical action, on October 26 he sent his first private message to President Kennedy with an implicit solution: he would withdraw the missiles merely in exchange for an American verbal promise not to attack Cuba.

Nikita Khrushchev never understood why Kennedy opted for the blockade instead of an invasion of Cuba. The blockade was in some sense more dangerous than an invasion, because it might put the United States in the position of having its warships fire at unarmed Russian merchant ships bound to Cuba, an evident act of piracy in the high seas. An invasion of Cuba seemed to Khrushchev less provocative because that way the American troops would only have to fight Cubans, while the Soviets could stand aside. Moreover, Khrushchev never understood why Kennedy, as he had done before during the Bay of Pigs invasion, had guaranteed again Castro's existence.[50]

The Cuban missile crisis was a typical example of the phenomenon Italian semiologist Humberto Eco calls "aberrant decoding." By placing the missiles in Cuba Khrushchev thought he sent a coded, but very clear message with a specific meaning to Kennedy. But, apparently the President decoded it erroneously and got a totally different meaning than the one Khrushchev intended. Whether Kennedy did so out of foolishness or out of cleverness, is a question to leave for honest historians to tell.

Far from criticizing the generals who allegedly had gotten him into a mess, Khrushchev called on them to rescue him. Marshal Budeny, who had been purged allegedly for his Stalinist connections, was symbolically restored to honor, and Voroshilov had appeared again at the tribune atop Lenin's mausoleum to review the troops parading across the Red Square on the anniversary of the October Revolution.[51]

The Cuban missile crisis had Khrushchev's unmistakable seal upon it; the typical imprint of a man who, throughout his life, had made bold moves to disentangle himself from dangerous situations. The crisis was just another of Khrushchev's monumental blunders, like the one which won him the disrespectful nickname of *Kukuruza*.[52]

The outcome of the crisis was a further irritant in Khrushchev's already threatened political situation. On October 13, 1964, he attended the Presidium meeting that turned out to be his trial. Though the single most important factor which led to his fall was the catastrophic failure of the Soviet economy, there is no doubt that his Cuban misadventure added weight to the cause of his "democratic" demotion.

Probably one of the most paradoxical aspects of the event, which apparently nobody has noticed, is that Khrushchev's plan, had it been successful, would had been an extraordinary step in the liberation of the Cuban people from the yoke of totalitarianism. Had Kudryavtsev, Escalante and the PSP communists managed to overthrow Castro and take power in Cuba in 1962, as Khrushchev had planned, they would have been able to keep themselves in power probably for no more than one or two years after being themselves overthrown by the Cuban people. If that would had been the case, Nikita Khrushchev would had become the unwilling liberator of the Cuban people.

During a conversation with his friend Ricardo Rojo, Che Guevara mentioned that when Castro heard the news that Khrushchev had reached and agreement with President Kennedy to remove the missiles from Cuba, Fidel was so furious that "he swore, kicked the wall and broke a mirror in his fury."[53] In a letter Khrushchev wrote to Castro on October 30, 1962, in an effort to calm him down, the Soviet Premier mentioned that "The main thing we have secured is preventing aggression on the part of your foreign enemy at present."

In an essay about the Cuban missile crisis, a Cuban intelligence defector mentioned the fact that, contrary to Soviet claims, the Cuban intelligence found no evidence that the U.S. was preparing for an invasion of Cuba, nor that it had plans to invade the Island.[54] Surprisingly, Castro ignored his own intelligence people and sided with the Soviets. Castro was totally sure that the U.S. was ready to invade Cuba. What most people ignore, is that, for forty-three long years, Fidel Castro has been preparing himself and waiting for an American invasion of Cuba. Not only waiting, it seems, but longing for the American invasion that will fulfill his prophecy. From Castro's perpective, Khrushchev had merely postponed what Fidel believes is his inevitable final confrontation with the United States. Perhaps Khrushchev never realized that the main reason for Castro's fury was not that Khrushchev had removed the missiles, but that he had prevented an American invasion of Cuba.

Khrushchev once told a fable about a Russian peasant who was so impoverished that he had to live with a goat in his home. As time passed he grew used to the animal's smell, but, though he knew he had no other choice, he never really enjoyed the arrangement.

In his forced retirement at his state-owned dacha in the village of Petrovo-Dalneye, twenty miles west of Moscow, honorary pensioner Nikita Sergeevich Khrushchev must have recalled the story of the poor peasant many times and also remembered the Cuban leader. Like the peasant's goat, Fidel had the beard... and the smell.[55]

PART TWO

This is *Not* a Missile

Chapter 10

A Missile is a Missile is a Missile

This is not a pipe.
—Caption in *The Treachery of Images*, a 1929 painting by René Magritte depicting a pipe.

The Cuban missile crisis is still a very elusive historical event. For forty years it has captured the imagination of the media, scholars, and the public alike, producing a veritable mountain of articles, scholarly essays, and books. Still, after so much effort by so many privileged minds, some aspects of the Cuban missile crisis continue to defy any logical explanation and are as puzzling today as they were at the time of the event. In this chapter, I will study the alleged evidence of the presence of strategic missiles and their associated nuclear warheads in Cuba in 1962 from the point of view of semiotics.

Is "Photographic Evidence" Evidence at All?

The official story, offered by the Kennedy administration, and accepted at face value by most scholars of the Crisis and later popularized by the American mainstream media, is that, though rumors about the presence of strategic missiles in Cuba were widespread among Cuban exiles in Florida since mid-1962,[1] the American intelligence community was never fooled by them. To American intelligence analysts, "only direct evidence, such as aerial photographs, could be convincing."[2] It was not until Sunday, 14 October, 1962, that a U-2, authorized at last to fly over the western part of Cuba,[3] brought the first high-altitude photographs of what seemed to be Soviet strategic missile sites, in different stages of completion, deployed on Cuban soil.

Once the photographs were analyzed by experts at the National Photographic Interpretation Center (NPIC), they were brought to President Kennedy who, after a little prompting by a photointerpreter who attended the meeting, accepted as a fact the NPIC's conclusion that Soviet Premier Nikita S. Khrushchev had taken a fateful, aggressive step against the U.S. by placing nuclear capable strategic missiles in Cuba. This meeting is considered by most scholars to be the beginning of the Cuban missile crisis.

Save for a few unbelievers at the United Nations[4] —a little more than a year before, U.S. Ambassador to the UN Adlai Stevenson had shown the very same delegates "hard" photographic evidence of Cuban planes, allegedly piloted by Castro's defectors, which had attacked positions on the Island previous to the Bay of Pigs landing— most people, including the members of the American press, unquestionably accepted the U-2 photographs as evidence of Khrushchev's treachery. The photographic "evidence," however, was received abroad with mixed feelings.

Senior CIA officer Sherman Kent recorded in detail the story of how the U-2 photographs were brought to some American allies, and what their reactions were. British Prime Minister Harold Macmillan, for example, just spent a few seconds examining the photographs, and accepted the proof on belief. The Prime Minister's Private Secretary, however, "expressed serious concern about the reception any strong government statement in support of the U.S. decision would have *in the absence of incontrovertible proof of the missile buildup.*"[5]

German Chancellor Adenauer accepted the photographic evidence, and apparently was impressed with it. General de Gaulle accepted President Kennedy's word initially on faith, though later he inspected the photographs in great detail, and was impressed with the quality of them. However, when the photographs were shown to French journalists, one of them, André Fontaine, an important senior writer for *Le Monde*, strongly expressed his doubts. Only circumstantial evidence he received later, not the photographs themselves, made him change his opinion. Canada's Prime Minister Diefenbaker questioned the credibility of the evidence of Soviet strategic missiles in Cuba.[6]

According to Kent, notwithstanding some of the viewers' past experience in looking at similar photographs, "All viewers, however, took on faith or on the say-so of the purveyors that the pictures were what they claimed to be: scenes from Cuba taken a few days past."[7]

Nevertheless, beginning with Robert Kennedy's classic analysis of the Crisis, the acceptance of the U-2's photographs as hard evidence of the presence of Soviet strategic missiles deployed on Cuban soil has rarely been contested.[8] CIA director John McCone reaffirmed the same line of total belief in a Top Secret post-mortem memorandum of 28 February 1963 to the President. According to McCone, aerial photography was "our best means to establish hard intelligence."[9]

THE NUCLEAR DECEPTION

This is not a pipe. René Magritte, *The Treachery of Images*, 1929.

These are not missiles. U-2 Photo (USAF). San Cristóbal, Cuba, October 14, 1962.

But both Robert Kennedy and John McCone were dead wrong. As Magritte's picture *The Treachery of Images* masterly exemplifies, a picture of a missile is *not* a missile. A photograph of a UFO is *not* a UFO. Clint Eastwood is *not* Dirty Harry. Charlton Heston is *not* Moses. A picture, by itself alone, can hardly be accepted as "hard" evidence of anything.[10] Linguist Alfred Korzybski masterly expressed it when he wrote, "The map is not the territory."[11] The fact is so obvious that no time should be wasted discussing it. It seems, however, that the very fact that it is so obvious —somebody said that the best way to hide something is by placing it in plain view— has precluded scholars from studying it in detail. Therefore, let's analyze the obvious.

A photograph is nothing more than a thin film of gelatine spread on top of a paper support. The gelatine has embedded in it very small grains of a light-sensitive substance. Once exposed to light, the grains suffer a chemical alteration. During the developing process with the right chemicals, some of the grains, in the form of very small dots, turn black, others remain white, and others take different gradations of gray. When observed by a trained individual, the dots, due to the integrating, holistic ability of the human mind, turn into a meaningful image.[12] This, both the material support and the mental image it creates, is what we call a photograph.

We are so used to dealing with photographs that most of the time we refer to them as if they were the real thing. A typical example is when a coworker pulls out of his wallet a photo of his family and says "this is my daughter, this is my wife, this is my dog, this is my house." Of course, what you see in the photograph are not the real things, just an *image* of the things.[13]

As nobody can smoke Magritte's pipe, no army can fire photographs of missiles against the enemy. Images appearing on photographs are not things, but *signs* of things. The inability to distinguish between a sign and the thing it signifies is one of the characteristics of primitive, magic thinking.[14]

Until relatively recent times the word semiotics appeared only in the field of medicine, in connection with the study of the symptoms of a particular disease. It was not until the beginning of the 20th century, however, that the Swiss linguist

Ferdinand de Saussure, and later the American philosopher Charles Sanders Peirce, created the scientific foundations of the discipline we now know as semiotics.[15]

Saussure saw signs as twofold entities, showing a signifier and a signified (or *sign-vehicle* and *meaning*). To him, "the sign is implicitly regarded as a communication device taking place between two human beings intentionally aiming to communicate or to express something."[16] Peirce, however, saw signs as threefold entities. In articulating the foundation of the science of semiotics, he stated, "By semiosis I mean an action, an influence, which is, or involves, a cooperation of three subjects, such as a sign, its object and its interpretant."[17] To Pierce, the interpretant was the mental image created in the mind of an interpreter.

According to Peirce, a sign is "something which stands to somebody for something in some respect or capacity."[18] As Italian semiotician Umberto Eco clearly puts it, "a sign can *stand for* something else to somebody only because this 'standing-for' relation is mediated by an interpretant."[19] The "something" can be anything: a material thing, a concept, an idea, a feeling; existing or non-existing, real or unreal.

Things are things. In some particular circumstances, however, a person can see (or hear, or smell, or touch) something and have similar impressions as if he were experiencing something different. Pierce called this process semiosis. To him, the process of semiosis in nothing but "a psychological event in the mind of a possible interpreter."[20] From the point of view of semiotics, the work of the technicians at the NPIC is basically a semiotic process. Surveillance photographs, by themselves alone, have no meaning. They become signs —that is, pointers to other real-life things— in the minds of skilled photointerpreters, who carefully compare apparently meaningless forms and shadows against their previous experiences, looking for meaningful relationships.

As Claude Lévi-Strauss put it, the science of semiotics is concerned with the different procedures used to transform nature into culture. This is roughly equivalent to the process of transforming raw data into intelligence.

Missiles and *Signs* of Missiles

Beginning with the concept of sign, Pierce created trichotomies of concepts, which sometimes extended almost *ad-infinitum*. According to him every sign is either an index, an icon, or a symbol.[21]

An index is a type of sign showing some relationship, usually of cause and effect, or antecedent to consequent, between a sign and a thing. Dark clouds are a sign indicating an approaching storm; high fever is an indexical sign of disease; smog is an indexical sign of air pollution. To Robinson Crusoe, footprints in the sand were the first indication that somebody else beyond him inhabited the island.

An icon is a type of sign which shows a relationship of formal or topological similarity or likeness between the sign and an object. Maps, diagrams, pictures,[22] and photographs are typical iconic signs. Usually, iconic signs stand for particular, specific things.

A symbol, however, is a type of sign which shows no physical, or visual, or any type of relationship between the sign and the thing it signifies. The relationship established in the mind of the interpreter is totally conventional and arbitrary, as the result of an explicit or implicit agreement among those who use the sign.[23] Language is the most extended system of symbols used by men to communicate ideas, though there are other important systems of symbols, like the ones used in mathematics, music, chemistry, etc.

Semiosis is just a mental process, and there are no physical ties whatsoever between something and its sign. Therefore, signs can be decoded differently by different people or by the same people under different circumstances. Moreover, something can act as an icon while, at the same time, acting as an index and a symbol. The American flag on top of my town's city hall is an object made out of red, white and blue pieces of cloth sewn together. An American flag on an American embassy abroad is an index that the building is owned by the U.S. government. A photograph of that particular American flag is an iconic sign of the particular flag it depicts. But the American flag also symbolizes all what America stands for. As such, it is the ultimate symbol of the American nation.

The famous photograph showing the footprints of an American astronaut on the moon's soil is an iconic sign depicting an indexical sign. With the passage of time, however, the photograph became a symbol (symbolic sign) of the advances of American space technology. The fact shows an important characteristic of signs: they are polysemic; they are always open to multiple interpretations.

Most studies about the Cuban missile crisis repeat the extended opinion that the U-2 photographs were the hard, irrefutable evidence provided by the photointerpreters at the NPIC as the ultimate, uncontrovertible proof that the Soviets had secretly deployed strategic missile bases in Cuba. But, as we have seen above, in order to become meaningful information, photographs need to be decoded (interpreted) by an interpreter.

Being a subjective process, however, semiosis is full of pitfalls. There is always the risk of erroneous interpretation, by which a sign is interpreted as something totally different from what the creator of the sign originally intended to communicate. The process is known as aberrant decoding.[24] In the case of the U-2 photographs, the NPIC photointerpreters incorrectly decoded the objects appearing in them as strategic missiles, instead of *images* of strategic missiles.[25] But accepting the images of missiles as the ultimate proof of the presence of strategic missiles in Cuba was a big jump of their imagination, as well as a semantic mistake. A more truthful interpretation of the things whose images appeared in the U-2's photographs would have been to describe them as "objects whose photographic image highly resemble the auxiliary equipment used in Soviet strategic missile bases." But the photointerpreters at the NPIC confused the images of the objects they saw in the photographs with the actual missiles.[26] Afterwards, like mesmerized children, the media and the scholarly community have blindly followed the pied piper of photographic evidence. But, as in Magritte's painting, a picture of a missile in not a missile.

With the advent of the new surveillance technologies pioneered with the U-2 plane, and now extensively used by imaging satellites, there has been a growing trend in the U.S. intelligence community to rely more and more on imaging intelligence and less and less on agents in the field (HUMINT).[27] But, as any intelligence specialist can testify, photography alone, though a very useful surveillance component, should never be accepted as hard evidence. Photographs, at best, are just indicators pointing to a possibility which has to be physically confirmed by other means, preferably by trained, qualified agents working in the field.

Moreover, even disregarding the fact that photographs can be faked and doctored,[28] nothing is so misleading as a photograph. According to the information available to this day, the photographic evidence of Soviet strategic missiles on Cuban soil was never confirmed by American agents working in the field. The highly quoted report of a qualified agent who saw something "bigger, much bigger" that anything the Americans had in Germany,[29] omitted the important fact that what he actually saw was a canvas-covered object resembling a strategic missile. Actually, the missiles were never touched, smelled, or weighed. Their metal, electronic components, and fuel were never tested; the radiation from their nuclear warheads was never recorded; their heat signature was never verified.

According to philosopher Robert Nozick, the main criteria for considering a fact objective is that it is invariant under certain transformations, and he gives three characteristics that mark a fact as objective:

> First, "an objective fact is accessible from different angles. Access to it can be repeated by the same sense (sight, touch, etc.), at different times; it can be repeated by different senses of the same observers. Different laboratories can replicate the phenomenon." Second, "there is or can be intersubjective agreement about it." Third, objective facts hold "independently of people's beliefs, desires, hopes, and observations or measurements."[30]

One of the golden rules of intelligence work is to treat with caution all information not independently corroborated or supported by reliable documentary or physical evidence.[31] Yet, recently declassified Soviet documents, and questionable oral reports from Soviet officials who allegedly participated directly in the event, have lately been accepted as sufficient evidence of the presence of strategic missiles and their nuclear warheads in Cuba in 1962. But one can hardly accept as hard evidence non-corroborated, non-evaluated information coming from a former adversary who has yet to prove he has turned into a friend.[32] Even if some day this becomes accepted practice in the historian's profession, I can assure my readers that it will never be adopted in the intelligence field.

Photographs are just information, and information is not true intelligence until it has been thoroughly validated. As a rule, most counterintelligence analysts believe that only information that has been secretly taken from an opponent and turned over is *bona fide* intelligence. But, if the opponent had intended it to be turned over, it is automatically considered disinformation.

One of the principles of espionage work is that what is really important is not that you know, but that your opponent doesn't know that you know. As Sherman Kent pointed out, once the U-2 brought [what seemed to be] photographs of strategic missile bases in Cuba, the main thing was to keep it secret. "Until the President was ready to act, the Russians must not know that we knew their secret."[33]

The fact that the Soviets had been so clumsy, failing to properly camouflage their missiles, surprised the American intelligence community. As it happens most of the time, however, American scholars found plausible explanations *a posteriori* for the Soviets' behavior. These explanations ranged from flawed bureaucratic standard operating procedures to political-military disagreements, and pure and simple carelessness. Nevertheless, still today the fact constitutes one of the most unexplainable Soviet "mistakes" during the crisis.

Probably one of the most known explanations was the one offered by Graham T. Allison. According to him, the failure to camouflage the missiles had a simple answer: bureaucratic procedures in the Soviet Army. Before the crisis, missile sites had never been camouflaged in the Soviet Union, so, the construction crews at the sites in Cuba did what they were used to do; building missile sites according to the installation manuals, because somebody forgot to retrain them before they were sent to work in Cuba.[34]

But, given the strict operational procedures of the Soviet Army, Allison's explanation seems a bit too simplistic to be credible. First of all, the personnel assigned to do the job of building the missile sites were not common soldiers, but specially trained personnel. Secondly, even without disregarding the bureaucratic procedures common to all armies, it is a naive assumption to suppose that the Soviets could have made this type of gross mistake, particularly if they were trying to deploy the missiles in Cuba using deception and stealth, as the U.S. official version of the event claimed. Of course, this is only a variation of the "the Russians are stupid" argument. This may also explain why the Soviet soldiers involved in Operation Anadyr (code name for the operation) were supplied with skis and cold weather gear and clothing before traveling to Cuba. But now we know that this was not because of an error, but part of the *maskirovka* procedures designed to disguise the operation.[35]

According to U.S. intelligence sources, missile sites had never been camouflaged in the Soviet Union. However, after Gary Power's U-2 was shot down, the flow of information about Soviet missiles almost stopped completely. Aside from the fact that, being in the so-called "denied areas," where no *in situ* verification by agents in the field was possible, we don't know if the U-2 photos never detected camouflaged sites because the camouflage was so effective it avoided the missiles from being detected. Also, there is the possibility that most of the missile sites photographed by the U2s on Soviet territory had actually been decoys.

One can safely surmise that, after the U-2 incident and the discovery of the high quality of its surveillance cameras, the Soviet Missile Forces would have changed their procedures and would have camouflaged their missile sites. Furthermore, Soviet military literature strongly emphasizes the importance of surprise (*udivlenie*) and deception (*loz'n*) in modern warfare. Among it, the literature on camouflage (*maskirovka*), is particularly abundant.[36] The Russian tradition of using camouflage to mislead goes back to the times of Grigori Aleksandrovich Potemkin. Consequently, it is difficult to avoid the conclusion that, if the Soviet personnel in charge of installing the missiles failed to camouflage them, it was not because they were stupid, but because they were specifically ordered to do so.

The lack of adequate camouflage to hide the missiles from American observation is such a gross mistake that author Anatol Rappoport concluded that it was part of a Soviet plan by which the missile sites were meant to be discovered by American spy planes.[37] During the height of the crisis, the *Wall Street Journal* reported that "the authorities here almost all accepted one key assumption: that Mr. Khrushchev must have assumed that his Cuban sites would soon be discovered." The report also added that, according to one authority who had studied the photographic evidence, "The Russians seem almost to have gone out of their way to call attention to them."[38]

Similarly, the Cubans were aware of the quality of American air surveillance technology. In 1961, *Life* magazine published a report about the anti-Castro guerrillas fighting in the Escambray mountains. Some of the photographs illustrating the article had been taken by the U-2s. On several occasions Castro asked the Soviets to give him SAMs, and let his people operate them, but the Russians were reluctant. Although most of the Cubans assigned to the SAM bases were engineering students from the University of Havana, the Soviets only allowed them to operate the radars.

To the evidence offered above of the Soviets' willingness to let the missiles be discovered, I can add some of my own. As a Cuban Army officer during the crisis I was assigned to headquarters and sent on inspection visits to several military units to assess their combat morale and battle readiness. One of these visits was to the Isle of Pines, where I visited a unit, deployed in an area close to the Siguanea peninsula, not far from a Soviet missile base located on the top of a nearby hill, close to the coast. The Cuban soldiers had aptly nicknamed the base *"el circo soviético,"* (the Soviet Circus), because of the canvas tarpaulins surrounding it. But the most interesting detail is that, though the tarpaulins precluded observers from seeing the base from the ground, the base itself remained uncovered on the top and in plain view of American spy planes. So, it seems that, though the Soviets apparently were eager to allow long-distance detection, they didn't want any short-range observation of the missiles by the Cubans.

In another inspection, I visited a Cuban Air Force base at San Antonio de los Baños, south of Havana. The visit occurred after president Kennedy had alerted the American public about the presence of missile bases in Cuba. Low-level American reconnaissance flights had begun, and Castro had ordered the antiaircraft batteries under his command to fire at American planes.

Once at the base, we drove our jeep to the runway, where I saw in the distance several MiG fighter planes, which looked to me like MiG 15 or 17 models, lying like sitting ducks on the apron. On close inspection, however, we discovered that the planes were clumsy dummies made out of wood, cardboard and painted canvas. An officer at the base told us that the real planes were well protected and camouflaged.

As we were talking to other officers at the end of the runway, the antiaircraft batteries received a phone call alerting them that American planes had entered Cuban airspace, and one of them was flying in our direction. A few minutes later, what seemed to me like a RF-101 Voodoo reconnaissance aircraft overflew us at treetop level, too fast for the inexperienced boys[39] manning the four-barreled antiaircraft guns to open fire.

Though the dummies on the runway were perhaps good enough to fool the high-flying U-2s, they were too clumsily made to fool low-flying reconnaissance planes. The fact, however, that the Soviets had used decoy planes (and probably other types of decoys) in Cuba during the Crisis has never been mentioned in any of the U.S. declassified documents pertaining to the Crisis. Also, it is difficult to believe, to say the least, that Soviet *maskirovka* had worked so well on other aspects of the Cuban operation, but failed on the most important part of it: covering the strategic missile bases from prying American eyes. Therefore, there is a strong possibility that the missiles deployed in Cuba, like the ones Khrushchev was displaying in Moscow's Red Square parades, were a *ruse de guerre;* nothing but empty dummies.[40]

It is known that, after Gary Powers' U-2 was shot down in May, 1960, the Soviets hurriedly began building dummy SAM silos. Dummy tanks, guns, and other types of war matériel were regularly deployed to confuse the sky spies.[41] According to some sources, as late as 1960, even some units of the newly created Soviet Strategic Rocket Forces were not getting real missiles, but dummies.[42]

This *not* a missile! This is a *photograph* of a Soviet MRBM, Sandal SS-4, like the ones Khrushchev sent to Cuba. Given the fact, however, that the Soviets would not run the risk of parading a real missile with its nuclear warhead and its highly unstable liquid propellant through Moscow's streets, this may not even be a photograph of a missile, but a symbol of Grigori Potemkin's motherland.

Camouflage in warfare can be used either passively, to conceal from the enemy the true thing, or actively, to mislead the enemy into accepting a false one. From the point of view of semiotics, camouflage is intentional false encoding with the purpose of deceiving the decoder. Furthermore, in semiotic terms, camouflage can be defined as the art of confusing the enemy to make him believe that a sign of a thing is the thing itself, that is, to induce the enemy into magical thinking.

Strategic Missiles as Symbols

The successful launching in 1957 of the first man-made earth satellite, the *Sputnik,* soon became a symbol of Soviet technological success. After that, the U.S.S.R. passed through a brief period of national pride and faith in a better future. Khrushchev's poorly chosen phrase "We will bury you," was most likely not intended as a threat to the West, but as an assertion of his confidence that, sometime in the near future, socialism, under the guidance of the Soviet Union, would replace decadent capitalism.

Though the Soviet Union had expressed support for the new revolutionary phenomenon developing 90 miles from American shores, it had been mostly rhetorical. Then, on July 9, 1960, Khrushchev told the U.S. to keep its hands off Cuba, backing his words with the famous threat of the Soviet nuclear missiles: *"Figuratively speaking,* in case of need, Soviet artillerymen can support the Cuban people with their rocket fire if the aggressive forces in the Pentagon dare to launch an intervention against Cuba."[43]

The precise nature of the Soviet military commitment to Cuba on Khruschev's speech of July 9 was later to be questioned, and the Soviets themselves immediately moved to de-emphasize Khrushchev's promise of "figurative" (symbolic) rocket support of Cuba.[44]

Just three days after Khrushchev made the symbolic offer of rocket support to Cuba, he backpedalled and said, "We don't need bases in Cuba. We have bases in the Soviet Union, and we can hit anything from here."[45] A week later, on July 16, *TASS* published an authoritative statement entitled "The Monroe Doctrine Ended Long Ago and Can No Longer Help the Imperialist Colonizer." But, a careful reading between the lines evidenced that in the event of an armed intervention against Cuba the only thing the Soviet Union was going to offer was its strong support. No mention was made of the symbolic missiles, which had suddenly disappeared from the picture as if they never existed.

After Khrushchev's symbolic *faux pas* about the missiles, Castro made several efforts to force him further into a strong commitment, but Khruschev ignored the Cuban leader's initiatives. Rumor ran that when the two leaders met in New York in September, 1960, Khrushchev told Castro to stop making references to Soviet missile support.[46]

Khrushchev pounding his shoe on his desk at the General Assembly was perhaps a symbolic, but ambiguous statement of support for Fidel. But the Cuban leader wanted more than symbols. That same month Castro sent Carlos Franqui, editor of *Revolución*, to Moscow on the pretext of interviewing Khrushchev, to find out how the Soviet leader could pass from figurative, symbolic language to direct statements. Franqui spent several hours in the Kremlin going over the subject with Khrushchev, but the most he obtained from the shrewd Soviet leader was a Solomonic statement, which was interpreted in contradictory fashion by the press services of the United States and the rest of the world.[47] Apparently Khrushchev had second thoughts about the responsibilities he had assumed with regard to Cuba. There are indications that he finally got tired of Castro's schemes and diplomatically told the Cuban leader to quit rattling the Soviet missiles against the United States.

It seems that, finally, Castro got it, because during a long speech on November 8, he told the Cubans to forget the idea that they were protected by Soviet nuclear missiles.[48] *Hoy*, the newspaper of the old pro-Soviet Cuban communist party, came to the rescue and denied that Khrushchev had told Castro to stop mentioning the Soviet missiles.[49] But The *New York Times* confirmed on November 19, that the Soviet leader had told Castro to moderate his violent attacks upon the United States, and in particular to stop rattling the Soviet nuclear missiles.

Premier Khrushchev used to complain about the American nuclear missiles deployed by some NATO countries around the Soviet borders. But the missiles the U.S. had deployed in Europe were no less symbolic than the ones Khrushchev had promised Castro. As Michael Mandelbaum rightly observed, "Tactical nuclear weapons became symbols of the American resolve to carry out its commitments to its NATO partners."[50] Another scholar has pointed out that, though the use of nuclear weapons has military value, "its symbolic political value can easily outweigh its military significance."[51]

In a private conversation with his British friend David Ormsby-Gore, Kennedy told him that the missiles in Turkey were "more or less useless."[52] They had been left there, however, because of their symbolic value. The phasing out of the American missiles in Turkey had been under consideration long before the crisis.[53] In any case, the Kennedy administration had decided the previous year to remove them because they were obsolete, clumsy liquid-fuel rockets. The American plan was to replace them with missile-bearing Polaris submarines stationed in the Mediterranean. Among the precautions which Kennedy took during the crisis to avoid a costly mistake by subordinates ignoring orders, was the bizarre fact that he reportedly ordered the removal of the fuses and warheads from the Jupiter missiles in Turkey, probably with the intention of making them fully symbolic.

In his life as a Russian leader, Khrushchev was to show that he was deeply addicted to the calculated risk, especially if it implied no real risk at all. Though not a trained semiotician, Khrushchev knew perfectly well the cardinal difference between a symbolic missile and a real one, and that the manipulation of symbols was a lot less riskier than the manipulation of things —particularly when the things in question were tipped with nuclear warheads.

We may safely surmise that, fully aware of the strong force of symbols, Khrushchev had realized that a dummy missile had the same symbolic value than a real one. As a matter of fact, symbolic missiles have the same deterrent power — and provocation power, for that matter— as the real ones, but without all of their inherent risks.[54]

The Treachery of Intelligence Images

According to Umberto Eco,

> Semiotics is concerned with everything that can be taken as a sign. A sign is everything which can be taken as significantly substituting for something else. This something else does not necessarily have to exist or to actually be somewhere at the moment in which a sign stands in for it. Thus *semiotics is in principle the discipline studying everything which can be used in order to lie.*[55]

Intelligence, espionage, and particularly counterintelligence, are semiotic activities *par excellence*; they deal mostly with all types of deception, and deception has always been an important component of the intelligence profession since its early days. I will use a relatively recent example to illustrate the point.

During World War II, the British intelligence services carried out an enormous disinformation exercise code-named Fortitude, as a part of a major deception operation code-named Bodyguard. The main goal of operation Fortitude was to fool the Germans about the place selected by the Allied armies for their coming invasion. Fortitude was extremely successful in creating a notional[56] American invasion force, the First U.S. Army Group (FUSAG), under the command of Lt. Gen. George Patton, which, according to German intelligence reports, was ready to land at Pas de Calais. More than 19 German divisions, including several armored ones, waited patiently for an attack that never materialized, while the invading forces secured their positions at Normandy, the true place of the invasion. The main mistake of the German Abwer and other intelligence services was that they apparently believed that aerial photographs were hard evidence.

German reconnaissance planes brought back to Berlin load after load of photographs showing two large Allied armies, one in Scotland, getting ready to invade Norway, and another getting ready for the assault on Pas de Calais. The aerial photographs depicted large concentrations of men, tanks, trucks, cannons, and all types of matériel associated with an invasion force.[57] What the Germans didn't know was that some of the tanks and trucks were inflatable rubber replicas, and the rest of the matériel was made out of plywood, cardboard and canvas. Some of the "cannons" hiding under camouflage nets consisted of an oil drum turned on its side with a telegraph pole resting on its top. Having in mind the quality of the photographic technology available at the time, the British intelligence was careful not to allow low flying planes to photograph the "armies," while high altitude

German reconnaissance flights were allowed to do their jobs unmolested.

In the case of the German intelligence, however, there are some alleviating circumstances which somehow explain their failure: the photographic illusion was supported by corroborating reports from their agents in the field. But the Germans ignored that the British intelligence services had managed to capture most of the German agents, "turning" some of them to feed controlled disinformation to the German intelligence.[58] At the end of the war, most German intelligence officers still believed that the invasion by the two large Allied armies never materialized only because of a late change of plans.

An interesting detail about the behavior of the American side during the Cuban missile crisis is that only three members of the U.S. government initially expressed doubts about the true existence of Soviet strategic missiles in Cuba: McGeorge Bundy,[59] General Maxwell Taylor and Deputy Secretary of State George Ball.[60] But, significantly, none of them were directly linked to the American intelligence services. On the other hand, no mention is made in the available literature of the Cuban missile crisis about any concern expressed by members of the American intelligence community about the possibility of Soviet deception, nor about what tradecraft tests were to evaluate the authenticity of the information they relied upon to reach the conclusion that the Soviets were deploying strategic missiles in Cuba.[61]

According to the CIA's internal tradecraft notes, a way to counter enemy deception is "to show increased respect for the deceiver's ability to manipulate perceptions and judgments by compromising collection systems and planting disinformation."[62] It seems, however, that during the Cuban missile crisis the NPIC analysts, ignoring all CIA's standard tradecraft practices, demonstrated a total lack of respect for the Soviets' disinformation abilities.

The fact that the American intelligence community apparently accepted the U-2 photos as hard evidence of the presence of missiles in Cuba could be interpreted as an indication not only of a gross violation of elementary intelligence practices but also of a high degree of incompetence. A simple evaluation of the information provided by the U-2 photos following the established procedures operating in the American intelligence services would have shown an appraisal close to a C5, that is, reliability of the source = C (fairly reliable), accuracy of information = 5 (improbable) (see Appendix 1). The problem I have with reaching the logical conclusion expressed above is that, first, I have a high opinion of the professionalism of American intelligence officers, and, secondly, that one of the axioms in the profession is that, in the field of intelligence and espionage, things are never what they seem to be.

Moreover, it seems that not all members of the American intelligence community accepted the U-2 photographs as hard evidence. Ten years after the crisis, in an article which appeared in *Studies in Intelligence*, a classified publication whose circulation was restricted to CIA officers and made available to the public only a few years ago, Sherman Kent affirms that, though he didn't know about any Ex Comm members who had doubts about the credibility of the U-2 photographs, he knew about a few very important officers at the Agency who did.[63]

Therefore, I have come to believe that, in the particular case of the unproved, but blindly accepted belief that the Soviets deployed strategic missiles and their nuclear warheads in Cuba in 1962, there is more than meets the eye. I base my doubts not only on a hunch, but on two facts. The first is that the U.S. didn't force an *in situ* inspection of the Soviet ships leaving Cuba —probably the only way to verify beyond any reasonable doubt that the missiles had actually been in Cuba and were now on their way back to the Soviet Union.[64] The second one is that, though a high number of American documents relating to the missile crisis —a great part of them dealing with anecdotal information about the *opinions* of the participants— have been declassified and made available to scholars, almost all signals intelligence (SIGINT), including communications, electronic and nuclear radiation intelligence (NUCINT), is still kept classified and held under a tight lid.

Gen. William Y. Smith, who was a Major and an assistant to Gen. Maxwell Taylor in the White House at the time, has reported a very interesting detail. While reviewing message traffic from U.S. intelligence sources on Soviet military activity, Gen. Smith discovered a report about a U.S. Navy ship which apparently had picked up suspicious levels of radioactivity emitted by a Soviet freighter, the *Poltava*. He suggested to Gen. Taylor that he ask Admiral Anderson if the emanations meant the ship was carrying nuclear warheads. At the next Joint Chief's meeting, Taylor posed the question to Anderson, who replied, somewhat embarrassed, that he had not seen the message. Later that morning, Anderson's office informed Smith that the report had little significance, that Smith had misread it.[65]

It makes sense to believe, therefore, that at the time the U.S. had the means to detect radiation from nuclear warheads leaving Cuba, without having to board the Soviet ships. But, again, no mention has been made of this important fact in any of the declassified documents on the Cuban missile crisis. Also, Admiral Anderson's behavior, as described by Gen. Smith, is strange, to say the least, because, contrary to Admiral Anderson's claims, that report was extremely significant.

There is a serious misconception which has become the gospel of many leftist and liberal American journalists: The CIA, like the gang that couldn't shoot straight, is inept and incompetent.[66] But you cannot take at face value everything you read or hear about how inept and stupid the CIA is.[67] The problem is that everything one ever hears about the CIA are its failures, but the very nature of intelligence work precludes them from announcing their successes. (This, added to the fact that one must take with extreme caution any intelligence services' claims about their successes or failures.) Thus, I think that, in the handling of the Cuban missile crisis, the CIA was not incompetent, but just deceitful —which, in the case of an intelligence service is not a criticism, but a compliment.

If this sounds too close to a conspiracy theory, I have to confess that I don't have a problem with that. At any rate, intelligence, espionage, and counterintelligence, ultimately are just key elements of a conspiracy to fool, confuse and eventually defeat the enemy.

A Logical Conclusion

My assertion that the presence of Soviet strategic missiles and their nuclear warheads in Cuba in 1962 is yet to be proved, is not a speculative, unsubstantiated hypothesis, but an uncontrovertible fact. Moreover, there is evidence showing that the photointerpreters at the NPIC used flawed methodological analyses in an effort to prove the existence of strategic nuclear missiles in Cuba in 1962.

Intelligence services could exist only by dealing in hard knowledge. Until now, however, the alleged evidence provided to substantiate the claims that the Soviets deployed strategic nuclear missiles in Cuba in 1962 is so flimsy that it makes it irrelevant.[68] As scientists like to say: extraordinary claims require extraordinary proof. In this case, the extraordinary proof has yet to appear. Up to this day, these claims seem to be more the product of theoretical, or perhaps ideological, considerations than direct observation.

In the case of seminal, but controversial events like the USS *Maine* explosion in Havana's bay, the sinking of the *Lusitania*, the Japanese attack on Pearl Harbor, and the Cuban missile crisis, just to mention a few, history has been manipulated through the suppression of data that challenges the prevailing interpretations. Moreover, it seems that the operant behavior for most scholars has been that if the facts do not agree with their theories, then such facts must be simply ignored.

What is simply amazing is that most of the American academic community, which firmly dismisses as nonsense UFOs, ESP, and astrology, accepted as models of scholarly research early studies of the Cuban missile crisis based almost entirely on highly questionable information provided by an administration that felt pride in its "management" of the news. The second generation of scholars is making a similar mistake, now based on questionable information coming from the Cuban and Russian governments, which are known for going way beyond mere news management in their total control of information. Scholars of the Cuban missile crisis should have treated the information coming from such unreliable sources with at least the same skepticism they reserve for claims of UFO abductions.

In the late 1960s, Neal D. Houghton said that recent American foreign policy had been so poorly conceived and so dangerous that it was unworthy of the dominant intellectual support it had received. Too much of what has been passing for political science scholarship, he added, has been little more than footnoted rationalizations and huckstering of that policy.[69] Most of the recent American scholarly studies about the Cuban missile crisis are evident proof that Houghton's observation is still valid. In a field that prides itself for detached analysis and intellectualism, dogma and extra-academic interests run rampant.

Despite all the U.S. photographic "hard" evidence (which constitutes no evidence at all); the assertions made by alleged participants in the Crisis (whose credibility is highly questionable); and the Soviet documentary evidence recently uncovered (which has not been corroborated by independently checked, unfriendly sources), the presence of Soviet strategic missiles and their nuclear warheads in Cuba in 1962 is, to this moment, just a figment of some people's imagination; a cargo cult which, like a malignant *meme*,[70] has become part of the American belief system. But, as Blight, Allyn, and Welch have rightly pointed out, "deeply rooted beliefs die hard."[71]

Chapter 11

Starry-eyed Historians VS. Hard-nosed Spies

The past telescopes into the present.
—James Jesus Angleton.

The Cuban missile crisis continues to attract the attention of historians, the media and the general public. Until recently, most of the information available about the crisis had come from the American side. Since the late 1980s, however, the study of the crisis expanded to the other two participants in the event, and included Cuban and Soviet scholars and government officials —Fidel Castro among them.

The international scholarly experiment, a five-year project organized first by Harvard University's Center for International Affairs and later by the Center for Foreign Policy Development at Brown University, relied mostly in what they called "critical oral history," which Raymond L. Garthoff defined as "the synthesis of recollections of participants with declassified documentation and the analyses of historians."[1]

The first meeting took place in Cambridge, Massachusetts, in March 1987, and involved mostly American scholars and government officials. Some recently declassified American documents were brought to the meeting for the participants to read. The second meeting, also held in Cambridge, was similar, except that three Soviets were able to attend. The third meeting was held in Moscow in January 1991, and a few Cubans joined the group. Finally, a three-day meeting took place in Havana in January, 1992, with the presence of Cuban, Soviet, and American scholars and officials, among them Robert S. McNamara. Fidel Castro himself was present during the three days of the meeting. New declassified documents of the crisis from the different parties involved were made available to the scholars. A new meeting in Havana has been scheduled for October 11-12, 2002. Cuban Vice President José Ramón Fernández, announced that Cuba will declassify all documents that could be fundamental in clarifying facts about the crisis.[2]

It was during the 1992 meeting in Havana that a Soviet officer, Army General Anatoly Gribkov, who allegedly was responsible for planning the missile operation in 1962, dropped a bombshell. According to Gribkov, who confirmed the presence of both strategic and tactical nuclear warheads on Cuban soil, Soviet Army General Pliyev, the Soviet military commander in Cuba, had been given authorization to fire nuclear missiles against an American invasion force if he considered it necessary, without further authorization from the Kremlin.[3]

Are Historians too Gullible to Write Spy Stories?

The meetings have stirred the interest of many scholars, and a spate of books and papers about the crisis has been published since. The Cambridge and Moscow meetings have been studied in detail in James G. Blight and David A. Welch, *On the Brink: Americans and Soviets Reexamine the Cuban Missile Crisis* (New York: Hill and Wang, 1989; rev. ed., Noonday Press, 1990). New studies about the crisis include Michael R. Beschloss, *The Crisis Years: Kennedy and Khrushchev, 1960-1963*; and Raymond L. Garthoff, *Reflections on the Cuban Missile Crisis* (Washington: Brookings Institution, 1987, rev. ed., 1989); Aleksandr Fursenko and Timothy Naftali, *"One Hell of a Gamble," The Secret History of the Cuban Missile Crisis* (New York: W.W. Norton, 1997); Richard Ned Lebow and Janice Gross Stein, *We All Lost the Cold War* (Princeton, N.J.: Princeton University Press, 1994); James G. Blight, Bruce J. Allyn, and David A. Welch, *Cuba on the Brink: Castro, the Missile Crisis and the Soviet Collapse* (New York: Pantheon Books, 1993); Bruce J. Allyn, James G. Blight, and David A. Welch, eds., *Back to the Brink: Proceeding of the Moscow Conference on the Cuban Missile Crisis, January 27-28, 1989*, CSIA Occasional Paper no. 9, Lathan, Md.: University Press of America, 1992; and James G. Blight and David A Welch, eds., *Intelligence and the Cuban Missile Crisis* (London: Frank Cass, 1998), just to name a few.

All of these studies show a high level of scholarship. What they lack, though, is a healthy amount of skepticism. Dealing with spies, intelligence and espionage, the authors of these books apparently ignore that a cardinal rule of the profession is that in the dark world of intelligence and espionage things are seldom what they seem. A curious characteristic of most of these books is that, though dealing with spies and espionage, their authors display an almost total ignorance of the craft of intelligence and espionage.

Upon reading many of these works, one feels that their authors apparently have accepted at face value most of the information in the form of declassified documents supplied by the parties involved, and apparently believe that most of the officials who attended the meetings have either told the truth or just made a few honest mistakes. The authors of these studies seem to ignore that most of the people they have dealt with in these meetings are intelligence operatives, that is, professional liars.[4]

Case officers whose job is recruiting and managing agents practice lying and deception as an art form and a way of life. They learn how to convince others that they are something very different from what they really are. Good deception combines the imagination of a fiction writer and the abilities of an actor. Intelligence agencies devote much of the training of their prospective case officers to lying.[5] Once the officers have successfully operated in the field for some time, lying becomes second nature to them, to the point that most of them don't know any longer when they are telling the truth or not.

But the authors I have mentioned above seem to ignore that espionage is a trade based on deception where cynicism and ruthlessness predominate. Nowhere in these works can one find a clear, unequivocal disclaimer alerting the reader about the potential disinformation value of the sources. A notable, and I would say unique, exception is Vladislav M. Zubok's paper "Spy VS. Spy: The KGB VS. the CIA."[6] Showing an uncommon in-depth knowledge of the spy's work, in the introduction to his paper Zubok warns his readers:

> For all their fascination, the internal KGB documents cited in this article should also be treated with a good deal of caution. They contain references to events, plans, individuals, and explicit or implicit relationships that are uncorroborated and should be carefully investigated and cross-checked with other evidence before their accuracy and significance can be confidently gauged. Many of the assertions contained in the documents will require, in particular, collation with relevant materials in the archives of other governments and intelligence agencies, especially the CIA, and analysis by specialists in the history of intelligence. ...those who evaluate the documents that do become available must keep in mind that evidence of crucial matters may have been deliberately destroyed, distorted, fabricated, or simply never committed to paper.[7]

But in the works I have mentioned above some participants are introduced to the unwary reader as former public servants who, by some chance of fate, played an important role in the event. This, however, is not always the case. As a typical example I can mention the case of Alexei Alexeev, the first Soviet official to arrive in Cuba after the advent of Fidel Castro to power. Even though his intelligence activities are not flatly denied, Alexeev is usually introduced as the former Soviet ambassador to Havana, without mentioning the important fact that his diplomatic position was just a cover for his true job.[8]

The fact that Alexeev, a senior KGB officer, was the first Soviet official selected to be sent to Havana clearly indicates that, from the very beginning, the Soviets saw Cuba and Castro essentially as an intelligence operation. Further proof of this is that most of the Soviet personnel sent to Havana for the first contacts with Castro and his people, including Nikolai Leonov and the first Soviet ambassador to Havana, Sergei M. Kudryavtsev, were also intelligence officers.

In a 1995 paper about a speech Castro allegedly gave in 1968, scholars Brenner and Blight mention that the document "is usefully read in conjunction with notes taken by the Soviet Ambassador to Cuba, Aleksandr Alekseev, during meetings immediately after the crisis between Soviet Deputy Premier Anastas Mikoyan and

Cuba's main leaders."[9] But, as we all know, or should know, ex-KGB officers are not free to share their notes —most likely used to file their secret reports— with scholars.

Ex-intelligence officers of any country must keep silence about any work they may have performed while on active duty. Often, an intelligence service calls on a retired employee to perform temporary or part-time work for which he is well qualified. The maintenance of discretion is inherent in the nature of an intelligence employee, whether he is on active duty or retired.[10] Like their CIA counterparts, KGB officers have a for-life bond of secrecy, and intelligence services don't take lightly any violation of it.[11] Therefore, it is misleading to tell the unwary readers that they are reading Alexeev's notes when what they are actually reading most likely is a version of Alexeev's notes carefully sanitized, or fabricated from scratch, by KGB disinformation specialists. Moreover, introducing KGB officer Aleksandr I. Shitov under his intelligence covers of *TASS* correspondent and Soviet Ambassador to Cuba and under his intelligence pseudonym Alekseev, without alerting the public that they are dealing not with a journalist or a diplomat, but with a highly efficient intelligence officer, is highly disingenuous, to say the least.

Historians and Intelligence Analysts

The goal of the historian and the intelligence analyst is basically the same: search for facts and establish the truth. Their approach, however, is totally different. Give a historian a document and he will do three things: check it for accuracy; evaluate its place in the context of his own knowledge of its subject matter; and try to exploit it for producing a finished paper or book.

Now give the same document to an intelligence officer. He will do four things, but quite different ones. First, he will examine it to verify that its source is the one it purports to be; second, he will try to know if its source has disseminated it wittingly or unwittingly, and, if unwittingly, if its source knows the fact that the document has been compromised; third, he will attempt to find, guess, or intuit the source's real motives for disseminating it; and, finally, he will try to use it —by divulging it, or by not divulging it— to influence somebody, either his employers or his employees.

The historian is trained to react *ad causam*, the intelligence analyst *ad hominem*. The historian focuses on subject matter and its relevance to understanding recorded events, the intelligence analyst focuses on people and their motives. The tools of the historian are quite different from the tools of the intelligence analysts and, therefore, the results of their research will show considerable differences. As a rule, intelligence analysts always keep in mind that some of their sources, particularly live ones, are going to try to intentionally deceive them. They take vulnerability to deception into account, and do so explicitly. Therefore, one can argue that intelligence analysts have better methodological tools than historians to successfully analyze intelligence operations, where deceit and disinformation play an important role.[12]

In the study of events like the Cuban missile crisis, we must always keep in mind that we are not dealing with innocuous aspects of history like the origins of New Orleans Jazz, or Roman architecture during the Republic. On the contrary, this is very recent history with a high content of intelligence and espionage and, therefore, deception. And, because of the fact that the basic principles of tradecraft don't change much among its different practitioners, intelligence services are reluctant to give their past, current, or potential opponents any feedback about the success or failure of their past operations. As a matter of fact their goal is to disinform their opponents as much as they can by keeping them in the dark. As a rule, most of what an intelligence service claims have been its successes are most likely its failures, and viceversa. In intelligence and espionage, things are seldom what they seem. Under this light, both the Bay of Pigs and the Penkovsky affair, respectively the CIA's worst failure and its greatest success, need to be reevaluated.

Contrary to intelligence analysts, most historians are wedded to the theory that "facts explain events" which, in the last resort, depends on the way in which you choose your facts. They seem to forget that facts are just information, and information is not true intelligence until it has been validated. As I mentioned in the previous chapter, only information that has been secretly taken from the enemy should be considered *bona fide* intelligence. But, if the opposition has voluntarily turned it over, it automatically becomes suspect of being disinformation.

For example, historians Philip Brenner and James G. Blight apparently felt highly honored that Fidel Castro made available to them a declassified portion of a secret speech he allegedly gave in 1968 to the Central Committee of his "Communist" Party.[13] Had Brenner and Blight being intelligence officers instead of scholars, their reaction would have been quite different. In the first place, they would have felt extremely concerned that Castro had selected precisely them as recipients of the scoop and would have tried to find the true reasons behind it. Secondly, had they not reported Castro's action immediately to their superiors as a subtle pitch to recruit them as his agents of influence, it would have generated concern and suspicion among their bosses regarding their true loyalties. Third, they would have tried to confirm the existence and the veracity of the speech by other independent, preferably Castro-unfriendly, sources. Finally, even after the true occurrence of the speech would had been confirmed, coming from an unreliable source such as Fidel Castro —a confessed, unashamed liar[14]— they would have doubted its veracity and, faced with the impossibility of confirming it, would have assigned very low intelligence value to the speech.[15]

Intelligence officers believe that intelligence can be distinguished from deception by judging how well it fits in with the rest of the intelligence reports. If it neatly dovetails with other validated reports, it is assumed to be valid intelligence. For example, General Gribkov's assertion that Soviet officers in Cuba had discretionary control over the use of nuclear weapons goes against what is known about Soviet military practices. Therefore, it would have been received by intelligence analysts with extreme skepticism and, just out of *déformation profesionelle*, with extreme suspicion.[16] The main question that would have crossed the mind of an intelligence officer after hearing General Gribkov's unsupported claims would not have been whether or not his assertions were true, which obviously they were not, but instead whether who Gribkov truly was and what were his true intentions for dropping that bombshell. Evidently, as I have shown in the two examples above, we are dealing here with two very different methodologies, both of them valid for different purposes, but which yield very different results.

The Spy With a Multiple Personality Disorder

A case which exemplifies the risks historians run by the indiscriminate acceptance of spies' stories, is evidenced in a recent book, *Intelligence and the Cuban Missile Crisis*, edited by James G. Blight and David A. Welch.[17] As the name indicates, the book offers a collection of studies about the Cuban missile crisis from the point of view of intelligence. An interesting innovation to the genre is that, previous to the publication, the authors of the different papers held a wide exchange of information about their papers in progress, and they quote each other extensively along the whole length of the book. Among the contributors are professor Raymond L. Garthoff, Aleksandr Fursenko and Timothy Naftali, James J. Wirtz, and Beth A. Fischer. Blight and Welch provided both the Introduction and the paper that closes the book.

As a bonus, the book offers a first: a paper by Domingo Amuchástegui, "Cuban Intelligence and the October Crisis." Amuchástegui is allegedly an ex-member of the Cuban intelligence services who played an important role during the crisis. According to him, his purpose is "to examine the role of the Cuban intelligence in the genesis, management, and resolution of the crisis."

In the introduction to his paper, Amuchástegui offers a disclaimer: "Readers should be aware that my account is based primarily upon my own recollections from my experiences with the General Staff, the Cuban Ministry of Foreign Affairs (MINREX), and the Intelligence Department of the Ministry of the Interior (MININT)." Notwithstanding his disclaimer, however, Amuchástegui's paper is extensively quoted by the rest of the authors collaborating in the volume. Being a primer in the exposition of the inner workings of the secretive Cuban intelligence services, it is no wonder that his paper is the one which has singlehandedly affected in the highest degree the papers produced by the rest of the writers.

There are, however, some things about Amuchástegui himself, that don't add up. In the Introduction to the book, Blight and Welch describe Amuchástegui as a person "who had recently come to the United States from Cuba."[18] But this, though perhaps is the story Amuchástegui told the editors of the book, is not exactly the truth. Domingo (Chomy) Amuchástegui did not come to the U.S. from Cuba. He came from Mexico, where he had defected several years ago.

Defectors are an important source of information about the inner workings of a rival intelligence service. Once a defector[19] is initially accepted as such by an intelligence service, he is put through a long process of exhaustive interrogation —which may range from friendly to extremely unfriendly and sometimes hostile— in order both to get the maximum information from him and to establish his *bona fides*. After the process ends, and the *bona fides* of the defector is established —something that usually is extremely difficult— he is usually relocated under a new name, to live a quite, unmolested life while receiving his paychecks from the country who accepted him, as a retribution for the services rendered.

But intelligence professionals have mixed feelings about defectors, because a defector is basically a traitor, and a person who committed treason against his own country is never to be fully trusted. Moreover, defectors are also the weapon of choice of rival intelligence services for planting disinformation. As such, they are seen with extreme suspicion. Some of them are not very successful in establishing their *bona fides*, and suffer the consequences. A typical example in the history of intelligence is the case of Yuri Ivanovich Nosenko.

Nosenko, a KGB officer who defected to the U.S., eventually became a prisoner of the CIA when his debriefers found anomalies in his disclosures about the KGB. James Jesus Angleton, the CIA's legendary Chief of Counterintelligence, became convinced that Nosenko was a disinformation agent. Nosenko was held for four years in solitary confinement in a small cell at Camp Peary, Virginia, under a harsh regimen of interrogations, sleep deprivation, and semistarvation. Though eventually he was released, his *bona fides* was never fully established.

I have brought the Nosenko case as an example to show that, contrary to historians, intelligence officers take very seriously the establishment of the *bona fides* of a defector. In the case of Amuchástegui, there are some intriguing aspects of his story which merit to be studied in detail.

In his paper, Amuchástegui claims that "I was with MINREX from 1959 to 1963 and from 1965 to 1966."[20] But this contradicts his previous assertion that he was with the General Staff, which, as ministries of foreign affairs have no General Staff, one may assume it is the Cuban Army. But how, one may ask, was he at the same time an Army officer and an official with the MINREX? Moreover, in an interview he gave to C-SPAN, he was introduced as a former "Cuban Revolutionary Armed Forces Political Officer." So, if one is to believe his claims, Amuchástegui was, at the same time, an official at the Ministry of Foreign Affairs, an intelligence officer at the Cuban intelligence, and a political officer in the Army.[21]

In his paper Amuchástegui gives the readers a detailed account of his long, successful career in Cuba:

> From 1978 to 1993 I held research and teaching positions in the University of Havana Higher College of Education Department of Social Sciences and History (1978-88), the Center for Studies of Africa and the Middle East of the Central Committee of the Communist Party of Cuba (1982-83), the Ministry of the Revolutionary Armed Forces (MINFAR) College

of National Defense (1991-93), and the MINREX Higher Institute of International Relations (1989-93).[22]

Like most defectors, however, Amuchástegui has a very selective memory. He fails to remember in his biography, among other things, the long period he spent in the mid-1970s in a Cuban military prison camp, undergoing "rehabilitation" after his conviction on charges of ideological diversionism and other political offenses against the Castro government. Of course, nobody expects a person, and particularly an ex-spy, to supply incriminating evidence against himself.

In his paper, Amuchástegui makes reference several times to his direct involvement at high levels of the Cuban intelligence during the Crisis. "To those of *us* working in the intelligence community ..."[23] "*We* discovered these ..."[24] "*We* received instructions ..."[25] "*Our* conclusion was ..."[26] "The reluctance of Soviet commanders to comply with Khrushchev's order was reported *to me* by Raúl Roa ..."[27] But, if he was with MINREX at the time of the missile crisis, how can he explain his presence at such high levels of the Cuban intelligence? Moreover, if he was at MINREX, at the Army's General Staff, and at high levels at the Cuban intelligence, how can he explain his claims that he was, at the same time, a political officer in the staff of the National School of Revolutionary Instructors Osvaldo Sánchez Cabrera?

Amuchástegui's paper offers to the naïve reader a lot of unheard stories about the inner workings of the Cuban intelligence during the crisis. Raymond Garthoff mentions in his paper one of the most controversial. "Domingo Amuchástegui reports that Castro saw his purge of the oldline Moscow Communists in Cuba as a preliminary clearing of the decks to allow closer collaboration with the Soviet Union." Adding, with evident surprise, that "There was no evidence at the time to support such a counterintuitive evaluation."[28] Professor Garthoff's surprise is justified, because there was no evidence at the time, nor does Amuchástegui brings any evidence now, to support his far-fetched assertion. And the main reason for Amuchástegui's lack of evidence is simply because the assertion is false, and if Castro ever said that, which I doubt, it was nothing but disinformation.

In his essay, Amuchástegui claims that "I have been aided in the preparation of this essay by individuals with extensive experience directly relevant to this topic who must, unfortunately, remain nameless, for personal security reasons."[29] In some cases, however, the reasons for his secrecy do not seem to be security, but unscrupulous use of sources. For example, his assertion of KGB allegations that they were leaking accurate information about the deployment of the missiles so as to mask it, was reported almost twenty years ago by former Cuban intelligence officer Juan Vivés.[30] Amuchástegui's claims seem too similar to Vivés' report to be just the product of a coincidence.

A common characteristic of most defectors is that they usually try to inflate their value by making exaggerate claims about their personal role in their previous job. This is not to say that all the information Amuchástegui brings up in his paper is not true. That, we don't know, even though one may safely assume that at least some of it is true, because he heard it, probably some time after the crisis, from some of his friends —like Paco Chavarri— at high levels in the MINREX. But his assertion that Raúl Roa, the Cuban Minister of Foreign Affairs, reported *to him* anything at all is pure baloney. Besides the fact that Amuchástegui was not with MINREX at the time, he was too unimportant, too wet behind the ears, to have access to Roa, much less to have Roa report anything to him.

Still, one cannot blame Amuchástegui for trying to sell himself as the high quality intelligence product he is not. Defection is not an easy thing to adjust to. It entails much more than catching a plane, flying abroad, and asking for political asylum. The psychological upheaval is excruciating, and it takes months before a person can decide himself to betray his own country. Life in exile is not easy, and people have to struggle hard for their survival. That is, if Amuchástegui is actually what he purports to be, and not a very different person.[31]

Domingo Amuchástegui defected in 1997 from his position in the Cuban government —whatever it was— while in Mexico during a government-sponsored visit. Following the typical behavior of intelligence defectors, he went into hiding for some time, until he resurfaced a few years ago in Miami. Just a few months after arriving in Miami he landed a well-paid job at *CUBANews*, a publication of the *Miami Herald*, and later became a Research Associate at the University of Miami's Institute for Cuban and Cuban-American Studies (ICCAS). After that, his name has been popping up in the media. This is quite unusual, because defectors normally hide themselves, or at least keep a very low profile, for long years, some of them for their whole life.

There are some other gray areas in Amuchástegui's cover story which don't add up. In the first place, intelligence officers, particularly high-level intelligence officers, as Amuchástegui claims to have been, just don't quit their jobs, walk away, and move to exotic lands. Secondly, a defector, as I expressed above, is basically a traitor,[32] and intelligence services don't take traitors lightly. The fact that Amuchástegui is living a normal life under his true name in Miami, and has become a sort of media star on the rise, is strange, to say the least. Finally, it is not a secret that Blight and Welch are sympathetic to Castro. Therefore, their enthusiastic acceptance of Amuchástegui, allegedly a traitor to the Castro government, as an important contributor to their book, is very difficult to swallow. Furthermore, in an article appeared in November, 2001, in which Wayne S. Smith tries to prove that the true terrorist is not Castro, but the anti-Castro Cubans in Florida, he calls Amuchástegui "a thoughtful Cuban defector."[33] Coming from Smith, a hyper Castro-friendly scholar, this strange recommendation may be an important clue as to where Amuchástegui's true allegiance is.

The main problem with Amuchástegui's paper is that what is true in it is not new, and what is new is not true. Yet, if one cannot blame Amuchástegui for his efforts to try to sell his dubious merchandise to the highest bidder, one can surely blame Blight and Welch for having accepted his unsubstantiated claims at face value, without previously having established his *bona fides*. The inclusion of Amuchástegui's paper in this book, and the fact that his claims have been extensively used by the rest of the contributors to reach conclusions and establish assessments of intelligence aspects of the crisis, has tarnished the value of what may have been an important scholarly contribution to the history of the Cuban missile crisis. This is the hard price well intentioned scholars pay when they try to play the dirty game of espionage —that is, if one accepts at face value that their intentions have been pure, which may not have been the case.

Chapter 12

The Blight, Allyn, Welch, *et al.*, Paper Mill

> *The amount of misinformation that has appeared in print and then elevated to history through constant repetition is appalling.*
>
> —David C. Martin, *Wilderness of Mirrors*.

In the previous chapter, I studied the possibility that some scholars may have been unwittingly duped by Castro's intelligence services to accept dubious, unfounded information as true historical evidence. In this chapter I am going to analyze the possibility that, at least some of them, may have been, wittingly or unwittingly, recruited by Castro's intelligence services as collaborators, agents, and agents of influence[1] to disseminate false or misleading information.

I know that analyses *ad hominem* are considered anathema in the academic community, but this particular group of scholars has been dealing with subjects heavily involved with the black arts of intelligence and espionage. In addition, while doing their research they have been heavily involved with intelligence agencies and former and active intelligence officers.

As I previously mentioned, the historian is trained to react *ad causam*, the intelligence analyst *ad hominem*. The historian focuses on subject matter and its relevance to understanding recorded events, the intelligence analyst focuses on people and their motives. Most people see academic books and papers as the ultimate product of the human intellect, totally removed from the daily life of passions, personal interest and pet peeves. They seem to forget, however, that behind every academic book and paper there is an author who is a living human being, with interests, political ideology, ego, biases, as well as aesthetic and sexual preferences. Also, the fact that a scholar is intelligent, bright and smart in his academic life does not mean that he cannot be a fool[2] or a maniac in other aspects of his personal life and, despite all claims of detachment and professionalism, the two aspects are inextricably linked.

In the last ten years, the Blight, Allyn, Welch, *et al.*, paper mill has been producing papers and books about Cuba just like Khrushchev claimed the U.S.S.R. was producing missiles: like sausages.[3*] However, given the fact that most of Khrushchev's missiles were actually dummies, I suggest that we take a second look not only at their books and papers but also at the authors, the same way a counterintelligence officer would have done when trying to disprove a defector's *bona fides*: with extreme distrust and skepticism, sometimes bordering on open hostility. There is nothing personal in this approach; it is only an established practice of tradecraft used by most intelligence services around the world.

If some of the scholars I am mentioning in this analysis get upset with this approach my only suggestion is that they should go back and get to study other subjects. If you cannot stand the heat, get out of the kitchen. But, if they continue to be interested in the subject of intelligence and espionage, and keep mixing themselves up with the practitioners of the black arts in such a carefree manner, the least they could expect is that, sooner or later, they would be judged by the standards of the trade.[4]

Scholars and Intelligence Services

In early 2001 an article by David N. Gibbs, an Associate Professor at the University of Arizona, ignited a debate about the collaboration of some American scientists with the CIA.[5] Gibbs' article, however, only brought new controversy over an old subject, because the close collaboration between scholars and intelligence agencies is not new.[6] In its issue of December 20, 1919, *The Nation* published an article by Franz Boas, one of the pioneers of academic anthropology in America, entitled "Scientists as Spies." In it, Boas accused Samuel Lothrop, Sylvanus Morley, Herbert Spinden, and John Mason, of having abused their professional research positions to conduct espionage missions in Central America during WWI.[7]

It is known that an American anthropologist worked closely with the CIA in providing intelligence for the CIA-sponsored operation that overthrew President Jacobo Arbenz in Guatemala in 1954. There is evidence that during the Vietnam war, documents from the private office of UCLA anthropologist Michael Moerman proved that several American anthropologists helped the war effort by sharing with the military their ethnographic investigations. In 1965, Norwegian sociologist Johan Galtung revealed the collaboration of some anthropologists with Project Camelot, a U.S. secret counterinsurgency program put in practice in Latin America.[8]

According to Gibbs, though the CIA-academia connection has been known for a long time, as well as the fact that during the 1940s and 1950s the CIA and the U.S. military intelligence were a major source of funding for many social scientists, it was commonly believed that those ties had been cut after the CIA scandals in the aftermath of the Vietnam war. However, an article by Chris Mooney, which appeared in the magazine *Lingua Franca,* asserts that, far from having disappeared, the CIA-academia links actually continued and have even flourished after the end of the Cold War.[9]

In his article, Mooney revealed that "A 1996 Directorate of Intelligence memo calls 'public outreach'[10] a top priority and targets academia in particular. According to experts on U.S. intelligence, the strategy has worked. Since the end of the Cold War, spies and scholars have grown more cozy than at any time...."[11]

Some scholars apparently do not agree with suggestions that their ties with the CIA might bias their scholarship. The fact, however, is so obvious that it is not easy to understand why some scholars refuse to see it —unless they are very naïve or are actually still working for the CIA. The failure of some scholars to see the danger involved in this collaboration is disturbing. According to Gibbs,

> Something is seriously wrong here. The CIA is not an ordinary government agency; it is an espionage agency and the practices of espionage, which include secrecy, propaganda and deception are diametrically opposed to those of scholarship. Scholarship is supposed to favor objective analysis and open discussion. The close relationship between intelligence agencies and scholars thus poses a conflict of interests. After all, the CIA has been a key party to many of the international conflicts that academics must study. If political scientists are working for the CIA, how can they function as objective and disinterested scholars?[12]

Gibbs' *LA Times* article elicited an e-mail by Francis A. Boyle, a Professor of Law and member of the American Political Science Association, arguing that members of the APSA who were working for the CIA were violating the Association's Ethical Rules and should be censured or expelled from the organization.[13]

But, in all the justified criticism generated against these American scholars who prostituted their prestige to justify the Cold War, there seems to be a blind spot. All criticism is directed against American scholars who have been recruited by American intelligence services, but no mention is made of American scholars who may have been recruited by foreign intelligence services.[14]

Mimicking Gibbs' argument quoted above, I would argue that the failure of some scholars and their critics to see the danger of collaborating with Fidel Castro is disturbing. Something is seriously wrong here. The Castro regime is not an ordinary government. It is a totalitarian dictatorship whose systematic use of espionage, propaganda and deception is totally opposed to the practices of scholarship. This close relationship between Castro's intelligence services and some American scholars thus poses an evident conflict of interests. After all, Castro and his intelligence services have been part of many of the international conflicts these academics study, like the Bay of Pigs, the Cuban missile crisis, and Castro's imperialist war in Angola, just to mention a few. If some political scientists have been collaborating with Castro and his intelligence services, how can they function as objective and disinterested scholars?

Unfortunately, neither Gibbs, nor the rest of the critics of the CIA-academia connection have mentioned the Castro-academia connection. This is a double standard that needs to be addressed.

Having spies and scholars working together presents some risks. It is like having sharks and sardines swimming together in the same tank. Scholars are no match for intelligence officers. They can be easily manipulated and used, wittingly or unwittingly, as channels for disinformation.

I will mention an example to illustrate my point. In the Preface to the Second Edition of their book *On the Brink*, Blight and Welch acknowledge the valuable assistance of several people and institutions, among them "the Center for the Study of the Americas (Havana)."[15]

Faced with such an innocuous mention, the unwary reader may guess that the Center for the Study of America is just another think tank, very similar to the American ones, probably attached to the University of Havana, and staffed by scholars from different fields. However, if Blight and Welch would have taken the time to do some simple research, it would have revealed that the *Centro de Estudios de America* (CEA) is not an independent research organization. Actually, the CEA is one of the many front organizations created by the Cuban intelligence services to conduct propaganda and disinformation operations.

In December of 1974, the National Liberation Directorate of the Cuban DGI (*Dirección General de Inteligencia*), was reorganized as part of the America Department (DA) under the Central Committee of the Cuban Communist Party. The DA centralized control over Cuban intelligence activities for supporting national liberation movements such as Nicaragua and Grenada. It was responsible for planning and coordinating Castro's secret guerrilla and terrorist training camps, and networks for the covert movement of personnel and war matériel from Cuba. It was also an efficient disinformation and propaganda apparatus.

The DA was organized into four regional sections: Central America, South America, the Caribbean, and North America. Attached to the DA, several front organizations were created: among them the Center for Latin American Studies (CEAL) and the Center for [North] American Studies (CEA) —the one Blight and Welch erroneously call the "Center for the Studies of the Americas." Intelligence officers in CEA's staff work under different covers, including diplomats, journalists for Cuba's *Prensa Latina* Agency, personnel of Cubana de Aviación airlines, the Institute for Friendship With the Peoples, and various Cuban front business companies.

El *Departamento America* (DA), for many years under Castro's direct control through his spymaster Manuel Piñeiro (barbarroja), was reportedly the most powerful branch of the Cuban intelligence services. In 1983 it had between 200 and 300 active officers. The DA draws on the expertise and support of the DGI, sharing manpower to conduct specific intelligence operations. It specializes in socioeconomic studies used as intelligence background for Castro's subversive plans in the region —a sort of Castroist Project Camelot.

In 1996, as a result of a long rivalry between the Army, under the command of Raúl Castro, and the intelligence services, under the command of Manuel Piñeiro and Juan Abrahantes, the CEA became the focus of a big scandal and a subsequent purge. Though some of the CEA officers were accused of different ideological weaknesses, the real motive was that, after the strange deaths of Abrahantes and Piñeiro, and the execution of Ochoa and Tony de la Guardia by firing squads, Raúl seized the opportunity to gain control over the Cuban intelligence apparatus.[16]

Historians involved in dealings with ex-spies, particularly during their visits to countries like Cuba and Russia, are apparently oblivious to the grave risks they run. One of the main goals of intelligence officers working in the field is the recruiting of agents.[17] Intelligence officers are carefully trained in this difficult ability which, once mastered, becomes second nature to them. Most historians involved in these projects see themselves as emotionally detached, objective scholars, far away from the world of lies and intrigue they are trying to disentangle. But, to spies —ruthless professionals with a peculiar idea of fair-play and ethics— these scholars are fair game.

Most historians dealing with intelligence officers in these countries[18] would be shocked if they were shown the extensive files the intelligence services have carefully compiled about them. These files include very personal aspects of their lives, including their sexual inclinations,[19] drinking habits, financial status, political leanings, and the like. No wonder the spies[20] historians have met during their trips to Cuba and Russia seem so nice and friendly. These intelligence officers know exactly what the scholars' likes and dislikes are and act consequently to gain their trust. Most scholars would be scared if they know of the extensive surveillance and scrutiny they have been under during their visits to these countries. The main reason for this is that, notwithstanding these scholars' impeccable academic credentials, foreign intelligence services will always see them as potential agents of the opposition and deal with them accordingly.

After a visit to a foreign country, an intelligence officer is thoroughly debriefed by trained counterintelligence specialists. To these specialists, the true intelligence is not the information obtained during official contacts and speeches or through declassified official documents. To them, there is more valuable intelligence in the informal contacts, apparently casual conversations and a multitude of minor details, seemingly bearing no connection whatsoever to the main purpose of the trip, which may pass unnoticed to the untrained eye.

In the case of scholars visiting Cuba, an intelligence officer would be very interested in knowing if they had any private meetings with Fidel Castro. The Cuban leader has shown an extraordinary ability to mesmerize and personally recruit visitors, who subsequently act as his unwitting agents of influence. He was successful in recruiting Alexeev,[21] a seasoned KGB officer, so it would be very easy for him to recruit an American scholar.

A well publicized incident last May indicates that Fidel Castro is not alien to resort to blackmail to force other people to do what he wants. Mexican President Vicente Fox discovered this the hard way when Castro released the tapes of a private conversation he had with the Mexican President, which Castro had secretly recorded notwithstanding his assurances to Fox that the conversation would remain private.

After the incident, some people speculated that perhaps Castro customarily keeps records of his dealings with other officials, just in case someday he needs to obtain some favors in exchange for compromising information. Among the possible victims of Castro's blackmail may have been President Bill Clinton, whose pro-Castro leanings during the Elián González incident may have had a more than just ideological explanation.[22]

Actually, President Fox's discovery was not unique. It has been experienced by many visitors to the Caribbean Island. It is widely known that Castro's Cuba operates one of the most efficient intelligence services in the world. Proof of the proficiency of the Cuban intelligence services is the way in which they have penetrated almost all the anti-Castro organizations abroad, as well as many branches of the U.S. government. Unknown to most visitors to the Island, Castro's intelligence services operate an efficient, first class section fully devoted to the entrapment and recruitment of agents, collaborators and agents of influence.[23]

High level defectors of the Castroist intelligence services have revealed an ambitious plan developed in the summer of 1997. The plan, one of Castro's pet projects, was code-named Operation Phoenix and placed under the direct command of General Abelardo Colomé Ibarra (Furry), Minister of the Interior. To accomplish the goals of Operation Phoenix, a special group of intelligence services —named Special Group 2— was created. Their job would be to penetrate the world of the rich and famous, mainly in the United States, to recruit agents of influence.[24] Cardinal in the operation was also the recruiting of visitors to Castro's Cuba.

Operation Phoenix was actually the offspring of "Plan Bravo," an operation that began in April, 1980, at the beginning of the Mariel boatlift. Another intelligence defector, Genaro Pérez, mentioned that, before defecting in mid 1981, he had worked many years undercover for Havanatur, a Miami-based travel agency —actually a front of the Castroist intelligence services— that maintained surveillance of visitors to the Island and recruited agents among them.[25]

But, among other things, Pérez revealed an even more sinister aspect of the operation. According to him, most rooms in Cuba's hotels frequented by foreign visitors have been rigged for audio and video, and DGI agents systematically make recordings for later use as powerful leverage in blackmailing the visitors who refuse to collaborate voluntarily.[26]

Some Castro-friendly authors and journalists have created the myth that pre-Castro's Havana was the sex capital of Latin America. Though this is not exactly true, it is evident that Havana under Castro's puritanical rule has become the sex capital of the Americas. In addition, Havana has become the *filmed* sex capital of the world. The secret vaults at the infamous Villa Maristas, one of the main MININT facilities, are the depository for thousands of video cassettes containing all types of sexual performances secretly recorded by the MININT's technicians.

Jorge Masetti, a former officer of Castro's intelligence services, now in exile in France, has described in detail the subtle methods used in the recruiting of agents of influence, in Cuba and abroad. Traditionally the most sought after potential agents are the ones with ideological sympathies for Castro's revolution.[27] Once a target has been identified as sympathetic to the Castro regime, an officer is assigned to his case, and he becomes in the Cuban intelligence jargon "an official contact under study by an intelligence officer." The case officer cultivates the target by invitations to lunch, or other apparently innocuous social contacts, and presents, like Havana cigars or Cuban rum on special occasions —in the case of a scholar researching a particular subject this may take the form of a visit to Cuba with all expenses paid and exclusive access to documents particularly difficult to obtain.

If the target shows responsiveness to these attentions, he is unknowingly promoted to the rank of "a subject of deep study." An elaborate dossier is opened and a careful process of information gathering about the target's background is put into action. The process may include direct visual surveillance and even sophisticated technical surveillance by eavesdropping devices. Every scrap of information is added to the target's dossier, and includes a psychological profile, family relations, habits, tastes, and sexual preferences.[28] All the data is carefully analyzed to unearth any telltale signs of vulnerability. The information is eventually used to entrap the target.

Entrapment may come in various forms, usually provoking the target into committing any type of minor criminal offense, like selling dollars in the black market or buying prohibited items. But the most effective method is usually sexual. Castro's MININT has made an art of using swallows,[29] ravens[30] and quiet ones[31] to sexually entrap and compromise visitors to the Island —including Castro-friendly American scholars.[32] Attending to apparently innocuous conferences in totalitarian police-states like Castro's Cuba is a risky business.

The process used for entrapment is relatively simple: First a trap is set up — usually a sexual encounter in a hotel room. Once the target is hooked and shown the incriminating photos or videos, he is forced to collaborate. Sexpionage is a brutal form of blackmail, and it is used to compromise persons of all sexual persuasions. Despite specific warnings, people generally show a strong need for local flesh. Standard operating procedure is to set a swallow, raven or quiet one after a target, according to his known sexual preferences —which of course, may include children of both sexes— and then set up a honey trap.

Over the years, thousands of tapes have been archived with the sexual performances of foreigners who have visited Cuba. Castro is an insatiable consumer of this type of product,[33] and no one, not even his close friend, Nobel Prize winner Gabriel García Márquez, has escaped from Castro's surveillance paranoia. According to a defector, Castro gave his friend García Márquez a luxurious mansion to live in, but the house had been secretly rigged for all types of video and audio recording.[34]

Modern tradecraft methods are shaped to a great extent by psychology. Modern intelligence work is about understanding vulnerabilities and predispositions, about knowing how to spot the particular traits that make one person a perfect recruit, and ultimately about using the positive and negative reinforcements that allow a human being to condition the behavior of another. This explains the extended use of the four principles of MICE (Money, Ideology, Compromise, Ego),[35] as powerful tools of tradecraft.

The point I want to make is that supposedly "objective" books and papers written by scholars who frequently visit totalitarian countries like Castro's Cuba, whose intelligence services are known for using entrapment techniques to compromise and recruit people, are not to be trusted, and their allegedly "objective" intellectual production must be read with caution and skepticism. If it happens that some of these authors follow propaganda lines known to have been developed by the disinformation departments of a particular intelligence service, their books and articles must be read with extreme caution.

Of course, this suspicion should apply not only to scholars who are suspected of having been recruited by the CIA, but also to the ones whose behavior indicate that they may have been recruited by other intelligence services. Doing otherwise is not only intellectually dishonest, but makes us witting accomplices in the dirty game of disinformation intelligence agencies like the CIA and Castro's DGI play on an unaware public.

The National Security "Archive"

According to information posted on its Web site, "the National Security Archive began a concerted campaign in 1987 to advance the historical record on the missile crisis." "The availability of previously classified material has enabled scholars both to challenge the conventional wisdom and to revise long-standing historical interpretation of the events that took place before, during, and after October, 1962."[36] But, as I have proved above, far from advancing, since 1987 the historical record on the Cuban missile crisis has moved backwards —among other things, thanks to the concerted disinformation campaign headed by the National Security Archive. Therefore, an analysis of the work of the National Security Archive is in order.

The first thing that calls the attention of an inquisitive reader is the name of this organization. I asked several educated persons, including several college professors and librarians, what was, according to their belief, the National Security Archive. All of them, with the single exception of an archivist who was familiar with it, thought that the National Security Archive was a government organization —which I myself believed for some time.

But, a close look at the Archive's Web site reveals that they are a non-governmental institution that receives no government funding. According to its own definition,

The National Security Archive was founded in 1985 by a group of journalists and scholars who have obtained documentation from the US government under the Freedom of Information Act and sought a centralized repository for these materials. Over the past decade, the Archive has become the world's largest non governmental library of declassified documents.

Therefore, one thing is certain: The name National Security Archive is misleading —it highly evokes "National Archives." It is also misleading that the above paragraph does not mention that the "group of journalists and scholars" who founded the Archive were mostly leftists and left-wing liberals.[37]

It is not a coincidence that the main goal of the Archive has been to obtain documents that prove the evil doings of the CIA, the Department of Defense and other government organizations, particularly about events that occurred during Republican administrations, or documents that show the evil intent of the right wingers in the Army and other branches of the military and intelligence during Democrat[38] administrations.

The second notable thing that calls one's attention about this non-governmental organization's name is the use of the word "archive." Reading on the Archive's Web site I found that it is called an archive, "Despite the Archive's non-traditional role (since the originals remain inside the government —hopefully)."[sic] A cursory view at some of the "documents" the National Security Archive allegedly keeps, shows that they are actually photocopies, not the original documents. Actually, they are not just photocopies, but photocopies of photocopies.[39]

Due to the fact that no mention is found in the site about any authentication procedure of the copies of copies of the documents they keep, one may safely surmise that the archivists at the National Security Archive have never seen, touched or scrutinized the original documents of which they keep alleged faithful copies.[40] This is simply amazing, because in the archival profession the process of authentication, that is, the evaluation of the physical veracity of a document, is a long, difficult and painstaking job. In the case of documents whose source is dubious or have a reputation for dissembling, extra care is taken. But, apparently, the persons in charge of the National Security Archive have trusted the certification of the copies of alleged documents whose originals —they hope— remain inside the government, to the very same organizations most of them despise because of their lying and cunning.

According to the *Random House Webster's College Dictionary*, 1977 edition, an archive is "a place where documents and other materials of historical importance are preserved; the documents and other materials preserved in such a place." This is more or less the definition of the word "archive" found in most dictionaries. No mention is made in any of the dictionaries I consulted, about an archive being a place for the preservation of *copies* of documents. Therefore, if an archive is a depository of documents, and the National Security Archive is actually the depository of photocopies provided by non-reliable sources, of alleged documents which, hopefully, remain in the government's possession, one has to reach the conclusion that the name National Security *Archive* is also misleading, because its role is so "non-traditional" that it is not an archive in the proper sense of the word.

Then, if it is not an archive, what is the National Security Archive? The National Security "Archive" is, at best, a hoax or a clever joke; at worst, an extraordinarily successful exercise in deception.

The Value of Documents

Intelligence professionals believe that all documents are suspect, particularly the ones purposely left as "historical evidence." As Daniel Ellsberg puts it, "The idea that official documents contain the real history of what transpires within the circles of power is a questionable assumption made by too many historians," adding that "So much of the official record is deception written as cover or justification for existing policy."[41]

Sir William Stephenson, the famous spymaster, once said that nothing deceives like a document. To intelligence analysts, all official recorded information is potential disinformation. This includes official records, memos, letters, photographs, etc., including audio recordings and, particularly after the advent of computer generated imaging, film, video recordings and all types of computer data.

It is useful to keep in mind that declassified documents are as untrustworthy as any other source. The fact that a document was labelled classified, and it has been declassified after some period of time, does not guarantee that what it says is the truth, nor that its original intent has not been disinformation.

It seems that, at least in the case of studies about the Cuban missile crisis, Stephenson was close to the truth. In the Introduction to a recent study of the missile crisis, Blight and Welch assert that "While an irreducible element of mystery enshrouds the event, and while imbalances in sources remain, the Cuban missile crisis remains the most thoroughly documented historical encounter of all time."[42] Paradoxically, the Cuban missile crisis remains full of unanswered key questions. Proof of it is that, after so many scholarly studies about the crisis, Blight and Welch's words closely resemble Castro's words when, less than six months after the crisis, he said, "This is a mystery. Maybe historians will be able to clarify this twenty years hence. I don't know."[43] But it is evident that, far from clarifying the event, some American scholars have been adding confusion to it. This doesn't speaks highly of their love for documents.

Not being trained in the black arts of intelligence and espionage, most scholars involved in the study of the Cuban missile crisis have been accepting raw data, that is, information, —i.e., documents, interviews, etc.— as if it were what in the field of intelligence and espionage is called intelligence. They seem to ignore that intelligence is not the product of the collection, but of the analysis of all types of data. It is not until the collected information has been thoroughly evaluated according to certain specific rules and criteria, that it becomes true intelligence. An important element in the evaluation process is the verification that the information has not been intentionally created for disinformation purposes, that is, that the persons who created it have intentionally lied. A close reading of the books produced by these scholars, however, show that the possibility that some of their sources may have intentionally lied for disinformation purposes seems to have been totally absent from their minds.

Documents, or Images of Documents?

As in Magritte's famous picture of a pipe mentioned in Chapter Ten, a copy of a document is *not* the document. Some naïve reader may think that my contention that some of the copies of the documents archived in the National Security Archive may not be a faithful rendering of the original, or that some of them may be total fabrications, is far-fetched. On the contrary, it is a totally justified concern.

My main objection to accepting copies of documents at face value is simply that, for obvious reasons, it has never been an accepted practice among archivists. Moreover, how can one accept without verification alleged copies of documents provided, among others, by the CIA, an organization that has a whole department devoted to the falsification of documents? How can we accept at face value the word of people from organizations whose main job is lying and deceiving?

My concern about the possibility that some of these "declassified' documents may be faked is not the product of a paranoid mind, but a legitimate one based on objective facts. It is widely known that some U.S. government agencies have falsified documents, and that he CIA makes considerable use of forged documents.[44] Just last year, an internal inquiry found that the very Pentagon agency charged with discovering and exposing fraud destroyed incriminating documents and replaced them with falsified ones to avoid embarrassment when its own operations were audited.[45] The Soviet (and now Russian) intelligence service has a department exclusively working full-time in the falsification of documents.[46] Some of the KGB cobblers[47] boasted that their falsifications were better than the originals. The Cuban DGI is proud of the quality of the works of its Technical Support Division, the department responsible for the production of false documents.[48]

Government officials would not accept a copy of a birth certificate or a certificate of naturalization *in lieu* of the original document. Why is one supposed to accept from this same government copies of documents instead of the originals? Americans have apparently become so fascinated with images that they have lost the dividing line between things and their images. But, despite general agreement of the contrary, a thing and its image are not the same thing. In the same fashion, a copy of a document is not the same as the document itself.

Have the signatures and other handwritten notations in these declassified "documents" undergone calligraphic analysis to verify that they are not forgeries? Have the watermarks on the paper been checked to make sure that they were typed on similar paper as the one used in similar documents typed at the same place and at approximately the same time?

For example, in the particular case of Castro's speech mentioned in the previous chapter, did Brenner and Blight actually listen to the original recording? Assuming that they did, did they electronically analyze the tape looking for alterations or forgeries? If what Castro gave them was a transcript of his speech, there is a strong possibility that they have been shortchanged. It is known that Castro heavily edits his own speeches before, and sometimes after, publication.[49] Therefore, if this was the case, what they actually got was not what Castro said, but what Castro would like to have said.

A historian may consider the physical analyses of documents I have mentioned above to be pure and simple paranoia, but they are standard operating procedure for intelligence professionals, who have been using them successfully for centuries.[50] The main reason for these precautions is that all intelligence services have whole sections devoted to the forging of documents. As a matter of fact, document forgery is an important specialization in the intelligence field.[51] Consequently, intelligence officers are very careful not to fall in the same traps they normally set for their opponents.[52]

Most scholars believe that true history only comes out of the study of original documents. Scholars are apparently satisfied when they verify the authenticity of a document. Intelligence officers, go a step further and try to verify its reliability, which is mostly given by the reliability of the person or persons who created it in the first place. Therefore, the last thing they would do would be to trust documents produced by opposing intelligence services —unless those documents, disregarding their truthfulness, help them to prove their point. For example, CIA officers would happily accept any declassified KGB document proving that Penkovsky was a traitor, while they would never accept a similar one proving that Penkovsky was a Soviet plant.

Intelligence officers are aware that, particularly in recent history, some of the documents have been left for the sole purpose of disinformation. Moreover, most scholars apparently ignore that a great part of dirty politics is based on orders never put to paper or never spoken, but merely "understood" by subordinates.[53] Therefore, an important part of modern history is systematically left out of the reach of scholarly work.

The comments above do not mean that I think that all the copies of the documents in possession of the National Security Archive are false. Most likely the majority of them are true copies of the original documents they claim to be — though probably some of them are not, and at least a few may be total fabrications.[54] The point I want to emphasize is that, because these copies have not been validated against the original documents, and there is no way they can be validated for the time being —hoping that they still exist somewhere in the government's archives— and that the original documents have not been authenticated,[55] the copies of documents in the possession of the National Security Archive are suspect and do not constitute a reliable source of information until they have been scientifically authenticated by qualified professionals. Moreover, all scholarly work based on information whose source has been these documents should be considered tainted and, therefore, unreliable. I think that, given the provenance of these documents, and the irregularities in their authentication (or lack of it), such skepticism is merely prudent.

This concern is even more justified when we see that, based on these "documents," some scholars have arrived at new explanations, sometimes diverging considerably from previous ones, about what really happened in some seminal historic events —like the Cuban missile crisis for example. The main danger I see in this trend of accepting spurious documents at face value is that studies based on them, which may be the product of erroneous data and, therefore, erroneous themselves, may one day be used by American leaders as a guide for future actions — the "lessons of the Cuban missile crisis" mentality. This is a mistake that may bring momentous consequences to America.

The Ouroboros of American Politics

According to the National Security Archive's web site, its close to $1.8 million yearly budget comes in part from private philanthropists. Among the organizations providing funds for the Archives are the Arca Foundation, the Carnegie Corporation, the John D. and Catherine T. MacArthur Foundation, the Ford Foundation, the Rockefeller Foundation, and the Rockefeller Family Fund, just to mention a few.[56]

What is difficult to understand is why the same people who made billions as the direct results of the evil doings of the CIA and other U.S. government agencies during the Cold War, are now out with the apparent intention of crucifying them. Like the medieval depiction of the ouroboros —a serpent biting its tail— they seem to be shooting themselves in the foot. This is highly suspicious. May it be that, contrary to appearances, this is precisely what they are trying to avoid?

A significant detail is that, though apparently damaging, most of the areas of interest of the National Security Archive do not deal with subjects which may be a cause of embarrassment for the people who are economically supporting the Archive. No documents in the National Security Archive mention the collaboration of some members of the U.S. government and their friends in the industry and banks with Nazi Germany and the Soviet Union. I particularly have not heard of any "document" in the National Security Archive mentioning the CIA's role in overthrowing Batista and helping Castro grab power in Cuba.[57] And this brings us to another obscure area of the "documents" in the National Security Archive.

Even though the role of the National Security Archive in the procuring of documents is a proactive one —usually they ask based on the Freedom of Information Act for a document they presume exists— the documents the different branches of the U.S. government eventually declassify are those that, for some reason, they believe are not smoking guns. Therefore, this is an obvious case of deception by omission. We can safely surmise that the truly damaging documents will never be made public.[58]

One of the most pernicious side-effects of the activity of the National Security Archive is that it has contributed to create the illusion that one can write truthful history based on the information provided by "declassified" documents provided by any government organization of any country —particularly intelligence organizations. But the idea is fallacious. In the first place, there is no guarantee that some of the key documents have not been doctored or fabricated from scratch. Secondly, the fact that some of the declassified documents have deletions shows that perhaps the most important bits of information are not provided. Finally, the declassification process itself, by which a government organization controls which documents are declassified and which are not, is a form of censorship which guarantees that the overall image that will come out is a distorted, slanted one tailored to benefit the interests of the declassifiers-cum-censors.

As I mentioned above, there is the possibility that the National Security Archive may be an exercise in deception. As Senator Daniel Patrick Moyniham has shown, the main goal of government secrecy is not keeping the documents out of the eyes of the enemy, but out of the eyes of their own people.[59]

It is highly suspicious that some of the people who created the CIA, like Allen Dulles, for example, were close associates with some of the people who control several of the organizations that are now bankrolling the National Security Archive. As professor Teresa Odendahl has pointed out, "contemporary American philanthropy is a system of 'generosity' by which the wealthy exercise social control and help themselves more than they do others."[60] One has to be a gullible fool to believe that the same people who created the CIA, and used it for the benefit of their businesses in Guatemala and Iran, just to mention two well-known examples, are going to fund an organization devoted to finding and exposing their dirty linen.

Some of the very foundations that provide the funds for the operation of the National Security Archive, "namely, Rockefeller, Ford and Carnegie, have been conscious instruments of covert U.S. foreign policy, with directors who can only be described as agents of U.S. intelligence."[60] The fact that Fidel Castro, who is everything but a fool, has been so eagerly cooperating with the National Security Archive folks, is perhaps an important clue to discover where their true allegiances really lie.

It would be a sad, but not surprising paradox, if some day it is found that, since the very beginning, the CIA has been behind the supposed efforts to unmask the CIA. That would be been the ultimate blowback operation, the consummation of the ouroboric goal.

In his well known novel *1984*, George Orwell wrote that he who controls the past controls the present, and he who controls the present controls the future. The intelligence services discovered a long time ago that he who controls the enemy controls the outcome of the battle. Thus, successful penetration of the opponent's ranks has always been the golden dream of all intelligence services.

Scholars or Spies?

There is a strong possibility that some of the scholars who have visited Cuba to attend conferences or do research work may have been, wittingly or unwittingly, recruited by Castro's intelligence services. It is evident that, since they began publishing books and papers about the Cuban missile crisis, Blight, Allyn, Welch, *et al.* have made a concerted effort to prove how close we were to nuclear Armageddon. Every new book and paper they have written on the subject of the Cuban missile crisis has tried to prove that we were a step closer to the brink than we actually thought when we read their previous book.[61] More and more dangerous missiles, menacing nuclear warheads, and reckless orders to trigger-happy Soviet officers have been piling up before the eyes of the terrified public.[62]

In a response to Mark Kramer's accusations of "their desire to portray the Cuban missile crisis in as dangerous a light as possible,"[63] Blight, Allyn, and Welch claimed that "We cannot even imagine what ends would be served by deliberately exaggerating the danger of the crisis."[64] Well, this statement only shows the authors' lack of imagination, because you don't need to be a rocket scientist to see why they may have a vested interest in making the crisis look much worse than it actually was. The key to the answer is very simple: follow the money.

According to authors Lebow and Stein, "We All Lost the Cold War." Granted, the assertion is true, but only from the point of view of the people of the nations involved in the Cold War. As the authors rightly point out, "The growing national debt, decaying infrastructure, and large trade imbalance are all attributable in part to decades of excessive military expending."[65] But the authors apparently forgot that expending and earning are two concepts inextricably linked which cannot exist separately. Somebody's expenditures are by force somebody else's earnings. Consequently, though it forced excessive spending upon the people of these nations, from the economic point of view of the ones who promoted it, the Cold War years were a very profitable period of time. Even if they did not win the Cold War militarily —they probably never wanted to win it— they made billions profiting from it.[66]

By the time of the Cuban missile crisis it was estimated that the United States had spent over a trillion dollars on arms since the beginning of the cold war.[67] What most people seem to miss, however, is that, for the U.S. government to have spent over a trillion dollars, somebody, by force, most have earned over a trillion dollars.

It is not by chance that the people who profited enormously from the Cold War —mostly Wall Street bankers who loaned the money to the debtor nations and owned the corporations involved in the production of war matériel— were the same ones who had previously profited enormously by doing business with both the Allies and Nazi Germany during WWII. They were the same people who covertly helped the development of both the Soviet and American military technology —particularly nuclear and missile technology. They were the same people who are now secretly helping the Chinese develop their intercontinental missiles. They are the same people who have secretly armed every single American enemy around the planet.

It is not by chance that the same people who made billions with the Cold War —which was mostly a propaganda product: remember the "missile gap"— are the same ones who control the non-profit foundations that are bankrolling most of the research whose main goal is to prove "how close we were to the brink" during the Cuban missile crisis. The reason for this is very simple: to these people our fear translates into their profit. It would lessen credibility to their plans for future fears if one day the people discover that the previous fears were unfounded.

Claiming that the Dullesses, the Rockefellers, the Bushes, Castro, Kissinger and McNamara, just to mention a few, lost the Cold War, is pure and simple nonsense. Using it as a title of a book, though, is tantamount to *dezinformatsia*. But, passing the old lies as truth guarantees that most people will accept the new lies without mental reservations.

Am I implying that all the scholars who have received grants from these foundations to do research on the Cuban missile crisis are told what they should write? Of course not. But, like rats in a psychologist's maze, scholars soon discover that some conclusions guarantee a constant input of grant money, while other conclusions dry it. It is extremely revealing that among hundreds of books and articles written about the Cuban missile crisis in the last fifteen years, dissidence is virtually nonexistent.[68] All revisionist historians seem to have died from natural causes. Most of the recent books about the Cuban missile crisis seem to be just variations of a single voice. The only thing that seems to change from one book to the next is the alleged number of nuclear warheads on Cuban soil. Like rabbits jumping out of a magician's hat, the nuclear warheads keep multiplying.[69] My only suggestion to these magicians of history is to be just a little cautious. If this trend continues, very soon we will discover that there were more nuclear warheads in Cuba than the total number made by the Soviet Union at the time.[70]

But, what about Fidel Castro, the alleged archenemy of the American capitalists? What have been his motivations for joining the fear-spreading crowd?

The fact is that, contrary to common belief, evidence indicates that Fidel Castro's claims of anti-Americanism have been highly exaggerated. As a matter of fact, and for different reasons that are difficult to understand, he always ends up, one way or another, playing the American card. The truth is that, despite his claims to the contrary, Fidel Castro is probably the best thing that ever happened to the American military-industrial-academic complex.[71]

The American military-industrial-academic complex craves for war, revolutions, low-intensity conflicts and terrorism, and Dr. Castro has been giving it precisely that medicine for many long profitable years. One can safely assume that, when Che Guevara sent his famous message to the Tricontinental Conference in Havana, asking for the creation of "two, three, ... many Vietnams,"[72] many presidents and CEOs of arms manufacturing American corporations and their friends in the Pentagon became extremely excited about their bright economic future. If one stops listening to Castro's rhetoric and looks closely at his actions, the unavoidable conclusion is that he may well qualify for the dubious honor of being one of the most pro-American leaders of all time in Latin America; a strong benefactor of the interests of the very American corporations he claims to hate.[73]

Oral History; But Whose?

Another thing that calls the attention of the skeptical reader is the treatment some of these scholars give to their subjects. After reading several of these books, the unaware reader may think that the people they have interviewed are just decent, honorable public servants and military and intelligence men who tried to do their best for their countries in a fair and honorable way. Granted, they may have made some errors, but they were made with the best of intentions.

But this is a total distortion of the truth. We are dealing here with a collection of politicians and spies very similar to a mafia. These people are far from being honorable men. Fidel Castro and his brother Raúl are known to have personally ordered the deaths of hundreds of people, are indirectly responsible for the deaths of several thousands, and have killed with their own hands quite a few.

Some of the interviewed, like Robert McNamara and Henry Kissinger, just to mention a few, are indirectly responsible for the deaths of several thousands of people —among them many American soldiers. In these books, however, the participants in these meetings are treated with the same respect as if they were mirror images of Mother Theresa. Nowhere in these books is the reader warned that most of these people are a bunch of liars whose word does not carry much weight. But, if one is to believe Blight and Welch, "all of the participants acted in perfectly good faith."[74] Lebow seems to agree, "We believe that most of these officials, Soviet, and American, told the truth as they understood it."[75] Unfortunately, they don't tell the reader how they reached that far-fetched conclusion. The only thing the opinion of these scholars seem to prove is that gullible people should not write history. At least a small dosis of skepticism should be required in the profession.

Moreover, as Cuban writer and ethnologist Miguel Barnet has pointed out, history is not only the product of the recollections of the elite, but it also appears through the significant, individual moments of marginalized persons. The goal of Barnet's concept of testimonial literature, his own version of oral history, is to "revise a mangled, deformed interpretation of the past."[76]

It seems, however, that Blight's concept of "critical oral history"[77] is an elitist one. The only people that apparently merit his investigative efforts are the rich and famous. I am still waiting to read one of his "oral interviews" with one of the Russian soldiers who manned the missile bases; one of the American sailors who participated in the blockade; or one of the Cuban soldiers who manned the SAM radars. But, looking at the cast of characters of his oral interviews, it is evident that Blight's purpose had never been to write the history of the "people without a history,"[78] but the history of the ones who believe they can rewrite history for their own benefit.

By the way, I think that, after such a long time and so much disinformation, the answers to some of the unsolved mysteries of the Cuban missile crisis may be found among these "people without a history" mentioned by Barnet. It is quite probable that some of the young technicians who were manning the SAM battery at Los Angeles, Cuba, that shot down Major Anderson's U-2, are still alive and living in Russia. I am sure that some of the peasants of the area around the missile bases are still alive in Cuba. It would be interesting to interview some of the Soviet soldiers and hear their version of who really shot down the plane, including why and how. Some of the Cuban peasants surely know what happened during these days and can confirm, or deny, that Cuban troops attacked the SAM bases. I would trust the stories of these people, who don't have a stake at changing history for their personal gain, much more than the cock and bull stories concocted by Castro, McNamara, Alexeev, and the rest of the professional liars who have been telling us their distorted version of the events for all these years.

Dezinformatsia, Inc.

One of the main forces behind this concerted effort to prove how close we were to the brink is Robert McNamara. Some years ago, McNamara found support for his theories from none other than his former target for executive action, Fidel Castro, and from a group of Russians, among them, Aleksandr Alekseev (Shitov), a retired KGB officer, and Sergo Mikoyan, a known KGB operative. The Castro, McNamara, Alexeev, Mikoyan *quartet,* has become the main source of disinformation since this new impetus on research on the Cuban missile crisis began about fifteen years ago. They have been the subject of several "critical oral history" interviews and have produced countless articles, speeches, and radio and tv programs where they have touted the new "discoveries." The problem with these characters is that none of them is a reliable source of information we can trust.

To the question of how reliable Robert S. McNamara is as a source, I would like to bring this example. In his book *Out of the Cold*,[79] in which he mentions some aspects of the Cuban missile crisis, McNamara claims that "The Soviet response of the following day [he is talking about October 23, 1962] was menacing: The Ministry of Defense placed its missile bomber and submarine forces on alert and canceled all leaves."[80] But one of the more striking things of the Cuban missile crisis is that, contrary to McNamara's assertion, the Soviets never placed their troops, nor the civilian defense, under alert. This astonishing fact is mentioned in most of the early accounts of the crisis.

A top secret CIA memo of October 25 clearly states that "We still see no signs of any crash procedure in measures to increase the readiness of Soviet armed forces."[81] A top secret memo of October 26 gives the first indications of a state of alert, but in some european satellite countries, not in the Soviet Union.[82] It is only on October 27 that a top secret CIA memo clearly acknowledges that "No significant redeployment of Soviet ground, air or naval forces has been noted. However, there are continuing indications of increased readiness among some units."[83]

Coming from a writer or scholar, such false information could be attributed to faulty or sloppy research. Coming from Robert McNamara, who had access to that classified information at the time of the crisis, it is simply a lie.[84]

Aleksandr Alekseev (Shitov) is a KGB officer who fell in love with Castro at first sight. Soon after, Castro recruited him as a double agent, and he has been working for the Cuban tyrant ever since. One of his main efforts has been directed at destroying Kudryavsetv's reputation through character assassination. Among his fabrications is the one claiming that Kudryavtsev was a physical coward who treated the Cubans "like one of Batista's generals."[85] Alexeev has published several accounts of the crisis, and has been the subject of several "oral history" interviews. Like McNamara, he is a totally unreliable source.

Now comes Fidel. Using Castro as a source of historical information is not a good idea. There is abundant proof that Fidel Castro is a pathological liar.[86] Moreover, he is not only a good liar, he is a shameless one. I will give just a few documented examples.

When Castro visited New York in 1996 to give a speech at the UN General Assembly, he paid an impromptu visit to the *CBS* studios, where he talked to his good friend Dan Rather and others. Just before he left, Mike Wallace asked him a tough question. "More than thirty years ago you came to New York to speak at the UN and, before leaving, you said you were going back to Cuba to restore democracy and to call for free elections. What happened?" To which Castro unabashedly answered: *"¡Eso fue hace mucho tiempo!"* ("That was a long time ago!") and, smiling, left the studio accompanied by his bodyguards.

In the Sierra Maestra manifesto published in July, 1957, Castro specifically promised that within a year after his provisional government took power there would be general elections, and he gave "absolute guarantee" that his government would grant individual and political rights specified in the 1940 Constitution. But, as Castro said, that was a long time ago.

In 1999 he visited the Dominican Republic to attend a summit of Caribbean leaders. The meeting's joint declaration included a provision to "reaffirm our commitment to preserve, consolidate and strengthen democracy, political pluralism and a state of law as the privileged backdrop that allows respect, defense and promotion of human rights."[87] Castro signed it without batting an eyelash.

However, at least once, Castro made the mistake of leaving written evidence that he is a liar. In 1954, he wrote a revealing letter to Melba Hernández, one of the women who participated in the assault of the Moncada garrisons and a close Castro associate. In it, Fidel advised her that, in order to outfox their opponents, she must use, "Much guile and smiles for everyone ... defend our points of view without creating problems. There will be ample time later to squash all the cockroaches together."[88]

A perfunctory reading of Castro's speeches shows dozens of instances in which he has admitted a posteriori that he has lied. An analyst of Castro's political behavior pointed out that "the Cuban dictator is a liar who confesses the truth —retroactively."[89] The fact explains why, writing about Castro's unbroken record of deceit, Cuban exile Mario Lazo called Fidel Castro "the great dissembler."[90]

Most of the production of the Blight, Allyn, Welch, *et al.*, paper mill is nothing but propaganda under a cover of legitimate scholarly work. But, propaganda, as David Gibbs rightly pointed out,[91] is an activity diametrically opposed to those of scholarship. When I affirm that the production of these scholars is equivalent to propaganda, I am not claiming that what they write is propaganda *per se*. The process is a little more sophisticated. Let me use an example to illustrate my point.

A joke running in the Soviet Union several years ago, told about this Moscow factory worker who, every Friday, walked out through the main gate pushing a wheelbarrow full of hay. The guard, suspecting he was stealing something, thoroughly searched through the hay, but he could not find anything. The process repeated itself for many months. One day, the intrigued guard told the worker: "Tomorrow I am moving to Kiev to a new job. I know you are stealing something. I will not tell anybody, but please, tell me what are you stealing." The clever worker answered: "Oh, I am stealing the wheelbarrows."

In the same fashion, these scholars' books and papers are the hay. The wheelbarrow is the fact that, by treating Castro's Cuba as a normal, democratic country, whose government declassifies documents and freely allows scholars access to them, they are creating a false image of legitimacy for an illegitimate government run by a bloodthirsty tyrant who has been in power for more than forty years and was never elected by the Cuban people. As in Marshall McLuhan's famous dictum, "The medium is the message."

Moreover, the fact that these scholars mix freely with Castro, and have *de facto* become his agents of influence, is repugnant, to say the least. As they perfectly know, but have never given the importance it merits, the only danger of a nuclear war during the missile crisis did not come from John Kennedy or Nikita Khrushchev, but from Fidel Castro. Not even Adolf Hitler or Joseph Stalin came as close as Castro to setting off a nuclear Armageddon which would have caused millions of civilian deaths in Cuba, America, Russia, and other parts of the world.[92] Fortunately, it did not happen, but it was not for Castro's lack of trying. Even more disturbing is the fact that Castro has never ceased in the pursuit of his most cherished dream: the annihilation of the American people he hates from the bottom of his heart.

It has been extensively documented that, after his efforts to develop a nuclear bomb ended in failure, Castro developed an outstanding capability for developing bacteriological warfare agents.[93] In May of 2001, Castro visited several anti-American Muslim countries, among them Algeria, Iran, Malaysia, Qatar, Syria and Libya.[94] Since 1993, Iran, Libya, and Syria, together with Cuba, Iraq, North Korea and

Sudan, have been in the U.S. Department of State yearly report "Patterns of Global Terrorism."

During his trip, Castro seized every occasion to pronounce inflammatory anti-American diatribes, among them, "the imperialist king will finally fall,"[95] "U.S. grandeur can be broken,"[96] the "American regime [is] an arrogant power,"[97] "Iran and Cuba, in cooperation with each other, can bring America to its knees,"[98] and the like. Of course, this may sound like heavenly music to anti-American American ears,[99] but perhaps they don't realize that they themselves and their families are among the hated Americans Castro dreams to annihilate some day. He is fully convinced that Americans are an infectious plague that must be eradicated in order to save planet earth and he is trying harder to do the job.

Castro is old, but he is not finished yet, and it is too early to tell his whole story. In 1961 Herbert Matthews called him "a prophet of doom."[100] He was right. As long as he is alive and in power in Cuba he will persist in his nuclear Armageddon dreams. Seemingly his grandiose plan is to go to the trash can of history with a big bang.

Like an ancient hero, Castro wants to go to his grave with human sacrifices. One of Castro's biographers, Georgie Anne Geyer, says that she has always believed that, "given his absolutist and apocalyptic personality, if he felt he was cornered or doomed, he would go down in an Armageddon end like Hitler in the bunker. It now looks as though that stage has begun."[101] Castro's own sister, Juana, said a long time ago that her brother's plans for Cuba are as sinister as Nero's for Rome.[102] Testifying before the House Committee on Un-American Activities, Juana Castro affirmed that "Fidel's feeling of hatred for this country cannot even be imagined by Americans. His intention, his obsession to destroy the U.S. is one of his main interests and objectives."[103]

Cuban writer Carlos Alberto Montaner provided one of the best characterizations of Dr. Strangelove Castro. To Castro, says Montaner, "the world is like a gigantic video game, and his role is to destroy the nasty aliens to the last one."[104]

PART THREE

Was There Ever a Cuban Missile Crisis?

PART THREE

Is There Ever a
Clean Missile Crisis?

Chapter 13

Decision-Making in the Kremlin and in the White House

> *This is my missile, this is my gun,*
> *One is for fighting, the other's for fun.*
> —Modified version of an army cadence.

It is said that Egypt's former Minister of War, Lieutenant General Mohammed Fawzi, called upon the spirit of a dead sheik in table-tapping seances to ask for advice on the best time to attack Israel.[1] Although that story most likely would make us laugh, it is also probable that the use of computers or some "scientific" decision-making theories could provoke laughter on people from some non-Western cultures. In any event, there is no substantiated proof that the spirits of dead sheiks, computers, or decision-making theories, can be of much help in the task of making decisions —particularly such complex decisions as the ones made by the leaders involved in managing events like the Cuban missile crisis.

The main problem with current mathematical and logical decision-making theories is that they apparently depart from the premise that all the players are rational human beings pursuing their own best interests. For these theories to work, you must assume, first, that you know what your opponents' best interests are — and very often they are not what *your* logic seems to indicate; secondly, that logical thinking, apparently good enough for machines, works equally well for human beings charged with feelings, biases, passions and prejudices. It is remarkable that there is no place in such theories, i.e., for a player trying unconsciously to punish himself with failure instead of striving to win. Yet, there is evidence of such personalities figuring prominently in world history. Was not Hitler, in some way, consciously or unconsciously, seeking his own destruction and the destruction of Germany and the German people?

Decision-Making and Decision-Makers

Graham T. Allison, one of the scholars who focused earlier on decision-making during the Cuban missile crisis, pointed out that, for some purposes, government behavior can be summarized as action chosen by a unitary, rational, centrally controlled, completely informed, and value maximizing decision-maker.[2] But this oversimplification often conceals the fact that a "government" consists of a conglomerate of individuals, each one on top of his organization. In the case of totalitarian nations, these organizations usually are only a few. In the case of a totalitarian dictatorship —like Hitler's or Castro's— the whole nation is a single pyramid-like organization with the dictator at its very top.

The striking similarity of results among analysts of various schools of thought when they are called to produce explanations about an event such as the Cuban missile crisis, arises from the fact that almost all of them assume that the player is a national government, and that the decisions are taken as a calculated response to a critical problem. A study of the work of most contemporary international relations analysts shows that they have had that assumption in mind when they have attempted to explain events in foreign affairs. For them, the idea that the occurrences in foreign affairs are the *acts of nations* is so fundamental that they are completely lost when faced with an event such as the Cuban missile crisis, which was, essentially, an *act of men*.

In confronting the problem posed by the installation of Soviet strategic missiles in Cuba, some analysts, as subscribers to the national policy model, have attempted to prove *a posteriori* that this was either a reasonable or an unreasonable act from the point of view of the Soviet Union, given Soviet strategic objectives. The fault with this type of analysis arises from the fact that, until now, no satisfactory answer has been given to explain, first, why the Soviets placed the missiles in Cuba, and, secondly, why they took them out so hastily.

American analysts who have studied the Cuban missile crisis have several theories to explain the Soviet move. For many years, the most widely accepted explanation of this bizarre incident was the one initially offered by Arnold Horelick and Myron Rush, two leading sovietologists at RAND, a California think tank. They concluded that the introduction of strategic missiles in Cuba "was motivated chiefly by the Soviet leader's desire to overcome... the existing margin of U.S. strategic superiority."[3] To support their conclusions, the authors cite several salient characteristics of the operation, and use these features as criteria to test alternative hypotheses about Soviet objectives. They seem to ignore, however, the vast amount of information which strongly suggests that the action was not a structured and calculated Soviet plan, but one of Khrushchev's pet projects, hastily conceived and planned by Khrushchev alone, and put into practice by him and a small group of his most trusted associates behind the backs of the Central Committee of the Soviet Communist Party.

To the initial "strategic superiority" theory, a new one has gained support in the last ten years. This theory, sometimes added to, and sometimes replacing the previous one, claims that Khrushchev's main goal was to protect Cuba from a U.S. attack.

However, a study by Eckart and White, in which they compare Kennedy and Khrushchev in a test of "mirror image" hypothesis, shows that American perceptions of the Soviet Union and Soviet perceptions of America were both fundamentally distorted in similar ways. The authors found that Khrushchev and Kennedy did not differ significantly from each other in any of various indices previously validated by Eckart as indicators of the use of war propaganda.[4]

Allison, for his part, cautioned about the tendency of some analysts to deduce Soviet objectives from American perceptions of what Americans saw as Russian intentions.[5]

Rational and Irrational Decision-Making

In his seminal study of the crisis,[6] Allison outlined three different models of decision-making: the rational actor (Model I), organizational process (Model II), and bureaucratic politics (Model III). Allison concluded that the second and third models produced better results in the analysis of the Cuban missile crisis. Apparently he was not bold enough to include the *irrational* actor (Model IV).

Virtually all analysts use, in some way or another, a conception of the decision-making process derived from the idea of rational choice. In its simplest version, the rational-choice hypothesis holds that a man acts to maximize his values under the constraints he faces. The basic rational choice hypothesis is rarely questioned and widely used, even though there is wide dispute over what values man typically pursues and over the interpretation of constraints.[7] Similarly, the writings of historians and foreign policy analysts, as well as the memoranda of government and intelligence officials, all seem to subscribe, in various degrees, to the hypothesis of rational choice and objective rationality.

The concept of objective rationality implies that the behaving subject molds all his behavior into an integrated pattern which implies: (a) viewing behavior alternatives prior to the decision in panoramic fashion, (b) considering the whole complex of consequences that would follow on each choice, and (c) having a system of values to be used as criteria to single out one from a whole set of alternatives.[8] From a decision-making point of view, knowledge is simply the means of discovering which one of all the possible consequences of a behavior will actually follow it.[9]

But, as Klaus Knorr pointed out, it is useful to distinguish among rational, emotional, technically mistaken, irrational, and apparently irrational behavior. Most of the times a complex behavior —as the one usually observed in international politics— is a mixture of all of them.[10].

In 1978 Herbert Simon received the Nobel Prize in economics for his theory of "bounded rationality" which challenges the central core of 20th-century economic theory by claiming that human behavior can't be logically defined. Simon's theory of "bounded rationality" —human behavior can't be logically explained— is perfectly applicable to the study of international politics and particularly to the analysis of the decision-making process.[11]

The central concern of administrative theory, as Simon has shown, lies along the boundary between the rational and non-rational aspects of human social behavior. According to Simon, administrative theory is actually the theory of intended and bounded rationality: a study of the behavior of human beings who *satisfice* because they do not have the wits —or the guts— to *maximize*.[12] Actual behavior falls short, in at least three ways, of objective rationality. First of all, rational vision requires a complete knowledge and anticipation of the consequences that will follow each choice —but knowledge of the consequences is always necessarily fragmentary. Secondly, since these consequences lie in the future, imagination must supply the lack of experienced feeling in attaching value to them — but values can be only imperfectly anticipated. And, finally, rationality requires a choice among all possible alternative behaviors —but in actual behavior only a few of all the possible alternatives ever come to mind.

Therefore, the first limitation upon rationality in actual behavior lies in the fact that rationality implies a complete, practically unattainable knowledge of the exact consequences of each choice. In real life, however, the decision-maker never has more than a fragmentary knowledge of the conditions surrounding his action, nor more than a slight insight into the regularities and laws that would permit him to imagine future consequences from a knowledge of present circumstances.[13]

It is obvious that the behaving subject cannot know directly the consequences that will follow as a result of his behavior.[14] Moreover, in order to determine the consequences of his actions, the behaving individual would need to know what will be the actions of the other actors, evidently another impossibility.[15] In real life, however, some decisions have the effect or outcome intended; others not —a fact commonly known as the law of unintended consequences. Moreover, some outcomes occur without a recognizable imputed decision to produce them.

Even though we never know what goes on in the mind of a person making decisions, there is evidence that the decision-making processes of executive systems can be reduced to the personality dynamics of its chief executives.[16] Henry Kissinger noted that whatever one's view about the degree to which choices of international affairs are "objectively" determined, the decisions are made by individuals who will be above all conscious of the seemingly multiplicity of options. Their understanding of the nature of their choice depends on many facts, including their experience during their rise to eminence.[17]

The idea of interpreting the outcomes of major historic events as expressions of the individual psychopathology of a particular national leader is not new; it was prefigured in Freud's work and Lasswell stressed its importance in the early thirties.[18] Yet, scholars in the field of international studies are only beginning to reassert the importance of national and international elites as causal agents of international behavior. But, as Kelman has observed, the study of political elites can be justified only if it can be proved that the single individual is a relevant unit of analysis for the study of international politics.[19] Some scholars, DeRivera among them, attach such an important role to elite actions as to assert that "(at least in the making of foreign policy), in at least one country (the United States), national action is determined by one individual (the President)."[20]

Foreign policy decision-making is strongly influenced by the belief system of the political leaders. Jeffrey Hart assumes that beliefs about the causal relationships among conceptual variables —which he calls "cognitive maps" and define as a set of casual beliefs and assertions which constitute a rather limited subset of the broader belief system on these individuals— can help to explain, and perhaps even predict, their policy choices.[21] Though Hart does not deny the probable effect of non-cognitive variables on the policy choice of individuals, he argues[22] that the behavior of political actors cannot always be explained in terms of "situational" determinants and that therefore psychological explanations may sometimes be useful.[23]

As we saw above, Hart defines cognitive maps as acts of casual belief or assertions, though some scholars use the term to stand for general beliefs about the fundamental characteristics of some aspects of a physical or social environment, whether or not such beliefs are casual. Other scholars are interested in sets of casual assertions as they are used in discussions and arguments among groups of policy makers. Such sets are more correctly called "rhetorical maps," because they do not assume that the individuals really *believe* the causal assertion that they make in order to persuade others to go along with a particular policy.[24]

Every individual's perceptions —and the actions based on those perceptions— are filtered through clusters of acquired concepts and beliefs. The process by which this is accomplished is called cognition. A belief system is a set of interrelated beliefs that help the individual to make sense out of what might otherwise be a confusing array of signals from his environment. A cognitive map is a representation of the causal beliefs or assertions of a specific individual. To the extent that the cognitive map represents beliefs, it may be considered a subset of the individual's subset system of beliefs.[25]

The way people —and leaders— perceive data is influenced not only by their cognitive processes (structure), and images (prejudices, biases) about other actors, but also by what they are concerned with at the time they receive the information. In addition, information is evaluated by just a small part of the person's memory that is presently active, what Robert Jervis calls the "evoked set."[26]

Shall we call a behavior "rational," Simon asks, when it is in error only because the information on which it is based is faulty? From a subjective point of view, it is rational for an individual to take medicine for a disease if he believes that it will cure his disease. From an objective point of view his behavior is rational only if the medicine is in fact effective.[27] Consequently, a decision may be called "objectively" rational, only if, in fact, it is the correct behavior for maximizing given values in a given situation.[28] Yet, no satisfactory treatment to the question of rational behavior has been found, a fact stated by Von Newmann and Morgenstern in 1947 which still remains unchallenged.[29]

Khrushchev's Pet Plan

The Cuban missile crisis was the boldest and riskiest of all of Nikita Khrushchev's foreign policy adventures. But what bypaths of political logic led him to undertake this staggering gamble, or what made him think it could succeed will probably never be known. To this day, most Western analysts have still offered no explanation for Khrushchev's "irrational" behavior.[30]

A more in-depth analysis, however, seems to indicate that Khrushchev's plan was no more farfetched than, for example, Kennedy's plan for the Bay of Pigs invasion. The available record suggests that, rather than trying to provoke a crisis of the international political system, and a nuclear confrontation with the U.S., Khrushchev was actually just trying to provoke Kennedy into a crisis in one of the political subsystems: Cuba. Though both the system and the subsystems were intimately related and both influenced each other, a Cuban crisis and a subsequent American invasion of the Island would not necessarily have provoked a nuclear confrontation between the United States and the Soviet Union —a fact that was fully understood by most of the American military leaders, though apparently not by President Kennedy and his close advisors.

It seems unlikely that Khrushchev's more conservative colleagues considered the plan sound —not even the distorted version of the plan Khrushchev must have given them. It is also unlikely that the Soviet Premier received much enthusiastic support from the Soviet military leaders for his Cuban project. No mastery of military strategy is necessary to see the risks of making strategic nuclear weapons so accessible to such an unreliable trigger-happy ally, in an exposed forward position. The whole plan only makes sense once one realizes that the missiles Khrushchev had in mind were not the real thing, but just iconic images of the real dangerous objects.

Soviet leaders liked to put forward the notion that scientific Marxism-Leninism provided a powerful key to the understanding of politics and gave them a sure path to act in any event. The reality of life, however, was quite different. Soviet statesmen, like all statesmen, were plagued by doubt and divided in counsel.[31] On the other hand, perhaps Khrushchev reasoned, sending missiles to Cuba technically broke no international law or established agreements among the powers. This had the advantage that, if the Americans were to react against the deployment of the missiles, it would force them to take "illegal" actions against Cuba. In addition, the Soviet move could be painted as the defense of a small, threatened ally from a bully, imperialistic superpower.[32]

Though it is scarcely necessary to emphasize the existence of disagreements within the Communist world —whether among Communist states or among members of the Soviet leadership— it should be pointed out that evidence showed again and again that conflicting pressures, internal tensions, and personal bitterness behind the scenes at high levels of government in the Soviet Union have been far greater than was apparent or suspected at the time. Even the incomplete evidence now available suffices to put to rest the official myth of a homogeneous ruling party in the Soviet Union.

These internal quarrels were never more evident than in the late fifties, when the mercurial versatility of Khrushchev had replaced the somber inflexibility of Stalin. Nikita S. Khrushchev, though then over 70, was still tough, devious, versatile. Short, bald and portly, wearing a poorly tailored suit, Khrushchev bore the well-deserved nicknames of "the hangman of the Ukraine" and "the butcher of Budapest."[33] But, paradoxically, he was also the one who had led the 208 million Soviet citizens to their greatest measure of liberty and prosperity since the Bolshevik Revolution.[34]

American journalists who visited the Soviet Union were impressed by Khrushchev's boundless energy, inner vitality and agile intelligence.[35] This blunt, aggressive little man[36] had a peculiar sense of humor[37] and was indefatigable and perspicacious.[38] He was not only one of the most loyal party men, but surely among the most astute.[39] What he lacked in formal education he made up in sheer energy and gall.[40] He appeared to sense in advance every major shift in policy, unerringly picking the right coattails to hang from.[41] He was also a consummate actor. He could be gay, sad, friendly, or downright furious according to what would serve him best.[42] "Life is a good school," Khrushchev once told reporters. "It thrashes you and bangs you about and teaches you."[43]

Contrary to external appearances, to Nikita Sergeevich, who had been illiterate until his midtwenties when he began attending school, Fidel Castro's personality and image must have been extremely distasteful. Castro was exactly the opposite of himself. The tall, young bearded rebel had been educated in the best religious schools in Santiago and Havana; his father was a wealthy landlord, and he never had to work to earn his bread.

By contrast, Nikita's childhood was as hard as it is possible to imagine. His grandfather was a serf. His father was a farmer and, occasionally, a coal miner. Nikita grew up as a typical Russian peasant. He drank too much, he talked too much, he was indiscreet, he lacked dignity, and he clowned. Sometimes he bullied. At times he was rough, uncouth, shrewd, entertaining, convivial and immensely talkative. From the very first moment they met, Khrushchev envied Fidel's pulsating humanity, his undeniable charm and warmth, his youth, his powerful charisma. This envy soon turned into hostility. Moreover, Fidel had outmaneuvered Escalante and Kudryavtsev and humiliated Khrushchev. But, surely, Fidel was not going to make a fool out of him.

There were three main schools of thought regarding the extent of Khrushchev's political power. One stressed the element of conflict in Soviet leadership politics.

To the advocates of this line of thinking, some signs of high-level conflict after 1957 evidenced that Khrushchev's leadership was not as stable and unchallengeable as was widely assumed. The other and more conventional school emphasized the stability of the Soviet leadership process once a political figure became the recognized leader of the regime. According to the supporters of this thesis, after Khrushchev overcame his challengers in June, 1957, the prevailing view was that he had become the new dictator of the party, something of a functional equivalent of Stalin minus the terror. This approach, however, did not stress the fact that conflict was a continuous and crucial fact of Soviet political life. The third school of thought was a variation of the conflict school. It asserted that, especially in the absence of a terror-imposed discipline in the leadership, the opposing tendencies toward oligarchy and dictatorship remained in constant interplay throughout the Khrushchev era.[44] Therefore, the two prevalent theories about the limits of Khrushchev's power were the one that saw him as the "first oligarch," fighting his way among powerful associates, and the one that saw him as a "dictator" with total control over Soviet events. It seems more likely, however, that none of the theories is totally correct, but both are partially correct. As a matter of fact, Khrushchev's power was always fluctuating between those two poles of power.

Evidence seems to indicate that, at the time of the Cuban missile crisis, Khrushchev had been temporarily freed from the forces of conventional morality and rationality, and was in a privileged position to influence political events. That meant he was able to command the necessary resources to intervene decisively and unilaterally in the political process in the Soviet Union. It was a situation that encouraged the expression of his personal talents for shaping events.[45]

When Vice-President Nixon visited the Soviet Union in mid-1959, he was reportedly impressed with the depth and stubbornness of Khrushchev's misconceptions about the United States.[46] On the other hand, George Kennan, an expert "sovietologist," said that he believed "the Soviets to be excellently informed about us." "I am sure," he affirmed, "that their information on the development of our economics, on the state of our military preparations, on our scientific progress, etc., is absolutely first-rate." But cautioned that "when it comes to the analysis of our motives, to the great things that make our life tick as it does, I think this whole system of intelligence-gathering breaks down seriously."[47] There was a lot of truth in Kennan's words, yet, most American analysts seemed to ignore that the reverse was also true. Kennan's appreciation of the virtues and defects of Soviet intelligence-gathering about the United States also may have been properly applied to American intelligence-gathering about the Soviet Union.

When Kennedy and Khrushchev met in Vienna, the main point of contention was the Berlin question. The American President had come to the summit prepared for a reasonable, rational discussion of the issues with the Soviet Premier. His hopes had been raised by an extensive report on Khrushchev compiled by psychologists and psychiatrists under the direction of the CIA —a report which eventually proved to be amazingly accurate.

According to the CIA report, Khrushchev was not the Machiavellian villain portrayed in the American press, but a predictable, pragmatic man. The Premier, the report said, was quick to grasp and utilize existing situations. Because he was flexible and impulsive, he could also exploit his opponents' weak spots as adroitly as a chess master. The President's advisors, however, felt that Kennedy could easily match the Soviet Premier's tactics. Khrushchev, the report continued, was an earthy, direct man who quickly came to the crux of the matter, particularly in personal relations. While he was not offended by a direct exchange of opposing viewpoints, he was not to be pushed. If Kennedy met a blank wall in his discussions with Khrushchev, he was advised to drop whatever they were discussing until a later time, particularly the Berlin question, because Khrushchev's fear of Germany was deadly and dangerous. Finally, the report emphasized that, despite Khrushchev's bluster, he was basically a man of peace.[48]

Unsound Theories

The most widely accepted hypotheses offered by the early analysts of the Cuban Missile Crisis have been that Khrushchev's objectives were: 1. Cold War strategy; 2. Cuban defense; 3. Bargaining chip; and, 4. Missile superiority. The problem with these hypotheses is that all of them seem to operate on the basis that the Soviet leader was just an unsophisticated, stupid peasant. For any of these hypothesis to be true, Khrushchev, first, would have had to have placed nuclear missiles —which he had denied to his closest allies—[49] into the hands of an unstable, self-proclaimed Marxist whom he had tried to overthrow by force less than six months before; secondly, he would have had to let his men commit dozens of major blunders, ranging from not camouflaging the missiles to deploying the very same type of missiles he knew the Americans had all the information about through Penkovsky and the U-2's; and, finally, after taking an action which undoubtedly would provoke Americans into a strong response, he would have failed to take the most elementary precautions at home in anticipation of the logical outcome of his action. Therefore, either Khrushchev was a total incompetent fool, and then these hypotheses are right, or he wasn't, and they are dead wrong.

The Cuban episode turned into a personal crisis for Nikita Khrushchev. The Soviet leader had not anticipated that Kennedy's move would be directed against the Soviet Union instead of Cuba. Khrushchev's behavior, particularly during the first days of the crisis, shows that he was surprised and unprepared for that turn of events. Direct, reliable evidence about time pressures and perceptions of threat as they were felt in the Kremlin during the week of October 22 to 28 is not available, but Soviet messages indicate the presence of these factors.

The threat of nuclear war became evident to the Soviet leader when the president's brother met Soviet Ambassador Dobrynin to convey a personal message from the American president. The message was a thinly disguised ultimatum setting a deadline for the next day and the threat that there was the possibility of a military take-over in the White House —an unlikely action to American minds, but a totally credible one to the Russians. Also, the fact that a U-2 plane had "lost" its course and for a few hair-raising minutes flew straight toward Moscow, undoubtedly increased the psychological pressure on the Russian leader's nerves.

Khrushchev's plan had been to impale Kennedy in the horns of a dilemma: either the American President would do nothing, discrediting himself and his country before the eyes of his allies, or he could invade Cuba and also be discredited in the eyes of the whole world. But on October 22, it was President Kennedy who impaled Khrushchev on one horn of his dilemma when he asserted that "..it will be the policy of this nation to regard any nuclear missile launched from Cuba against any nation in the Western Hemisphere as an attack by the Soviet Union on the United States requiring a full retaliatory response upon the Soviet Union."[50]

The Soviet leader's decision of sending whatever he actually sent to Cuba was based on some assumptions. He was aware of the broad outlines of American military strategy as expressed by President Kennedy. The main concepts of this strategy had been developed in the Pentagon under the aegis of Secretary of Defense Robert McNamara and had been accepted *in toto* by Kennedy.[51] By increasing American conventional forces and by making less vulnerable both strategic bombers and missiles, the new military strategy intended to achieve a more wide range of strategic options available to U.S. leaders. The new Kennedy military doctrine developed the concept of flexible, selective and controlled responses to face any type of warfare at whatever level, forcing on the enemy the onus of striking the first nuclear blow and risking a retaliatory blow which could inflict unacceptable loses. Of course, this flexible response theory needed not only second strike forces capable of fighting a limited nuclear war, but highly efficient conventional forces capable of meeting limited war necessities below the nuclear threshold. A provocation like the one Khrushchev had mounted in Cuba would necessarily be over the American political threshold, and therefore unacceptable for Kennedy, but at the same time well below the American nuclear threshold, and could be solved with limited conventional forces only, especially in an area where Americans had ample tactical superiority. In addition, the establishment of "the most powerful military force in human history," often cited as one of Kennedy's great achievements, was a clear proof to Khrushchev of the American president's tendency to see the world's problems in military, not political terms.[52]

There is also another explanation for Khrushchev's reasoning vis-à-vis American policy. According to his scale of values, when the Soviet Union acted against Hungary in 1956 it was only acting the way a great power should in drastically eliminating a pressing threat. His analysis of what he called "capitalist nations" led him to believe that the Americans would act similarly if confronted with a comparable challenge. Khrushchev expected the United States to take similar steps should it ever be confronted with a dangerous threat in its own back yard. He hardly anticipated that the U.S. would sit idly by, while a Communist government was taking over in Havana. Nor did Khrushchev, with his pragmatic view of things, expect that the U.S. would allow Cuba to become a Soviet satellite before their very noses. Despite the unexplainable American failure at the Bay of Pigs, Khrushchev still had enough respect for the U.S. as a great power to believe that they would act in their own best interests should a necessity arise.[53]

The Soviet Premier firmly believed that Americans would not shy from taking all measures, including unpopular ones, to safeguard their security. In Latin America especially, Khrushchev would have liked to fish in troubled waters and hope for the best. While the Cuban venture was apparently in blatant contradiction to his own détente policies, it nonetheless bore the earmarks of the classic Khrushchevian tactics —the sudden and bold initiative aimed at setting his opponents off balance and producing a quick and decisive advantage in his political struggle.[54]

Kennedy's "Irrational" Behavior

Probably the one who better summarized the prevalent feelings among the Kennedy apologists was Morton H. Kaplan. According to him, "The handling of the Cuban missile crisis was John F. Kennedy's shining hour. Those who make abominable criticism of him for his handling of the crisis need to have both their heads and their hearts examined."[55] But apologists don't make good historians, and make very bad intelligence officers. So, let's study President Kennedy's behavior during the crisis with a skeptic's eye.

A few minutes before nine o'clock in the morning of October 16, McGeorge Bundy took the U-2 photographs, which allegedly depicted medium-range ballistic missiles on Cuban soil, to President Kennedy who was still in his bedroom in pajamas and robe, reading the morning papers. After taking a look at the photographs, Kennedy quickly dictated a list of government officials who were to be called immediately to the White House. At 11:45 the group —later to be named the Ex Comm (short for Executive Committee of the National Security Council)— gathered in the Cabinet Room for the first of a running series of meetings during the next two weeks.

It is interesting to note that when the crisis erupted and a dangerous confrontation with the Soviet Union seemed imminent, it was not the elected representatives of the American people whom the President called together, but the representatives of the *real* power in the United States, namely, big business.[56] Among the members of that inner circle of Kennedy advisers who formed the Ex Comm were: Lyndon Johnson, representative of oil interests; Dean Rusk, former president of the Rockefeller Foundation; Robert McNamara, former president of Ford Motor Co.; Douglas Dillon, former president of Dillon, Read; Roswell Gilpatrick, a corporation lawyer from New York; John McCone, a multi-millionaire industrialist from San Francisco; Dean Acheson, a corporation lawyer and former Secretary of State; General Maxwell Taylor, a former chairman of the Mexican Light and Power Company; George Ball, a Washington corporation lawyer; and, of course, his brother Robert, like him a multi-millionaire from Boston. Actually, the elected representatives of the people, the Congressional leaders and the Foreign Relations Committee were left in the dark an told of the decisions only *after* they had been made.[57]

During the Cuban missile crisis Kennedy not only ignored the cabinet but even broadened the National Security Council —the President, the vice-President, the Secretary of State, and the Secretary of Defense. As a result, the national policy of the United States was directed by an *ad hoc* "executive" committee composed of men in whose judgement he had an unusually high degree of confidence.

A common statement that appeared in most early books and articles about the crisis was that the discovery of the strategic missiles in Cuba came as a surprise to the U.S. government. Robert Kennedy described the dominant reaction at the first Ex Comm meeting as one of "stunned surprise."[58] One wonders, however, how come after all the reports from the press and U.S. congressmen, the administration was so unprepared for the discovery of Soviet missiles in Cuba? Was the surprise only for public consumption?

At that time, Kennedy faced one of his greatest decisions in history. He had to determine the fullest implications from the evidence at hand. He could have asked himself: Is the threat coming from Khrushchev, in which case the Soviet withdrawal must be his aim? Or does the central threat to American security stem specifically from Castro's regime? If this was the case, could that mean that Castro himself had to be driven out? But, as Theodore Sorensen has observed, "Presidents rarely, if ever, make decisions —particularly in foreign affairs— in the sense of writing their conclusions on a clean slate... The basic decisions, which confine their choices, have all too often been previously made."[59] Obviously, dictators in totalitarian countries are much more free to make decisions than presidents in democratic states.

Some scholars have made studies about the amount of consultation sought by decision makers and the speed with which decisions are taken, and apparently there is a close relationship between these two variables involved in the process of decision making.[60] Kennedy's decision to force the removal of the missiles appears to have been made in less than a half hour, and by all accounts just a few minutes after he was convinced that the photographic "evidence" was conclusive.[61] For some reason, since the very beginning President Kennedy raised the issue of the missiles in Cuba from a confrontation between the U.S. and Cuba to a confrontation with the Soviet Union. In the same unilateral way, and against the generalized opinion of his advisers, he made the decision to implement a blockade around Cuba.

To some members of Congress and the military, the President's sudden decision to impose a blockade on Cuba instead of invading the Island was surrounded by considerable mystery. The question arose as to whether the intelligence data that the administration must have been collecting throughout the summer about the missile build-up in Cuba was accurately evaluated, or whether policy dictated the intelligence estimates or turned them aside.[62]

According to the official version, the option of a sudden air strike against the missile sites, with the possibility of an eventual invasion of the island, initially had strong support among most of the Ex Comm members, and, according to Sorensen, even the President.[63] After numerous discussions, however, the idea of a blockade emerged with a majority in the group. Yet it is also well known that there was a dominant trait in Kennedy's White House staff: an overwhelming desire among them to serve the President's political interests and goals. That is, perhaps, nothing new for American presidents, but there are indications that under Kennedy this emphasis on personal loyalty was pronounced.

"Our loyalty to Kennedy transcended everything. There wasn't anything we wouldn't do for him," expressed Myer Feldman. "Presidential assistants are of course always loyal to their bosses," he added, "but our feelings were so unique, it made those other staff people look like a bunch of Judases."[64] Thus, one could easily surmise that the sudden change in opinion from pushing for an invasion to supporting a blockade was just a way of following the President's expressed (or assumed) desires. This was not, however, the tone of the President's military advisers. Throughout the crisis, the Joint Chiefs of Staff continued to press for a military attack, correctly assuming that the Soviets would do nothing in response.

Those in the Ex Comm who were against the invasion were later reinforced in their position when Secretary McNamara reported on Wednesday, October 24, that a surprise attack against the missiles alone —a surgical air strike— was militarily impractical.[65] In the view of the Joint Chiefs of Staff, any such military action would have included all military installations in Cuba, eventually leading to a full invasion by U.S. forces.[66] Those who argued for the military strike instead of a blockade, however, pointed out that a blockade would not, in fact, remove the missiles, and would not even stop the work from going on at the missile sites themselves. The missiles were already in Cuba, and all that the blockade could do would be to close the door after the horse had left the barn. Furthermore, they argued, America would be risking a confrontation with the Soviet Union by stopping their ships, when the logical thing to do would be to concentrate on Cuba and Castro instead.[67]

The members of the Joint Chiefs of Staff were unanimous in calling for immediate military action. They forcefully presented their view that the blockade would not be effective. General Curtiss LeMay, Air Force Chief, argued strongly with the President that a military attack was essential. When the President questioned him about what the Soviet response might be, General LeMay assured him that there would be no reaction at all.[68] Former Secretary of State Dean Acheson made his arguments that an air attack and invasion represented the only alternative to the U.S. He said that the President of the United States had the responsibility for the security of the American people and of the whole world, that it was his duty to take the only action which could protect that security, and that this meant destroying the missiles in Cuba.[69]

But, from the very beginning, and for reasons still unknown, President Kennedy deliberately moved from a preconceived idea to a predetermined decision. Everything else was just a smoke screen.

Shortly before his tv speech to inform the nation of his decision to impose a blockade on the Soviet ships bound for Cuba, President Kennedy met with the members of the Cabinet and informed them of the crisis for the first time. Then, he met with leaders of Congress. According to Robert Kennedy, this was the President's most difficult meeting. Many congressional leaders were sharp in their criticism. They complained that the President should take more forceful action —a military attack or an invasion of Cuba— and that the blockade was far too weak a response.[70]

When Senators Richard Russell and William Fulbright were informed of the situation in Cuba and the presidential decision to blockade the Island, they argued that a blockade could not be effective in the short time remaining before the missile sites became operational. In fact, if one assumed that the nuclear warheads were already in Cuba, as it was logical to suppose, a blockade of the Island seemed to be a foolish decision. Prior to the meeting, Senator Fulbright had advocated the invasion of Cuba as a wiser course than the "quarantine" —the less belligerent name Kennedy chose to name the blockade. Fulbright's point was that the blockade, by involving a direct confrontation with Soviet ships, would be more likely to provoke a nuclear war than an invasion that would place Americans fighting against Cubans.[71]

Dean Acheson, one of the most acerbic critics of President Kennedy's decisions during the crisis, later wrote that, though the American strategy during the crisis was wrong, it succeeded in obtaining the withdrawal of the missiles simply by "dumb luck."[72] Acheson's recommendation for decisive military action, namely an air strike over Cuba, was flatly rejected by Kennedy. But Acheson was not the only one with little praise for Kennedy's decision-making abilities. General Douglas McArthur, though crediting Kennedy with political cunning, called the President "just dumb when it comes to decision making."[73]

In a conversation with Schlesinger on Sunday, October 20, Kennedy said that no one in the intelligence community had anticipated the Soviet move because everyone had assumed that the Russians would not be so stupid as to offer the U.S. this pretext for intervention.[74] But, with the benefit of hindsight, one can only wonder if Kennedy's reluctance to invade the Island was actually based on the suspicion —or the knowledge— that the missiles were just a trap set for the American President by Nikita Khrushchev.

It is known that though Kennedy appeared to be open to advice, he preferred to ignore the information his advisors give him, especially when his "ignorance" was politically expedient. For example, during his presidential campaign he repeatedly criticized President Eisenhower for having allowed the Soviet Union to surpass the United States in the development of missiles —what was later known as the "missile gap." During his campaign Kennedy promised that, once elected, he would close the gap. A short time after he was elected, however, Kennedy ordered Defense Secretary McNamara to investigate the problem and, to everybody's surprise, McNamara soon "discovered" that there was no such thing as a "missile gap," nor had there ever been one.

But McNamara made the big mistake of announcing his discovery to the media, provoking the displeasure of the newly elected president. Kennedy's immediate reaction was to issue a White House statement claiming that McNamara was mistaken. Kennedy's claim was apparently based only on his conviction that his administration should not admit the absence of such a helpful "missile gap."

Why did Kennedy act in such an apparently irrational way? Probably because of two reasons. First, because a public statement by his brand new administration admitting that his claims of the existence of a "missile gap" were not true would have diminished his credibility in the eyes of a public which evidently had been manipulated during Kennedy's political campaign to believe that the lack of action of a Republican administration had endangered national security. But there was probably a second and more important reason for disclaiming McNamara's findings: the presence of a "missile gap" would be a major justification for Kennedy's expanding defense program. Without the "missile gap" it should have been more difficult to explain to the American taxpayers the massive increases in the military budget.[75]

Some writers have asserted in the reverential language typical of the President's biographers and court historians that the Cuban missile crisis was John F. Kennedy's greatest triumph. Several revisionist authors, however, have disagreed with that widely accepted version of the event, and believe that the President's decision to go to the brink of nuclear war was irresponsible and reckless. They also believe that Khrushchev's decision to place strategic nuclear missiles in Cuba was just as irresponsible and reckless because he must have known that his provocation would certainly invite a nuclear catastrophe. Still, one wonders if perhaps both Kennedy and Khrushchev were more clever than anyone imagined, and that the apparently risky confrontation implied in fact no risk at all. Although Kennedy is reported to have said during the crisis that the possibilities of a nuclear confrontation were "somewhere between one out of three and even," there is evidence that he knew all along that the United States was not in any immediate danger. Furthermore, as he publicly expressed in a television interview on December 17, 1962, he was entirely confident that Khrushchev had neither the intention nor the desire —and perhaps not even the capability— to use the missiles in Cuba.

Kennedy was reasonably confident that the missiles didn't represent a threat to American security and that the Russians would not go to war. Henry Brandon wrote the inside story of Kennedy's reaction when, on Saturday, October 27, Roger Hilsman told the President that a U-2 plane had apparently lost its way, wandered into Soviet territory, and was headed for Moscow. It is highly revealing that, after listening to Hilsman's report, Kennedy did not lose his temper, nor did he panic about what the Russians might or might not do. Instead, at this blackest point of the crisis, Kennedy broke into laughter and said: "There is always somebody who does not get the word..."[76]

In addition, when a U-2 plane was shot down over Cuba the same day, although the Ex Comm had earlier agreed to take out one of the SAM missile sites if this happened, Kennedy waited for Khrushchev's response instead of ordering the retaliatory attack. Was his restraint the product of sober judgement, as it has been said, or out of fear? Or could it be that he knew some top secret information that prevented him from ordering an attack against Cuba? Why was he so bold against Khrushchev and so restrained against Castro? If, as Robert Kennedy pointed out, courage was the virtue that President Kennedy most admired, it is very difficult to understand why he lacked the courage to properly avenge the humiliation of having an American plane shot down over Cuba.

Some characteristics of John Kennedy's reactions have puzzled even his admirers. Theodore Sorensen mentioned Kennedy's ability to view his own actions with detached amusement.[77] But his behavior facing grave issues sometimes seemed to have gone beyond cold blood detachment. Some people commented that Kennedy lacked emotional commitment. Others mentioned that the only things he enjoyed were rationality and intelligence.

Psychologist Roy Wise of Concordia University in Montreal, pointed out that neurons that release dopamine —a neurotransmitter— seem to be involved in behavioral arousal or motivational states in some fundamental way. They influence motor activity and are the cells that die in Parkinson's disease. With their dopamine producing cells gone, parkinsonian patients seem not to respond to events and other stimuli that most people find rewarding.[78]

Though rumors that John F. Kennedy was suffering from Parkinson's disease have never been confirmed, it is know, as was made public in 1972 by the *New York Times*, that he was among the patients treated by Dr. Max Jacobson, aka "Dr. Feelgood," who dispensed amphetamine "peppills," better known as "speed," to patients in highly competitive jobs who needed to fight fatigue and depression. According to the *NYT* report, Kennedy's reliance on the drug had actually begun early in his administration. But only some years later concern began within physicians about potential side effects of the hyperactivity-inducing drug, which included addiction and psychiatric complications.[79]

Little Brother Was Watching Them

In his laudatory review of Robert Kennedy's *Thirteen Days*, John Kenneth Galbraith went as far as to claim that, despite the advice of some "hawkish" members of the U.S. military, the moral forthrightness of President Kennedy and his brother saved Cuba from invasion.[80] Nice story. But it is not easy to forget that these Kennedys were the same "heroes" who sent the Cuban Brigade to fight at the Bay of Pigs only to betray them, leaving them in the lurch to die on the beaches, and the same ones who, like common criminals, had been planning Castro's assassination. If, as Galbraith claimed, they truly opposed the invasion of Cuba, they were either acting out of character, or they had something quite different in their minds.

Robert Kennedy was the man who had called anyone unwilling to attack Castro a "gutless bastard."[81] Despite being the highest law enforcing official in the U.S. government, he obviously knew about CIA plots to assassinate Castro, and apparently encouraged them. Therefore, it is difficult to believe that he was the one who, from the very first moment, raised the moral questions about an attack on Cuba and who became the strongest force within the administration for a negotiated settlement of the crisis. As the story tells us, it was at the Ex Comm meeting on Wednesday, October 17, when George Ball made a sustained argument against the air-strike proposal, on the grounds that it was inconsistent with American traditions. Robert Kennedy seconded him immediately, saying that he didn't want his brother to become the Tojo of the 1960s.[82]

According to some versions, the President pushed for assurances that an air strike would work, and no one opposed him, except his brother Robert. Some have tried to explain Robert Kennedy's behavior on the grounds of ethical and moral considerations: Robert did know how much the crisis owed to prior provocation on the CIA's part. It is difficult to believe, however, how men whose behavior had proved to be beyond any ethical or moral considerations can change so suddenly. After the Bay of Pigs Chester Bowles wrote: "The Cuban fiasco demonstrates how far astray a man as brilliant and well-intentioned as President Kennedy can go when he lacks a basic moral reference point." But, as Charles Frankel pointed out, "morality, however cynically we may be about it, has at least this much real efficacy: one must appear to be moral, or at least to be persuading oneself that one is moral, to exercise power successfully."[83]

It is known that in the aftermath of the Bay of Pigs invasion, Robert Kennedy became the President's representative in Operation Mongoose, the CIA-led secret campaign to overthrow Castro by force. In January, 1962, Robert Kennedy, acting as Attorney General, the highest law enforcement official in the country, assembled the Mongoose planners at the Justice Department, and urged them to give top priority to the operation, and spare no time, money, effort or manpower in the process.[84] The effect of the Bay of Pig's debacle was to increase Robert Kennedy's determination to "get Castro."[85] As late as mid-1962, Robert Kennedy was the driving force behind the clandestine effort to overthrow Castro. Inside accounts depict him as a wild man putting pressure on the CIA to get rid of the Cuban leader. He was ardent about the Green Berets project and even more in pursuing the program of the Special Group, Augmented, a special body set up to handle top priority plots, whose highest priority assignment was the overthrow and assassination of Fidel Castro.

When Defense Secretary McNamara testified before the committee investigating President Kennedy's assassination, he acknowledged that many people in the Administration were hysterical about Castro at the time of the Bay of Pigs and thereafter, and that there was pressure from the President and the Attorney General to do something about Castro.[86] In 1983, Richard Helms confirmed the President's anti-Castro feelings: "There are those who for some reason write that President Kennedy really didn't mind about the Cuban thing. Hell, he minded a great deal. He was *wild* with Castro, and the whole government was pushed hard to see if there wasn't some way to unseat him."[87]

With all respect for the Kennedy brothers and their admirers and eulogists, this author firmly believes that the Tojo remark was just a well rehearsed piece of histrionics for The Jack & Bob Show to justify the President's *a priori* decision of not to invade Cuba and get rid of Castro.

Eyeball to Eyeball *Machismo*

Many political commentators, especially those who were directly involved in the decision-making process, later pointed to the Cuban missile crisis as President Kennedy's finest hour. "It was the moment when his tenacity, his "machismo," was expressed for all to see and respect.[88] Apparently, some believe, Khrushchev's actions stirred the Irish in John F. Kennedy. For columnist William S. White, the real issue was "manhood." Failure to have confronted Khrushchev "would have been an unmanly betrayal to this nation."[89]

Though machismo, that perpetual assertion of masculinity, is usually attributed to underdeveloped Latin Americans, it certainly was a characteristic of the Kennedys. "The combination of intellectuality and machismo was the hallmark of the New Frontier," affirmed Christopher Lash.[90]

In their analysis of how the Kennedy Administration formulated its policy during the Cuban missile crisis, Alsop and Bartlett recounted the now famous offhand comment by Secretary of State Dean Rusk: "We're eyeball to eyeball, and I think the other fellow just blinked."[91] Most American analysts agree that Rusk's phrase captured the essence of the situation.

Yet Rusk's comment reveals a lot about how widespread in the American psyche is Hollywood's "cowboy mentality." The moral of the tale is that Kennedy finally won because he had more guts than the other guy, the one who blinked. Apparently none of the eulogists of President Kennedy have taken the time to observe that in real life people act more out of fear than out of courage. One wonders what would have happened if, out of fear, Khrushchev had ordered a spasm nuclear attack. It would have been interesting to see the reaction of the "macho men" in Washington after they would had been informed that the Russian missiles had been launched.

It should be a cause for great concern to realize that the American love for images is not limited just to the common people, but to all levels of the population, including their political leaders. During the Cuban missile crisis most American leaders and policy makers acted as if they were not living a real crisis that threatened the entire world with destruction, but a fictitious crisis on their tv screens. To many, it was not John Kennedy who won; it was John Wayne.

It seems that one of the main concerns of President Kennedy during the crisis was not to appear "chicken." Also typical of the American cowboy mentality is that the so called "game of chicken" is studied in the most prestigious American universities as one of the variations of decision theory. According to this theory, an international crisis can take on the appearance of a game of chicken if a player is anxious to persuade the other that he is willing to go to the brink of war, even if both are desperately anxious to avoid a nuclear exchange.[92]

It is somehow difficult to agree with Thomas Mongar in his belief that Kennedy made policy decisions for psychotherapeutic reasons.[93] Yet, the record seems to indicate that he made most of his decisions following the dictates of his heart —or his guts— rather than his brain. Obsessed by his image, Kennedy feared that Khrushchev would not take him seriously if he again backed down in Cuba. Kennedy apparently believed that if Nikita Khrushchev questioned his courage it could tempt the Russian leader to pursue a policy of adventurism, perhaps in Central Europe.

Those who advised Kennedy against the Bay of Pigs invasion, Harris Wofford recalled, were mocked by the President for "grabbing their nuts" in fear.[94] When somebody told him that his appointment of Robert Kennedy as Attorney General would cause a storm of protest, he turned to his brother and said: "Let's grab our balls and go."[95] Ballsiness was a quality as important to John F. Kennedy as to Hemingway and Mailer, or Castro. He must have been delighted when Joseph Alsop began referring to him at Washington dinner parties as "a Stevenson with balls."[96]

William Styron said that, after the Cuban Missile Crisis, Kennedy must have felt that his *cojones* were in good shape.[97] Aside for offsetting the humiliation of the Bay of Pigs fiasco, the showdown with Khrushchev gave the President the opportunity to show that he could hang tough, face such powerful adversary and emerge the glorious, undisputed winner.[98] Styron also has the distinction of being the first American writer to perceive that, apart from their hateful and irreconcilable differences and the animosity that separated them, Castro and Kennedy were temperamentally and intellectually alike.[99] Both men ruled by mesmerizing their subjects, and both Kennedy and Fidel smoked cigars, phallic symbols of male potency and power.[100]

Gary Wills observed, however, that Kennedy's ballsiness had conspicuous exceptions. The Kennedy Administration, which fearlessly took on the bureaucrats, was seemingly timid in its dealings with the oldest bureaucrat entrenched in Washington: J. Edgard Hoover.[101] Yet Wills failed to notice an even more conspicuous lapse: Fidel Castro. Both Hoover and Castro, though despised, were strangely immune from the wrath of the Kennedys. In the case of Hoover the mystery had an explanation: President Kennedy was certain that the FBI had recordings of him[102] making love to a woman suspected of espionage —his father had told him to beware of Hoover's use of such recordings.[103] But, how about Castro? What did Castro know that made Kennedy fear him so much? In Castro's case this behavior is difficult to explain, because Kennedy's preoccupation with the Cuban leader constituted a concern so deep as to justify the word "obsession."

Throughout his campaign and presidency, Kennedy spoke as if Castro was America's Public Enemy Number One. As Gary Wills wrote, "Kennedy's Bay of Pigs target was a man who obsessed him." It was a chess game "played mind to mind, macho to macho, charisma to charisma."[104] Still, the known fact of Kennedy's obsession to "get Castro," makes it much more difficult to understand why he saved his enemy's life both during the Bay of Pigs and the Missile Crisis.

The "ballsy" President would take on U.S. Steel —on the sons o'bitches businessmen— and Khrushchev, but both Castro and Hoover kept doing outrageous things and both of them remained in power. There was no "ballsiness" in Kennedy's behavior toward either Hoover or Castro.

The central thesis of the book *Apocriphos,* by Czech writer Karel Capek, is that, from palaeolithic times to the 20th century, man has remained essentially the same. The only difference, if any, is that modern man knows how to disguise his feelings, hatreds, and passions, in a better way. I cannot agree more with Capek. Computer simulation and decision-making theories are just useful tools which modern man employs to disguise the fact that, like his Neanderthal ancestor, he still makes decisions out of his balls.

Chapter 14

The Missile Crisis that Never Was

> *"Mire vuestra merced"* —respondió Sancho— *"que aquellos que allí se parecen no son gigantes, sino molinos de viento."*
> —Miguel de Cervantes, Don Quijote de la Mancha.

> *"Both you and me understand what kind of weapons these are."*
> —Nikita Khrushchev, Message to President Kennedy, October 28, 1962.

Western analysts who initially studied the Cuban missile crisis, generally agree that the Soviet attempt to deploy 42 medium-range and some 24 to 32 intermediate-range nuclear ballistic missiles in Cuba in the early fall of 1962 triggered the most dangerous crisis of the Cold War. Never before, or since —went the conventional wisdom— had the Soviet Union and the United States been so close to the brink of a shooting war, one that could easily have escalated into a thermonuclear exchange. To many people, the Cuban missile crisis marks the closest the world has come to nuclear Armageddon.

Robert S. McNamara, who closely watched the dangerous confrontation from the privileged perspective of U.S. Secretary of Defense, stated some years later: "The world was faced with what many of us felt then, and what since has been generally agreed, was the greatest danger of a catastrophic war since the advent of the nuclear age."[1]

The imminence of danger became evident for all when Kennedy concluded his presidential address to the nation on October 22 with these dramatic words:

> My fellow citizens, let no one doubt that this is a difficult and dangerous effort on which we have set out. No one can foresee precisely what course it will take or what costs or casualties will be incurred.[2]

As Kennedy himself pointed out afterward, it was the first direct test between the Soviet Union and the United States in which nuclear weapons were the issue. Yet, after forty years of continuous study, no American analyst is certain as to what specific and general benefits the Soviet Premier hoped to derive directly or indirectly from the deployment of nuclear missiles in Cuba.

Senator Les Aspin pointed out that, in order to maintain credibility within the bureaucracy, intelligence analysts like to have a high degree of confidence in their findings. They are, therefore, weary of advancing conclusions based on anything other than hard information. For this reason, the U.S. intelligence community traditionally focused on Soviet technical capabilities rather than intentions.[3]

If, many years after the Cuban missile crisis, American analysts still know next to nothing about what is going on inside Russian minds —as proved by their surprise with the collapse of the Soviet Union— Senator Aspin's words are even more accurate when we think about an event like the Cuban missile crisis.

The most commonly accepted version of the event is that Khrushchev's action took everyone in the U.S. intelligence community by surprise. The fact, if true, would indicate that, if the U.S. intelligence community never lacked HUMINT and ELINT,[4] they surely lacked what Andrew Cockburn pejoratively called IMAGININT,[5] that is, imagination.

Some of the decision-makers at the time, and a large number of analysts and scholars, accept as the most satisfactory explanation of Khrushchev's action what has been called the "quick fix" theory. This theory states that Khrushchev's move was an attempt to close the "missile gap" with the United States, since the missiles in Cuba amounted to a doubling of Soviet first strike capabilities. Khrushchev's account of the crisis in his memoirs —published posthumously in 1970— seems to confirm that theory when he asserted that, while the main goal was to defend Cuba, another consideration was that "our missiles would have equalized what the West likes to call the 'balance of power.'"[6] The available evidence, however, shows that, on the contrary, as I have shown above, the missiles were not intended to protect Cuba and, in fact, were actually jeopardizing the security of the Island even further. Khrushchev also lied when he affirmed that the missiles would have brought military advantages to the Soviet Union. Most military experts, East and West, agree that the missiles in Cuba would not have given the Soviets even a short-term strategic superiority.

The logical positivist philosophers stated long ago that when two people don't agree, it is either because they are calling two different things by the same name, or because they are using two different names to call the same thing by. Therefore, in order to avoid the semantic trap, an analysis of the very concept of crisis is in order.

What is a "Crisis"?

The word *crisis* comes from the Greek *krinein*, to separate. In traditional medical terms a crisis denotes that change in a disease which indicates whether the outcome is to be recovery or death. From among several uses of the word crisis, the medical term seems to be the most analogous for purposes of international conflict. Broadly, the term "crisis" refers to that point in time when it is decided whether an affair or course of action will go on unmodified or be changed to reach termination point.

Oran Young has defined crises as situations which have important implications for the stability of some pattern of interaction, system, or subsystem. Stability means, in this context, the ability of a system, subsystem, or pattern of interaction, to undergo a disruptive sequence of events without breaking down or suffering qualitative changes of nature.[7]

Though the antecedents of a crisis are seldom easy to isolate, we might identify them in general as the issues in conflict with the normal coping mechanisms of society. As with many physical diseases, we assume those coping mechanisms to be present at all times, in some form and degree, in the international system. When there is a weakening of the coping mechanisms to the point that the issues in conflict overwhelm them; or new issues arise for which the coping mechanisms are inadequate, a crisis comes about.[8] Typical coping mechanisms are diplomacy, international law, public international institutions such as the United Nations, and so forth.

The field is hardly lacking in definitions of crisis,[9] but perhaps the most widely accepted definition of the term is the one advanced by Charles Hermann. Professor Hermann has defined a crisis as a situation that (1) threatens high-priority goals of the decision-making unit; (2) restricts the amount of time available for response before the decision is taken, and (3) surprises the decision-maker by its occurrence. Consequently, extreme threat, short decision-making time, and surprise are —following Hermann's definition— the most commonly accepted characteristics of a crisis.[10]

To make his definition more clear, Hermann uses a situational cube to illustrate what he calls the three dimensions of a crisis: threat, decision-making time, and awareness.

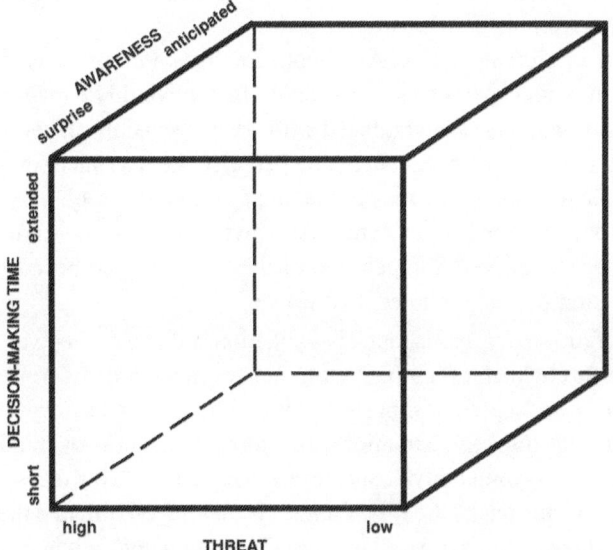

(From Hermann, "Some Issues in the Study of International Crisis," in Charles F. Hermann, edit., *International Crisis: Insight from Behavioral Research* (New York: The Free Press, 1972), p. 14.)

Hermann places surprise in one extreme of an awareness dimension in order to permit a construction parallel to that for threat and decision-making time. Thus, decision-making time can be short or extended; the threat can be high or low; and the complete absence of awareness is surprise, anticipation being the other extreme. Yet, when he offers his definition, he feels himself forced to make clear that, because awareness refers to a condition of the decision-maker (i.e., his perception), the term is less satisfactory when one deals with the observer's estimation of the properties present in the situation. Therefore, Hermann assumes that decision-making time and threat, in opposition to awareness, are objective dimensions of crisis, not affected by the decision-maker's perceptions.

Yet, it is evident from the available information about international crisis that decision-making time and threat are dimensions as subjective as awareness. Threat has no physical magnitude. People don't perceive threat the same way they perceive heat or light.

Also, the deadline for making a decision can be arbitrarily set down. Both threat and decision-making time, as well as awareness, refer, rather than to an objective characteristic of a situation, to a subjective condition of a decision-maker (i.e., his perception), and have nothing to do with the reality of the situation.

Nevertheless, what is known about international crisis confirms W.I. Thomas' much quoted aphorism: "If men define situations as real, they are real in their consequences."[11] But the sole fact of admitting that a crisis situation is real for somebody doesn't imply that it has to be real for everybody. Yet, in most of the scholarly literature about crises, we find implicit the idea that crises are radically separated from the decision-maker, as if they were objective organisms with their own life set apart from those who are living it.

But there are no crises *per se*. An event turns into a crisis when somebody (i.e., the decision-maker) perceives it as such. In fact, it would be inappropriate to talk about decision-makers (leaders) faced with crisis. Decision-makers don't face crises; they turn events into crises when they perceive them as such (or when they want other people to believe that they are facing a crisis). Consequently, if a decision-maker feels compelled to act when faced with an event he perceives as a crisis, it is not because it is an imperative of the situation, but because his own mental organization forces him to act that way.[12]

My own definition of crisis is that it is a situation suddenly perceived as threatening by somebody who feels compelled to act (to make a decision) before the arrival of a deadline accepted or arbitrarily set by himself. According to this definition, crises are not objective situations, but subjective states of mind. A crisis always is something to somebody. Inspector Clouseau, i.e., never faces any crisis: he is never aware of the tricks the Pink Panther is playing on him and therefore he never perceives them as threats. Similarly, not all of Kennedy's advisors perceived the situation in Cuba to be more threatening to the United States than it had been in the past. McNamara's highly quoted words: "A missile is a missile. It makes no great difference if you are killed by a missile fired from the Soviet Union or from Cuba," makes a good argument for the subjectivity of threat in a given situation.

Also, conspicuously absent in most of the theoretical analyses of the term crisis is the possibility of a pseudo-crisis; a crisis artificially created in order to obtain political, economic, military or psychological gains. It is a well-known fact that some leaders —Hitler and Castro among them— have used the practice of concocting continuous "crises" in order to mobilize their people to back their politics of frantic nationalism, fiery xenophobia, and ideological megalomania. One wonders why in the extensive scholarly literature concerning crisis the possibility of an artificially provoked crisis is never mentioned. Given the proverbial cunning of politicians and the dirty tricks abounding in a field where lies and deception are commonly used weapons, this possibility should have been considered and analyzed. Apparently, however, most American scholars take at face value statements made by decision-makers —particularly the ones whom they sympathize

The Notorious September Estimate

On its now famous September Estimate, the United States Intelligence Board (USIB) predicted that, though the Soviet Union could derive considerable military advantage from the establishment of medium and intermediate range ballistic missile bases in Cuba, this possibility was very low because it "would be incompatible with Soviet practice to date and with Soviet policy as we presently estimate it."[13] Since then, there has been considerable debate over alleged American "intelligence failures" in the Cuban missile crisis.[14] The National Intelligence Estimate of September 19, 1962, became a *cause célèbre* because it continued to express the conviction that the Soviets would not place strategic nuclear missiles in Cuba.

Several analysts have tried to prove, sometimes using the wrong arguments, that the American intelligence community, though obviously acting a little sluggish at the beginning of the crisis, nevertheless discovered the missiles just in time. Others, mainly the critics of the Kennedy administration, have tried to prove exactly the contrary, but the problem is still a subject to debate.

As we have seen above, throughout the Spring of 1962 Castro had been pressing the Soviets for commitments they were reluctant to give him. In April and May the strains in Cuban-Soviet relations reached a peak, highlighted by the failed coup d'ètat to overthrow Castro, the Escalante and PSP purges, and the detention and expulsion from Havana of Soviet ambassador Kudryavtsev. Khrushchev was furious with the insolence of his self-declared Marxist "ally." Therefore, it makes no sense at all that Khrushchev would have selected precisely that moment to place nuclear missiles in Cuba to protect Fidel Castro, a person he had abundant reasons to hate and despise, from an American invasion.

According to Robert Kennedy, the American leaders had been deceived by Khrushchev, but they had also fooled themselves. No official within the government had ever suggested to President Kennedy that the Russian buildup in Cuba would include nuclear missiles. The President had asked the intelligence community on several occasions for a specific evaluation on what they felt to be implications for the U.S. of the Soviet buildup in Cuba. On each of the four occasions in 1962 when the intelligence community and its National Estimate of the future course of events had furnished him with official reports on Cuba, they had told the President that the Russians most likely would not make offensive weapons available to Cuba.[15]

The American intelligence community had been following the developments in Cuba most carefully. Two estimates were produced. The first, in August, concluded that the Russians would not place strategic missiles on the Island. The second one, the now notorious September Estimate, approved by the United States Intelligence Board (USIB) on September 19, 1962, reached the conclusion that the Soviet Union would not introduce nuclear missiles into Cuba.

When the U.S. Intelligence Board met on September 19 to consider the question of Cuba, they had the following information available: 1, the arrival in the port of Mariel of two large-hatch Soviet lumber ships, which were riding high in the water as if they carried an oversized, low weight cargo, a fact that had not passed unnoticed to American shipping analysts;[16] 2, a report that Castro's private pilot, after a night of heavy drinking, had boasted that Cuba would have atomic weapons very soon;[17] 3, countless reports by Cuban refugees about sightings of missiles in the Pinar del Río province;[18] 4, a sighting by a qualified CIA agent of the rear profile of a strategic missile;[19] and, 5, U-2 photos taken on August 29, September 5 and 17, showing SAM sites under construction.[20]

The Estimate conceded that even if the Russians might be tempted to place strategic missiles in Cuba, it was nevertheless highly unlikely that they would be sent in, because the Soviets would be deterred by their awareness of the violent reaction that such a move would provoke on the part of the United States. Charles E. Bohlen and Llewellyn Thompson, Jr., both former U.S. ambassadors to Moscow and chief Kremlinologists in the State Department, agreed with the conclusions reached in the Estimate.[21]

The Estimate took into consideration the fact that the Soviet Union had never before displayed a willingness to take steps that so significantly raised the risk factor in Russo-American relations. The Soviet leaders would undoubtedly had foreseen that the installation of strategic nuclear weapons in Cuba would bring about the unwanted outcome of a prompt, and almost surely violent reaction of the American public and its government.[22]

But probably the consideration that added most weight to the Estimate's conclusions was the fact that the Soviet Union had never given nuclear missiles to other nations. Actually, until the Cuban missile crisis there was no indication that the Soviets had any intention of changing that policy. When Randolph Hearst, Jr., asked Khrushchev in December, 1957, if Russia would supply the Warsaw forces with missiles and nuclear weapons, the Soviet Premier answered that the Soviet Union had designed its rockets to be used from its own territory and therefore had no need to place launching sites on the territory of these countries.[23] In his final speech at the U.N. on October 12, 1959, the Soviet Premier pointed out once more, that if the world did not disarm soon, the possession of atomic weapons would spread to perhaps a dozen additional nations, the arms race would be stepped up and disarmament would be impossible.[24]

Ulam rightly pointed out that the Soviets realized that the effectivity of nuclear arms as a *political* weapon was not necessarily dependent on the size of the stockpile but on the ruthlessness and *apparent* disregard of the consequences of using it.[25] Therefore, the prospect of nuclear arms in a Communist state other than the Soviet Union, even in one of its own satellites, would have been a most unwelcomed one.

Not even faced with the possibility of nuclear weapons in West Germany the Soviet Union hinted about the possibility that the Russians would provide nuclear arms to East Germany. Moreover, though the Soviet Union began in 1957 to give some help to China in the development of nuclear technology for peaceful uses, by 1959, apparently fearing the Chinese could develop their own nuclear weapons capabilities, the Soviets went back on their promises.[26]

According to Ulam, by the 1960s the decision of helping China develop its nuclear technology was the most bitterly regretted Soviet policy decision since World War II.[27] Though it was not known to the world until very much later, in mid-1959 Khrushchev refused to give the Chinese samples of the atomic bombs and nuclear know-how. By late 1959 the Soviets withdrew their technicians from China, with catastrophic effect on the Chinese economy. Therefore, it was highly improbable that Khrushchev, given the peculiar characteristics of Fidel Castro and his "Communist" regime, would make the same mistake again.

A lot of biases affect *post hoc* explanations of warning failures. One of the essential characteristics of strategic warning is that it is concerned with the predictions of a single event —e.g., enemy surprise attack— dichotomizing the possibility of its occurrence and the probability of its non-occurrence.[28] Warning forecasts attempt to reduce the uncertainty of what is essentially defined as a dichotomous pair of alternatives —the negative event will occur soon or it will not.

But, given the costs involved, warning forecasts seek to drive the probability of one side of the dichotomy as close to unity as possible. This usually means the negative alternative, since no forecast (special stimulus) is needed for the non-occurrence alternative. The dichotomy burdens the warning forecasts with refuting all alternative explanations of the information which leads to issuing a warning. This is particularly true because, given the "bad news" nature of warning, strong motivations are at work to find alternative explanations and thus deny the probable occurrence of the unwanted event. Accordingly, for warning forecasts to be valid they must be durable in a demanding number of ways. First, independent sets of information must converge in the same conclusion. Secondly, these sets must seem inherently most trustworthy indicators of what is to come than all other sets of available information. Third, the forecasts must have a well established record for not providing false information.[29]

On September 20, the day after the Estimate was handed down, a reliable eyewitness report of a missile too big to be a SAM reached Ray Cline, the CIA's deputy director of Intelligence. Apparently a CIA informer had spotted a missile on a highway as early as September 12, but had trouble in getting his information out of Cuba. Missile experts in Washington, who had rejected hundreds of prior reports by Cuban refugees, concluded that the agent's description checked out against the known features of some Soviet MRBMs. In retrospect, the CIA decided that the missile had arrived in a shipment of Soviet cargo on September 8.[30]

But the Soviet experts of the U.S. Department of State were firm in their advice that Khrushchev would never place nuclear missiles in Cuba, because he had never placed such weapons in the territory of other satellites. Therefore, when they were presented with photographs showing what looked like Soviet strategic missile bases in Cuba, the entire staff was, according to one diplomat, "in a state of shock." They would not believed that the pictures seemed to indicate was true until there had been a retake.[31]

The White House would confess later that American intelligence had been a little drowsy. It had been lulled into that state by the constant reassurances of the Soviet affairs experts in the State Department that it was highly unlikely that the Russians would take strategic nuclear missiles outside their territory. There was no precedent for such action and no indication that they would change their habits at this time.[32]

There is a question of cardinal importance in the Cuban missile crisis that has consistently failed to yield a satisfactory answer, namely: Why did Nikita Khrushchev place nuclear missiles in Cuba? As I stated in the Prologue, the question has eluded a satisfactory answer because it has been erroneously formulated, and it is impossible to find the right answer when the question itself is wrong. As I have shown above, the Soviet Union *never* placed strategic nuclear missiles in Cuba. As a matter of fact, they have never placed nuclear missiles outside their own borders —neither before the Cuban missile crisis nor after. Even 25 years after the crisis, all the Soviet SS-4s, SS5s, and SS-20s, as well as half their FROG and SCUD tactical nuclear weapons, which had too short a range to reach NATO territory without being moved forward several hundred miles, were based inside the U.S.S.R. borders. The Soviet Union provided its Eastern European allies some FROG and SCUD missiles but, consistent with its policy, the nuclear warheads were retained by the U.S.S.R. in Soviet territory.[33]

Consequently, the predictions of the American intelligence community in their evaluation of the situation in Cuba were confirmed by the facts. They forecasted that the Soviets would never place nuclear missiles in Cuba, and they didn't. The only thing that would have proved the Estimate wrong would have been actual proof of the presence of nuclear warheads in Cuba in 1962.[34] This would have been the smoking gun. But, contrary to repeated unsubstantiated claims to the contrary, as of today the presence of nuclear warheads in Cuba in 1962 has never been proved. No smoking gun has been found for the simple reason that it was never there. Consequently, the September Estimate could not had been more accurate. Sherman Kent and the rest of the people at the USIB proved their worth to the American intelligence community.[35]

But the September Estimate concluded that the Russians would not risk deploying strategic missiles in Cuba because, among other reasons, they were fully aware that the Americans would have little difficulty in discovering the missiles, and that the U.S. reaction would be violent. In this respect the September estimate proved to be wrong. Even though American intelligence rapidly detected the missiles, the American response could not have been weaker. No American invasion of Cuba was carried out. On the contrary, Castro emerged fortified from the crisis with an American commitment to guarantee and preserve his regime, and protecting him from the anti-Castro Cubans in the United States. In that sense the American intelligence community proved to know the Soviet Union better than its own government.

Why did President Kennedy fail to seize the opportunity to get rid of his supposed archenemy? This is the real question to be answered if one is to solve this forty-year-old riddle called the Cuban missile crisis.[36]

In a *post mortem* analysis of the alleged causes of the Estimate's failure, Assistant Director for National Estimates Sherman Kent, Chairman of the Board of National Estimates, though reluctantly admitting that they had come down on the wrong side, could not restrain himself from pointing out what he considered the "incredible wrongness of the Soviet decision to put missiles in Cuba."[37] Of course, Kent was absolutely right in believing that, if Khrushchev actually did what he seemed to have done, he was dead wrong. Even more, something that perhaps Kent might have thought, but didn't put in writing, by doing what he apparently had done, the Soviet Premier had proved to be a stupid, incompetent fool and a madman. But, as I have shown above, this was not the case.

Now, there is an elementary rule of tradecraft which states that when there is an unexpected, unexplainable change in the opponent's behavior, the first thing to suspect is deception.[38] I cannot explain myself why so many senior CIA officers committed such an obvious breach in their established tradecraft practices. Nevertheless, I have a theory.

Just a few hours after President Kennedy had been informed of the U-2 photos, the Ex Comm met for the first time. Arthur Lundahl, head of the National Photographic Interpretation Center had been invited to the meeting. Robert Kennedy's recollection of the moment is so descriptive that it is worth reproducing it in detail:

> At 11:45 that same morning, in the Cabinet Room, a formal presentation was made by the Central Intelligence Agency to a number of high officials of the government. Photographs were shown to us. Experts arrived with their charts and their pointers and told us that if we looked carefully, we could see there was a missile base being constructed in a field near San

Cristobal, Cuba. I, for one, had to take their word for it. I examined the pictures carefully, and what I saw appeared to be no more than a clearing of a field for a farm or the basement of a house. I was relieved to hear later that this was the same reaction of virtually everyone at the meeting, including President Kennedy. Even a few days later, when more work had taken place on the site, he remarked that it looked like a football field.[38]

So confused was the President with the "evidence" presented by Lundahl, that he asked him point blank: "Are you sure these are Soviet MRBMs?" Lundahl's cryptic answer was "as sure of this as a photointerpreter can be sure of anything."[39] Unfortunately, none of the presents had the knowledge, or the guts, to translate Lundahl's answer to the President. In plain English it meant, "I haven't the slightest idea!"[40]

With the benefit of hindsight, I have reached the conclusion that Lundahl wittingly disinformed the President.[41] My contention is based in the fact that the Cuban missile crisis marked the primacy of TECHINT (Technical intelligence)[42] over HUMINT (human intelligence)[43] in the CIA —in my opinion with disastrous consequences.[44] Therefore, an explanation of Lundahl's behavior may be that he was motivated just by bureaucratic politics inside the CIA. After the success of the technical intelligence means during the Cuban missile crisis the TECHINT area grew enormously and its budget was highly increased.[45] By early 1970s, close to 85 percent of all information collected by the various U.S. intelligence agencies was coming from ELINT (Electronic intelligence), PHOTINT (Photographic intelligence), RADINT (radar intelligence) and all the "hardware" based sources, as opposed to information obtained by spies and agents in the field (HUMINT).

On the other hand, I suspect that President Kennedy either knew all along, or eventually discovered, that the estimate produced by the American intelligence community was essentially correct. After the missile crisis was over, CIA director John McCone was urged to make Sherman Kent the scapegoat for the bad guess. But McCone refused to fire him, despite repeated reminders from the White House that the September Estimate was wrong. Evidently, Kennedy didn't press the issue too hard. Kennedy's behavior may also explain why he did not order the U.S Navy to board the Soviet ships in the high seas to physically verify that the canvas-covered objects on deck were actually 42 missiles on their way back to the Soviet Union.

Was the Cuban Crisis a Real Crisis?

At the time of the Cuban Missile Crisis President Kennedy reportedly estimated the probability of nuclear war as "somewhere between one out of three and even." Yet, though the crisis was undoubtedly a dramatic confrontation, some analysts have questioned the accepted notion that it was the most dangerous crisis of the Cold War.[46] How much of the actual Cuban Missile Crisis was a "scenario"?[47] Was it a pseudo event?

So, in order to find out if the Cuban missile crisis was a true event or just a pseudo-event, let's go back to Hermann's definition of a crisis as an unanticipated situation of short decisionmaking time and severe threat,[48] and use it as criteria against which to test the widely accepted assumption that the Cuban missile crisis was a true crisis.

The place Hermann gives to the Cuban Missile Crisis in his situational cube demonstrates his belief that the Cuban crisis was a real crisis indeed:

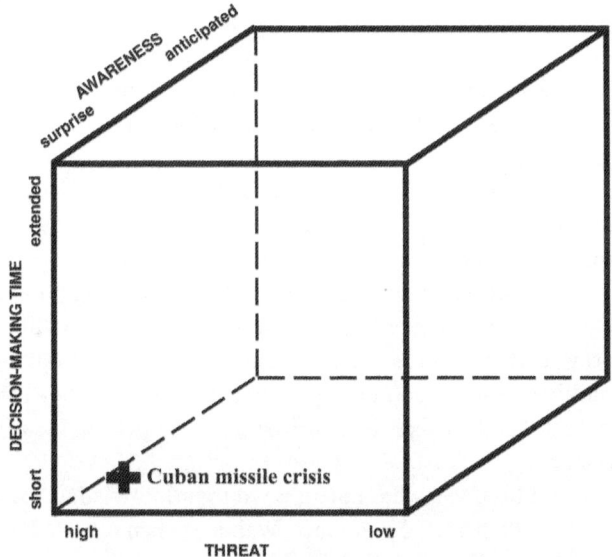

(From Hermann, "Some Issues in the Study of International Crisis," in Charles F. Hermann, edit., *International Crisis: Insight from Behavioral Research* (New York: The Free Press, 1972), p. 14.)

But Hermann based his analysis on some questionable information available at the time. Now, let's analyze the Cuban event from a different perspective, in the light of both re-evaluated new evidence, and of some old evidence which was discarded at the time.

Awareness

Was the discovery of what seemed to be Soviet strategic missiles in Cuba really a surprise to Kennedy? If one is to believe Robert Kennedy, the President was "surprised and stunned" by the news of Soviet missiles in Cuba. However, as early as October 6, 1960, at an electoral speech in Cincinnati, Ohio, Kennedy the candidate had warned Americans not to close their eyes to Castro's rattling of red rockets and alerted them to a potential enemy missile base only ninety miles from American shores.[49] Why, then, was the President so shocked when faced with an event so foreseeable that he had considered it a possibility 2 years before when he had used it as an element of his campaign?

Despite the consensus among American intelligence against the possibility that Khrushchev would dare to place strategic missiles in Cuba, John McCone, who, after the Bay of Pigs, had succeeded Allen Dulles as Director of the CIA, had conveyed to Kennedy on August 22 what he said was only a "hunch" that long-range strategic missiles were being brought into Cuba. His theory was that SAMs were being installed to protect the coming missile bases, since missile bases that were not safe from conventional attack were of little value.[50] Yet McCone's theory that the only reason for installing SAM batteries in Cuba was to eventually protect the long-range missile bases from conventional air attack has little credibility, because the Soviets had already supplied SAMs to Indonesia and Iraq, and no one ever suspected the Russians were going to install nuclear missiles in any of these countries. So, was McCone's suspicion really just a "hunch," as he claimed, or did the CIA director know more than he admitted?

Moreover, on October 10, Senator Kenneth Keating had challenged the Kennedy Administration to deny that there were intermediate-range missile bases in Cuba, affirming that "construction has begun on at least a half dozen launching sites for intermediate range tactical missiles."[51] Though Keating produced no evidence other than his own statement, the oncoming events proved him right. The Senator never revealed the source of such accurate information, but —if one discards Soviet intelligence— his source may only have been American intelligence. Could it be that both McCone and Senator Keating were getting their information from the same source?

But Keating and McCone were not alone in their knowledge about developments in Cuba. On September 10 columnist Walter Trohan reported that the Russians already had missile bases on the Island.[52] It is also interesting to note that by the end of September General Curtis LeMay ordered supplies to be flown to Florida. That mission had to be completed by October 10, and the Tactical Air Command was to be combat-ready by October 20. Henry Pachter rightly wonders if these moves were just precautionary or whether the dates indicate that the Air Force Chiefs of Staff expected a crisis at the end of October?[53]

Also, Representative Bob Wilson of California, the Chairman of the Republican Congressional Committee, insisted that the Administration knew in late September that Russian missiles were in Cuba, but had delayed announcing the fact in order to go into the election in a time of crisis.[54] Wilson also said that administration officials had held a secret briefing for him and other members of the CIA Subcommittee in the House six weeks before the election and had disclosed that long range missiles were then in Cuba.[55] The Administration denied Wilson's claims, but it is interesting to remember that, just after the crisis, Arthur Sylvester, Assistant Secretary of Defense for Public Affairs, made a series of statements which suggested that the Administration might have been manipulating the facts through its official announcements and its "leaks" to the press.[56]

According to the Kennedy administration's version of the event, it was not until October 14 that the U-2 took the photographs that discovered the missiles.

But the Defense Department continued denying after that date that there were any strategic missiles in Cuba. The President continued campaigning as if nothing had happened until October 20, when he was ready to make his decision. Because of his previous secrecy, which the press contributed to keep for the sake of alleged American vital interests, Kennedy's coast to coast prime-time tv and radio message to the American people was a total success in terms of audience.

From the very first day, President Kennedy directed that the Ex Comm work in the most extreme secrecy so as not to alert the Russians to the American discovery of the missiles. But one may guess that the Russians should have known that the missiles were in Cuba —of course, they were installing them— and also that they were aware that American spy planes had detected the missile sites —of course, they have seen the planes in their radar screens. Therefore, who was Kennedy trying to keep in the dark?

Simply because the most elementary logic cannot sustain the idea that the presence of strategic missiles in Cuba was a threat to the United States (or, to say it properly, a greater threat than missiles inside Soviet territory) —the U.S. had strategic missiles even closer to the Soviet borders and had denied that they constituted a threat— the main argument of the Administration was that the Russians had brought their weapons in "surreptitiously, using deceit and stealth." But, as I have shown above, the knowledge of the existence of strategic missiles in Cuba — mainly due to Soviet "mistakes"— was a "secret" known to everybody. Thus, it is difficult to believe that the only people in the U.S. who ignored the existence of the missiles were the President and his administration. It is very hard, then, to accept the President's claim that the situation was unanticipated.

Decision-Making Time

According to Hermann, short decision-making time is another characteristic of crises. But information not made public at the time of the crisis makes one wonder if Kennedy really was compelled to act in a short time.

One of the reasons offered by some analysts to explain why Kennedy made no effort toward a diplomatic solution before ordering the blockade was that the President feared losing time in negotiations while the missiles could be put into operational readiness.[57] According to the official story, the Administration had set a deadline for the dismantling of the bases *before* the missiles reached full operational status. When Kennedy spoke to the American people on October 22, he gave the impression that none of the MRBMs or IRBMs, and perhaps not even the SAMs, were operational. That explained the rush to force the Soviets to dismantle the sites, or to destroy them by force, before they could reach a dangerous operational condition.

On Wednesday, October 24, Khrushchev suggested a summit conference with Kennedy to discuss the missile issue. Though some of the President's advisors considered it a useful idea, Kennedy turned it down flat. According to his logic,

Khrushchev was just playing to gain time enough to put the missiles in operational status and then present the Americans with a *fait accompli*.

In mid-week during the crisis, U.N. Secretary General U-Thant suggested a brief relaxation of tensions during which the Soviets would stop its arms shipments to Cuba and the U.S. would suspend its quarantine of the island. Khrushchev rushed to agree with U-Thant's suggestion, but Kennedy again refused. When asked why he had not accepted U-Thant's proposed delay to permit negotiations, some spokesmen of the administration explained that it was unacceptable because the delay would allow the Soviets to finish the work on the sites, put the missiles into operational readiness, and thereby make more difficult their eventual removal.[58] In the meantime, administration officials continued warning about the imminence of the missile sites becoming operational and the danger this would imply.[59] To emphasize the imminent danger and put pressure on Khrushchev, a State Department declaration underscored Kennedy's words in the sense that if the Soviet build up continued, the U.S. would be forced to take further action.[60]

The information that the administration supplied to the press and to the American public prompted the widely accepted theory that Kennedy had to set a deadline in order to keep the missiles from becoming operational. Yet, as Professor Barnton Bernstein pointed out, the "operational missile" theory, which assumes that the missiles in Cuba were not operational until the 29th of October, is very questionable.[61] A CIA report dated October 23, 1962, but kept classified until fifteen years after the crisis, points to the astonishing fact that, as early as October 22, six of the MRBM missile sites in Cuba were "fully operational" —whatever this meant— and two more could be made operational in an emergency.[62]

Professor Bernstein concluded that earlier CIA reports presumably had forecasted the rate of progress on the site installations. Therefore, President Kennedy must have known by the 19th or the 20th, or perhaps earlier, that most of the sites seemingly had reached operational status or were soon to reach it.[63] The fact reported by the CIA was later confirmed by Juan Vivés, a former Cuban intelligence officer now living in France. According to Vivés, some MRBMs were ready to fire by the first days of October, and some SAM installations in the western part of Cuba were ready by the beginning of August.[64] Therefore, it is hard to believe that a deadline implicit in the situation forced President Kennedy to make his decisions in such a short time.

Threat

The third characteristic of crises according to Hermann is threat. The Administration emphasized the fact that the missiles in Cuba were a great threat to the U.S., but not everyone agreed with the President. Sorensen believed that although such missiles would offer certain advantages to the U.S.S.R., "these Cuban missiles alone, in view of all the other megatonnage the Soviets were capable of unleashing upon the U.S. did not substantially alter the strategic balance."[65] Deputy Secretary of Defense Roswell Gilpatric was of the same opinion. While on a television program two weeks after the crisis, he stated: "[I] don't believe that we were under much greater threat from the Soviet Union's power, taken in totally, after this than before."[66]

Now, with the benefit of a broader and in depth analysis, we can assert that, as Defense Secretary Robert S. McNamara correctly pointed out when he affirmed that a missile was a missile independently of where it was fired from, the missiles in Cuba would not have affected the strategic balance —although perhaps not for the reasons McNamara had in mind at the time.

Immediately after Kennedy's October 22 speech to the nation, McNamara gave a not-for-attribution backgrounder emphasizing the extremely dangerous situation created by the possibility of a Soviet-Cuban use of nuclear weapons on the Island. But McNamara significantly avoided giving details about the type of Soviet missiles installed in Cuba. Nor did he give any information about the number of missiles and sites. The Secretary of Defense produced just one picture, taken by a U-2 plane flying over Cuba, which showed what looked like "scars" on the ground —totally meaningless to the reporters— which according to some photo-interpretation experts were IRBM sites in their early phase of installation.

Though McNamara admitted that the administration did not know at that time if any IRBMs were actually in Cuba, he explained, pointing to a chart, that the missiles covered an extensive area whose inner ring included Washington D.C. and most of Central America, and whose outer ring included almost all of the United States and the northern part of South America.[67]

At the time, almost everybody accepted the administration's claims about the range of the missiles in Cuba at face value. But not much time passed before some analysts questioned the figures. The Kennedy administration claimed a range of over 1,000 miles for the MRBMs, and more than 2,000 miles for the IRBMs. But, less than a month after the crisis was over, an editorial in the highly respected magazine *Aviation Week and Space Technology* seriously questioned the range which the U.S. government officials attributed to the missiles. The editorial is so revealing that it is useful to quote it in detail:

> There is considerable skepticism that the MRBMs in Cuba have the 1,000-mile range claimed for them by the US official spokesmen and a strong suspicion that this alleged intelligence was tailored to fit political goals. The same MRBMs, displayed in Moscow parades for a number of years, were never previously credited with much more than 500-mile range. Using alcohol fuel and red fumic nitric acid as an oxidizer, their propulsion efficiency makes even this range with a fractional megaton warhead optimistic.
>
> However, the alleged threat posed by 1,000-mile range IRBMs would have become genuine with the arrival of the 1,200-mile range IRBMs for

which launching pads were being constructed in Cuba. Why the IRBM that has been carried in the official U.S. appraisal of the Soviet inventory for many years as roughly a 1,200-mile weapons was suddenly stretched to a 2,200-mile weapon has never been satisfactorily explained by any of the Pentagon or White House spokesmen making these claims, ...

Some Washington observers cynically claimed that these Soviet missile ranges were deliberately stretched before the November election to include more states in the potential target areas.[68]

It is interesting that, though the *Aviation Week's* editorial appeared just after the crisis, and Neville Brown mentioned the fact again in 1964,[69] no one seemed to notice it. It was not until 1979, when David Detzer published his book *The Brink*, that the official figures were questioned.[70]

Even more startling is that, as late as October 27-28, 1962, American intelligence sources apparently had been unable to determine the exact number of missiles in Cuba. Thirty-three SS-4 missiles allegedly had been identified and it was supposed that there might also be some SS-5s, because the NPIC photointerpreters had identified their distinctive launchers and some supporting equipment unique to them, but the exact number was not known. Nevertheless, when Khrushchev revealed that the Soviet Union had only forty-two SS-4s in Cuba, the figure offered by the "Russian liars"[71] was accepted at face value and nobody seemed to have taken much care in verifying the actual number of missiles on the Island.

President Kennedy mentioned medium-range missiles which can reach points as far as 1,000 nautical miles and intermediate-range missiles capable of striking points as far as 2,200 nautical miles. But *Newsweek* also found some evidence that the range of the missiles in Cuba was exaggerated. Previous military intelligence estimates of Soviet MRBMs were 400 to 700 nautical miles, and IRBM no more than 1,130 to 1,300 nautical miles.[72] According to Neville Brown, the Soviet IRBMs were at the time large clumsy weapons with unstorable liquid fuel that were operated from static emplacements with elaborate ground support, including concrete bunkers.[73] Though the Kennedy administration credited them with a range of 2,100 miles, these missiles have been credited before with a range of just 1,200 miles.[74] Therefore, one has to conclude that, given the lack of care shown by the Kennedy administration, it is hardly likely that any severe threat emanated from the missiles in Cuba.

If we accept Hermann's definition of crises as unanticipated situations of severe threat and short decision-making time,[75] it is easy to see that, given the facts analyzed above, the events of October 1962, were either a mild crisis[76] or no crisis at all. The threat was highly exaggerated, the situation was anticipated, and the short decision-making time was arbitrarily set. If one is to place the Cuban missile crisis in Hermann's situational cube, it would be more accurately placed this way:

THE NUCLEAR DECEPTION

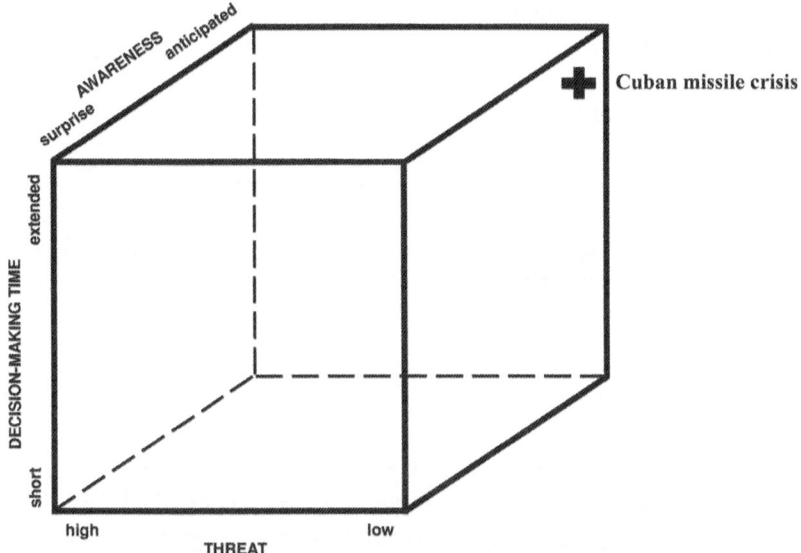

(Adapted from Hermann, "Some Issues in the Study of International Crisis," in Charles F. Hermann, edit., *International Crisis: Insight from Behavioral Research* (New York: The Free Press, 1972), p. 14.)

But there are even more facts supporting this thesis.

The Incredibly Shrinking Nuclear Warheads

At his news conference on August 29, President Kennedy was asked about the rumors concerning the presence of Soviet strategic missiles on Cuban soil. His answer is revealing:

> We cannot base the issue of war and peace on a rumor or report which is not substantiated, or which some member of Congress refuses to tell us where he heard it.[77] ... To persuade our allies to come with us, to hazard ... the security ... as well as the peace of the free world, we have to move with hard intelligence.[78]

According to William Colby, though he was aware that the CIA had been getting reports about the preparations the Russians were making to place strategic missiles in Cuba, the agency analysts tended to discount these reports as exaggerations or figments of overheated imaginations. But when the definitive intelligence finally came from the U-2 and its photographs, this "hard" undisputable intelligence convinced them that the Russians were in fact deploying offensive missiles on Cuban soil.[79] Also, in a joint statement made on the 20th anniversary of the crisis, Rusk, McNamara, Ball, Gilpatric, Sorensen, and Bundy, six of Kennedy's key men, asserted that, in order to assure the support of U.S. allies and the readiness of the Soviet government to withdraw, Americans needed to show proof of

Soviet misconduct that simply could not be refuted. According to this line of reasoning, no evidence less explicit and authoritative than that of photography would have been sufficient.[80]

But there is more than meets the eye in this *roman à clef* called the Cuban missile crisis. The White House tapes of October 16 have Secretary of Defense Robert S. McNamara concluding that since photography revealed land still unfenced, the warheads were probably still not in place.[81] Moreover, in a session with newsmen in the Pentagon on the night of October 22, less than an hour after Kennedy's speech, McNamara was asked by journalists if the U.S. knew whether the nuclear warheads were in Cuba too. McNamara's answer was quite intriguing:

> "We don't know. Nuclear warheads are of such size that it is extremely unlikely we would ever be able to observe them by the intelligence means open to us."[82]

Was Secretary McNamara trying to say that Russian technology was so advanced that their nuclear warheads were microscopic? Didn't he know about the resolution power of optics and film of American surveillance planes? Several years before, in order to make sure President Eisenhower understood just how revolutionary the U-2 was, CIA officials arranged for one of the U-2s reconnaissance photographs taken during a test flight in 1955 be shot from 55,000 feet over one of Eisenhower's favorite golf courses in Augusta, Georgia. As Eisenhower noted smilingly, the picture clearly showed golf balls lying on a putting green. Was McNamara trying to make the American public believe that the Soviet nuclear warheads were smaller then golf balls?

Even French President Charles DeGaulle, who at the time of the Missile Crisis was shown U-2 photos of Cuban airfields, was forced to utter a loud *"C'est formidable"* as he looked over the pictures with a magnifying glass and picked out individual planes parked on the runway. Was Secretary of Defense McNamara unaware of the state of the art of American surveillance technology?

The U-2 spy plane had a very sophisticated system of high-technology cameras. The heart of the U-2's photo imagery system was the "B-Camera's" lens. This device was the result of work done by Harvard University astronomer Dr. James Baker. It consisted of a 36" focal length unit, with resolving power unmatched by any other lens in the world at the time. Its acuity was rated at nearly 60 lines per millimeter —no less than four times the maximum power obtained from comparable lenses developed less than a decade earlier during WWII. At 65,000 feet, surface objects less than 2 feet in diameter were discernible and interpretable.[83]

It is, therefore, difficult to accept McNamara's claims that the nuclear warheads were of such a size that it was extremely unlikely they would ever be able to observe them by the intelligence means open to the U.S. As we have seen above, the U.S. intelligence had at the time the technical means capable of detecting the nuclear warheads —provided they were there!

THE NUCLEAR DECEPTION 265

Russian soldiers unloading a nuclear warhead in the Ukraine. *Spektrum der Wissenschaft*, October 1992.

As an example, I have brought the photo above. As you can see, nuclear warheads are big enough to be detected by the sophisticated U-2's cameras. We may safely guess that Soviet-made nuclear warheads forty years ago may have been even larger —even today, miniaturization is not a strong characteristic of Russian technology. So, it seems that Mr. McNamara was perhaps talking about some microscopic nuclear warheads, not very big Russian-made ones.

When somebody asked him if the type of missiles already in Cuba had nuclear capability, McNamara made some enigmatic statements:

> It is inconceivable to me that it would be used with another type of warhead. The photographs I showed you were the typical missile exclusive of the warhead. Normally the warhead would be mated at the last moment as the missile was put on the launcher, and erected into position. Those particular photographs do not show the warheads. As I stated earlier, we have not detected the location of the warheads. I think it is fair to say we may never by the means of the intelligence open to us. But it is absolutely inconceivable to those of us who have worked on the problem and have been exposed to it that this equipment, in this state of readiness, a high state of operational capability, would have been placed in Cuba without warheads close to the missiles themselves.[84]

When asked if the administration had any intelligence reports before the beginning of the crisis that indicated that there were strategic missiles in Cuba, McNamara categorically answered:

No. There have been rumors off and on —I have noticed some of them in the press, as a matter of fact, I suppose coming from refugees— of a variety of types of equipment in Cuba. But we had no, what I would call "hard" intelligence until, I said Monday midnight, maybe it was 10 o'clock Monday night.[85]

Aside from the fact that Secretary McNamara did not try to hide that U.S. intelligence never detected nuclear warheads in Cuba, two points of his argument are inconsistent. First of all, he stressed the point that it was inconceivable that there were no nuclear warheads for the missiles in Cuba. But, if one is to believe his own story, less than three weeks before, American intelligence had estimated that it was inconceivable that the Russians would place strategic missiles in Cuba, and they apparently did —or, to put it more accurately, they deployed some canvas-covered objects which resembled the crates that may have contained strategic missiles. Therefore, why not accept another "Russian impossibility?" Secondly, why did the Kennedy administration need "hard" intelligence to accept the fact of missiles in Cuba, but only needed such "soft" intelligence as McNamara's "inconceivability theory" to believe that there were also nuclear warheads in the Island? Why this inconceivable double standard of credibility? What seems inconceivable is that Robert S. McNamara, whom many people considered one of the most rational and sharp American minds,[86] had mistaken —like Dr. Sack's patient who mistook his wife for a hat— canvas-covered objects for strategic nuclear missiles.

I am aware of recent claims that nuclear warheads were actually in the Island, and that more were bound for Cuba in Soviet ships. But CIA reports at the time consistently denied the presence of nuclear warheads in Cuba. A CIA report on October 23, 1962, offering an estimate of the operational readiness of the missiles in Cuba stated in very clear terms: "We are unable to confirm the presence of nuclear warheads."[87] Indeed, American planes, flying low over the missile sites and the Soviets ships, apparently never detected any of the radiation that could be expected from nuclear warheads. Nor any of the American warships sailing close to Soviet ships and submarines reported any radiation. As a matter of fact, almost no mention to NUCINT[88] is made in the hundreds of thousands of pages that have been written about the crisis. This is remarkable, because the technology to detect radiation already existed at the time. In the 1960s the NEDS 900 series of radiation detectors had been developed and deployed in the Dardanelles as a way to monitor the presence of nuclear weapons aboard Soviet warships transiting the strait from the Black Sea.

Gen. William Y. Smith, who was a Major and an assistant to Gen. Maxwell Taylor in the White House at the time, has reported a very interesting detail. While reviewing message traffic from U.S. intelligence sources on Soviet military activity, Gen. Smith found out a report that a U.S. Navy ship had picked up suspicious levels of radioactivity emitted by a Soviet freighter, the *Poltava*. He suggested to

Gen. Taylor that he ask Admiral Anderson if the emanations meant the ship was carrying nuclear warheads. At the next Joint Chief's meeting, Taylor posed the question again to Anderson, who replied, somewhat embarrassed, that he had not seen the message. Later that morning, Anderson's office informed Smith that the report had little significance; that Smith had misread it.[89]

Therefore, it makes sense to believe that the U.S. had the means to detect radiation from nuclear warheads leaving Cuba, without having to board the Soviet ships. But, again, no mention is made of this important fact in any of the available declassified documents on the Cuban missile crisis. Also, Admiral Anderson's behavior, as described by Gen. Smith, is strange, to say the least, because that report was extremely significant. I hope that it has not mysteriously disappeared.

It seems that the subject of radiation from nuclear warheads during the crisis is somehow touchy. During the Havana meeting, Raymond Garthoff mentioned that "Well, we never confirmed that there were warheads in Cuba." To what Scott Sagan, another participant in the meeting, asked "Did you have unusual radioactivity detections?" Garthoff's answer was sort of enigmatic: "We had some indications from inside the Soviet Union that preparations were under way to move warheads to Cuba. This movement was, however, interdicted by the quarantine. *I'm afraid I shouldn't say more than that.*"[90]

Therefore, either the Americans detected no radiation from the Soviet ships, and they kept the fact secret, or they simply forgot that they had the means to check indirectly the presence of nuclear warheads, or they never tried to detect radiation from nuclear warheads in Cuba because they were pretty sure there were never any in the Island. This may explain the strange behavior of the Kennedy administration in not forcing on the defeated Soviets the physical inspection of their ships who allegedly were bringing the missiles and their nuclear warheads back to the Soviet Union.

The Metamorphosis of the Soviet Missiles

In his October 22 tv address, President Kennedy stated that the Soviet armaments in Cuba, "included medium-range ballistic missiles *capable* of carrying a nuclear warhead," and also "jet bombers *capable* of carrying nuclear weapons."[91] Also, Adlai Stevenson, in his request to convene the U.N. Security Council dated that same day, made reference in the first paragraph of the document to "long-range ballistic missiles *capable* of carrying thermonuclear warheads."[92] This terminology is evidently misleading. As I mentioned above, almost any vehicle is in principle capable of carrying a nuclear warhead, from a B-52 to a Jeep. The real issue in this case is obviously not capability, but the reality of nuclear warheads actually installed on the tip of the missiles or, at least, very close to the missiles and ready to be installed. But, some paragraphs later, Stevenson suddenly jumps from assertions of "capability" to assert "the fact of nuclear missiles and other offensive weapons in Cuba"[93] —a "fact" that nobody has been able to confirm.

A U.S. draft resolution presented the same day to the UN Security Council, expressed American concerns that "nuclear missiles and other offensive weapons have been secretly introduced into Cuba."[94] However, a statement by Secretary Rusk to the Organization of American States (OAS) on October 23, mentions missiles in Cuba "*capable* of carrying nuclear warheads."[95] But, a few paragraphs below, it asserts that the U.S. quarantine will prevent further additions to soviet offensive nuclear military power in our midst."[96]

A resolution adopted by the OAS the next day, October 23, jumps back again and refers to middle-range missiles in Cuban territory, "*capable* of carrying nuclear warheads."[97] A statement by Ambassador Stevenson to the UN Security Council, also on October 23, expresses that several installations in Cuba, "include medium-range ballistic missiles *capable* of carrying nuclear warheads," and also that "jet bombers, *capable* of carrying nuclear weapons are now been uncrated and assembled in Cuba."[98] But, just a few paragraphs below, Stevenson affirms that the missiles in Cuba "introduce a nuclear threat into an area now free of it," and that their installation results in "the most formidable nuclear base in the world outside existing treaty systems."[99] Stevenson also observes how "this once peaceful island is being transformed into a formidable missile and strategic air base armed with the deadliest, far-reaching modern nuclear weapons."[100] However, some paragraphs below, Stevenson accuses the Soviet Union of sending to Cuba "jet bombers *capable* of carrying atomic warheads."[101] And, by the end of the statement, some mentions are made about the Americans now being "under the nuclear gun,"[102] and to the "dreadful question of nuclear arms."[103]

A statement made by Stevenson to the press on October 23, as a reply to Soviet declarations, asserts that, "it is now apparent that President Dorticós of Cuba was admitting the existence of long-range nuclear weapons in Cuba."[104] Next day, October 24, Sir Patric Dean, British Ambassador to the UN, made a statement to the UN Security Council affirming that his government strongly believed that no one can legitimize the installation in Cuba of "nuclear missiles."[105] The same day, the Irish Ambassador joined the chorus stating to the U.N. Security Council that we "have reached the stage when the extension of nuclear bases and the spread of nuclear weapons" are unacceptable.[106] A statement by French Ambassador Roger Seydox, also the same day, mentions "the appearance of foreign nuclear missiles on Cuban soil."[107] A more cautious statement by British Prime Minister Harold Macmillan, on October 25, observes that, "All these [missiles in Cuba] are designed to carry and must be presumed to carry, nuclear bombs."[108] Like Kafka's character Gregorio Samsa, the missiles in Cuba had metamorphosed from being *capable* of carrying nuclear warheads to actual carriers of nuclear warheads nobody saw.

In a statement to the UN Security Council, dated October 25, Stevenson mentions the word "nuclear" twelve times.[109] However, in a second statement to the UN Security Council the same day, Stevenson, though still mentioning the word "nuclear" twice, by the end of the document affirms that near the town of Guanajay, southwest of Havana, close to a missile site there is a building in construction with a heavy arch which "may well be intended as the storage for the nuclear warheads." But he has to concede that "The installation is not yet complete, *and no warheads are yet visible.*"[110]

It is particularly significant that, although administration officials were now talking freely about nuclear weapons in Cuba, in all his successive statements President Kennedy stuck to the original version of the "capability" of the missiles rather than affirming that there were actually nuclear warheads in the island.[111]

Also, in Kennedy's message to Khrushchev acknowledging the Soviet leader's information about his orders to dismantle the missile sites —one of the last official documents that originated during the crisis— the President encourages Khrushchev to devote attention to the problem of disarmament and that "we should give priority to questions relating to the proliferation of nuclear weapons, on earth and in outer space, and to the great effort for a nuclear ban."[112] But, conspicuously, he did not relate, not even indirectly, his nuclear reference to the Cuban issue.

Still, in a statement read by President Kennedy at a press conference held on November 20, three weeks after the crisis ended, he asserted, "the Soviet government has stated that all nuclear weapons have been withdrawn from Cuba." This was, of course, a misstatement, because, during his messages to Kennedy, the Soviet leader deliberately refrained from referring to the missiles in Cuba as nuclear. Particularly in Khrushchev's message of October 28, informing Kennedy of his order to dismantle the missile sites and to return the missiles to the Soviet Union, the Soviet Premier went to great pains to avoid mentioning the word "nuclear."[113] Moreover, Soviet diplomats consistently denied that nuclear weapons were on the Island and, at the regular meeting of the U.N. Security Council held on October 24, the Soviet Union delegates categorically denied they had armed Cuba with nuclear weapons.[114] The most interesting thing about Kennedy's statement, however, is that it is the Soviets, not him, who were quoted as mentioning *nuclear* weapons.

McCone reasoned that the Russians had never installed nuclear missiles of substantial range in Europe because they feared they might be turned against them. But, even though the missiles in Cuba had sufficient range to reach much of the United States, they would have never been able to reach the Soviet Union.[115] Yet, McCone failed to consider that Khrushchev should have been fully conscious that if just a single nuclear missile fired from Cuba hit the United States, it most probably would have triggered an all-out nuclear response by the Americans, not only against Cuba, but also against the Soviet Union. Therefore, it is very improbable that Nikita Khrushchev would have placed the fate of the Soviet Union so close to the trigger-happy Fidel Castro. Therefore, Soviet leaders may have taken special precautions to avoid even the remotest possibility of such a disastrous occurrence.

It has been mentioned that, at the time of the crisis, the Soviets lacked the sophisticated PAL (Permissive Action Links) technology to have full control over their nuclear missiles. But most people seem to miss the fact that Khrushchev actually had an even better way to fully avoid the unauthorized use of the Soviet nuclear missiles by any person, particularly Castro. The real joke of the Cuban missile crisis, said Carlos Franqui, "is that the nuclear warheads were never installed in the missiles."[116]

But, even if the American media raised no objection to the dubious arguments of the Kennedy administration, not everybody accepted their claims about "nuclear" missiles in Cuba. Schlesinger recalled that the British received the President's speech denouncing the missiles in Cuba with great skepticism. Some even questioned whether nuclear missiles really were on the Island.[117]

According to authors George and Smoke, the capability of fast deployment of the Russian MRBMs probably encouraged the Soviets to think that the missiles could be made operational and would serve to deter a U.S. attack while additional missiles, including IRBMs, were being readied.[118] But this reasoning has some weak points. First of all, the Soviet leader must have supposed that once the missiles were discovered —and, given Khrushchev's knowledge of American surveillance techniques after a U-2 had been shot down in the Soviet Union two years before, he would have guessed that it would not take too long— the first thing Americans would do would be to blockade the Island to stop the introduction of more war matériel. Therefore, the most elementary logic dictated that each missile must be accompanied by its assigned nuclear or conventional warhead in order to guarantee its immediate readiness. Yet when the missiles finally seemed to be ready for firing, there were no signs anywhere of nuclear warheads —or any other type of warhead, for that matter— for them.

On August, 1962, Arthur Krock of the *New York Times* criticized Kennedy's August 29 press conference in which the President had made adverse comments to those who favored invading Cuba. According to Krock, a naval patrol around the Island was the most effective means of keeping Cuba from acquiring Soviet missiles and it would not involve military invasion at all.[119] The next day a dispatch was brought to the *Times* with word that, in fact, the administration already had a "naval patrol" around the island. Consequently, unless the nuclear warheads had been brought to Cuba by air —a not too probable occurrence— one must assume that the naval patrol checking what the Soviets were sending to Cuba would have detected at least some clues of the presence of nuclear warheads in the Soviet ships bound for Cuba. But no such detection was ever reported.

Most analysts who studied the Cuban missile crisis during the first twenty years after the event, ascribed either very little,[120] or relatively high[121] military value to the missiles in Cuba. However, since the available evidence shows that it has never been proved that nuclear warheads were ever in Cuba —a fact that most analysts seem to ignore or to forget— one must certainly conclude that the military value of the Soviet missiles in Cuba was close to zero. The military value of the missiles, *if* the Soviets had sent the nuclear warheads to Cuba, and *if* they finally had installed them on the missiles, is a worthless speculation that has nothing to do with the historical facts. In retrospect, it seems clear that Khrushchev never ordered the nuclear warheads to be sent to Cuba, and that he never intended to do such a foolish thing.

Therefore, either the best and the brightest fooled themselves into assuming[122] that the nuclear warheads were actually in Cuba, or they fooled the rest of us. Frankly, the more I read about the Cuban missile crisis the less I think that they fooled themselves.

Kennedy's Politics

In the election time days of September and October, 1962, Republicans charged that the U.S. was not taking the necessary steps to protect its national security. Some critics of the Kennedy administration, such as Senator Homer E. Capehart of Indiana, even suggested that the U.S. should take military actions against Cuba.[123] On August, the Gallup poll indicated that President Kennedy's popularity had slumped to 61 points, the lowest rating he had received during his tenure.[124]

By September, 1962, many American were in an angry mood about Cuba: according to a Gallup Poll of September 18, 1962, 71 percent of the persons interviewed wanted some kind of action against Castro's Cuba. The poll indicated a large rise in public concern compared with a poll taken three months earlier.[125] The Kennedy administration was acutely aware of the Cuban issue and its negative impact on the public, and kept track of it through the public opinion polls since the Bay of Pigs. Cuba had become, according to Theodore Sorensen, Kennedy's "Achilles' heel."

In early October, 1962, the Cuban issue had become the main political concern. The *Washington Post* reported on October 17 and 18 that 344 editors and members of Congress considered it the primary campaign issue, and that the GOP campaign chiefs had said that Cuba was the top issue.[126] Early in October Joseph Alsop reported President Kennedy's concern about the power of the Cuban issue to attract votes for the Republicans. Apparently, Kennedy feared more the potential danger of losing votes than the Soviet build up in Cuba.[127]

American politicians realized long ago that national emergency situations have great potential for the expansion of the power of national leaders —a fact that has become even more evident after the attacks of September 11th, 2001. Kennedy's announcement of a national emergency, and the fact that the nation was virtually on a war footing, had the immediate effect that the press avoided embarrassing questions or criticizing the administration's interpretation and the facts it made available to the press. As it always happens when similar situations arise, the function of the press in the American democratic society was neutralized.[128]

The very fact that the removal of the American missiles in Turkey had been considered previously to the Cuban crisis raises questions about the very necessity of a crisis at all. President Kennedy could have given Khrushchev an ultimatum in private before disclosing the presence of the missiles in Cuba, as normal diplomatic procedures indicate.[129] As a matter of fact, that was exactly what Adlai Stevenson said Kennedy should do.[130] The fact was also observed by James Reston, who wrote, "The new Kennedy style of diplomacy is now operating in the Cuban crisis. It is highly personal and national." ... "[The President] did not follow the normal diplomatic practice of giving his antagonist a quiet escape from fighting or withdrawing..."[131]

The President, however, made no effort to use diplomatic means to solve the crisis but instead precipitated a perhaps avoidable confrontation with the Soviet Premier. Some critics of the President's actions suggested that his reaction had nothing to do with the missiles in Cuba, but that he had the forthcoming congressional elections in mind.

After the missile crisis, the results of the congressional elections turned out much better than Kennedy had hoped. He had expected to lose ten or fifteen seats in the House and perhaps gain one or two in the Senate, but the Democrats lost only four in the House and gained that many in the Senate. Whereas the Republicans had been exploiting the Cuban issue before October 22, they had been obviously hurt by it thereafter. What had been a major liability for the Democrats had turned into a major advantage after Kennedy's "victory."[132]

With Khrushchev's retreat there came a sense of triumph. President Kennedy's popularity, down sharply in the summer, rose dramatically as the press hailed him as the architect of a great diplomatic victory. His courage, his coolness, and his carefully calculated combination of firmness and restraint, won him the applause of the press. And the American people responded by giving him a Democratic Congress in the mid-term elections, which were held only nine days after the crisis had ended. Though at the time a few dissidents raised questions about the veracity of Kennedy's victory, the vast majority of Americans accepted the Cuban missile crisis as JFK's finest hour.[133]

The removal from Cuba of what looked like Soviet missiles neutralized the internal political threats against the Kennedy administration, endangered because of the widespread domestic dissatisfaction with its policies toward Cuba. According to Representative Bob Wilson of California, the outcome of the crisis cost the Republicans as many as twenty seats. Wilson, Chairman of the Republican Congressional Committee, insisted that the administration knew in late September about the Soviet missiles in Cuba, but delayed announcing it in order to provoke a crisis at election time, having in mind that the nation traditionally rallies around the President in a time of crisis.[134]

It is known that at the time of the crisis, many people believed Kennedy had domestic rather than international politics in mind. Even Eisenhower was skeptic when McCone informed him about the missiles. Perhaps he also suspected that Kennedy might be playing politics with the Cuba issue on the eve of Congressional elections. The thought was shared also by British Ambassador David Ormsby-Gore, a friend of Kennedy. When told about the crisis, the Ambassador thought that the British people must somewhat be needed to be persuaded that the missile crisis was real and not a political trick played by Kennedy to get votes for his party.[135] No wonder Roger Hilsman, head of intelligence in the State Department and then Assistant Secretary of State for the Far East, asserted that if the missiles were not important enough to justify a confrontation with the Soviet Union, as McNamara initially believed, then the U.S. might not be in mortal danger, but the Kennedy administration most certainly was.

How Close to the Brink?

One aspect consistently emphasized in earlier revisionist analyses of the Cuban missile crisis was President Kennedy's "irresponsible" and "reckless" behavior in deciding to go to the brink of nuclear war just to prove to the world that he was a tough guy.[136] Walton argued that "Kennedy, without sufficient reason, consciously risked a nuclear catastrophe."[137] Louise Fitzsimmons observed how, "in order to force Soviet missiles off the island of Cuba, John F. Kennedy risked a nuclear war that might have meant the destruction of all life on earth ..."[138] Louis Heren pointed out that, though Khrushchev agreed to remove his missiles from Cuba if Kennedy took similar steps with the American missiles in Turkey, the President refused to accept the exchange and "the world was taken close to the nuclear brink."[139] The Cuban missile crisis "brought the nation as close to an all-out nuclear war as it ever has been," observed Sidney Lens.[140]

In his summary of the event made a few weeks later, President Kennedy admitted that, though it was questionable whether the missiles would have changed the strategic balance of power, "It would have appeared to, and appearances contribute to realities."[141] Many doubted, however, that appearance and political costs alone were worth a nuclear war whose risk the President himself estimated between one-in-three.[142] Yet, there are strong reasons to believe that President Kennedy actually never brought the United States near the brink of nuclear war, as the revisionist historians of the old school claimed. Even Allison observed that it was difficult to think that Kennedy actually felt that the chances of nuclear Armageddon were one-in-three.[143] Nor there is any proof that Premier Khrushchev brought the world any closer to the brink. But the controversy still remains, therefore it is worthwhile to analyze more in depth the facts surrounding Kennedy's behavior during the crisis.

It is interesting to remember how Kennedy tried to exercise absolute control even over the smallest details of the crisis. The President's micromanagement style sharply contrasts with his apparent recklessness relating to broader issues involving Khrushchev. Did Kennedy really believe he was bringing the world to the brink of nuclear Armageddon or did he actually know more than he admitted? Was he just taking a controlled risk, and not a big one at that? One possible explanation of Kennedy's efforts to control all aspects of the action may have been that, though he was sure that the Soviet Premier was not going to risk nuclear war just because of Cuba, he feared that an accident caused by the reckless behavior of an overly patriotic member of the American armed services could trigger a spasm nuclear response from the Soviets.

A little known incident that occurred during the crisis clearly illustrates the point. President Kennedy became alarmed after discovering that the Navy, unbeknownst to the White House, had engaged in wartime pursuit of Soviet submarines in the North Atlantic. Perhaps Kennedy had more to fear from his own military than from Khrushchev.[144]

Among the precautions which Kennedy took to avoid a costly mistake by subordinates ignoring orders was the bizarre fact that he reportedly ordered the missiles in Turkey to be defused. Strange behavior indeed for a commander-in-chief of a nation supposedly at the brink of nuclear war.

Also, it is known how he went to great pains trying to control all aspects of the blockade and the frictions this aroused from Navy officers. One explanation for his apparently bizarre behavior is that Kennedy was fully aware that Soviet missiles in Cuba lacked nuclear warheads, and, therefore, nothing was to be feared from them. Another significant detail is that, even though during the crisis the U.S. and all federal agencies went to DEFCON 3, a very serious condition of defense readiness, the local civil defense organizations were not notified officially of this condition.[145]

Moreover, the Emergency Command Center at Mt. Weather was never placed on alert.[146] Even more significative is the fact that, according to a close witness, "President Kennedy never paid much attention to the football. Even during the Cuban missile crisis he never considered reaching for the briefcase."[147]

Kennedy's certainty also explains why he accepted at face value the Soviet claims about the number of missiles in Cuba and why he finally contented himself with just an aerial verification of the Russian ships performing a strip-tease on the high seas. This is also why he never pressed for the *in situ* verifications originally stated in U.S. official documents. He knew very well that there never had been any nuclear warheads on Cuban soil.

President Kennedy knew all the time that the United States was not in any immediate danger. Furthermore, as he publicly expressed in a television interview, he was entirely confident that Khrushchev had neither the intention, nor the desire, to use the missiles in Cuba.

Let's accept for a moment the hypothesis, advanced both by Khrushchev and by several American analysts, that the Soviet Premier's goal was either to protect Castro's Cuba from an American invasion or to equalize the "balance of power" or both. But, for this hypothesis to be correct, we must also accept that Khrushchev made the following mistakes:

1. He deployed in Cuba the same type of missiles he knew Penkovsky had given the Americans all the information about,

2. The missile sites were built in such a way as to be easily discovered by U.S. spy planes in an early phase of installation,
3. Breaking with all previous usage, he ordered nuclear missiles to be installed in a country far beyond the Soviet military sphere of influence,
4. The country where he deployed the missiles was controlled by an unreliable ally, whom he had tried to overthrow by force just a few days before,
5. He totally miscalculated what the American reaction would have been when faced with the foreseeable discovery of the missiles,
6. He failed to bring the nuclear warheads to Cuba before the also foreseeable American blockade of the Island,
7. Once the missiles were discovered, he was not prepared to face a strong American military response against the U.S.S.R.

The weakness of this hypothesis is that in order to accept it you have also to accept that Nikita Khrushchev and his military advisors were a bunch of incompetent idiots, a fact that cannot be inferred from their previous behavior

Neville Brown pointed out that, "warheads were never seen in Cuba," adding that, "so we don't know what the Soviets had in mind."[148] But now we know what Khrushchev had in mind. He had set up a trap to catch Kennedy and, as a bonus, get rid of his arrogant, suspicious ally. Had the Americans invaded Cuba, they would have found no nuclear warheads, and most likely not even strategic missiles. After such a discovery, which the Soviets would have immediately publicized, President Kennedy and the United States would instantly have become the laughing stock of the whole world. As a matter of fact Khrushchev enjoyed setting up those kind of traps. The one he set up for Eisenhower when he announced that the Soviets had shot down a U-2 plane, but kept secret the fact that the pilot had been captured alive, is proof that he was not alien to this type of scheme.

In the first hours after the discovery of the missiles someone in the Ex Comm said that "Even a gigantic hoax had to be guarded against."[149] Well, it *was* a gigantic hoax. Like in Miguel de Cervantes' *Quixote*, the ferocious giants aggressively moving their arms ended up being peaceful windmills. Whether Kennedy's refusal to invade Cuba and fall into Khrushchev's trap was a result of blind dumb luck or of extreme cleverness is something we may know someday.

Was the Crisis a Pseudo-event?

According to Eliot Cohen, the Cuban missile crisis had all the characteristics of a soap opera summer mini-drama. Essentially it was a simple plot studded with movie-star personalities. The whole incident unfolds and is resolved in just under two short weeks. Major players such as the handsome, young U.S. President John F. Kennedy, the pugnacious and thuggish Soviet Premier Nikita Khrushchev, and the mysterious revolutionary guerrilla leader Fidel Castro provide dramatic performances in the crisis scenario. Khrushchev deploys missiles into Cuba, Kennedy confronts him and demands their removal, Khrushchev ultimately relents and withdraws the missiles. Several sub-plots, like the downing of a U-2 plane over Cuba, add just enough interest and complexity to complete the thespian similitude, and, "Like any good play, the crisis has an easily discerned beginning, middle, and end."[150] In other words, the crisis was a made-for-television show; a pseudo-event.

Daniel Boorstin coined the word "pseudo-event" —using the prefix *pseudo* that comes from the Greek word meaning false or deceiving— to denote the new kind of synthetic novelty which lately has flooded the American experience.[151] According to Boorstin a pseudo-event is a happening that possesses the following characteristics: (1) It is not spontaneous, but comes about because someone has planned, planted or incited it; (2) it is planted primarily (though not always exclusively) for the immediate purpose of being reported or reproduced. Therefore, its occurrence is arranged for the convenience of the reporting or reproducing media. Its success is measured by how widely it is reported; (3) its relation to the underlying reality of the situation is ambiguous. Its interest arises largely from this very ambiguity. Without some of this ambiguity a pseudo-event cannot be very interesting; and (4) actually it is intended to be a self-fulfilling prophesy.[152]

If we analyze from this perspective the event known as the Cuban missile crisis, it becomes evident that it largely meets Boorstin's requirements for pseudo-events. As I have shown, the crisis was not spontaneous, but was planned in detail by President Kennedy and his advisors. Furthermore, the evidence indicates that Kennedy had the means to avoid the crisis, but instead he let it develop and even magnified it.

On October 22, President Kennedy addressed the nation in a prime-time, coast-to-coast speech somebody called a "television spectacular."[153] As David Wise observed, few Americans can emotionally resist the dramatic, sudden appearance of the President on television, particularly if it is in the midst of a foreign policy crisis.[154] Consequently, American presidents have learned to use television as a way to attract public attention and to enhance their political images.[155]

Boorstin also observed that, because of the power and prestige of his position and due to the influence of the Washington press corps, the American president has direct access to the world of pseudo-events.[156] In its effort to convince the press about the reality of the crisis, the Kennedy administration resorted to the melodramatic ploy of telling some of the Washington reporters not to be more than fifteen minutes from the White House, because they had been selected to go with the President to some caves in Virginia in case of nuclear war. Even the most hard-core skeptics among the reporters took this directive seriously. Almost all of them, particularly those whose lives were to be spared, tacitly consented to the Administration's control of the news.

Some critics of the Kennedy administration have argued that the crisis was of Kennedy's own making, because he initially relied on armed force instead of normal diplomatic channels to force a withdrawal of the Soviet missiles from Cuba.[157] Moreover, in a series of remarkable articles appearing on October 20, 22, and 24,

1962, the *New York Times* analyst C.L. Zultzberg gave further evidence that the motives behind the American action in the crisis were dynamic and not responsive in character. Four months later James Reston summarized Zultzberg's conclusions when he affirmed that the Administration had decided, some weeks before the Cuban confrontation, to have a showdown with the Soviet Union at a time and place of its own choosing. What puzzled Reston was that Khrushchev had chosen a time, October, and a place, Cuba, that seemed more suited to Kennedy than to himself.[158]

In retrospect, it is highly significative that less than one year after the Soviet Union and the United States apparently were on the brink of nuclear war, the American media was enthusiastically talking of a "new era" in Soviet-American relations, and both governments were exploring new areas of accommodation in a surprisingly quick defrosting of the Cold War. As Charles Lerche pointed out, such rapid transformation in the relations between two countries which less than a year before were allegedly on the brink of mutual annihilation is a picture which defies common sense.[159] Even in an era of rapid change it is unlikely that such total reorientation of foreign policy —almost a complete reversal— can occur in less than twelve months. One logical explanation for this apparent nonsense is that much of the crisis was just a "scenario;" a pseudoevent that passed for a real event just because it made as much noise as a real event.

Epilogue

More Questions than Answers

It is not uncommon in history to see men and governments set out to achieve a goal, and end up achieving something they neither expected nor desired —what some people call the law of unintended consequences. For example, Khrushchev's plan to get rid of Castro and discredit the Americans, brought prestige to the American President, helped make Castro stronger, and involved the Soviet Union in Castro's destiny even more. In addition, Khrushchev's attempt to lure Kennedy into doing the dirty work on his behalf, resulted in having the U.S. protecting Fidel from his enemies. Moreover, by backing down in the crisis, Khrushchev provided a major impetus to those in the Soviet government who were becoming increasingly restless with his leadership.

There was a peculiar series of developments during the years prior to Khrushchev's fall that have been considered to be among the main causes for his demotion. Among them was his decision not to support China in its border war with India; a growing discontent among the military over resource allocations; the agricultural stagnation and the continuing decline in the rate of economic growth; and unrest, and even rioting, among urban workers over rising food prices. Yet there are good reasons for believing that the embarrassing withdrawal of his "nuclear missiles" from Cuba irretrievably undermined Khrushchev's position. His last years in power were wasted; spent in non-productive, peevish fights with the Chinese and with the Soviet intellectuals and artists.

From 1958 on, Soviet relations with Communist China were bad, but they worsened rapidly and extensively after the Cuban affair. The Soviet Premier's poor performance when faced with Kennedy's stratagems confirmed Mao Tse-tung's opinion that Khrushchev was not only a coward, but also a traitor to the international Communist movement. That led Mao to hope that he could gain further support from other Communist and radical nationalists, like Castro and Ho Chi Minh, who shared the virulent anti-Americanism of the Chinese. Yet the fall of Khrushchev deprived Americans of a Soviet leader who in the long run proved to be easier to deal with than his successors.

The "Lessons" of the Cuban Missile Crisis

The Cuban missile crisis was hardly over when some members of the Kennedy administration, including President Kennedy himself, cautioned against the temptation to generalize from its outcome. The American media, however, engraved upon the public's minds the idea that Kennedy's success in forcing Khrushchev to remove the "nuclear" missiles from Cuba demonstrated the potentialities of a strong stand with the Soviets. The major lesson of the Cuban missile crisis, as most of them saw it, was that it proved that success in such situations was largely a matter of national will; of "guts." No one, however, knew better than Kennedy how different the real outcome was from the one publicized by the American media.

But the lauding of President Kennedy was not confined to the media. Soon after, the American academic community followed suit. In 1977, James Schlesinger, then Secretary of Defense, stated at a press conference that the United States stand on the Cuban missile crisis was the model to follow in American foreign policy. Few American political scientists have refrained from writing about the "lessons" of the Cuban missile crisis.

Yet, after having studied in detail the event known as the Cuban missile crisis I have arrived at the conclusion that the only lesson we can derive from it is that there are no lessons at all. And there are no lessons from the Cuban missile crisis for the same reasons that there are no great historical lessons.

In the sense that it can be used to predict the future, History has proved to be useless. But, if useless in predicting the future, could History at least be useful in preventing others from predicting the future? I have to confess that, in this sense, I am a pessimist. The reason for this is that all historical studies that draw lessons based on false premises and faulty data —as it seems to be the case in most studies of the Cuban missile crisis— are doomed to draw the wrong "lessons."

The Spanish-American philosopher George Santayana is often quoted as saying that those who cannot remember the past are condemned to repeat it. The problem with Santayana's dictum is that, before remembering the past, one must ask oneself: Which past? Which History? It is evident that there are as many histories as there are groups, or even individuals. To one group, for example, the Vietnam War means to never lose another war to communism. To another group, it means to never fight another war against a Third-World country. To me, it means that sending your sons to fight a war to defend the interests of transnational corporations is not a good idea.

To know if History repeats itself it would be necessary, as Arturo Uslar Petri has observed, to have a complete inventory of all human actions. But such a task is as impossible as the map of the Earth that Jorge Luis Borges imagined, so complete and exact in detail that it ended up being the same size as the Earth.

That explains why some historians, faced with the impossibility of creating history, just create myths. And myths, as Theodore Draper once observed, are notoriously hard to die. They can flourish, subside, and flourish again. But, if the official myth to be presented is particularly unbelievable, it is necessary to have honorable men study it and proclaim that they have found it to be true. This is not as difficult as it sounds, because there is nothing which honorable men, joined in an honorable cause, will not do in the name of duty —particularly if duty is supported by generous funds. As a general rule of thumb, the more unbelievable the story, the more honorable should be the men assigned to prove its veracity.[1]

For example, one of the undying myths about the U.S. inability to tame Castro was for many years the existence of the Kennedy-Khrushchev Pact —or "agreement," or "understanding," as some people liked to call it. But, contrary to the popular belief, the famous Kennedy-Khrushchev Pact never existed.

The problem with the existence of such a document, or even with such an "agreement" or "understanding," is that in any compromise both parties agree to do something. According to the prevalent myth, Khrushchev agreed to remove the nuclear missiles from Cuba in exchange for the American promise not to invade the Island. But, as we have shown above, the available evidence shows that no Soviet nuclear missiles were ever on the Island, and no one is going to believe that President Kennedy was so naïve as to exchange something for nothing.

In 1970, Secretary of State Henry Kissinger, concerned over the submarine base the Soviets were building in Cienfuegos, a port on the Southern coast of Cuba, hunted through the State Department's files looking for the written agreement he was sure President Kennedy had signed with Khrushchev. He discovered, to his utter amazement, that there was none. Furthermore, if the agreement ever existed, it has the dubious honor of being one of the few international agreements to have been applied long before it was signed, because the U.S. government's harassment of the anti-Castro Cuban-Americans began a year and a half *before* the Cuban missile crisis, just after the Bay of Pigs invasion.

The Kennedy-Khrushchev Pact was nothing but a U.S. government's concoction to justify the unjustifiable. If, despite rhetoric on the contrary, American presidents from John F. Kennedy to George W. Bush have proved unwilling to get rid of Fidel Castro, it is not because a non-existent pact forbids them to do so, but because of some hidden motives unknown to us.[2]

If it is proclaimed in Havana or Peking tomorrow that the moon is made of green cheese, a phalanx of honorable men can be produced to attest to that fact. If it is proclaimed in Washington tomorrow that 20,000 angels can dance on the head of a pin, a horde of honorable experts will rush to confirm it. Anyone rash enough to question these official verities can expect to be exposed as a traitor or a fool. The name of the game, both East and West, has never been truth, but power.

Entrenched in research centers quite apart from real life, like the Hudson Institute and the RAND Corporation, and with plenty of monetary resources and scientific hardware, an elite group of mathematicians, economists, historians, and political scientists spent their time using game theory, higher mathematics, and the most advanced computers to find the hidden rationality of the irrational future of nuclear war. Confronted with a book like Herman Kahn's *On Thermonuclear War*, the mathematician James R. Newman rhetorically asked if there was really such a person as Herman Kahn, because no one could exist who thought like this. Science without conscience is the rain of the soul, wrote Rabelais.

To be sure, some philosophers of science would agree that there is no sharp line separating science from pseudoscience. But it is a verifiable fact that most of the studies about the Cuban missile crisis produced by the American scholarly community are of the GIGO type (garbage in, garbage out). First, the analyst builds upon confirmed "facts" and preconceived assumptions; then, he does some impeccable analysis; and, finally, arrives at absurd conclusions.[3]

The official slogan of super-states should be "who controls the past controls the future." In the super-state it is regarded as a self evident truth that the control of history is an inalienable right of government. Because of their relations with the Establishment the media has a vested interest in maintaining public ignorance, thus their continued "failures" in conducting an effective inquiry. "Don't rock the boat" is their motto. Peace of mind is better than knowledge.

Soon after the Cuban missile crisis had ended, Assistant Secretary of Defense Arthur Sylvester was unusually frank when he spoke about "the inherent right of the government to lie to save itself when faced with nuclear disaster..." Several times during the crisis Sylvester affirmed that news was a "weapon" in the hands of the government and that "information is power." His candid admission of the government's right to lie unleashed a heated controversy between the press and the Kennedy administration. James Reston observed, however, that the whole controversy arose not when the government lied, but when Sylvester made the government's intention explicit. As long as the officials merely didn't tell the whole truth, said Reston, very few of us complained; but as soon as Sylvester told the truth, the editors fell on him like a fumble.

Most people around the world, particularly Latin Americans, have always taken for granted that their governments lie to them. Americans, however, prefer to avoid the fact that their government lies. The very idea of duplicity in the high levels of government is inconsistent with the American ideal of a democratic society. To suggest that what the government says may be more myth than reality elicits the most antagonistic reactions. Although Americans, by choice, deny the fact that the government lies, a few times they have been forced to admit it, faced with such events as the shot down of the U-2 over the Soviet Union, the Bay of Pigs, the Tonkin Gulf incident, Watergate, or the secret sale of arms to Iran. Denial of the existence of lying may save the consciences of some people, but to repress the facts because they are distasteful and incongruent with cherished values may lead to consequences even more serious than those we are trying to escape by putting fantasy in place of reality.

Admittedly, the United States is still one of the most democratic countries in the world.[4] Most American presidents, however, act as if they don't trust the Constitution. They are duplicitous, they sneak, they deny, they lie to their own people.

Like their opposite numbers in Peking or Havana, they seem to prefer unilateral decisions and secret negotiations rather than letting the people know the truth.

In testimony before a Subcommittee on National Security, Professor Richard Newstadt pointed out how presidential decision-making in the nuclear age involves, "the risk of irreversibility," namely, the possibility that a presidential action could provoke a nuclear or biological Armageddon. We are poised in a moment in history when the future of the human race is in danger, a moment when the judgment of a single person could decide whether life or death will prevail on planet Earth. That it is even possible to make such a decision is frightening. That people like Nikita S. Khrushchev, Fidel Castro, or John F. Kennedy, had the power to make such momentous decisions is even more frightening. Perhaps the time is right to take such an important and now vital thing as politics away from the politicians.

For many years, the American military apparently believed that it was possible to fight, survive, and win a nuclear war. They probably still do. What is known of Russian and Chinese military doctrine indicates that their opinion is not too different. Some time ago, historian Barbara Tuchman questioned the real desire of the American and Soviet governments to limit nuclear arms: "They go on talking about it as they are talking now in Geneva, but the intention behind the talks is questionable." It is not by chance, she wrote, that governments have always been the paramount field of folly. In his essay *Fable*, William Golding summarized his observations about war: "Anyone who moved through these years without understanding that man produces evil as a bee produces honey, must have been blind or wrong in the head."

The Aftermath of the Crisis

After Khrushchev's defeat, most people thought that Kennedy's balls, badly hurt during the Bay of Pigs, were in good shape again. The confrontation gave Kennedy the opportunity to prove he was the tough guy in the White House, capable of defeating a powerful and clever adversary and emerging the undisputed winner of the showdown in the tradition of the best of Hollywood's Western films.

With the passage of time, however, and particularly with the growing disillusionment over the war in Vietnam, some observers began to take a more critical look at the President's performance in the Cuban missile crisis. Right-wingers, who saw Castro's dominance of Cuba as a continuing threat to American security, attacked Kennedy for the price paid by the U.S. to have the Soviets withdraw their missiles, namely, a spurious agreement not to invade Cuba. Some critics observed that Kennedy had missed a golden opportunity to remove a dangerous enemy who was much too close to the shores of the U.S. Nixon went as far as affirming that, by turning a sure victory into a stalemate, Kennedy and the White House doves caused the United States "to pull defeat out of the jaws of victory."[5] As for the liberal writers, they soon began questioning Kennedy's decision to forego traditional diplomacy in dealing with the event, particularly when he refused to consider the sound idea of a swap of obsolete American missiles in Turkey for the

Soviet missiles in Cuba —which eventually it was discovered it had been exactly what Kennedy had done. The radical New Left went a step further and charged that perhaps Kennedy's allegedly great victory was no mere accident, but the result of a trap laid by him to catch Khrushchev.

Whatever the case, President Kennedy's apparent success in forcing Khrushchev to dismantle the bases and withdraw the missiles was unquestionably compromised by Castro's refusal to allow U.N. specialists to inspect the missile bases on-site. Republicans seized the opportunity to suggest that Castro's refusal was a sign that the Russian military buildup in Cuba had resumed and that not all the "nuclear" missiles had been removed —an argument that found an echo among some Cuban-Americans in Florida.[6]

In the end, and against all advice, Kennedy not only did nothing to penalize a Soviet move apparently aimed at inflicting a mortal blow upon the United States, but also made an unheard-of non-invasion pledge, denying Americans even the *status quo ante*. Kennedy the candidate had proclaimed several times during his presidential campaign what he thought a new administration could do to stop Castro's drift to Communism. After the Cuban missile crisis, President Kennedy ended up doing the very things he had condemned when he was a candidate, and continued harassing the anti-Castro Cubans in Florida even more.

As for Fidel, he felt he had come out the real winner of the missile crisis. He had rejected the demands of the United States, the Soviet Union and the United Nations, and there had been no inspection of Cuba.

Following the crisis, Khrushchev, in order not to lose all his assets, bit the bullet and went to considerable lengths to patch up his relations with Fidel. Cuba received additional aid and promises of support. After Castro's visit to the Soviet Union, in April-May 1963,[7] an apparent harmony in their relations was established. Cuba was finally admitted as a full member of the Communist community, while Fidel stopped criticizing the Soviets, at least in public, for their handling of the missile affair, and the pro-Soviet Communist parties in Latin America for their inaction vis-à-vis the U.S. But this harmony was to be short-lived. Castro was still determined to show his independence and to promote *Fidelismo* in Latin America. Much to the Kremlin's annoyance, he exploited the dispute between China and the Soviet Union by proclaiming his intentions to maintain ties with all socialist states. To add insult to injury, on October 7, 1963, the Cuban delegate to the U.N. informed the General Assembly that Cuba would not sign the Nuclear Test Ban Treaty, thus defying the Soviets' expectations for Cuban support of the treaty. This action must not be seen just as an attempt to mortify the Soviets. In fact, Castro had clearly expressed on several occasions that he would never renounce his right to have all types of weapons of mass destruction.[8]

Signs of tension increased as Castro continued rejecting the Soviet policy of peaceful coexistence. To counter it, Castro launched, in May, 1966, his own new thesis of the parallel construction of Socialism and Communism. As a countermeasure, the Russians tightened the Island's economy even more. In the same month the Cuban people were alerted that, if aggression were to occur, they were alone to defend themselves. One more sign of the tightening Russian grip was that the commercial treaty for 1967 between both nations was not satisfactory to Cuba, and the Soviet Union refused to increase vital oil shipments to the Island.

Faithful to his self-appointed role as the Jiminy Cricket of the Communist camp —Fidel has always seen himself as the revolutionary conscience of the Communist world— and despite his economic and military dependence on the U.S.S.R., Castro picked quarrels not only with the Latin American Communist parties and with China, but with the Soviet Union itself. He expelled Volodia Teitelboim, one of the most respected leaders of the Chilean Communist Party, from the third Afro-Asian People's Solidarity Organization (AAPSO) conference which was held in Havana. He criticized both the Chinese and the Soviets for their policies with relation to Vietnam and on several occasions offered to send Cubans to fight in the war —an offer the cautious Vietnamese declined with much diplomacy. Moreover, Castro used the French writer Regis Debray as a mouthpiece to promulgate his own fascist-inspired theory of revolution which was even more extremist than that of the Chinese and, of course, totally unacceptable to the Russians.

The role Castro has played in foreign affairs is a very complex one. Over the years he followed the Chinese line that advocated armed struggle as the only means to attain political power. But, paradoxically, the Chinese never understood why he supported the Soviets in some issues, and always considered him Moscow's man. Evidence of the Sino-Cuban differences emerged during the Tricontinental Conference held in Havana in January, 1966, when Castro denounced the Chinese refusal to raise the amount of rice shipments to Cuba.

Further signs of his resentment toward the Soviet policy line were offered by Castro himself in a speech at the time of the Latin American Solidarity Organization (OLAS) Conference in Havana in 1967. Reaching new heights in his innuendo, he referred to a "Mafia of slanderers and defamers of the Cuban Revolution" within the Communist movement, in clear allusion to both the pro-Soviet Cuban Communists, the old-guard Communists in Latin America, and the U.S.S.R. and its Eastern European satellites.

Coinciding with the worsening of Sino-Cuban relations, Castro disagreed even more seriously with the Russians over the means to promote communism in Latin America. Both the Soviets and their puppet Latin American Communist parties opposed violence, while Castro furiously advocated armed insurgency. By 1967 Castro virtually had wrestled control of the Communist movements in Latin America from the hands of the discredited pro-Soviet Latin American Communist parties. As for the Russians, they could not do anything overtly against their new competitor without compromising their prestige, now so heavily committed to support the Castroite regime which naïve revolutionaries and third worldites considered to be the only Marxist regime in the West.

In January-February, 1968, Fidel went a step further and openly attacked an anti-Castro faction, allegedly formed by "old resentful sectarians," within his

"Communist" Party (PCC, *Partido Comunista de Cuba*). He clearly identified them as a group of old-guard Cuban Communists, followers of Moscow's line, and endowed it with the name "microfraction." The group, headed again by the indefatigable Aníbal Escalante, was expelled from the PCC and tried before a revolutionary court, accused of conspiracy against the Cuban government and of passing information about the Cuban economy to a Soviet diplomat,[9] and finally condemned to sentences ranging from 5 to 15 years in prison. Simultaneous with the "microfraction" incident, the PCC declared it would not send any representative to the meeting of Communist parties to be held in Budapest in February, 1968, which the Russians called to discuss preparations for an international Communist conference. Later on, in May, 1968, the Cuban government, in accordance with Castro's policy of not renouncing to the possession of nuclear weapons, announced its refusal to sign the Nuclear Nonproliferation Treaty that was sponsored by the Soviet Union and the United States.

It is true that the Soviets supplied Cuba for many years with heavy arms and military equipment. But to see Castro as a mere pawn for the Russians is to deny him his own power-seeking abilities. A brief analysis of the Cuban foreign policy since 1959 shows that it is a mirror image of the American one. Castro envies America's strength and use of force as a means to get results. He envies American imperialism. As a matter of fact, most Americans don't realize, and don't even seem to understand, that Castro has always treated them exactly the same way the U.S. usually treats the rest of the world: with total contempt. As political science scholar Jorge Dominguez pointed out, "Cuba is a small country, but it has a big country's foreign policy."[10] The fact was also noted by professor Irving Louis Horowitz, who observed that, ". . . at least with respect to participation in the affairs of other nations, Cuba scores higher than any nation in the Western hemisphere other than the United States."[11] In fact Cuba's foreign policy has been just the political expression of Castro's *delusions de grandeur*.

Both scholars are absolutely right. Cuba's foreign policy under 43 years of Castro's rule has been a carbon copy of the American foreign policy, with imperialistic wars, military intervention, support of corrupt tyrants, covert action, executive action,[12] development of weapons of mass destruction, and the like. Castro's envy of America has turned him into a copycat of the United States. Unfortunately, he has copied only the worst aspects of America, the ones he seems to love from the bottom of his heart.

Though Castro has not been too effective in promoting his revolutionary objectives in Latin America, it has not been for lack of trying. Apparently he firmly believed that the time had arrived for leftist anti-American movements to seize power in Latin America. Yet the Soviets, as well as most of the leaders of the Latin American Communist parties, not only did not share the idea, but also feared that Castro was not promoting the Soviet version of communism, but his own brand of *Fidelismo* —which is nothing but a tropical version of fascism.[13] In order not to be criticized by the left, however, the Soviets were forced, at least rhetorically, to get along with their self-appointed Caribbean associate.

It is very significant that not since Hitler has a national leader talked so openly as Fidel Castro about his ambitions for power, about his historical duty to conduct the destiny of some part of the world, about the way to destroy his enemies, and about his plans to achieve his goals. Yet Hitler's threats and fateful deeds were mainly considered the work of an irresponsible psychopath while Castro's words still seem to make sense to millions of gullible Latin Americans and Arabs blinded by their understandable anti-Americanism. The most curious fact is that most of Castro's followers and advocates, both in Latin America and in the U.S., call themselves either leftists or liberals, and they label themselves as "progressives." They don't seem to be aware that, by supporting Castro, they are in fact defiling the philosophies of leftism and liberalism. How a person who calls himself a leftist, and is anti-Pinochet, can also be pro-Castro? The only conclusion to be drawn is that something is wrong with the American Left.

Since Che Guevara left Cuba —with Castro's approval or encouragement— to die in Bolivia in 1968, there has been no one in Cuba who has even tried to contest Castro's personal, iron rule. Castro himself has been careful not to allow anyone who has the slightest potential for leadership to climb the ladder of power on the Island. Not even his brother Raúl, his designated successor, reputedly an unscrupulous and aggressive man of energy and cunning, possesses the personal magnetism required to continue mesmerizing the Cuban people the way Castro has done for almost half a century.

Henry Kissinger observed that victorious leaders, who have spent several years risking their lives in a revolutionary struggle, are not likely to favor a system of government which makes them dispensable. Indeed the strong attraction communism exerts on many of these leaders —Castro among them— is not Marxist-Leninist philosophy or economics, but the legitimization of totalitarian rule which it provides. The roads open to totalitarianism in the second half of the 20th century were two: communism and fascism. Fascism, however, is so discredited that, in fact, the only way open for a not-too-scrupulous political leader willing to stay forever in power is communism. Philip Bonsal, a former U.S. Ambassador to Cuba said rightly that what best characterizes Fidelismo is "the eccentric, sweepingly revolutionary, wholly arbitrary exercise of absolute personal power made possible by Castro's phenomenal charisma and by his talent as a leader."[14]

Two, Three... Many Vietnams

Some years ago, during my research on the Cuban missile crisis, I was at the library of the San Francisco State University when I ran across a book titled *The Cuban Crisis as Reflected in the New York Press*. When I opened it, I discovered to my utter surprise that the book was about the Cuban crisis of 1895-1898! That book is a reminder that the Cuban missile crisis is not a unique event in the history of Cuban-American relations, but just one more incident in a long history of crisis after crisis.

Some author observed that when there is a sufficiently prolonged period of interaction between two states, they tend to behave like a single system with respect to their transactions, that is, they tend to seek a maximum level of mutually rewarding activity at the lowest feasible level of punishment and maintain a reciprocally tolerable steady state of interaction. Whether Castro and the United States like or despise one another it is difficult to say; what the available record clearly proves, is that they developed a tacit working partnership against the Soviet Union. Nothing exemplifies this partnership better than the case of Angola.

In 1975, ostensibly because the "legitimate government" of Angola had asked for Cuban military aid and it was Cuba's "duty" to assist a Third World country, Castro sent thousands of Cuban troops to that African country. It is interesting to note, as Irving Louis Horowitz did, that this argument —intervention to help a legitimate government— is exactly the same one used by other imperial powers, such as the U.S., which justified its intervention in Korea and Vietnam to maintain "legitimate governments."

Contrary to the prevalent view, the decision to send Cuban troops to Angola was entirely Castro's. He did not ask the Soviets for permission nor even consult them about his decision. The first Cuban soldiers traveled to Angola disguised as civilians, with their weapons hiding in their luggage, in civilian planes of the Cuban airline.[15] The military units that followed were sent in Cuban cargo ships. The Soviets gave no logistic or military support to the initial phase of the operation.

By a strange coincidence, the U.S. government, who had been encouraging South Africa to support Savimbi in fighting the MPLA, suddenly withdrew its political support just before the arrival of the Cuban troops, when the South African and Savimbi's forces were at the gates of Luanda. It was not until the Cuban troops had the situation under control that the surprised Russians, who had expected Castro's adventure to end in a disastrous failure, joined the band wagon and began sending economic and military aid to the country.

Two years later, when the Soviets tried to overthrow Agostinho Neto —a "Marxist," but certainly not a pro-Soviet one— and put in his place Nito Alves, of the pro-Soviet faction of the MPLA, the Cubans took side with Neto against the pro-Soviets and drowned the attempt in blood.

Ten years and 30,000 Cuban soldiers later, the picture in Angola was, to say the least, confusing. Chase Manhattan Bank, Bankers Trust, Morgan Guaranty and Citybank, all were lending money to Angola. General Tire operated a plant there, and General Motors was trying to sell them vehicles. Boeing provided spare parts for Angola's national airline, and installed an airtraffic control system for Luanda's Airport which was later used by Cuban and Angolan MiGs. Lockheed sold C-130s and trained pilots for the government. A Louisiana sugar manufacturer was helping to manage a major sugar mill. Caterpillar, IBM, NCR, Pfizer, and Xerox were doing business in Angola. Texaco, Mobil, Conoco, Marathon, and Cities Service were all operating in the country.

But the largest operation by far was the Cabinda Gulf Oil Company, a subsidiary of Chevron. In the decade of Castro's intervention, Gulf expanded its operations as never before. At the time, its investments in Angola totalled $1.3 billion. Cabgulf, as Chevron's company is called in Angola, was pumping about 70 percent of the country's oil —190,000 barrels a day. In 1985 the company paid the Angolan government $580 million in taxes and royalties, which were mainly used to help pay Castro's army for the war against Savimbi and his UNITA forces. Part of this money also went to Cuba, the estimates of which range between $300 and $800 million. As none of the money was invested in the welfare of the Cuban people, one may guess that most of it found its way to Castro's numbered accounts in Zürich.

Contrary to the popular image of Angola as a Soviet satellite, the country under Castro's patronage became a great source of profit and plunder for Western multinationals. The diamond mines were under indirect control of the De Beers consortium. At least 95 percent of Angola's oil ended up in the West; half of Gulf's production found its way into U.S. refineries. After 10 years of Castro's imperial domination, the United States was Angola's largest trading partner.

On the other hand, the Soviets reaped very little in return for their military and financial investment. They received virtually none of Angola's oil. At most, what they gained was the dubious pride of having another country that they could say was in their orbit.

The relations between Fidel Castro and the Soviet Union were a typical case of common but conflicting goals. Undoubtedly, Castro's actions in some way helped communism and, therefore, also the Soviet Union, but there is a vital difference between Castro being a pro-Communist in effect and being a pro-Communist in intention.

For example, when Castro sent his troops to Angola in 1975, the result was pro-Soviet in effect; but, since he did so by his own will and against Soviet advice, it was hardly by design. When in 1959 Castro included the formation of cooperatives in his Law of Agrarian Reform, he committed an act that was ultimately pro-Communist in effect; but, considering that the Cuban and Russian Communists were annoyed by his haste, his act was hardly pro-Communist by design. When in 1961 he delivered the Second Declaration of Havana, which officially encouraged guerrilla warfare in Latin America, he was certainly committing a profoundly anti-American act and therefore pro-Communist in effect. But, if we remember that at that time the Soviets were engaged in a policy of peaceful coexistence and therefore opposed Castro's adventurism, Castro's action was hardly pro-Communist by design. When he affirmed that he was a Marxist-Leninist and created a totalitarian society guided by a Communist party, Castro was most certainly doing something that was pro-Soviet in effect. But, in the light of the evidence that shows that Castro's Cuban Communist Party was never oriented toward Moscow, but is instead an instrument of power in his hands, one must conclude that his actions were not pro-Soviet in design.

Paradoxically, Fidel Castro has been most successful in alerting Latin America to the danger of communism, and provided the U.S. with an excuse for large-scale intervention in the hemisphere.[16] Not only did Castro make the potential for autonomous revolution in Latin America remote, but he put a special emphasis on fighting autonomous revolutionary movements. His fiery polemic with Douglas Bravo and the Venezuelan guerrillas is a good example to illustrate the point. Even more, by encouraging, supporting, and fomenting subversive activities, he intensified in the area the fear of communism, one of the main causes for the flight of Latin American capital to U.S., thus directly benefitting the United States.

The U.S.-imposed economic blockade, though highly ineffective, gave Castro an excuse to justify the self-provoked economic difficulties of his regime and also to justify the increased cost to the Soviet Union of aiding Cuba. In addition, Castro's economic reversals, while serving as a drain on Soviet resources, made the Cuban example less appealing to Latin America. Moreover, because of its supposed identification with Soviet interests, Castro's revolution actually made the possibilities of Soviet-friendly anti-American revolutions in Latin America more difficult.

What Nikita Khrushchev feared so much happened at last: the Soviet Union became overextended. The cost of maintaining allies such as Cuba, and of holding onto Eastern Europe and fighting in Afghanistan while continuing the arms race, exhausted the always scarce Soviet resources. Evidence of Soviet fears of even more involvement in areas they could not control was the meager Soviet aid to Nicaragua and to leftist African states. Thanks mainly to Fidel Castro, the U.S.S.R. overextended, militarily and economically, well beyond its own capabilities, and found itself in a dangerous situation.

The Soviet Union had the capability to strike targets in the United States, both with ICBMs launched from its territory and from submarines operating off American coasts. Cuba was not strategically indispensable to the Soviet Union. The Island was too far from the Soviet military sphere of tactical influence, and not even essential for the operation of Soviet submarines equipped with nuclear missiles, which have long been operating in the Atlantic from northern Soviet ports. Though Cuba could have been a convenient location for servicing Soviet submarines, no strategic Russian military activity of that kind was ever observed in Cuba. One might speculate that the reason for this was that the Soviets always feared Castro's long, nuclear-grabbing hands.

For many years the Soviet Union continued posing as the protector of the Castro regime and tried to give the impression that it would defend Cuba if the Island were attacked by the United States. But the Russians were very careful not to commit themselves formally to do so. Cuba's exclusion from the Warsaw Pact was not an accident, but a planned omission.

Though nobody can blame Castro alone for the fall of the Soviet Union, it is an unquestionable fact that he contributed to some extent to its demise. It is known that the Reagan administration relentlessly pursued a secret plan to bring about the bankruptcy of the Soviet Union by creating a false image of heavy spending by the American military, which in turn provoked a similar attempt from their Soviet counterparts.[17] Added to the heavy spending in their military development, the Soviets had the extra burden of having to financially support Castro's ever-crumbling economy, which, by 1982, was running close to $11 million per day, and they were paying four times the world price for Cuban sugar. By the mid-eighties, Castro's debt to the Soviet Union had reached $9 billion, without counting the value of military aid. Undoubtedly, the amount of money they were dumping into the Cuban black hole, added to the cost of the increased investment in armaments, proved to be too high a bill for the Soviets to foot.[18]

The Pentagon loved to portray Soviet soldiers as 10 feet tall. It was in the Pentagon's interest to exaggerate Russian military power. According to *Soviet Military Power*, a U.S. Department of Defense publication, year after year the Soviets had the best planes, the largest submarines, the greatest number of tanks, and the fastest helicopters. Such publications contributed to an atmosphere of perpetual panic —the reds-under-the-beds syndrome— in which spending increases were routinely approved.

In 1962, President Kennedy confessed that the only real reason given for the resumption of nuclear testing was the fear that the engineers could not find work, that America wouldn't be able to keep the labs going. Apparently the U.S. had built a technological force that didn't have any place to go, that did not fit into the business or commercial side of the economy, except by producing means of destruction. The American Security State had developed its own pension classes — large groups of people directly dependent on expenditures voted by Congress for the maintenance of old wars and the creation of new ones. A substantial part of the educated class depended on the national security structure; even the universities operated in part as its instruments.

Though successive American presidents initially looked like opponents of the "Castro-Soviet aggression," the evidence indicates that they actually stimulated it. From the study of Soviet documents, it has been established that prior to the Bay of Pigs the Soviet Union considered Latin America not ripe for communism. But the manifest American lack of interest in the region, added to its "failure" to tame Castro, created a power vacuum which gave the Soviets an opportunity for intervening on a large scale in this hemisphere. Likewise, the Castroist and Russian intervention eventually gave the United States an excuse for large-scale military intervention in Latin America —and the corresponding military spending increases.

The American interests that profited from the war in Vietnam would not look kindly upon anyone who would try to eliminate the person who promised to create "two, three..., many Vietnams." Low-intensity conflicts were the new panacea to cure all the maladies of capitalism, and Doctor Castro was diligently prescribing them the very medicine they were begging for.

The real danger threatening the American military-industrial-academic complex was not the threat of communism, but the danger of not finding enough enemies. The business of America never was anti-communism, as it is not anti-terrorism either. The business of America is business. Seen from this perspective,[19] Americans should be thankful to Fidel Castro —maximum promoter of anti-gringo little wars around the world— for contributing so much to the well-being of capitalism in America.

A Few Conclusions

As I mentioned in the Preface, the main questions of the Cuban missile crisis have eluded satisfactory answers because the fundamental question about the crisis, namely, why Khrushchev installed strategic nuclear missiles in Cuba, has been erroneously formulated: Nikita Khrushchev *never* installed strategic nuclear missiles in Cuba. Moreover, he never intended to do so. Consequently, it has been impossible to find the right answer to a question when the question itself is wrong.

Even though there are still many unanswered questions about the Cuban missile crisis, at least I have shown that the answers provided to some of the questions are false. Let's take a look at some of the main issues:

1. As the Escalante-Kudryavtsev affair clearly indicates, Cuba's defense against a U.S. invasion was *not* among Khrushchev's motives for his actions.
2. Far from loving Castro, Khrushchev was strongly suspicions of Fidel's *bona fides*, and there is evidence that, particularly after the Escalante-Kudryavtsev affair, he hated the arrogant Cuban leader. Castro's behavior during the crisis, shooting down a U-2 plane and asking the Soviet leader to launch a preemptive nuclear attack against the U.S., confirmed Khrushchev's fears that Castro was an irresponsible maniac.[20]
3. Castro's true motive for accepting the missiles was not to strengthen the socialist camp, as he has claimed, but to fulfill his secret death wish of grabbing the missiles and using them to annihilate the hated Americans.
4. Khrushchev never thought that placing what looked like strategic missiles in Cuba was not going to provoke a strong American response —most likely and invasion of the Island. In this sense, he did not miscalculate.
5. Instead of being directed against Cuba, however, Kennedy's response was directed against the Soviet Union. In this sense Khrushchev miscalculated badly. He was not alone in his miscalculation. Many American officials in the Kennedy administration, the U.S. Congress, and the military, not to mention the American public, also miscalculated badly.
6. Lundahl and the officers at the NPIC willingly disinformed President Kennedy when, bypassing the appraising step of the intelligence cycle, directly presented him the U-2 photos as hard evidence of the presence of strategic Soviet missiles in Cuba.
7. Sherman Kent and the CIA analysts who forecasted the low possibility that the Soviet Union would deploy strategic nuclear missiles in Cuba were right.

8. Oleg Penkovsky was most likely a plant, an important part of a Soviet strategic disinformation exercise.
9. The U-2 that entered Soviet air space during the crisis was most likely part of a psychological warfare exercise whose goal was to scare Khrushchev to death. It was eminently successful.
10. There is still no clear answer about who was really in command of the Soviet SAM battery that shot down Major Anderson's U-2 and under what conditions it really happened.
11. No satisfactory answer has been provided to explain why President Kennedy opted for a blockade instead of invading Cuba to get rid of the missiles and Castro. It was seemingly a preconceived decision, not based on the opinion of his advisors.
12. To this day, the presence of strategic missiles in Cuba and their nuclear warheads has never been proved. All the "evidence" provided to support the assertion that Soviet strategic missiles and their nuclear warheads were in Cuba in 1962 has been based on hearsay, spurious documents, and assumptions. Until solid evidence is presented, these claims are totally unsubstantiated. Like Adlai Stevenson, I am prepared to wait for the proofs until hell freezes over.
13. The only thing that may explain Kennedy's strange refusal to force an *in situ* inspection of the Soviet ships leaving Cuba was that he knew, or at least suspected, that no missiles or nuclear warheads were on the ships.
14. Most of the conclusions made by the Ex Comm members were based on assumptions. In fact, "assume" is the highest frequency word appearing on the Ex Comm tape transcripts, and the word is repeated over and over by former Ex Comm members in the recent meetings about the crisis. If you delete the word "assume" from these texts, what remains is close to nothing. It boggles my mind that a group of people, who many considered the best and the brightest, made such important decisions based on totally unfounded assumptions.
15. Recent claims that Soviet commanders in Cuba had been given discretionary power to use nuclear weapons without specific orders from Moscow [21] are so far-fetched and stupid that, out of respect for the intelligence of my readers, I have not even bothered to discuss them in detail.[22]
16. Far from shedding light on the event, the new declassified "documents," combined with recent "critical oral interviews" provided by Soviet, Cuban, and American officials, has thrown a dark mantle of disinformation over the historical record of the crisis.
17. Most of what has been published by the Blight, Allyn, Welch, *et al.* paper mill, is nothing but propaganda under a cloak[23] of scholarly work.

The Cuban missile crisis was basically an intelligence operation. As I mentioned in the Preface, in writing this book I used a new research and analysis methodology I have developed, which I call "historical tradecraft." It is a combination of the research methodology of the historian with the approach of the intelligence analyst.[24] One of the cardinal premises of the intelligence analyst is that in the field of intelligence and espionage things are seldom what they seem. This book is a proof that, when applied to historical events which basically have been intelligence operations and where the historian's traditional research and analysis tools are not enough,[25] this methodology works at least to some extent.

Calling something a fact does not make it one. Consequently, most claims about the Cuban missile crisis, particularly the ones made by some of the participants during the discussion meetings that have taken place in the last fifteen years, are nothing but wild assertions, with no foundation whatsoever. The role of both the historian and the intelligence analyst is not to pass unconfirmed, unevaluated data as if it were intelligence, but to evaluate the data against established criteria in order to change it into usable intelligence. But, until now, the lack of disproof of wild assertions that strategic missiles and its nuclear warheads were in Cuba in 1962 has been accepted as sufficient proof.

It seems that, after so much uncontested propaganda work, the folks running the paper mill have lost all sense of shame. Philip Brenner and James Blight's latest book, scheduled to appear in October of 2002 coinciding with the 40th anniversary of the crisis, is titled *Sad and Luminous Days: Cuba's Struggle with the Superpowers After the Missile Crisis*. The book's title comes from a letter Che Guevara wrote to Castro in 1962. The authors apparently forgot that the maniac they are honoring is the one who wanted to fire the Soviet missiles to destroy New York. The infamous Che Guevara, who sent hundreds of prisoners to the firing squads based only on suspicions, was the very same man who created the first concentration camp in Castro's Cuba. The camp was located in the Guanahacabibes peninsula, an inhospitable place near a mosquito-infested coast, in the Pinar del Río province, west of Havana. The lack of sensitivity of these authors is not only offensive to all democratic-minded people; it is also repugnant.

A Personal Note

As the reader by now may have guessed, this book is the result of my inner anger[26] after seeing, day after day, the history of both Cuba and the United States distorted by a bloodthirsty tyrant, unscrupulous spies, corrupt politicians, and naïve or compromised scholars, to serve spurious interests.[27] As I mentioned above, most of what has been written in the last fifteen years as the result of meetings where alleged participants in the crisis have been "orally interviewed" and declassified "documents" have been produced, is nothing but propaganda under a cover of legitimate scholarly work. But, whatever the reasons these American scholars have for risking their prestige to justify the actions of a tyrant who has destroyed his country and its people, it is evident that they are evidencing their low moral stature.

Since the advent of Castro's era, Cubans are not citizens any more, but subjects of an absolute monarch. Cubans belong to the state, and, as such, are Castro's private property. He has total power of life and death over them. He decides what they read, what they hear, what they eat, how they dress, where and how they live. As farmers take good care of their chickens and their cows, because they are their private property, Castro was interested in keeping his human property in relatively good health. Slave masters were known for their concern for their slaves' health, because sickness would surely lower the value of their human property.[28]

Like a modern slave master, King Castro is selling the work force of his slaves to foreign investors in Cuba and unscrupulous businessmen abroad, who are not only exempt from the normal labor codes, but pay him market prices in dollars while he pays his subjects low salaries —sometimes as low as the equivalent of 12 dollars a month— in devaluated Cuban pesos. As Humberto Fontova brilliantly put it,

> Havana recently topped Bangkok as "child-sex capital of the world." Consider the tragedy, the desperation of poor people driven to such things in such numbers, and after 43 years of "liberation" and "national dignity."
>
> 18,000 riddled by firing squads. Half a million incarcerated. 50,000 drowned or ripped apart by sharks in the Florida Straits. Thousands more slaughtered in Africa for Moscow. Two million exiled. And we wind up with a nation that in 1959 had a higher living standard than Belgium or Italy, had a lower infant mortality rate than France, had net immigration, as child-sex capital of the world.
>
> Friends, are you beginning to understand why we get a trifle "emotional" or "unreasonable" when we hear some imbecile professor or bonehead politician yapping about "the good things" Castro has done for Cuba?[29]

Only moral morons can rejoice in the company of a tyrant while the people on the streets show evident symptoms of malnutrition[30] and mental illness, as a result of long years of hopelessness and despair. Only moral morons can believe that Cubans, who risk their lives every day escaping from Castro's prison island, are a happy people. Only moral morons can enjoy the privileges of power as personal guests of the tyrant, while honest people in the streets are forced to prostitute themselves and their children in order to bring food to their mouths. Only moral morons who see themselves as "progressives," can help legitimize a reactionary regime that makes the dictatorships of Batista, Somoza, Trujillo or Pinochet, look like glowing examples of democracy, freedom, and respect for human rights.

But the time is ripe for adding a little cognitive dissonance to the discussion. Like Howard Beale, Paddy Chayefski's character in the film *Network*, I am sticking my head out of my window and yelling with all the force of my lungs: I am mad as hell, and I am not going to take this any more!

Appendix 1

The Evaluation of Information

Also known as appraisal, the evaluation of information has to do with the analysis of a piece of information in terms of credibility, reliability, pertinency, accuracy, and the use of an item of information, an intelligence product, or the performance of an intelligence system. The evaluation of information is accomplished at several stages within the intelligence cycle with progressively different contexts.

The evaluation or appraisal of a particular item of information is indicated by a conventional letter-number system.

Reliability of the Source
A Completely reliable
B Usually reliable
C Fairly reliable
D Not usually reliable
E Unreliable
F Reliability cannot be judged

Accuracy of Information
1 Confirmed by other reliable sources
2 Probably true
3 Possibly true
4 Doubtful
5 Improbable
6 Accuracy cannot be judged

The evaluation simultaneously takes into consideration both the credibility of the information itself—a process involving a check against information already in hand and an educated guess as to the accuracy of the new information—and the reliability of the source based on its previous performance. Though independent, the two aspects cannot be totally separated from each other. The authoritativeness of the source, which may not necessarily coincide with its reliability, can never be ignored, though it is sometimes overrated in the light of the credibility of the information, something that has to do with the expectations of the people involved in the evaluation process. Most people, however, including intelligence analysts, tend to believe what they suspect or expect to be true, or what better fits their personal needs.

It must be emphasized that both evaluations should be entirely independent of each other, and they are indicated in accordance with the system shown above. Thus, information judged to be "probably true" received from a source considered to be "usually reliable" is designated "B2".

The question of what is authoritative and what is not is very relative. A highly authoritative source may produce credible information, but the intelligence officer must always ask himself the question "Why?" The higher the authoritativeness of the source, the higher the possibility that it may be biased or had been compromised and, therefore, the higher the danger of disinformation. Highly authoritative sources from totalitarian governments may not always tell the truth, to say the least, but highly authoritative sources from democratic countries may not be very reliable either. There is evidence that the CIA has been involved in recruiting scholars at the most prestigious American universities, and journalists in the most influential American media. Also, there is suspicion that the KGB, the Mossad, and even the Cuban intelligence services, among others, have done a good job penetrating American universities and media.

From the point of view of intelligence, a stolen document is often more valuable than a gratuitously conveyed secret one from whatever source, since it diminishes, though not totally eliminates, the risk of deliberately misleading information. The "why?," however, applies not only to the danger of planted disinformation. It must also be asked of the source whose *bona fides* is beyond question. The danger here is of an intelligence service believing what it wants to believe —a problem that has affected all the world's intelligence services at one time or another. The problem of the bias of the evaluator is one that is unavoidable in intelligence; it extends even to information of fullest credibility from the most reliable sources.

Bias in evaluation can never be fully overcome in an intelligence service and, more importantly, in high government circles, and it can only be compounded by creating evaluators to evaluate the evaluators. Within the intelligence establishment, the only effective safeguard lies in the individual competence and quality of its members as well as their intellectual honesty and personal courage to face pressures from above.

One must always bear in mind that no source can ever be regarded as infallible, and no single bit of information can ever be regarded as totally accurate. Whatever the case, the chances for error, misinterpretation, misunderstanding and deceit are too high to blindly trust any information.

Superpatriots, doctrinaire partisans, court historians, bureaucratic climbers, people of provincial outlook —all are potential dangers to sound information evaluation. Perspective, perspicacity, worldliness, a soundly philosophical outlook, the knowledge and sense of history, and perhaps a bit of skepticism and a sense of humor— these are the individual qualities which minimize error in the interpretation and evaluation of information.

Notes

Preface

1 Paul Seabury, *The Rise and Decline of the Cold War* (New York: Basic Books, 1967), p. 126.

2 "Our Unswerving Objective," *Time*, November 2, 1962. p. 15.

3 Most of the questions were originally made by Harold MacMillan in a Foreword to Robert Kennedy's *Thirteen Days*. In an interview made 20 years ago with most of the surviving American participants in the crisis, they emphasized the fact that the riddles remained. "20 years After Missile Crisis, Riddles Remain," *The New York Times*, October 23, 1982. Today, forty years after, the main riddles still remain.

4 See, Robert C. North, , Ole R. Holsti, M. George Zaninovich and Dina A. Zinnes, *Content Analysis: A Handbook with Applications for the Study of International Crisis* (Chicago: Northwestern University, 1963), p. 19.

5 A.J.P. Taylor, *The Struggle for Mastery in Europe, 1848-1918* (London: Oxford, 1954), p. 569.

6 (New York: Vintage, 1961), pp. 3-35.

7 An excellent example is Robert Kennedy's efforts to produce a totally disingenuous memo in order to leave a paper track proving that, contrary to his actions, he actually opposed the ongoing assassination attempts on Castro. See, Gus Russo, *Live by the Sword* (Baltimore: Bancroft Press, 1998), pp. 72-73.

8 Tradecraft: The methods and techniques of the intelligence and espionage business, in other words, its *modus operandi*. According to CIA veteran William Hood, tradecraft, though mysterious to outsiders, is just a "little more than a compound of common sense, experience, and certain almost universally accepted security practices . . ." *Mole* (New York: Ballantine Books, 1982), p. xiv.

9 "Things are seldom what they seem." From *H.M.S. Pinafore*; music by Sir Arthur Sullivan, script by W.S. Gilbert.

10 Since biblical times, intelligence, counterintelligence, espionage and counterespionage have played an extraordinarily important role in historical events. For unknown reasons, however, few historians seem to bother looking at these aspects.

11 According to Eco, "semiotics is in principle the discipline studying everything that can be used in order to lie." *A Theory of Semiotics* (Bloomington: Indiana University Press, 1979), p. 7. Given the fact that both politicians and spies are liars, somebody should initiate the study of the semiotics of politics and espionage

12 In one of the initial Ex Comm meetings, Attorney General Robert Kennedy, whose main job was allegedly enforcing the law, suggested that, in order to have a pretext to get militarily involved in Cuba, the U.S. should "sink the *Maine* again, or something." The revealing remarks about the *Maine* are in "White House Tapes

and Minutes of the Cuban missile crisis," Excerpts from Off-the-Record Meeting on Cuba, October 16, 1962, 6:30-7:45 p.m., p. 191, Kennedy Library. According to Evans Thomas,"[Robert] Kennedy had been toying with the idea of provocation for months." "Bobby at The Brink," *Newsweek,* August 14, 2000, p. 51.

In most accounts of the Ex Comm meetings, Robert Kennedy is mentioned as having raised the ethical issue of a sneak attack on Cuba, alleging that he didn't want his brother to be remembered as another Tojo —General Hideki Tojo was the Japanese officer who planned the Pearl Harbor attack. However, given the contradictory ethical principles involved in the *"Maine"* and "Tojo" arguments, one cannot escape the conclusion that one of them came from the bottom of his heart and the other was made for public consumption only.

Self-provocation, however, is nothing new among American leaders. A recent book by James Bamford, *Body of Secrets* (New York: Random House, 2001), tells about Operation Northwoods, the code name for a proposed series of sabotages, provocations and assassination attempts. The plan, detailed in a recently declassified Joint Chiefs of Staff document from 1961, outlined U.S. plans to covertly fabricate various pretexts that would justify an American invasion of Cuba. The plan included staging the assassination of Cubans living in the U.S., simulating an attack of the Guantánamo base, and blowing a U.S. ship in Cuban waters to create a "Remember the Maine" type of incident.

Bamford believes that Operation Northwoods is perhaps the most corrupt plan ever created by the U.S. government. I fully concur. Moreover, the military men who created the anonymous document, consciously dishonored their uniforms, their branch of service, and their country

13 The mental mechanism may be something like "If we, the good guys, are so wicked, what can we expect from the others?" This can easily be used as a self-justificatory argument.

14 As Christopher Lash has pointed out, "Historians, like other scholars, need to become more conscious of the social conditions under which they work," adding that, "The established premises of historical interpretation, from which scholars are beginning to dissent, are the product, in part, of the intellectual's identification of himself with the interests of the modern state —interests he serves even while maintaining the illusion of detachment." "The Cultural Cold War: A Short History of the Congress for Cultural Freedom," in Barton J. Bernstein, ed., *Towards a New Past* (New York: Pantheon, 1968), p. 22.

15 "'Most Experts Don't Know More Than the Average Person,' A Conversation with Richard Feynman," *U.S. News and World Report,* March 18, 1985, p. 79. During WWII some natives in the South Seas saw cargo airplanes drop lots of goods, and they wanted it to happen again. So they arranged to make things like in the past: they started fires, made a wooden hut for a man to sit in, with two wooden pieces on his ears like headphones and bars of bamboo sticking out like antennas —he was a radio operator. Then they waited for the airplane to drop the goods, but it never came. They were doing everything right. The form was perfect, but it

didn't work. Feynman calls a similar attitude among scientists "cargo-cult science" because they follow all the apparent precepts and forms of scientific investigation, but they are missing something essential.

16 James A. Robinson, Editor's foreword to Robert C. North, Ole R. Holsti, M. George Zaninovich and Dina A. Zinnes, *Content Analysis: A Handbook with Applications for the Study of International Crisis* (Chicago: Northwestern University, 1963), p. IX.

17 David L. Larson, "Objectivity, Propaganda, and the Puritan Ethic," in David L. Larson, ed., *The Puritan Ethic in the United States Foreign Policy* (Princeton, N.J.: D. Van Nostrand, 1966), p. 4.

18 See, Margaret G., and Charles F. Hermann, "A Look Inside the 'Black Box.' Building on a Decade of Research," in Gerald Hopple, ed., *Biopolitics, Political Psychology and International Politics* (New York: St. Martin Press, 1982), p. 1.

19 Adam B. Ulam, *The Rivals: America and Russia Since World War II* (New York: The Viking Press, 1971), p. 325.

20 See Anthony Brandt, "Truth and consequences," *Esquire,* October 1984.

21 See K.C. Cole, "Is there such thing as Scientific Objectivity," *Discover,* September 1985, p. 98.

22 "La historia como mentira," entrevista con Mario Vargas Llosa, *El País,* October 27, 1984, p. 26.

23 The sight of Janet Reno's black clad troops storming a house in Miami in the wee hours and kidnapping a child at gun point was an eye-opener to some Cuban-Americans. Unfortunately, most of them still refuse to see what they don't want to see.

24 *That Noble Dream: The "Objectivity Question" and the American Historical Profession* (Cambridge, Mass.: Cambridge University Press), 1988.

25 See, i.e., Richard Ned Lebow and Janice Gross Stein, *We All Lost the Cold War* (Princeton, New Jersey: Princeton University Press, 1994), p. 5.

26 As an example I can mention the far-fetched claims that Soviet officers in Cuba had discretionary power to fire nuclear missiles without specific authorization from the Kremlin.

One of the unexpected outcomes of the end of the Cold War is that the liars from both sides have joined efforts in their disinformation activities, and one should be very careful in accepting their claims. But, in a typical snowballing effect, most of the authors of books on the Cuban missile crisis written in the last fifteen years have made their analyses based on information obtained from these declassified "documents" and "oral history," with the result that their research has been contaminated by the original disinformation.

27 Maurice Halperin, *The Rise and Decline of Fidel Castro* (Berkeley: University of California Press, 1972), p. 125.

28 I will show in this book how most of what has been offered as documents relating to the Cuban missile crisis, particularly the ones that have appeared in the last fifteen years through declassification by the countries involved, has low or no value at all and must be taken with a huge mountain of salt.

29 For example, I don't think that we will ever know if there were actually Soviet nuclear warheads in Cuba in 1962. As in a perfect crime, where the criminal in cahoots with a corrupt police destroys all the evidence, factual proof of what really happened during the crisis is now almost impossible to obtain.

30 Arthur S. Hulnick, Conference on U.S. Intelligence, June 6, 1984, quoted in Loch K. Johnson, *America's Secret Power: The CIA in a Democratic Society* (New York: Oxford University Press, 1989), p. 96

31 For typical examples of how Castro literally makes decisions from his balls, see Servando González, *The Secret Fidel Castro: Deconstructing the Symbol* (Oakland: InteliBooks, 2001), pp. 230-231.

Introduction

1 Following the Cuban usage in Spanish, I have capitalized the word *Island* when it stands for Cuba.

2 The Russians always refer to the crisis as the "Caribbean Crisis." Some Western analysts have tried to see under that denomination some obscure ideological motivations. But this is not the case. Cubans, for example, always call it the "October Crisis" (*La crisis de Octubre*). In the same fashion Cubans call the Bay of Pigs invasion *Playa Girón*. Definitely, Americans don't have a world monopoly for naming historical events. For a good beginner's introduction to the mythical version of the Missile Crisis see Abel, 1966; Daniel and Hubbel, 1963; and Detzer, 1970. For probably the best compendium on the crisis see Larson, 1963.

3 Although several interpretations have been made, the Cuban missile crisis, as Harold MacMillan observed, still remains a "strange and still scarcely explicable affair." Harold MacMillan, Introduction to Robert F. Kennedy, *Thirteen Days: A Memoir of the Cuban Missile Crisis* (New York: Signet Books, 1969), p. 17.

4 According to Theodore C. Sorensen, the most probable ones, as discussed in the Ex Comm meetings, were: 1. bargaining barter; 2. diverting trap; 3. Cuban defense; 4. Cold War politics; and, 5. missile power. *Kennedy* (New York: Bantam, 1966), pp. 762-64.

5 *Niekulturnyi*, literally "uncultured," is the Russian word for "uncouth," "boorish," "ill mannered."

6 Khrushchev interrupted MacMillan's speech before the U.N. Assembly by shouting loudly and surprised the seemingly imperturbable delegates by banging his shoe on the table at an Assembly session.

7 David Wise and Thomas B. Ross, *The Invisible Government* (New York: Bantam, 1965), pp. 310-311. Apparently McCone was not the first. Some people have seen allusions to the Cuban missile crisis in certain quatrains of Nostradamus. See *The Prophecies of Nostradamus*, translated and introduced by Erika Cheetham (New York: Perigee, 1973), p. 172. Also, James Wilkie, a Toronto Hospital orderly

with some attributed psychic powers, apparently predicted the crisis on September 13, 1962. See, Allen Spraggett, *The Unexplained* (New York: New American Library, 1967), p. 26. It seems, however, that McCone's ability to predict the deployment of Soviet missiles in Cuba had nothing to do with his psychic abilities but with more mundane ones, like his personal contacts in the dark world of espionage.

Even more surprising, as early as January, 1961, Fidel made a surprising prediction. According to Castro, CIA Director Allen Dulles already had everything ready for an invasion. "The excuse would be the assertion that Cuba was allowing rocket pads to be constructed on its territory." See *Revolución*, January 2, 1961.

8 "Spying From High," *Time*, April 7, 1980, p. 77.

9 Robert Kennedy, *Thirteen Days* (New York: W.W. Norton, 1971), p. 5.

10 In 1950 the CIA created the Office of National Estimates, to produce high-level national intelligence estimates, a sort of forecasts of possible Soviet behavior.

11 See Kennedy, Robert. *Thirteen Days*. New York: W.W. Norton, 1971), p. 6; Hugh Sidey, *John F. Kennedy, President* (Greenwich, Conn.: Crest Books, 1963), p. 298; Also Klauss Knorr, "Failure in National Intelligence Estimates, The Case of the Cuban Missiles," *World Politics*, Vol. XVI No. 3 (April, 1964); and Arnold Horelick, "The Cuban Missile Crisis. An analysis of Soviet Calculations and Behavior," *World Politics,* Vol. XVI No. 3, April 1964.

12 On the apparent failure of the U.S. intelligence community to predict the deployment of the Russian missiles in Cuba, see *Investigation of the Preparedness Program*, Interim Report on the Cuban Military Buildup by the Preparedness Investigating Committee, Committee on armed Services, U.S. Senate, 88 Congress, 1st Session, Washington, 1963. The Report is usually called the Stennis Report because Senator Stennis was chairman of the subcommittee.

13 Dexter Perkins, *The Evolution of American Foreign Policy* (New York: Oxford University Press, 1966), p. 135.

14 Graham T. Allison, "Conceptual Models and the Cuban missile crisis," in Morton H. Halperin and Arnold Kanter, eds., *Readings in American Foreign Policy* (Boston: Little, Brown and Company, 1973), p. 80.

15 Robert Kennedy, *Thirteen Days*, p. 33.

16 Actually, this was not the first time that American ships blockaded the island of Cuba. In April 22, 1898, following President McKinley's orders, American ships proceeded to blockade five of Cuba's main ports, thus beginning the war with Spain.

17 See, Ronald Steel, "The Kennedys and the Missile Crisis," in Morton H. Halperin and Arnold Kanter, eds., *Readings in American Foreign Policy* (Boston: Little, Brown and Company, 1973), p. 204. The Kennedy eulogists had repeated over and over that the Bay of Pigs failure was the price Kennedy paid in his learning process at the White House. So many times it has been repeated that it is now a kind of orthodoxy. But the evidence seems to point out that if the President learned something it was not evidenced in his later behavior. Just after the Bay of Pigs

defeat Kennedy gave orders to expand guerrilla warfare and counterinsurgency tactics, and there is circumstantial evidence supporting the fact that he persisted in his actions to assassinate Castro. Yet, if Kennedy learned nothing from the Bay of Pigs failure, how did he apparently respond so wisely in the Cuban missile crisis? The common orthodoxy is that his wisdom could only have been derived from lessons of his earlier mistake. But the orthodoxy also assumes that the Cuban missile crisis ended in a victory for the President, and that assumption needs to be re-evaluated in detail.

18 Henry Kissinger, "Reflections on Cuba," *The Reporter*, November 22, 1962.

19 Their failure to provide an answer to the most important question about the crisis after 42 years of continuous study, may indicate that the methodology these noted scholars have been using to analyze their subject is not the right one.

20 James G. Blight and David A. Welch, *On the Brink: Americans and Soviets Reexamine the Cuban Missile Crisis* (New York: The Noonday Press, 1990), p. 34.

21 Blight and Welch, *On the Brink*, p. 352.

22 Blight and Welch, *On the Brink*, p. 28,

23 Arnold L Horelick and Myron Rush, *Strategic Power and Soviet Foreign Policy* (Chicago: University of Chicago Press), 1966.

24 Blight and Welch, *On the Brink*, p. 36.

25 Hugh Sidey, *John F. Kennedy, President* (Greenwich, Conn.: Crest Books, 1963), p. 318. The fact that Sidey's words are today as valid as thirty-nine years ago when he wrote them, is sufficient proof that the riddles remain.

Chapter One

1 See, i.e., Nikolai V. Sivachev and Nikolai N. Yakovlev, *Russia and the United States* (Chicago: The University of Chicago Press, 1979), p. 244.

2 *Hoy*, December 13 and 14, 1962.

3 See Adam B. Ulam, *The Rivals: America and Russia Since World War II* (New York: The Viking Press, 1971), p. 328.

4 Ulam, *The Rivals,* p. 332.

5 See "The Cuban Missile Crisis," in Arnold Horelick and Myron Rush, eds., *Strategic Power and Soviet Foreign Policy* (Chicago: University of Chicago Press, 1966), pp. 127-136.

6 Hilsman, *To Move a Nation,* (Garden City, N,Y.: Doubleday, 1967), pp. 161-165; and 201202.

7 Ulam, *Expansion and Coexistence: The History of Soviet Foreign Policy* (New York: Praeger, 1968), pp. 668-677.

8 See Richard Ned Lebow and Janice Gross Stein, *We All Lost the Cold War* (Princeton, New Jersey: Princeton University Press, 1994), p. 27.

9 Lebow and Stein, *We All Lost*, p. 28.

10 Secretary of Defense McNamara testified that the program to remove the obsolete Thor and Jupiter missiles dated from early 1961. See, Defense Intelligence Agency, *Department of Defense Appropriations for 1964*, Hearing Before a Subcommittee of the Committee on Appropriations, House of Representatives, 88 Congress, 1st Session (Washington, D.C., 1963), Part I, p. 57.

11 Turkey announced on January 23, 1963, that it has agreed to the removal of the Jupiters.

12 *Izvestia*, October 28, 1962.

13 The SS-20 —the missile some people believed Khrushchev planned to deploy in Cuba in a later date— was nothing more than a slightly updated, upgraded replacement for SS-4 and SS-5 ballistic missiles that had been around since the late fifties and into the sixties. See Strobe Talbot, *Deadly Gambits* (New York: Knopf, 1984), p 29.

14 See James Daniel and John G. Hubbel, *Strike in the West* (New York: Holt, Rinehart and Winston, 1963), p. 51.

15 Nikita Khrushchev, *Khrushchev Remembers*, translated and edited by Strobe Talbot (Boston: Little, Brown and Company, 1970), p. 511.

16 See Michel Tatu, *Power in the Kremlin: From Khrushchev to Kosygin* (New York: Viking, 1970), pp. 230-231; also, Richard J. Walton, *Cold War and Counter-Revolution: The Foreign Policy of John F. Kennedy* (New York: The Viking Press, 1972), p. 141.

17 Eventually Gromyko only admitted the installation of one type of missile, presumably the one with the shorter range, since this is all that would have been needed to make the Americans "think twice" about attacking Cuba.

18 The author was present during some of these exchanges at the University of Havana when Castro discussed the subject with the students. Unfortunately no report of these evenings at the University has been published.

19 See Adolfo Gilly, *Inside the Cuban Revolution* (Westport, Connecticut: Greenwood Press, 1964), p. 54.

20 In Cuba, *conga* is not the name of a musical instrument (generically called *tumbadora*), but of a street dance.

21 *Revolución*, January 3, 1963.

22 *Le Monde*, March 22 and 23, 1963. Almost twenty years later, Carlos Franqui, who was at the time the editor of *Revolución*, confirmed Julien's version of Castro's words and also gave an interesting account about how Fidel concocted the whole episode and used Julien to put pressure on Khrushchev, using the opportunity to criticize the Russians. See, Carlos Franqui, *Retrato de familia con Fidel* (Barcelona: Seix Barral, 1981), pp. 424-433.

23 Alexei Adzhubei was a sort of unofficial deputy for Khrushchev on Foreign Affairs. On several occasions Khrushchev took steps in personal and private diplomacy through Adzhubei as, for example, when in late 1964 he decided, without consulting his colleagues of the Presidium, to send him to Bonn trying to come with an understanding with West Germany. During the Cuban missile crisis he

played an important role as Khrushchev's personal emissary abroad, well above the Soviet Foreign Minister Gromyko and of the Soviet ambassadors, who most of the time were not informed about Adzhubei's whereabouts. See Roy A. Medvedeev and Zhores A. Medvedeev, *Khrushchev, The Years in Power* (New York: W.W. Norton, 1978), p. 141.

24 Jean Daniel, "Castro Explains Request for Soviet Missiles," *The Washington Post*, December 11, 1963, pp. A-12-13. Later Castro himself, having being caught in the web of his own inconsistencies, provided either the "mutual consent" or the "Soviet interest" explanation.

For more details on this see, Jean Daniel, "Unofficial Envoy," *The New Republic*, December 14, 1963, pp. 15-20, and Castro's "denial" to *Prensa Latina*, March 23, 1963; also Herbert Matthews, *The New York Times*, October 12 1963; Matthews, "Return to Cuba," *Hispanic American Review*, Special Issue, January, 1964, p. 16; K.S. Karol, *Guerrillas in Power* (New York: Hill and Wang), 1970. pp. 261-262; Frank Mankiewicz and Kirby Jones, *With Fidel* (New York: Playboy Press, 1975), p. 174; and Juanita Castro, "Speech to the World Affairs Council," Los Angeles, February 8, 1965.

25 Lee Lockwood, *Castro's Cuba, Cuba's Fidel* (New York: Macmillan, 1967), p. 200.

26 Tad Szulc, "Friendship is Possible, But...," *Parade*, April 1, 1984, pp. 5-6.

27 Carlos Lechuga, *Cuba and the Missile Crisis* (Melbourne: Ocean Press, 2001), p. 2, (emphasis mine).

28 Khrushchev, *Khrushchev Remembers*, p. 493.

29 Arthur M. Schlesinger, Jr., *A Thousand Days* (New York: Fawcet Books, 1975), 731.

30 *The New York Times*, September 12, 1962.

31 This point was clearly explained by Arnold L. Horelick, "The Cuban Missile Crisis. An Analysis of Soviet Calculations and Behavior," *World Politics*, Vol. XVI, No. 3 (April 1964), p. 368.

32 Statement by a spokesman of the Chinese Government, September 1, 1963. Quoted in John Gittins, *Survey of the Sino-Soviet Dispute* (London: Oxford University Press, 1968), pp. 181182.

33 Among the most popular explanations about Khrushchev's motivation offered at the time, there is one that stated that he hoped to panic the U.S. into an invasion of Cuba —which would bog down U.S. combat divisions and incur world-wide enmity. This perhaps explains why, while some members of the Kennedy administration liked the idea of declaring war and invading Cuba, other members were more cautious. "Our Soviet experts believe that this is exactly what Khrushchev wanted us to do," said a Presidential aide. "An invasion of a nation of 7 million by one of 180 million wouldn't sit well." See, "Showdown-Backdown," *Newsweek*, November 5, 1962, p. 30.

Also, referring to Khrushchev, Dean Acheson believed that, "His aim in Cuba was threefold: first, to increase his nuclear first-strike capacity against the United

States by about 50 percent; second, to discredit the United States completely in the Western Hemisphere; and, third, to force the United States to pay so high a price for the removal of the Cuban missiles as to discredit us in Europe and Southeast Asia. See, Dean Acheson, "Dean Acheson's Version of Robert Kennedy's Version of the Cuban Missile Affair," *Esquire*, (February 1966), pp. 76-77. Moreover, Sorensen mentioned that the President was concerned "about the possibility that Khrushchev hoped to provoke him into another entanglement in Cuba which would make a martyr out of Castro and wreck our Latin American relations while the Soviets marched in on West Berlin." Theodore Sorensen, *Kennedy* (New York: Bantam, 1965), p. 756). "Even a gigantic hoax had to be guarded against," advised Sorensen, *Kennedy*, p. 761.

Chapter Two

1 Hugh Thomas, Foreword to Mario Llerena, *The Unsuspected Revolution* (Ithaca, New York: Cornell University Press, 1978), p. 11.

2 Theodore Draper, *Castro's Revolution* (New York: Praeger, 1962), p. 3. My book *The Secret Fidel Castro: Deconstructing the Symbol* (Oakland: InteliBooks, 2001), is not only dedicated to Draper but, as I mention in the Introduction, the book is my attempt to answer Draper's questions. See p. xxv.

3 Draper, *Castro's Revolution, p.* 196.

4 Carlos Franqui, *Family Portrait with Fidel* (New York: Random House, 1984), p. 22.

5 H. Michael Erisman, *Cuba's international Relations* (Boulder, Colorado: Westview Press, 1985), p. XIII.

6 Herbert S. Dinerstein, *The Making of a Missile Crisis* (Baltimore, Md.: Johns Hopkins University Press, 1976), p. 24.

7 See, for example, Foy D. Kohler, "Cuba and the Soviet Problem in Latin America," in Jaime Suchlicki, ed.; *Cuba, Castro, and Revolution* (Coral Gables, Florida: University of Miami Press, 1972), p. 121.

8 See, William Benton, *The Voice of Latin America* (New York: Harper and Row, 1965), p. 83.

9 Foy D. Kohler, "Cuba and the Soviet Problem in Latin America," in Jaime Suchlicki, ed., *Cuba, Castro and Revolution* (Coral Gables, Fl.: University of Miami Press, 1972), p. 121.

10 Robert J. Alexander, "Soviet and Communist Activities in Latin America," in DeVere E. Pentony, ed., *Red World in Tumult: Communist Foreign Policies* (San Francisco: Chandler, 1962), p. 240.

11 In February, 1957, Herbert Matthews wrote 3 articles for *The New York Times* about Fidel Castro. Matthews' story contributed to Castro's success in more than one way: not only was it a refutation of the Batista propaganda, which claimed that Castro was dead, but it presented Castro as a firm believer in democracy,

liberty and social justice. The image that Matthews evoked appealed to the idealism of the noble, but gullible American people and, for a time, they were quite willing to accept this appraisal at face value. There is no doubt that Matthews helped Castro to win the revolution. The *NYT* articles accomplished a shift in public opinion both outside and inside Cuba that Castro could not have provoked by himself. See, Gerhard Masur, *Nationalism in Latin America* (New YorK: The Macmillan Co., 1966), p. 206.

12 Though widely ignored by Castro's official media, there was also an attack against the military barracks in the city of Bayamo, also in the Oriente province.

13 *Daily Worker*, New York, August 5, 1953. It is interesting to see that the Cuban communists kept hammering the word "putschist" in all their references to Castro.

14 Luis Dam, "El grupo 26 de julio en la cárcel", *Bohemia*, July 8, 1956.

15 The deceased leader of the *Ortodoxo* Party.

16 Two well-known PSP leaders.

17 "¡Basta ya de mentiras!", *Bohemia*, July 15, 1956. Castro's article is quoted in length in Rolando E. Bonachea and Nelson P. Valdes, eds., *Revolutionary Struggle, 1947-1958* (Cambridge, Massachusetts: The MIT Press, 1972), p. 323. I corrected a few minor inaccuracies in the above mentioned translation.

18 Theodore Draper, *Castroism, Theory and Practice* (New York: Praeger, 1965), p. 28.

19 "Cuba —'Long Live the Revolution'," *The New Republic*, November 3, 1962, p. 15.

20 Ernesto Che Guevara, Letter to Daniel (cover name of René Ramos Latour), Sierra Maestra, December 14, 1957, cited in Carlos Franqui, *Family Portrait with Fidel* (New York: Random House, 1984), p. 149.

21 Carlos Franqui, *Family Portrait*, pp. 152-153. *History Will Absolve Me* was in fact the retouched, heavily edited version of Castro's self-defense speech at the trial for attacking the Moncada garrisons. The document circulated later in *samizdat* fashion all over the island. Some people claim that the core of the document was not written by Castro himself, but by his university professor Dr. Jorge Mañach, then an undercover anti-Batista conspirator. See, Guillermo Cabrera Infante, Introduction to Carlos Franqui, *Family Portrait*, p. XIII.

22 *The New York Times*, March 28, 1982. Of course, one must take the words of professional liars with extreme skepticism.

23 Robert D. Crasweller, *Cuba and the U.S.: The Tangled Relationship* (New York: Foreign Policy Association, 1971), p. 22.

24 For a strong statement on Castro's democratic and anti-communist views, see the interview with Castro by Andrew St. George which appeared in *Look,* in April of 1958.

25 On Castro as a pathological liar see Servando González, *The Secret Fidel Castro: Deconstructing the Symbol* (Oakland: InteliBooks, 2001), pp. 203-207.

26 See, Lionel Martin, *The Early Fidel* (Seacaucus: Lyle Stuart, 1978), p. 118.

27 See, Nathaniel Weyl, *Red Star Over Cuba* (New York: Hillman/Macfadden, 1961), pp. 73-85, 92-97.

28 Hugh Thomas, *Cuba: The Pursuit of Freedom* (New York: Harper and Row, 1971), p. 829.

29 Ramón Eduardo Ruiz, "The Impact of the Cuban Revolution," in Neal D. Houghton, ed., *Struggle Against History* (New York: Clarion, 1968), p. 135.

30 Claude Julien, *La Révolution Cubaine* (Paris: Maspero 1961), p. 166.

31 Franqui *op. cit.*, p. 153.

32 Andrés Valdespino quoting from *Carta Semanal* in a public polemic with Carlos Rafael Rodríguez, a PSP leader (*Bohemia*, June 26, 1960, p. 43). Rodríguez didn't challenge the assertion in his answer to Valdespino.

33 Though it was later denied, there is evidence that until late 1958 Castro did not consider guerrilla fighting as a fundamental method of struggle. Apparently his hopes when he landed in Oriente Province in 1956 were to prompt urban uprisings which could develop into an insurrection, but the very few that actually occurred were quickly crushed by Batista's army. Even then, Castro, who took not a single measure in the event of a prolonged guerrilla warfare in the Oriente mountains, still believed that Batista would be defeated by some kind of general strike or mass action —like Mussolini's March on Rome. But the Cuban people — especially the poor farmers and city workers— remained indifferent to his struggle.

34 Claude Julien, *La Révolution Cubaine* (Paris: Maspero, 1961), p. 81.

35 *Hoy*, La Habana, January 11, 1959.

36 Hugh Thomas, Cuba, p. 981.

37 "Note from K. Voroshilov to Manuel Urrutia, January 10, 1959," *Pravda*, January 11, 1959.

38 Edwin Leuwen, *Arms and Politics in Latin America* (New York: Praeger, 1961), p. 276.

39 Carlos Rafael Rodríguez to Herbert Matthews. See Herbert Matthews, *Fidel Castro* (New York: Simon & Schuster, 1969), p. 176.

40 "*Guía del pensamiento político-económico de Fidel*," In *Diario Libre*, La Habana, 1959, p. 48.

41 "Conclusiones del pleno del Comité Nacional del PSP, realizado en los días 25 al 28 de mayo de 1959", *Hoy*, June 7, 1959.

42 Since his University days many people feared that Fidel Castro was an *agent provocateur*.

43 "Conclusiones del pleno del Comité Nacional del PSP," *Hoy*, June 7, 1959.

44 "El peor camino," *Hoy*, January 13, 1959.

45 The Cuban communists' distrust for Castro has been confirmed by sources behind the iron curtain. See, i.e., Markus Wolf, *A Man Without a Face: The Autobiography of Communism's Greatest Spymaster* (New York: Public Affairs,1997), pp. 343-344.

46 "The Cuban Revolution in Action," *World Marxist Review*, II, No. 8 (August, 1959), p. 17.

47 *Revolución*, May 22, 1959.

48 *Bohemia*, June 14, 1959.

49 Theodore Draper, *Castro's Revolution* (New York: Praeger, 1962), pp. 116-117.

50 *Documents on International Affairs, 1960* (London, 1964), p. 534.

51 *Hoy,* May 24, 1960.

52 *Documents on International Affairs, 1960* (London, 1964), p. 563.

53 *Documents on International Affairs, 1960* (London, 1964), p. 564.

54 *Revolución*, July 11, 1960.

55 Gerhard Masur, *Nationalism in Latin America* (New York: Macmillan, 1966), p. 215.

56 Max Frankel, "Extent of Red Grip in Cuba is Related by Party Chief," *The New York Times*, November 27, 1960, p. 1.

57 News Conference, December 10, *Department of State Bulletin*, December 28, 1959. p. 937.

58 The full text of Fidel's confession of Marxist faith was published in *Hoy*, December 2, 1961, and in the evening edition of *Revolución*, December 2, 1961. Usually Fidel's speeches first published in the evening edition of *Revolución* were reprinted the following day in the morning edition. For unknown reasons it was not done this time. There are several slightly different versions of the speech: the *Hoy* version; two versions published in the first and second edition of *Revolución*; one abridged version in *Bohemia* on December 10; and one in a pamphlet edition in *Obra Revolucionaria*. For an excellent analysis of Fidel's "I am a Marxist" speech, see Loree Wilkerson, *Fidel Castro's Political Programs from Reformism to Marxist Leninism* (Gainesville, Florida: University of Florida Press, 1965).

59 Loree Wilkerson, *Fidel Castro's Political Programs from Reformism to Marxist Leninism* (Gainesville, Florida: University of Florida Press, 1965). p. 81.

60 An illegal is an intelligence operative placed in a foreign country with false identity to operate independently from any of his embassies or consulates. Illegals are not covered by diplomatic immunity, therefore they normally operate under deep covers and use false documentation. A sleeper is an agent or intelligence officer who has been implanted into a country under a false identity and has been living a normal life for a rather long amount of time, waiting to be roused into action. The main job of a sleeper is to wait, as unnoticed as possible, until he receives the wake up order, regardless of the length of time required.

61 *Editorial Research Reports* July 9, 1967.

62 Thomas, *Cuba*, p. 1489.

Chapter Three

1 According to Carlos Franqui, Castro's nickname "The Horse" was the creation of Beny Moré. It was past midnight, says Franqui, and the popular

musician was singing at a party when, unexpectedly, Castro showed up. When he saw Fidel approaching, Beny yelled: "Hey, guys! Here comes The Horse!"

When the people at the party heard Beny they cried out: "Horse! Horse! Horse!" Castro's reaction, however, was not a happy one. When he heard the people calling him "Horse," Fidel became furious and threw one of his famous tantrums. But the nickname stuck, and, after some time, he got used to it and ended up by accepting the nickname as a sign of the people's affection. See, Franqui, *Family Portrait with Fidel* (New York: Random House, 1984), p. 25. For more information about Castro's nickname and its connections to *Santería*, see Servando González, *The Secret Fidel Castro: Deconstructing the Symbol* (Oakland: InteliBooks, 2001), pp. 260-266.

2 "Khrushchev's answer to the questions of Brazilian journalist Murilo Marroquin de Souza," *Mezhdunarodnaia Zhizn* (International Affairs), No. 11, 1985, p. 5. Cited in Dinerstein, *The Making of a Missile Crisis*, p. 35.

3 See, for example, K. M. Obyden, "The Victory of the Cuban People," *Agitator* 2 (February, 1959); M. Kremionov, "In Cuba," *New Times* 22, (May 1959); Severo Aguirre, "The Revolution in Cuba," *Mirovaia ekonomika i mezhdunarodnye otnoshenia* 5, (May 1959); Juan Marinello, "Chto proizoshlo na Kube," (What has happened in Cuba), *Ogonek* (March 22, 1959); K. M. Obyden, *Kuba V bor'be za avovodu i nezavisimost* (Cuba in the Struggle for Freedom and Independence), (Moscow: Iz. Politiceskoi Literatury, 1959.

4 See, *The New York Times*, November 12, 1959, p. 12. On October 21, 1959, Major Pedro Luis Díaz Lanz, former Chief of the Cuban Air Force who had defected to the United States a few weeks before, flew a plane over Havana dropping leaflets calling on Castro to eliminate communism from his government. Some anti-aircraft batteries from across the bay opened fire against the plane, the shrapnel causing injuries among the civilian population. Immediately radio stations began spreading the news that at least two planes had flown over Havana dropping bombs. The final toll was two dead and forty-five wounded.

The following morning *Revolución*, Castro's official newspaper, proclaimed that *two* planes from the United States had bombed the city and machine-gunned people on the streets The next night, October 23, Castro went on tv announcing that the "bombing of Havana" was a "graver incident" than Pearl Harbor or the sinking of the *Maine* battleship in Havana's harbor in 1898. He added that the planes took off from Florida and therefore the United States had either "consented" to the "bombing" or was "completely defenseless" if planes could take off without its knowledge.

5 Herbert S. Dinerstein, *The Making of a Missile Crisis* (Baltimore, Md.: The John Hopkins University Press, 1976), p. 51.

6 Robert J. Alexander, "Soviet and Communist Activity in Latin America," *Problems of Communism* X, No. 1 (January-February, 1961), p. 8.

7 See, Herbert S. Dinerstein, "Soviet Policy in Latin America," *The American Political Science Review*, LXI, No. 1 (March, 1967), pp. 80-90; see also, J. Gregory

Oswald, "Soviet Strategy in Latin America since 1962," *Communist Affairs*, 4, No. 5 (September-October, 1966), pp. 3-6.

8 Dinerstein, *The Making*, p. 1.

9 See, David J. Dallin, *Soviet Foreign Policy After Stalin* (Philadelphia: J. B. Lippincott, 1961). pp. 228 ff.

10 Richard P. Stebbins, *The United States in World Affairs, 1959* (New York: Vintage, 1960), pp. 373-374.

11 Stebbins, *The United Sates*, p. 105.

12 Stebbins, *The United States*, p. 373.

13 Stebbins, *The United States*, p. 373.

14 *Current Digest of the Soviet Press*, February 18, 1959, pp. 13, 15; same, March 11, 1959, pp. 17-18.

15 *Current Digest of the Soviet Press*, February 18, 1959, pp. 15-19.

16 See, "Khrushchev's Report to the 20th Congress of the Soviet Communist Party," February 14, 1956, in *Documents in American Foreign Relations, 1956* (New York: Harper, 1957), pp. 188-195.

17 This, i. e., was the opinion of Frank J. Barnett, "Overview of Soviet Strategy," *Naval War College Review*, (June 1971).

18 Herbert S. Dinerstein, "The Soviet Union and the Communist World" *Survey*, Spring 1973, p. 147.

19 Dean Rusk, *As I Saw It*, ed. Daniel S. Papp (New York: Norton, 1990), p. 245. It seems that Mikoyan, despite all his cunning, apparently forgot that when something seems too good to be true, it most likely is.

20 Almost unknown to the Soviet and Cuban public, however, the Soviet Union had bought from Cuba, from 1955 to 1959 inclusive, without any agreement, 1,924,320 tons of sugar for $139,581,096, for an annual cash income to Cuba of more than $27 million. Under the touted Cuban-Soviet agreement, however, the Soviet Union will pay Cuba in dollars for only 200,000 tons per year, at approximately 3.25 cents per pound, or $75 per ton, with an income of $15 million per annum, or $75,000,000 for five years. Since Russia had paid Cuba $139 million dollars in the last five years without any formal agreement, and would pay only $75 million in the next five years, this "splendid" agreement meant in fact a loss of $64 million to Cuba. One way or another, the U.S.S.R. would have bought the same or similar amount of sugar from Cuba in the years to come without any agreement. See, Fulgencio Batista, *Cuba Betrayed* (New York: Vantage Press, 1962), pp. 284-285.

21 See, for example, S. Utegonov, "Cuba on the Path to Strengthening its Independence," *Partinaia Zhizn'Kazahstana* 5 (May 1960), pp. 58-61; A.I. Kalinin, "Cuba is a Revolutionary Democratic State," *Sovetskoe gosudarstvo i pravo* 9 (September 1960), pp. 54-61; K.M. Obyden, *Kuba v bor'be za svobody i nezavisimost* (Cuba in the Struggle for Freedom and Independence) (Moscow: Iz. Politicheskoi Literatury, 1959); I. Altman, "The Banner of the Cuban Revolution Waves over Cuba," *Kommunist* (Vilnyus) 1, (January 1961), pp. 60-63; Yurii A.

Fadeev, *Dva goda vorby i pobed* (Two Years of Struggle and Victories) (Moscow: Iz. Znanie, 1961).

22 Though Khrushchev's alcoholic consumption had been severely cut in the late fifties on the order of his doctors and the insistence of his wife, he was publicly drunk in Belgrade on at least one occasion during his visit in 1955. See, William Randolph Hearst, Jr., B. Considine and F. Coniff, *Khrushchev and the Russian Challenge* (New York: Avon, 1961), p. 59. References to Khrushchev stumbling after too many toasts were not uncommon in the Western press, see, i. e., N.H. Mager and Jakes Katel, eds., *Conquest Without War* (New York: Cardinal, 1961), p. 16.

23 In his speech at the Twenty-First Congress of the Communist Party of the Soviet Union, Defense Minister Rodion Y. Malinovsky asserted that Soviet rockets were "very accurate" and could carry their hydrogen warheads "precisely to any point of the globe" —a statement that sounded to President Eisenhower like pure propaganda. See, *The New York Times*, February 4 and 5, 1959. We now have positive proof that Malinovsky was bluffing and that the only "very accurate" thing about the Soviet missiles was Eisenhower's remarks.

24 *Pravda,* July 10, 1960, translated in *Current Digest of the Soviet Press*, August 10, 1960, p. 5.

25 See, Ronald R. Pope, *Soviet Foreign Affairs Specialists: An Evaluation of their Direct and Indirect Impact on Soviet Foreign Policy Decision-Making Based on their Analysis of Cuba, 19581961, and Chile, 1969-1973*, Ph.D. Dissertation, University of Pennsylvania, 1975, pp. 64-65, 111-112.

26 Quoted in Alexander Werth, *Russia Under Khrushchev* (New York: Fawcett, 1961), p. 319.

27 *Khrushchev's Foreign Speeches, 1960*, Vol. 2, p. 382, quoted in Michael Tatu, *Power in the Kremlin: From Khrushchev to Kosygin* (New York: Viking, 1970), p. 231.

28 Carlos Franqui, *Family Portrait with Fidel* (New York: Random House, 1984), pp. 184-185; also in Fidel Castro, "Speech to the General Assembly of the United Nations," (September 26, 1960), in Robert F. Smith, *What Happened in Cuba* (New York: Twayne Publishers, 1963), p. 294.

29 Robert D.Crasweller, *Cuba and the U.S.: The Tangled Relationship* (New York: Foreign Policy Association, 1971), p. 23.

30 See Adam B. Ulam, *The Rivals: America and Russia Since World War II* (New York: The Viking Press, 1971), pp. 292-93.

31 See, John Thomas, "The Limits of Alliance: The Quemoy Crisis of 1958," in Raymond L. Garthoff, ed., *Sino-Soviet Military Relations* (New York: Praeger, 1966), pp. 114-149.

32 "Message from Nikita S. Khrushchev, Chairman of the Council of Ministers of the Union of Soviet Socialist Republics to President Kennedy, Concerning Cuba," April 18, 1961, *Department of State Bulletin*, May 8, 1961, p. 662.

33 John Guerassi, *The Great Fear in Latin America* (New York: Collier, 1965), p. 403.

34 Carlos Franqui, *Family Portrait with Fidel* (New York: Random House, 1984), p. 185.

35 *The New York Times*, November 19, 1960, p. 1.

36 *The New York Times*, November 23, 1960, p. 11.

37 Frank Gibney, *The Khrushchev Pattern* (New York: Duell, Sloan & Pearce, 1960), p. 63.

38 I have extrapolated almost verbatim to the case of Cuba, Adam Ulam's excellent analysis of Khrushchev's policy in the Middle East. Though the situation in both cases was not exactly the same, a parallel can easily be drawn. See Adam B. Ulam, *Expansion and Coexistence: The History of Soviet Foreign Policy* (New York: Praeger, 1968), pp. 613-616.

39 Adam B. Ulam, *The Rivals: America and Russia Since World War II* (New York: The Viking Press, 1971), p. 274.

40 Herbert S. Dinerstein, *Fifty Years of Soviet Foreign Policy* (Baltimore, Md.: The John Hopkins University Press, 1967), p. 80.

41 Dinerstein, *Fifty Years*, p. 80.

42 Dinerstein, *Fifty Years*, p. 80.

43 See, *The New York Times*, 5 January, 1982. The Second Declaration of Havana, adopted on February 4, 1962, was Castro's fiery response to a pronouncement — most likely U.S. inspired— by the Organization of American States condemning Cuba's adherence to Marxism-Leninism and expelling the country from the organization.

44 "Radio Interview of Fidel Castro with the Editors of *Pravda* and *Izvestia*," January 29, 1962.

45 According to Carlos Franqui, not even Che Guevara considered Fidel to be a Communist at the time of the Sierra Maestra struggle. In a letter Che wrote in 1957, he asserted that he considered Fidel's movement motivated by the eagerness of the bourgeoisie to free itself from the economic chains of imperialism. And Che added that he always considered Fidel to be "an authentic left-wing bourgeois leader, although his figure is glorified by personal qualities of extraordinary brilliance that set him far above his class." See, Guevara's Letter to Daniel (René Ramos Latour), Sierra Maestra, December 14, 1957, cited in Carlos Franqui, *Family Portrait with Fidel* (New York: Random House, 1984), p. 149.

46 See Leon Goure and Julian Winkle, "Soviet-Cuban relations. The Growing Integration," in Jaime Suchlicki, ed., *Cuba, Castro and Revolution* (Coral Gables, Florida: University of Miami Press, 1972), p. 148.

47 Maurice Halperin, *The Rise and Decline of Fidel Castro* (Berkeley: Univ. of California Press, 1972), p. 125.

48 Edward Crankshaw, *Khrushchev: A Career* (New York: Viking, 1966), p. 276.

49 Crankshaw, *Khrushchev*, p. 277.

50 See Adam Ulam, *Expansion and Coexistence: The History of Soviet Foreign Policy* (New York: Praeger, 1968), p. 574.

51 See H.I. Dinerstein, "Moscow and the Third World," *Problems of Communism*, (JanuaryFebruary, 1968), pp. 52-56; also, Edward Taborsky, "The Communist Parties of the Third World in Soviet Strategy," *Orbis*, XII, No. 2 (Summer 1968), pp. 128-148.

52 See Cole Blasier, *The Giant's Rival: the U.S.S.R. and Latin America* (Pittsburgh: University of Pittsburgh Press, 1982), p. 37.

53 See, Alfred G. Meyer, *Communism* (New York: Random House, 1962), p. 169.

54 See Ulam, *Expansion and Coexistence*, p. 544.

55 Blasier, *The Giant's Rival*, p. 38.

56 See B.F. Denno, "Sino-Soviet Allies Toward Revolutionary War," *Orbis* XI, No. 4 (Winter, 1968), pp. 1193-1207.

57 See Philip W. Bonsal, *Cuba, Castro and the United States* (Pittsburgh. Penn.: University of Pittsburgh Press, 1971), p. 144.

58 "Statement of President Eisenhower on the Reduction of Cuba's Sugar Quota for 1960, July 6, 1960," *Department od State Bulletin*, July 25, 1960, p. 140.

59 See Philip W. Bonsal, *Cuba, Castro and the United States* (Pittsburgh. Penn.: University of Pittsburgh Press, 1971), p. 156.

60 See Franqui, *Family Portrait*, p. 78.

61 The full text of Fidel's confession of Marxist faith was published in *Hoy*, December 2, 1961, and in the evening edition of *Revolución*, December 2, 1961. Usually Fidel's speeches first published in the evening edition of *Revolución* are reprinted the following day in the morning edition. For unknown reasons it was not done this time. There are several slightly different versions of the speech: the *Hoy* version, two versions published in the first and second edition of *Revolución*, one abridged version in *Bohemia* on December 10, and one in a pamphlet edition in *Obra Revolucionaria*. For an excellent analysis of Fidel's "I am a Marxist" speech, see Loree Wilkerson, *Fidel Castro's Political Programs from Reformism to Marxist Leninism* (Gainesville, Florida: University of Florida Press, 1965).

62 Halperin, *The Rise and Decline*, p. 137.

63 *Revolución*, November 3, 17, 1961.

64 According to Mikoyan it was Khrushchev himself who granted him permission to visit the Island. See Mikoyan's toast in "Reception in the Embassy of the Republic of Cuba," *Pravda*, November 5, 1960.

65 Nikita S. Khrushchev, *Khrushchev Remembers*, translated and edited by Strobe Talbot (Boston: Little, Brown and Company), 1970), p. 492.

66 See, David D. Catell, "Soviet Policies in Latin America," *Current History*, November 1964, p. 288.

67 Robert D. Crasweller, *Cuba and the U.S.; The Tangled Relationship* (New York: Foreign Policy Association, 1971), p. 23.

68 *The New York Times*, February 15, 1960, pp. 1-2.

69 Crasweller, *Cuba and the U.S.*, p. 20.
70 Crasweller, *Cuba and the U.S.*, pp. 25-26.
71 Crasweller, *Cuba and the U.S.*, p. 23.
72 I have made the distinction because there is the possibility that Castro's true purpose was quite different from what even the most suspicious Russian had ever guessed. I will explore the subject in detail in my forthcoming book *Fidel Castro Supermole: Walking Back the Cat in the Cuban Operation*.
73 Crasweller, *Cuba and the U.S.*, p. 24.
74 See Ulam, *The Rivals*, p. 156.
75 See Halperin, *The Rise and Decline*, p. 127-128.
76 As early as January 31, 1959, Severo Aguirre, a representative of the Executive Committee of the PSP, told the Soviet Party Congress in Moscow that the Communist underground forces had been "in the first rank of the rebellion that overthrew Batista." *The New York Times*, February 1, 1959, p. 22.
77 Crasweller, *Cuba and the U.S.*, p. 21.
78 Halperin, *The Rise and Decline*, p. 138.
79 Halperin, *The Rise and Decline*, p. 138.
80 Halperin, *The Rise and Decline*, p. 138.
81 *Cuba Socialista*, 2, No. 7 (March 1962), p. 21.
82 Carla Anne Robbins, *The Cuban Threat* (New York: McGraw-Hill, 1983), p. 263.
83 *Time*, January 26, 1959.
84 Characteristics that Zevedei Barbu observed also in Adolf Hitler. See "Democracy and Dictatorship," in Gordon Wright and Arthur Mejia, Jr., eds., *An Age of Controversy* (New York: Dodd, Mead and Company, 1963), p. 262. On the uncanny parallel between Castro and Hitler see, Servando González, *The Secret Fidel Castro: Deconstructing the Symbol* (Oakland: InteliBooks, 2001).
85 *Time*, January 26, 1959.
86 On psychological analysis of political leaders see, T. Abel, "Is a Psychiatric Interpretation of the German Enigma Necessary?," *American Sociological Review* No. 10 (1945), pp. 457-464; G. M. Gilbert, *The Psychology of Dictatorship* (New York: Ronald, 1960); J. N. Knutson, ed., *Handbook of Political Psychology* (San Francisco: Jossey-Bass, 1973); P. Kecskemeti and N. Leites, "Some Psychological Hypotheses on Nazi Germany," Washington, D.C.: The Library of Congress Document No. 60, 1945; H. D. Lasswell, *Psychopathology and Politics* (Chicago: University of Chicago Press, 1930); R. E. Money-Kyrle, *Psychoanalysis and Politics* (London: Gerald Duckworth, 1951; A.A.Rogow, "Psychiatry as a Political Science," *Psychiatric Quarterly*, No. 40 (1960), pp. 319-332; and "Toward a Psychiatry of Politics," in A.A.Rogow, ed., *Politics, Personality and Social Science in the Twentieth Century* (Chicago: University of Chicago Press, 1969). For an in-depth analysis of Fidel Castro from the point of view of intelligence and espionage, see Servando González, *The Secret Fidel Castro: Deconstructing the Symbol* (Oakland: InteliBooks, 2001).

87 Ulam, *Expansion and Coexistence*, pp. 599.
88 Documents on American Foreign Relations, (New York: Harper, 1960), p. 500.
89 Enrique Oltusky, "Gente del llano," in *Cuba: una revolución en marcha* (Madrid: Ruedo Ibérico, 1967); Also, Ernesto Che Guevara, "Cuba: ¿Excepción histórica o vanguardia en la lucha anticolonialista?," *Verde Olivo*, March 9, 1961, pp. 22-29.
90 See Alexander Dallin, "Long Divisions and Five Fractions," in DeVere E. Pentony, ed., *Red World in Tumult* (San Francisco: Chandler, 1962), p. 189.
91 Robin Blackburn, "Prologue to the Cuban Revolution," *New Left Review*, Vol. 21, No. 4, 1963, reprinted in Eric R. Wolf and Edward C. Hansen, eds., *The Human Condition in Latin America* (New York: Oxford University Press, 1972), p. 308.
92 Robin Blackburn, "Prologue to the Cuban Revolution," *New Left Review*, Vol. 21, No. 4, 1963, reprinted in Eric R. Wolf and Edward C. Hansen, eds., *The Human Condition in Latin America* (New York: Oxford University Press, 1972), p. 309.
93 See Jose M. Illan, *Cuba: Facts and Figures of an Economy in Ruins* (Miami: Editorial ATP, 1964), p. 10.
94 U.S. Department of Commerce, Investment in Cuba, (Washington, D.C.: 1956), p. 4.
95 Luis V. Manrara, *Cuba Disproves the Myth that Poverty is the Cause of Communism* (Miami: The Truth About Cuba Committee, 1963), p. 7.
96 See, for example, Eric Williams, *From Columbus to Castro* (New York: Harper and Row, 1970), p. 479.
97 Leland L. Johnson, "U.S. Business Interests in Cuba and the Rise of Castro," *World Politics*, April 1965, p. 457.
98 See Robert F. Lamberg, "The Cuban Economy and the Soviet Bloc, 1963-1968: A Commentary," in J. Gregory Oswald and Anthony J. Strover, *The Soviet Union and Latin America* (New York: Praeger, 1970), p. 116.
99 Frank Tannenbaum, *Ten Keys to Latin America* (New York: Vintage, 1966), p. 218.
100 Raymond Aron and Alfred Grosser, "A European Perspective," in John Plank, ed., *Cuba and the United States* (Washington, D.C.: The Brookings Institution, 1967), p. 153.
101 Franqui, *Family Portrait*, pp. 165-166.
102 Personal communication to the author by JLPA, a former member of the Board of Directors of Guevara's Ministry of Industries. According to him, usually after dealing with the meeting's work agenda, Che asked the members of the Board to hide paper and pens and then proceeded to criticize the Soviets in detail in his typical unhumorous, acid way.
Guevara, the second most important man in the revolution, apparently was a self-instructed Marxist, but never had been a Party man. Although he was certainly

pro-Soviet at that time and had been pro-PSP at the beginning of the revolution, he felt more attracted now by the Chinese and had begun reading Trostkyist literature. See Franqui, *Family Portrait*, p. 22-23.

103 "Bolo" is reputedly slang for Bolshevik, though most Cubans most likely ignored the original meaning. The original Mauser "broom handle" pistol, most favored by Boshevik revolutionaries, is also called the "Bolo" Mauser.

104 Lit.: Socialism with *Pachanga*. Pachanga is a rhythm which originated in Cuba in the 1950s and quickly spread to New York via Miami. Pachanga rhythm is played by a *charanga* band; an orchestra consisting of a wood flute, violins, piano, güiro, and various percussion instruments, but not brass. See, John A. Luchesse, *Pachanga* (New York: Avon, 1961), p. 7.

105 *The New York Times*, January 10, 1962, p. 49.

106 Rationing in Cuba is still in force after more than forty years of Fidelismo.

107 *The New York Times*, March 14, 1962, p. 38.

108 See Victor Lasky, *The Ugly Russian* (New York: Trident Press, 1965), pp. 292-293.

109 *Kubyshka*, a jar in which Russian peasants bury money. The joke is mentioned in a letter attributed to Alexandr Dimitriyevich Morozov, a Soviet attaché in Havana, in June, 1963.

110 See, *The New York Times*, March 15, 1962, p. 8.

111 There is evidence, however, that the destruction of Cuba and its people by Fidel Castro has not been by mistake, because of Castro's adoption of communism, or by force, because of the American embargo, but by a conscious, carefully planned design. This will be the subject of another book I plan to write.

112 *Cuba Socialista*, March 1962, p. 33.

113 Draper, *Castro's Revolution*, p. 227.

114 *The New York Times*, April 16, 25, 27, 28, 1962. There is circumstantial evidence indicating that most of the sabotage was due to self-provocations by the Castro government in order to have a pretext for blaming the U.S. See, Servando González, *The Secret Fidel Castro*, pp. 89-93.

115 *The New York Times*, April 29, 1962, p. 12.

116 *The New York Times*, editorial, May 19, p. 26.

117 John Guerassi *The Great Fear in Latin America* (New York: Collier, 1965), pp. 402-403.

118 See, M. Michael Kline, "Castro's Challenge to Latin American Communism," in Jaime Suchlicki, ed., *Cuba, Castro, and Revolution* (Coral Gables, Florida: University of Miami Press, 1972).

119 See Leon Goure and Julian Weinkle, "Soviet-Cuban Relations: The Growing Integration," in Jaime Suchlicki, ed., *Cuba, Castro, and Revolution* (Coral Gables, Florida: University of Miami Press, 1972), p. 149.

120 Franqui, *Family Portrait*, p. 36.

121 Or so Castro claimed. But there is evidence that most of the time Castro provoked the U.S. in order to elicit a reaction which in turn he claimed was a

provocation and used it as a pretext to act against the U.S. —a truly symbiotic relationship.

122 See, Franqui, *Family Portrait*, p. 73.

123 Among the many nicknames Fidel had since an early age was *"el loco Fidel"* (crazy Fidel). The descriptive nickname followed Fidel to the Colegio de Belén, and later to the University of Havana. Undoubtedly, Fidel's actions and day-to-day behavior usually make his close associates question his mental sanity. For more about Castro's madness see Servando González, *The Secret Fidel Castro*, pp. 215-216.

124 See Guerassi, *The Great Fear*, pp. 394-395.

125 Franqui, *Family Portrait*, pp. 196-197.

126 Franqui, *Family Portrait*, p. 5.

127 For an analysis of Castro's fascist inclinations see Servando González, *The Secret Fidel Castro*, pp. 274-295.

128 Alexandra Obrenovich, *Who is Responsible?* (New York: Carlton Press, 1962), pp. 244-245.

129 Henry A. Kissinger, "Domestic Sources of Foreign Policy," in Robert L. Pfaltzgraff. Jr., ed., *Politics and the International System,* Second Edition (New York: Lippincot, 1972), p. 402.

130 Louis J. Halle, "Lessons of the Cuban Blunder," *The New Republic*, CXLVI, No. 13 (June 5, 1960), p. 15.

Chapter Four

1 For example, in one of the best studies of the Escalante affair, professor Maurice Halperin, who knew of the facts first-hand while living in Cuba, barely mentions Ambassador Kudryavtsev. See, *The Rise and Decline of Fidel Castro* (Berkeley: Univrsity of California Press, 1972).

2 See, i. e., Herbert Matthews, *Revolution in Cuba* (New York: Charles Scribner's Sons, 1975), p. 228.

3 For a detailed story of the political aspects of the Escalante affair, see Maurice Halperin, *The Rise and Fall of Fidel Castro* (Berkeley: University of California Press, 1972); Andrés Suárez, *Cuba: Castroism and Communism, 1959-1966* (Cambridge, Mass.: The M.I.T. Press, 1967); Hugh Thomas, *Cuba: The Pursuit of Freedom* (New York: Harper and Row, 1971); and K. S. Karol, *Guerrillas in Power* (New York: Hill and Wang, 1970). The military and intelligence aspects of the incident are much less known.

4 Richard Lowenthal, "The Logic of One-Party Rule," in Abraham Brumberg, ed., *Russia Under Khrushchev* (New York: Praeger, 1962, p. 36.

5 Castro's destruction of Cuba and its people has not been by mistake, but by design. I will study the matter in detail in the third volume on my trilogy on Fidel Castro. The first volume, *The Secret Fidel Castro: Deconstructing the Symbol,*

appeared in 2001. The second volume, *Fidel Castro Supermole: Walking Back the Cat in the Cuban Operation* will appear by mid-2003.

6 See John Barron, *KGB* (London: Corgi Books, 1979), p. 201. Some people have mentioned the Brezhnev doctrine of irreversibility of Communism to argue that Khrushchev would never have tried to get rid of Castro. But the Brezhnev doctrine should not be overgeneralized. It is not certain that other leaders before Brezhnev and Kosygin would have responded in the same way to Castro's challenges. Stalin obviously felt no hesitation about cutting Tito off completely from Soviet support —even if that meant forcing Yugoslavia into the capitalist camp. Similarly, Khrushchev —despite the lessons of Yugoslavia— did not hesitate to withdraw support from China in an equally hostile and abrupt manner when the Chinese leadership dared to challenge his control on the international revolutionary movement. See, i. e., Carla A. Robbins, *The Cuban Threat*, pp. 167-68. See also, Edgar Snow, *The Other Side of the River* (New York: Random House, 1962), p. 665.

When Khrushchev retired in 1960 nearly all Soviet technicians from China, in a power move that considerably disrupted the country's economic development programs, the Chinese published their strong indictment against the U.S.S.R.: "You bully those fraternal countries whose economies are less advanced, oppose their policy of industrialization and try to force them to remain agricultural countries and serve as your sources of raw materials and as outlets for your goods." From a 1964 letter of the Chinese Communist Party's Central Committee to the Communist Party of the U.S.S.R., quoted in Zbigniew Brzezinski, *The Soviet Bloc* (Cambridge, Mass.: Harvard University Press, 1971), p. 421.

7 Thomas, *Cuba*, p. 1372.

8 Halperin, *The Rise and Fall* , p. 132.

9. See, "Discurso de Aníbal Escalante en Pekín," *Hoy*, October 21, 1959.

10 "Extent of Red Grip in Cuba is Related by a Party Chief," *The New York Times,* November 27, 1960, p. 35. During a visit to Havana in May, 1960, Morris Child, an FBI agent infiltrated at the highest levels of the American Communist Party, met Aníbal Escalante, who informed him about the web of ties the pro-Moscow communists had woven around Castro and the inroads they had made into his government. See John Barron, *Operation SOLO: The FBI's Man in the Kremlin* (Washington, D.C: Regnery, 1996), p. 63.

11 Karol, *Guerrillas in Power*, p. 234.

12 Halperin, *The Rise and Fall*, p. 143.

13 Matthews, *Revolution*, p. 230.

14 *Revolución,* December 2, 1961.

15 Suárez, *Cuba: Castroism and Communism*, p. 230.

16 On ORI's organization see *Bohemia*, October 8, 1961.

17 *Bohemia*, October 8, 1961.

18 Suárez, *Cuba: Castroism and Communism,* p. 139.

19. Tad Szulc, *The Cuban Revolution and Latin America* (New York: Praeger, 1964), p. 131.

20 Among the casualties the PSP sectarians created in the *Fidelista* ranks was writer Gabriel García Márquez who some years later received a Nobel Prize. García Márquez was at the time a reporter for *Prensa Latina*, the Cuban news agency, headed by Argentinean Jorge Ricardo Massetti. Massetti and Márquez fought the Communists as best as they could, but finally had to yield. Massetti and a group of *Fidelistas* tendered their resignations, among them García Márquez. See, Gabriel García Márquez, *El olor de la guayaba* (Bogotá: Editorial La oveja negra, 1982), p. 72.

21 Franqui, *Family Portrait*, p. 180.

22 Halperin, *The Rise and Fall*, p. 132.

23 Goldenberg, *The Cuban Revolution and Latin America* (New York: Praeger, 1965), p. 262.

24 Matthews, *Revolution in Cuba* (New York: Charles Scribner's Sons, 1975). p. 156.

25 The fact that Castro had appointed a well known anti-communist as his first ambassador to Moscow was interpreted at the time as Fidel's way to penalize Chomón for some disagreements he had had with Castro. With the benefit of hindsight, however, it is clear that Chomón's appointment is a good example of Castro's conspiratorial abilities: due to Chomón's visceral anti-communism, Fidel was confident that the KGB would never be able to recruit his ambassador as a double-agent.

Actually, most, if not all, of the Cubans who were sent to the Soviet Union to study in military or espionage schools were approached by the Soviet intelligence services. While some of them were recruited, most of them informed Castro of the pitch. It makes sense, then, that General Arnaldo Ochoa, executed by Castro on false charges of drug dealing, was one of the Cubans originally recruited as an agent by the Soviets. Ochoa had spent several years in the Soviet Union, graduated from the prestigious Frunze Military Academy, and spoke Russian fluently. An interesting detail is that, during the kangaroo trial that ended up with his conviction, Raúl Castro accused him of being "too friendly" to Russian officers in Angola.

Further indications that Ochoa may have been the man the Soviets selected to replace Castro have been offered by Ileana de la Guardia, Tony de la Guardia's daughter, now living in exile. In a book recently published in France, *Le nom de mon Pre* (My Father's Name), Ileana mentions a conversation late in the evening among Tony, his twin brother Patricio, and Ochoa. After many military anecdotes and perhaps too many drinks, the subject veered into Cuba's economic disaster. After discussing what was needed to fix the problems —which to them was perhaps the *perestroika* way— Ochoa said the words that became his death sentence: "Qué hacemos con el loco?" ("What are we going to do with the madman?"). See, Plinio Apuleyo Mendoza, "El testimonio de Ileana," *El Nuevo Herald*, August 25, 2002.

Among the many nicknames Fidel had since an early age was *"el loco Fidel"* (crazy Fidel). The descriptive nickname followed Fidel to the Colegio de Belén, and later to the University of Havana. See, Servando González, *The Secret Fidel Castro*, pp. 215-216.

26 Halperin, *The Rise and Fall*, pp. 151-152.

27 *The New York Times,* February 24, 1962, p. 36.

28 *The New York Times*, Feb 25, 1962, p. 36.

29 *The New York Times*, February 26, 1962, p. 12.

30 Many years later it became known that, in his typical fashion, Castro orchestrated the whole event by previously deleting the word "God" from the document, to use it as a pretext to attack the PSP communists.

31 Halperin, *The Rise*, pp. 152-153.

32 Tad Szulc, *The Winds of Revolution* (New York: Praeger, 1965), p. 262.

33 Halperin, *The Rise and Fall*, pp. 152-153.

34 Franqui, *Family Portrait with Fidel,* p. 180.

35 I am thankful to Jaime Figueras for background information on Sánchez.

36 U.S. Senate, Committee on Foreign Relations, *Soviet Bloc Latin American Activities and their Implications for the United States Foreign Policy*, 86th Congress, 2nd. Sess., February 28, 1960, p. 22.

37 David Atlee Philips, "Castro's Spies," *Soldier of Fortune*, November 1983, p. 66.

38 Thomas, *Cuba*, p. 1273.

39 Phillips, "Castro's Spies," p. 66.

40 Plane "accidents" have been extremely useful to Castro. On October, 1959, Fidel sent Major Camilo Cienfuegos to Camagüey to detain Major Huber Matos. On his way back to Havana, Cienfuegos' plane mysteriously disappeared forever without leaving the slightest trace.

Camilo Cienfuegos, one of the most colorful characters among the Rebel Army leaders, had fought valiantly against Batista. He, rather than Che Guevara, was responsible for the victory in the battle of Santa Clara. In January, 1959, Fidel made Camilo head of the Rebel Army, with Raúl subordinate to him as head of the army of Oriente province. Once in Havana Camilo's charming personality gained him a wide popularity —perhaps too wide for Fidel's peace of mind. See Rufo López-Fresquet, *My 14 Months with Castro* (Cleveland, Ohio: World Publishing Co., 1966), p. 66; also Manuel Urrutia Lleó, *Fidel Castro and Company, Inc.* (new York: Praeger, 1964), pp. 80-82.

41 *Prensa Latina's* report was not published in the Cuban media.

42 Prensa Latina's report available at <http://lanic.utexas.edu/la/cuba/castro/1962/19620601>.

43 There is conflicting information about what Soviet intelligence service Kudryavtsev represented. Barron always refers to him as a KGB operative. See, *KGB: The Secret Work of Soviet Secret Agents* (London: Corgi, 1979), p. 20. On the other hand, Christopher Andrew and Oleg Gordiewsky identify him as a GRU

officer. See *KGB: The Inside Story* (New York: Harper Perennial, 1991), p. 255. Given the intense animosity between the KGB and the GRU, and the fact that Castro recruited Alexeev, a KGB officer, as his double-agent, it makes sense that Kudryavtsev may have been a GRU officer.

44 Kudryavtsev is probably one of the most important clues to understand this historical puzzle we call the Cuban missile crisis. Most authors, however, have totally ignored the key role he played in the events previous to the crisis. To me, Kudryavtsev is a sort of acid test for checking the value of the books written about the crisis. If he is not mentioned, as it happens with most of the books about the crisis written in the last fifteen years, you can rest assured that the book has no value at all. On the other hand, the fact that a book on the Cuban missile crisis mentions Kudryavtsev is no proof that it is has any value either. A typical example of this is Aleksandr Fursenko and Timothy Naftali, *"One Hell of a Gamble": The Secret History of the Cuban Missile Crisis* (New York: W.W. Norton, 1997), pp. 62-63, 89, 91. 167, where many pages are devoted to a hatchet job, mostly by Castro's double agent Aleksandr Alexeev, directed at discrediting Kudryavtsev.

The failed Escalante-Kudryavtsev operation was not, though, the last attempt the Soviets made to overthrow Castro. I will study the subject in detail in my forthcoming book *Fidel Castro Supermole: Walking Back the Cat in the Cuban Operation*.

45 Though most people still believe the CDRs were Castro's idea, it seems that he got his inspiration for them right from the *blockwarts*, a very similar institution created by Hitler in Nazi Germany.

46 John Barron, *KGB: The Secret Work of Soviet Secret Agents* (London: Corgi, 1979), pp. 201-202.

47 The *New York Times*, June 5, 1962, p. 3.

48 Theodore Draper, *Castroism: Theory and Practice* (New York: Praeger, 1965), p. 149.

49 Lisa Howard, "Castro's Overture," *War/Peace Report,* September 1983, p. 4. Other sources, however, claim that actually Castro detained Kudryavtsev and placed him under military custody until he was embarked on a Moscow-bound Soviet plane. See, Domingo Amuchástegui, "Cuban Intelligence and the October Crisis," in James G. Blight and David A. Welch, eds., *Intelligence and the Cuban Missile Crisis* (London: Frank Cass, 1998), p. 92.

50 Barron, *KGB*, p. 26.

51 *"Este Kudryavtsev me tiene más cansado que Bonsal,"* evidence of writer Guillermo Cabrera Infante, at the time the Editor of *Revolución's* weekly literary magazine *Lunes de Revolución*, who overheard Castro. Quoted in Thomas, *Cuba*, p. 1381. Bonsal (Philip), was the last U.S. Ambassador to Cuba.

52 It would be interesting to know what shooting Khrushchev was talking about. I have found no reference to any shooting at that time in either the Cuban or Soviet Press.

53 Nikita S. Khrushchev, *Khrushchev Remembers* (Boston: Little, Brown and Company, 1970), p. 490.

54 Nikita S. Khrushchev, *Khrushchev Remembers*, pp. 490-491, (emphasis added).

55 For a fictional plot where the KGB tries to kill Castro while the CIA protects him, see Juan Arcocha, *Operación Viceversa* (Madrid: Ediciones Erre, 19760).

56 Fursenko and Naftali, *"One Hell of a Gamble"*, p. 62.

57 John Barron, *KGB: The Secret Work of Soviet Secret Agents* (London: Corgi, 1979), p. 20.

58 Andrew Tully, *White Tie and Dagger* (New York: Pocket Books, 1968), pp. 74-75.

5959. Barron, *KGB*, p. 26; also Thomas, *Cuba*, p. 1279.

60 Tully, *White Tie*, pp. 74-75.

61 Christopher Andrew and Oleg Gordiewsky, *KGB: The Inside Story* (New York: Harper Perennial, 1991), p. 255.

62 Tully, *White Tie*, pp. 74-75.

63 Strangely, the Kudryavtsev-Escalante affair, a key element needed to fully understand the Cuban missile crisis, has been barely mentioned in the series of meetings where alleged participants in the crisis have compared notes and remembrances. The fact that neither the Cuban nor the Russian participants in the meetings can claim ignorance of the event, indicates a conscious effort to disinform the public.

64 Tully, *White Tie*, pp. 74-75.

65 Rufo López-Fresquet, *My 14 months with Castro* (Cleveland, Ohio: World Publishing Co., 1966), p. 23.

66 See, U.S. Department of State, *Cuba,* Inter American Series No. 66, Washington, D.C., 1961, in Robert F. Smith, *What Happened in Cuba?* (New York: Twayne, 1963), p. 314.

67 Fidel Castro, "Elogió Fidel el heroísmo de nuestros combatientes," *Revolución*, May 8, 1961, pp. 1, 3-7.

68. Fidel Castro speech quoted in "Escuela de Instructores Revolucionarios 'Osvaldo Sánchez Cabrera'," *Verde Olivo*, June 18, 1961, pp. 3-5.

69 See Draper, *Castroism*, pp. 36-37.

70 The author graduated from the first course of the "Osvaldo Sánchez" school and later was appointed professor of History and Marxist Philosophy at the School. For an interesting view of the role of the Revolutionary Instructors in Cuban Army and politics, see Marta San Martín and Ramón L. Bonachea, "The Military Dimension of the Cuban Revolution," in Irving Louis Horowitz, ed., *Cuban Communism, Fourth Edition* (New Brunswick, N.J.: Transaction Books, 1981); also, but with a somehow distorted perspective, see William Leogrande, "A Bureaucratic Approach to Civil-Military Relations in Communist Political Systems," in *ibid*.

71 Cuban History was taught in a shortened version, with especial emphasis on the Cuban patriot's struggle for national independence from Spain first and later from "American imperialism." The textbook was the *Manual de Capacitación Cívica,* written by Lt. Carlos Díaz, now the school's Director, and edited by the *Departamento de Capacitación Cívica* (Department of Civic Instruction) of the Rebel Army. For Political Economy the textbook was the outdated *Manual de Economía Política,* by Konstantinov et. al., edited by the Soviet Academy of Sciences, but already discredited in the Soviet Union. The textbook for Marxist Philosophy was the *Manual de Filosofía Marxista,* by Otto Wilhelm Kuusinen. Other mainly used texts were Paul Sweezy's *Los bienes terrenales del hombre* (Man's Earthly Goods); *Principios de Filosofía,* by Georges Politzer; Blas Roca's *Los fundamentos del socialismo en Cuba* (a hastily updated version of the old text, which now emphasized the role of the proletariat in the Castroist revolution); and, last but not least, Castro's latest speeches.

72 See K. S. Karol, *Guerrillas in Power* (New York: Hill and Wang, 1970), p. 242.

73 See, William Leogrande, "A Bureaucratic Approach to Civil-Military Relations in Communist Political Systems," in Irving Louis Horowitz, ed., *Cuban Communism, Fourth Edition* (New Brunswick, N.J.: Transaction Books, 1981), p. 610.

74 Marta San Martín and Ramón L. Bonachea, "The Military Dimension of the Cuban Revolution," in Irving Louis Horowitz, ed., *Cuban Communism, Fourth Edition* (New Brunswick, N.J.: Transaction Books, 1981), p. 534.

75 See Escalante's report to the general assembly of the ORI in Oriente province, *Revolución,* December 9, 1961; also Edward González, *Cuba Under Castro* (Boston: Houghton Mifflin, 1974), p. 103.

76 Halperin, *The Rise,* p. 160.

77 Halperin, *The Rise,* p. 161.

78 The group included Lázaro Peña, Blas Roca y César Escalante, Anibal's younger brother.

79 Carlos Franqui, *Family Portrait,* p. 86.

80 Vladislav Zubok and Constantine Pleshakov, *Inside the Kremlin's Cold War* (Cambridge, Mass.: Harvard University Press, 1996), p. 207.

81 Aleksandr Fursenko and Timothy Naftali, *"One Hell of a Gamble": Khrushchev, Castro, and Kennedy, 1958-1964* (New York: W.W. Norton, 1997), p. 306. It seems that the hatred was mutual. Many years later, while talking to Lee Lockwood, Castro mentioned that after the missile crisis their personal relations "had reached their lowest point." Lee Lockwood, *Castro's Cuba, Cuba's Fidel* (New York: Vintage, 1969), p. 226. But, being a master in the subtle arts of hypocrisy and tartuffery, Castro was all smiles during his trip to the Soviet Union in 1964.

82 Both Castro and Khrushchev had a peasant's background and the cunning and craftiness of the peasant's character. As little boys in the countryside, both may have noticed how the man who was going to slaughter a pig kept the knife

hidden from the animal until the very instant he was going to give the mortal stab. They learned the lesson.

83 I seems that, like Castro, Khrushchev didn't take humiliations lightly. According to Lebow and Stein, "Khrushchev's reaction to the U-2 was a striking example of his propensity to personalize events. He was humiliated and enraged by the intrusion of the spy planes." *We All Lost the Cold War*, p. 90.

84 Thomas, *Cuba*, p. 1381. See also Andrés Suárez, *Cuba: Castroism and Communism, 19591966* (Cambridge, Massachusetts: The MIT Press, 1967), p. 157

85 Currently known as "active measures" (*aktivnye merppriati*), the term *dezinformatsia* is used to describe a whole set of overt and covert techniques directed at influencing events and behavior in, and the actions of, foreign countries. See, Richard H. Shultz and Ron Godson, *Dezinformatsia: The Strategy of Soviet Disinformation* (New York: Berkley Books, 1984), p. 2.

86 According to Khrushchev's son Sergei, "When Fidel Castro took power in Cuba, the Russians did not know who he was. They were sure Castro was a CIA agent and was working together with the United States." See Carrie Linin, "Khrushchev Outlines Missile Crisis," *The Collegian*, <www.spub.ksu.edu/issues/v099b/sp/n116/cam-cuban-linin.html>

87 For an interesting argument on how the Soviet Union would have gained with an American invasion of Cuba, see John N. Plank, "Monroe's Doctrine —and Castro's," *The New York Times Magazine*, October 7, 1962.

Chapter Five

1 See, Adam B. Ulam, *Expansion and Coexistence: The History of Soviet Foreign Policy* (New York: Praeger, 1968), pp. 573-574.

2 Michel Tatu *Power in the Kremlin: From Khrushchev to Kosygin* (New York: Viking, 1970).

3 Lee Lockwood, *Castro's Cuba, Cuba's Fidel* (New York: Vintage, 1969), p. 225.

4 Most recently, some of the people who were close to Khrushchev admitted that the whole idea was Khrushchev's alone, and the whole operation was carried out following his orders. See, Lebow and Stein, *We All Lost the Cold War*, p. 19.

5 Though in the strictest sense most likely the photos were not fakes, they were not "hard evidence" either. I will study this in detail in Chapter Ten.

6 Samuel L. Sharp, "National Interest: Key to Soviet Politics." in Abraham Brumberg, ed., *Russia Under Khrushchev* (New York: Praeger, 1962).

7 I will study this issue in greater detail in Chapter Twelve.

8 Short for Executive Committee of the National Security Council, and ad hoc group of high-level advisors created by President Kennedy to help him manage the crisis.

9 *We All Lost the Cold War*, p. 62.

10 See Karol, *Guerrillas*, p. 293.

11 As a matter of fact, though it seems that the Americans had no immediate plans to invade Cuba, Khrushchev's lies at least may have had a grain of truth. In the autumn of 1961 the Kennedy administration had formulated a plan, named Operation Mongoose, to get rid of the Castro regime. Also, during the month of October 1962 the marines were to be engaged in an invasion exercise, code-named Phibriglex 62, in the island of Vieques, off the south coast of Puerto Rico. The main goal of the war game exercise was to invade the island and overthrow its fictitious tyrant, significantly named "Ortsac" (Castro spelled backwards).

12 Contrary to the alarming news provided by the Soviets, the Cuban intelligence had concluded that the evidence suggested exactly the opposite: no U.S. invasion was likely at the time. See Domingo Amuchástegui, *Intelligence and the Cuban Missile crisis*, p. 96. According to Amuchástegui, by the spring of 1962 the Cuban intelligence services had concluded that the Soviets were deliberately providing Castro with false, alarmist assessments of the possibility of an American invasion. The only explanation for this is that the Soviets were trying to scare Castro to convince him of the need of the missiles.

Surprisingly, Castro ignored his own intelligence officers and sided with the Soviets. Allegedly, Castro was totally convinced that the U.S. was ready to invade Cuba. What most people ignore, however, is that, for forty-two long years, Fidel Castro has been preparing himself and waiting for an American invasion of Cuba. Not only waiting, it seems, but longing for the American invasion that would fulfill his prophecy and allow him to enjoy his secret desire of killing American soldiers on Cuban soil.

13 A rule of intelligence and espionage is that disinformation cannot be generated in a vacuum, but must be based on the target's expectations. Usually, intelligence services use disinformation to fully convince the target of something about which he is already half-convinced. In this particular case, the target, Fidel Castro, was ripe for disinformation —that is, if we accept that Castro actually is what he purports to be.

14 Hilsman, *To Move,* p. 159.

15 Alexeev story in interview conducted by WGBH-tv, Boston, for the PBS series, quoted in Michael R. Beschloss, *The Crisis Years: Kennedy and Khrushchev, 1960-1963* (New York, HarperCollins, 1991), p. 389.

16 Guevara quoted in James Monahan and Kenneth O. Gilmore, *The Great Deception* (New York: Farrar, Strauss, 1963), p. 212).

17 For a detailed account of Castro's efforts to develop nuclear and other weapons of mass destruction, see Servando González, *The Secret Fidel Castro*, pp. 53-73.

18 Lockwood, *Castro's Cuba*, p. 1967, (emphasis mine).

19 The thesis that the deployment of Soviet missiles in Cuba was intended solely or primarily at deterring a U.S. attack on the island, as Khrushchev claimed, has been rebutted, among others, by Hilsman, *To Move a Nation,* pp. 161-165;

Horelick and Rush, *Strategic Power*, pp. 127-136; and Ulam, *Expansion and Coexistence*, pp. 668-677.

The main reason for these authors' rejection of Khrushchev's claims that the missiles were mostly intended to defend Cuba is that the presence of IRBMs as well as MRBMs was a far redundant force to be used for deterrent purposes. The only major analyst who accepted Khrushchev's claims at the time was Allison. His explanation was that the IRBMs may have been included as a result of bureaucratic organizational goals and routines within the Soviet government. See, Allison, *Essence of decision*, pp. 113, 247.

Allison's analysis, however, has serious flaws. It requires us to accept the incredible fact that the Soviet leaders ignored that some subordinates had taken the risky initiative of adding, without their superior's approval, IRBMs to the missile force to be deployed in Cuba —a quite improbable occurrence. Moreover, this fully contradicts his previous explanation of "bureaucratic procedures" as an explanation for the failure to camouflage the missile sites.

20 See, Address by Fidel Castro, Prime Minister of Cuba, before the U. N. General Assembly, on the purpose of the Revolution in Cuba, September 26, 1960, United Nations General Assembly, *Official Records*, 15th Session, Part I, Vol, I (1960).

21 Halperin, *The Rise*, p. 167.

22 See, Richard Smith Beal, *System Analysis of International Crises* (Washington, D.C.: University Press of America, 1979), p. 199.

23 *Cuba: Castroism and Communism, 1959-1966* (Cambridge, Massachusetts: The MIT Press, 1967), p. 163.

24 Crassweller, *Cuba and the U.S.*, p. 26.

25 Franqui, *Family Portrait*, p. 188-189.

26 Franqui, *Family Portrait*, p. 129.

27 *Tass* communiqué, September 2, 1962, quoted in Henry M. Pachter, *Collision Course*, pp. 175-176, (emphasis added).

28 The sense of humiliation is extremely strong in Fidel Castro. Like many easily humiliated people, Castro is likely to become upset by actions and events that most people either don't notice or see as too unimportant to merit any emotional involvement.

Any person familiar with Castro's speeches may testify that the word "humiliation," is a sort of mantra he repeats over and over; and when he feels humiliated he will do everything to recover his self-esteem, including engaging in risky or heroic deeds, like the Moncada attack, or acts of sheer *bravado*, like shooting down a U-2 plane during the Cuban missile crisis. This complicated mechanism of psychological survival when faced with perceived loss of self esteem explains the irrationality of most of Castro's policy decisions.

Evidence indicates that most of the time Castro makes policy choices not for political, but for psychological reasons. The incident in which he ordered two civilian planes of the Miami-based Brothers to the Rescue organization to be shot down is an example of the above. According to Castro he did so because the planes were violating Cuban air space and he felt "humiliated."

29 See Aleksandr Fursenko and Timothy Naftali, *"One Hell of a Gamble" The Secret History of the Cuban Missile Crisis* (New York: W.W. Norton, 1997), pp. 194-195.

30 Proof that my theory is not far-fetched at all is the fact that Dean Rusk suggested to use a back channel to tell Castro that the Soviets were actually planning to betray him and destroy Cuba. Moreover, it seems that somebody in the U.S. government even wrote a draft of a twenty-four-hour ultimatum to Castro telling him that "to serve their interests," the Soviets had "justified the Western Hemisphere countries in making an attack on Cuba which would lead to the overthrow of your regime." See Michael Beschloss, *The Crisis Years: Kennedy and Khrushchev, 1960-1063* (New York: HarperCollins, 1991), p. 432.

31 In 1980 Mariel captured again the world's headlines when Castro selected it as an exit port to send an "invasion" of Cuban refugees desperately escaping from his proletarian paradise to the Florida beaches. The Machiavellian Castro introduced hundreds of hardened criminals from Cuban jails among the honest people trying to flee the Island. Those criminals, who soon after were known as *Marielitos*, became famous for their activities in the American underworld.

32 Soviet special forces, considered the toughest and meanest in the world.

33 Franqui, *Family Portrait*, p. 188.

34 Briefing Paper, "Cuban Missile Crisis and Aftermath, "Department of State, *Foreign Relations of the United States, 1961-1963*, Volume xi, Washington, D.C., October 1, 1962.

35 Franqui, *Family Portrait*, p. 189.

36 Juana Castro, "My Brother Fidel," *Life*, Vol. 57, No. 9 (August 28, 1964), p. 32. Apart from the fact that most of the Russian soldiers disguised as civilians were wearing only two different types of shirts, the Russian drivers displayed a strange driving habit. Perhaps in an effort to avoid the intense heat, instead of driving normally, looking at the road through the windshield, most of them drove with their bodies contorted and their heads and left arm out of the driver's window. No wonder there was a rise in car accidents.

37 The fine art of "cratology" —deducing from the shape and size of a container (crate) what is inside— began in the mid-1950s, though, when the practice of reading crates began, senior intelligence officers were critical of its usefulness.

Former CIA analyst Victor Marchetti, one of the pioneers of the art of "cratology" said that during the Cuban missile crisis he and a handful of other analysts poured through the mass of photographs from reconnaissance flights and found that the Soviets indeed were bringing in intermediate-range nuclear missiles to Cuba.

The reason for their conclusion was that, while the Russians normally designated certain freighters to carry military equipment, this time the ships had larger hatches and had not been previously used for military transport. This, according to Marchetti, was highly unusual, because the Soviet pattern of supplying military freight had been previously fairly predictable: the same ships and the same crews generally transporting the same equipment." See Knut Royce, "How CIA Sees Through Soviet Shipping Crates," *San Francisco Examiner*, November 11, 1984.

There is, however, a big flaw in the application of "cratology" to the Cuban missile crisis. One of the main assumptions of the spy business is that, more important than what you know, it is that the opposition doesn't know that you know. But there is evidence of Soviet efforts to disguise the shape of their crates in order to disinform the opposition. Therefore, it is safe to assume that they knew of the existence of the CIA cratologists.

Consequently, in this particular case, in which the Soviets were making an extraordinary effort to let the Americans know what they wanted them to know, because they knew that the Americans had the technical means to know, cratology played into Russian hands, becoming a useful tool for disinformation. See, Anatoly Gribkov and William Smith, *Operation Anadyr* (Chicago: edition q, 1994), pp. 30, 56. Moreover, from a skeptic's point of view, cratology seems fairly stupid. It is like making a census of cars by counting garages.

To me, cratology was the creation of arrogants who apparently were convinced that the Soviets were stupid. After the end of the Cold War, stories about Soviet "stupidity," particularly in books and papers about the Cuban missile crisis, have turned into a cottage industry in which the Russians have gladly contributed to enhance the image of their own supposed stupidity. This collaboration has proved to be profitable for both sides: in exchange for hard currency, so scarce in Russia in the early years after the fall of the Soviet Union, some clever, greedy Russians will always tell the Americans what they love to hear.

38 Robert kennedy, *Thirteen Days*, pp. 6-7.

39 Philippe Thyraud de Vosjoli, "A Head that Holds Some Sinister Secrets," *Life*, Vol. 64, No. 17 (April 26, 1968), p. 35.

40 Keating quoted in Robert A. Divine, ed., *The Cuban Missile Crisis* (Chicago: Quadrangle, 1971), pp. 7-8.

41 Walton, *Cold War*, p. 107.

42 Walter Trohan, "Kennedy on Cuba," the *Chicago Tribune*, September 6, 1962, p. 16.

43 "Report From Washington," the *Chicago Tribune*, September 10, 1962, p. 2.

44 See, "Khrushchev's Threat," the *Chicago Tribune*, September 12, 1962, p. 16.

45 "Kennedy's Patience," September 15, 1962, p. 10. See also "Be it Resolved," September 28, p. 12; "The Senators Huff and Puff," September 21; and "Our Baby," September 26, p. 12. Kennedy's critics had enough reasons to be upset. The distinction between "defensive" and "offensive" weapons is probably one of the most stupid concepts a human mind can conceive.

46 See Richard H. Rovere, "Letter from Washington," the *New Yorker*, October 6, 1962, pp. 148-167.

47 See, Nikita S. Khrushchev, *Khrushchev Remembers,* translated and edited by Strobe Talbot (Boston: Little, Brown and Company, 1970), p. 495.

48 Hilsman, *To Move a Nation*, pp. 159-161.

49 Briefing by John Hughes, Defense Intelligence Agency, *Department of Defense Appropriations for 1964*, Hearing Before a Subcommittee of the Committee on Appropriations, House of Representatives, 88th Congress, 1st Session (Washington, 1963, Part I, p. 7.

50 For an interesting analysis of events as words or deeds, see Richard Smith Beal, *System Analysis of International Crises* (Washington, D.C.: University Press of America, 1979), pp. 106108.

51 On September 4, Soviet Ambassador Anatoly Dobrynin told Robert Kennedy that the military equipment the Soviets were sending to Cuba was "defensive in nature and did not represent any threat to the security of the United States." Quoted in Sorensen, *Kennedy*, p. 668; also in Hilsman, *To Move*, p. 165.

52 Robert Kennedy, *Thirteen Days*, pp. 2-4.

53 Robert Kennedy, *Thirteen Days*, p. 4.

54 Some members of the Kennedy administration called it the "New Frontier."

55 Ulam, *Expansion and Coexistence*, p. 671. The diplomat who made the remarks was Georgi Bolshakov, nominally press attaché of the Soviet Embassy, but seemingly a sort of personal representative of Khrushchev in Washington. Bolshakov was believed to be a KGB officer.

56 Schlesinger, *Robert Kennedy and his Times*, pp. 501-502.

57 See Crankshaw, *Khrushchev's Russia*, p. 52.

58 Richard M. Nixon, *Leaders* (New York: Warner, 1982), p. 177.

59 Official English translation supplied by *Tass* as reprinted in the *New York Times*, September 12, 1962, p. 16.

60 The *New York Times*, September 12, 1962, p. 16 (emphasis added).

61 See, Ronald R. Pope, *Soviet Views on the Cuban Missile Crisis* (Washington, D.C.: University Press of America, 1982), 99-100.

62 Nathan Miller, *Spying for America: The Hidden History of U.S. Intelligence* (New York: Dell, 1989), p. 429.

63 Bartlett to Robert Kennedy, October 26, 1962, RFK Papers.

64 See, Harry Hodkinson, *Double Talk, The Language of Communism* (London: George AllenUnwin. 1956), p. 5.

65 Hugh Sidey, *John F. Kennedy, President* (Greenwich, Conn.: Crest Books, 1963), p. 304305.

66 K.S. Karol, the *New Statesman*, November 2, 1962.

67 Dino A. Brugioni, *Eyeball to Eyeball: The Inside Story of the Cuban Missile Crisis* (New York: Random House, 1991), p. 150.

68 Hilsman, *To Move a Nation*, p. 201.

69 David Detzer, *The Brink* (New York: Thomas Y. Crowell, 1979), p. 72

70 There is, however, more than meets the eye in McCone's "hunch." According to the available documentation, McCone based his hunch on some technical

considerations about the tactical use of SAMs as a cardinal element in the protection of MRBMs and IRBMs. But McCone was a newcomer to the intelligence field, and there is nothing indicating that he had any previous knowledge of the profession. Yet, the arguments he used are the ones that only an expert could have used. Therefore, this seems to indicate that McCone was actually the mouthpiece of some experts at the CIA. The question is, why did they use McCone as their unofficial mouthpiece? Did they thought that the Kennedy administration would have paid no attention to their suspicions? Or, even worse, did they fear that expressing their suspicions may have brought reprisals from the Kennedys?

71 McCone's suspicions are told in detail in Arthur Crock, *Memoirs* (New York: Funk and Wagnalls, 1968), pp. 378 ff.; also in Weintal and Bartlett, *Facing the Brink*, pp. 60-71. For a declassified Memorandum where McCone relates the whole story and refers several times to his suspicions, see John A. McCone, Memorandum, "Soviet MRBMs in Cuba," 31 October 1962, in Central Intelligence Agency, *The Secret Cuban Missile Crisis Documents* (Washington, D.C.: Brassey's, 1994), pp. 13-17.

72 Khrushchev, *Khrushchev Remembers*, p. 495.

73 Cuba is 780 miles in length from east to west, and some to 25 to 125 miles in width.

74 See, Hilsman, *To Move a Nation*, p. 201.

75 Juan Vivés, *Los amos de Cuba* (Buenos Aires: Emecé, 1982), p. 122.

76 Aside from the Russians-are-stupid commonly advanced explanation.

77 Allison, *Essence of Decision*, 110-111.

78 Allison, *Essence of Decision*, 110.

79 This, by the way, was the conclusion reached by Harold W. Rood, "Cuba: Payment Deferred," *National Review,* November 27, 1981, p. 14).

80 Never forget that Russia is the motherland of Grigori Potemkin, a pioneer in the art of *maskirovka*.

81 See Sidey, *John F. Kennedy*, p. 305.

82 Hilsman, *To Move*, p. 165.

83 Anatol Rappoport, *The Big Two: Soviet-American Perception of Foreign Policy* (New York: Pegasus, 1971), p. 183.

84 The *Wall Street Journal*, October 24, 1962.

85 Lyman B. Kirkpatrick, Jr., *The U.S. Intelligence Community* (New York: Hill and Wang, 1973), pp. 91-92.

Chapter Six

1 Intelligence services distinguish between a *defector*, a member of the opposition who asks for asylum in the opponent's country, and a *defector-in-place*, a member of the opposition who changes allegiances but remains in his position and begins acting as a spy for his previous opponents, mostly passing them secret information.

2 Chapman Pincher, *Their Trade is Treachery* (New York: Bantam, 1982), p. 363.

3 John Barron, *KGB* (London: Corgi Books, 1975), p. 395.

4 Ray S. Cline, *The CIA Under Reagan, Bush and Casey* (Washington, D.C.: Acropolis Books, 1981), p. 221.

5 p. Jerrold L. Schechter and Peter Deribin, *The Spy Who Saved the World* (Washington, D.C.: Brassey's, 1992), p. 334.

6 Establishing a defector's *bona fides* is not an easy job. A typical example is the case of Yuri Nosenko, a KGB officer who began spying for the CIA in 1962 when he offered his services while serving in Geneva under a diplomatic cover, and eventually defected to the U.S. in 1964. Almost immediately after his defection, some senior CIA officers began expressing their doubts about Nosenko's *bona fides*. But, after many years of friendly and hostile interrogation, careful research, and investigation, Nosenko's *bona fides* was never proved, nor disproved. For an excellent study of the Nosenko case see Richards J. Heuer, Jr., "Nosenko: Five Paths to Judgment," in H. Bradford Westerfield, ed., *Inside Cia's Private World: Declassified Articles from the Agency's Internal Journal, 1955-1992* (New Haven, Ct.: Yale University Press, 1995), pp. 379-414. But be prepared for a dissappointing experience: it reads like a modern version of Akutagawa's *Rashomon*.

7 Pincher, *Their Trade is Treachery*, p. 184.

8 Victor Marchetti and John D. Marks. *The CIA and the Cult of Intelligence* (New York: Knopff, 1974), p. 209.

9 Marchetti and Marks. *The CIA*, p. 254.

10 Pincher, *Their Trade*, p. 184.

11 Intelligence lingo for true, but inconsequential or outdated information an intelligence service provides to a plant in order to help him prove his value and *bona fides*. In order to disguise the key bits of disinformation, chicken feed can have a high percentage of true, even valuable information.

12 Thomas Powers, *The Man Who Kept the Secrets: Richard Helms and the CIA* (New York: Alfred A. Knopf, 1979), p. 127.

13 Powers, *The Man Who Kept the Secrets*, p. 362.

14 Powers, *The Man*, p. 422.

15 See, Raymond L. Garthoff, *Intelligence Assessment and Policy Making: A Decisive Point in the Kennedy Administration* (Washington, D.C.: The Brookings Institution, 1984), p. 8.

16 Pincher, *Their Trade*, p. 184.

17 Powers, *The Man*, p. 422.

18 Marchetti and Marks, *The CIA*, p. 182).

19 Interview with Joe Bulik, January 31, 1998, in *Spies*, Episode 21, aired on March 14, 1944. <www.gwu.edu/~nsarchiv/coldwar.interviews.episode-21/bulik2.html> Contrary to common lore, I think that actually the Bay of Pigs was the CIA's best success and Penkovsky its worst failure. A detailed study of the Bay

of Pigs operation will appear in my forthcoming book *Fidel Castro Supermole: Walking Back the Cat in the Cuban Operation.*

20 See also Edward Jay Epstein, *Deception: The Invisible War Between the KGB and the CIA* (New York: Simon and Schuster, 1989), pp. 79-80.

21 Interview with Joe Bulik, January 31, 1998, in *Spies*, Episode 21, aired on March 14, 1944. <www.gwu.edu/~nsarchiv/coldwar.interviews.episode-21/bulik2.html>

22 Pincher, *Their Trade*, p. 183.

23 Marchetti and Marks. *The CIA*, p. 183.

24 Marchetti and Marks, *The CIA*, p. 182-183.

25 For this section I am relying heavily on an excellent analysis by British author Chapman Pincher, *Their Trade is Treachery* (New York: Bantam, 1982).

26 Peter Wright, *Spy Catcher* (New York: Dell, 1987), p. 263.

27 Pincher, *Their Trade*, p. 183.

28 See Victor Marchetti and John D. Marks, *The CIA and the Cult of Intelligence* (New York: Dell, 1974), p. 214.

29 Wright, *Spy Catcher*, p. 265.

30 Pincher, *Their Trade*, p. 183.

31 Pincher, *Their Trade*, p. 183.

32 Pincher, *Their Trade*, p. 183-184.

33 Pincher, *Their Trade*, p. 184.

34 Pincher, *Their Trade*, p. 185.

35 Pincher, *Their Trade*, p. 185-186.

36 Pincher, *Their Trade*, p. 186. The rule-of-thumb is that, if he is to be trusted and believed, a plant must provide at least 95 percent true information. In response to an article by Thomas Powers in which he brought the issue of doubts of Penkovsky's *bona fides*, Jerrold L. Schechter countered that "none of Penkovsky's material was ever proven to be false or fabricated." "A Very Important Spy," *The New York Review of Books*, June 24, 1993. But, as we have seen above, the issue is not if the material provided by a plant is true, but if it is really relevant.

37 Pincher, *Their Trade*, p. 128. In fact, as history has shown once and again, an intelligence service will go to almost any extreme to protect and maintain a valuable source of either information or disinformation. One of the most famous known cases is Winston Churchill allowing German bombs to fall on Coventry rather than warn the inhabitants and risk exposure of the Allies most carefully held secret: that the British had broken the German military code. It is also known that George Blake who, like Kim Philby, was a Soviet penetration inside the British intelligence services, revealed to the Russians the details of the tunnel dig under the Berlin Wall to install listening devices. But, instead of acting against the operation, the Russians allowed valuable, but controlled information to continue flowing from the CIA's tunnel operation for over a year rather than jeopardize Blake's position in London by letting the East Germans know about the tunnel.

38 Pincher, *Their Trade*, p. 186.

39 Peter Deriabin, quoted by Thomas Powers in reply to Jerrold L. Schechter, "A Very Important Spy," *The New York Review of Books*, June 24, 1993.

40 Pincher, *Their Trade*, p. 186.

41 Central Intelligence Agency, *A compendium of Analytic Tradecraft Notes*, Washington, D.C. February 1997.

42 Jerrold L. Schechter and Peter S. Deriabin, *The Spy Who Saved the World* (Washington, D.C.: Brassey's, 1992), p. 324.

43 Schecter and Deriabin, *The Spy Who Saved the World*, p. 351.

44 Tom Mangold, *Cold Warrior. James Jesus Angleton: The CIA's Master Spy Hunter* (New York: Touchstone, 1991), p. 98

45 At one point Penkovsky told his controllers that he wanted to have a personal meeting with both Queen Elizabeth II and President Kennedy. The Queen didn't fall for the pitch, but Wynne claimed that Penkovsky was flown to Washington D.C. by the CIA, where he had a brief meeting with President Kennedy in the Oval Office. See Nathan Miller, *Spying for America: The Hidden History of American Intelligence* (New York: Dell, 1989), p. 430. If this actually happened, I can only imagine the bouts of laughter it caused at Dzhershinsky square and the Kremlin.

46 Pincher, *Their Trade*, p. 186-187.

47 One of the most successful disinformation operations accomplished by the Soviet intelligence services was the "Trust." In the 1920s, the Soviet services created a false anti-Soviet underground organization operating inside the Soviet Union to carry out spying and sabotage missions in coordination with anti-Soviet groups operating outside the U.S.S.R. The Soviet intelligence arranged a series of initial successes for the supposed anti-Soviet underground to prove the efficacy and establish the Trust's *bona fides*. Once the fake anti-Soviet underground established its reputation as the mainstay of the anti-Soviet resistance movement, the Soviet intelligence agents running it began spoon-feeding Western intelligence agencies with information (actually disinformation) supposedly obtained from defectors-in-place at the highest levels of the Soviet government. Those fabricated reports were later confirmed by other false anti-Soviet groups set up by the Soviet intelligence services. This disinformation campaign helped Moscow confuse Western governments about its real plans for world revolution and convinced them that the Soviet Union was moving more toward nationalism than Communism. See Edward Jay Epstein, *Legend: The Secret World of Lee Harvey Oswald* (New York: McGraw-Hill, 1978), p. 277, n. 7.

The technique has been successfully used by many intelligence services. For example, it is known that both Omega 7 and Alpha 66, two violent, organizations of virulent anti-Castro Cubans in exile, were successfully penetrated by Castro's intelligence services.

48 Pincher, *Their Trade*, p. 128.

49 Pincher, *Their Trade*, p. 128, 187.

50 Pincher, *Their Trade*, p. 187.

51 Pincher, *Their Trade,* pp. 188-189. Victor Marchetti claimed that, after Penkovsky allegedly had been executed, someone at the CIA had said, "Why don't we try to contact him?" and that this suggestion had led to the agency's becoming "involved with mediums." (Marchetti on Penkovsky in Martin Ebon, *Psychic Warfare* (New York: McGraw-Hill, 1983), 193-194. But, after knowing the particularities of the Penkovsky case, one may guess that, instead of talking about contacting Penkovsky through any psychic with mediumnistic abilities, perhaps what the CIA guy really meant was contacting Penkovsky directly in Russia.

52 Thomas Powers, answer to Jerrold L. Schechter, "A Very Important Spy," *The New York Review of Books,* June 24, 1993.

53 Pincher, *Their Trade,* p. 189.

54 See, Edward Crankshaw, Foreword to Oleg Penkovsky, *The Penkovsky Papers* (Garden City, New Jersey: Doubleday, 1965), p. viii.

55 Radio Moscow went as far as to claim that Penkovsky had been deserted by the CIA. See, *The Washington Post,* May 8, 13, and 17, 1963, and Joseph Alsop, "A Soviet Hiss Case," April 29, 1963.

56 See Greville Wynne, *Contact on Gorky Street* (New York: Atheneum, 1968); also Richard Helm's speech reported in *The New York Times,* April 14, 1971.

57 Evan Thomas, *The Very Best Men: Four Who Dared: The Early Years of the CIA* (New York: Simon and Schuster, 1995), p. 192

58 Some amount of paranoia is a necessary condition for counterintelligence work.

59 Powers, *The Man,* p. 362.

60 Pincher, *Their Trade,* p. 189.

61 Just to have an idea of the intricacies and the degree of complexity of counterintelligence thinking, as well as the complex personality of James Jesus Angleton, see Ron Rosenbaum's masterpiece, "The Shadow of the Mole," *Harper's,* October 1983.

62 *Mole*: intelligence lingo for an enemy agent that has bored his way into an opposing intelligence service. The correct intelligence term to describe this type of activity is "penetration agent."

The term "mole" was introduced by writer David Cornwell (better known by his *nom de plume,* John le Carré) in one of his spy novels, and it has been widely adopted by the intelligence community —an outstanding example of the two-way link between reality and fiction.

63 Wright, *Spy Catcher* , pp. 263-265.

64 Wright, *Spy Catcher* , p. 264.

65 Wright, *Spy Catcher* , p. 265; also, Richard Deacon, *"C, " A Biography of Sir Maurice Oldfield* (London: Macdonald, 1985), p. 131.

66 Wright, *Spy Catcher* , p. 265.

67 Wright, *Spy Catcher* , p. 265-266.

68 Unwittingly, they played right into the greedy hands of the Pentagon and their friends in the military-industrial-academic complex. Harvard economist

Sumner Slichter mentioned that, unknowingly, Khrushchev had some allies on the American side, who maybe were thanking him for helping make capitalism in the U.S. work better than ever. See, *The New York Herald Tribune*, October 26, 1959.

Some experts in the U.S. government—most notably the Air Force specialists—claimed that they were extremely concerned with the growing Soviet strategic threat. Yet, it is easy to see that the most pessimistic, alarmist estimates of Soviet capabilities were not always based on a legitimate interpretation of the uncertain evidence, but were directed at developing a stronger case for the expansion of American forces.

69 Ronald Kessler, *Inside the CIA* (New York: Pocket Books, 1992), p. 100.

70 Strategic deception can take two forms: deceive the enemy to make him believe one is strategically superior, when not, as when Khrushchev boasted about Soviet missile superiority from 1959 on, or deceive him to make him believe one is strategically inferior when not, as when in 1969 two Soviet plants informed American intelligence that the U.S.S.R. was on the verge of embarking in a crash program to develop chemical and biological weapons in fact already developed. As Sun Tzu advised, "when capable, feign incapacity; when active, inactivity." *The Art of War* (London: Oxford University Press, 1963), p. 66.

71 Wright, *Spy Catcher*, p. 267.

72 Hugh Sidey, *John F. Kennedy, President* (Greenwich, Conn.: Crest Books, 1963), p. 305. One wonder if perhaps they actually were the *same* missiles photographed in Moscow during the May Day parade, which, knowing the scarcity of real missiles at the time, one may safely assume were dummies.

What is unexplainable is that the CIA officers who read the reports made by the photo interpreters never raised questions about their violation of so many elementary rules of tradecraft. A basic rule of espionage is that even more important than what you know is that the enemy doesn't know that you know it. Only the suspicion that the enemy knows that you know makes all information acquired through any source suspect. But here, senior American intelligence officers, with years of experience in the profession, were accepting, without raising any objections, clandestine information from a source —the U-2— they positively knew had been compromised because the Russians knew of the U-2s overflights and of its technological capabilities. This is such an incredible demonstration of incompetence that makes one wonder if it actually was what it seems to have been and not a different thing.

Chapter Seven

1 Henry Pachter, *Collision Course: The Cuban Missiles and Coexistence* (New York: Praeger, 1963), p. 8. A post-mortem "Summary of Major Findings" by the Senate Preparedness Subcommittee on the Soviet build-up in Cuba concluded that the CIA evaluations were based on preconceived ideas about Soviet policy and a tendency to discredit Cuban refugees' reports. *The New York Times*, May 10, 1963.

There is a possibility, however, that the CIA's motives may have been more convoluted.

2 Ralph de Toledano, *R. F. K., The Man who would be President* (New York: Signet Books, 1968), p. 278.

3 At the time of the Cuban missile crisis the U-2's imagery collection capabilities was top secret, and only the ones directly involved with the operation of the plane, and a small group people at the highest levels of the intelligence community, knew its extraordinary capabilities, particularly the use of infrared photography. But the Russians, who had carefully studied Gary Powers' U-2, were better informed than the American public: In order to defeat infrared photography, they put special shielding inside some of the crates of military equipment they were sending to Cuba. See Anatoli I. Gribkov and William Y. Smith, *Operation Anadyr* (Chicago: edition q., inc., 1994), p. 56.

4 Hillsman, *To Move*, p. 159.

5 Hillsman, *To Move*, pp. 104-105, 159.

6 The creation of the concept of "defensive" and "offensive" weapons is perhaps the most stupid legacy of the Kennedy administration in the field of international politics.

7 See, i.e., President Kennedy's address to the nation, *Department of State Bulletin*, XLVII (1962), p. 716; Stevenson's statement to the U.N. Security Council, *United Nations Review*, IX (September, 1962), p. 80; and the resolution adopted by the Organization of American States, October 23, 1962, in David L. Larson, ed. *The "Cuban Crisis" of 1962: Selected Documents and Bibliography* (Boston: Houghton-Mifflin, 1963), p. 66.

8 See, Clifton E. Wilson, "The Use and Abuse of International Law," in N. D. Houghton, ed. *Struggle Against History* (New York: Clarion, 1968), pp. 240-241.

9 *The New York Times*, September 5, 1962.

10 David Wise and Thomas B. Ross, *The Invisible Government* (New York: Bantam, 1965), p. 310.

11 There is probably some basis for these claims. The actual route flown by the U-2, now under SAC command, differed slightly from the original one initially planned by the CIA. For the declassified official map showing both routes see CIA, *The Secret Cuban Missile Crisis Documents* (Washington: Brassey's, 1994), p. 4.

11 See, Subcommittee on Department of Defense Appropriations, *Hearings*, pp. 66-67.

12 John Dille, "Course of the Russian Build-up, Our Choices," *Time*, September 21, 1962, p. 36.

13 See, Dino A. Brugioni, *Eyeball to Eyeball: The Inside Story of the Cuban Missile Crisis* (New York: Random House, 1991), p.155.

14 Wise and Ross, *The Invisible Government*, p. 312.

15 Wise and Ross, *The Invisible Government*, p. 311.

16 Wise and Ross, *The Invisible Government*, p. 321.

17 See *The New York Times*, November 3, 1962.
18 Congress, Senate, *Interim Report*, pp. 3, 8-9.
19 Congress, House, *Defense Appropriations*, pp. 25, 27-28, 45-46, 67-71, and 362-363.
20 Pachter, *Collision Course*, p. 8.
21 Roger Hilsman, "The Cuban Crisis: How Close We Were to War," *Look*, 28 (August 25, 1964).
22 Klaus Knorr, "Failure in National Intelligence Estimates, The Case of the Cuban Missiles," *World Politics*, Vol. XVI No. 3 (April, 1964), pp. 458-59.
23 Sorensen, *Kennedy*, 1965, p. 672.
24 Wohlstetter, Roberta,"Cuba and Pearl Harbor: Hindsight and Foresight," *Foreign Affairs* 43 (July 1965).
25 *The Missile Crisis*, 1967
26 *To Move a Nation*, 1967
27 Brugioni, *Eyeball to Eyeball*, p.164.
28 Brugioni, *Eyeball to Eyeball*, p.144. Brugioni describes in some detail Rusk's and Bundy's strange behavior. See, pp. 134-164. Rusk's machinations, however, come as no surprise. Since the time of the infamous Sumner Welles, to the time of the obnoxious Collin Powell, not to mention the mysterious William Wieland, State Department folks have shown a penchant for carrying out their own private Cuban policy, sometimes quite different from the policy dictated by the U.S. president and Congress.
29 Carl A. Linden, *Khrushchev and the Soviet Leadership, 1957-1964* (Baltimore, Md.: The Johns Hopkins University Press, 1966), p. 53
30 It is not a surprise that the "inept Khrushchev" theory was the creation, just a few weeks after the end of the crisis, of none other than the master disinformer: Henry Kissinger. According to him, it was Khrushchev's ineptness and lack of predictability what caused the whole incident. See, Henry Kissinger, "Reflections on Cuba," *The Reporter*, November, 22, 1962, pp. 21-24.
31 Schlesinger, *A Thousand*, pp. 750, 752.
32 Schlesinger, *A Thousand*, p. 752.
33 Schlesinger, *A Thousand*, p. 752.
34 Schlesinger, *A Thousand*, p. 750.
35 Robert Kennedy, *Thirteen Days*, p. 36.
36 Robert kennedy, *Thirteen Days*, p. 36
37 Pachter, *Collision Course*, p. 55.
38 See Leon Goure, *Civil Defense in the Soviet Union* (Berkeley: University of California Press, 1962). See also P.T. Yegorov, et. al., *Civil defense (Grazhdanskaya Oborona)*, (Moscow: Vysshaya Shkola, 1966); and Joanne L. Gailar, "Seven Warning Signals: A Review of Soviet Civil Defense," *Bulletin of the Atomic Scientists*, December 1969, pp. 18-22. Ms. Gailar points out that unclassified literature in the Soviet Union evidenced a massive effort on civil defense dating back from 1961.

39 Jan F. Triska and David D. Finley, *Soviet Foreign Policy* (New York: Macmillan, 1968), p. 126.

40 Crankshaw, *Khrushchev's Russia*, p. 53.

41 "The Showdown," *Time*, November 2, 1962.

42 Linden, *Khrushchev and the Soviet*, p. 154.

43 Sorensen, *Kennedy*, p. 709. Herbert Dinerstein made a persuasive case for the existence of significant differences within the Soviet leadership, especially at the height of the crisis. See Dinerstein, *The Making*, p. 187 ff.

44 The *Washington Post*, December 18, 1962.

45 Richard Ned Lebow and Janice Gross Stein, *We All Lost the Cold War* (Princeton, N.J.: Princeton University Press, 1994), p. 62, (emphasis added). I am using Lebow and Stein for no particular reason, just as a good example of the formulation of the "miscalculation" theory. But it has been repeated over and over in most books about the Cuban missile crisis.

46 Lebow and Stein, *We All Lost the Cold War*, p. 64.

47 Lebow and Stein, *We All Lost the Cold War*, p. 65.

48 Memorandum of a Conversation at the Vienna Meeting Between the President and Chairman Khrushchev, 3 June 1961, 12:45 P.M., John F. Kennedy Library, POF:CO: U.S.S.R., box 126, folder 12, p. 1.

49 Memorandum of a Conversation at the Vienna Meeting Between the President and Chairman Khrushchev, 3 June 1961, 12:45 P.M., John F . Kennedy Library, POF: CO: U.S.S.R., box 126, folder 12, p. 6. The exchange has been reproduced also in Michael R. Beschloss, *The Crisis Years, 1960-1963* (New York: HarperCollins, 1991), pp. 196-197.

50 Whose characterization in Kevin Costner's film is shamefully inaccurate.

51 Halperin, *The Rise*, p. 174.

52 Arthur M. Schlesinger, Jr., *Robert Kennedy and his Times* (Boston: Houghton Mifflin Co., 1978), p. 498.

53 Arthur M. Schlesinger, Jr., *A Thousand Days* (Greenwich, Conn.: Crest Books, 1965), p. 296.

54 Walton, *Cold War*, p. 115.

55 Pachter, *Collision Course*, p. 29.

56 Robert Kennedy, *Thirteen Days*, pp. 14, 126.

57 Sorensen, *Kennedy*, p. 687.

58 Johnson's spicy remarks were reported in the *Arizona Daily Star*, October 7, 1962, p. 1A.

59 Schlesinger, *A Thousand*, p. 739.

60 Schlesinger, *A Thousand*, p. 736.

61 Schlesinger, *A Thousand*, p. 738.

62 Schlesinger, *A Thousand*, p. 743.

63 Schlesinger, *A Thousand*, pp. 749, 752.

64 See, "Showdown-Backdown," *Newsweek*, November 5, 1962, p. 34.

65 See, Thomas M. Mongar, "Personality and Decision Making: John F. Kennedy in Four Crisis Decisions," in Gordon J. DiRenzo, ed., *Personality and Politics* (Garden City, New York: Anchor Books, 1974), p. 358.

66 *Pravda*, January 17, 1963.

Chapter Eight

1 *U.S. Senate, Committee of the Judiciary, Subcommittee to Investigate the Administration of Internal Security Act*, "Castro's Network in the United States," Hearing, 88th Congress, First Session, Part 6, February 8, 1963.

2 "What Castro Planned: Destroy U.S. Cities," *U.S. News and World Report*, December 24, 1962, pp. 36-38. The most virulent parts of Guevara's words were suppressed by the *Daily Worker*, but a full version of the interview was obtained by *United Press International*.

3 *Verde Olivo*, December 22, 1968. An interesting detail is that, although Guevara wrote the editorial in 1962, it was not published until 1968, when the Cuban-Soviet differences over armed struggle had finally come out in the open.

4 For an analysis of Castro's dreams of nuclear and biological Armageddon, see Servando González, *The Secret Fidel Castro*, pp. 65-75.

5 Servando González, "Bomba y Paranoia," *Observando,* Segunda Edición (San Francisco: El Gato Tuerto, 1986), pp. 53-54.

6 See, Document 45,: Prime Minister Fidel Castro's letter to Premier Khrushchev, October 26, 1962, in Laurence Chang and Peter Kornbluh, eds., *The Cuban Missile Crisis, 1962: A National Security Archive Documents Reader* (New York: The New Press, 1992), p. 189. (Letter reprinted from the international edition of *Granma*).

7 See, Document 57,: Premier Khrushchev's letter to Prime Minister Fidel Castro, October 30, 1962, in Laurence Chang and Peter Kornbluh, eds., *The Cuban Missile Crisis, 1962*, p. 243. Contrary to what Khrushchev thought, he didn't understand Castro's motivations. Had he understood them, he would have shivered in terror.

8 Sometimes it is not easy to understand what Castro says he said.

9 See, Document 58,: Prime Minister Fidel Castro's letter to Premier Khrushchev, October 31, 1962 in Laurence Chang and Peter Kornbluh, eds., *The Cuban Missile Crisis, 1962*, p. 244. (Letter reprinted from the international edition of *Granma*).

10 Nikita Khrushchev, *Khrushchev Remembers: The Glasnost Tapes* (Boston: Little, Brown and Company, 1990), p. 177.

11 Nikita Khrushchev, *Khrushchev Remembers:*, p. 183.

12 More on the National Security "Archive" and Castro's forging abilities in Chapter 12.

13 See, Juan Vivés, *Los amos de Cuba* (Buenos Aires: Emecé Editores, 1982), pp. 181-182.

14 See, Ernesto Betancourt, *"Is Castro Planning a Preemptive Strike Against the U.S.?"* (Washington, D.C., 1996), p. 4.

15 See, Jeanne Kirkpatrick, "Is a stubborn Castro testing U.S. defenses?," the *Miami Herald*, March 31, 1991, p. 3C.

16 See, Joseph B. Treaster, "Defecting General Says Cuba Has Plan to Raid Base in the U.S. if It Is Attacked," the *New York Times*, October 11, 1987.

17 *Granma Weekly Review*, December 22, 1963.

18 Andrés Suárez, *Cuba: Castroism and Communism, 1959-66* (Boston: MIT Press, 1967), p. 94.

19 *Le Monde*, November 24, 1997; also in "Castro Fond of Missiles," *AP* report, August 16, 1997.

20 *Le Monde*, November 24, 1997.

21 For a controversial analysis of the missiles in Cuba see Servando González, "A Missile is a Missile is a Missile," *Sumeria*, http://www.sumeria.net/politics/amissile.html.

22 González, "A Missile," *Sumeria*.

23 U.S. Senate, Committee on Foreign Relations, "Cuban Realities: May 1975," a Report by Senator George S. McGovern to the Committee on Foreign Relations, August 1975, p. 14.

24 Andrew Tully, *White Tie and Dagger* (New York: Pocket Books, 1968), pp. 74-78. Tully mistakenly believes the plot was a Soviet idea, but it was Castro's. The plot is also mentioned in Andres Oppenheimer, *Castro's Final Hour* (New York: Simon and Schuster, 1992).

25 Amuchástegui, "Cuban Intelligence and the October Crisis," p. 101.

26 Amuchástegui, "Cuban Intelligence and the October Crisis," p. 101.

27 Juan Vivés, *Los amos de Cuba* (Buenos Aires: Emecé, 1982), p. 122. Of late, however, Fidel Castro seems to have reached the conclusion that the Soviets wanted the missiles to be discovered.

28 Daniel Ellsberg, "The Day Castro Almost Started World War III," The *New York Times*, October 31, 1987, p. A7.

29 Dinerstein, *The Making*, p. 229.

30 See, "Bad Boys and Good," *Newsweek*, November 12, 1962.

31 See, Louis L. Wizmitzer, "Sino-Soviet Rivalry in Latin America," the *New Republic*, December 1, 1962, p. 18.

32 Pope, *Soviet Views*, p. 63.

33 *Khrushchev Remembers*, p. 499.

34 Frank Mankiewicz and Kirby Jones, *With Fidel* (Chicago: Playboy Press, 1975), p. 171.

35 Castro customarily uses the royal "we" when is talking about himself.

36 Nikita S. Khrushchev to Fidel Castro, October 28, 1962.

37 *Khrushchev Remembers*, p. 499.

38 Nikita S. Khrushchev, *The Glasnost Tapes* (Boston: Little, Brown and Company, 1990) p. 178.

39 U-Thant, *View From the U.N.* (Garden City, N.J.: Doubleday, 1978), p. 188.

40 Tad Szulc, "Friendship is Possible, But ...," *Parade*, April 1, 1984, p. 6.

41 Dino A. Brugioni, *Eyeball to Eyeball: The Inside Story of the Cuban Missile Crisis* (New York: Random House, 1991), pp. 462, 463.

42 *Hoy*, May 2, 1964.

43 *Family Portrait With Fidel* (New York: Vintage, 1984), p. 193.

44 Seymour Hersh, "Was Castro Out of Control in 1962?" in the *Washington Post*, October 11, 1987; Adrián Montoro, "Moscow Was Caught Between Cuba and U.S.," the *New York Times*, November 17, 1987; Rodríguez Menier in personal communication to the author, December 20, 1994. Menier claims he heard the story from Gen. José Abrahantes.

45 James Blight and David Welch, *On the Brink* (New York: Hill and Wang, 1989), p. 56.

46 Scott Armstrong and Phillip Brenner, "Cuba Crisis: No Hits But Many Errors," the *Los Angeles Times*, November 1, 1987.

47 The messages exchanged between Castro and Khrushchev were published by the Cuban government in 1990 and copies of them exist at the Kennedy Library. Soviet sources have verified the accuracy of the messages.

48 Del Pino interview in the *Milwakee Journal*, October 23, 1987.

49 Bruce J. Allyn, James G. Blight, and David A. Welch, eds., *Back to the Brink: Proceedings of the Moscow Conference on the Cuban Missile Crisis, January 27-28, 1989*, CSIA Occasional Paper no. 9 (Lanham, Md.: University Press of America, 1992), pp. 30-31.

50 Fidel Castro, letter to Nikita S. Khrushchev, October 31, 1962, Folio 3, List 65, File 907, pp. 137-137, reproduced in James G. Blight et. al., *Cuba on the Brink: Castro, the Missile Crisis and the Soviet Collapse* (New York: Pantheon Books, 1993), pp. 489-91.

51 James G. Blight, Bruce J. Allyn, and David A. Welch, *Cuba on the Brink* (New York: Pantheon Books, 1993), p. 79.

52 Szulc, *Fidel*, p. 46. On Castro's incredible mesmerizing powers see Servando González, *The Secret Fidel Castro*, pp. 31-43.

53 See Blight and Welch, *On the Brink*, p. 311.

54 Blight, Allyn, and Welch, *Cuba on the Brink*, p. 359.

55 After an exhaustive study of Fidel Castro, I arrived at the inevitable conclusion that Castro "is a monster, and he is evil." See, Servando González, *The Secret Fidel Castro*, p. 309.

56 Hilsman, *To Move a Nation*, p. 220.

57 See Detzer, *The Brink*, p. 246; also Hilsman, *To Move a Nation*, p. 221.

Chapter Nine

1 Foy D. Kohler, "Cuba and the Soviet Problem in Latin America," in Jaime Suchlicki, ed., *Cuba, Castro and Revolution* (Coral Gables, Florida: University of Miami Press, 1972), pp. 125126.

2 Robert Kennedy denied this: "There was no question that the letter had been written by him personally. It was very long and emotional. But it was not incoherent," *Thirteen Days* (New York: W.W. Norton, 1971), p. 64

3 The tone of the letter was its most important feature. "It was a plea for peace almost eloquent," said one White House aide. According to Hugh Sidey, the letter transmitted a secret feeling; "a feeling of the horror of nuclear war." *John F. Kennedy, President* (Greenwich, Conn.: Crest Books, 1963), p. 317.

4 *Strike in the West* (New York: Holt, Rinehart and Winston), p. 150.

5 *The Missile Crisis* (Philadelphia: Lippincott, 1966), p. 178.

6 *A Thousand Days*, p. 755.

7 *Collision Course*, p. 50.

8 "What Happened in the Kremlin," *Newsweek*, November 12, 1962, p. 26.

9 Pachter, *Collision Course*, p. 50-51.

10 *Department of State Bulletin*, November 19, 1973, pp. 640-645.

11 Robert Shelby Frank, *Linguistic Analysis of Political Elites: A Theory of Verbal Kinesics* (Beverly Hills: Sage, 1973).

12 Frank, *Linguistic Analysis*, p. 27.

13 For my analysis, I have used the official translation provided by the U.S. Department of State. "Chairman Khrushchev's message of October 26, 1962," (Official translation) *Department of State Bulletin*, November 19, 1973, pp. 643-645.

14 "Chairman Khrushchev's message," p. 643.

15 "Chairman Khrushchev's message," p. 644.

16 "Chairman Khrushchev's message," p. 645.

17 "Chairman Khrushchev's message," p. 645.

18 "Chairman Khrushchev's message," p. 645.

19 Pachter, *Collision Course*, p. 67-68.

20 Nikita S. Khrushchev, *Khrushchev Remembers*, translated and edited by Strobe Talbot (Boston: Little, Brown and Company, 1970), pp. 497-498.

21 *The Louisville Times*, January 20, 1961, quoted in Victor Lasky, *JFK, The Man and the Myth* (New York: Dell, 1966), p. 24.

22 See, Henry Brandon, "An Untold Story of the Cuban Crisis," *Saturday Review*, March 9, 1963, p. 56. See also Anthony Lewis, "Plane Veers Over Soviet, Kennedy Voices Regrets," *The New York Times*, October 29, 1962.

23 See, i.e., Ole R. Holsti, *Crisis, Escalation, War* (Montreal: McGill University Press, 1962), pp. 225-226.

24 Brandon, "An Untold Story of the Cuban Crisis,", p. 57, emphasis added.

25 There is a seven hour time difference between Moscow and Washington, therefore the U-2 overflight actually took place on October 27, Washington time.

26 Chairman Khrushchev's Message of October 28, 1962, *Department of State Bulletin*, November 9, 1973, pp. 652-654. The Russian text was delivered to the American Embassy in Moscow at 5:10 p.m. on October 28, 1962, and broadcast over Moscow radio in Russian and English beginning at 5 p.m. Moscow time on

the same date. This is the official translation prepared subsequently by the U.S. Department of State.

27 The system of alert warning used by the U.S. Armed Forces and all other federal agencies is a system of graded warning, signifying different grades of danger. The system uses five defense readiness conditions, abbreviated as DEFCON (Defense Condition). Normal operating peaceful status is designated as DEFCON 5. A the other extreme, DEFCON 1 specifies a condition of tactical alert, imminent attack or actual war. In between these two extremes there are three other conditions of readiness, graded according to the degree of danger.

28 Robert A. Divine, ed., Introduction to *The Cuban Missile Crisis* (Chicago: Quadrangle, 1971), pp. 3-4.

29 Khrushchev, *Khrushchev Remembers*, p. 498.

30 According to Henry Pachter, "Some time during Thursday, October 25, Khrushchev must have decided that Kennedy was not bluffing." *Collision Course: The Cuban Missiles and Coexistence* (New York: Praeger, 1963.),

31 William Randolph Hearst, Jr., B. Considine and F. Coniff, *Khrushchev and the Russian Challenge* (New York: Avon, 1961), p. 121.

32 Quoted in Fred J. Cook, *The Warfare State* (New York: Collier, 1962), p. 177.

33 Nikita S. Khrushchev, *Khrushchev Remembers*, translated and edited by Strobe Talbot (Boston: Little, Brown and Company, 1970), p. 496.

34 "What Happened in the Kremlin," *Newsweek*, November 12, 1962, p. 25.

35 Raymond L. Garthoff, *Intelligence Assessment and Policy Making: A Decision Point in the Kennedy Administration* (Washington, D.C.: The Brookings Institution, 1984), p. 30.

36 Konrad Lorentz, *On Aggression* (London: Methuen, 1966).

37 See, "The Lessons of the Cuban Missile Crisis," *Time*, September 27, 1982, p. 85.

38 See, *Report of the Special Inter-Department Committee on Implications of NIE 11-8-62 and Related Intelligence*, II, para. 6, reproduced in Raymond L. Garthoff, *Intelligence Assessment and Policy Making: A Decision Point in the Kennedy Administration* (Washington, D.C.: The Brookings Institution, 1984), p. 44.

39 Robert Kennedy, *Thirteen Days*, p. 36.

40 See, Theodore C. Sorensen, *Kennedy* (New York: Bantam Books, 1966), p. 272.

41 Montague Kern, Patricia W. Levering and Ralph B. Levering, *The Kennedy Crises: The Press, the Presidency, and Foreign Policy* (Chapel Hill, N.C.: The Univ. of North Carolina Press, 1983), p. 131. The book shows that John F. Kennedy's idea of freedom of the press was perhaps not too different from Khrushchev's.

42 Robert Kennedy, *Thirteen Days*, pp. 75-76, 79. The Kennedy eulogists have always tried to surround the actions of the Kennedy brothers and the Ex Comm members with an aura of grandiosity. This is also reflected in the made-for-

propaganda photos of the Kennedys and the Ex Comm during the crisis days. But Dean Acheson, for one, was never convinced of the grandiosity of the Kennedys or the effectivity of the Ex Comm. See, Dean Acheson, "Dean Acheson's Version of Robert Kennedy's Version of the Cuban Missile Affair," *Esquire* 71 (February 1969). See also, Dean Acheson, "Homage to Plain Dumb Luck," in Robert A. Divine, ed., *The Cuban Missile Crisis: The Continuing Debate* (New York: Markus Wiener Publishing, 1988).

43 Allison, *Essence of Decision*, p. 46.

44 Many Americans would smile faced with that line of thought, but I am not analyzing here an American, but a Russian mind. Anyway, Khrushchev had valid reasons to be scared. As of today, the U.S. is the only nation that has dropped atomic bombs on open cities.

45 Allison, *The Essence*, p. 64, (emphasis mine).

46 U.S. Congress, House of Representatives, Committee of Appropriations, SubCommittee on Department of Defense Appropriations, *Hearings*, 88th Congress, 1st Session, 1963, p. 31.

47 See U.S. Department of State *Bulletin*, vol. 47, no. 1220, November 12, 1962, pp. 740-741.

48 Edward Jay Epstein,"Incorporating Analysis of Foreign Governments' Deception into the U.S. Analytical System," in Roy Godson, ed., *Intelligence Requirements for the 1980's* (Washington, D.C.: National Strategy Information Center, 1980), p. 124

49 See, Frederick S. Feer,"Incorporating Analysis of Foreign Governments' Deception into the U.S. Analytical System, II" in Roy Godson, ed., *Intelligence Requirements for the 1980's* (Washington, D.C.: National Strategy Information Center, 1980), p. 141.

50 I will study this in detail in my forthcoming book, *Fidel Castro Supermole: Walking Back the Cat in the Cuban Operation.*

51 Pachter, *Collision Course*, p. 23.

52 One of the wildest of Khrushchev's policies was the cultivation of corn on the largest scale ever seen in Russia. The maize campaign, which eventually proved to be disastrous to the economy, was overdone to the point of absurdity, such that people began calling him *Kukuruza* —which is Russian for corn. See Crankshaw, *Khrushchev's Russia*, p. 85.

53 Ricardo Rojo, *Mi amigo el Che* (Buenos Aires: Jorge Alvarez, 1968), p. 130.

54 See Domingo Amuchástegui, "Cuban Intelligence and the October Crisis," in James G. Blight and David A. Welch, *Intelligence and the Cuban Missile Crisis* (London: Frank Cass, 1998), pp. 96-98. Though Amuchástegui's claims about his personal participation in the event are highly exaggerated, it seems likely that he heard the story from some of his friends at high levels in the Castro government. More on Amuchástegui in Chapter 11.

55 Contrary to the Cuban habit of cleanliness, Castro has never been too much concerned about daily showers or clean clothes. During his student days at Havana

University he often smelled so bad that he earned the nickname *bola de churre* (grease ball). He has not reformed.

Chapter Ten

1 The word that there were Soviet missile sites in Cuba was so widespread that *Time* ran an article on September 21 showing a map of Cuba clustered with Soviet ground-to-air missiles, mainly in the western part of the island, west and south of Havana.

2 The quote is from Raymond L. Garthoff, "U.S. Intelligence in the Cuban Missile Crisis," in James G. Blight and David A. Welch, eds., *Intelligence and the Cuban missile crisis* (London: Frank Cass, 1998), p. 23.

Like the majority of the people, the President and his close advisors most likely were convinced that "seeing is believing." But, actually, seeing should never be used as a basis for believing, because many things we see every day are misleading, or not real, or outright false. From watching magicians we know how easily one can be misled by visual images. See, Arthur Asa Berger, *Seeing is Believing: An Introduction to Visual Communication* (Mountain View, California: Mayfield Publishing Company, 1989), pp. 15, 17.

3 Though most alleged sightings coming from Cuban exiles located the missiles in the western part of the island, U-2 planes had concentrated their efforts on spying in the *eastern* part of Cuba. It was not until October 9, 1962, that the interagency Committee on Overhead Reconnaissance (COMOR) gave authorization to fly over the western part of Cuba.

4 When U.S. Ambassador Stevenson displayed the photographs of what he claimed were Soviet strategic missile sites in Cuba at the U.N. Security Council meeting in October 25, Soviet Ambassador Zorin countered that the photographs were a fake. Evidence indicates that Zorin, like most Soviet diplomats, was left out of the loop by his own government about the events developing in Cuba. Therefore, his doubts about the credibility of the photographs most likely were not faked.

5 Sherman Kent, "The.Cuban Missile Crisis of 1962: Presenting the Evidence Abroad," *Studies in Intelligence*, Spring 1972. (Emphasis added.)

6 Kent, "The.Cuban Missile Crisis of 1962."

7 Kent, "The.Cuban Missile Crisis of 1962."

8 The only exceptions I am aware of, are my own "El Gran Engaño," a series of 6 articles in Spanish published in New York's *El Diario-La Prensa*, on October 21-27, 1982; Ralph Epperson, *The Unseen Hand* (Tucson: Publius Press, 1985), 120-121; and Epperson's "Russia Has Wooden Missiles!," a two-hour videotape of a lecture he gave in 1988.

It seems, however, that some time after the crisis James Jesus Angleton had his own doubts about the objects appearing in the U-2 photos. Perhaps suspecting Russian foul play, he asked to see all the documents prepared by the NPIC during the crisis.

Unfortunately, the results of his study —if he ever did one— were never published. See Brugioni, *Eyeball to Eyeball*, p. 563. Brugioni mentions that most people at CIA regarded Angleton as eccentric and paranoid. It is easy to understand why Angleton came to be so hated by some of his CIA colleagues.

9 McCone memo in *CIA Documents on the Cuban Missile Crisis* (Washington, D.C.: Central Intelligence Agency History Staff, 1992), note 6, p. 374.

10 In an interesting article enigmatically titled "DC Power and Cooling Towers," Henry Rubenstein shows how high tech aerial photography, though a valuable means of detection of enemy activity, requires the support of other means of collection and analysis to become true intelligence. See H. Bradford Westerfield, ed., *Inside CIA's Private World* (New Haven: Yale University Press,1995), p. 3-26. Rubenstein's article originally appeared in CIA's internal publication *Studies in Intelligence*, vol. 16, no. 3 (Fall 1972), and was classified "Secret." Given the fact that Rubenstein's article appeared in 1972, ten years after the Cuban missile crisis, and it is safe to assume that during these years the quality of aerial surveillance advanced considerably. Still, the inability of photographs, by themselves alone, to serve as a source of true intelligence, persists.

11 *Science and Sanity: An Introduction to Non-Aristotelian Systems and General Semantics* (1933). The following story is further proof of the validity of Korzybski's extensively quoted dictum.

General George Lee Butler, commander of U.S. Strategic Command from 1990 to 1994, was the man responsible for developing the whole strategy for nuclear war with the U.S.S.R. In that capacity he had carefully studied the Soviet Union at a level of detail matched by only a few others in the West. He had studied the footage of the military parades at the Red Square, pored over thousands of satellite surveillance photos, and scrutinized the deployments of Soviet missiles and other armaments. His mental image of the Soviet Union was a fearsome superpower with a highly developed military machine capable of using the most advanced sophisticated military technology. But then, he had the opportunity of visiting the Soviet Union for the first time. His first surprise was the uneven, pockmarked runway at Sheremetievo airport, which from the air resembled an open field. The taxiways were still covered with snow from a storm two days earlier, and dozens of the runway lights were broken. As he rode into downtown Moscow he noticed that the streets were ragged and most of the big buildings lacked paint and were crumbling. After poring over thousands of satellite photos and thirty years worth of classified reports, Butler had expected to find a modern, advanced country. What he found let him realize that what he had been watching all these years was actually a caricature. See R. Jeffrey Smith, "The Dissenter," *Washington Post Magazine*, December 7, 1997, pp. 18-20.

12 As members of technologically advanced cultures —or so we believe— we are so used to decoding photographic images that we fail to recognize that this is not an inborn or intuitive process, but a learned one. Some anthropologists have recorded the impressions of members of primitive tribes after they have been shown

a photograph for the first time in their lives. Usually they have taken the puzzling object from the hands of the person conducting the experiment, smelled it, looked for something on its back, and returned the photograph without being able to decode the meaning of the small dots appearing on its surface.

In the early 1960s, the Cuban Institute of Cinema (ICAIC) produced a documentary film, *Por primera vez* (For the First Time), which records the impressions of farmers in the Sierra Maestra mountains after they saw the projection of a film for the very first time in their lives. The farmer's comments about their impressions are quite revealing, not too different from the anthropologists' experiments described above.

13 It seems, however, that NPIC Director Arthur Lundahl didn't have a clear distinction between things and their photographic images. During a briefing at the White House on Thursday, October 18, in which he presented some of the U-2 photographs, he kept referring to pictures as if they were the real objects they represent. See, i.e., "There are two pads, here —and here. They are separated by 750 feet. There's a control bunker with cable scars going up into small buildings inboard for each of the pads." Ernest R. May and Philip D. Zelikov, eds. *The Kennedy Tapes: Inside the White House During the Cuban Missile Crisis* (Cambridge, Massachusetts: Harvard University Press, 1997), p. 123.

14 In his monumental work *The Golden Bough*, Sir James Frazer analyzed the main principle on which magic is based. Basically, magic operates on the principle that similar objects share the same properties. According to it, there is no difference between an object and its photograph. Science, on the contrary, operates on the opposite principle, which is best expressed in Einstein's Principle of Locality.

15 Ferdinand de Saussure, *Cours de linguistique générale* (Paris: Payot, 1916). Charles Sanders Peirce, *Collected Papers* (Cambridge: Harvard University Press, 1931-1958).

16 Saussure's quote in Umberto Eco, *A Theory of Semiotics* (Bloomington: Indiana University Press, 1979), p. 15.

17 Peirce, *Collected Papers*, p. 484.

18 Peirce, *Collected Papers*, Vol. II, p. 228.

19 Eco, *A Theory of Semiotics*, p. 15.

20 Eco, *A Theory of Semiotics*, p. 15.

21 Peirce's theories were further advanced by some of his followers, particularly Charles Morris in his "Foundations of the Theory of Signs" *International Encyclopaedia of Unified Science 1-2* (Chicago: University of Chicago Press, 1938); *Signs, Language and Behavior* (New York: Prentice-Hall, 1946); and *Writings on the General Theory of Signs* (The Hague: Mouton, 1971). Though Peirce's original trichotomy of signs has been improved, modified, and contested (see works by Umberto Eco, Thomas A. Sebeok, and others), it is still a good introduction for the beginning semiotician.

22 Not all pictures, however, are iconic signs. Contrary to common belief, most of the small pictures appearing on the Macintosh interface are actually *symbols*, not icons.

23 For example, after the emergence of Nazism, the swastika became to many people in the Western culture a symbol of war, hatred and evil. For many centuries, however, the swastika has been a symbol of peace, love, and good luck for many people around the world, including some American indians.

24 The concept of aberrant decoding was introduced by Umberto Eco in "Lignes d'une recherche sémiologique sur le message télévisuel," a paper written in 1968 and later published in his *Recherches sur les systèmes signifiants* (The Hague: Mouton, 1973). For humorous examples of aberrant decoding see Daniel Meyerowitz, "Symbol Game," *Whole Earth Review*, Spring 1994, pp. 48-49.

25 Actually, it seems that they never saw missiles on Cuban soil, but "canvas covered" objects and other things which in similar U-2 photos taken over Soviet territory were seemingly related to strategic missile bases.

26 In an interview for the "Secrets of War" a documentary series produced by The Documedia Group in Los Angeles, CA, Dino A. Brugioni, of the NPIC, stated: "Okay, this is the picture that started the Cuban Missile Crisis. This is when we found uh, the missiles in Cuba, and if you look close[ly] you can see it's annotated that we not only have the missiles, and uh, but we also have the erectors [are] in place. And this is the photograph that was shown to President Kennedy that began the Cuban Missile Crisis." See Transcript of interview #S3181 conducted late in 1997 with Mr. Brugioni for "SECRETS OF WAR," http://www.secretsofwar.com/experts/brugioni4.html. But, as I will show below, Brugioni and the photo-interpreters at the NPIC actually never found any missiles in Cuba.

In *Eyeball to Eyeball: The Inside Story of the Cuban Missile Crisis* (New York: Random House, 1991), a book whose only purpose seems to have been the aggrandizing of himself and his bosses at the NPIC, Brugioni devotes a couple of paragraphs to describe Soviet *maskirovka* and deception, (pp. 89-90). Unfortunately, however, it seems that he learned about *maskirovka* too late in his career, because nothing of what he wrote in his book was applied by him during the missile crisis.

27 HUMINT, ELINT, IMINT, etc., are actually misnomers, because all these activities actually deal with data collection, and data is not true intelligence. The product of these activities sometimes is called "raw intelligence," but this is also a misnomer. Raw intelligence is a contradiction in terms. Intelligence is the sum of the conclusions based on raw data after it has been processed and evaluated by qualified intelligence analysts. Therefore, intelligence is a very elaborate product of the human intellect. As such, it is a very well cooked product, with nothing raw in it.

28 See Servando González, "De William Randolph Hearst a Adobe Photoshop: ¿Adónde fue a parar la realidad fotográfica?," *Lateral* (Barcelona), Año V No. 47 (November 1998), p. 12; also Kenneth Brower, "Photography in the Age of Falsification," *The Atlantic Monthly*, May 1998, pp. 92-111. By the way, the photo of a missile parading through the Red Square I used in the cover of this book has been doctored. The original picture shows two missiles. I removed one of the missiles using Adobe Photoshop. I purposely did it in a clumsy way to avoid disguising the fact that the photo has been doctored.

See also, Dino A, Brugioni, *Photo Fakery: The History and Techniques of Photographic Deception and Manipulation* (Dulles, Virginia: Brassey's, 1999). Brugioni devotes several pages (116-121) to visual deception in warfare. Unfortunately, it seems that Brugioni learned the use of decoys in warfare too late in his career, because during the Cuban missile crisis he never mentioned the possibility that the canvas-covered object appearing in the U-2 photos may have been decoys.

29 Philippe L Thyraud de Vosjoli, *Lamia* (Boston: Little, Brown and Company, 1970), p. 296

30 Colin McGinn, "An Ardent Fallibilist," *The New York Review of Books*, June 27, 2002, p. 39. McGinn's article is a review of Robert Nozick's book *Invariances: The Structure of the Objective World* (Harvard: Belknap Press/Harvard University Press, 2002). In order to provide some theoretical justification for their gross mistake, the photointerpreters at the NPIC and their supporters created a posteriori the so-called "triangulation theory." According to it, the NPIC photointerpreters were so confident about their belief that the Soviets had deployed strategic missiles in Cuba because they had three different types of information which have confirmed their judgement. But, as professor Nosick rightly affirms, in order to be considered objective, a fact has to be confirmed by different people, using different senses, at different times.

According to the proponents of the triangulation theory, the three alleged angles of the triangle are: 1, the U-2 photos of canvas-covered objects on Cuban soil resembled the ancillary equipment used in strategic missile sites in the U.S.S.R., which, 2, were known thanks to U-2 and Corona satellite photos of SS-4 and SS-5 sites in the Soviet Union, and, 3, further confirmed by the operating manuals and blueprints of their installations provided by Penkovsky. But the triangulation theory is fallacious. In the first place, U-2 photos of Cuba and the Soviet Union, and the Corona satellite photos, are just variations of the same sense, photography. Therefore the "triangulation" is actually a biangulation. But the strong doubts about Penkovsky's *bona fides*, added to gross violations of the most elementary rules of tradecraft in his handling, indicate that the information he provided is not reliable. Consequently, the triangulation theory is not even a biangulation, and it has no value at all. (Thanks to Professor Brian Latell for reminding me of the triangulation theory in a personal communication in which he criticized an early draft of this chapter.)

31 One of the ways intelligence analysts may use to counter deception is basing their conclusions "on *reliable* all source information." See Central Intelligence Agency, *A Compendium of Tradecraft Notes*, Volume I, Washington D.C., February 1997, Note 10, Tradecraft and Counterintelligence. It seems, however, that, contrary to some people's claims, the intelligence provided by the NPIC analysts was based on unreliable, single-source information —namely, only the photographs taken by the U-2s.

32 Moreover, intelligence officers believe that there is no such thing as a friendly intelligence service. Israel is a traditional American friend, yet, one of its agents,

Jonathan Pollard, is in an American prison convicted of espionage. In November, 1996, after the dissolution of the "evil empire," Harold Nicholson, a former CIA chief of station, was charged with treason when it was discovered that he had been recruited by the Russian intelligence services to spy on the U.S. See, "Update - Spy Catching," Jim Lehrer's *Online Newshour* (November 19, 1996), http://www.pbs.org/newshour/96/fed agencies/spy-11-19.html.

33 "The Cuban Missile Crisis of 1962: Presenting the Photographic Evidence Abroad," *Studies in Intelligence*, Spring 1972.

34 Graham T. Allison, *Essence of Decision: Explaining the Cuban Missile Crisis* (Boston: Little, Brown, Co., 1971), pp. 110-111.

35 Anatoli Gribkov and William Smith, *Operation ANADYR: U.S. and Soviet Generals Recount the Cuban Missile Crisis* (Chicago: Edition q, Inc, 1994), p. 15.

36 See, i. e., M. I. Tolochkov, *Maskirovka na Voine* (Moscow: Izdatelsvo DOSAAF, 1958); Col. Iu. "Maskirovka -delovazhoe," *Voennyl Vestnik* 12 (1979); Gen. V. S. Popov, *Vnezapnost' i neozhidannost' v istorii voin* (Moscow: Voenno Izdatelsvo Ministersva Oborony SSSR, 1955); A. A. Bulator and V. G. Prozorov, *Takticheskaia vnezapnost'* (Moscow: Voenno Izdatelsvo Ministersva Oborony SSSR, 1965); M. M. Kirian, "Vnezapnost'," *Sovetskaya Voennaia Entsiklopedia*, Vol. 2 (Moscow: Voenno Izdatelsvo Ministersva Oborony SSSR, 1976); V. A. Efimov and S. G. Chemashentsev, "Maskirovka," *Sovetskaya Voennaia Entsiklopedia*, Vol. 5 (Moscow: Voenno Izdatelsvo Ministersva Oborony SSSR, 1976). See also David M. Glantz, *Soviet Military Deception in the Second World War* (London: Frank Cass, 1989).

37 *The Big Two: Soviet-American Perception of Foreign Policy* (New York: Pegasus, 1971), p. 183.

38 *The Wall Street Journal*, October 24, 1962.

39 I vividly remember that the soldiers manning the antiaircraft guns were very young.

40 See Mark Lloyd, *The Art of Military Deception* (London, Leo Cooper, 1997), p. 122.

41 Lloyd, *The Art of Military Deception*, p. 123. In *Russia Has Wooden Missiles!*, a provoking video of a conference given by A. Ralph Epperson in 1988, he mentions, among other interesting facts, that, on November 17, 1985, he interviewed Abraham Shifrin, ex-chief advisor for the Soviet Ministry of Defense, at the time a Russian emigré living in Israel. Shifrin told him that he had heard from other Russian Jews that most ICBM silos in the forests of Krasnoyarski Kai and other places were faked. Such silos had been deliberately camouflaged less carefully, so that they would not be missed by the American surveillance planes and satellites. Shifrin is not the only who heard such rumors. Georgi Arbatov, of the U.S.-Canada Institute in Moscow, mentioned having heard that the Soviets had "phony missile launch sites" and inflatable dummies of submarines. See, Beschloss, *The Crisis Years*, p. 372. There are reasons for believing that the rumors were true. During WWII the Soviets built a huge factory hidden in the Ural mountains, solely dedicated to the production of all types of military dummies and decoys.

42 See Viktor Suvorov (pseud.) *Inside the Soviet Army* (New York: Berkley Books, 1983), p. 69. For unknown reasons, the American intelligence services have apparently ignored the important place deception plays in warfare, particularly strategic deception.

In the mid-1980s, however, Kenneth de Graffenreid, the National Security Council staffer on intelligence specialized in counterintelligence, turned his attention to CCD (Camouflage, Concealment and Deception), a new-fad hypothesis which focused in the Soviets' efforts to deceive. De Graffenreid wanted to study the possibility that some of the data collected by American technical means, particularly satellite imagery and communications intercepts, could have been part of a vast Soviet hoax. He argued that it was logical that the Soviets had conducted deception operations, but the U.S. had never uncovered one. Therefore, he concluded, it was important to examine the possibility that some larger, successful deception may have been under way and had been missed. See, Bob Woodward, *Veil: The Secret Wars of the CIA, 1981-1987* (New York: Pocket Books, 1987), p. 219. Not surprisingly, de Graffenreid made a lot of enemies in the intelligence community, among them Bobby Ray Inman, the National Security Agency director.

43 *Pravda*, July 10, 1960. Translated in *Current Digest of the Soviet Press*, August 10, 1960, p. 5 (emphasis added).

44 See, Ronald R. Pope, *Soviet Foreign Affairs Specialists: An Evaluation of their Direct and Indirect Impact on Soviet Foreign Policy Decision-Making Based on their Analysis of Cuba, 19581961, and Chile, 1969-1973*, Ph.D. Dissertation, University of Pennsylvania, 1975, pp. 64-65, 111-112.

45 Quoted in Alexander Werth, *Russia Under Khrushchev* (New York: Fawcett, 1961), p. 319.

46 Robert D. Crassweller, *Cuba and the U.S.* (Headline Series) (New York: Foreign Policy Association, October 1971), p. 23.

47 See Carlos Franqui, *Family Portrait with Fidel* (New York: Random House, 1984), p. 185.

48 The *New York Times*, November 19, 1960, p. 1.

49 *NYT*, November 23, 1960, p. 11.

50 *The Nuclear Question: The United States and Nuclear Weapons, 1946-1976* (London: Cambridge University Press, 1979), p. 105.

51 Paul Bracken, *The Command and Control of Nuclear Forces* (New Haven: Yale University Press, 1983), p. 92. The perception of missiles as phallic symbols is evidenced in the title of Helen Caldicott's book *Missile Envy* (New York: Bantam, 1986).

52 Sir David Ormsby-Gore to Prime Minister Harold Macmillan, October 23, 1962, Public Records Office, Kew, England, quoted in Aleksandr Fursenko and Timothy Naftali, *"One Hell of a Gamble": Khrushchev, Castro, and Kennedy 1958-1964* (New York: W.W. Norton, 1997), p. 236.

53 Secretary of State McNamara testified that the program to remove the obsolete Thor and Jupiter missiles dated from early 1961. See *Defense Intelligence Agency,*

Department of Defense Appropriations for 1964, Hearing Before a Subcommittee of the Committee on Appropriations, House of Representatives, 88 Congress, 1st Session (Washington D.C., 1963), Part I, p. 57.

54 Castro himself discovered some years later that Che Guevara's symbol was more useful and less risky than the real Che.

55 Eco, *A Theory of Semiotics*, p. 7.

56 In the lingo of intelligence and espionage, the word notional is used to design things that only exist in your opponent's mind. A notional mole, for example, is sometimes more useful than a real one. The main advantage over the real one is that the notional mole is impossible to discover for the very reason that it does not exist. Some people have speculated that Angleton's search for a Soviet mole inside the KGB, which eventually cost him his career and almost destroyed the CIA, was actually a wild goose chase after a notional one. See Ron Rosenbaum, "The Shadow of the Mole," *Harper's*, October, 1983.

57 See Seymour Reit, *Masquerade: The Amazing Camouflage Deceptions of World War II* (New York: Signet, 1978; also Martin Young and Robbie Stamp, *Trojan Horses: Deception Operations in the Second World War* (London: Mandarin, 1991).

58 The whole story is told in detail in Sefton Delmer, *The Counterfeit Spy* (New York: Harper & Row, 1971).

59 On October 16, Bundy briefly raised the issue of whether the Soviet leaders were bluffing about the nuclear warheads. See Marc Trachtenberg, ed. "White House Tapes and Minutes of the Cuban Missile Crisis: Ex Comm Meetings, October 1962," *International Security*, 10/1 (Summer 1985), note 13, p. 178.

60 At a morning Ex Comm meeting on 17 October, Gen. Taylor and George Ball expressed some doubts about the missiles and wondered if they might be a Soviet deception to provoke the U.S. into some sort of action. Their speculation was quickly rejected by the majority of the Ex Comm members. See MacCone's notes on the morning Ex Comm meeting of 17 October in Mary S. McAuliffe, ed., *CIA Documents on the Cuban Missile Crisis* (Washington, D.C.: Central Intelligence Agency History Staff, 1992), note 6, p. 159.

61 The need for tradecraft tests to evaluate the authenticity of information is expressed in Central Intelligence Agency, *A Compendium of Tradecraft Notes*, Volume I, Washington D.C., February 1997, Note 10, Tradecraft and Counterintelligence.

62 See Central Intelligence Agency, *A Compendium of Tradecraft Notes*, Volume I, Washington D.C., February 1997, Note 10, Tradecraft and Counterintelligence.

63 "The Cuban Missile Crisis of 1962: Presenting the Photographic Evidence Abroad," *Studies in Intelligence*, Spring 1972.

64 Amazingly, the American military who had boarded and inspected the *Marucla*, a cargo ship bound to Cuba which they positively knew was carrying no military matériel, abstained themselves to board and inspect the Soviet ships who allegedly were bringing the missiles and their warheads back to the Soviet Union. Another mystery to add to the long list of mysteries surrounding the Cuban missile crisis.

On the other hand, one can only imagine the scenario of an American search team boarding a Soviet ship only to find out that the missiles and their warheads were actually decoys. The U.S. would have instantly become the laughing stock of the whole world.

65 See Anatoli Gribkov and William Smith, *Operation Anadyr* (Chicago: Edition q, 1994), pp. 139-40.

66 See, i. e., Edward G. Shirley, "Can't anybody Here Play This Game?," *The Atlantic Monthly*, February 1998, pp. 45-61.

67 Recently declassified articles from CIA's secretive publication *Studies in Intelligence* show an extremely high level of scholarly work and competence. Even more surprising, they show an unexpected freedom of opinion and criticism of the Agency's own operation. For a collection of recently declassified articles originally appeared in *Studies in Intelligence*, see, H. Bradford Westerfield, *Inside CIA's Private World* (New Haven: Yale University Press, 1995). Other declassified articles are available on-line at the Center for the Study of Intelligence.

68 I am not mentioning here the claims that Soviet officers in Cuba in 1962 had been authorized to use tactical nuclear weapons at their discretion, without direct orders from the Kremlin. Even if a mountain of declassified Soviet documents were provided as proof (not a single one, to this moment), one has to be very gullible not to laugh in the face of anybody making such a far-fetched claim.

69 Neal D. Houghton, ed., *Struggle Against History* (New York: Clarion, 1968).

70 "Meme" (pronounced to rhyme with "gene") is a neologism, coined by analogy to "gene," by zoologist Richard Dawkins in his book *The Selfish Gene* (New York: Oxford University Press, 1976). Dawkins defines a meme as a replicating information pattern that uses minds to get itself copies into other minds, in a virus-like fashion.

The meme is the basic unit of replication and selection in the ideosphere. According to Dawkins, memes, like viruses of the mind, float about in the soup of human culture where they grow, replicate, mutate, compete, or become extinct. As Nazism and Marxism have shown, however, a meme doesn't need to be true to be powerful.

71 James G. Blight, Bruce J. Allyn, and David A. Welch, "Kramer VS. Kramer: Or, How Can You Have Revisionism in the Absence of Orthodoxy?" *Cold War International History Bulletin* No. 3 (Fall 1993), p. 41.

Chapter Eleven

1 See Raymond L. Garthoff, "The Havana Conference On the Cuban Missile Crisis: Tactical Weapons Disclosure Stuns Gathering," *Cold War International History Project Electronic Bulletin*, No. 1 (Spring 1992).

2 Lilliam Riera, "Cuban Missile Crisis: A Political Vision 40 Years Later," *Granma Internacional Digital*, English Edition, June 21, 2002. Also "Cuba to Declassify Documents on Cuban Missile Crisis," *Sun-Sentinel*, June 13, 2002.

3 Garthoff, "The Havana Conference."

4 I am not using the term "liar" in a pejorative sense, but just to indicate that, as it is expected from seasoned intelligence professionals, lies and disinformation are essential aspects of their profession. As a matter of fact, learning how to lie convincingly is an important part of the training of intelligence officers all around the world. Some of them, particularly the Soviets and Cubans, have made an art of beating the polygraph (commonly known as lie detector).

5 Jefferson Mack, *Running a Ring of Spies: Spycraft and Black Operations in the Real World of Espionage* (Boulder, Colorado: Paladin Press, 1996), p. 51.

6 *Cold War International History Electronic Bulletin*, No. 4 (Fall 1994)

7 Zubok, "Spy VS. Spy,"*Cold War International History Electronic Bulletin*, No. 4 (Fall 1994).

8 Alexandr Ivanovich Alexeev arrived in Havana in November 1959, less than a year after Fidel Castro took power in Cuba, ostensibly as a correspondent for the Soviet *TASS* agency. But Alexeev, whose real name is Alexandr I. Shitov, had other duties to perform. He was also a senior KGB officer with a long, successful career. As a Soviet intelligence officer Alexeev had been previously deployed, under different covers, in France (1946-51), the Netherlands (1951-54), and finally in Argentina (1954-58). References to Shitov's career in John Barron, *KGB* (London: Corgi, 1974), 534.

9 See "The Crisis and Cuban-Soviet Relations: Fidel Castro's Secret 1968 Speech," *Cold War International Project Electronic Bulletin*, No. 5 (Spring 1995).

10 See Marcelo Fernández-Zayas, "Once Inside Never Out," *Intelligence Report From Washington*, 14 (March 21, 2001).

11 Former CIA officer David Atlee Philips mentions how, on joining the Agency, he "signed the Secrecy Oath, a covenant required of all CIA personnel; it bound one not to reveal, even after resignation or retirement, classified information learned while working for United States intelligence." See *The Night Watch* (New York: Ballantine, 1977), p. 72.

Ex-CIA officer Frank Snepp made the mistake of writing a book, *Decent Interval*, about the fall of Saigon. Though the book was based entirely on unclassified materials, the CIA took reprisals and moved in to punish him. The Justice Department, on CIA's behalf, sued Snepp for violation of his oath, managing to deprive him from all his book's earnings and obtaining a gag on him, allowing the CIA to censorship all his writings, including fiction works, with the exception of cook and gardening books. Many years later, Snepp told his ordeal in detail in his memoirs, *Irreparable Harm* (New York: Random House, 1999).

12 As a critic of the *ad causam* methodology when applied to the analysis of intelligence events, I will not fall in my own trap by using it in this book, which deals mostly with spies and espionage. Therefore, I am consciously using the *ad hominem* methodology as a valid, scholarly alternative. If some of the scholars I mention in this paper feel upset because of my treatment, I would like to make it clear that I have no personal animosity against any of them. They should not expect,

however, to delve into the spy world and be dealt with as scholars. If some of them feel hurt and complain about my treatment, it will be further proof that they are too naïve to be involved with spies.

Conversely, in the case of the spies I mention in this paper no disclaimer is needed. My approach is standard operating procedure in the trade, and they, as practitioners of the second oldest profession, not only are used to it but take it for granted. Moreover, they don't feel any professional respect for people who don't treat them the way they expect to be treated.

13 Brenner and Wright, *Cold War International Project Electronic Bulletin*, No. 5 (Spring 1995). Their enthusiasm is evidenced in the overall tone of the paper, and also by the fact that, perhaps unconsciously, they have adopted Castro's discourse, i.e., calling the anti-Castro guerrillas in the Escambray mountains "counter-revolutionaries" and accepting at face value the tyrant's claims about saboteurs burning the fields —there is strong evidence that most of the acts of sabotage were orchestrated by Castro himself as self-provocations he used later to justify his anti-American policies. See, Servando González, *The Secret Fidel Castro*, pp. 89-93.

14 Just a perfunctory reading of Castro's speeches shows dozens of instances in which he has admitted a posteriori that he has lied. Mark Falcoff, an analyst of Castro's political behavior, pointed out that "the Cuban dictator is a liar who confesses the truth—retroactively." See "How to Think about Cuban-American Relations," in Irving Louis Horowitz, *Cuban Communism, Fifth Edition* (New Brunswick, N.J.: Transaction Books, 1984), 547.

15 See Appendix 1, The Evaluation of Information.

16 Though Gribkov's claims apparently have been accepted by the academic community at large, there is a notable exception. In his paper "Tactical Nuclear Weapons, Soviet Command Authority, and the Cuban Missile Crisis," *Cold War International History Project Bulletin*, No. 3 (Fall 1993), Professor Mark Kramer expertly "deconstructs" Gribkov's assertions and strongly criticizes the scholars who uncritically accepted Gribkov's claims. A rather incoherent and bland rebuttal of Kramer's analysis appeared in the same issue of the publication. See James G. Blight, Bruce J. Allyn, and David A. Welch, "Kramer VS. Kramer: Or, How Can You Have Revisionism in the Absence of Orthodoxy?," *Cold War International History Project Bulletin*, No. 3 (Fall 1993).

17 (London: Frank Cass,1998).

18 James G. Blight and David A. Welch, *Intelligence and the Cuban Missile Crisis* (London: Frank Cass,1998), p. 9.

19 I am talking here about a true defector, not a defector-in-place.

20 "Cuban Intelligence and the October Crisis," in James G. Blight and David A. Welch, *Intelligence and the Cuban Missile Crisis* (London: Frank Cass, 1998), n. 3, p. 112.

21 Contrary to the common usage in most communist countries, where they were called Political Commissars, political officers in the Cuban Army were called *"Instructores Revolucionarios"* (Revolutionary Instructors).

22 Ibid, n. 3, page 112.

23 Ibid, p. 95. (Emphasis added.)

24 Ibid, p. 100. (Emphasis added.)

25 Ibid, p. 95. (Emphasis added.)

26 Ibid, p. 102. (Emphasis added.)

27 Ibid, p. 118, n. 52. (Emphasis added.)

28 Ibid, p. 55, n. 3.

29 Ibid, p. 112, n. 3.

30 See, *Los Amos de Cuba* (Buenos Aires: Emecé Editores, 1982), p. 118. Vivés is a former officer of the Cuba intelligence who defected to France. His book originally appeared in French under the title *Les Maitres de Cuba* (Paris, Opera Mundi, 1981).

31 The fact that Castro's intelligence services have successfully penetrated most of the anti-Castro organizations in the U.S. has been extensively documented. According to Alfonso Tarabocchia, of Florida's Dade County sheriff's intelligence unit, "The [Cuban] exile community has been penetrated to the fullest degree." See also David Corn, *Blond Ghost* (New York: Simon and Schuster, 1994), p. 85. More recently, Juan O. Tamayo, a *Miami Herald* staff writer, reported that some people estimate Castro maintains about 300 trained intelligence officers on South Florida alone to spy on the Cuban exile community. See "Spies Among Us: Castro Agents Keep Eye on Exiles," the *Miami Herald*, April 11, 1999.

Since the mid-1990s, however, the Castro government implemented a new plan of penetration, in the cultural field, of the Cuban exile community. Some key figures of the Castroist intelligentsia have been allowed to move abroad, mostly to Spain, Mexico, and Venezuela, without breaking ties with the Castro government, and very quickly have reached prominent and influential positions. Among them are Lisandro Otero, now director of a section of *Excelsior*, one of the most important Mexican newspapers, and Daniuska González, whose articles frequently appear in the most important publications of Venezuela. See Angel Cuadra, "El gobierno cubano y sus planes contra el exilio," *Diario Las Américas* (electronic edition), November 27, 1998. Other prominent pseudo-defectors are Writers Norberto Fuentes, now living in exile in the U.S., and Jesús Díaz, editor of *Encuentro* magazine, who died mysteriously a few months ago in his apartment in Madrid. I will study the subject of the pseudo-defectors in detail in my forthcoming book, *¿Intelectuales o espías? Los servicios de inteligencia castristas en la batalla de las ideas*.

32 The CIA's definition of a defector is "an individual who has committed treason, a person who first accepted identification with a regime and then betrayed his allegiance to cooperate with a hostile intelligence service." See Wilhem Marbes, "Psychology of Treason," in H. Bradford Westerfield, ed., *Inside CIA's Private*

World: Declassified Articles From the Agency's Internal Journal, 1955-1992 (New Haven Connecticut: Yale University Press, 1995), p. 70.

33 See, Anya K. Landau and Wayne S. Smith, "Keeping Things in Perspective: Cuba and the Question of International Terrorism," *Center for International Policy*, November 6, 2001.

Chapter Twelve

1 Agents of influence: Suborned or ideologically committed people —not directly under control of an enemy intelligence organization, but willing to work for them— occupying positions within a country where they can affect policies or public opinion in favor of another country. Agents of influence usually are, or have access to, influential official and media leaders, though basically any person with the ability to influence public opinion could be a potential target for turning him into an agent of influence. For many years, Castro's intelligence services have mastered the art of recruiting and controlling agents of influence.

2 Living proof that a person can be both a noted scholar and a political idiot at the same time is the case of Arthur M. Schlesinger, Jr. Schlesinger was one of the American scholars who attended the meeting about the Cuban missile crisis in Havana in 1992. During one of the sessions at the end of the meeting, he criticized Castro for his treatment of dissidents, and mentioned the case of María Elena Cruz Varela, a Cuban poet in jail at the time. See Blight, Allyn, and Welch, *Cuba on the Brink*, p. 398.

In 1989, Varela had won Cuba's National Award for Poetry, a prize awarded to her by the Union of Cuban Writers. But in 1991, as Varela's dissident posture became widely known, the Union expelled her from its ranks. That same year, *Criterio Alternativo*, a group of Cuban intellectuals led by Varela, published a manifesto calling for democratic and economic reforms and denouncing the Castro government. A few days later some members of a Fast Action Brigade broke into her apartment and dragged her downstairs into the street, where they cursed and beat her. Then, they attempted to force her to eat a copy of her manifesto. Finally, the police, who had witnessed the whole event without intervening to stop it, arrested Varela and sent her to prison for two years. In any event, physical aggression against defenseless women, as in the Varela case, is a common occurrence in Castro's Cuba. See, i.e., Servando González, *The Secret Fidel Castro*, p. 283.

The infamous *Brigadas de Acción Rápida* (Fast Action Brigades), another of Castro's fascist abominations, are groups of government-sponsored gangs composed of thugs and common criminals, apparently inspired by Mussolini's street fighters, the *squadristi*. The Brigadas, were Castro's invention for the brutal repression of Cuban dissidents.

Schlesinger's lame criticism, however, was not motivated by the fact that a human being's human rights had been violated in the most outrageous way by a tyrannical government. No. His main concern, according to his own words, was that, by not committing these type of actions, Castro "... would in turn make it easier for those in the U.S. who want what I believe you and Cuba want, which is rapprochement with the U.S. and the lifting of the anachronistic embargo." See Blight, Allyn, and Welch, *Cuba on the Brink*, p. 399.

Apparently Castro was so surprised by such an extemporaneous criticism that he could not find a good answer to it. Used to order the killing of people by the hundreds, forcing a poet to eat her poems may look like an insignificant act. But, true to his role as Cuba's absolute King, he cannot let pass unchecked Schlesinger's impertinence and seized the opportunity to make a not-so-veiled threat: "You know, Professor Schlesinger, you say we have taken a hard line, that we permit no dissent from some supposed "line" that must be followed. But let us take your own case. We have not arrested you, in spite of what you have said. We have not mistreated you in any way, in spite of your having accused Cuba of being —I believe you said we are "uncivilized," or words to that effect. In fact, we are very tolerant here, very tolerant! We are often criticized for being *too* tolerant!" Blight, Allyn, and Welch, *Cuba on the Brink*, pp. 398-399. I am sure that Dr. Schlesinger, and perhaps some other American participants in the meeting, had trouble falling sleep that night.

Moreover, Schlesinger's mentioning of rapprochement with the U.S. and the lifting of the embargo as the things Castro want, when these are precisely the ones the Cuban tyrant does *not* want, must have confirmed Castro's poor opinion of his American friends. No wonder in Castro's inner circle his leftist and liberal supporters, particularly the American ones, are commonly called *comemierdas* (literally "shit eaters").

3 See, i.e., James G. Blight and David A. Welch, *On the Brink: Americans and Soviets Reexamine the Cuban Missile Crisis* (New York: Farrar, Strauss, 1989, (rev. ed., Noonday Press, 1990); James J. Blight, *The Shattered Crystal Ball: Fear and Learning in the Cuban Missile Crisis* (Savage, MD: Rowman and Littlefield, 1990); James G. Blight, Bruce J. Allyn, and David A. Welch, *Cuba on the Brink: Castro, the Missile Crisis and the Soviet Collapse* (New York: Pantheon Books, 1993); Bruce J. Allyn, James G. Blight, and David Al Welch, eds., *Back to the Brink: Proceeding of the Moscow Conference on the Cuban Missile Crisis, January 27-28, 1989*, CSIA Occasional Paper no. 9, Lathan, Md.: University Press of America, 1992; and James G. Blight and David A Welch, eds., *Intelligence and the Cuban Missile Crisis* (London: Frank Cass, 1998), just to name a few. Among their many articles are Allyn, Blight, and Welch, "Essence of Revision: Moscow Havana and the Cuban Missile Crisis," *International Security*, 1989/1990 (vol. 14, no. 3), pp. 136-172.

4 Among the ex-intelligence officers who have participated in some of the meetings about the Cuban missile crisis are Samuel Halpern, Ray Cline, Robert Reynolds, Fabián Escalante, Sergio del Valle, Alexandr (Shitov) Alexeev, Nikolai Leonov, Fyodor Burlatsky, Georgi Bolshakov, and Sergo Mikoyan, just to mention a few.

5 David N. Gibbs, "Academic and Spies: The Silence That Roars," *Los Angeles Times*, January 28, 2001. Other books that had dealt recently with the subject are Robin Winks, *Cloak and Gown* (New York: William Morrow, 1987); and Frances Stonor Saunders, *Who Paid The Piper?: The CIA and the Cultural Cold War* (London: Granta, 1999).

6 See. i.e., Sigmund Diamond, *Compromise Campus: The Collaboration of Universities with the Intelligence Community, 1945-1955* (New York: Oxford University Press, 1992); also Robert Witanek, "The CIA on Campus," *Covert Action Information Bulletin*, Winter 1989, pp. 25-28; Ernest Volkman, "Spies on Campus," *Penthouse*, October 1979; also Warren Hinckle, Robert Scheer, and Sol Stern, "The University on the Make," *Ramparts*, April 1966.

7 David Price, "Anthropologists as Spies," *The Nation*, November 20, 2000, p. 24.

8 Price, "Academic and Spies", p. 26.

9 Chris Mooney, "For Your Eyes Only: The CIA Will Let You See Classified Documents —But at What Price?," *Lingua Franca*, November 2000, pp. 35-43.

10 Most likely CIA lingo for recruiting in the academic field.

11 Mooney, "For Your Eyes Only", p. 35.

12 Gibbs, "Academic and Spies."

13 E-mail from ownerrpalist@southwestern.edu, February 3, 2001, disseminating an original message from fboyle@lawuiuc.edu.

14 This is, for example, the case of Frances Stonor Saunders' *Who Paid the Piper? The CIA and the Cultural Cold War* (London: Granta, 1999), a hypocritical book full of moral indignation against the CIA. As expected, no mention is made of similar activities conducted by the KGB or other intelligence services. For an interesting review of the book see Peregrine Worsthorne, "How Western Culture Was Saved by the CIA," *Literary Review*, July 1999.

15 Blight and Welch, *On the Brink*, p. xvi.

16 Background information on CEA in Pablo Alfonso, "Cuba hizo purga contra académicos," *El Nuevo Herald*, May 4, 2002; Orlando Pérez, "Dirigentes cubanos endurecen la línea," *Revista del Sur*, June 1996. The CEA's purge is the subject of *El caso CEA*, a book by Italian author Maurizio Giuliano.

17 For a revealing view of KGB's recruiting efforts and techniques, see Christopher Andrew and Oleg Gordievsky, *Comrade Kryushkov's Instructions: Top Secret Files on KGB Foreign Operations, 1975-1985* (Stanford, California: Stanford University Press, 1993), 29-51.

18 I am not trying to demonize Cuba or Russia. The CIA, Mossad, and other Western intelligence services keep an eye on foreign scholars visiting their countries, and work hard in trying to recruit them —successfully in many cases.

19 As an example of this I can cite the case of Wayne S. Smith, whom an observer of Cuban events called "the dean of Fidel Castro's American apologists." See Charles Lane, "TRB From Washington: Fidel and Mr. Smith," *The New Republic*, March 25, 1996.

Smith represented President Carter's administration when it opened a U.S. Interests Section in Havana. At the time, this was seen as a first step in the "normalization" of relations with Cuba. Smith's tenure at the U. S. Interest Section in Havana was characterized by a total contempt for the suffering of the hundreds of Cubans desperately trying to obtain visas to leave the country as well as by his friendly attitude towards the Cuban tyrant.

After meeting Castro, Mr. Smith became a strong supporter of his regime and, after he ended his tenure as a diplomat in Havana, was often seen on *CNN*'s Crossfire and other talk shows, usually advocating that the U.S. extend diplomatic recognition to the Castro government. But, during one of his heated arguments in favor of Castro, Smith made the mistake of badmouthing the Cuban American National Foundation, and its chair, Jorge Más Canosa, decided to fight back, bringing him to court and accusing him of defamation —a case Canosa easily won. But, during the trial, some interesting details about Smith came to light.

According to documents made public during the trial, Smith, as a diplomat in the 1960's, was approached by the Soviet intelligence services in an effort to recruit him into spying for the Soviet Union. Apparently Mr. Smith had some sexual inclination the KGB considered exploitable, and they tried to use it as leverage to recruit him. Allegedly Smith immediately reported the Soviet's recruiting attempt to the State Department and avoided being fired. There is the possibility, however, that Castro's intelligence services may have done a better job than the KGB, and Castro got an ally for life. Soviets trying to recruit Wayne Smith as an agent in Soren Triff, "Los extremists en la academia," *El Nuevo Herald*, August 22, 1996.

In a long answer to Triff's article, Smith tried his best to disprove Triff's allegations one by one —most of them resorting to arguments *"ad hominem."* But there was an important exception: no mention is made to Triff's assertion that the Soviet intelligence services tried to recruit Smith using his sexual proclivities as leverage. See Wayne Smith, "Mi respuesta a Soren Triff," *El Nuevo Herald*, September 1, 1996.

In Cuba prostitution and homosexuality are criminal offenses that can bring jail terms. This may explain the sudden conversion to Castroism of some scholars, writers, journalists, tv anchors, film makers, actors, UNESCO officials, businessmen and politicians, after visiting Castro's Cuba. On Cuban intelligence sexual blackmailing activities, particularly the ones directed against personnel of the U.S. Interests Section in Havana, see Norberto Fuentes, *Dulces Guerreros cubanos* (Barcelona: Seix Barral, 1999), pp. 132-133.

Smith's name popped up again in connection with Castro's intelligence services during the case of Ana Belen Montes, a Defense Intelligence Agency senior analyst for Cuban issues who pleaded guilty on charges of spying for Castro. According to information appeared on the press, Montes was member of an unofficial study group at Georgetown University, of which Smith also was member. Smith was also quoted as saying "One of the Cubans at the Interest Section was saying the other day, 'you have people you run [as spies] in Cuba, We have to know what your plans are. We have to know what kind of operations you are running against us.'" See Larry Daley, "Did Castro's Pentagon Spy have Help, Details, Assessment of Damage, and Who Was Helping Her Get These Fast Promotions." www.amigos-pais-guaracabuya.org. It is a know fact that most Cuban diplomats, particularly the ones assigned to the U.S., are intelligence officers. The fact that Mr. Smith was able to overheard one of them saying something, indicates that he is in friendly terms with some of Castro's intelligence officers in the U.S.

20 There is no such thing as a "retired" intelligence officer. Once a spy, forever a spy.

21 As a senior Soviet intelligence officer deployed in the field, Alekseev's main mission in Havana was to act as control to run self-recruited "agent" Fidel Castro. Alekseev, however, proved to be incapable of running Castro, who was not only running himself but sometimes seemed to be the one actually running Alekseev. Reports began piling up in KGB files informing that the Soviet intelligence officer had even become Castro's personal friend. They had been seen drinking and womanizing together and apparently Alekseev had fallen under the spell of the Cuban leader. See Arkady N. Shevchenko, *Breaking with Moscow* (New York: Ballantine, 1985), 187.

Alekseev, one of the first Soviet officials to meet Castro in 1959, recalls that during their first meeting he was very much taken aback by Castro's ability to quote Marx, Engels and Lenin by heart. Alekseev's surprise was total, because the information he had been given in Moscow about Castro firmly stated that he was not a Communist and that his knowledge of Marxism was very limited. What Alekseev ignored was that, in order to fool him as he has done to many others, the previous night Castro had spent several hours reading whole chapters of books by Marx, Engels and Lenin. Thanks to Castro's prodigious photographic memory, he just regurgitated whole chunks of Marxist texts. On castro's eidetic or photographic memory, see Servando González, *The Secret Fidel Castro*, pp. 164-165.

Alexeev, however, was not the only Soviet to fall under Castro's power of fascination. In April 13th, 1990, Gorbachev's envoy Leonid Abalkin arrived in Havana to discuss new economic terms with the Cubans. Abalkin, deputy chairman of the Soviet Union's Council of Ministers, was a reformist economist known for his drastic views about a substantial cut in Soviet aid to Cuba. But Castro gave him the royal treatment and the tough Abalkin inexplicably mellowed his attitude substantially. According to witnesses, Fidel never left Abalkin's side, using all his powers of persuasion to convince him that Cuba had a great economic potential and a lot to offer the Soviet Union. Abalkin's visit ended with the signing of a one-year trade protocol for 1990 that was incredibly better than the one the Russians had in mind. Yuri Pavlov, the Soviet Foreign Ministry's Latin American Department director at the time, had an explanation for what happened to Abalkin in Cuba: "Fidel charmed him. The agreement Abalkin came back with was seen by us as unrealistic." See Andres Oppenheimer, *Castro's Final Hour* (New York: Simon & Schuster, 1992), 236-237.

Proof that Castro's mesmerizing abilities are strong is that he used them to win a seemingly unapproachable Russian character. According to Ken Alibek, a Soviet Colonel who was in charge of developing bacteriological weapons for the Soviet Union, Premier Leonid Brezhnev was the one who provided Castro with the necessary technology to produce bacteriological weapons. Alibek recalls that most Soviet officers were against providing Castro with the technology, but Brezhnev "was in love with Castro," and authorized the technology transfers. See Roberto Fabricio, "Las instalaciones cubanas de biotecnología `están llenas de zonas cerradas y secretas'" *El Nuevo Herald*, June 20 1999.

22 See, "Havana's Linda Tripp?," *NewsMax.com*, April 24, 2002. According to the article, there is the possibility that any calls Clinton made to Castro during the Elián González affair may have been recorded by the Cuban tyrant. If this is true, the article suggests, "The answer to why Clinton threw his legacy away over Elián may ultimately reside in Fidel's audio library."

23 It is a well-known fact in the intelligence business that the best agent is the one who doesn't know he has been recruited. As a typical example I can mention the case of Peter Kornbluh, a leftwinger who has an active role in the National Security Archive. Kornbluh was the chief organizer of a meeting in Cuba to discuss the Bay of Pigs invasion. This was the overt purpose. The covert one, according to a critic, was trumpeting Castro's genius and vilifying America.

During the Havana meeting, the Castro government offered to the participants a scoop of newly declassified documents about the invasion. But a few days after the end of the meeting, Miguel Angel Sánchez, a Cuban writer now in exile in the U.S., discovered that all of the allegedly declassified documents had been already published in his book *Girón no fue sólo en abril* (La Habana: Editorial Orbe, 1979). See, Wilfredo Cancio Isla, "Las 'revelaciones' de Castro son una farsa," *El Nuevo Herald*, April 1, 2001. It seems, therefore, that a main characteristic of these meetings is that what has been offered to participants as true is not new, and what is new is not true.

Some Castro-friendly authors have been making an extraordinary effort trying to prove that, far from hating Kennedy, at the time of the assassination Castro actually had begun an effort to seek an accommodation with the U.S. See Peter Kornbluh and James Blight, "Our Secret Dialogue With Castro: A Hidden History," *The New York Times Review of Books*, October 6, 1994. For a detailed account of how this alleged accommodation never took place see Carlos Ripoll, "Kennedy y Castro: el abrazo imposible," www.eddosrios.org/obras/politica/kennedy.htm.

A typical example of this type of argument is Peter Kornbluh's "JFK & Castro: The Secret Quest for Accommodation," *Cigar Aficionado*, September/October 1999. To support his thesis, Kornbluh brings a series of declassified documents showing that, unbeknownst to all but his brother and a few close advisors, President Kennedy had begun in 1963 a secret path towards a rapprochement with Castro. Kornbluh also offers some declassified documents proving that Castro had made some overtures in the same direction.

Apart from the inconsistencies between those documents and the actual behavior of Castro and the Kennedys, Kornbluh's article is too close for comfort to the official Castroist line developed by the Cuban intelligence services. Both Carlos Lechuga, a former Cuban ambassador to the U.N., and Fabián Escalante, a senior counterintelligence officer, have been producing this type of disinformation for many years.

Moreover, Kornbluh's article is reminiscent of the main theme of a disinformation campaign orchestrated by the Soviet intelligence services in the late 1970s. In 1977, for example, the Soviet *New Times*, a KGB chosen vehicle for spreading disinformation abroad, published a two-part lengthy article accusing the CIA and the military of being the "sinister forces" behind the President's assassination. See "On the Trail of a President's Killers," *New Times*, No. 2, 1977, pp. 26-30. Kornbluh's article may have been a case of protracted blowback.

In his article Kornbluh admits that "John F. Kennedy would seem the most unlikely of presidents to seek an accommodation with Fidel Castro." I fully agree. The reason for this, which Kornbluh seems to ignore, is because at the time of his alleged moves to rapprochement, JFK and his brother actually were aggressively planning the assassination of Fidel Castro, a fact that not even a thousand dubious declassified documents can deny.

Kornbluh has also written a book and several papers and articles about the Bay of Pigs invasion. As expected his point of view is totally slanted to offer a distorted, Castro-friendly vision of the event. Some people have interpreted Kornbluh's love for Castro as a proof of the power of the Cuban tyrant's charisma. Granted, there is a possibility that Kornbluh may just be a bleeding heart liberal who sincerely believes Castro is a true anti-American hero. But there is also the possibility that he has been recruited by Castro's intelligence services.

But proving that Kornbluh is or is not one of Castro's agents of influence is irrelevant. He writes like one, speaks like one, and acts like one, therefore, to all practical effects it is safe to assume that either he has been, wittingly or unwittingly, recruited by Castro's intelligence services or, even worse, he recruited himself. See, Ronald Radosh, "Human Rights and Foreign Policy: How to Deal with the Totalitarian Remnant," FrontPageMagazine.com, March 27, 2001; also "Richard Cohen Reminds the Left Why Castro Must Go," Publications of the Center for Security Policy, No. 01-F 25, March 27, 2001.

24 Eugenio Rodríguez Chaple, "El espía que me amó," *Interview* (Spain), No. 1,298, March 12, 2001.

25 Daniel James, "Castro Plan to Destabilize U.S. May Be Broadening," the *Chicago Tribune*, August 23, 1981.

26 James, "Castro Plan to Destabilize." This information has been corroborated by other defectors, among them Delfín Fernández, and Jorge Masetti.

27 Jorge Massetti, *El furor y el delirio: Itinerario de un hijo de la Revolución cubana* (Barcelona: Tusquets, 1999), p. 68.

28 Homosexuality in Castro's Cuba, as mentioned in article 203 of the Cuban Penal Code, is a criminal act punishable with up to one year in prison.

29 Swallows: beautiful women sexually trained to entrap any men whom an intelligence service wants to blackmail.

30 Ravens: attractive men used to sexually entrap women for blackmailing purposes.

31 Quiet ones: homosexuals used for homosexual entrapment and subsequent blackmail. The long list of homosexuals involved in spy scandals is a proof of the effectivity of this technique.

32 According to Norberto Fuentes, every important visitor who has visited Cuba, *without exception*, has a dossier and compromising videos at the Villa Marista vaults. *Dulces guerreros*, p. 133. (emphasis in the original).

33 Norberto Fuentes, *Dulces guerreros cubanos* (Barcelona: Seix Barral, 1999), p. 132-133. According to Fuentes, Castro enjoys watching the tapes, particularly of important people, not because of the sexual images but just because of the bits of gossip he may obtain from them. According to some sources, most hotels catering for foreign tourists have several rooms rigged for secret recording of video, audio and even infrared pictures. Among the main ones are: Habana Libre (ex-Hilton), 10 floors with 200 rooms; Riviera, 3 floors with 50 rooms; Capri, 6 floors with 85 rooms. Most of the rooms of the Nacional and Deauville hotels, which cater only for tourists, as well as most hotels in Varadero beach, are part of the extensive secret surveillance system.

34 The story was told by Delfín Fernández (Otto), an officer of Castro's intelligence service who defected to Spain in early 2001. See "Prensa en España revela operativo de inteligencia cubana contra personas conocidas y sus relaciones sexuales en Cuba," Madrid, March 15, 2001, *CNB*.

35 Some tradecraft experts argue that there is only one motivation that really matters, and that is ego. That is what leads someone to become a spy, to defect, to betray his country. He may rationalize it in other terms. He may see himself as serving a higher cause. Or he may think he wants all the money he's been promised. But these are merely conscious expressions of something deeper. Ideology is not a deep motive. It may be how an agent rationalizes his treason, but the real motivation is something more basic, involving response to authority, superiority complex or fear that his moment of weakness, now preserved on tape, may be revealed. Due to their inflated egos, scholars, university professors, writers, artists and intellectuals in general are easy prey for trained recruiters.

The approach in the recruiting process, however, is dictated by the characteristics of the target. If he is an out-and-out rogue, willing to betray his country or his organization just for money, the questions to be resolved are only "How much?" and "How?" But even the allegedly ideologically motivated agent is first persuaded to accept expenses, then "payment for your time." Some intelligence services, like the CIA and the KGB, are very strict in enforcing the pay principle. They believe that an agent who works without being paid may feel too independent and can give up his spying activities whenever he wants, or he may reconsider his decision and reveal his activities to the authorities, minimizing his guilt by stressing his "idealistic motives."

A paid agent, however modest his remuneration, becomes a serving person, a subordinate, a dependent individual. He is expected to follow orders, to be humble, obedient, and silent; his decision and moves must be discussed and approved before he can take any action; receipts bearing his signature, or video recordings of him receiving the money, can be produced and used to coerce him if he should try to desert the recruiting service. Once he is paid, he is hooked firmly in the hands of his employer.

Contrary to most intelligence services, however, the Cubans boast that ideology, not money, has always been their most powerful recruiting tool. The case of Ana Belén Montes, Castro's spy inside the Defense Intelligence Agency, is a proof that their technique works.

Showing a large amount of stupidity incredible for a seasoned KGB officer, soon after meeting Castro for the first time Alexeev tried to recruit him. The process, as described by Alexeev himself in detail to his bosses in Moscow, shows a by-the-book recruiting approach as specified in KGB standard tradecraft practices. See, Fursenko and Naftali, *"One Hell of a Gamble,"* p. 45. According to Alexeev's own recollection, Castro had the time of his life making fun of the Russian fool. Eventually, it was Castro who made rings around the inept KGB spy and recruited Alexeev, who apparently saw himself as serving a higher cause.

The funny part of the story is that there are indications that Castro actually recruited Alexeev under a false flag, a technique by which an ideologically motivated individual is recruited by an agent of an intelligence service posing as a member of a rival organization. I will study the Alexeev case in detail in my forthcoming book *Fidel Castro Supermole: Walking Back the Cat in the Cuban Operation.*

36 www.gwu.edu/~nsarchive/nsa/cuba_mis_cri/declass.html.

37 This, of course, is no surprise. Paradoxically, the American Left has always been indirectly bankrolled by the most reactionary elements of the Right. See, i.e., Evan Gahr, "Looking at Philanthropy — The Gift of Giving: Paymasters of the PC Brigades," *The Wall Street Journal*, Jan 27, 1995; Joyce Price, "Media Give Liberal Causes Millions More, Study Says," *The Washington Times*, Nov. 14. 1993; Marshall Robinson, "The Ford Foundation: Sowing the Seeds of a Revolution." Environment, v. 35 n. 3 (April 1993) 10-20; Goldie Blumenstyk, "New Head of Ford Fund's Education Program is Champion of Women and Minority Students," *The Chronicle of Higher Education*, v. 39 n. 16 (Dec 9, 1992), A27; Daniel Brandt, "Philanthropists at War," NameBase NewsLine, No. 15 (October-December, 1996). The fact perhaps explains why the American Left is perhaps one of the most reactionary Lefts in the world. Of course, they see themselves as "progressives."

38 I refuse to use the word "democratic" when I mention the Democratic Party because, as it fits to this era of semantic deception, the Democratic Party is not democratic. Moreover, I think that it is time to begin talking about the Repucrat (or Demoblican, if you wish) party, the one that truly controls American politics.

39 Unfortunately, even serious scholars apparently believe that the National Security Archive is in possession of the actual documents. After mentioning some documents, Richard Ned Lebow affirms that, "All documents, unless otherwise noted, are found in the National Security Archive." See, Richard Ned Lebow and Janice Gross Stein, *We All Lost the Cold War* (Princeton, N.J.: Princeton University Press, 1994), p. 377, note 9.

40 Some of the documents show deleted areas, so one can safely guess that the deletions have been made on copies, not on the originals.

41 Ellsberg quoted in Michael Parenti, *History as Mystery* (San Francisco: City Lights, 1999), p. 153.

42 "What can Intelligence tell us about the Cuban missile crisis, and what the Cuban missile crisis tell us about Intelligence?," in James G. Blight and David A Welch, eds., *Intelligence and the Cuban missile crisis* (London: Frank Cass, 1998), p. 3.

43 Fidel Castro in interview with Claude Julien, *Le Monde*, 22 March 1963.

44 In 1973, during the investigations of the Watergate scandal, E. Howard Hunt, one of the burglars, was questioned about his forgery of a State Department cable linking the Kennedy administration to the assassination of President Ngo Dinh Diem of South Vietnam. Hunt told the federal prosecutor that he had been given some training in his past CIA career to do just this sort of thing "... floating forged newspapers accounts, telegrams, that sort of thing." Victor Marchetti and John D. Marks, *The CIA and the Cult of Intelligence* (New York: Dell, 1974), p. 170.

In his book *The Master of Disguise: My Secret Life in the CIA* (New York: William Morrow, 1999), ex-CIA officer Antonio Mendez offers a candid behind-the-scenes view of his career as CIA's foremost specialist in disguises. He also explains in some detail the artistic abilities and state-of-art techniques to forge official documents.

45 See, "Anti-Fraud Agency Fakes Documents," *Associated Press,* Washington, June 5, 2001.

46 Ladislav Bittman, *The KGB and Soviet Disinformation* (Washington, D.C.: Pergamon-Brassey's, 1985). See particularly Chapter 5, The Art of Forgery, pp. 91-107. See also "Soviet Covert Action: The Forgery Initiative," *Hearings Before the Subcommittee on Oversight of the Permanent Select Committee on Intelligence*, House of Representatives, 96th Congress, 6,19 February, 1980, Washington, D.C., U.S. Government Printing.

47 In spy lingo, a passport is a "shoe." Hence the name "cobbler" for the person who falsifies passports.

48 See, Manuel Cereijo, "Cuba's Adversary Foreign Intelligence Operations," INGMCA@aol.com, July 2001; also Domingo Amuchástegui, "Cuban Intelligence and the October Crisis," in Blight and Welch, *Intelligence and the Cuban Missile Crisis*, p. 98. In May 1967, after a dispute with American black leader Robert Williams, the Cuban intelligence forged an issue of William's publication *The Crusader*, and mailed thousands of copies to the U.S. and Africa. In the forged issue, Williams accused the Chinese of various political crimes. See Daniel Tretiak,

Cuban Relations with the Communist System (Waltham, Mass.: Advanced Study Group, June 1940 [monograph 4), cited in Carlos Moore, *Castro, The Blacks, and Africa* (Los Angeles: Center for Afro-American Studies, University of California, Los Angeles, 1988), pp. 265-266. (Thanks to Lázaro Cañizares for this info.)

49 Usually, after giving a speech Castro goes directly to *Granma*, the official newspaper, and personally edits his speech before it gets printed. When he is too tired to do it, *Granma's* presses wait patiently until he comes by or approves the printing over the phone. In the case of his speech at the trial for the Moncada attack (later published under the title "History Will Absolve Me") and his famous "I am a Marxist" speech, so many different versions have been officially published that it is almost impossible to know what he actually said.

50 One must keep in mind that, long before we had historians, there were spies. Sun Tzu is still considered obligatory reading by many intelligence officers. Blight and Welch's criticism about the Russian and American intelligence services reluctance to declassify SIGINT and HUMINT information "that would compromise certain by-now-surely-defunct sources and methods," only shows their lack of understanding of the essential work of intelligence services. The basic practices of tradecraft, particularly HUMINT, don't change much over the years, and intelligence services keep information about it under tight control. See "What can Intelligence tell us about the Cuban missile crisis, and what the Cuban missile crisis tell us about Intelligence?," in James G. Blight and David A Welch, eds., *Intelligence and the Cuban missile crisis* (London: Frank Cass, 1998), p. 2.

51 According to Amuchástegui, "Cuban intelligence became very adept at falsifying identities, forging documents, and other techniques of deception." See, Domingo Amuchástegui, "Cuban Intelligence and the October Crisis," in *Intelligence and the Cuban Missile Crisis*, James G. Blight and David A Welch, eds. (London: Frank Cass, 1998), 98.

52 Proof of it is their preoccupation about forgery and document integrity. *Studies in Intelligence*, a CIA scholarly publication with a very restricted circulation among members of the American intelligence community, has published several articles and book reviews about graphology and scientific examination of documents.

53 Norberto Fuentes points out that, once the Castroist regime disappears, no one will be able to find any compromising documents in the DSE (Department of State Security) archives. The reason for this is that "Castro has never dictated to his secretaries any assassination order, or a guerrilla landing or the kidnapping of an American diplomat in Central America. Those papers, of course, do not exist. Fidel Castro has won his main battles "whispering to the ears of his Antonios de la Guardia." *Dulces guerreros cubanos*, p. 153. Col. Antonio de la Guardia was Castro's main hit man, who boasted of having killed more than forty people abroad following Castro's direct orders. Eventually Fidel had his assassin assassinated.

54 For example, I bet that Castro's letter to Khrushchev, published by *Granma*, is a toned down fabrication. See, Prime Minister Fidel Castro's letter to Premier Khrushchev, October 26, 1962 (reproduced from the international edition of Granma), *The Cuban Missile Crisis, 1962, A National Security Archive Documents*

Reader, Laurence Chang and Peter Kornbluh, eds. (New York: The New Press, 1992) p. 189.

The original letter was written in Spanish, not in English as the one published by the NSA. In it, the Cuban maniac, excited about the possibility of provoking a nuclear holocaust which may have caused the death of half of the world's population, urged the Soviet Premier to launch a preemptive nuclear attack on the United States. Faithful to their role as propagandists of the Castro regime, the folks at the National Security Archive published the false letter, disingenuously purporting it as the real document. Of course, the NSA folks don't want the rest of us to discover that their hero is actually an evil monster. For a detailed analysis of Castro as an evil monster, see Servando González, *The Secret Fidel Castro,* pp. 306-318.

55 The authentication of a document whose source is suspect may involve verifying that the signature or any hand writing on them really corresponds to the persons who produced the document, as well as the typewriters in use at the time. But, as the Hitler Diaries hoax proved, none of them is conclusive. If an organization with the technical means and know-how were intent in forging a document, the most rudimentary precautions they would take would be to find the proper typewriter and use a paper of the same size. The only way to really be certain is to have chemical tests made on the paper and its age, and the ink, looking for inconsistencies like, for example, the use of synthetic fibers in papers purporting to have been made at a time when this had not been yet introduced in paper manufacturing.

56 It is interesting to see that some of the foundations contributing to the National Security Archive are the same ones author Christopher Simpson identified as those that, working close with the US military and intelligence services, provided the largest single source of funding for major scientific research in the 1950s —a research sponsored by the CIA. See, Simpson, *Universities and Empire: Money and Politics in the Social Sciences During the Cold War* (New Press, 1968), quoted in Mooney, "For Your Eyes Only," p. 36.

57 Out of unavoidable oversimplification, people always refer to actions taken by intelligence services as "the CIA knew," "the KGB acted," "the Mossad believed," etc., forgetting that intelligence services are not homogeneous entities. Due to the application of the need-to-know and compartmentation principles, a common characteristic of intelligence services is that the right hand doesn't know what the left hand is doing, and vice versa. Therefore, when one says "the CIA knew," it actually means "some people at the CIA knew." In the case of critical operations, as in the case of assassination attempts on a foreign leader, it is likely that most people at CIA, including very senior officers, were left out in the dark about the operation. On the other hand, there is some evidence that, since the sixties, the CIA has been not only teeming with liberals but it has had some crypto-leftists among its ranks. Contrary to what most people think, Castro always has had many secret admirers among CIA officers. Some CIA defectors, like Philip Agee, are notoriously pro-Castro.

Given the strange coincidence of interests between Castro and the CIA, there is the remote possibility that both of them may just be different sides of the same coin. The strange coincidence of interests between Castro and the CIA will be the subject of my next book, *Fidel Castro Supermole: Walking Back the Cat in the Cuban Operation*.

58 As an example I can bring the case of Paul Wolf, who has been for many years engaged in a legal battle with the CIA trying to obtain through the Freedom of Information Act the release of documents related to the assassination of Colombia's leader and presidential candidate Jorge Eliécer Gaitán. But the Gaitán case has many ramifications, and is a potential can of worms the CIA does not want to unlid. Therefore, it is not surprising that the CIA folks, so eager to comply with the requests filed by the National Security Archive, have not been cooperative at all with Wolf's requests. For a detailed account of this legal battle and interesting details of the Gaitán case, see www.derechos.net/paulwolf/gaitan/gaitan.html.

Some people, myself included, suspect that some of the documents related to the Gaitán case, so secretly kept in the CIA files, may contain incriminating information about the CIA's early dealings with Fidel Castro. On Castro's magnicidal inclinations see Servando González, *The Secret Fidel Castro*, pp. 96-131.

59 Daniel Patrick Moynihan, *Secrecy* (New Haven: Yale University Press, 1998).

60 Teresa Odendahl, *Charity Begins at Home: Generosity and Self-Interest Among the Philanthropic Elite* (New York: Basic Books, 1990), p. 245. See also Francie Ostrower, *Why the Wealthy Give: The Culture of Elite Philanthropy* (Princeton, N.J.: Princeton University Press, 1995). The classic of all these studies still is Rene Wormser, *Foundations: Their Power and Influence* (New York: Devin-Adair, 1958).

60 Daniel Brandt, "Philanthropists at War," *Namebase NewsLine*, No. 15 (October-December, 1996).

61 I will study the subject in detail in a book I plan to write some day: *Brinking the Brink: More BS on the Cuban Missile Crisis*.

62 Some of the frightening "discoveries" brought up in these meetings have immediately been reproduced by the mainstream media, usually not before adding one or two scary touches of their own creation.

63 Mark Kramer, "Tactical Nuclear Weapons, Soviet Command Authority, and the Cuban Missile Crisis," *Cold War International History Bulletin* 3 (Fall 1993).

64 James G. Blight, Bruce J. Allyn, and David A. Welch, "Kramer VS. Kramer: Or, How Can You Have Revisionism in the Absence of Orthodoxy?," *Cold War International History Bulletin* 3 (Fall 1993).

65 Richard Ned Lebow and Janice Gross Stein, *We All Lost the Cold War* (Princeton, N.J.: Princeton University Press, 1994), p. 3.

66 As a good example I can mention that after Gary Powers' U-2 was shot down over the Soviet Union —most likely the result of Pentagon-CIA sabotage— the price of shares of arms manufacturing companies rose sharply in the New York Stock Exchange, and government military-contract awards increased substantially. Just two months after the incident, the Eisenhower administration allocated the biggest military appropriations ever approved at that time, $48.3 billion for fiscal

1960-61. See V. Cherniavsky, "U.S. Intelligence and the Monopolies," *International Affairs* (January 1965).

In the same fashion, the US defense budget for the fiscal year that began July 1, 1962, was $56.6 billion. Of these, $15.4 was designated for purchasing new weapons, $11.5 to operations and maintenance, and $6.7 to research and development. In the decade of mid-1953 to mid-1963, the US spent more than $400 billion in defense. *U.S. News and World Report*, October 8, 1962, p. 50. Fear has always been good for business, and everybody knows that the business of America is business.

67 Theodore C. Sorensen, *The Kennedy Legacy* (New York: Macmillan, 1969), p. 358.

68 Professor Mark Kramer is a notable exception.

69 McNamara mentioned an article published in the Russian press which stated that "at the height of the crisis the Soviet forces in the island possessed a total of 162 nuclear warheads, including at least 90 tactical warheads." Robert S. McNamara, "The Nuclear Emperor has no Clothes," *New Perspectives Quarterly*, Summer 95, Vol. 12 Issue 3.

70 Faced with conflicting reports in the American press about the number of Soviet missiles in Cuba, Deputy Secretary of Defense Roswell Gilpatric had to admit in a television interview: "We never knew how many missiles were brought to Cuba. The Soviets said there were forty-two. We have counted forty-two going out. We saw fewer than forty-two. Until we have so-called on-site inspection of the island of Cuba we could never be sure that forty-two was the maximum number that the Soviets brought into Cuba." Gilpatric was interviewed by *ABC* correspondents Bob Clark and John Scali, on *Issues and Answers*, November 11, 1962. Unfortunately, there was no on-site inspection of Cuba.

71 Contrary to what some people may think, the concept of the American military-industrial complex is not Marxist-inspired. It was coined by President Eisenhower in his farewell speech to the nation. The idea of the existence of a military-industrial-academic complex does not imply that all officers in the armed forces, all academics, or all executives working for the corporations that produce war matériel are corrupt. But it is obvious that some high brass, as well as some academics involved in military research, have a stake in the war economy. Also, it is known that there is a revolving door by which many Pentagon top brass, after retiring, become advisors to the very same corporations they helped to secure contracts.

People in positions of power in the world of business and finance successfully penetrated the Department of Defense. For example, James Forrestal, Charles E. Wilson (of General Electric), Neil McElroy, Robert McNamara (of Ford), Clark Clifford, Robert A. Lovett, David Packard, just to mention a few, were all Wall Street lawyers.

In the same fashion, retired officers landed well-paid jobs with industry, i.e., General Lauris Norstad, former Allied Commander in Europe, became president of Owens-Corning Fiberglas; Admiral William M. Fechteler, former Chief of Naval Operations, became a consultant for General Electric; Admiral Arleigh Burke, another Chief of Naval Operations, was appointed director of many corporations and head of a think-tank at Georgetown University; and scientists such as Herbert F. York, Harold Brown, and John S. Foster, Jr., became directors of Research and Engineering for the Pentagon after having worked in similar positions at the Livermore Laboratory in California. See, Sidney Lens, *The Day Before Doomsday: An Anatomy of the Nuclear Arms Race* (Boston: Beacon Press, 1977), pp. 162-163.

The record shows that, after retirement, thousands of former military officers have gone to work for the very same large defense corporations that they had been instrumental in adjudicating large defense contracts. Once working for the corporations, they have continued the practice by arranging contracts through men in the Pentagon who were their former subordinates.

72 John Guerassi, ed., *Venceremos! The Speeches and Writings of Ernesto Che Guevara* (New York: Macmillan, 1968), p. 422.

73 A long time ago I pioneered the concept of Fidel Castro as a benefactor of the American monopolies in my *Historia herética de la revolución fidelista* (San Francisco: El Gato Tuerto, 1986) pp. 138-139, 152. Many people at the time saw it either as a joke or a far-fetched idea. Now, however, it seems that some people are arriving at the same conclusion. See, for example, what Castro's daughter Alina Fernández wrote: "I left the [presidential] Palace with the bitter conviction that my conscience had been swindled, and that the Yankees were delighted to have Fidel ninety miles away, planting subversion in the rest of the world. As long as Fidel was there, the United States could always find employment for its blond, gum-chewing army, idle since Vietnam and Korea." *Castro's Daughter* (New York: St. Martin's Press, 1998), p. 129.

74 Blight and Welch, *On the Brink*, p. 7.

75 Lebow and Stein, *We Almost Lost the Cold War*, p. 10. Again, Lebow and Stein forget to mention the spies among the Soviet, Cuban, and American "officials."

76 Miguel Barnet, *Biography of a Runaway Slave* (Willimantic, CT: Curbstone Press, 1994), p. 204.

77 On the shortcomings of oral history, with specific references to the Cuban missile crisis, see Mark Kramer, "Remembering the Cuban Missile Crisis: Should We Swallow Oral History?," *International Security*, vol. 15 no. 1, (Summer 1991), pp. 212-218.

78 Barnet, *Biography*, p. 206.

79 (New York: Simon and Schuster, 1989).

80 McNamara, *Out of the Cold*, p. 64.

81 CIA, *The Secret Cuban Missile Crisis Documents* (Washington, D. C.: Brassey's, 1944), p. 304.

82 CIA, *The Secret*, p. 316.

83 CIA, *The Secret*, p. 328.

84 For a few more examples of McNamara lying through his teeth see Seymour M. Hersh, *The Dark Side of Camelot* (Boston: Little, Brown and Company, 1997), pp. 373-374.

85 Fursenko and Naftali, *"One Hell of a Gamble,"* p. 62. This accusation, of course, plays with the implied assumption that Batista's generals were criminals and assassins. Granted, some of Batista's generals were not pure, and participated in the corruption and graft of Batista's administration. None of them, however, had a record which can bring them even closer to, say, General Raúl Castro, Cuba's for-life chief of the Castroist armed forces. Raúl Castro's documented record of crimes —some of them committed with his own hands— corruption and graft has no parallel to anything seen in previous Cuban history. As the saying goes, even in Hell there are hierarchies.

86 For an analysis of Castro as a pathological liar see Servando González, *The Secret Fidel Castro*, pp. 203-207.

87 Mireya Navarro, "Caribbean Unity? Bananas Are Getting in the Way,? the *New York Times*, April 19, 1999, p. A4.

88 Castro's letter to Melba Hernández, 17 April 1954, in Luis Conte Agüero, *Cartas del presidio* (Havana: Ed. Lex, 1959), p. 38.

89 Mark Falcoff, "How to Think about Cuban-American Relations," in Irving Louis Horowitz, ed., *Cuban Communism, Fifth Edition* (New Brunswick, N.J.: Transaction Books, 1984), p. 547.

90 Lazo, *Dagger in the Heart* (New York: Twin Circle, 1968), p. 182. For an insightful analysis of the deep roots of lying from a non-conventional perspective, see M. Scott Peck, *People of the Lie* (New York: Simon and Schuster, 1983).

91 "Academic and Spies: The Silence That Roars," *Los Angeles Times*, January 28, 2001.

92 See, Paul Greenberg, "Springtime For Old Dictators," *The Washington Times*, May 6, 2001.

93 See, Servando González, *The Secret Fidel Castro*, pp. 59-75.

94 See, "Fidel meets with Portuguese authorities before returning from extensive tour," *Granma Internacional Digital*, May 21, 2001. Curiously, just a few hours after the September 11 attack, *Granma Internacional Digital* purged its databases of all the information related to Castro's close links to the anti-American Muslim world.

95 *AFP*, May 10, 2001.

96 *AFP*, May 10, 2001.

97 *AFP*, May 10, 2001.

98 *AFP*, May 10, 2001.

99 In every country there are people who, for some reasons, don't like their country, or at least some aspects of their country. But the case of people who hate their country so much that they would like to see it destroyed seems to be a unique American phenomenon.

100 Herbert Matthews, *The Cuban Story* (New York: George Brazillier, 1961), p. 172.

101 Georgie Anne Geyer, "Anti-Reforms are evidence the Cuban revolution is over," *Mobile Press Register*, June 6, 1994, 13-A.
102 Jesús Conte Agüero, *Fidel Castro: Psiquiatría y Política* (Mexico, D.F.,: Editorial Jus, 1968), p. 105.
103 Report of the Committee of Un-American Activities, House of Representatives, June 1965.
104 *Fidel Castro y la revolución cubana* (Madrid: Playor, 1983), p. 117.

Chapter Thirteen

1 The *New York Times*, June 4, 1971.
2 Graham T. Allison, "Conceptual Models and the Cuban Missile Crisis," in Morton H. Halperin and Arnold Kanter, eds., *Readings in American Foreign Policy* (Boston: Little, Brown and Company, 1973), p. 55.
3 Arnold Horelick and Myron Rush, *Strategic Power and Soviet Foreign Policy* (RAND, 1965), page 154, based on an article by Horelick, "The Cuban Missile Crisis: An Analysis of Soviet Calculations and Behavior," originally appeared in *World Politics*, April 1964.
4 W. Eckart and R.K. White, "A Test of the Mirror-Image Hypothesis: Kennedy and Khrushchev," *Journal of Conflict Resolution*, II (1967), 213-239.
5 Graham T. Allison, *Essence of Decision: Explaining the Cuban Missile Crisis* (New York: HarperCollins, 1971), p. 237.
6 *Essence of Decision: Explaining the Cuban Missile Crisis* (New York: HarperCollins, 1971).
7 See, i.e., John D. Steinbrunner, *The Cybernetic Theory of Decision* (Princeton, N.J.: Princeton University Press, 1974), p. 8.
8 Herbert Simon, *Administrative Behavior* (New YorK: Macmillan, 1957), 80.
9 Simon, *Administrative Behavior*, p. 77.
10 See "Failure in National Intelligence Estimates, the Case of the Cuban Missiles," *World Politics*, Vol. XVI, No. 3, April, 1964, pp. 458-59.
11 Herbert Simon, *Administrative Behavior* (New York: Macmillan, 1957).
12 Simon, *Administrative Behavior*, p. xxiv.
13 Simon, *Administrative Behavior*, p. 81. On the narrow limits of the human mind to choose among alternatives, see G.A. Miller's classic, "The Magical Number Seven, Plus or Minus Two: Some Limits of Our Capacity for Processing Information," *Psychology Review*, no. 63, 1956.
14 Simon, *Administrative Behavior*, p. 68.
15 Simon, *Administrative Behavior*, p. 71.
16 See, i.e., Thomas M. Mongar, "Personality and Decision Making: John F. Kennedy in Four Crisis Decisions," in Gordon J. DiRenzo, ed., *Personality and Politics* (Garden City, N.Y.: Anchor Books, 1974), p. 353.
17 Henry A. Kissinger, "Domestic Choices of Foreign Policy," in Robert L. Pfaltzgraff, Jr., ed. *Politics and the International System, Second Edition* (New York: J.B. Lippincott, 1972), p. 394.

18 See Robert Jay Lifton, "On Psychohistory," in Robert Jay Lifton and Eric Olson, eds., *Explorations in Psychohistory* (New York: Simon and Schuster, 1974), p. 26.

19 H.C. Kelman, ed., *International Behavior: A Social-psychological Analysis* (New York: Holt, Reinehart, and Winston, 1965), p. 587.

20 J. DeRivera, *The Psychological Dimensions of Foreign Policy* (Columbus, Ohio: Charles E. Merrill, 1968), p. 105.

21 Jeffrey A. Hart, "Cognitive Maps of Three Latin American Policy Makers," *World Politics* 30 (October 1977), pp. 115-116.

22 As Fred Greenstein does in *Personality and Politics* (New York: Norton, 1975), pp. xvii-xix.

23 Hart, "Cognitive Maps," p. 116.

24 Hart, "Cognitive Maps," pp. 115-116.

25 Hart, "Cognitive Maps," p. 116.

26 Robert Jervis, "Hypothesis on Misperception," in Morton H. Halperin and Arnold Kanter, eds., *Readings in American Foreign Policy* (Boston: Little, Brown and Company, 1973), p. 132.

27 Simon, *Administrative Behavior*, p. 76.

28 Simon, *Administrative Behavior*, p. 76.

29 J. Von Newmann and O. Morgernstern, *Theory of Games and Economic Behavior* (Princeton, New Jersey: Princeton University Press, 1947).

30 See, i.e., Klaus Knorr, "Failure in National Intelligence Estimates: The Case of the Cuban Missiles." *World Politics*, Vol. XVI No. 3 (April, 1964), pp. 458-59.

31 Dinerstein, *The Making*, p. xi.

32 Carl A. Linden, *Khrushchev and the Soviet Leadership, 1957-1964* (Baltimore, Md.: The Johns Hopkins Univ. Press, 1966), p. 153.

33 Khrushchev personally conceived and executed the plan for the mass starvation and liquidation of six to eight million people in the Ukraine in the early 1930s. He was the chief executioner for the bloody Moscow kangaroo purge trials in 1936. He personally supervised the killing of thousands. In 1937-38, during a second two-year reign of terror in the Ukraine, he supervised the slaughter of another 400,000 people. In the post-Ukraine purge, he had an active role in the liquidation or exile of hundreds of thousands in the gulags. See, U.S. Congress, House Committee on Un-American Activities, *Crimes of Khrushchev*, Part II, p. 2, Part I, pp. 7, 1.

34 *Time*, September 21, 1959.

35 William Randolph Hearst, Jr., B. Considine and F. Coniff, *Khrushchev and the Russian Challenge* (New York: Avon, 1961), p. 39.

36 Hearst and Coniff, *Khrushchev*, p. 39.

37 Hearst and Coniff, *Khrushchev*, p. 42.

38 Hearst and Coniff, *Khrushchev*, p. 92.

39 Hearst and Coniff, *Khrushchev*, p. 65.

40 Hearst and Coniff, *Khrushchev*, p. 59.

41 Hearst and Coniff, *Khrushchev*, p. 65.

42 Hearst and Coniff, *Khrushchev*, p. 229.

43 Crankshaw, *Khrushchev*, p. 13.

44 See, Linden, *Khrushchev*.

45 See, F.I. Greenstein, "The Impact of Personality in Politics: An Attempt to Clear Away Underbrush," *American Political Science Review*, No. 61, 1967, pp. 629-641. On the principle of strategic intervention see T. Kotarbinsky, *Praxiology: An Introduction to the Science of Efficient Action* (New York: Pergamon, 1965).

46 Richard P. Stebbins, *The United States in World Affairs, 1959* (New York: Vintage, 1960), p. 125.

47 George Kennan, *Russia, the Atom and the West* (New York: Harper and Row, 1957), p. 2122.

48 CIA's report quoted in Bryant Wedge, "Khrushchev at a Distance: A Study in Public Personality," *Transaction* 5 (October 1968), pp. 24-28.

49 I will study this in more detail in the next chapter.

50 The *New York Times*, October 23, 1962.

51 See, U.S. President, *Recommendations Relating to Our Defense Budget*, U.S. House Document no. 123 (Washington: Government Printing Office), 1961.

52 See, Walton, *Cold War*, p. 60.

53 See, Hearst, *Khrushchev*, pp. 208-209.

54 Linden, *Khrushchev*, p. 152.

55 Review of Robert Kennedy's Thirteen Days, *Political Science Quarterly*, vol. LXXXV, no. 4 (December, 1970), p. 656.

56 Felix Greene, *The Enemy* (New York: Vintage, 1970), p. 304.

57 Greene, *The Enemy*, pp. 304-305.

58 Kennedy, *Thirteen Days*, p. 2.

59 Theodore Sorensen, "You Get to Walk to Work," The *New York Times Magazine*, March 19, 1967.

60 See, Thomas M. Mongar, Personality and Decision Making: John F. Kennedy in Four Crisis," in Gordon J. DiRenzo, ed., *Personality and Politics* (Garden City, N.Y.: Anchor Books, 1974), p. 361. I have used the term "consultation" in reference to a situation in which a decision-maker asks another person what response should be made to a given situation.

61 Schlesinger, *A Thousand*, p. 733.

62 Hanson Baldwin, the *New York Times*, International Edition, November 1, 1962.

63 Theodore C. Sorensen, *Decision Making in the White House: The Olive Branch and the Arrows* (New York: Columbia University Press, 1963), p. 771.

64 Lewis J. Paper, *The Promise and the Performance* (New York: Crown, 1976), p. 148.

65 This was found later to be incorrect.

66 Kennedy, *Thirteen Days*, p. 12.

67 Kennedy, *Thirteen Days*, pp. 12-13.

68 Kennedy, *Thirteen Days*, p. 14.
69 Kennedy, *Thirteen Days*, p. 16.
70 Kennedy, *Thirteen Days*, p. 31-32.
71 See, *Congressional Record*, December 10, 1973, S22289; also, interview with R.W. Howe and Sarah Trott, *Saturday review*, January 11, 1975.
72 Dean Acheson, *Present at the Creation* (New York: W.W. Norton, 1969), p. 411.
73 Quoted in Richard Nixon, *Leaders* (New York: Warner Books, 1982), p. 93.
74 Schlesinger, *A Thousand*, p. 742.
75 See, Paper, *The Promise*, p. 137.
76 Henry Brandon, "An Untold Story of the Cuban Crisis," *Saturday Review*, March 9, 1963, pp. 56-57. Kennedy's *sang froid* highly contrasted with McNamara's reaction. According to General David Burchinal, the Director of Plans of the Air Staff in 1962, when McNamara heard the news about the U-2 he "turned absolutely white and yelled hysterically, 'This means war with the Soviet Union. The President must get on the hot line to Moscow,' and he ran out of the meeting in a frenzy." McNamara later said he didn't recall the incident.
77 See, *The Kennedy Legacy* (New York: Macmillan, 1969), p. 158.
78 See Signe Hammer and Lesley Hazleton, "Cocaine and the Chemical Brain," *Science Digest*, October 1984, pp. 58-60.
79 The *New York Times*, December 4, 1972.
80 John Kenneth Galbraith, "Storm Over Havana: Who Were the Real Heroes?," *Book World*, January 19, 1969, p. 16.
81 Harris Wofford, *Of Kennedys and Kings: Making Sense of the Sixties* (New York: Farrar, Strauss, Giroux, 1988), p. 386.
82 Elie Abel, *The Missile Crisis* (Philadelphia: Lippincot, 1966), p. 64.
83 Charles Frankel, *Morality and U.S. Foreign Policy* (New York: Foreign Policy Association, Headline Series No. 224, February 1975), p. 4
84 Wofford, *Of Kennedys and Kings*, p. 398.
85 Wofford, *Of Kennedys and Kings*, p. 386.
86 U.S. Congress, Senate, *Alleged Assassination Plots Involving Foreign Leaders*, 94th Congress, 1st. Session, Report 94-465 (Washington, D.C.: U.S. Government Printing Office, 1975), p. 141.
87 *Newsweek*, November 28, 1983, p. 75. On the Kennedy administration's hysteria about Castro see also "The CIA's Secret Army," *CBS* report, 1977; rebroadcasted on Bill Moyers' *Journal* (PBS), February 13, 1981.
88 Paper, *The Promise*, p. 92.
89 William S. White, *San Francisco Examiner,* October 23, 1984. See also White, "Finally the U.S. Draws the Line," *San Francisco Examiner*, October 25, 1962.
90 Christopher Lash, "The Life of Kennedy's Death," *Harper's*, October 1983, p. 40.
91 Stewart Alsop and Charles Bartlett, "In Time of Crisis," The *Saturday Evening Post*, December 8, 1962, pp. 15-21.

92 In an article in the *Saturday Evening Post* in March, 1962, Stewart Alsop had mentioned John Kennedy's belief that Khrushchev must not be certain that the United States will never strike first.

93 Thomas M. Mongar, "Personality and Decision Making: John F. Kennedy in Four Crisis Decisions," in Gordon J. DiRenzo, ed., *Personality and Politics* (Garden city, N.Y.: Anchor Books, 1974), p. 355.

94 Gary Wills, *The Kennedy Imprisonment* (Boston: Little, Brown and Company, 1982), p. 35.

95 Wills, *The Kennedy,* p. 35

96 Wills, *The Kennedy,* p. 35

97 William Styron, "The Short, Classy Voyage of JFK," *Esquire*, December 1983, p. 129.

98 Styron, "The Short, Classy Voyage of JFK," p. 129.

99 Styron, "The Short, Classy Voyage of JFK," p. 129.

100 Nancy Gager Clinch, *The Kennedy Neurosis* (New York: Grosset and Dunlap, 1973), p. 73.

101 Wills, *The Kennedy*, p. 35.

102 It is known that Hoover had a secret archive with compromising information on most politicians and important people in the U.S., including members of Congress. This is known in intelligence and espionage as "biographical leverage."

103 Wills, *The Kennedy*, p. 34.

104 Wills, *The Kennedy*, p. 35.

Chapter Fourteen

1 Robert S. McNamara, Introduction to Robert F. Kennedy, *Thirteen Days* (New York: Signet, 1969), p. 13.

2 Address by President Kennedy, October 22, 1962, in David L. Larson, ed., *The "Cuban Crisis" of 1962* (Boston: Houghton Mifflin, 1963), p. 45.

3 Les Aspin, "Misreading Intelligence," *Foreign Policy*, no 43, Summer 1981, p. 166.

4 HUMINT, human intelligence; ELINT, electronic intelligence.

5 Andrew Cockburn, "Tinker With Gadgets, Taylor the Facts," *Harper's*, April 1985, p. 70.

6 Nikita S. Khrushchev, *Khrushchev Remembers* (Boston: Little, Brown and Company, 1970), p. 494.

7 Oran Young, *The Politics of Force* (Princeton, N.J.: Princeton University Press, 1968), pp. 615.

8 Robert C. North, *Content Analysis* (Chicago: Northwestern University Press, 1963), pp. 4-5.

9 For other definitions of crisis see Anthony J. Wiener and Herman Kahn, eds., *Crisis and Arms Control*, Hudson Institute, Advanced Research Projects Agency Contract no. SD-105, October 9, 1962, p. 12; Kenneth E. Boulding, *Conflict and*

Defense (New York: Harper and Row, 1963), p. 250; Jan F. Triska and David D. Finley, *Soviet Foreign Policy* (New York: Macmillan, 1968), p. 317; Oran R. Young, *The Intermediaries: Third Parties in International Crisis* (Princeton, N.J.: Princeton University Press, q967), p. 10; also, Kent Miller and Ira Iscoe, "The concept of Crisis: Current Status and Mental health Implications," *Human Organization*, xxii (1963), pp. 195-201.

10 For a thorough analysis of these characteristics, see Charles F. Hermann, "Some Consequences of Crisis Which Limit the Viability of Organizations," *Administrative Science Quarterly*, 8, no. 1 (1963); Charles F. Hermann, *Crises in Foreign Policy: A Simulation Analysis* (Indianapolis: Bobbs-Merrill, 1969); also Hermann, "Some Issues in the Study of International Crisis," in Charles F. Hermann, ed., *International Crisis: Insights From Behavioral Research* (New York: The Free Press, 1972).

11 Quoted in Robert Merton, *Social Theory and Social Structure* (New York: The Free Press, 1957), p. 421.

12 See, i.e., G. Matthew Bonham and Michael J. Shapiro, eds. *Thought and Action in Foreign Policy* (Basel: Birkhaüser Verlag, 1977), p. 6.

13 Special National Intelligence Estimate number 85-3-62, "The Military Buildup in Cuba," September 19, 1962, in Central Intelligence Agency, *The Secret Cuban Missile Crisis Documents* (Washington, D.C.: Brassey's,1994), p. 93.

14 See, U.S. Congress, Senate Committee on Armed Services Preparedness Investigations Subcommittee, *Interim Report on Cuban Military Build-up*, 88th Congress, 1st. sess., 1963; Hanson Baldwin, "Growing Risks of Bureaucratic Intelligence, *The Reporter* (August 15, 1963); Roberta Wohlstetter, "Cuba and Pearl harbor: Hindsight and Foresight," *Foreign Affairs*, July 1965; "Intelligence Gap on Cuba? The Senate Gets the Report," *U.S. News and World Report*, May 20, 1963; Klauss Knorr, "Failures in National Defense estimates," *World Politics*, April 1964.

15 Robert Kennedy, *Thirteen Days*, pp. 5-6.

16 Roger Hilsman, *To Move a Nation: The Politics of Foreign Policy in the Administration of John F. Kennedy* (New York: Doubleday, 1967), p. 186.

17 Abel, *The Missile Crisis*, p. 24.

18 Abel, *The Missile Crisis*, p. 24.

19 Department of State Appropriations, *Hearings*, p. 64.

20 Department of State Appropriations, *Hearings*, pp. 1-30.

21 Wise and Ross, *The Invisible Government*, pp. 311-312.

22 Lyman B. Kirkpatrick, Jr. *The U.S. Intelligence Community* (New York: Hill and Wang, 1973), p. 88.

23 Hearst, Jr., *Khrushchev*, pp. 121-122.

24 Hearst, Jr., *Khrushchev*, p. 249.

25 Ulam, *Expansion and Coexistence*, p. 610 (emphasis mine).

26 William A. Griffith, *The Sino-Soviet Rift* (Cambridge, Massachusetts: Harvard University Press, 1964), p. 351.

27 Ulam. *Expansion and Coexistence*, p. 611.

28 See, Steve Chan, "The Intelligence of Stupidity: Understanding Failures in Strategic Warning," *American Political Science Review* 73 (March 1979), p. 171.

29 David B. Bobrow, "Criteria for Valid Forecasting," Paper presented at the International Relations Forecasting Conference, Cambridge, Mass., 1973, pp. 17-18.

30 Wise and Ross, *The Invisible Government*, p. 312.

31 "Washington Whispers," *U.S. News and World Report*, November 5, 1962, p. 26.

32 Sidey, *Kennedy*, p. 229.

33 Jonathan Steele, *Soviet Power* (New York: Simon and Schuster, 1983), p. 45. Professor Mark Kramer criticized Peter Jennings for saying that the Soviet Union had "never before moved missiles *capable* of delivering nuclear warheads outside its own borders." In fact, wrote Kramer, the Soviet Union had shipped nuclear-*capable* Frog and Scud missiles to the East European members of the Warsaw Pact before 1962. "Tactical Nuclear Weapons, Soviet Command Authority, and the Cuban Missile Crisis," *Cold War International History Project Bulletin* 3 (Fall 1993), n. 14 (emphasis mine).

The problem with Kramer's statement resides in his use of the word "capable." The fact that something is "capable" of doing something is almost meaningless. In the strictest sense, with current technology a Volkswagen Beetle is capable of carrying a nuclear warhead and delivering it to its designated target. On September 11, 2001, Americans suddenly discovered that box cutters were capable of serving as hijackers' weapons and that commercial jet planes were capable of destroying skyscrapers. The problem, thus, is not capability, but actual existence of the nuclear warhead, and there is no evidence that the Soviets had ever brought any nuclear warhead outside of its borders.

Furthermore, in an excellent paper in which he studies how the Cuban missile crisis experience may have affected the Soviet command and control of nuclear devices in Warsaw Pact operations, Kramer offers several revealing facts. In the first place, "the East European governments were denied any say in the use of the Pact's 'joint' nuclear arsenal." Secondly, "all nuclear warheads for the delivery systems remained under exclusive Soviet control." Finally, and this is probably the most interesting fact, the East European Army officers had no "control over the reinforced storage bunkers for nuclear warheads" (or even the housing for elite units assigned to guard the bunkers). A Senior Czech army officer later confirmed to Kramer that "the procedures for the defense and protection of these special-purpose storage centers for nuclear warheads were such that no one from our side had permission to enter, and even Soviet officials who were not directly responsible for guarding and operating the buildings were not allowed." See Mark Kramer, "'Lessons' of the Cuban Missile Crisis for Warsaw Pact Nuclear Operations," *Cold War International History Project Bulletin* 5 (Spring 1955), pp. 59, 110, 112-115.

Consequently, with the available information, it is almost impossible to determine if the extraordinary security procedures had been designed to avoid any unauthorized use of the nuclear warheads, or to keep the Soviet allies from discovering that there were no nuclear warheads whatsoever in the bunkers. Likewise, we don't know if what looked like Frog and Scud missiles in East Europe were not actually dummies —a common Soviet *maskirovka* practice. The fact is that, despite all the tight security provided by specialized units, no army officer is sure that he can stop a frontal attack by an opposing army equipped with heavy weapons. But nuclear warheads are very dangerous toys. In the wrong hands they can create a very serious problem. Even a single possibility in a thousand that they can be taken by force is a risk too high to be acceptable. Therefore, the best way to avoid this possibility is by keeping them as far as possible from power hungry hands —even from the hands of friends who, as it happened with Castro in 1962, may one day become adversaries. And this reasoning applies to everybody, East and West. For any country, bringing such powerful weapons out of strict, total control is very unlikely.

It is for the reasons expressed above that, of lately, I have come to suspect that the U.S. missiles in Italy and Turkey never had nuclear warheads available, and perhaps even the missiles may have been dummies. This may explain the funny stories claiming that they were almost useless because they could have been easily disabled by a boy with a .22 rifle. The bottom line is that no country wants to commit nuclear suicide, particularly with somebody else pulling the trigger.

34 When asked during an interview at the Kennedy Library in 1970 about the presence of nuclear warheads in Cuba in 1962, Deputy Secretary of Defense Roswell Gilpatric clearly expressed: "We never had any positive evidence" [that Soviet warheads were in Cuba]. "If you ask my own belief, I don't think that there were." ... "I think there were plans for flying them in, but I don't think they were actually matched up ... with the launchers." Quoted in Seymour Hersh, *The Dark Side of Camelot* (Boston: Little, Brown and Company), p. 355

35 Men of strong convictions, some of the authors of the September estimate, notably Sherman Kent, Abbot Smith and John Huizenga never recanted. Faced with their apparent failure, their conclusion was that it had been Khrushchev, not the Estimate, who had been wrong. I cannot agree more. If Khrushchev had done what he seemingly did, he would have been wrong. Information on Kent, Abbot and Huizenga in Raymond L Garthoff, "US Intelligence in the Cuban Missile Crisis," in Blight and Welch, *Intelligence in the Cuba Missile Crisis*, p. 21.

36 I will partially answer this question in my forthcoming book *Fidel Castro Supermole: Walking Back the Cat in the Cuban Operation,* to be published by mid-2003.

37 Sherman Kent, "A Crucial Estimate Relived," *Studies in Intelligence*, Spring 1964. Kent was not alone in his conclusions. Both deputy chairman Abbot Smith, and board member John Huizenga, agreed with Kent that the Estimate had been correct and that is was Khrushchev who had been mistaken. See Raymond L. Garthoff, "US Intelligence in the Cuban Missile Crisis," in Blight and Welch, *Intelligence in the Cuban Missile Crisis*, p. 21.

38 According to the CIA's own prescribed tradecraft practices, there are warning signs to detect enemy deception which address the likelihood that a country or organization is engaged in a disinformation attempt. The first set of warnings has to do with the likelihood that a country may be engaged in an attempt to distort the analyst's perceptions: (I have added between brackets the known facts which prove that every single one of the six warning signs was present during the crisis and was ignored by the CIA analysts.)

1. **Means**. The country being assessed has the experience and means to undertake sophisticated deception operations. [*Maskirovka*, a common Soviet practice.]
2. **Opportunity**: When the country is known to have knowledge of the periodicity and acuity of technical collection vehicles that pass over an area it wishes to protect, analysts have to be aware that the resultant information may be incomplete if not also deliberately distorted. [The knowledge was provided by Power's U-2.]
3. **Motive**. A motive to deceive is believed to be present. [Khrushchev's motive was his desire to get rid of the unreliable Castro. But he wanted the Americans to, unwittingly, do the dirty job for him.]

The second set of warnings focuses on anomalies in the information available to the analysts. These warning signs include:
4. **Suspicious gaps in collection**. The analysts are not receiving the range and volume of information they would expect if there was no deliberate tampering with sources and collection platforms. [The collection black out after the shot down of Powers' U-2.]
5. **Contradictions to a carefully researched pattern**. The new information does not match with the opponent's previously observed priorities and practices. [The Soviets never had deployed nuclear weapons beyond their borders.]
5. **Suspicious confirmation**. A new stream of information from clandestine sources or technical collection seems to reinforce the rationale for the action. [The confirmation provided by Penkovsky.]

Source: Central Intelligence Agency, *A compendium of Analytic Tradecraft Notes*, Washington, D.C. February 1997. The author of the *Notes* was Jack Davis, a retired officer who spent 40 years as practitioner, teacher, and critic of intelligence analysis. Though the *Notes* were published in 1997, they just summarized tradecraft practices that have been standard operating procedures in the CIA for many years, including during the Cuban missile crisis. Therefore the gross failures in tradecraft by the CIA analysts and the CIA officer's inability to detect the Soviets' deception efforts cannot by any stretch of the imagination be attributed to lack of knowledge or "errors," but to a willful desire to mislead the American decision-makers.

38 Kennedy, *Thirteen Days*, pp. 2-3.

39 Dino Brugioni, *Eyeball to Eyeball: The Inside Story of the Cuba Missile Crisis* (New York Random House, 1991), pp. 197-198.

40 It seems, however, that, like lemmings, some crisis scholars have stopped thinking and are just following the disinformation leaders. See, i.e., Ernest R. May and Philip D. Zelikow, *The Kennedy Tapes: Inside the White House During The Cuban Missile Crisis* (Cambridge, Massachusetts: Harvard University Press, 1997). In the very first line of the Introduction, the authors affirm that "On the morning when he first saw photographs of Soviet missiles in Cuba ..." Either the authors have privileged information they have not shared with the readers, or they simply still don't get it. Not only did President Kennedy not see any missiles in the photos, but nobody saw any missiles in them for the simple reason that no photograph taken by the U.S. at the time showed even the image of a single strategic missile in Cuba —and this is an undisputable fact that anybody can easily verify just by taking a look a the U-2 photos, most of then now available on the Web. These authors' affirmation is such a gross distortion of the historical record that it raises doubts about their professional competence.

In the same fashion, in his Prologue to Central Intelligence Agency, *The Secret Missile Crisis Documents* (Washington: Brassey's, 1994, Graham T. Allison, Jr., in a section entitled "The Facts," asserts that on 14 October, 1962, "A U.S. high-altitude U-2 overflight of Cuba took photographs that provided clear evidence of an ambitious Soviet deployment of 48 medium-range ballistic missiles (MRBMs, range 1,100 nautical miles) and 24 intermediate-range ballistic missiles (IRBMs, range 2,2000 nautical miles) at four separate sites in Cuba." (p. vi). Allison's statement is remarkable, because a careful reading of the documents offered in the very same book he is prologuing, provides no evidence whatsoever to substantiate his affirmation. The references found in some of the documents offered to the reader are to "eight canvas-covered, missile-type trailers," (p. 71); "six canvas-covered trailers of 80 feet in overall length which are of the general size and configuration of those used to transport the Soviet SS-3 (700 n.m. ballistic missile) and SS-4 (1,100 n.m. ballistic missile)." (p. 140); "14 canvas-covered missile trailers" and "8 canvas covered missile trailers." (p. 155). Only on page 255 is found a direct reference to actual missiles in an Area near San Cristóbal, in western Cuba, "We have identified six of the launchers and seven of the sixteen missiles," but, just a few lines below it is explained that the identification is not based on direct visual confirmation but that "The keys to these identifications are the size of the missile body." (p. 255). Further proof of this is that a few pages later, a description of the San Cristóbal sites reports "seven canvas covered missiles," (p. 263) as well as "six canvas-covered missiles" in the San Cristóbal area. On page 176, one of the document states that "Detailed photointerpretation shows that the missiles are canvas-covered, have a blunt nose, and are 66 feet, plus or minus two feet in length" According to my view, the only thing this statement shows is that the photointerpreters at the NPIC were very gullible.

Under the title "The Real Thirteen Days: Reconnaissance Photo," The National Security Archive has posted some of the U-2 photos taken during the crisis. See

THE NUCLEAR DECEPTION 383

www.gwu.edu/~nsarchiv/nsa/cuba_mis_cri/photos.html. I challenge my readers to visit the site and try to find in any of the photos, particularly in the ones taken between October 14, 1962 and January 27, 1963, any object that even slightly resembles a strategic missile or a nuclear warhead.

Following the same trend, at the end of a chapter entitled "Nuclear Warhead Postmortem," Dino Brugioni wrote, "Statements by responsible U.S. officials, and articles written subsequent to the crisis, maintaining that nuclear weapons were never seen in Cuba simply weren't true." *Eyeball to Eyeball*, p. 548. However, after reading Brugioni's chapter twice, I could only find the following type of references: "There was no evidence of a nuclear warhead storage facility, but it was *assumed* that there were nuclear warheads in Cuba, *probably* near the missile sites." (p. 538); "A number of nuclear warhead storage bunkers were found under construction near other missile sites in Cuba," (p. 539); "It was therefore *believed* that there *would be* a communication center near any nuclear weapons storage area." (p. 541); "It was generally *agreed* that nuclear warheads for the SS-4 missiles *would be* guarded..." (p. 541); "The warheads *would be* mated to the missiles only when ..." (p. 541); Since it was *assumed* that the warheads were under control of the KGB, it also was *assumed* that the warheads *would be* stored in a ..." (p. 541); "There was no doubt, however, that if the Soviet missile units in Cuba moved into an operational posture, the warhead and support elements *would be* observed at the launch pads on aerial photography." (p. 541); "The Soviets attempted to conceal the *nose cone containers*..." (p. 546); "Further postmortem reviews of all previous photography over Cuba revealed that, indeed, the nuclear warheads were stored in the 'unidentified' vans." (p. 545); "There were at least twenty-three netcovered coffin-shaped warhead containers in two separate rows, so that at least twenty-three warheads were present in Cuba." (p. 546); "One of the coffin-shaped warhead containers was open." (p. 546); "One of the vans had its rails extended and *appeared* to be transferring a warhead to a truck..." (p. 547).; "The postcrisis review of past photography *made it obvious* that the Soviets had fueled and mated the warheads ..." (p. 547); "It has to be *presumed* that the warheads were also mated to the missile." (p. 547), (emphasis added).

Most likely I am missing something here. But, even disregarding the fact that a photo of a nuclear warhead is *not* a nuclear warhead, after reading Brugioni's arguments supporting his unsubstantiated, far-fetched assertion that responsible U.S. officials and people who wrote that nuclear weapons were never seen in Cuba were wrong, as well as his claims that there were nuclear warheads in Cuba in 1962, I can only say that I have to join the group of unbelievers who maintain that nuclear weapons were never seen in Cuba. Actually, the NPIC folks could not even provide us with a single candid snapshot of a nuclear warhead on Cuban soil. Perhaps they have the photos, but have kept them secret all these years to avoid the Soviets from discovering that they had nuclear warheads in Cuba. Or probably the CIA psychics found the nuclear warheads using remote viewing. That, if confirmed, would be by far the greatest unpublished story of the Cuban missile crisis.

41 I think that Lundahl broke his line of command when he brought the U-2 photos directly to President Kennedy, bypassing the normal process of data evaluation analysis. An essential part of the CIA's work is based on the so-called intelligence cycle. The CIA defines the cycle as "the process by which information is acquired, converted into intelligence, and made available to policymakers." Central Intelligence Agency, *Fact Book on Intelligence* (Washington, D.C.: CIA, 1983), p. 17. The cycle has five phases: planning and direction, collection, processing, production and analysis, and dissemination.

Though all aspects of the cycle are important, it is in the fourth phase, production and analysis, when information is changed into intelligence. Obviously, the work of the NPIC is part of the collection and perhaps processing phases, but it has nothing to do with analysis. Proof of this is that in a review of David T. Lindgren's book *Trust But Verify: Imagery Analysis in the Cold War*, Jeffrey Richelson notices that "Strangely, despite the subtitle of the book and the author's experience, Lindgren devotes very little attention to the analytic process." See, *Bulletin of the Atomic Scientists*, www.thebulletin.org/issues/2001/jf01/jf01reviews.html.

But Lundahl violated the intelligence cycle and bypassed the fourth step, undertaking analysis and dissemination activities that were totally out of his job content and beyond his knowledge and experience. Why he did such a thing, and, more important, why he was allowed to do it, is something that merits to be investigated. I think that the CIA senior officers who allowed Lundahl to commit such a violation of the line of command committed themselves a dereliction of duty worse than Lundahl's.

Moreover, Lundahl's failure to consider the possibility of enemy deception was not the product of ignorance. In his book *Photo Fakery* (Dulles, Virginia: Brassey's, 1999), Dino Brugioni mentions that "Lundahl always loved to tell the story that the British discovered a German decoy airfield in North Africa during World War II. They subsequently sent a lone bomber over the field, which dropped a wooden bomb," pp 120-121. Therefore, Lundahl's failure to explore the possibility that the canvas-covered objects appearing in the U-2 photos may have not been what they seemed, cannot be explained by ignorance or incompetence, but to a conscious effort to disinform the President.

42 TECHINT: the gathering of intelligence through technical means, including computers, electronic sensors, satellites and overhead photography.

43 HUMINT: intelligence collected by people acting in the field, usually intelligence officers acting under different covers, illegals, and recruited agents (spies).

44 The fact was noted by intelligence analyst Walter Laqueur. In *A World of Secrets*, he pointed out that the need for HUMINT had not decreased, but it had become fashionable to denigrate the importance of human assets because technical means are politically and intellectually more comfortable.

45 There is, however, another, more convoluted explanation *à la* Angleton. Since its creation the CIA has never been an organization serving the interests of the United States or the American public, but the interest of the American military-

industrial-academic complex, particularly its Wall Street friends. Of course, 99 percent of CIA employees are true American patriots who firmly believe they are working for America. But the very essence of the CIA's organization, with its characteristics of compartmentation and need-to-know, preclude their gaining of an overall view of the inner workings of the organization they are working for. Consequently, what appears to be the CIA's incredible blunders have been mostly attributed to "mistakes."

But, despite compartmentation and need-to-know, CIA officers in the field — the HUMINT people— sooner or later get a better overall picture, and eventually begin suspecting that there is something fishy going on and that not all blunders are actually the result of honest "mistakes." It is no coincidence that most CIA dissidents and whistler blowers have come from the HUMINT area. Therefore, the anti-HUMINT push, which began after the Cuban missile crisis, may well have been nothing but a cleverly disguised effort to curb dissidence inside the CIA.

46 See, i.e., Raymond L. Garthoff, "The Cold War and the Changing Communist World," in Roger Hilsman and Robert C. Good, eds., *Foreign Policy in the Sixties* (Baltimore, Maryland: The Johns Hopkins Press, 1965), pp. 6-7/

47 Charles Lerche, Jr., *The Cold WAr and After* (Englewood Cliffs, N.J.: Prentice-Hall, 1965), p. 112.

48 Hermann, *Crisis in Foreign Policy*, pp. 29-36.

49 Kennedy quoted in Walton, *Cold War*, p. 36.

50 Walton, *Cold War,* p. 108.

51 Congressional Record, vol. 18, p. 22957. Also "Inside Story on Cuba... Why the U.S. Almost Got Caught. Interview with Senator Kenneth B. Keating," *U.S. News & World Report*, November 19, 1962, pp. 86-89.

52 Walter Trohan, "Report From Washington," *The Chicago Tribune*, September 10, 1962, p. 2.

53 Pachter, *Collision Course*, p. 7.

54 Wise and Ross, *The Invisible Government*, pp. 317-318.

55 Was he referring to the eyewitness report of a missile part which had reached the CIA on September 11?

56 See, *Hearings*, House Foreign Operations and Government Information Subcommittee, March 19, 1963, p. 15; also, Arthur Sylvester, "The Government Has the Right to Lie," *The Saturday Evening Post*, November 18, 1967, p. 10.

In a book written in James Bond fashion, author Robert D. Morrow claims that in the Spring of 1961 there were already launching facilities for intermediate ballistic missiles in the Sierra de Cubitas mountains north of Camagüey province in the eastern part of Cuba. See Robert D. Morrow, *Betrayal* (Chicago: Henry Regnery, 1976, pp. 16-17, 34. He also affirms that the Kennedys' knew about the missiles in Cuba long before October 14, 1962. Morrow's weird story, however, seems to have been confirmed to some extent five years later by Juan Vivés, an officer of the Cuban intelligence who defected to France. See, Juan Vivés, *Los amos de Cuba* (Buenos Aires, Emecé, 1982), pp. 131-132.

57 Schlesinger, *A Thousand Days*, pp. 801-813; Sorensen, *Kennedy*, pp. 682-699; Hilsman, *To Move a Nation*, pp. 198-206; and Robert Kennedy, *Thirteen Days*, pp. 32, 72.

58 See, The *New York Times*, October 26, 1962, p. 1; also, The *New York Times*, October 27, 1962, pp. 1, 7.

59 See, The *New York Times*, October 26, 1962, p. 18, October 27, pp. 1, 6; and October 28, p. 1.

60 The *New York Times*, October 26, 1962, pp. 16, 30.

61 Barnton J. Bernstein, "The Week We Almost Went to War," *Bulletin of the Atomic Scientists*, February, 1976, p. 17.

62 CIA, "Readiness Status of the MRBM Missile Sites in Cuba," October 23, 1962, NSF Countries: Cuba, Kennedy Library. There is no agreement, however, as to what the CIA meant by "fully operational."

63 Bernstein, "The Week We Almost," p. 17.

64 Vivés, *Los amos de Cuba*, p. 124, 127.

65 Sorensen, *Kennedy*, p. 121.

66 The *New York Times*, November 12, 1962.

67 Pentagon Background Briefing on Cuban Situation," 22 October, 8:00 P.M. Kennedy Library.

68 Robert Holtz, Editorial, *Aviation Week and Space Technology,* November 12, 1962, p. 21.

69 Neville Brown, *Nuclear War* (New York: Praeger, 1964), pp. 80-81.

70 For a discussion of the range of the missiles in Cuba, see David Detzer, *The Brink: Cuban Missile Crisis, 1962* (New York: Thomas Y. Crowell, 1979), pp. 72-73.

71 I put the words "Russian liars" inside quotes to imply that this was literally the way President Kennedy referred to them in his speech of October 22. By the way, he was right. Actually, most of the politicians of the three countries involved in the crisis, including Kennedy himself, were liars.

72 "How Much Censorship? How Much Distortion?," *Newsweek*, November 12, 1962, p. 28.

73 Which apparently were never seen in Cuba.

74 Neville Brown, *Nuclear War* (New York: Praeger, 1964), p. 80.

75 Hermann, *Crises in Foreign Policy: A Simulation Analysis* (Indianapolis: Bobbs-Merrill, 1969),

76 This was, i.e., the opinion of Thomas Schelling, *Arms and Influence* (New York: Yale University Press, 1966), p. 242.

77 He was apparently referring to Senator Keating.

78 Sorensen, *Kennedy*, p. 755.

79 William E. Colby and Peter Forbath, *Honorable Men: My Life in the CIA* (New York: Simon and Schuster, 1978), pp. 188-189.

80 "The Lessons of the Cuban Missile Crisis," *Time*, September 27, p. 86.

81 See, David Burner and Thomas R. West, *The Torch is passed* (New York: Atheneum, 1984), p. 136.

82 "Red Missiles in Cuba: Inside Story from Secretary McNamara," *U.S. News and World Report*, November 5, 1962, p. 45.

83 See Jay Miller, *Lockheed U-2* (Austin, Texas: Aerofax, 1983), p. 65.

84 "Red Missiles in Cuba", p. 50.

85 "Red Missiles in Cuba", p. 47.

86 However, after reading some of McNamara's previous and recent statements about the crisis, it is not easy to disagree with Castro's candid opinion that "McNamara was an idiot —still is!" See, Arthur Allen, "Che and Diana: The Shocking Untold Story," http://www.salon.com/media/1997/10/14castro.html.

87 CIA, Office of Current Intelligence, "Readiness Status of Soviet Missiles in Cuba," October 23, 1962, NSF, Countries, Cuba, Kennedy Library.

88 NUCINT: nuclear intelligence; the intelligence obtained from the collection and analysis of radiation emitted by different radioactive sources. A web search in Google under the heading "Cuban missile crisis" brought about 55,400 entries. But a search under "Cuban missile crisis" AND "NUCINT" does not match any documents in the Web. A search under "Cuban missile crisis " AND "radiation" brings about 2,330 entries, all of them irrelevant to the aim of the research with the exception of my own article "Thirteen Lies ... and Perhaps a Single Truth," which appeared in *lewrockwell.com*, *The New Australian*, and other Web sites.

Now, one must be aware that radiation, though a much more reliable indicator of the actual presence of nuclear warheads than photographs, should not be fully trusted. During the development of the MX missile, which never went into production, the initial plan contemplated building close to 200 missiles and making them difficult to pinpoint by using a Multiple Protective Shelter System —which was commonly referred to as the "shell game" system.

The shell game system consisted in creating thousands of MX identical dummies and rotating them through more than 4,600 shelters. To completely eliminate the MXs, the enemy would have to destroy thousands of MX look-alikes in order to destroy the hundreds of real MX's. In order to fool the enemy, the dummies and the missiles were not only similar in shape and color, but they had exactly the same weight, heat and magnetic signatures as the real missiles. Moreover, the dummy nuclear warheads on the look-alikes had been designed to emit the same amount and type of radiation as the real ones.

To accomplish this, the scientists at Raytheon designed a set of coils for the canisters containing the dummy missiles that would make them produce the same magnetic signature as a real canister loaded with a real missile. I have not found information about how they faked the radiation, but it may have been even simpler; just by putting inside the dummy warhead some amount of radioactive, gamma-ray emitting material which produce a similar amount of radiation as a real nuclear warhead.

To have an idea of the technical aspects involving the detection of radiation from nuclear warheads, see "Steve Fetter, Thomas B. Cochran, et al., "Gamma-

Ray Measurements of a Soviet Cruise-Missile Warhead," *Science*, vol. 248, May 1990, pp. 828-834.

89 See Anatoli Gribkov and William Smith, *Operation Anadyr* (Chicago: Edition q, 1994), 13940.

90 Blight and Welch, *On the Brink*, p. 45. (emphasis mine).

91 David L. Larson, ed., *The "Cuban Crisis" of 1962: Selected Documents and Bibliography* (Boston: Houghton-Mifflin, 1963), p. 41 (emphasis added).

92 Larson, *The "Cuban Crisis,"* p. 46 (emphasis added).

93 U.S. Department of State, *Bulletin*, vol. XLVIII, no. 1220 (November 12, 1962).

94 U.S. Department of State, *Bulletin*, vol. XLVIII, no 1220 (November 12, 1962), p. 724.

95 Larson, *The 'Cuban Crisis,'* p. 61 (emphasis added).

96 Larson, *The 'Cuban Crisis,'* p. 63.

97 Larson, *The 'Cuban Crisis,'* p. 66 (emphasis added).

98 Larson, *The 'Cuban Crisis,'* p. 67 (emphasis added).

99 Larson, *The 'Cuban Crisis,'* p. 76.

100 Larson, *The 'Cuban Crisis,'* p. 78.

101 Larson, *The 'Cuban Crisis,'* p. 79 (emphasis added).

102 Larson, *The 'Cuban Crisis,'* p. 79.

103 Larson, *The 'Cuban Crisis,'* p. 81.

104 U.S. Department of State, *Bulletin*, vol. XLVII, no. 1220 (November 12, 1962), p. 734.

105 The *New York Times*, October 25, 1962, p. 25.

106 The *New York Times*, October 25, 1962, p. 23.

107 The *New York Times*, October 25, 1962, p. 23.

108 The *New York Times*, October 26, 1962, p. 19.

109 U.S. Department of State, *Bulletin*, vol. XLVII, no. 1220 (November 12, 1962), p. 734737.

110 U.S. Department of State, *Bulletin*, vol. XLVII, no. 1220 (November 12, 1962), pp. 737740 (emphasis added).

111 See, i.e., "Letter of President Kennedy to Acting Secretary General U Thant," White House press release dated October 25, 1962, US Department of State, *Bulletin*, vol. XLVII, no. 1220 (November 12, 1962), p. 740; "White House Statement on Confirmation of Missile Build-up in Cuba, October 26, 1962, *Bulletin*, p. 740-741; "White House Statement on Soviet Proposals," October 27, 1962, *Bulletin*, p. 741; "Letter from President Kennedy to Chairman Khrushchev, October 27, 1962, *Bulletin*, p. 743; "Statement by President Kennedy on Receipt of Chairman's Khrushchev Letter," October 28, 1962, *Bulletin*, p. 745; "Letter From President Kennedy to Chairman Khrushchev, October 28, 1962, *Bulletin*, pp. 745-746; "Brief Address from White House by radio and television by President Kennedy, November 2, 1962, *Bulletin*, p. 762; and "Statement Issued by Assistant

Secretary of Defense Arthur Sylvester on removal of Soviet Missiles from Cuba," November 8, 1962, The *New York Times*, November 9, 1962, p. 3.

112 U.S. Department of State, *Bulletin*, (November 19, 1973), pp. 654-655.

113 U.S. Department of State, *Bulletin*, December 10, 1962), pp. 834-875.

114 U.N. Security Council, Official records, 1024th meeting (October 24, 1962), pp. 12-13.

115 Walton, *Cold War*, p. 108; Abel, *The Missile Crisis*, p. 18.

116 Carlos Franqui, *Family Portrait with Fidel* (New York: Random House, 1984), p. 201. I corrected the translation following the original in Spanish.

117 Schlesinger, *A Thousand Days*, p. 747.

118 Alexander L. George and Richard Smoke, *Deterrence in American Foreign Policy* (New York: Columbia University Press, 1974), p. 463.

119 Arthur Krock, "But a Naval Patrol is not an 'Invasion,'" *The New York Times*, August 30, 1962, p. 28.

120 See, i.e., Roger Hagan and Barnton Bernstein, "Military Value of Missiles in Cuba," *Bulletin of the Atomic Scientists*, vol. 19 (February, 1963), pp. 8-13.

121 See, i.e., Allison, *Essence of Decision,* pp. 53-55; also, Albert Wohlstetter and Roberta Wohlstetter, *Controlling the Risks in Cuba,* Adelphi Paper 17 (London: International Institute for Strategic Studies, April, 1965), pp. 10-12.

122 According to the old military dictum, assumption is the mother of all fuck-ups. However, any person who has read the official American documents produced during the crisis, the White House transcripts, and the oral interviews made many years later by some participants in the crisis, will surely agree with me that "assumed" is one of the most frequently used words appearing in these texts.

123 Robert Kennedy, *Thirteen Days*, p. 3

124 Hugh Sidey, *John F. Kennedy, President* (New York: Atheneum, 1963), p. 222, 297.

125 Montague Kern, Patricia W. Levering and Ralph B. Levering, *The Kennedy Crises* (Chapel Hill, N.C.: The University of Carolina Press, 1983), p. 100.

126 "GOP Campaign Chief Says Cuba Is Top Issue," the Washington Post, October 17, 1962, p. 5; also, "Congressmen and Editors Choose Cuba as the Main Campaign Issue," the *Washington Post*, October 18, 1962, p. 2.

127 Victor Lasky, *JFK: The Man and the Myth* (New York: Macmillan, 1963), p. 562.

128 Kern, Levering and Levering, *The Kennedy Crises*, p. 140.

129 See, David Horowitz, *The Free World Colossus* (New York: Hill and Wang, 1965), p. 380.

130 Henry Pachter, *Collision Course: The Cuban Missiles and Coexistence* (New York: Praeger, 1963), p. 30.

131 The *New York Times*, International Edition, October 26, 1962.

132 See Walton, *Cold War*, p. 143.

133 Robert A. Divine, Introduction to Robert A. Divine, ed., *The Cuban Missile Crisis* (Chicago: Quadrangle, 1971). p. 4.

134 Wise and Ross, *The Invisible Government,* pp. 317-318.

135 See, Ronald Steel, "The Kennedy's and the Missile Crisis," in Morton H. Halperin and Arnold Kanter, eds., *Readings in American Foreign Policy* (Boston: Little, Brown and Company, 1973), p. 207.

136 New studies by Blight, Allyn, Welch and others have only translated the blame to Nikita Khrushchev, but the alarmist emphasis in trying to prove at all costs how close we were to the brink has only been increased.

137 Richard J. Walton, *Cold War and Counter-Revolution: The Foreign Policy of John F. Kennedy* (New York: The Viking Press, 1972), p. 104.

138 Louise Fitzsimmons, *The Kennedy Doctrine* (New York: Random House, 1972), p. 126.

139 Louise Heren, *No Hail, No Farewell* (New York: Harper, 1971), p. 251.

140 Sidney Lens, *The Military-Industrial Complex* (Philadelphia: Pilgrim Press, 1970), p. 91.

141 *Public Papers of the Presidents, John F. Kennedy,* 1962, p. 848.

142 Allison, *Essence of Decision,* p. i.

143 Allison, *Essence of Decision,* p. 218.

144 See, John Steinbruner, "National Security and the Concept of Strategic Stability," *Journal of Conflict Resolution,* vol. 22, no. 3 (September 1978), p. 424.

145 Thomas L. Martin, Jr., and Donald C. Lathan, *Strategy for Survival* (Tucson: University of Arizona Press, 1972), p. 194

146 *Time,* August 10, 1992, p. 36.

147 Col. David H. Hackworth, U.S. Army (ret.), "Hell in a Handbasket," *Maxim,* January 2001, p. 132. Commonly called "the football," this is a titanium-made, ordinary looking briefcase carried 24 hours a day by a military officer who must stay as close as possible to the President. The briefcase carries the secret codes to give the launch orders for a nuclear attack.

148 Neville Brown, *Nuclear War* (New York: Praeger, 1964), p. 80.

149 Sorensen, *Kennedy,* p. 675. The possibility that Khrushchev's move had been a hoax was explored by Richard Ned Lebow in "Was Khrushchev Bluffing in Cuba," *Bulletin of the Atomic Scientists,* April 1988, pp. 38-42. I talked to Professor Lebow over the phone in 1993 or 1994 (I don't remember exactly the date), and I got the impression that he had recanted what he originally wrote in the *Bulletin.*

150 Eliot A. Cohen, "Why We Should Stop Studying the Cuban Missile Crisis," *The National Interest,* Winter 1985-86, p. 4.

151 Daniel J. Boorstin, *The Image* (New York: Atheneum, 1962), p. 9.

152 Boorstin, *The Image,* pp. 11-12.

153 The phrase is from R.H. Ferell, *American Diplomacy: A History* (New York: W.W. Norton, 1975), p. 779.

154 David Wise, *The Politics of Lying* (New York: Random House, 1973), p. 29.

155 Wise, *The Politics of Lying,* p. 29.

156 Boorstin, *The Image,* p. 40.

157 See. i.e., Lewis J. Paper, *The Promise and the Performance* (New York: Crown Publishers, 1975), p. 194.

158 James Reston, The *New York Times*, February 25, 1963.
159 Charles O. Lerche, Jr., *The Cold War... and After* (Englewood Cliff, N.J.: Prentice-Hall, 1965), p. 112.

Epilogue

1 The fact was discovered a long time ago by intelligence services all around the world. See Appendix 1, The Evaluation of Information.

2 By the way, everything Mr. Bush is now accusing Sadam Hussein of, without changing a single comma, can be applied to Castro, plus the fact that Castro and Hussein have a very close anti-American collaboration. Why, then, are we after Hussein, half-way around the globe, when his twin brother Fidel, just ninety miles away from our shores, is ignored? A big mystery indeed.

For a detailed study of Castro's efforts to develop atomic, chemical and bacteriological weapons, see Servando González, *The Secret Fidel Castro*, pp. 53-75. For an analysis of Castro's probable role in the September 11th, 2001, attacks, see Servando González, "A Sad Day For Fidel Castro?," *Pravda* online, English edition, October 2001.

3 Roberta Wohlstetter's well-known study of the Cuban missile crisis is a good example of the above-mentioned type of analysis. The conclusions she arrives at, come out of totally erroneous premises. After reading John Toland's *Infamy*, one even wonders about the value of her conclusions on Pearl Harbor.

4 It seems, however, that this is changing rapidly.

5 Richard M. Nixon, "Cuba, Castro, and John F. Kennedy," *Reader's Digest*, November 1964, p. 297.

6 See, i.e., Néstor T. Carbonell, *And the Russians Stayed: The Sovietization of Cuba* (New York: William Morrow, 1989).

7 Apparently, the ever distrustful Castro initially suspected Khrushchev would attempt to poison him during his visit to the Soviet Union. In order to overcome his fears, Alekseev had to tell him that he could bring his own drinking water from Cuba. See Fursenko and Naftali, *"One Hell of a Gamble,"* pp. 326-327. I recall that, at the time of the Escalante-Kudryavtsev affair, rumors ran in Cuba that Khrushchev had plans to invite Castro to visit the Soviet Union and, once there, commit him by force to a mental institution. With the benefit of hindsight I confess that it would have brought great benefits, both for the Russian and Cuban people.

8 On Castro's long dream to possess nuclear and other weapons of mass destruction, see Servando González, *The Secret Fidel Castro*, pp. 53-75

9 The fact that, just a few days after Castro destroyed the plot, he expelled from Cuba several KGB officers, indicates that the "microfraction" was another Soviet-concocted plot to overthrow Castro. Among the Soviet intelligence officers expelled from Havana were Rudolf P. Shlyapnikov, second secretary of the Soviet embassy; Mikhail Roy, of the press agency *Novosti*; Vadim Lestov, another "journalist;" and several KGB advisers to the DGI. See, John Barron, *KGB: The Secret Work of*

Soviet Secret Agents (London: Corgi, 1979), p. 204. The fact also indicates that the Soviet's suspicions about Castro, and the plan to get rid of him, didn't die with Khrushchev's demotion.

Raúl Martín, a Cuban journalist who worked for more than 10 years for *Prensa Latina*, Castro's press agency, affirms that during 1987 to 1989, a special KGB team explored the possibility of overthrowing Castro by force. According to Martín, Mikhail Gorbachev himself ordered the team to explore anti-Castro feelings among the Cuban military. To this end, a Soviet military group, under the cover of a "historical investigation" of the Cuban armed forces, visited dozens of army and MININT units and schools all around the Island. Martín claims that, because of his pro-perestroika feelings, he was recruited in 1987 by KGB officers working under cover for *Novosti*. For a full account of Martín's story, see, Olance Nogueras, "Periodista cubano dice KGB quiso derrocar a Castro," *El Nuevo Herald*, June 27, 1998.

The fact that the Soviets had intentions to overthrow Castro by force was not alien to the U.S. intelligence services. During the missile crisis, CIA director John McCone speculated that one of the reasons for such a large number of Soviet troops in Cuba may have been "to insert sufficient Soviet specialists and military leaders to take Cuba away from Castro and establish it as a true Soviet controlled satellite." See, "Memorandum of Discussion with the President's Special Assistant for National Security Affairs (Bundy)," Department of State, *Foreign Relations of the United States, 1961-1963*, Volume xi, Washington, D.C., October 5, 1962, 5:15 p.m.

10 Jorge I. Dominguez, "Cuban Foreign Policy," *Foreign Affairs* 57 (Fall 1978), p. 83. See also Jorge I. Dominguez, "Cuba as Superpower," *Cold War International History Project Electronic Bulletin*, Nos. 8-9 (Winter 1996-1997).

11 "Military Outcomes of the Cuban Revolution," in Irving Louis Horowitz, ed., *Cuban Communism, Fourth Edition* (New Brunswick: Transaction Books, 1981), p. 590.

12 Executive action: CIA's euphemism for political assassination. In a recent book, *Dulces guerreros cubanos* (Barcelona: Seix Barral, 1999), Cuban writer Norberto Fuentes deals in detail with aspects of the military career of Colonel Tony de la Guardia, probably the best of Castro's hit men, who ended his life facing a firing squad. But, while he was still Castro's hit man, de la Guardia boasted of having assassinated, following Castro's direct orders, more than forty of Fidel's real and imagined enemies, mostly abroad, some of them in the U.S.

13 On Castro's fascist proclivities, see Servando González, *The Secret Fidel Castro*, pp. 274-295

14 Philip Bonsal, *Cuba, Castro and the United States* (Pittsburgh. Penn.: University of Pittsburgh Press, 1971).

15 On this, Fidel copied Hitler's idea of sending Nazi soldiers disguised as "tourists" to Austria and Czechoslovakia before the German invasion.

16 A common joke told in Cuba in the late 1960s was that Castro's revolution was actually a top secret CIA operation to stop the spread of communism in Latin America.

17 The fact that Reagan's Star Wars was an intelligence hoax used to destroy the Soviet economy is explained in Alvin A. Snyder, *Warriors of Disinformation: American Propaganda, Soviet Lies, and the Winning of the Cold War* (New York: Arcade Publishing, 1995), pp. 120-125.

18 Richard J. Payne, *Opportunities and Dangers of Soviet -Cuban Expansion* (Albany, N.Y.: State University of New York Press, 1988), p. 9; also in W. Raymond Duncan, *The Soviet Union and Cuba* (New York: Praeger, 1985), p. 1.

According to some U.S. government estimates based on official Cuban and Soviet sources, from 1961 to 1983 the Soviets threw $34.290 billion U.S. dollars down into Castro's Cuban black hole. See U.S. Congress, *Cuba Faces the Economic Realities of the 1980s* (Washington, D.C.: U.S. Government Printing Office, 1982, p. 16; also Directorate of Intelligence, *The Cuban Economy: A Statistical Review*, Reference Aid ALA 84-10052 (Washington, D.C., June 1984).

19 Full of cynicism, I admit, but nevertheless very close to the truth.

20 See, Fursenko and Naftali, *"One Hell of a Gamble,"* p. 325.

21 The only reason for this to be true —if the order actually was given— was that Khrushchev had an extraordinary sense of humor.

22 As I mentioned before, after the end of the Cold War, stories about Soviet "stupidity," particularly in books and papers about the Cuban missile crisis, have turned into a cottage industry in which the Russians have gladly contributed to enhance the image of their own supposed stupidity. This collaboration has proved to be profitable for both sides: in exchange for hard currency, so scarce in Russia in the early years after the collapse of the Soviet Union, and invitations with all costs paid to attend conferences in the U.S., some clever, greedy Russians have been telling American scholars what they love to hear.

23 And perhaps not just cloak, but also dagger.

24 The main cause for the catastrophic failure of the "critical oral interview" methodology used by James Blight and his followers, is that it passes raw data as finished intelligence. No wonder why, after fifteen years of continuous research and dozens of books published on the subject, the main questions of the Cuban missile crisis remain unanswered —forcing historians to continuously resort to the Khrushchev-stupid-fool hypothesis and to use the word "assume" hundreds of times— and the event looks more obscure than never before. What Blight, Allyn, Welch, *et al.* have written is, wittingly or unwittingly, tantamount to *dezinformatsia*.

25 As an example of the limitations of the traditional historian's research and analysis tools I can mention Angelo Codevilla's *Informing Statecraft: Intelligence for a New Century* (New York: The Free Press, 1992). This potentially excellent book lost most of its value because the author applied the historian's tools to the analysis of intelligence and espionage. This is particularly difficult to understand in the case of Codevilla, who has a substantial training and experience in the field

of intelligence and espionage. He was a senior staff member of the Senate Intelligence Committee from 1977 to 1985.

26 I believe that American-style scholarly "detachment," a standard by which Anglo-Saxon scholars judge the rest of the scholarly work, is not only hypocritical, but, as when they try to impose it upon other cultures, also a manifestation of cultural imperialism.

27 Granted, most of the American scholars who have participated in the meetings about the crisis are persons of proved honesty and integrity whose only fault is perhaps to have been too naïve in dealing with spies and corrupt politicians. But there are some participants who have shown a conscientious effort to confuse, distort and disinform. Prominent among them are Robert McNamara, Aleksandr Alexeev, Sergo Mikoyan, and, last but no least, Fidel Castro. I only mention Castro among the Cuban participants, because the rest of them are just Castro-clones, living in terror under the watchful eye of the trigger-happy tyrant.

Also important is the role of the scholars who have been instrumental in the occurrence of these meetings, particularly the ones in Havana. Prominent among them are James G. Blight, Bruce J. Allyn, David A. Welch and Peter Kornbluh. Some day, probably sooner than they expect, the secret archives in Havana — particularly the ones at the MININT and the DGI— will be truly opened, and we will discover their true intentions and motivations for wittingly distorting the historical record.

28 In this sense —and only in this sense— Secretary of State Colin Powell was right when he claimed that Castro has "done some good things for his people." Actually Castro has done also some good things for *his* cows, *his* chickens, *his* dogs and for most of the things he owns, hence his initial interest in public health. As a feudal lord, Castro takes good care of *his* property —which now comprises the whole island of Cuba and its inhabitants. On Powell's words see Jay Nordlinger, "Castro and 'His People,'" *National Review*, April 26, 2001. Nordlinger found Powell's words "alarming and repugnant."

29 Humberto Fontova, "Yankee Doodle Castro," *NewsMax.com*, September 3, 2002.

30 Evidence indicates that Cuban slaves in the 19th century were better fed than Castro's subjects. A comparison between the average caloric content of a slave's daily food intake and what an average Cuban can buy with his meager salary shows that, though both diets lack variety and flavor, the slaves were by far better fed. For information about the Cuban slaves' diet see Manuel Moreno Fraginals, *El Ingenio*, Tomo I (La Habana: Editorial de Ciencias Sociales, 1978).

Select Bibliography

Books

Abel, Elie. *The Missile Crisis*. Philadelphia: Lippincot, 1966. Abel's analysis of the Cuban missile crisis follows the Liberal Establishment version of the events as told by the Kennedy administration officials, sycophants and court historians. Notwithstanding its lack of objectivity this book became a classic on the Cuban missile crisis.

Acuña, Juan Antonio. *Cuba: revolución traicionada*. Montevideo, Uruguay: Imp. Ed. Goes, 1962. Useful analysis of Castro's efforts to join the Soviet block and the pressures he pu on the Soviets to reach his goal.

Adomeit, Hannes. *Soviet Risk-Taking and Crisis Behavior: A Theoretical and Empirical Analysis*. New York: George Allen and Unwind, 1984. Knowledgeable analysis of the decisionmaking process in the high echelons of the Soviet government.

Alexander, Robert J. *Communism in Latin America*. New Brunswick, N.J.: Rutgers University Press, 1957. A useful book to understand the activities of the Soviet controlled Communist parties in Latin America and particularly the Partido Socialista Popular, the Cuban Communist party. See pages 278-285 for an interesting analysis of the relations between Batista and the Cuban Communists.

Allen, Robert Loring. *Soviet Influence in Latin America: The Role of Economic Relations*. Washington, D.C.: Public Affairs Press, 1959.

Allison, Graham T. *Essence of Decision: Explaining the Cuban Missile Crisis*. Boston: Little, Brown, Co., 1971. Interesting analysis, now turned into a classic on the subject, about the decision-making process in the American government. Its weak side, however, is that its takes at face value the American version of the facts, as told by President Kennedy and his coterie, without any attempt to a critical analysis.

_____. "Conceptual Models and the Cuban Missile Crisis." in Morton H. Halperin and Arnold Kanter, eds., *Readings in American Foreign Policy*. Boston: Little, Brown and Co., 1973

Alsop, Stewart. *The Center: People and Power in Political Washington*. New York: Popular Library, 1968. Useful study to better understand the people aound President Kennedy during the Cuban missile crisis.

Alvarez Díaz, José R. *La trayectoria de Castro*. Miami, Fla.: Ed. AIP, 1964. A strongly biased analysis of Castro's motives to joining the Cuban communists. Evidence points to the fact that the communists were the ones who joined Castro.

___. *Un estudio sobre Cuba.* Coral Gables, Florida: University of Miami Press, 1963.

Andrew, Christopher M., and Oleg Gordievsky. *KGB: The Inside Story.* New York: Harper Collins, 1990.

Arnault, Jacques. *Cuba et le Marxisme.* Paris: Editions Sociales, 1963. Idealized study of Castro's Marxist(?) inclinations, seen from a European leftist perspective.

Art, Robert J., and Kenneth N. Waltz, eds. *The Use of Force: International Politics and Foreign Policy.* Boston: Little, Brown, 1971. Real macho men don't eat quiche: they play with big guns!

Ball, Desmond. *Politics and Force Levels: The Strategic Missile Program of the Kennedy Administration.* Berkeley: University of California Press, 1981.

Barnet, Richard J. *Intervention and Revolution.* New York: World, 1968.

Barnet, Richard J. *Roots of War.* Baltimore, Maryland: Penguin Books, 1973. The militaryindustrial-academic complex in action.

Barron, John. *KGB: The Secret World of Soviet Secret Agents.* London: Corgi, 1975.

Beal, Richard Smith. *System Analysis of International Crises.* Washington, D.C.: University Press of America, 1979. Useful information about the Cuban missile crisis on pages 199206.

Beggs, Robert, ed. *The Cuban Missile Crisis.* London: Longman Group Limited, 1971.

Bender, Lynn Darrell. *The Politics of Hostility: Castro's Revolution and United States Policy.* Hato Rey, P. R.: Inter American University Press, 1975. A repetition of the old story that American mistakes were the cause of Fidel antiamericanism.

Benton, William. *The Voice of Latin America.* New York: Harper and Row, 1965. Useful information about Communist advances in Cuba prior to 1959.

Bernstein, Barton J. "The Cuban Missile Crisis." in Lynn H. Miler and Ronald W. Pruessen, eds., *Reflections On the Cold War.* Philadelphia: Temple Univ. Press, 1974.

Beschloss, Michael R. *The Crisis Years. Kennedy and Khrushchev, 1960-1963.* New York: HarperCollins, 1991. Excellent documentation in a well-written (sometimes too poetic), nonadulatory view of the Kennedy administration. Unfortunately the chapters dealing with the Cuban missile crisis just repeat the old witches and elves stories found elsewhere. Also, the painstaking accuracy the author shows when dealing with Soviet and American sources is not evidenced when he deals with Cuban ones. One example is calling Castro's son Felix. (Fidel Castro's only recognized son is Fidel Castro Díaz, a nuclear engineer). Another is the story about

Castro's demands that Khrushchev fire the Soviet ambassador Kudryatsev. (Castro summarily expelled Kudryatsev from Cuba without asking for Khrushchev's permission.)

Beschloss, Michael R. *Mayday: Eisenhower, Khrushchev and the U-2 Affair.* New York: Harper, 1986. Another conspiracy story that is true.

Bethel, Paul D. *The Losers.* New Rochelle, New York: Arlington House, 1969. This book, that claims to be the definitive report, by an eyewitness of the Communist conquest of Cuba, is another futile attempt to build a Communist past for Fidel. The background information in it, however, is very good.

Blackstack, Paul W., and Frank L. Schaf, Jr. *Intelligence, Espionage, Counterespionage, and Covert Operations.* Detroit, Mich.: Gale Research, 1978. A useful guide to intelligence bibliography and sources.

Blasier, Cole. *The Giant's Rival: the USSR and Latin America.* Pittsburgh: University of Pittsburgh Press, 1982.

Bloomfield, Lincoln P., Walter C. Clemens, Jr., and Franklyn Griffiths. *Khrushchev and the Arms Race: Soviet Interests in Arms Control and Disarmament, 1954-1964.* Cambridge, Mass.: The MIT Press, 1966.

Bobrow, Davis. "New Approaches: Decision Making and the Cuban Missile Crisis." in Davis Bobrow, ed., *International Relations.* New York: The Free Press, 1972.

Bogush, E. Iu., *Mif ob "Eksporte Revoliutsii" i Sovetskaya Vneshniaia Politika.* [The Mith of "Export of Revolution" and Soviet Foreign Policy]. Moscow: Izdatel'stvo "Meszhdunarodnye Otnosheniia", 1965. Soviet point of view about exporting revolution, containing veiled criticism to Castro's policies toward Latin America.

Bohlen, Charles. *Witness to History, 1929-1969.* New York: W.W. Norton, 1973.

Bonsal, Philip W. *Cuba, Castro and the United States.* Pittsburgh. Penn.: University of Pittsburgh Press, 1971. Bonsal was the last American ambassador in Havana before the U. S. broke diplomatic relations with Cuba in Jannuary, 1961. He searches in vain for American policy mistakes that justify Castro's anti-American reaction. Good information about the first months of the revolution and how Castro took total control of it.

Boorstein, Daniel. *The Image: A Guide to Pseudo Events in America.* New York: Atheneum, 1972. Was the Cuban missile crisis a pseudo event?

Borisov, Oleg B., and B. T. Koloskov. *Soviet-Chinese Relations, 1945-1970.* Bloomington, Ind.: Indiana Univ. Press, 1975.

Bottone, Edgar M. *The Missile Gap: A Study of the Formulation of Military and Political Policy.* Cranbury, N.J.: Fairleigh Dickinson Univ. Press, 1971. The famous "missile gap" was actually a "missile crap."

Brams, Steven. *Game Theory and Politics.* New York: The Free Press, 1975. See pp. 39-50 for an interesting study of the "chicken game," which may well be applied to the analysis of the Cuban missile crisis.

Brockriede, Wayne, and Robert L Scott. *Moments in the Rhetoric of the Cold War*. New York: Random House, 1970.

Brodie, Bernard. *War and Politics*. New York: Macmillan, 1973.

Brown, Neville. *Nuclear War*. New York: Praeger, 1964. Interesting technical data about the Soviet missiles in Cuba. See reference on p. 81 to the fact that nuclear warheads were never seen on the island, nor the radiation from nuclear warheads was ever detected.

Brown, Thomas. *JFK: History of an Image*. Bloomington, Ind.: Indiana University Press, 1988.

Bruck, H. W., and B. M. Sapin, eds. *Foreign Policy Decision-Making: An Approach to the Study of International Politics*. New York: The Free Press, 1962.

Brumberg, Abraham, ed. *Russia Under Khrushchev*. New York: Praeger, 1962. Collection of essays giving a good idea of Khrushchev's power at the time of the Cuban missile crisis.

Brune, Lester H. *The Missile Crisis of October 1962: A Review of Issues and References*. Claremont, Calif.: Regina Books, 1985.

Brzezinsky, Zbygniew. *The Soviet Bloc: Unity and Conflict, Revised Edition*. Cambridge, Mass.: Harvard Univ. Press, 1967. Probably one of the most lucid analysis written about the Soviet Bloc. Useful to get a good idea of the problems Khrushchev was facing at the time of the Cuba missile crisis.

———. "U.S. - Soviet Relations." in Henry Oven, ed., *The Next Phase in Foreign Policy*. Washington, D.C.: The Brookings Institution , 1973.

Brzezinsky, Zbygniew and Samuel P. Huntington. *Political Power: USA/USSR*. New York: Viking, 1963.

Bureau of Intelligence and Research. *Key Khrushchev Missile Statements*. Intelligence Report no. 8288, 1 July 1960.

Burks, David D. *Cuba Under Castro*. Headline Series # 165, Foreign Policy Association, New York, June 29, 1964. Short study about the first years of Castro in power. Well documented.

———. "Soviet Policy for Castro's Cuba." in John J. TePaske and Sydney Nettleton Fisher, eds., *Explosive Forces in Latin America*. Columbus, Ohio: Ohio State University Press, 1964

Burner, David, and Thomas R. West. *The Torch is Passed: The Kennedy Brothers and American Liberalism*. New York: Atheneum, 1984. And the myth goes on!

Burns, James MacGregor. *John Kennedy: A Political Profile*. New York: Hartcourt, 1960.

Burrows, William E. *Deep Black: Space Espionage and National Security*. New York: Random House, 1986.

Carpozzi, George, Jr. *Red Spies in Washington*. New York: Trident Press, 1968.

According to this author, the American capital has always been a fertile soil for Russian espionage activities.

Cassel, Christine, Michael McCally and Henry Abraham, eds. *Nuclear Weapons and Nuclear War.* New York: Praeger, 1984.

Casuso, Teresa. *Cuba and Castro.* New York: Random House, 1961. Interesting information about Castro strange rush to become a "Communist." First-hand account of his visit to the U.S. in 1959.

Cave Brown, Anthony, ed. *Dropshot: The United States Plan for War with the U.S.S.R. in 1957.* New York: Dial Press, 1978. Khrushchev had enough reasons to be scared in October, 1962.

CBS. *A Conversation with President Kennedy.* 17 December 1962, mimeo.

Center for Cuban Studies. *The U.S. Blockade: a Documentary History.* New York, 1979.

Chayes, Abram. *The Cuban Missile Crisis: International Crises and the Role of Law.* New York: Oxford University Press, 1974. A stydy of the crisis from the point of view of international law.

Chayes, Abram, Thomas Erlich, and Andreas F. Lowenfeld. "The Missile Crisis." in *International Legal Process*, 2 vols. Boston: Little, Brown, 1969, Vol. II, pp. 1057-1149.

Clinch, Nancy Gager.*The Kennedy Neurosis*.New York: Grosset and Dunlap, 1973.

Cline, Ray S. *Secrets, Spies and Scholars: Blueprint for the Essential CIA.* Washington, D.C.: Acropolis Press, 1976.

Clissold, Stephen, ed. *Soviet Relations with Latin America 1918-1968: A Documentary Survey.* New York: Oxford University Press, 1970.

Collins, John M. *American and Soviet Military Trends Since the Cuban Missile Crisis.* Georgetown: Center for Strategic and International Studies, 1978.

Conquest, Robert. *Power and Policy in the U.S.S.R.* New York: St. Martin's Press, 1961. Important work to understanding the extent of Khrushchev's power.

_____. *Russia After Khrushchev.* NewYork: Praeger, 1965. A study of the infighting among different factions in the CPSU and the inherent instability of the Soviet leadership.

Conte Agüero, Luis. *Los dos rostros de Fidel Castro.* Mexico, D.F.: Editorial Jus, 1960. Conte Agüero, a former close friend and associate, brings important information portraying Fidel as the Great Dissembler.

Cook, Fred J. *The Cuban Missile Crisis, October 1962: The U. S. and Russia Face a Nuclear Showdown.* New York: Franklin Watts, 1972. The myth goes on.

Cousins, Norman. *The Improbable Triumvirate: John F. Kennedy, Pope John, Nikita Khrushchev.* New York: Norton, 1972.

Crankshaw, Edward. *Khrushchev's Russia.* Baltimore, Md.: Penguin Books,

1959.

_____. *Khrushchev, A Career*. New York: Viking Press, 1966. Insightful study on the Soviet Premier.

Crassweller, Robert D., *Cuba and the U.S.; The Tangled Relationship*. New York: Foreign Policy Association, 1971.

Crisp, Norman. *The Brink*. New York: Pocket Books, 1983.

Dallin, Alexander, and Alan F. Westin, eds. *Politics in the Soviet Union*. New York: Harcourt, Brace and World, 1966.

Daniel, James, and John G. Hubbel. *Strike in the West*. New York: Holt, Rinehart and Winston, 1963.

Deadline Data on World Affairs. *Cuban Crisis*. New York: Keynote Publications Inc, 1963.

Deakin, James. *Straight Stuff: The Reporters, the White House and the Truth*. New York: William Morrow, 1984. It seems that the Kennedys shared with Castro a totalitarian dislike for a free press.

Deane, Michael J. *Political Control of the Soviet Armed Forces*. New York: Crane, Russak, 1977. Revealing insights of the relations between Khrushchev and the Soviet military.

Delmas, Claude. *Crises à Cuba: 1961-1962*. Bruxelles: Editions Complexe, 1983.

DeRivera, J. *The Psychological Dimension of Foreign Policy*. Columbus, Oh.: Charles E. Merril, 1968. Key work to understanding the decision-making process in the United States government.

Destler, I. M., Leslie H. Gelb and Anthony Lake. *Our Own Worst Enemy: The Unmaking of American Foreign Policy*. New York: Simon and Schuster, 1984. As Pogo said: We have met the enemy and he is us!

Detzer, David. *The Brink: Cuban Missile Crisis, 1962*. New York: Thomas Y. Crowell, 1979. Useful information about the Soviet missiles in Cuba, whose range was much shorter that the Kennedy administration's claimed, and about the role of the U-2 spy plane in discovering them.

Deutsch, Karl W. *The Nerves of Government: Models of Political Communication and Control*. New York: The Free Press, 1966. See pages 107-109 for an interesting introduction to Deutsch's original study of the parallels between cybernetics and politics.

Devlin, Kevin. *The Soviet-Cuban Confrontation: Economic Reality and Political Judo*. Research Department of Radio Free Europe, 1 April, 1968. Analysis of Soviet-Cuban relations after the missile crisis.

_____. "The Castroist Challenge to Communism." in J. Gregory Oswald and Anthony J. Strovel,eds., *The Soviet Union and Latin America*. New York: Praeger, 1970.

Dinerstein, Herbert S. *War and the Soviet Union*. New York: Praeger, 1962.

_____ *The Making of a Missile Crisis*. Baltimore, Md.: The John Hopkins University Press, 1976. Interesting and well documented analysis of the different elements involved in the crisis. Basically it follows the "good-boys-vs-bad-boys" U.S. government official line.

Divine, Robert A., ed. *The Cuban Missile Crisis*. Chicago: Quadrangle, 1971.

Domhoff, G. William. "Who Made American Foreign Policy, in David Horowitz, ed., *The Corporations and the Cold War*. New York: Monthly Review Press, 19969. A true eye-opener.

Donald, Aida DiPace, ed. *John F. Kennedy and the New Frontier*. New York: Hill and Wang, 1966.

Draper, Theodore. *Castros Revolution: Myths and Realities*. New York: Frederick A. Praeger, 1962. Perceptive, useful study of Castro's first years in power. Though unfriendly to Castro, it avoids commonplace, unjustified criticism.

_____. *Castroism: Theory and Practice*. New York: Praeger, 1965. Draper studies the relations between Fidel and the Cuban communists. He is one of the first authors to question the accepted wisdom that Fidel Castro was, or has been at any time in his life, a Communist.

_____. *Abuse of Power*. New York: Viking, 1967. Interesting study abou how the U.S. government lies to the American people.

Driver, M. J. *Crisis and Reciprocity in Soviet-American Interaction*. Los Angeles: University of Southern California, School of International Relations, August, 1969.

Dulles, Allen. *The Craft of Inteligence*. New York: New American Library, 1965. A classical study in the field of intelligence. Useful information about the American intelligence agencies involvement in the Bay of Pigs operation and their role in the Cuban missile crisis. But, written by a spymaster, don't expect much truth on its pages.

Dumont, René. *Cuba: Socialism and Development*. New York: Grove Press, 1970. First-hand analysis by a leading economist of Castro's economic blunders in the first years of the revolution.

Duncan, W. Raymond, ed. *Soviet Policy in Developing Countries*. Waltham, Mass.: GinnBlaisdell, 1970.

Duncan, W. Raymond. *The Soviet Union and Cuba: Interests and Influence*. New York: Praeger, 1985. Was Fidel a Soviet pawn; an independent actor pursuing his own interests that not always coincide with the Soviet ones; or none of the above?

Earl T. Smith. *The Fourth Floor*. New York: Random House, 1962. A former U. S. Ambassador to Havana expresses his views about CIA and US State Department officers who helped Castro to take power in Cuba. Revealing inside information about how the U. S. government orchestrated Batista's downfall.

Edmonds, Robin. *Soviet Foreign Policy 1962-1973: The Paradox of Superpower*. London: Oxford University Press, 1975. Useful information about the Soviet-Cuban troubled relations after the crisis.

Epperson, A. Ralph. *The Unseen Hand*. Tucson, Arizona: Publius Press, 1985. Epperson is one of the few authors who noticed the obvious fact that the presence of strategic missiles and their nuclear warheads in Cuba in 1962 was never proved. See pp. 120-122.

Epstein, Edward Jay. *Deception. The Invisible War Between the KGB and the CIA*. New York: Simon and Schuster, 1989. Insightful report on the world of double agents, moles, dangles, disinformation, and deception loops. Interesting first-hand information on James Jesus Angleton, the man who was never convinced of Penkovsky's bona fides.

⎯⎯⎯. "Incorporating Analysis of Foreign Governments' Deception into the US Analytical System." in Roy Godson, ed., *Intelligence Requirements for the 1980's*. Washington, D.C.: National Strategy Information Center, 1980.

Erisman, H. Michael. *Cuba's International Relations*. Boulder, Colorado: Westview Press, 1958.

Evans, Stanton M. *The Liberal Establishment*. New York: The Devin-Adair Co., 1965. Intersting details about John F. Kennedy's singular idea of freedom of the press

Facts on File. *Cuba, The U.S. and Russia, 1960-63*. New York: Facts on File, 1964.

Fainsod, Merle. *How Russia is Ruled*, rev. ed. Cambridge, Mass.: Harvard Univ. Press, 1963. Useful work to understanding the power structure in the Soviet Union.

Fitzsimmons, Louise. *The Kennedy Doctrine*. New York: Random House, 1972. Useful for its analysis of how national politics affected Kennedy's decision-making process during the crisis.

Foreign Policy Research Institute, Univ. of Penn. *Khrushchevs Strategy and its Meaning for America*. Washington, D.C.: U.S. Government Printing Office, 1960.

Frank, Robert Shelby. *Linguistic Analysis of Political Elites: A Theory of Verbal Kinesics*. Beverly Hills, Calif.: Sage Publications, 1973. Useful in the analysis of Khrushcev's famous letter to Kennedy during the Cuban missile crisis.

Frankel, Charles. *Morality and U.S. Foreign Policy*. New York: Foreign Policy Ass., Headline Series No. 224, February, 1975.

Frankland, Mark. *Khrushchev*. New York: Stein and Day, 1967.

Franqui, Carlos. *Family Portrait with Fidel*. New York: Random House, 1984. Interesting details, from a personal point of view, of Fidel's personal life in the first years of the revolution. Includes anecdotical information about how Fidel himself allegedly shot down a U-2 plane during the missile crisis. Excellent prologue by Guillermo Cabrera Infante.

Freedman, Laerence. *U.S. Intelligence and the Soviet Strategic Threat*. London: Macmillan, 1977. Good information about the "missile gap" that never was.

Freeman, Thomas, (pseud.). *The Crisis in Cuba*. Derby, Conn.: Monarch Books, [1963].

Freemantle, Brian. *CIA*. New York: Stein and Day, 1985.

Frei, Daniel. *International Crises and Crisis Management*. Westmead, U.K.: Grover Ltd., 1981.

Fromm, Erich. *May Man Prevail? An Inquiry into the Facts and Fictions of Foreign Policy*. Garden City: Doubleday & Co., 1964.

Fuller, Hellen. *Year of Trial: Kennedy's Crucial Decisions*. New York: Hartcourt Brace, 1962.

Gaddis, John Lewis. *Russia, the Soviet Union and the United States: an Interpretive History*. New York: John Wiley and Sons, 1978.

Gadney, Reg. *Kennedy*. New York: Holt, Rinehart and Winston, 1983.

Garthoff, Raymond L. *Soviet Strategy in the Nuclear Age*. New York: Praeger, 1958.

_____. *Reflections on the Cuban Missile Crisis*. Washington D.C.: Brookings, 1987.

George, Alexander L., and Richard Smoke. *Deterrence in American Foreign Policy: Theory and Practice*. New York: Columbia University Press, 1944.

_____. "The Causal Nexus Between Cognitive Beliefs and Decision Making Behavior." in L.S. Falkowski, ed., *Psychological Models in International Politics*. Boulder, Colorado: Westview, 1979.

Guerassi, John. *The Great Fear in Latin America*. New York: Collier, 1965.

Gerosa, Guido. *I missili a Cuba*. Milano: Mondadori. 1974.

Geyer, Georgie Anne. *Guerrilla Prince*. Boston: Little, Brown and Co., 1991. Thoughtful study about Castro's personality which wipes out with most myths about the bearded Caribbean dictator. Geyer was one of the firsts in noticing Castro's fascist makeup.

Gibney, Frank. *The Khrushchev Pattern*. New York: Duell, Sloan & Pearce, 1960.

Goldenberg, Boris. *The Cuban Revolution and Latin America*. New York: Praeger, 1965.

González, Servando. *Observando*. San Francisco: Ediciones El Gato Tuerto, 1986. Collection of articles and essays about Cuba, the Unites States, and the Soviet Union. Humorous and/or revisionists.

_____. *Historia herética de la revolución fidelista*. San Francisco: Ediciones El Gato Tuerto, 1986. Humorous study of Castro's early days, his Fascist persuasion and the strange circumstances under which he took power in

Cuba. An original, revisionist hypothesis explaining why Khrushchev placed strategic missiles in Cuba. (Published in Mexico by Editorial Dante under the title *Fidel Castro para herejes y otros invertebrados*).

———. *The Secret Fidel Castro: Deconstructing the Symbol*. Oakland: InteliBooks, 2001.

Gouré, Leon, and Morris Rothenberg. *Soviet Penetration in Latin America*. Miami: University of Miami Press, 1975.

Gouré, Leon. *Civil Defense in the Soviet Union*. Berkeley, Calif.: University of Californis Press, 1962.

Green, Felix. *The Enemy*. New York: Vintage Books, 1971.

Gregory, Oswald J., and Anthony J. Estrover, eds. *The Soviet Union and Latin America*. New York: Praeger, 1970.

Griffiths, John. *The Cuban Missile Crisis*. Vero Beach, Fl.: Rourke Enterprises, 1987.

Gromiko, Anatolii A. *Through Russian Eyes: President Kennedy's 1036 Days*. Washington, D.C.: International Publishers, 1973.

Halberstam, David. *The Best and the Brightest*. New York: Random House, 1972. Useful information about the men around Kennedy in his administration and how they influenced the President in his decision-making process.

Halle, Louis J. *The Cold War as History*. New York: Harper & Row, 1967.

Halper, Thomas. *Foreign Policy Crises: Appearance and Reality in Decision Making*. Columbus, Ohio: Charles E. Merrill, 1971.

Halperin, Maurice. *The Rise and Decline of Fidel Castro*. Berkeley: Univ. of California Press, 1972. Halperin lived in Cuba throughout most of the events he studies in his book. It is particularly accurate in his analysis of the internal struggle between Castro and the Cuban communists.

Headline Series, No. 157. *The Cuban Crisis: A Documentary Record*. New York: Foreign Policy Association, January 20, 1963. Major papers on the missile confrontation of 1962.

Hearst, Jr., William Randolph, B. Considine and F. Coniff, *Khrushchev and the Russian Challenge* (New York: Avon, 1961).

Heath, Jim F. *Decade of Disillusionment: The Kennedy-Johnson Years*. Bloomington, Ind.: Indiana Univ. Press, 1975.

Hermann, Charles F. *Crises in Foreign Policy*. Indianapolis: Bobbs-Merrill, 1969.

———. ed. *International Crises: Insights from Behavioral Research*. New York: The Free Press, 1972.

Hermann, M. G. *Describing Foreign Policy Behavior*. Beverly Hills, Calif.: Sage, 1982.

Hilsman, Roger. *To Move a Nation: The Politics of Foreign Policy in the Administration of John F. Kennedy*. New York: Doubleday, 1967.

Horelick, Arnold L., and Myron Rush. *Strategic Power and Soviet Foreign Policy*. Chicago: University of Chicago Press, 1966.

Hughes, Thomas L. *The Fate of Facts in a World of Men: Foreign Policy and Intelligence-Making*. New York: Foreign Policy Association, Headline Series No. 233, December 1976.

Hyland, William, and Richard W. Shryrock. *The Fall of Khrushchev*. New York: Funk and Wagnalls, 1968.

Infield, Glenn B. *Unarmed and Unafraid*. New York: Macmillan, 1970. Information about the U-2 plane and the Cuban missile crisis.

Institute for the Study of Conflict. *Annual of Power and Conflict (1962-1963)*. London: Institute for the Study of Conflict, 1963. Interesting analysis of the Cuban missile crisis.

Ion, Edmund S., ed. *The Politics of John F. Kennedy*. London: Routledge and Kegan Paul, 1964.

Jackson, D. Bruce. *Castro, the Kremlin and Communism in Latin America*. Baltimore, Md.: The Johns Hopkins University Press, 1969.

Jacobsen, Carl G. *Soviet Strategy-Soviet Foreign Policy: Military Considerations Affecting Soviet Policy-Making*. Glasgow: The University Press, 1972.

James, Daniel. Cuba: *The First Soviet Satellite in the Americas*. New York: Aron Books, 1961. A wealth of information about Castro's early days and about the first years of his regime.

James, Daniel. *Red Design for the Americas*. New York: John Day Co., 1954. Fidel's design for the Americas?

Jane's. *All the World's Aircraft, 1963-64*. New York: MacGraw-Hill, 1963. Useful information about Soviet strategic missiles like the ones they allegedly deployed in Cuba in 1962.

Janis, Irving L., and Leo Mann. *Decision Making: A Psychological Analysis of Conflict, Choice, and Commitment*. New York: Free Press, 1977.

Janis, Irving L. *Victims of Groupthink: A Psychological Study of Foreign-Policy Decisions and Fiascoes*. Boston: Houghton Mifflin Co., 1972. Interesting, though a little far-fetched, scientific analysis of the American decision-making process during the Bay of Pigs and the Cuban missile crisis. When the raw data is faulty you most probably end up by getting what computer people call GIGO (garbage in, garbage out).

Jervis, Robert. *The Logic of Images in International Politics*. Princeton, N.J.: Princeton Univ. Press, 1970.

———. *Perception and Misperception in International Politics*. Princeton, N.J.: Princeton Univ. Press, 1976.

Johnson, Loch K. *America's Secret Power. The CIA in a Democratic Society*. New York: Oxford University Press, 1989. An illuminating picture of the Central Intelligence Agency and its major missions in the fields of

intelligence gathering and analysis, counterintelligence, and covert action.
Joxe, Alain. *Socialism et crise nucleaire*. Paris: Editions de l'Herme, 1973. A European view of th crisis.
Karol, K. S. *Guerrillas in Power*. New York: Hill and Wang, 1970. An excellent study of Castro's economic blunders. A revealing analysis of Fidel's early relations with the Cuban communists.
Katz, Amron. *The Soviets and the U-2 Photos - An Heuristic Argument*. Santa Monica, Calif.: The RAND Corporation, RM-3584-PR, March 1963. The author argues that the Soviets must have known about U-2 flights over Cuba in October, 1962, and about the early discovery of the missiles.
Kellen, Konrad. *Khrushchev, a Political Portrait*. New York: Praeger, 1961. Useful to have an idea of the measure of Khrushchev's power.
Kelman, Herbert C., ed. *International Behavior*. New York: Holt, Rinehart & Winston, 1965. Analysis of decision-making processes.
Kennan, George F. *On Dealing with the Communist World*. New York: Harper & Row, 1964. A classic study on the Soviet World. Fortunately not useful any more!
Kennedy, Robert. *Thirteen Days*. New York: W.W. Norton, 1971. The well known, though highly idealized, account of the crisis from the Kennedy administration point of view. Politicians never make good historians!
Kent, Sherman. *Strategic Intelligence*. Princeton, N.J.: Princeton Univ. Press, 1966.
Kern, Montague, Patricia W. Levering and Ralph B. Levering. *The Kennedy Crises: The Press, the Presidency, and Foreign Policy*. Chapel Hill, N.C.: The Univ. of Norh Carolina Press, 1983. A useful study of crises faced by John F. Kennedy, and his particular idea of freedom of the press.
Khrushchev, Nikita S. *Khrushchev Remembers,* translated and edited by Strobe Talbot. Boston: Little, Brown and Company, 1970. Be careful about politicians trying to (re)write history. Very useful if you know how to read between the lines.

_____. *Khrushchev Remembers. The Last Testament*, translated and edited by Strobe Talbot Boston: Little, Brown and Company, 1974. Second part of Khrushchev attributed memoirs.

_____. *The Present International Situation and the Foreign Policy of the Soviet Union*. New York: Crosscurrents Press, 1963.

_____. *On Peaceful Coexistence*. Moscow: Foreign Languages Publishing House, 1961. Collection of Khrushchev's speeches on peaceful coexistence.

_____. *Speeches and Interviews on World Problems*. Moscow: Foreign Language Publishing House, 1958.

Kintner, William R. *A Study on Crisis Management*. Philadelphia: University of Pennsylvania Press, 1966. McNamara affirmed a posteriori that there is no such thing as "crisis management." I fully concur.

Kirk, Grayson, and Nils H. Wessen, eds. *The Soviet Threat: Myths and Realities*. Proceedings of the Academy of Political Science, v. 33, No. 1, 1978.

Kirkpatrick, Lyman B. *The U.S. Intelligence Community*. New York: Hill and Wang, 1973.

_____. *The Real CIA*. New York: Macmillan, 1968. The irreal CIA!

Kissinger, Henry A. *Nuclear Weapons and Foreign Policy*. New York: Harper and Brothers, 1957. Nuclear weapons as great equalizers!

Kolko, Joyce, and Gabriel Kolko. *The Limits of Power: The World and United States Foreign Policy*. New York: Harper and Row, 1972.

Kolkowicz, Roman. *Conflicts in Soviet Party-Military Relations: 1962-1963*. Santa Monica, Calif.: The RAND Corporation, RM 3760-PR, August, 1963. An revealing analysis of Soviet politico-military relations in the period following the Cuban missile crisis.

Kulski, W.W. *The Soviet Union in World Affairs*. Syracuse, N.Y.: Syracuse Univ. Press, 1973.

Kurland, Gerald. *The Cuban Missile Crisis*. Charlottevile, N. Y.: Story House Corp., 1973.

Kwitny, Jonathan. *Endless Enemies. The Making of an Unfriendly World*. New York: Penguin, 1986. The data is accurate and the information excellent, but the analysis is faulty. Kwitny's point of view is that American interventionist activities abroad have undermined U.S. foreign policy goals. A different, revisionist point of view is that America (the American militaryindustrial-academic complex) badly needs that unfriendly world.

Lafeber, Walter. *America, Russia and the Cold War, 1945-1966*. New York: John Wiley & Sons, 1967.

Lane, Thomas A. *The Leadership of President Kennedy*. Idaho: The Caxton Printers, 1964.

Langley, Lester D. *The Cuban Policy of the United States: A Brief History*. New York: John Wiley & Sons, 1968.

Langley, Lester D. *The United States, Cuba, and the Cold War: American Failure or Communist Conspiracy?* Lexington, Mass.: D. C. Heath, 1970. Most likely none of the two hypotheses are true.

Langley, Lester D. *The United States and the Caribbean in the Twentieth Century*, rev. ed. Athens, Georgia: The Univ. of Georgia Press, 1985.

Langley, Lester D. *Cuba: A Perennial Problem in American Foreign Policy*. St. Charles, Mo.: Forum, 1973.

Lapp, Ralph E. *Arms Beyond Doubt: The Tyranny of Weapons Technology*. New York: Cowles, 1970.

Lapp, Ralph E. The Weapons Culture. New York: Norton, 1968. Larson, David L., ed. *The "Cuban Crisis" of 1962: Selected Documents and Bibliography*. Boston: Houghton-Mifflin, 1963. A valuable collection of documents and a useful bibliography.

Larson, David L. *The Puritan Ethic in United States Policy*. Princeton, N. J.: D. Van Nostrand, 1966.

Larson, Thomas B. *Soviet-American Rivalry*. New York: W.W. Norton & Co., 1978. See particularly p. 223. Lasky, Victor. *JFK: The Man and the Myth*. New York: Macmillan, 1963. Lasky, Victor. *Robert Kennedy: The Myth and the Man*. New York: Trident, 1968.

Lathan, Earl, ed. *J. F. Kennedy and Presidential Power*. Lexington, Mass.: Heath, 1972.

Lazo, Mario. *Dagger in the Heart*. New York: Twin Circle Pub., 1968. Interesting facts about Castro's early days and about Cuban-American relations before and during the first months of the revolution.

Lebow, Richard N. *Between Pace and War: The Nature of International Crisis*. Baltimore, Md.: The Johns Hopkins University Press, 1981.

Lee, William T. *Understanding the Soviet Military Threat: How CIA Estimates Went Astray*. New York: National Estrategy Information Center, Agenda Paper No. 6, 1977.

Lee, Asher, ed. *The Soviet Air and Rocket Forces*, Second Edition. London: G. Dyckworth, 1962. Useful information about Soviet missiles similar to the ones allegedly deployed in Cuba in 1962.

Leighton R. *The Cuban Missile Crisis of 1962: A Case in National Security Crisis Management*. Washington, D.C.: National Defense University, 1978.

Leites, Nathan. *Kremlin Thoughts: Yielding, Rebuffing, Provoking, Retreating*. Santa Monica, Calif.: The RAND Corporation, RM-31618-ISA, May 1983. Insightful study in the analysis of Soviet decision-making process.

Lens, Sidney. *The Military-Industrial Complex*. Kansas City: Pilgrim Press, 1970. There is a military-industrial complex in America, and it was not a Soviet fabrication.

Lerche, Charles O. *The Cold War and After*. Englewood Cliffs, N.J.: Prentice-Hall, 1965.

Levesque, Jacques. *The USSR and the Cuban Revolution: Soviet Ideological and Strategical Perspectives, 1959-77*. New York: Praeger Publishers, 1978. Useful information about the Soviet Union's troubled relations with Castro and how they got involved in a mess they weren't looking for.

Lieber, Robert J. *Theory and World Politics*. Cambridge, Mass.: Winthrop Publishers, 1972. See chapter on politics and cybernetic theory.

Linden, Carl A. *Khrushchev and the Soviet Leadership, 1957-1964*. Baltimore, Md.: The Johns Hopkins Univ. Press, 1966. Useful analysis of the limits of Khrushchev's power.

Llerena, Mario. *The Unsuspected Revolution*. Ithaca, N. Y.: Cornell University Press, 1978. Interesting facts about Fidel' early days at the Sierra Maestra mountains and about his relation with the Movimiento 26 de Julio and with the Cuban communists. Excellent information about the men surrounding Fidel at the beginning of the revolution. With an excellent foreword by Hugh Thomas.

Lockwood, Lee. *Castro's Cuba, Cuba's Fidel*. New York: Macmillan, 1967. See Castro's intertesting remarks about the Cuban missile crisis.

Lord, Donald C. *John F. Kennedy: The Politics of Confrontation and Conciliation*. Woodbury, N.Y.: Barron's, 1977.

Lukacs, John. *A New History of the Cold War*. New York: Anchor Books, 1966.

MacGaffey, Wyatt, and Clifford R. Barnett. Twentieth-Century Cuba: The Background of the Castro Revolution. New York: Doubleday & Co., 1965.

MacGregor Burns, James. *John F. Kennedy: A Political Portrait*. New York: Hartcourt, Brace and World, 1959.

Mackintosh, J. M. *Strategy and Tactics of Soviet Foreign Policy*. New York: Oxford Univ. Press, 1963.

Macmillan, Harold. *At the End of the Day*. London: Macmillan, 1973.

MacSherry, James E. *Khrushchev and Kennedy in Perspective*. Palo Alto, Calif.: Open-Doors Press, 1971.

Madariaga, Salvador de. *Latin America Between the Eagle and the Bear*. New York: Praeger, 1962.

Mallin, Jay. *Strategy for Conquest*. Coral Gables, Fla.: University of Miami Press, 1970.

Manchester, William. *Portrait of a President: John F. Kennedy in Profile*. Boston: Little, Brown, 1967.

Mandelbaum, Michael. *The Nuclear Question*. New York: CAmbridge University Press, 1979.

Mankievicz, Frank, and Kirby Jones. *With Fidel: A Portrait of Castro and Cuba*. New York: Playboy Press, 1975.

Manrara, Luis V. *Betrayal Opened the Door to Russian Missiles in Red Cuba*. Miami: The Truth About Cuba Committee, 1968. Version of the Cuban missile crisis from a highly biased, Miamian-style "anticommunist" perspective.

March, James G, and Herbert A. Simon. *Organizations*. New York: John Wiley and Sons, 19958. Herbert Simon's classical analysis of the decision-making process shows that it is not always as rational as it seems to be.

Marchetti, Victor, and John D. Marks. *The CIA and the Cult of Intelligence*. New York: Knopff, 1974.

McGarvey, Patrick J. CIA: *The Myth and the Madness*. New York: Saturday Review Press, 1972.

McSherry, James E. *Khrushchev and Kennedy in Retrospect*. Palo Alto, Calif.: Open-Door Press, 1971.

Medvedev, Roy A., and Zhores A. Medvedev. *Khrushchev: The Years in Power*.

New York: W.W. Norton, 1978.
Medvedev, Roy A. *Khrushchev.* Garden City, N.Y.: Anchor Press, 1983.
Metcalf, Lawrence E. *The Cold War and Beyond.* New York: Random House, 1975.
Meyer, Alfred G. *Communism.* New York: Random House, 1962.
Mezerik, A. G. *Cuba and the United States* (2 vols.) New York: International Review Service, 1963. Useful chronology and documents.
Miller, Lynn H., and Ronald W. Pruessen. *Reflections on the Cold War.* Philadelphia: Temple Univ. Press, 1974.
Miller, Jay. *Lockeed U-2.* Austin, Tx.: Aerofax, Inc., 1983. One of the most thorough studies with detailed technical information about the marvelous U-2 spy plane.
Miroff, Bruce. *Pragmatic Illusions: The Presidential Politics of John F. Kennedy.* New York: David McKay, 1976.
Mitchell, R. Judson. *Ideology of a Superpower.* Stanford, Ca.: Hoover Institution Press, 1982.
Monahan, James, and Kenneth O. Gilmore. *The Great Deception.* New York: Farrar, Strauss, 1963. An interesting, but somehow biased (that is, more biased than it is normally acceptable) account of the first years of Castro's revolution. A wealth of almost unknown information.
Moore, Carlos. *Castro, the Blacks, and Africa.* Los Angeles: Center for Afro-American Studies, Univ. of Calif., 1988.
Moreno Fraginals, Manuel. *La historia como arma. Barcelona*: Editorial Crítica, 1983. This paper "History as a weapon", written by my professor and friend Moreno Fraginals, was first published in *Casa de las Américas* magazine as a result of a polemic with another historian, Julio LeRiverend.
Mosely, Phillip E., *The Kremlin and World Politics.* New York: Vintage, 1960.
NBC. "Cuba: The Missile Crisis." 9 February, 1964, mimeo.
Neustadt, Richard E. *Presidential Power: The Politics of Leadership.* New York: John Wiley & Sons, 1960.
_____, and Graham T. Allison. *"Afterword"* to Robert F. Kennedy, *Thirteen Days: A Memoir of the Cuban Missile Crisis.* New York: W. W. Norton, 1971.
Newfield, Jack. *Robert Kennedy: A Memoir.* New York: Bantam Books, 1970.
Nicholas, William (Pseud.) [William Johnson and Nick Thimmesh]. *The Bobby Kennedy Nobody Knows.* Greenwich, Conn.: Fawcet Books, 1967.
Nixon, Richard M. *Six Crises.* Garden City: Doubleday, 1962.
Novick, Peter. *That Noble Dream: The "Objectivity Question" and the American Historical Profession.* Cambridge, Mass.: Cambridge University Press, 1988.
O'Donnell, Kenneth P., and David F. Powers. *Johnny, We Hardly Knew Ye.* New

York: Pocket Books, 1972. It is very difficult to know him through this idealized vision.

Oswald, J. Gregory, and Anthony J. Strover, eds. *The Soviet Union and Latin America*. New York: Praeger, 1970.

Pachter, Henry. *Collision Course: The Cuban Missiles and Coexistence*. New York: Praeger, 1963. Very informative study of the Cuban missile crisis.

Page, Martin. *The Day Khrushchev Fell*. New York: Hawthorne Books, 1965.

Pálóczi-Horváth, George. *Khrushchev, the Road to Power*. Boston: Little, Brown, 1960. Interesting analysis of Khrushchev's personality. Nikita Sergeevitch was no fool!

Paper, Lewis J. *The Promise and the Performance*. New York: Crown Publishers, 1975. Interesting analysis of the Kennedy administration.

Parmet, Herbert S. *JFK: The Presidency of John F. Kennedy*. New York: The Dial Press, 1983. Partido Socialista Popular.

Payne, James L. *The American Threat: The Fear of War as an Instrument of foreign Policy*. Chicago: Markham Publishing Co., 1970.

Penkovsky, Oleg. *The Penkovsky Papers*. New York: Doubleday, 1965. If, as some intelligence specialists affirm, Penkovsky was a Soviet penetration, these papers are CIA-made hogwash.

Plank, John. *Cuba and the United States; Long Range Perspectives*. Washington, D.C.: The Brookings Institution, 1967.

Ploss, Sidney. *Conflict and Decision-Making in Russia: A Case Study of Agricultural Policy, 1953-1963*. Princeton, N.J.: Princeton University Press, 1965. A useful study about the decision-making process in the Soviet Union.

Pope, Ronald R. *Soviet Views on the Cuban Missile Crisis*. Washington, D.C.: University Press of America, 1982.

Poppino, Rollie, E. *International Communism in Latin America*. London: Collier-Macmillan, 1964.

Popular Socialist Party of Cuba. *The Cuban Revolution*. New York: New Century Publisher, 1961.

See pp. 26, 38-39. Powers, Thomas *The Man Who Kept the Secrets: Richard Helms and the CIA*. New York: Alfred A. Knopf, 1979.

Prouty, L. Fletcher. *The Secret Team: The CIA and its Allies in Control of the World*. New York: Ballantine, 1973. A collection of examples of carefully planned and executed acts of deviousness by the Central Intellignce Agency, written by a person who served for nine years as Pentagon focal point officer —all CIA military activities were channelled through him.

Quester, George H. *Nuclear Diplomacy: The First Twenty-Five Years*. New York: Dunellan, 1970.

R. Hart Phillips. *The Cuban Dilemma*. New York: Ivan Obolensky, 1962

Radvanyi, Janos. *Hungary and the Superpowers*. Stanford, Ca.: Hoover

Institution Press, 1972.
Ranson, Harry Howe. *The Intelligence Establishment.* Cambridge: Harvard Univ. Press, 1970.
Rapoport, Anatol. *The Big Two: Soviet American Perceptions of Foreign Policy.* New York: Pegasus, 1971. The author argues that failure to camouflage the missile construction sites was due to a plan by which they were meant to be discovered by American spy planes.
Reford, Robert W. Canada and Three Crises. Lindsay, Ont.: John Deyell, 1968. Interesting analysis of American intelligence reports and the September estimate.
Reshetar, John S. Problems of Analyzing and Predicting Soviet Behavior. Garden City, N.Y.: Doubleday, 1955.
Roberts, Chalmers M. *The Nuclear Years: The Arms Race and Arms Control 1945-70.* New York: Praeger, 1970.
Robin, G. *La crise de Cuba.* Paris: IFRI, Economica, 1984.
Robinson, James A. *The Concept of Crisis in Decision-Making.* Washington, D.C.: National Institute of Social and Behavioral Science, 1962.
Rositzke, Harry. *The CIA's Secret Operations.* New York: Reader's Digest Press, 1977.
Rubinstein, Alvin Z., ed. *The Foreign Policy of the Soviet Union.* New York: Random House, 1966.
Rush, Myron. *The Rise of Khrushchev.* Washington, D.C.: Public Affairs Press, 1958.
Salinger, Pierre. *With Kennedy.* New York: Avon Books, 1966.
Sampson, Ronald V. *The Psychology of Power.* London: Heineman, 1965.
Sauvage, Leo. Autopsie du Castrisme. Paris: Flammation, 1962.
Schelling, Thomas C. *Arms and Influence.* New Haven, Conn.: Yale University Press, 1966. A wild west classic!
Schlesinger Jr., Arthur M. *A Thousand Days.* Greenwich, Conn.: Crest Books, 1965. A detailed account of the crisis and the American decision-making process by one Kennedy's court historians. Plenty of useful, though idealized iformation.
Schlesinger Jr., Arthur M. *The Imperial Presidency.* Boston: Houghton Mifflin, 1973. Useful to understanding the limits of Kennedy's powers.
_____. *Robert Kennedy and his Times.* Boston: Houghton Mifflin Co., 1978.
Schwab, Peter, and J. Lee Scheidman. *John F. Kennedy.* New York: Twayne Publications, 1974.
Schwartz, Morton. *Soviet Perception of the United States.* Berkeley: University of California Press, 1978. Highly speculative, but useful analysis of Soviet official expectations about the possible American reaction after the discover of strategic missiles in Cuba.
Seabury, Paul. *The Rise and Decline of the Cold War.* New York: Basic Books,

1967.

Semidei, Manuela, ed. *Kennedy et la révolution cubaine, un apprentissage politique?* Paris: Julliard, 1972.

———. *Les États-Unis et la révolution cubaine, 1959-1964.* Paris: Libraire A Colin, 1968. Insightful analysis of Cuban-American relations from a European perspective.

Seton-Watson, Hugh. *From Lenin to Khrushchev.* New York: Praeger, 1960.

Shultz, Richard H., and Roy Godson. *Dezinformatsia: Actives Measures in Soviet Strategy.* Washington, D.C.: Pergamon-Brassey's, 1984. If you believed the story that the Soviets did not camouflage the missiles in Cuba because the Russians are stupid, be ready for a big surprise!

Sidey, Hugh. *John F. Kennedy, President.* Greenwich, Conn.: Crest Books, 1963.

Simon, Herbert. *Administrative Behavior.* New YorK: Macmillan, 1957. Simon's theory of "bounded rationality" (human behavior can't be logically explained) is very useful in the analysis of the decision-making process.

Sivachev, Nikolai V., and Nikolai N. Yakovlev. *Russia and the United States.* Chicago: The University of Chicago Press, 1979. Interesting for an official Soviet view of the Cuban missile crisis.

Smith, Malcolm E., Jr. *Kennedy's Thirteen Greatest Mistakes in the White House.* New York: The National Forum of America, 1968.

Smith, Robert F. What Happened in Cuba? A Documentary History. New York: Twayne Publishers, 1963.

Snyder, Richard C., H. W. Bruck, and B. Sapin, eds. Foreign Policy Decision Making. New York: The Free Press, 1962. Sobel, Lester A., ed. Cuba, The U. S. and Russia, 1960-1963. New York: Facts on File, 1964.

Sorensen, Theodore C. *Kennedy.* New York: Bantam Books, 1966. Sorensen, Theodore C. *Decision Making in the White House: The Olive Branch and the Arrows.* New York: Columbia University Press, 1963.

Steel, Ronald. *Imperialists and Other Heroes: A Chronicle of the American Empire.* New York: Random House,1971.

———. *Pax Americana.* New York: The Viking Press, 1967. See pp. 25-27 and 219-231.

Steinbruner, John D. *The Cybernetic Theory of Decision: New Dimensions of Political Analysis.* Princeton: Princeton Univ. Press, 1974.

Stockwell, John. *In Search of Enemies: A CIA Story.* New York: W. W. Norton, 1978. This books is perhaps the key to understand the strange symbiotic alliance between Castro and the CIA. The CIA needs enemies, and Dr. Castro has been eager in providing them.

Stoiko, Michael. *Soviet Rocketry: Past, Present and Future.* New York: Holt, Rinehart and Winston, 1970.

Stone, I. F. *In a Time of Torment.* New York: Random House, 1964.

Stone, Ralph A., ed. *John F. Kennedy: 1971-1963*. Dobbs Ferry, N.Y.: Oceana Publications, 1971.
Strauss, Lewis L. *Men and Decisions*. Garden City, N.Y.: Doubleday, 1967.
Strausz-Hupe, Robert, William R. Kintner, and Stefan T. Possony. *A Forward Strategy for America*. New York: Harper And Brothers, 1961.
Suarez, Andrés. *Cuba: Castroism and Communism*, 1959-1966. Cambridge, Mass.: M. I. T. Press, 1967. Perceptive study of Castroism. An excellent analysis of Castro-URSS relations.
Suchlicki, Jaime. *Cuba: Continuity and Change*. Miami: North-South Center for the Institute of Interamerican Studies, Univ. of Miami, 1986.
_____. *Castro, Cuba, and Revolution*. Coral Gables, Fl.: University of Floridda Press, 1972.
Sutherland, Elizabeth. *The Youngest Revolution*. New York: Dial Press, 1969.
Szulc, Tad. *Fidel: A Critical Portrait*. New York: William Morrow, 1986. It is unbelievable that an experienced writer and journalist like Szulc had passed verbattin so much junk as told by Fidel himself.
Szulc, Tad. The Winds of Revolution. New York: Praeger, 1964.
Taber, Robert. *M 26: The Biography of a Revolution*. New York: Lyle Stuart, 1961.
Tannenbaum, Frank. *Ten Keys to Latin America*. New York: Vintage, 1966.
Tatu, Michel. *Power in the Kremlin: From Khrushchev to Kosygin*. New York: Viking, 1970.
Taylor, Maxwell D. *Swords and Plowshares*. New York: Norton, 1972.
Tetlow, Edwin. *Eye on Cuba*. New York: Hartcourt, Brace and World, 1966.
Thant, U. *View from the U. N.* Garden City, N.Y.: Doubleday, 1978.
Thomas, Hugh. *Cuba: The Pursuit of Freedom*. New York: Harper and Row, 1971. Excellent study of Cuban history and the origins of Castroism. Thomas is one of the first scholars who noticed Fidel's fascist inclinations.
Thomas, John R. *Soviet Foreign Policy and Conflict within Political and Military Leadership*. RAC-P-61. McLean, Va.: Research Analysis Corp., 1970.
Thornton, Thomas P. *The Third World in Soviet Perspective*. Princeton, N.J.: Princeton Univ. Press, 1964.
Toledano, Ralph de. *R. F. K., The Man who would be President*. New York: Signet Books, 1968.
Torres Ramírez, Blanca. *Las relaciones cubano-soviéticas (1959-1968)*. Mexico, D. F.: El Colegio de Mexico, 1969.
Triska, Jan F., ed. *Soviet Communism: Programs and Rules*. San Francisco: Chandler, 1962.
Triska, Jan F., and David D. Finley. *Soviet Foreign Policy*. New York: Macmillan, 1968.
Tully, Andrew. *CIA, The Inside Story*. New York: William Morrow, 1962. Tully,

Andrew. *The Super Spies*. New York: Pocket Books, 1969.
Tutino, Saverio. *L'ottobre cubano*. Turin: Einaudi, 1968. Interesting anecdotical information about the crisis by a Castro apologist.
Ulam, Adam B. *The Rivals: America and Russia Sice World War II*. New York: The Viking Press, 1971.
⎯⎯⎯. *The New Face of Soviet Totalitarianism*. Cambridge, Mass.: Harvard University Press, 1963. Essays on Soviet foreign policy and politics under Khrushchev.
⎯⎯⎯. *Expansion and Coexistence: The History of Soviet Foreign Policy*. New York: Praeger, 1968. Excellent study of Soviet foreign policy. Insightful analysis of the Castro-Khrushchev relations and the Cuban missile crisis.
United States Department of State. *Events in the United States-Cuban Relations: a Chronology, 1957-1963*. Washington, D.C.: U.S. Government Printing Office, 1963.
Valkenier, Elizabeth Kridl. *The Soviet Union and the Third World: An Economic Bind*. New York: Praeger, 1984.
Verrier, Anthony. *Through the Looking Glass*. New York: W. W. Norton, 1983. Interesting information about Penkovsky.
Volkman, Ernest, and Blaine Baggett. *Secret Intelligence*. New York: Doubleday, 1989. A history of American espionage in our century and its role in the American society, which nevertheless values openness over secrecy in matters of government.
Walton, Richard J. *Cold War and Counter-Revolution: The Foreign Policy of John F. Kennedy*. New York: The Viking Press, 1972. An interesting analysis suggesting that Kennedy's actions during the crisis were mostly motivated by national politics.
Warner, III, Edward L. *The Military in Contemporary Soviet Politics*. New York: Praeger, 1977.
Weintal, Edward, and Charles Bartlett. *Facing the Brink: An Intimate Study of Crisis Diplomacy*. New York: Scribner's, 1967.
Welch, William. *American Images of Soviet Foreign Policy*. New Haven, Conn.: Yale University press, 1970.
Werth, Alexander. *Russia Under Khrushchev*. Westport, Conn.: Greenwood Press, 1975.
Wesson, Robert G. *Soviet Foreign Policy in Perspective*. Homewood, Ill.: The Dorsey Press, 1969.
Weyl, Nathaniel. *Red Star Over Cuba*. New York: Devin-Adair, 1960. Interesting information about Castro's early days and his guerrilla activities. The author, however, seems to be paranoid about Communism and sometimes twists the facts more than what it is socially acceptable in order to prove his thesis that Fidel had been a communist stooge all the time.

Wicker, Tom. J. F. K. and L. B. J. *The Influence of Personality Upon Politics.* New York: Morrow, 1968.
Wicker, Tom. *Kennedy Without Tears: The Man Beneath the Myth.* New York: Morrow, 1964.
Wilkerson, Loree. *Fidel Castro's Political Programs from Reformism to "Marxism-Leninism."* Gainesvile, Fl.: Univ of Florida Press, 1965. Interesting, in depth analysis of Castro's "I am a Marxist" speech.
Williams, Phil. Crisis Management: Confrontation and Diplomacy in the Nuclear Age. New York: John Wiley & Sons, 1976.
Williams, William Appleman. *The United States, Cuba and Castro.* New York: Monthly Review Press, 1962.
_____. *Some Presidents: Wilson to Nixon.* New York: Vintage Books, 1972.
Wills, Gary. *The Kennedy Imprisonment.* Boston: Little, Brown and Co., 1982.
Wise, David, and Thomas B. Ross. *The Espionage Establishment.* New York: Random House, 1967.
_____. *The Invisible Government.* New York: Bantam Books, 1965. Useful analysis and information about CIA attempts to control American foreign policy.
Wofford, Harris. *Of Kennedys and Kings: Making Sense of the Sixties.* New York: Farrar, Strauss, Giroux, 1988.
Wohlstetter, Albert, and Roberta Wohlstetter. *Controlling the Risks in Cuba.* Adelphi Paper No. 17. London: Institute for Strategic Studies, April 1965. Classical GIGO (garbage in, garbage out) study on Cuba by the same author who wrote the classical GIGO on Pearl Harbor.
Wolfe, Thomas. *Soviet Strategy at the Crossroads.* Cambridge, Mass.: Harvard University Press, 1964. Describes tension between Khrushchev and the military in the 1962-63 period.
Wynne, Greville. *The Man from Moscow.* London: Arrow Books, 1968. Interesting information on Penkovski.
Yarmolinsky, Adam. *The Military Establishment.* New York: Harper & Row, 1971.
Young, Oran R. *The Politics of Force: Bargaining During International Crises.* Princeton, N.J.: Princeton Univ. Press, 1968.

Articles and Papers

ABC News. "John Scali, ABC News." August 13, 1964.
Abel, Elie. "The Khrushchev Version of the Cuban Missile Crisis." *Washington Post*, January 4, 1971.

Acheson, Dean. "Dean Acheson's Version of Robert Kennedy's Version of the Cuban Missile Affair." *Esquire* 71 (February 1969).
Alexander, Robert J. "Soviet Communist Activities in Latin America." *Problems of Communism*, X, No. 1, (January-February, 1961), pp. 8-13.
Alexander, Robert J. "Latin American Communism." *Survey*, August 1962, p. 100.
Alexander, Robert J. "Latin America and the Communist Bloc." *Current History*, Vol. 44, No. 258, February 1963.
Alexander, Robert J. "Old Quarrels in Havana." *New Politics*, 33, Fall 1964.
Alsop, Stewart, and Charles Bartlett. "In Time of Crisis." The *Saturday Evening Post*, December 8, 1962, pp. 15-21.
Armstrong, Scott, and Philip Brenner. "Cuba Crisis: No Hits But Many Errors." *Los Angeles Times*, Novemebr 1, 1987, p. V-3.
Baber, Asa. "Killing Us Softly With Their Song." *Playboy*, March 1984, p. 50.
Booda, Larry. "U. S. Watches for Possible Cuban IRBMs." *Aviation Week and Space Technology*, October 1, 1962, pp. 20-21.
Castro, Fidel. Television speech delivered on Nov. 1, 1962. Peking: Foreign Languages, 1962.
_____. Interview by Lee Lockwood. *Playboy*, January 1967.
Castro, Juana. "My Brother Fidel." *Life*, August 28, 1964, pp. 22-23.
CBS. "A Conversation with President Kennedy." 17 December 1962, mimeo.
Cole, K. C. "Is there such thing as Scientific Objectivity?" *Discover*: September 1985, p. 98.
Cooper, Chester L. "The CIA and Decision Making." *Foreign Affairs*, V. 50, No. 2. January 1972. p. 223.
Crosby, Ralph D., Jr. "The Cuban Missile Crisis: Soviet View" *Military Review*, Vol 56, No. 9, (September 1976) pp. 58-70.
Devlin, Kevin. "The Soviet-Cuban Confrontation: Economic Reality and Political Judo." Research Department of Radio Free Europe, 1 April, 1968.
Driver, M. J. "Crisis and Reciprocity in Soviet-American Interaction." Los Angeles: University of Southern California, School of International Relations, August, 1969.
Ellsberg, Daniel. "The Day Castro Almost Started World War III." The *New York Times*, October 31, 1987, p. 7.
Epstein, Edward J. "Incorporating Analysis of Foreign Governments' Deception into the US Analytical System." in Roy Godson, ed., *Intelligence Requirements for the 1980's*. Washington, D.C.: National Strategy Information Center, 1980.
George, Alexander L. "The Causal Nexus Between Cognitive Beliefs and Decision Making Behavior." in L.S. Falkowski, ed., Psychological Models in International Politics. Boulder, Colorado: Westview, 1979.
George, Alexander L. "Presidential Control of Force: The Korean War and the Cuban Missile Crisis." Paper presented at the 1967 Annual Meeting of the American Sociological Association.
Gerberding, William P. "International Law and the Cuban Missile Crisis." in Lawrence Scheimann and David Wilkinson, eds., *International Law and*

Political Crises. Boston: Little, Brown, 1968.
Geyer, Georgie Anne. "El fascismo reaparece bajo disfraz del comunismo en la América Central." *El Universal* (Caracas), viernes 8 de julio de 1983.
González, Servando. "El gran engaño." *El Diario/La Prensa* (New York), Octubre 21-27, 1982.
Gouré, Leon, and Morris Rothenburg. "Latin America." in Kurt London, ed., *The Soviet Union in World Politics*. Boulder, Co.: Westview Press, 1980.
Hermann, ed., *International Crises: Insights from Behavioral Research*. New York: The Free Press, 1972.
Hersh, Seymour. "Was Castro Out of Control in 1962?" The *Washington Post*, October 11, 1987.
Holsti, Ole R. "Perceptions of Time, Alternatives, and Patterns of Comm. as Factors in Crisis Decision-Making." Paper read at the International Peace Research Conference, Chicago, Nov. 17, 1964.
Kirkpatrick, Jeanne. "Is a stubborn Castro testing U.S. defenses?" The *Miami Herald*, March 31, 1991, p. 3C.
Knorr, Klaus. "Failure in National Intelligence Estimates, The Case of the Cuban Missiles." *World Politics*, Vol. XVI No. 3 (April, 1964), pp. 458-59.
Knox, William E. "Close-Up of Khrushchev During a Crisis." The *New York Times Magazine*, November 18, 1962.
Kramer. Mark, "Tactical Nuclear Weapons, Soviet Command Authority, and the Cuban Missile Crisis," *Cold War International History Bulletin* 3 (Fall 1993).
McDonald, Kim A. "Cuba Said to Have Nuclear Warheads During 1962 Crisis." *The Chronicle of Higher Education*, Jan 29, 1992.
McNamara, Robert S. Interview on "All Things Considered." *National Public Radio*, January 14, 1992.
Milza, Pierre. "La crise de Cuba". *L'Historie*, No. 151, January 1992, pp. 140-145.
Montaner, Carlos Alberto. "¿Quiere Castro abandonar a los soviéticos?" *La Estrella de Panamá*, 22 de febrero de 1985.
Montoro, Adrian G. "Moscow Was Caught Between Cuba and U. S." The *New York Times*. November 17, 1987.
Morrow, Lance. "When Artists Distort History." *Time*, December 23, 1991, p. 84.
Muggeridge, Malcolm. "On the Brink: America in the Shadow of the Cuban Missile Crisis." The *New Statesman*, August 2, 1991.
NBC. "Cuba: The Missile Crisis." 9 February, 1964, mimeo.
Nixon, Richard M. "Cuba, Castro, and John F. Kennedy." *Reader's Digest*, November 1964, pp. 282-300.
Pike, Otis. "Do Americans want the Truth?" The *Times-Picayune*, February 6, 1991, p. B-7.
Riccards, Michael P. "Dangerous Legacy: John F. Kennedy and the Cuban Missile Crisis." Address presented at the Fourth Annual Presidential Conference, Hofstra University, March 2830, 1985.

Robinson, Linda. "Weird Story." *U.S. News and World Report*, Jan 20, 1992.
Rogers, Warren Jr. "Reflections on the Bob and John Show." The *New Republic*, February 23, 1963, pp. 10-11.
Rosenbaum, Ron. "The Shadow of the Mole." *Harper's*, October 1983, pp. 45-60.
Ross, Stanley. "We Were Wrong About Castro." *American Weekly*, June 12, 1960, pp. 4-5.
Rowley, Anthony. "Les fusées soviétiques, une mystification!" *L'Historie*, No. 151, January 1992, pp. 136-138.
Schultz, Donald E. "Kenedy and the Cuban Connection." *Foreign Policy* 26 (Spring 1977), pp. 57-64, 121-139.
Talbott, Strobe. "High Noon Minus the Shoot-Out." *Time*, February 10, 1992, p. 39.
Tolchin, Martin. "U.S. Underestimated Soviet Force in Cuba in '62." The *New York Times*, Jan 15, 1992.
Treaster, Joseph B. "Defecting General Says Cuba Has Plan to Raid Base in U.S. If Is Attacked." The *New York Times*, October 11, 1987, p. 12.
Turner, Stanfield. "Secrecy and Democracy." *Newsweek*. May 20, 1985.
Vargas Llosa, Mario. "La historia como mentira." (Interview) *El País*, 27 de octubre de 1984, p. 26.
Wohlstetter, Roberta,"Cuba and Pearl Harbor: Hindsight and Foresight," *Foreign Affairs* 43 (July 1965), 691-707.

Index

Abel Elie, 140, 162.
Abrahantes, José, 93, 206-207
Acheson, Dean, 145-146, 238-240
Adenauer, Konrad, 178
Adzhubei, Alexei, 31, 34-35, 109-110
Alekseev (Shitov), Aleksandr,
    badmouths Kudryavtsev,
    discredits Kudryavtsev,
    disinformation agent,
    friendship with Castro
    recruited by Castro,
    tries to recruit Castro,
Allison, Graham, 121, 140, 170-171, 183
Allyn, Bruce J., 160, 192, 194, 203-204, 217, 222, 293
Amuchástegui, Domingo (Chomy), 198-202
Anderson Jr., Rudolf, 111, 121, 156-158, 160, 167, 190, 220, 267, 292
Angleton, James J., 126, 131, 193, 199
Angola,
    Cuban military assistance to, 205, 287; Soviet involvement in, 287; Western corporations in, 288
Arbenz, Jacobo, 42, 50, 59, 204
Arca Foundation, 215
Aviation Week, 261-262

Baker, Dr. James, 264
Ball, George, 169, 189, 238, 243, 263
Barnet, Miguel, 219-220
Bartlett, Charles, 118, 244

Batista, Fulgencio, 42-44, 47-48, 50, 52, 58, 63, 75, 79, 81, 84, 92, 97, 99-101, 275, 294
Bay of Pigs, 24, 34, 55, 72, 98-99, 101, 107-108, 116, 172, 178, 197, 205, 232, 237, 243, 244, 255, 271, 280, 244, 255, 271, 280, 281, 282; US intelligence and, 116, 121, 126; Khrushchev and, 65, 71, 290
Beale, Howard, 294
Bernstein, Barnton, 260
Bissell, Richard M., 131
Blake, George, 128
Blight, James G., 161, 192, 194,-195, 197-198, 201-204, 206, 212, 214, 217, 219, 222, 293
blockade of Cuba, U.S., 34, 82, 84, 141, 146-147, 171-172, 219, 238-240, 259, 270, 274-275, 289,292
Board of National Estimates, 255
Bohlen, Charles E., 143, 252
Bogotazo, 104
Bohemia, 45, 52
Bolshakov, Georgi, 118
"bomber gap," 133
Bonsal, Philip, 96, 286
Boorstin, Daniel, 276
Borges, Jorge Luis, 279
Bowles, Chester, 243
Brand, Anthony, 18
Brandon, Henry, 242
Bravo, Douglas, 289
Brenner, Philip, 195, 197, 214
Brezhnev, Leonid, 187

Broz (Tito), Josif, 68, 70, 74, 76
Brugioni, Dino, 23, 141
Bundy, McGeorge, 141, 169, 184, 237, 263
Bush, George W., 280

camouflage, 119-122, 137-138, 153, 183-186, 188
Camp Peary, 246
Capek, Karel,
cargo-cult science, 17
Carnegie Corporation, 216
Carpentier, Alejo, 18
Carr, Edward H., 14
Castro, Fidel (Fidel Alejandro Castro Ruz)
  Angola, war in, 205, 287-288; anti-Americn feelings, 32, 68, 70, 218, 222; arrogance of, 55, 83,-84, 96, 103, 112, 275, 91; asks Kkrushchev to launch missiles, 149-152, 161, 2; assassination plots against, 243-244; and *Bogotazo*, 104; charisma and, 233, 246, 286; decision-making, 21; *dellusions de grandeur,* 86, 11, 223, 205; envy and, 285; expells Kudryavtsev, 96-97, 103-104; fascims and, 44-45, 284 fights "sectarianism," 91-93, 95, 101-102; hatred of Americans, 76, 85, 223- 291; sense of humiliation, 113; Jesuit education, 103-104 Marxist claims, 46-47, 55 56, 62, 68, 71-74, 89-90, 92-93, 235, 251, 284, 288; Muslims and, 222; physical appearance of, 233, 273; stinkiness of, 173; terrorism and, 89, 154, 201, 206, 218, 222; at the university, 33, 44-47, 68, 83, 85, 92, 101, 109; and U-2 shot down, 111, 121, 156, 157, 158-159, 160, 165, 220
Castro Ruz, Juana, 223
Castro Ruz, Raúl, 35, 37, 52, 92, 94, 112, 114, 152, 155, 200-201, 206
Central Intelligence Agency (CIA), 20, 23, 34, 94, 104, 114, 120, 123-124, 126, 129-132, 136, 139-140, 142, 148, 154, 178, 190, 195-196, 199, 204-205, 210-211, 213-216, 220, 235
Centro de Estudios de America (CEA), 247,
Cervantes, Miguel de, 247
Chayefski, Paddy, 294
Chicago Tribune, 115
China, People's Republic of, 23, 65-66, 69-70, 73, 74, 82, 106, 139, 253, 278, 283, 284
Chomón, Faure,
Churchill, Winston,
CIA, see Central Intelligence Agency
Cienfuegos, Camilo, 52
Cline, Ray, 124, 254
Clinton, Bill, 208
Clouseau, Inspector, 250
Colby, William, 263
Cold War, 13, 31, 41 43, 78, 80, 127, 144, 146, 194, 204-205, 217-218, 235, 247, 256, 272
Colomé Ibarra (Furry), Abelardo, 205
Comités de Defensa de la Revolución (CDRs), 95
Communist Party of Cuba (Castro's), 57, 153, 197, 253, 285
Communist Party of Cuba (PSP), pro Soviet, 43-44, 47-53, 55-56, 63, 67, 70-72, 74-75, 83-85, 87-94, 98-104, 173, 251; Batista and, 44, 47; Castro and, 44, 47,

48, 49-56, 63, 67, 70-72, 74-75, 83-85, 88-994, 98, 99-100, 251; Khrushchev and, 70-72, 74-75, 83-85, 88-94, 98, 99-100, 251
Cuba
  economy of, 50, 55, 71, 77-78, 80-83, 89; before Castro, 50, 54, 75, 79; Soviet Union and, 89, 102, 253, 283, 385, 290
Cuban-Americans, 19, 280, 287
Cubanology
Curbelo, Maj. Raúl,

Daily Worker (newspaper), 44, 111, 149
Dam, Luis, 45
Daniel, Jean, 162
Debray, Regis, 284
Díaz, Carlos, 98
Dinerstein, Herbert S., 40
Dorticós, Osvaldo, 74, 114, 268
Draper, Theodore, 40, 45, 81, 95, 279
Dulles, Allen, 42, 46, 216, 218, 258

ECO, UMBERTO, 172, 178
Ellsberg, Daniel, 159, 212
Escalante, Aníbal, 49, 88, 91-93, 100, 102, 105, 111-112, 173, 233, 251, 285, 291
espionage, see intelligence and espionage
exiles (Cuban) in U.S., see Cuban-Americans

Fast Action Brigades, 283
Feynman, Richard, 17
Fernández, Marcelo, 91
Ford Foundation, 215-216
Franqui, Carlos, 33, 40, 46-47, 66, 93, 112, 114, 155-159, 187, 270
Fulbright, William, 147, 240

García Márquez, Gabriel, 209
Gaulle, Charles de, 170, 264
Geyer, Georgie Anne, 223
Gibbs, David, 204-205
Gómez Abad, José, 154
Granma (yacht), 47

Granma (newspaper), 52
GRU (Glavnoye Razvedyvatelnoye Upravieniye), 96, 124, 127-129, 132
Guantánamo Naval Base, 64, 167
Guardia, Antonio (Tony) de la, 207
Guevara, Ernesto (Ché), 35, 37, 39, 41, 46, 52-55, 74, 77, 80-83, 93, 109, 11-114, 149, 152, 155, 167, 173, 218, 243, 286, 288

historical tradecraft, 16, 298
history, oral, 20, 25, 29, 193, 217, 220-221
Hitler, Adolf, 76, 79, 222-223, 227-228, 251, 286
Hollis, Roger, 131
Holmes, Sherlock, 18
Homestead AFB (Florida), 152
Hoover, J. Edgard, 246
Horelick, Arnold, 25, 29, 109, 228
Horowitz, Irving Louis, 285, 287
Hoy (Cuban Communist's newspaper), 42, 44, 49-50, 53, 66, 72, 93, 187
Hudson Institute, 280

Intelligence and espionage, terms of
  agent, 24, 94, 97, 104, 114, 126-128, 131-132, 152, 182-183, 194, 199, 203, 207, 252, 256; agent of influence, 197, 203, 207-209; *agent provocateur*, 63, 127; appraisal of information, see evaluation of information asset, 98; blowback, 216; *bona fides*, agent's, 69, 124, 126-1130, 199, 202, 204, 281; chicken feed, 125; cobbler, 213; controller, 118, 125, 128-129, 132; counterespionage, 127; counterintelligence, 131-132, 182, 188, 191, 197,

204, 207; deception, 16, 107, 113, 121-122, 129, 12-134, 137, 171, 183, 184, 188-189, 194-1197, 205, 212, 215-216, 251, 255;
defector, 128, 131, 152, 160, 178, 198-201, 205, 212, 215-216, 251, 255;
disinformation, 14-15, 20, 29, 109-110, 126-127, 130, 133-134, 150, 161, 165, 183, 188-189, 195-197, 199-200, 206, 210, 212-214, 220, 292-293;
dezinformatsia; 104, 130;
double agent, 96, 221, 218
doubled agent, 189; ELINT, 248, 256; espionage, 14-16, 97, 127, 131,134, 183, 188-191, 194-195, 197, 202-205, 212, 246, 293; evaluation of information, 16, 182, 212, 251, 239, 257, 293; forgery, 152, 214;
HUMINT, 131, 182, 248, 256;
illegal, 56;
intelligence, 15-16, 124, 127-128, 132-134, 139-140, 178, 180, 182-183, 188-191, 194-197, 199, 202-207, 212, 256, 263-266, 293;
intelligence cycle, 292;
legend, 55;
maskirovka, 122, 183-185;
MICE, 210;
NUCINT, 190, 266;
PHOTINT, 256;
plant, 125-128, 130-131, 214, 292
propaganda, 48, 52, 65, 84, 130, 205-206, 210, 218, 222, 229, 293
psychological warfare, 165-166, 236, 292
quiet one, 209
RADINT, 256

rezident, 97;
recruitment, 94, 97, 197, 207-209;
SIGINT, 190;
sleeper, 56;
swallow, 209;
TECHINT. 256;
tradecraft, 16, 127, 129, 132, 189, 197, 204, 210, 255, 293;
Izvestia, 31, 109

Johnson, Lyndon B., 146, 237
Jiminy Cricket, 83, 284
Julien, Claude, 22, 33, 48

Kafka, Franz, 268
Kahn, Herman, 280-281
Kaplan, Morton, 237
Karamessines, John,
Keating, Kenneth,
Kennan, George, 178, 183, 190, 255-256, 292
Kent, Sherman, 13, 178, 190, 255-256, 292
Kennedy, John F., 13, 22-23, 25, 65-66, 86, 107-110, 113, 115-117, 124-126, 134, 136, 137, 139-141, 229, 232, 236, 237, 292, 273; and "bomber gap," 133; and Bay of Pigs, 107-108, 126, 145-146, 148, 244-246, 271; decision-making, 17, 23, 25, 138, 144, 245; against invading Cuba, 146, 148, 168, 171-172, 240, 260; and missiles in Turkey, 30, 187; does not enforce inspection, 190, 267, 283, 292; does not retaliate after U-2 shot down, 161, 168, 170; orders blockade, 146-147, 171, 238, 240, 292; creates Green Berets, 244; Khrushchev and, 22, 24, 33, 37-38, 39, 65, 85-86, 108,

142-143, 145, 162-165; and *machismo*, 244; and "missile gap," 31, 126, 132-134, 218, 241, 245; sees U-2 photos, 23, 184, 255, 258;
Kennedy, Robert F., 16, 25, 32, 116-118, 126, 140; *Maine, USS* and, 16, 191; and Pearl Harbor analogy, 16, 191;
KGB (Komitet Gosudarstvennoy Bezopasnosti), 93-98, 110, 126-132, 155-156, 158, 195, 199-200, 207, 209, 214, 220221;
Khrushchev, Nikita S., 13-14, 18, 29, 42, 53-54, 58-59, 60-64, 67, 69-71, 73, 78, 84, 88, 97, 108, 113-114, 116-117, 131-133, 169-170, 172, 178, 184, 186, 204, 228, 232-235, 248, 259-260, 262, 278, 296; tries to overthrow Castro, 88-103; hates Castro, 72, 86, 89, 112-113, 251, 291; meets Castro, 33, 54-55; suspects Castro is CIA agent, 104; decides to send missiles to Cuba, 18, 21, 22, 29-30; dispute with China, 65-66, 68-70, 72, 247, 253, 278, 283 and Cuba, 18, 21-22, 29-30; demotion of,29, 107; "errors," 114, 116, 119-123; and Kennedy, 22, 24, 33, 37-38, 39, 65, 85-86, 108, 142-143, 145, 162-165; letters to Kennedy, 22, 24, 31, 162-165; "miscalculations," 143-148, 161, 275, 281; offer missiles to Castro, 35, 36, 63-64, 104, 107, 109-112; in retirement, 173; sends Adzhubei to U.S. and Cuba, 31, 34-36, 109-110, 165; scared to death,

30, 162-165, 168, 171, 292;
Kirkpatrick, Lyman, 123
Kissinger, Henry, 35, 86, 218-219, 280, 286
Knorr, Klauss, 140, 229
Korzybski, Alfred, 179
Kosygin, Alexei, 29, 107
Kotchergin, Vadim, 94
Kramer, Mark, 217
kremlinology, 108
Krock, Arthur, 270
Kudryavtsev, Sergei,

Latin America, 32, 34, 37, 40-41, 43, 48, 51-51, 55, 58-60, 62, 67-68, 70, 73-80, 84-86, 89, 92, 130, 204, 208, 219, 237, 244, 281, 283, 288-290
Lazo, Mario, 222
Lechuga, Carlos, 36
L'Express, 34
LeMay, Curtis, 146, 153, 239, 258
Le Monde, 22, 33, 34, 149, 153, 178
Lenin, Vladimir I., 61, 78, 143
Lévi-Strauss, Claude, 180
Lingua Franca, 204
Lockwood, Lee, 35-36, 107, 111, 157
Lorentz, Konrad, 142, 169
Lundahl, Arthur, 235, 256, 292
HMS *Lusitania, 16, 191*

McArthur, Douglas, 240
McArthur Foundation, 215
McCone, John, 23, 120-121, 138-139, 142, 145, 178-179
McDill AFB,
MacMillan, Harold, 178, 268
McNamara, Robert S., 24-25, 32, 120, 139-140, 145, 147, 169-170, 193, 218-221, 236-237, 239, 241, 247, 520, 261
Mao Tse-tung, 68, 74-75, 110, 278
Maine, USS (battleship), 16, 191

Mankiewicz, Frank, 157
Marchetti, Victor, 130
Magritte, René, 177, 179, 182, 213
Mariel, 113, 130, 208, 252
Martin, David C., 203
Martin, Lionel, 46
Marx, Karl, 14, 56-57, 59, 61-62, 70-74, 85, 90, 92-93, 98-99, 101, 105, 232, 235, 251, 284, 286-287
Matos, Huber, 52
Matthews, Herbert L., 91, 104, 223
Maury, Jack, 130-131
meme, 192
The Miami Herald, 201
Mikoyan, Anastas, 53, 60, 62-63, 79-72, 107, 117, 161, 195
Mikoyan, Sergei (Sergo), 161, 220
military-industrial-academic complex, 218, 291
militia, Cuban, 33, 41, 66, 101, 113
Ministerio del Interior (MININT), 93, 198, 208, 209
"missile gap," 31, 126, 132-134, 218, 241, 248,
missiles (American) in Turkey, 22, 30, 38, 97, 116, 126, 152, 161, 167, 187, 271, 274, 282
missiles (Soviet) in Cuba, MRBMs (SS-4, Sandal), 115-116, 119-120, 134, 256, 259, 261-262, 270; IRBMs (SS-5 Skean), 115-116, 119-120, 134, 256, 259, 261-262, 270; nuclear warheads, 13, 36, 118, 177, 194, 217-218, 240, 261, 264-268;radiation from, 182, 266-267, 270; PALs, 269; Soviet policy on, 254; range

of, 31-32, 37, 125, 254, 261-262, 268-269; SAMs; 111, 115, 126, 121, 139-140, 156-161, 170, 184-184, 219-220, 242, 252, 254, 258-260, 292; San Cristóbal site, 114-115, 124, 139; as symbols, 186-188, 245;
Montaner, Carlos Alberto, 223
Montoro, Adrián, 159
Mooney, Chris, 204-205
Morgenstern, Oskar, 292
Moyniham, Daniel P., 216

Nasser, Gamal Abdel, 43, 74
National Estimate, U.S., 133-134, 140, 146, 154, 217, 239, 251-252, 254-256, 262, 266, 273, 288
National Photographic Interpretation Center (NPIC), 124, 134-135, 178, 180-181, 189, 171, 262, 292
National Security Archive, 152, 210-216
Newman, James R., 291
Newman, John von, 232
New York Times,
Nitze, Paul, 145
Nixon, Richard,
Novomody, Jaime,
Nozick, Robert, 182

Ochoa, Arnaldo, 162, 207
Oldfield, Maurice, 127
Oltuski, Enrique, 91
Operation Bodyguard, 188
Operation Fortitude, 188
Operation Phoenix, 208
Ormsby-Gore, Davis, 187, 272
Organizaciones Revolucionarias Integradas (ORI), 74, 89-93, 100
Orwell, George, 216
ouroboros, 215

Pachter, Henry, 140, 163, 258

Patton, George, 188
Pearl Harbor, 16, 191
Peirce, Carles Sanders, 180
Penkovsky, Oleg, 119, 123-132, 134, 197, 214, 235, 274, 292
Pérez, Faustino, 91
Philby, Kim, 131
Pino Díaz, Rafael del, 152, 160
Piñeiro Losada, (barbarroja) Manuel, 44-45, 206-207
Pliyev, Issa A., 157, 194
Powers, Francis Gary, 122
Prensa Latina 94-95
Project Camelot, 204-206
pseudo-events, 256-257, 276-277
PSP. See Communist Party of Cuba (PSP),

quarantine, see blockade,

Rabelais, François, 201
Ramos, Sidroc Melquisidec, 98, 102
RAND Corporation, 228, 280
Rather, Dan,
Reagan, Ronald, 290
Revolución (M-26-7's newspaper), 33, 40, 49, 51, 66, 72, 89, 92, 95-96, 158, 187
Roa, Raúl, 200-201
Roca, BIas, 44-45, 51, 53, 70, 90, 93-94
Rockefeller Family Fund, 215
Rockefeller Foundation, 215-216, 237
Rodríguez, Carlos Rafael, 48, 50, 55, 89
Rodríguez Menier, Juan Antonio, 159
Roosevelt, Franklin D., 16
Rostow, Walt Whitman, 78
Rush, Myron, 29, 228
Rusk, Dean, 62, 85-86, 149, 163, 169, 237, 249, 263, 268; stalls U-2 fligts, 141;
Russell, Bertrand, 141, 169

Russell, Richard, 147, 240
Salinger, Pierre, 137, 166
Sánchez Cabrera, Osvaldo, 48, 93-94, 98
Sánchez Cabrera, Osvaldo (school) 97-102, 200
Sánchez Manduley, Celia, 92
Sánchez, Miguel Angel,
Santayana, George, 279
Santiesteban Casanova, Roberto,
Saussure, Ferdinand de, 180
Schlesinger Jr., Arthur M., 72. 109, 142, 163, 240, 279,
semiotics, 116, 179-180, 186, 188
September Estimate, 23, 251-256
Shitov, Aleksandr, see Alekseev, Aleksandr
Sierra Maestra mountains, 43, 46-51, 75-76, 91-92, 97, 102, 221
Simon, Herbert, 229-231
Smith, William Y., 190, 266-268
Smith, Wayne S., 201
Sorensen, Theodore, 251, 108-109, 140, 143, 189, 238-239,
Sputnik, 42, 136
Stalin, Joseph V., 41, 52, 59, 61, 69-70, 89, 98, 100, 172, 222, 233-234
Stephenson, William, 212
Studies in Intelligence, 189
Suárez, Andrés, 111
Suárez, Rafael (pseud.), 93
Suslov, Mikhail, 90, 107
Sylvester, Arthur, 258, 281
Szulc, Tad, 36, 156-158, 161

TASS (Soviet press agency), 23, 37, 58, 64, 66, 89-90, 97, 112, 117-118, 186, 196
Tatu, Michel, 106
Taylor, A.J.P., 14
Taylor, Maxwell, 145, 167, 189,

190, 238, 266-267
Teitelboim, Volodia, 284
Time magazine, 13, 76, 138
Thomas, Hugh, 40, 56, 79
Thompson, Jr., Llewellyn, 252
Tojo, Hideki, 243-244
Touze, Vincent, 153
Tonkin Gulf incident, 16, 281
Trohan, Walter, 115, 258
Tuchman, Barbara, 282

Ulam, Adam B., 18, 29, 253
UNESCO, 96
United Nations Organization,
United States Intelligence Board (USIB), 23, 251-252, 255
University of Havana, 33, 44-47, 68, 83, 85, 92, 101, 109
Uslar Petri, Arturo, 279
U-Thant, 141, 157, 169, 260
U-2 (spy plane),
    cameras, 119, 122-123, 134, 137, 139, 264-265, 270;
    flights over Cuba, 117, 121, 123-124, 136, 138-139, 155-156, 177, 237, 252, 255, 258, 261, 263; flights over the U.S.S.R., 122-123, 133, 235; photographic gap, 136, 138, 139, 140, 141; shot down in Cuba, 13, 111, 121, 156-161, 165, 170, 220, 242; shot down in the U.S.S.R., 64, 70, 270, 275, 281; strays over Chukotski peninsula, 165-166, 168, 236, 242, 292; takes photos of sites, 23, 119, 147, 178-179, 181-185, 189-190, 292

Valdés, Maj. Ramiro, 94, 114
Vargas Llosa, Mario, 19
Verde Olivo (magazine), 149
Vietnam, 17, 64, 204, 218, 279, 282, 284, 286-231, 290
Villa Maristas, 208
Vivés, Juan, 152, 200, 260

Wallace, Mike, 221
Washington Post, 34, 271
Welch, David A., 161, 192, 194, 198, 201-204, 206, 212, 217, 219, 222, 293
Wieland, William, 104
Wills, Gary, 246
Wilson, Bob, 258
Wise, David, 276
Wise, Roy, 242
Wofford, Harris, 295
Wright, Peter, 131--132, 134
Wynne, Greville, 124, 127-128, 130

Zorin, Valerian, 107, 142, 147
Zubok, Vladislav M., 195

In Place of a Colophon

A President, a Dictator, and a Prime Minister are on their way to the United Nations building
by FGC

after Geoffrey Chaucer's Canterbury Tales

There was a dictator, a crazy one at that,
He wasn't too skinny, but not too fat.
An olive-green uniform was his choice of dress,
And he always smoked a cigar, whether at work or rest.
Bola de churre, they called him when he was young,
I believe it meant "greaseball" in his native tongue.
You see, he had a huge smelly beard which he never shaved,
Mixed with the cigar and the uniform, the stink came in waves.
Just like the waves of those who tried to flee
His island; many to be swallowed by the sea.

This Dictator collaborated with the Prime Minister, many years back,
To destroy the President's country; his plan of attack.
Missiles were his weapons of choice,
Everyone condemned this; whoever had a voice.
This dictator had broken every rule,
But not one was surprised by the actions of this insane fool.
This was part of the "revolution" which he held so dear,
His followers agreed with him, yet they dreaded each coming year.
Scratching their heads at why he'd stayed in power so long,
Wondering when he would kick the bucket, or sing his last song.
Yet he gave weekly speeches in the capital square,
Condemning his enemies; if they made sense that would be rare.
Called "The Devil" by many because he didn't seem to die,
He was in power for so long, all one could ask was "why"?

www.ingramcontent.com/pod-product-compliance
Lightning Source LLC
Chambersburg PA
CBHW031228290426
44109CB00012B/205